Race and Partisanship in California Redistricting

Race and Partisanship in California Redistricting

From the 1965 Voting Rights Act to Present

Olivier Richomme

LEXINGTON BOOKS
Lanham • Boulder • New York • London

Published by Lexington Books
An imprint of The Rowman & Littlefield Publishing Group, Inc.
4501 Forbes Boulevard, Suite 200, Lanham, Maryland 20706
www.rowman.com

6 Tinworth Street, London SE11 5AL, United Kingdom

British Library Cataloguing in Publication Information Available

Library of Congress Cataloging-in-Publication Data

Names: Richomme, Olivier, year- author.
Title: Race and partisanship in California redistricting : from the 1965 Voting Rights Act to present / Olivier Richomme.
Description: Lanham, Maryland : Lexington Books, [2019] | Includes bibliographical references and index.
Identifiers: LCCN 2019011413 (print) | LCCN 2019015388 (ebook) | ISBN 9781498585934 (electronic) | ISBN 9781498585927 (cloth) Subjects: LCSH:
California. Legislature—Election districts. | Election districts—California—History. | Apportionment (Election law)—California | Minorities—California—Politics and government. | Political participation—California.
Classification: LCC JK8768 (ebook) | LCC JK8768 .R53 2019 (print) | DDC 328.794/07345—dc23
LC record available at https://lccn.loc.gov/2019011413

In memory of Tim Hodson

Contents

Acknowledgments ix

Introduction 1

1 "One Person, One Vote":
How Minorities Benefitted from the End of Malapportionment 33

2 Gridlock over One (Latino) Seat in 1971 69

3 The Battle for the Latino Vote and the Burton Plan of 1981 105

4 Race and Redistricting in Los Angeles County:
Garza v. County of Los Angeles 139

5 Strategic Gridlock of 1991:
Republicans Bet on the Judiciary 165

6 The Status Quo Gerrymander of 2001:
MALDEF Sues the Democrats 223

7 The California Civil Rights Act:
Latinos End at-Large Districts 269

8 Tenth Time Is a Charm:
The Citizens Redistricting Commission 289

9 Conjoined Polarization in California and the
Evolution of Redistricting 341

Conclusion 367

Bibliography 375

Case List 411
Index 415
About the Author 421

Acknowledgments

This book has been a long time in the making. The sudden passing of Tim Hodson in 2011, who was the director of the Center for California Studies at California State University Sacramento (CSUS), was the impetus for this undertaking. But in retrospect the book had probably been in the making since I had met Tim, many years before, as a young graduate student at CSUS, when he shared his experience supervising the 1991 California Senate redistricting. As great professors do, he passed on his passion for politics and redistricting. I think he would have enjoyed this book.

But Tim is not the only person I'm intellectually indebted to and I would like to thank some of the people who helped me make this book possible. I am extremely grateful to Morgan Kousser who reviewed the first draft of my manuscript and his feedback was thorough and tremendously helpful. I also need to thank Bruce Cain for pointing me in the right direction when I needed it. The statewide database is a wonderful source of information and its terrific staff helped me a great deal with the practical and technical aspects of redistricting. I also need to thank the people who accepted to be interviewed for this book: Kathay Feng, Karin Mac Donald, Doug Johnson, Joaquin Avila, Denise Hulett, Leland Saito, and Eric McGee. I want to thank the colleagues who have helped me in many other ways with their suggestions, comments and encouragements: Bernie Grofman, Dick Engstrom, and particularly Andy Rudalevidge, Ray La Raja, Vincent Michelot, and Marie Plassart. At Rowman and Littlefield I wish to thank Emily Roderick for believing in my project right away, along with Alison Keefner and Courtney Morales for their editorial assistance and patience. Scholars can do no good work without good libraries and librarians. I wish to express my gratitude to the staff of the IGS library at UC Berkeley for their dedication even when I requested archive boxes at the last minute on Christmas Eve. The staff at the Rose Institute

Library made my life easier with the digitalization of much of the Rose Institute's redistricting archives. I was also very fortunate to have benefitted from a sabbatical from the *Conseil National des Universités* in France. Jacob Pacheco provided much needed assistance in gathering some of the material. Last but not least, I wish to thank my wife Danna for her many comments and her constant support in what is very often a lonely process.

Finally, it is common for academics to acknowledge that all the remaining errors are theirs and theirs only. While I take full responsibility for any remaining mistakes or omissions, a part of me can't help but think that some of the blame should fall on the Golden State Warriors who, in the past four years, have done everything in their power to distract me from my work. Or so it seems.

Introduction

This book attempts to analyze redistricting and its evolution in the state of California since the passage of the 1965 Voting Rights Act (VRA) and the judiciary's jump into the "political thicket." The goal is to evaluate the role played by race and partisanship in the voting rights revolution and its ensuing redefinition of the meaning of political representation in the past half-century. As explained further in the chapter, redistricting can be defined as the process by which a territory gets partitioned into a set of electoral constituencies from which one or more representatives are to be elected.[1]

This book aims to demonstrate that race and partisanship are intertwined in modern US redistricting and have been inseparable for half a century. Since the passage of the Voting Rights Act in 1965, redistricting is done with one eye on partisanship and the other on race representation. Most studies usually focus exclusively on one redistricting cycle, providing a partial view of the redistricting process. Most redistricting negotiations do not occur in a vacuum, meaning that every redistricting round is, to some extent, a reaction to the previous one. They are very often led by the same protagonists (i.e., politicians hiring the same consultants). The same minority organizations, with at times, the same staff, try to take part in the political bargaining process. Each redistricting session brings with it the weight of previous deals, calculations, and grievances. Previous maps are never entirely scraped off to start anew. Incumbency is, to some degree, always part of the equation. In other words, the redistricting process is political as much as it is historical; and it is as much of a partisan fight for political power as it is an ethno-racial struggle for political empowerment. In particular, this book takes a closer look at the dynamics of redistricting in California to show it is neither post-racial nor post-partisan but rather that ethno-racial interests and partisan interests overlap so much that differentiating one from the other has become a quixotic quest. The tortuous US Supreme Court jurisprudence on the matter suggests that a different approach might be needed to respond to the twenty-first-century challenge posed by fair political representation.[2]

> The principal difficulty lies, and the greatest care should be employed in constituting this Representative Assembly. It should be in miniature, an exact portrait of the people at large. It should think, feel, reason, and act like them.[3]

Democracy is most commonly taken in its traditional etymological meaning: the power or the rule of the people. Through the voting process citizens elect the leaders that will act according to the preferences expressed by the majority. As these leaders are perceived as agents of the people and thus acting on their behalf, representative democracy is often understood as designing institutions that will result in the closest expression of the will of the people. This is the reason why direct democracy has such a great appeal to many voters: it is perceived as the "real" expression of the people. However, this populist conception of democracy can fall prey to the passions of the electorate. History has shown that some sort of delegation of power creates, at times, the necessary buffer to solve society's problems due to the lack of expertise of the people. However, as modern representative democracies have swayed between these two forms of democracies, what James Madison referred to as republic and democracy in Federalist Paper No. 10, one feature remains constant. Both the direct and indirect forms of representation have been defended as necessary to truly reflect the will of the majority. Some have argued that the best way to reflect the will of the people is for the body of representatives to be like a society in miniature. The political theory of representation implies that any citizen can serve as an agent of the people. However, and this is especially true over the past half century, homogeneous representative bodies have become politically unacceptable. Many countries have put in place mechanisms to increase the number of political minorities in their legislatures or other representative bodies.[4] Minorities, components of society that were politically and historically marginalized, fought hard to benefit from reforms designed specifically to make sure their representation increased. These minorities were for the most part women and ethno/racial/religious groups. Their increased presence in the representative body was to guarantee that their interests were heard by the political majority. The diversity of interests of the people should be reflected in the body of representatives. According to this theoretical framework the optimum form of representation would come from a legislative or governing body that closely mirrors society in its diversity. For historical reasons, race has been a central feature of the political compromises that led to the creation of the United States. Race is consubstantial to the birth of what is now known as the United States and its institutions. It is therefore no surprise that several centuries later the question of political representation still revolves around race.

In the 1960s, the United States embarked on a voting rights revolution. It was not the first attempt at political equality. After the American Revolution in the 1780s, and the failure of Reconstruction a century later, the civil rights movement of the 1960s can be seen as another phase in the same quest to live up to the Founding Fathers' ideal of political equality expressed in the Declaration of Independence most revolutionary of sentences: "We hold these truths to be self-evident that all men are created equal." The 1960s Minority Rights Revolution,[5] coupled with the passage of the 1965 Voting Rights Act, completely upended the electoral landscape and changed the way Americans perceived political representation. The absence of non-Anglo elected officials became the symbol of institutional discrimination that delegitimized the entire political system and threatened the very core of the political compromise the nation was believed to have been built upon. As long as the US Congress, state legislatures, and other governing bodies were only composed of older Anglo males the American democracy would not be representative of the entire country. A diverse population required a diverse body of representatives. Furthermore, the United States could not be a democracy without an unhindered right to vote. The franchise was meaningless if it did not translate into the election of representatives that carried the voices of the historically marginalized minority groups. Otherwise many political communities' interests were not represented and their grievances would not be heard and addressed.

The voting rights revolution impacted many aspects of the American political system. None was more important to the emergence of minority elected officials than redistricting. While the first goal of the civil rights movement was access to the ballot and enforcement of the Fifteenth Amendment of the US Constitution,[6] it soon became clear that enfranchisement alone could not achieve political representation in a racially polarized environment and in a winner-take-all electoral system. Racial polarization, or racial bloc voting, can simply be defined as members of a community voting systematically for candidates they perceive as a member to their own racial group. Using racial polarization and residential segregation, redistricting had been used to keep racial minorities out of office. After the 1960s, thanks to federal legislation and court intervention, one solution was to use redistricting to help minorities get elected to office in a majoritarian system. Instead of opting for a form of proportional representation to guarantee that minorities might have a chance to elect a candidate representing their interest, American reformers opted to keep a winner-takes-all system in which some electoral districts would be composed of large numbers of ethno-racial minorities.

Redistricting might be the most political activity in America.[7] Electoral district boundaries are drawn every ten years in a jigsaw puzzle of competing interests, one of which is partisanship. The modern phase of redistricting in the US is at the crossroads of race and partisanship. To understand this, we need to go back to the beginning of the twentieth century.

The Minority Rights Revolution and the Republican "southern strategy" completed a racial partisan realignment that has its roots in President Roosevelt's coalition of the 1930s.[8] The Democratic Party came to champion minority rights as its electoral base was reshaped by the integration of minority groups, starting with African Americans. Therefore the issue of minority political representation, understood as necessarily including some sort of descriptive representation, became intertwined with partisanship.[9] Most Anglo voters prefer to vote for Anglo candidates. Most African Americans (and to some extent other ethno-racial minorities), when given the option, prefer to vote for an African American candidate. Racial polarization rates are especially high in the US South but this phenomenon is by no means limited to this region.[10] The Democratic Party has become the party of minority rights, thereby preferred by ethno-racial minorities, in particular among African Americans. As many scholars have observed, "it is often difficult to untangle racial consideration from partisan consideration."[11] After all, as Professor Rick Hasen remarked: "Liberal and conservative scholars have long recognized that the Voting Rights Act's enforcement and interpretation can have partisan implications and motivations."[12] Since the 1980s at least, over 90 percent of African Americans and about two-thirds of Latinos have consistently supported the Democratic Party for presidential or congressional elections. By contrast the Democratic Party has not won the White vote in a presidential election for more than fifty years, that is since the civil rights movement and the voting rights revolution reached its apex.[13] Partisan polarization is extremely high[14] and racial polarization of the vote is still very pronounced. So much so that Professor Bruce Cain considered that racial and partisan polarization are now "two sides of the same coin."[15] The interconnection between race and partisanship is such that Cain and Zhang have called this phenomenon "conjoined polarization":

> Racial sorting and party sorting trends have been closely intertwined. Civil rights policies gave socially conservative white Democrats reason to defect to the Republican Party. Immigration policies also enabled the nonwhite and non-European population to grow and eventually enter a coalition with liberal whites. At the same time, both parties became more ideologically consistent, with more within-party conformity in social and economic policy. This undercut the ideological heterogeneity that in the immediate post World War II era had limited the polarization of activists, donors, and representatives in both parties.

> The Democratic and Republican parties became more ideologically consistent and racially distinctive.[16]

This conjoined polarization has tremendous electoral consequences. Scholars seem to have reached a consensus on the partisan implications of majority-minority districts.[17] Creating districts that contain a majority of minority voters, as is often required by the Voting Rights Act, is obviously intended to help minority candidates get elected in those districts but it harms the Democratic Party overall by packing Democratic supporters into too few districts.[18] Besides, the Voting Rights Act as it is enforced by the executive branch can be used as a partisan tool for electoral gain, independent of the party in control. Scholars suggest that when either party oversees the Department of Justice they seem to enforce the Voting Rights Act in partisan ways.[19] Republicans openly complain about the Voting Rights Act infringement of states electoral rights but seem to find that majority-minority districts, especially if they contain large Democratic majorities, are a source of electoral gains in other districts. Democrats, on the other hand, have pushed for the creation of those districts to help minority candidates get elected, especially African Americans, as these candidates are almost exclusively Democrats. However, these sure-shot elections put them at a disadvantage in adjacent districts. Consequently, when Republicans in Congress supported that reauthorization of the Voting Rights Act in 2006 it was perceived as a simple strategic calculation being in their partisan interest.[20] The Republican Party did not necessarily support minority groups voting rights and interest representation but only saw majority-minority districts as a way to concentrate, and therefore weaken, Democratic voters. Any written work on redistricting is fundamentally about representation, or more precisely "fair and effective representation," and this debate shows that in the US this implies a questioning of the interaction of race and politics.

The thesis of this book is that race and partisanship are intrinsically intertwined when it comes to redistricting and that political battles of the previous decades inform the strategies and political fault lines of the following redistricting cycles. This book proposes the first comprehensive approach of the last half century of redistricting in one state (California) in order to fully grasp the interaction of race and partisanship during this highly political process that is so central for the American democracy. The narrative of the book intends to show the numerous connections between several redistricting cycles and their interaction with major political reforms and events. Some connections are obvious such as the one between the special masters' redistricting of the 1970s and 1990s, in which a conservative majority on the California State Supreme Court used the same consultants. Another connection is the one between courts intervention in the late 1960s following the "one, person, one vote" doctrine that ended malapportionment, that is the population discrepancies between electoral districts, and the election of minority officials in metropolitan areas. If minorities had not been elected to positions of power they would not have been able to fight for more minority representation and make the process more inclusive. Another obvious link is the one between the incumbent gerrymander of 2001 and the passage of the California Citizens Redistricting Commission (CRC) in 2008. Minority defense groups' lawyers were so frustrated with both parties during the 2001 round of redistricting that they eventually teamed up and authored an initiative to take redistricting "out of the hands of politicians." Other connections are more subtle. For instance, few scholars mention the parallels between the risk-averse gerrymanders of the 1980s and 2000s, both involving political consultant Michael Berman, Congressman Howard Berman's brother. The numerous referenda promising to "take politics out of redistricting" influenced party leaders' strategies as much as court decisions and informed the strategy that led to the creation of the Citizens Redistricting Commission. Also, early successes in the Voting Rights Act Section 2 litigations in the 1980s and the *Garza* case dealing with the Los Angeles County Board of Supervisors help explain the content of the California Voting Rights Act in 2001 and the reason civil rights lawyers felt compelled to change the law of the state to compensate for what they perceived as the shortcomings of the Federal Voting Rights Act.

The comprehensive depiction of fifty years of redistricting in California will try to convince the reader that redistricting, at least since the Civil Rights Revolution, is as much a partisan activity as it is a political battle for ethno-racial minority representation. And that this phenomenon is not limited to the South. In California the degrees of both partisan and racial polarization are such that treating partisan and ethno-racial factors separately in redistricting, as the US Supreme Court jurisprudence has done for decades, does not make much political (or historical) sense. Actually trying to disconnect one from the other may not even be desirable because it only gives a truncated, partial vision of the political dynamics of the state and of the redistricting process. A new approach is needed, one in which race and partisanship are considered together rather than separately in order to not get a disjointed understanding, or jurisprudence, of redistricting.

OVERVIEW OF THE 1965 VOTING RIGHTS ACT

During the period that is sometimes called the second Reconstruction,[21] due to the fact that southern states and local governments resisted attempts to remove obstacles that prevented African Americans from voting, Congress enacted the Voting Rights Act (VRA) in 1965 to try and make the Fifteenth Amendment a reality.[22] The VRA is a unique piece of legislation that contains permanent and temporary sections. Section 2 is permanent: it outlaws electoral procedures that "result in the denial or abridgement of the right of any citizen of the US to vote on account of race or color." Sections 4 through 9 are temporary and need to be renewed regularly. Out of its sections Section 5 is probably the most controversial, and also the most efficient. It created an exception to federalism and was decried, especially by Southerners, as an attack on state sovereignty. Through Section 5, the VRA specifically targeted certain state and local government jurisdictions in the South. Southern states used tests or devices, such as literacy tests, as a prerequisite for voter registration. Section 4 of the VRA created a triggering formula that measured voter registration and turnout levels in states and local governments that used these mentioned prerequisites. The VRA ultimately forbade the use of these tests or devices in these jurisdictions for a five-year period. Section 5, sought to prevent the implementation of any change affecting the right to vote unless federal approval, was obtained from the US Attorney General in an administrative proceeding or in a judicial action from the US District Court for the District of Columbia. The revolutionary aspect of Section 5 is that it placed the burden of proof on the covered jurisdiction that submitted the proposed voting change. The jurisdictions covered by Section 5 had to demonstrate that the proposed voting change did not have a *discriminatory effect* on minority voting strength and that the change was not adopted with a *discriminatory purpose*. In 1965, the covered jurisdictions where those in which less than 50 percent of persons of voting age were registered on November 1, 1964, or in which less than 50 percent of persons of voting age voted in the presidential election of 1964.[23]

US Congress then prolonged and amended the 1965 VRA several times. In order to extend the temporary provisions of the VRA, Congress modified the triggering formula found in Section 4. In 1970, Congress extended the regional ban on tests or devices to the entire nation and not only in the South.[24] Moreover, Congress prolonged Section 5 preclearance requirement, as well as the national ban on tests or devices, for another seven years. In 1975, Congress permanently banned tests or devices and extended the Section 5 preclearance requirement for an additional seven years. In addition, Congress realized that voting discrimination was not limited only to African Americans, but also applied to other ethno-racial groups, such as Latinos and Asians.[25] Consequently, Congress expanded the definition of a test or device to include English-only elections in those jurisdictions where more than 5 percent of the eligible voters were members of an applicable language minority group (such as Spanish or Chinese in California). Thus, if a jurisdiction

(1) either had less than a 50 percent voter registration rate or less than a 50 percent voter turnout rate; (2) had English-only elections in a state, county, or jurisdiction that conducted voter registration; and (3) had more than 5 percent of the eligible voters as members of an applicable language group, then the jurisdiction was subject to Section 5 preclearance requirements. This extended definition mainly concerned states with an important Latino population, such as Arizona and Texas, or a large Native American population, such as Alaska. The 1975 amendments also aimed to help limited-English proficiency citizens to vote. Furthermore, the newly enacted Section 203 provided language assistance during elections in jurisdictions that met certain criteria.[26] Under the 1975 VRA amendments, a jurisdiction could simultaneously be subject to the language assistance provisions of Section 5 and Section 203. This was particularly consequential for a state such as California with many linguistic minorities.[27] Only 4 out of 58 counties in California were covered by Section 5 (Kings, Merced, Monterey, and Yuba) but many more are covered by Section 203.[28]

The Voting Rights Act went under another drastic change when in 1982 Congress was faced with its prolongation. In 1980, the US Supreme Court had held, in a plurality opinion on the case *City of Mobile v. Bolden* that invalidating an at-large method of election on the basis of violation of the Fourteenth and Fifteenth Amendments or Section 2 of the VRA required proof of a discriminatory intent.[29] In response, Congress amended Section 2 to eliminate the *discriminatory intent* requirement. The newly amended Section 2 required proof only of a *discriminatory effect* on minority voting strength.[30] This is a good example of the back-and-forth between the legislative and the judiciary branches in the field of voting rights enforcement. The Senate Report accompanying the 1982 VRA amendments further defined the standard: Section 2 is violated when it is demonstrated that, under the "totality of circumstances," minority voters did not have an equal opportunity to participate in the political process and elect "candidates of their choice."[31] That same year Congress also extended the preclearance requirement of Section 5 for twenty-five years. In addition, Congress established a new mechanism to create an incentive for covered jurisdictions to comply with Section 5 of the VRA. Congress provided an expanded "bail-out" mechanism that permitted Section 5–covered jurisdictions to be exempt from Section 5 preclearance upon meeting certain criteria. The language assistance provisions in Section 203 were extended for a ten-year period until 1992; and then, Congress extended the language assistance provisions to 2007. As a result of these amendments, the triggering formula was modified.[32] The language assistance provisions have been instrumental in California in providing citizens who are not proficient in English with an opportunity to register to vote and to exercise that right in elections, but they go beyond the scope of this particular book.

As the VRA was up for renewal in 2007, Congress prolonged it for twenty-five years in 2006 and amended it significantly again as a reaction of a US Supreme Court jurisprudence that appeared contrary to its initial legislative intent. In another fascinating example of the inter-branch dialogue between the legislative and the judiciary branches on voting rights enforcement, proponents of the VRA tried to correct three Supreme Court cases, two that dealt with Section 5 and one that dealt with expert witness fees:

1. The first case, *Reno v. Bossier Parish School Board*, 528 US 320 (2000) (known as *Bossier II*) dealt with Section 5 requirement. Before *Bossier II* the standard was that any change that had a discriminatory purpose or intent would not be approved. In *Bossier II* the US Supreme Court ruled that Section 5 only outlawed "retrogressive dilution," that is, voting changes that made things worse for minorities. After *Bossier II*, simply maintaining the status quo passed constitutional muster. Section 5 of the VRA was amended by Congress to replace the phrase "does not have the purpose and will not have the effect," with "neither have the purpose nor will have the effect." Congress also added a subsection that forbade preclearance of any voting change "that has the purpose or will have the effect" of discrimination. The word "purpose" was defined to include "any discriminatory purpose."
2. The second Supreme Court case was *Georgia v. Ashcroft*, 539 US 461 (2003). Before this decision the standard for Section 5 preclearance was whether an election procedure had the potential to dilute minority voting strength.[33] The 2003 Supreme Court decision lowered this standard in granting approval by simply giving minorities the capacity to influence elections even if they were not able to elect the candidate of their choice. Congress responded to this ruling by amending Section 5 to specify that the purpose of this section was to protect the ability of minority citizens to "elect their preferred candidates of choice."
3. The third, less famous case was *West Virginia University Hospitals, Inc. v. Casey*, 499 US 83 (1991). Private Section 2 challenges can be very complex, long, and expensive. Section 14 of the VRA allowed private parties that prevailed in court to recover attorney' s fees, but in 1991 the Supreme Court limited it to legal fees excluding expert witness fees. Congress added language into the act covering "reasonable expert fees."

The Act was renewed by a majority Republican Congress and signed by a Republican president but with a strong Republican opposition that appeared in a rare post hoc report of the Senate Judiciary Committee.[34] This opposition materialized in 2 subsequent US Supreme Court decisions. In *Northwest Austin Municipal Utility District No. 1 v. Holder*, 557 US 193 (2009), known as NAMUNDNO, the conservative Supreme Court majority declined to rule on the constitutionality of Section 5 but some justices strongly indicated that they were bothered by Section 5 as it stood. In *Shelby County v. Holder*, 570 US 2 (2013) the Court ruled, by a 5 to 4 vote, that Section 4(b) is unconstitutional because the coverage formula is based on data more than forty years old, making it no longer responsive to current needs and therefore an impermissible burden on the constitutional principles of federalism and equal sovereignty of the states. The Court did not strike down Section 5, but without Section 4(b), no jurisdiction will be subject to Section 5 preclearance unless Congress enacts a new coverage formula.

Prior to Shelby, 9 states (mostly, but not exclusively, in the South) were entirely covered by Section 5. Counties and townships in 7 additional states were also covered. The state of California was not subject to Section 5 but 4 of its 58 counties were: Kings, Merced, Monterey, and Yuba. Counties, just like states, resented being covered by Section 5 and some applied for "bail out" relief.[35]

IMPACT OF THE 1965 VOTING RIGHTS ACT

There are several ways one can measure the impact of the VRA. Statistics depicting the increase of minority voting and political participation in the years following the passage of the law are nothing but spectacular. In the 7 states covered by the VRA in 1965,[36] the average African American registration rate was 29.3 percent before the Act and reached 52.1 percent by 1967. African American voting registration rates in the 11 states of the former Confederacy increased from 43.1 percent in 1964 to 62 percent in 1968. In Mississippi, the discrepancy between the Anglo and African American voter registration rates went from 63.2 percent in 1965 to 6.3 percent in 1988.[37] African American turnout also increased tremendously as a result. For instance in Alabama and Mississippi, between the 2 presidential elections of 1964 and 1968, African American turnout increased by respectively 19.3 percent and 16.8 percent.[38]

There were only 1,469 African American officeholders in the US in 1970. By 2002 there were 9,430 of them.[39] According to the National Association of Latino Elected Officials (NALEO) figures, there were 4,004 Latino elected official in the US in 1990. By 2004, that number had reached 4,853 and by 2014 it was at 6,084.[40] The first *National Asian Pacific American Political*

Almanac printed in 1976 listed just over 100 Asian Americans who were elected or appointed to public office in only 4 states: California, Hawaii, Oregon, and Washington. The 2015 issue lists more than 4,000 in the US and its territories.[41] All these figures are not all attributable to the VRA but its impact on all types of voting statistics is undeniable.

For instance, in 1965, the number of African Americans elected in the US House of Representatives was 6. In 1995 that number had ballooned to 41. In 2005 and 2015 it reached its peaks of 44.[42] Most of these gains were due to redistricting. Most congressional minority elected officials represent majority-minority districts. By contrast, in statewide elections ethno-racial minorities usually struggle to get elected. In 2016, no African American governor held office and by then, there had only been 4 in American history. That same year there was a grand total of 4 non-Anglo governors.[43] The same is true in the US Senate where minorities have historically been exceptions, sometimes the result of appointments. In 2017, a historic year for diversity in Congress, there were 4 African Americans, 2 Asian Americans, and 4 Latinos in the Senate.[44] Therefore minorities represented a record 10 percent of the US Senate.[45] Between its two chambers Congress reached a new historical high for ethno-racial diversity with 19 percent of legislators being non-Anglo. In the House of Representatives, 22 percent of all members belonged in 2017 to an ethno-racial minority. Between the 2 chambers the total breakdown of minority members was: 50 African Americans, 39 Latinos, 15 Asians, and 2 Native Americans.[46] In 2001, minorities accounted for 12 percent of all members (compared to 31 percent of the population).[47] In 1981, only 6 percent of Congress members were from ethno-racial minority groups, while these groups represented 20 percent of the American population. These figures suggest that the VRA was a success in reforming the American political system. Yet it also raises the issue of substantive versus descriptive representation and the conundrum of proportional representation.

Does the election of an African American candidate (descriptive representation) guarantee that the interests of the African American community be adequately represented (substantive representation)? Should not a skillful Anglo candidate that accumulates seniority in the legislature and sits on powerful committees be more likely to deliver tangible results for this community? Some studies have suggested that African Americans that are elected in very safe majority-minority districts operate too far left on the political spectrum and therefore end up being marginalized in the legislative bargaining process that usually takes place at the center.[48] Would not a form of proportional representation solve, in part, the issues raised by majority-minority districts in a winner-take-all system? If minority representation is so crucial for the American society should not the electoral system be designed to achieve such a goal?

In spite of the disclaimer included in Section 2 by Congress, and despite numerous reiteration by the US Supreme Court that the Constitution does not guarantee proportional representation to minorities, one can clearly see that ethno-racial minorities advocacy groups are not satisfied by levels of descriptive representation that are lower than their proportion the general population. The debate over the VRA has revolved around the determination, a process that is by nature a political bargain, of how much disproportionality mandates corrective action in a winner-take-all and geographical district-based electoral system.

REDISTRICTING IN THE US

As a foreigner who lived in the United States for many years, I sometimes find myself reminding American colleagues how exceptional the US form of democratic government is.[49] The main characteristic of the American electoral system is its reliance on single member districts with a plurality vote. In the US, most districts use single-member plurality systems (SMD) and not some form of proportional voting (PR). This has tremendous implications since many groups try to achieve through redistricting some form of proportional representation and feel frustrated with the system when they do not reach their goal. Redistricting is therefore quite different from what happens in most other democracies. Other countries in the world also use single member districts yet "American practice has diverged more and more from those employed elsewhere."[50] A number of prominent American scholars have supported some form of proportional representation.[51] Nevertheless, one of the most striking features of American electoral reform is the absence of proportional representation and the unwillingness to experiment with such electoral systems. The irony of redistricting in the US is that as the jurisprudence on racial representation has evolved toward an implicit norm of ethno-racial proportionality[52] as the proof of a "fair and effective representation," proportional electoral system have not gained much traction.

Another important difference with other countries is that, in most states in the US, redistricting is still in the hands of the legislature. In many nations this was considered a clear conflict of interest. Many Americans seem to agree if we judge by opinion polls or the increasing number of attempts at creating independent redistricting commissions. Political parties see redistricting as a way to assert their power. Incumbents see it as an opportunity to stay in office. Minority groups see an opportunity to increase their descriptive, or substantive, representation. Reform groups worry about the fairness of this key procedure for any representative democracy. The fact that redistricting is done by legislatures means that every other legislative activity takes a back seat to line-drawing negotiations, while it consumes all the political oxygen. Some scholars have referred to it as "war,"[53] "the bloodsport of politics,"[54] Butler and Cain sum up the unspoken motto of line-drawing negotiations as "redistricting überalles."[55] Important policy matters or impending legislation become engulfed in the process and every political dispute becomes fair game in redistricting negotiations. Redistricting can also be used for retaliation against a member that refuses to follow his or her leadership or the party's line. One needs to note that redistricting does not necessarily bring about incumbent protection in a way that can easily be measured by registration rates. For instance, incumbents may obtain advantages in the form of opponent neutralization or fundraising capacity. Keeping some big donors or good fundraising areas in one district or, on the contrary, keep the home of a competitor out of the district are sometimes more valuable for a candidate with name recognition or an established record.[56] This information only appears when one looks into the detail of negotiation between lawmakers and line drawers. This is why this book looks closely at the legislative history of the State of California.

Another feature of redistricting in the US is the degree to which plans are litigated in the courts. As mentioned, court intervention in the 1960s quickly focused on the redistricting process. The first generation of voting rights cases broadened the electorate and made the process more open than ever before in American history. The amended Voting Rights Act has subjected line-drawers decisions to judicial review. In the 1940s, the US Supreme Court considered that the US Congress, not the courts had the authority to supervise states' political activity such as redistricting. In *Colgrove v. Green* Justice Frankfurter warned the judiciary not to enter the "political thicket" by ruling on redistricting and vote dilution claims.[57] As a political endeavor it was, according to him, not justiciable. However, in the early 1960s in *Gomillon v. Lightfoot* the same justice wrote the majority opinion that struck down the new district in the city of Tuskegee, Alabama, not because of vote dilution claim but because the new map denied Tuskegee African American residents a vote in municipal elections.[58] Frankfurter held that the legislature's law did violate the provision of the Fifteenth Amendment. Justice Whitaker concurred but wrote in his opinion that he believed the law should have been struck down under the Equal Protection Clause of the Fourteenth Amendment. As it turns out *Gomillon* was the bridge between *Colgrove* and *Baker v. Carr*, a Tennessee malapportionment case, with which the Court plunged into the political thicket.[59] *Baker* required state legislatures to redistrict based on population, in order to reflect demographic changes and enable representation of urban populations. *Baker* opened the door to more litigation such as *Gray v. Sanders,* 372 US 368 (1963) which established the principle of "one person, one vote" under the Equal Protection Clause.[60] In *Wesberry v. Sanders*, 376 US 1 (1964), a case involving US Congressional districts in the state of Georgia, the US Supreme Court required each state to draw its congressional districts so that they would be approximately equal in population. In the related case, *Reynolds v. Sims*, 377 US 533 (1964), the US Supreme Court held that seats in both houses of a bicameral state legislature must also represent districts as equal in population as practicably possible. At the same time that the US Supreme Court started its redistricting revolution, Congress passed the 1965 Voting Rights Act. Section 5 of the VRA established the process of preclearance which required that covered jurisdictions receive federal approval before implementing changes to their election laws. This allowed federal entities such as the Department of Justice or the District Court for the District of Columbia to block state legislatures from implementing discriminatory election changes.[61] Passed on a temporary basis the VRA was renewed in 1970, 1975, and 1982 for twenty-five years and again in 2006 for twenty-five years. In 1975, it was amended to protect language minorities which broadened its application to new areas of the country and other minorities, specifically Latino, Asian, and Native Americans. In 1982, it was amended to broaden the definition of discrimination: plaintiffs no longer had to prove intent to establish discrimination.[62] Therefore the passage of the VRA and the courts intervention involving the Fourteenth and the Fifteenth Amendments changed everything in the sense that it created what does not exist in many other countries: minority vote dilution and racial gerrymandering.[63] Both stem from a tension inside American law between group-based harm and individual-based harm. The conflict between the two has been at the heart of the fight over the definition of the Equal Protection doctrine. The intervention of the courts has had two important consequences. First, because the American judiciary is quite politicized (some judges are elected, appointed by partisan elected officials, subject to recall in some states), it is often accused of partisan bias.[64] Second, the willingness of the courts to review redistricting cases has led to the expectation of strict statistically measurable standards.[65] This approach has shown its limits in partisan gerrymandering cases since the US Supreme Court has been incapable on agreeing on a workable standard.[66] For thirty years after *Baker v. Carr* the courts used racial vote dilution doctrine focused exclusively on group rights, that is to say the ability of a racially defined community to participate in the political processes and to elect legislators of their choice, instead of addressing the rights of individual voters. As a result, voting rights were administered by equal protection standards that differed markedly from those applied in other areas. Then in 1993, in the new jurisprudence following the case *Shaw v. Reno*, the US Supreme Court tried to "merge the analysis governing race-conscious districting back into general-purpose equal protection doctrine."[67] Trying to administer voting rights cases through its already tortuous affirmative action framework, emphasizing individual rights versus competing state interest, led the Court to establish an especially meandering jurisprudence when it came to race.[68] The crux of the matter is that under current jurisprudence partisan gerrymandering is permissible while racial gerrymandering is inherently suspect and may be subjected to strict scrutiny.[69] As Cain and Zhang have observed: "Such a distinction between race and party is meaningless in the context of conjoined polarization. Nearly every decision to discriminate against racial minorities in voting has an electoral purpose. Considered in that light, all manipulations of the electoral process are partisan at heart."[70] One of the most interesting consequences of the absence of standard for partisanship and a strict standard for race is that racial gerrymandering claims or equal population deviation claims have therefore been used as a proxy for partisan vote dilution claims.[71] Third, court intervention changed the nature of redistricting because legislators and governors now had to take into consideration what types of maps the judiciary might draw in case of gridlock and took the habit of hedging their bets. Or as Professor Gary Cox puts it: "Endowing the lower courts with the power to set the reversion meant that the courts became players in all subsequent redistricting actions. The possibility always existed that a state's plan would be litigated. Thus, those devising new redistricting plans had to consider which court would hear the case and its likely view of matters."[72] In California, starting in the 1960s, the courts capacity simply to set deadlines, or even to set revisions, and the inevitable political fight over the partisan control of the judiciary are an integral part of the redistricting wars.

While constitutional constraints are now much greater, it seems the stakes are still as high for people involved in redistricting, be it parties, elected officials, ethno-racial minorities, political activists, "good government" groups. Malapportionment has been banned by the courts since *Baker v. Carr* so now the fight over boundaries is between equally populated districts.[73] But redistricting can still advantage one group over the other, usually one party over the other (partisan gerrymandering) or one ethno-racial group over the other (racial gerrymandering). Both have become intertwined to the point that most of the time it is illusory to attempt to differentiate between the two. When can race be considered "a predominant factor"? When is race used as a proxy for partisanship and vice-versa?[74] The US Supreme Court maintains the theoretical distinction between the two because its view of racial gerrymandering is derived from its individual rights approach on race in affirmative action jurisprudence. Yet this approach, quite opaque in affirmative action cases, seems ill equipped to deal with the questions raised by democratic representation whether one takes a group-rights approach, a structuralist approach or even an individual-rights approach.[75] The example of California shows how race and politics are intertwined and more precisely that the partisan fight over redistricting is inseparable from the struggle over minority representation.[76]

Starting in the 1990s, technological changes in turn have opened the redistricting process to a broader set of activists and to the public eye. Because American institutions are Madisonian in design, actors in the political system are not supposed to be neutral or disinterested. Americans expect different groups to lobby for their interest. Institutions expect people to be interested and therefore, in a way, encourage people to behave in a self-interested manner and not for the public welfare. Redistricting follows this norm deeply engrained in the political culture. Redistricting is the product of various interests competing against one another. Over the years, the number of competing factions has increased. While redistricting became a more open process, a constantly growing number of interests needed to be satisfied.

One of the main characteristics of American political dynamics is the centrality of race. For understandable historical reasons, interest groups coalesce around ethno-racial identities, which put great emphasis on ethno-racial statistics in the context of redistricting. As a foreigner who grew up in a country where those statistics are illegal (for historical reasons, the occupation of Nazi Germany being one of them), it is always striking to see that these statistics are usually presented as the main demographic characteristics without discussing the creation or the evolution of these statistical categories. One needs to notice that some of these ethno-racial categories, often taken for granted, did not exist when the VRA was passed, such as the Hispanic category. Besides, as is the case with affirmative action policies, there is an inherent tension between the ever growing number of identity claims and the need for statistical categories to remain stable over time. If Professor David Hollinger's "ethno-racial pentagon" has proven to be quite resilient to the creation of new categories (Arab American, multi-racial, etc.) it is because the entire anti-discrimination legal framework can only operate with a finite stable number of categories. Race-conscious public policies are often in conflict with the multiplication of identity claims. The more minorities there are the more difficult it is to monitor discrimination evolution over time. Reforming institutional discrimination and measuring progress has limited the increase of ethno-racial identities and their accompanying statistics. In theory, the diversity of any given society is endless (religious freedom in the US goes in this direction) but there are also political forces that keep minority groups from multiplying. In the case of ethno-racial groups what is striking is the fairly stable nature of these statistical categories or at least the presence of mechanism to make those statistics appear as stable over time and space.

The sum total of all these factors is a redistricting process under greater pressure, under greater public scrutiny and judicial oversight, and still unable to deliver the promise of five decades of Supreme Court jurisprudence about fair political representation. These unrealized expectations are now more obvious than ever and are ultimately destabilizing to the redistricting process.[77] Renewed attention to alternatives and redistricting reform attempts have come to respond to this frustration. California is a good illustration of this evolution.

STATE-LEVEL IMPACT: THE CASE FOR CALIFORNIA

One of the reasons to study California is that every redistricting process is specific to each state because it is determined by state laws or constitutions. Article I, Section 4, of the United States Constitution delegates authority to conduct federal elections to the state legislatures; the Constitution is silent on the conduct of state and local elections, reserving those responsibilities to the states because they are one of the pillars of state sovereignty. Redistricting schemes not only differ across states, but may diverge for congressional and state legislative redistricting even within the same state. Therefore, focusing on the national level only gives a partial picture of the complexity of the process. National and state constitutions have been amended, interpreted by the courts, and have, therefore, placed constraints on map drawers. These constraints are the environment under which law makers operate. They cannot be ignored and play a major role. But in the end all redistricting is local.

As the fiftieth anniversary of the 1965 VRA was celebrated in 2015 many books and scholarly articles were published discussing the great achievements of the law and its uncertain future. Yet, studies that intend to look at the impact of the voting rights revolution at the state level in a comprehensive manner and over a fifty-year period are much more seldom.[78] Most studies focus on the GOP-controlled South and how blue and Black political interests have converged and have been pitted against red and White interests.[79] Since the *Shelby* decision in 2013, and understandably so, the political science and legal fields have been focused again on the South because of the impact the disappearance of Section 5 could have on this region.[80] This book is trying to tell the story of redistricting in the West (of the US) and what is now considered one of the bluest (most Democratic) states.[81] The alignment of racial, partisan, and ideological interests is not limited to the US South. In California, liberal and minority rights forces have coalesced under the Democratic umbrella as the Republican Party has become the party of Anglo conservatives. California is the most populous and one of the most diverse states in the Union. It has a large Latino population (40 percent of the state's residents) and a substantive Asian American population (15 percent), the two fastest growing ethno-racial groups in the Union. As a consequence, California may represent the future of American demographics and the increased complexity of representational issues raised by redistricting. It, therefore, seems like an ideal candidate for anyone interested in the interaction between race and politics.[82]

Additionally, California's institutions make it an interesting case study for redistricting. The state has an extremely professionalized political system. In the mid-1960s, California embarked on a professionalization program that resulted in full-time sessions and full-time legislators, large expert staff and significant salaries and perks.[83] After the 2010 census, California had by far the largest number of seats in the House of Representatives with 53. This number is so high that California is always in any discussion dealing with congressional majorities. Its legislature has 40 Senate seats and 80 Assembly seats. As of 2011, each state Senator represents almost a million people, twice as many as an Assembly member. So California is atypical in the sense that it has, compared to its population, a low number of representatives in comparison to other states.[84] It means that every senator and Assembly member has a lot of political clout and the stakes for their elections are high. The Senate also has fairly long terms of four years which also increases the power of state senators.[85] In other large states, redistricting fights are dominated by congressional seats. By contrast, in California, the stakes are heightened in the legislature as career professional politicians compete for a comparatively smaller number of seats with longer terms in the Senate.

Furthermore, California is a particularly interesting example because of its political tradition to take reform to the next level. In particular, California's initiative system is quite transformative. California puts more citizen initiatives on the ballot than any other state and it takes another initiative to undo one once it is passed. Which lead Eric McGee and Jack Citrin to describe California political system as "not quite a republic in the way the nation's the founding fathers imagined; it is more an ancient Athenian democracy writ large, with citizens making and breaking policy and the state' s elected officials often struggling to keep up."[86] This penchant for electoral reforms is also visible in the field of redistricting with, for instance, the passage of the California Voting Rights Act in 2001 and the California Redistricting Commission in 2008. California is therefore appealing because the state has often experimented with policies and institutions that far exceed what other states regard as the realm of possible reform.

OUTLAY OF THE BOOK

The book logically (but also symbolically) starts in 1965 when the California legislature was forced by the courts to redraw district lines to abide by the new "equal population" standard set by the *Baker v. Carr* line of jurisprudence. This marks the end of malapportionment in California and ushers in the modern era of redistricting. The strict "equal population" standard placed great restraint on the legislature in its attempt to protect incumbents or gain partisan advantage. However, 1965 also marks the beginning of the minority voting rights revolution. The Federal Voting Rights Act was in its infancy and its effect could not be felt yet even tough from a symbolic standpoint, its passage sent an important message especially to the segregated South as it precipitated the ideological and geographical realignment of the two major parties. But before Section 2 or Section 5 could take effect, "equal population" had tremendous consequences for minorities in California. Malapportionment gave rural areas disproportional political power. "Equal population" corrected this bias and gave metropolitan areas their true electoral weight. Because ethno-racial minorities are overwhelmingly concentrated in urban centers they finally were able to make their ballots count. And, because of residential segregation, some urban areas concentrated so many minorities that candidates had no choice but to take minorities' vote into consideration. In some districts they were even able to elect minority candidates, mostly African Americans, for the first time. "Equal population" was therefore responsible for the first wave of post–civil rights movement minority elected officials in the legislature and in Congress. They, in turn, were able to pressure their colleagues into creating more opportunities for other minorities.

Chapter 2 starts only a few years later. During the 1971 round of redistricting a political impasse revolving around one seat led to the intervention of the Supreme Court. This political crisis was directly linked to the issue of minority representation. With a Republican governor and two thin majorities in the Assembly and the Senate the redistricting plan should have been a bipartisan incumbent protection affair maintaining the status quo. But both parties dug their heels in when an Anglo Republican upset a Latino Democrat in an Assembly special election. Richard Alatorre was supposed to become the third Latino in the Assembly in a Los Angeles district that was racially diverse and heavily Democrat. Republicans demanded that their new incumbent be protected while Democrats argued they should honor the deal that had previously been agreed upon. Governor Reagan refused to support the deal struck by the legislative leaderships and vetoed all three redistricting plans which had the consequence to put the Supreme Court in charge of redistricting. Therefore a bitter partisan feud started when Republicans tried to prevent the Democrats from increasing the number of Latino elected officials from 2 to 3 in the Assembly. Partisan battles are inseparable from minority representation questions and even one seat can escalate confrontation to gridlock. The Supreme Court appointed a special master to draw new maps. In 1991, Republicans had rather take their chances with the judiciary than bargaining with the Democrats and their bet paid off as the new maps were drawn by the same expert consultants.

Chapter 3 deals with what is sometimes considered a strong partisan gerrymander on the part of the Democrats who had total control of the redistricting process with a Democratic governor and two majorities in both legislative chambers. Yet, the 1981 round of redistricting is also the story of the wooing of the Latino community. This growing minority group had not yet aligned itself with any of the major parties. Republicans assisted Latino activists with the technology and training to propose districts that could increase the number of Latino elected officials. This helped the Republicans prove that the GOP and Latinos interests were converging. This move was also a shrewd political tactic because it put the Democrats in a difficult position because creating Latino districts meant collapsing Anglo incumbent districts. But the Democrats smartly put minority officials in charge of the redistricting process. With Assembly Speaker Brown, an African American, and Richard Alatorre, a Latino, as the chairman of the Election and Reapportionment Committee, Democrats were able to increase the number of Assembly districts in which Latinos had an opportunity to influence the election while at the same time protecting their partisan interest. Alatorre and Brown also made sure that the Senate and congressional plans were fair to minorities. Having minorities in such high positions proved invaluable for the Democrats in their negotiations with incumbents and minority activists. Democrats protected their majority for almost a decade but also helped minorities elected a few new Latino representatives before the Voting Rights Act was amended in 1982. These gains (2 more Latinos in the legislature and 2 more in the congressional delegation) helped the Democrats win over Latinos who now had joined African Americans inside the California Democratic coalition.

Empowered by these gains and by the strengthened VRA, Latinos took their fight for representation to the local level. Chapter 4 takes a quick detour to look at one of the most important redistricting battles in the 1980s. California is such an interesting case study because of its size. Some counties are larger and more populated than some states of the Union, making local redistricting a very high stakes game. And the stakes are never higher than in Los Angeles County. This county of 10 million people is ruled by a 5-member Board of Supervisors. That is about 2 million constituents per representative, the most populated electoral districts in the US. In 1988 Mexican American

Legal Defense and Educational Fund (MALDEF) and the American Civil Liberties Union (ACLU) (later joined by the Justice Department) sued the Board of Supervisors arguing members had put in place a redistricting process that intentionally discriminated against ethno-racial minorities. In spite of the difficulty of proving intent, a federal court sided with them and forced the Board to create a Latino-majority district for the 1990 election and Latinos were able to elect the first Latina in the history of the county. Because a large majority of Latinos in Los Angeles County were registered with the Democratic Party, creating a Latino district meant creating a majority Democrat district and therefore electing a Democrat to the Board. Because electing a Latina meant electing a Democrat separating partisan from racial animosity became very difficult.

The power of judges in redistricting cases was now obvious and chapter 5 deals with another involvement of the courts in 1991. After being in the minority in the 1980s and having watched the Democrats redistrict as they pleased, Republicans used the tools at their disposal in response: direct democracy. Republicans financed referendums submitting redistricting plans to the vote of the people and launched campaigns to recall California Supreme Court Justices in hopes of regaining a conservative majority. While referendums were unsuccessful, the recalls were. With a Republican governor in place, conservatives were able to change the partisan majority on the Court. This new majority weighted heavily on the redistricting negotiation. Because no party controlled the redistricting process, the 1991 round of redistricting should again have been a bipartisan agreement. Democrats with two majorities in both chambers were in charge of redistricting and proposed three different types of plans that preserved minority group interests and each plan was aimed at a faction of the Republican minority to obtain some bipartisan support and possibly a veto proof two-third majority. However, the GOP was not really interested in negotiating. When Republican Governor Wilson did not obtain what he wanted, and when his redistricting commission project tanked, he quickly decided to take his chances with the California Supreme Court, convinced that a conservative majority would give him a better deal than what the Democratic leadership was willing to concede. While the court-drawn maps were favorable to the GOP, the power of the VRA was at its apex and it was used to create many majority-minority districts instead of influence districts as in 1981. Majority-minority districts concentrate minorities and therefore Democratic voters therefore making adjacent districts more Republican. These changes, however, were not enough to save the GOP from the demographic evolution of the state. 1994 was a good Republican year nationally but during the rest of the decade the Latino electorate greatly increased at the same time as voters approved term limits. Latino candidates took advantage and the number of

Latinos dramatically augmented especially in the Assembly. As more Latinos were elected, Democratic majorities increased.

In 2001, the Democrats were in complete control of redistricting and yet decided to strike a bipartisan deal. They feared another special masters' redistricting and believed they had maximized their partisan gains. As a consequence, Democrats chose to protect every single incumbent to make sure they reached a referendum proof majority in order to not get dragged again in a long-lasting redistricting battle. However, by protecting many incumbents the Democrats limited their potential partisan gains during the following decade as Republican registration continued to drop throughout the state. The Democrats also limited minorities' potential electoral gains as their percentage of the electorate kept increasing. Consequently, by unabashedly protecting so many incumbents they angered minority group activists. MALDEF unsuccessfully sued and was astonished to lose because the longtime Democrat consultant Michael Berman openly explained that he had greatly lowered the number of Latinos in his brother's district, Congressman Howard Berman, in order to save him from a Latino challenger. Redistricting is always about race, always partisan, and always very personal. The most long-lasting and unanticipated effect of the 2001 incumbent gerrymander is that the Democrats' consultants also brushed aside Asian American groups grievances. One of these young lawyers for the Asian Pacific American Legal Center, Kathay Feng, became the director of Common Cause California in 2005. She teamed up with Steve Reyes, a former MALDEF attorney in 2001, to author the propositions that created the California Redistricting Commission and took redistricting out of the hands of the legislature.

But before dwelling in the California Redistricting Commission and its consequences, the reader ought to take one more detour to look at the local level because a quiet revolution took place at beginning of the 2000s and is described in chapter 7. Latino Civil Rights Attorney Joaquin Avila was able to convince Latino Senate Majority Leader Polanco to sponsor his proposal of a California Voting Rights Act (CVRA) which was signed into law in 2002 and took effect in 2003. The CVRA supplements the federal VRA as it is designed to force jurisdictions to abandon at-large elections and switch to district elections. It was extremely successful as many cities, school boards and other jurisdictions either voluntarily switched to districts or were forced to do so after they lost expensive lawsuits. At-large elections, that have been for a long time associated with minority discrimination, are disappearing in California. Yet, district elections on their own are no guarantee that minorities might be elected or that these districts will lead to minority representation that is proportional to their electoral weight. Community outreach, mobilization, and other mechanisms to increase registration and turnout are essential.

Chapter 8 deals with the creation of the California Redistricting Commission. As mentioned, minority group advocates who believed they had been marginalized during the 2001 round of redistricting teamed up with "good government" groups, and the Republican Party, to create an independent redistricting commission. Ironically, the plans designed by this independent body had originated inside Republican circles and in the end resulted in more minority elected officials and a two-third Democrat majority in both houses of the legislature. This last redistricting episode demonstrates again that partisan calculations always have racial implications. Democrats reached their largest majorities as the legislative body and the congressional delegation become the most diverse in the state's history.

Chapter 9 explores how redistricting has evolved over the past half-century and how conjoined polarization has changed California redistricting. Today, racial, partisan, and ideological interests have aligned to the point that any increase in minority representation is now synonymous with increases in Democratic majority. In a majority-minority state, conjoined polarization means that it has become extremely difficult to differentiate Republican partisan opposition from racial antagonism when one can be used as a proxy for the other. In its modern form redistricting is as much about racial representation as it is about partisan representation. They need to be considered together as part of the same representative democracy paradigm. This is the conundrum that California redistricting commissioners will have to deal with in 2021.

NOTES

1. Even though those terms tended to be used synonymously in American political science I will distinguish redistricting from (re)apportionment: the calculation of how many representatives any administrative unit will be entitled to elect.

2. Richard L. Hasen, "Race or Party, Race as Party, or Party All the Time: Three Uneasy Approaches to Conjoined Polarization in Redistricting and Voting Cases," *William and Mary Law Review* 59 (2018): 1837.

3. John Adams, *Thoughts on Government*, Paper 4, April 1776. http://press-pubs.uchicago.edu/founders/documents/v1ch4s5.html.

4. Andrew Reynolds identifies thirty-two of them. Reynolds, "Reserved Seats in National Legislatures: A Comparative Approach," in *Redistricting in Comparative Perspective*, edited by Lisa Handley and Bernard Grofman (Oxford University Press, 2008), 117.

5. John D. Skrentny, *The Minority Rights Revolution* (Cambridge, MA: Harvard University Press, 2002).

6. The Fifteenth Amendment states that the "right of citizens of the United States to vote shall not be denied or abridged by the United States or by any State on account

of race, color, or previous condition of servitude." It also gives Congress the power to "enforce this article by appropriate legislation."

7. Charles S. Bullock III, *Redistricting: The Most Political Activity in America* (Lanham, MD: Rowman & Littlefield, 2010).

8. Eric Shickler, *Racial Realignment: The Transformation of American Liberalism, 1932–1965* (Princeton, NJ: Princeton University Press, 2016).

9. According to Hanna Pitkin's definition, descriptive representation is concerned with representing the identity of a voter, while substantive representation is concerned with representing the interests of a voter. Hanna Fenichel Pitkin, *The Concept of Representation* (University of California Press, 1967), chapter 4.

10. For recent comprehensive figures about racial polarization in the US, see Stephen Ansolabehere, Nathaniel Persily, and Charles Stewart III, "Regional Differences in Racial Polarization in the 2012 Presidential Election: Implications for the Constitutionality of Section 5 of the Voting Rights Act," *Harvard Law Review Forum* 126 (2013): 205–20.

11. Richard H. Pildes, "Voting Rights The Next Generation," in *Race, Reform and Regulation of the Electoral Process*, edited by Guy-Uriel E. Charles, Heather Gerken, and Michael Kang (Cambridge, MA: Cambridge University Press), 30.

12. Richard L. Hasen, "Racial Gerrymandering's Questionable Revival," *Alabama Law Review* 67 (2016): 365.

13. "Election Polls: Vote by Groups, 1960–1964," Gallup, accessed September, 21 2018, http://www.gallup.com/poll/9454/election-polls-vote-groups-19601964.aspx.

14. James E. Campbell, *Polarized: Making Sense of a Divided America* (Princeton, NJ: Princeton University Press, 2016); James A. Thurber, and Antoine Yoshinaka, eds., *American Gridlocked: The Sources, Character, Impact of Political Polarization* (Cambridge: Cambridge University Press, 2016).

15. Bruce Cain, "Moving Past Section 5: More Fingers or a New Dike," *Election Law Journal* 13, no. 2 (2013): 338–40.

16. Bruce E. Cain and Emily R. Zhang, "Blurred Lines: Conjoined Polarization and Voting Rights," *Ohio State Law Journal* 77, no. 4 (2016): 867–904.

17. For an exception, see for instance example Richard L. Engstrom, "Race and Southern Politics: The Special Case of Congressional Districting," in *Writing Southern Politics: Contemporary Interpretations and Future Directions*, edited by Robert P. Steed and Laurence W. Moreland (Lexington: University of Kentucky Press, 2006), 110; Kenneth W. Shotts, "The Effect of Majority-Minority Mandates on Partisan Gerrymandering," *American Journal of Political Science* 45 (2001): 121; Adam B. Cox and Richard T. Holden, "Reconsidering Racial and Partisan Gerrymandering," *The University of Chicago Law Review* 78, no. 2 (Spring 2011): 553–604.

18. See for instance David T. Canon, *Race, Redistricting, and Representation: The Unintended Consequences of Black Majority Districts* (Chicago, IL: University of Chicago Press, 1999); David Lublin, *The Paradox of Representation: Racial Gerrymandering and Minority Interests in Congress* (Princeton, NJ: Princeton University Press, 1997); Carol M. Swain, *Black Faces, Black Interests: The Representation of African Americans in Congress* (Cambridge, MA: Harvard University Press, 1993); Kimball Brace, Bernard Grofman, and Lisa Handley, "Does Redistricting Aimed to

Help Blacks Necessarily Help Republicans?," *Journal of Politics* 49 (1987): 183; Daniel D. Polsby and Robert D. Popper, "Ugly: An Inquiry into the Problem of Racial Gerrymandering under the Voting Rights Act," *Michigan Law Review* 92 (1993): 682: Charles Cameron, David Epstein, and Sharyn O' Halloran, "Do Majority-Minority Districts Maximize Substantive Black Representation in Congress?" *American Political Science Review* 90 (1996): 794–95; David L. Epstein and Sharyn O' Halloran, "Trends in Minority Representation, 1974 to 2000," in *The Future of the Voting Rights Act*, edited by David L. Epstein et al. (New York: Russell Sage 2006), 77; Kevin A. Hill, "Does the Creation of Majority Black Districts Aid Republicans? An Analysis of the 1992 Congressional Elections in Eight Southern States," *Journal of Politics* 57 (1995): 384; David Lublin and D. Stephen Voss, "Racial Redistricting and Realignment in Southern State Legislatures," *American Journal of Political Science* 44 (2000): 793.

19. "In other words, both Texas and Georgia show that Democrats enforce voting rights differently from Republicans. Often this means that Democrats enforce voting rights more expansively and aggressively than do Republicans, but as Georgia shows, not always. More consistently, Democrats enforce voting rights in ways that tend to advance Democratic interests while Republican-led enforcement tends to produce benefits for Republicans." Ellen D. Katz, "Democrats at DOJ: Why Partisan Use of the Voting Rights Act Might Not Be So Bad After All," *Stanford Law and Policy Review* 23 (2012): 417.

20. Nathaniel Persily, "The Promises and Pitfalls of the the New VRA," *Yale Law Journal* 117 (2007): 174–253.

21. Morgan Kousser, *Colorblind Injustice: Minority Voting Rights and the Undoing of the Second Reconstruction* (Chapel Hill, NC: North Carolina Press, 1999); Richard Vallely, *The Two Reconstructions: The Struggle for Black Enfranchisement* (Chicago, IL: University of Chicago Press, 2004).

22. For a more detailed discussion of the Voting Rights Act see for example David L. Epstein, Richard H. Pildes, Rodolfo the Garza, and Sharyn O' Hallaran, eds., *The Future of the Voting Rights Act* (New York: Russell Sage 2006); Daniel McCool, ed., *The Most Fundamental Right: Contrasting Perspectives on the Voting Rights Act*, (Bloomington: Indiana Press University, 2012).

23. Voting Rights Act of 1965 § 4(c).

24. Voting Rights Act Amendments of 1970, Pub.L. No. 91–285, 84 Stat. 314 (1970).

25. I use the expression ethno-racial to emphasize the conflation of race and ethnicity as in David Hollinger's expression the "ethno-racial pentagon." David Hollinger, *Postethnic America: Beyond Multiculturalism* (New York: Basic Books, 1995).

26. According to Section 301 of the 1975 amendments, any state or political subdivision that met the following criteria had to provide language assistance during elections: more than 5 percent of the eligible voter population was members of a language minority group and the illiteracy rate for this language minority group had to be higher than the national illiteracy rate. Illiteracy was defined as the failure to complete the fifth grade. See id. § 203(b) (ii). These language assistance provisions

were to be in effect for a period of ten years—until August 6, 1985. See id. § 203(b). For more information see the very comprehensive James Thomas Tucker, *The Battle over Bilingual Ballot: Language Minorities and Political Access under the Voting Rights Act* (Burlington, VT: Ashgate, 2009).

27. According to the census, 43 percent of California residents speak another language than English at home. The top five languages spoken are Spanish, Chinese, Tagalog, Vietnamese, and Korean.

28. In 2016 the entire state of California was covered for the Latino language minority and eleven counties were covered for one or several language minorities. https://www.gpo.gov/fdsys/pkg/FR-2016-12-05/pdf/2016-28969.pdf.

29. *City of Mobile v. Bolden*, 446 US 55, 60–62, 66–67 (1980).

30. Voting Rights Act Amendments of 1982, Pub.L. No. 97–205, 96 Stat. 131 (1982).

31. Senate Report No. 97-417 (1982), 28. In *Thornburg v. Gingles*, 478 US 30 (1986) the Supreme Court further refined Section 2 in a case involving a challenge to multimember and single-member legislative districts in North Carolina. The majority opinion established a three-pronged test to analyze vote dilution claims in parallel to the "totality of circumstances" test. First, the minority group must be "sufficiently large and geographically compact to constitute a majority of a single member district." Second, the minority group must be "politically cohesive." And third, the "white majority votes sufficiently as a bloc" to enable it to "usually defeat the minority's preferred candidate," *Thornburg v. Gingles*, 50–51. The precise definition of these new concepts (geographical compactness, political cohesion, candidate of choice, racial bloc voting) was not given by the Court.

32. Under the formula, a jurisdiction is subject to the language assistance provisions if the following criteria are met: (1) 5 percent of the voting-age population or 10,000 voting-age citizens must consist of members of a single language minority group; (2) the members of this single language minority group must be of limited English proficiency; 48 (3) for those political jurisdictions that contain all or part of an Indian reservation, more than 5 percent of the total number of eligible voters within the Indian reservation must be eligible voters of a single language minority group who are of limited English proficiency; and (4) "the illiteracy rate of the citizens in the language minority as a group [must be] higher than the national illiteracy rate."

33. *Beer v. US*, 425 US 130 (1976).

34. James Thomas Tucker, "The Politics of Persuasion: Passage of the Voting Rights Act reauthorization Act of 2006," *Journal of Legislation* 33, no. 2 (2007): 205–67; Persily, "The Promises and Pitfalls."

35. One can take Merced County as an example. In 1975 when Merced County became subject to its provisions, a jurisdiction was covered if (1) certain voting practices (i.e., literacy tests and use of all-English ballot materials where the jurisdiction had more than 5 percent of the population speaking another language as their primary language) were in use within the jurisdiction on November 1, 1972, and (2) less than 50 percent of eligible voters were registered or voted for president during the November 1972 election. County officials argued that the County met the first prong of the test (i.e., use of a literacy test and all-English ballot materials)

because those voting practices were prescribed by California State law, not County policy. And according to opponents of Section 5, the second prong was met as a result of methodological errors by the Census Bureau because a large military population on Castle Air Force Base was treated as eligible to vote in Merced County, even though most of them voted absentee in their home counties. Even with those exceptional factors, Merced County just barely missed the 50 percent turnout mark; 49.6 percent of eligible voters voted in November 1972. The argument is that if the precincts that covered Castle AFB had been excluded, well over 50 percent of eligible voters voted.

36. The states of Alabama, Georgia, Louisiana, Mississippi, South Carolina, and Virginia were covered in their entirety, along with 40 counties in North Carolina.

37. Lisa Handley and Bernard Grofman, "The Impact of the Voting Rights Act on Minority Representation: Black Officeholders in Southern State Legislatures and Congressional Delegations," in *Quite Revolution in the South*, edited by Chandler Davidson and Bernard Grofman (Princeton, NJ: Princeton University Press, 1994), 335–50.

38. Bernard Grofman, Lisa Handley, and Richard G. Niemi, *Minority Representation and the Quest for Voting Equality* (New York: Cambridge University Press, 1992), 22.

39. "Black Elected Officials by Office, 1970 to 2002, and State, 2002," US Census Bureau, Statistical Abstract of the US 2011, table 413, p. 258, http://www2.census.gov/library/publications/2010/compendia/statab/130ed/tables/11s0413.pdf.

40. The 1990 numbers cited by Luis Ricardo Fraga and Sharon A. Navarro, "Latinos in Latino Politics," in *Latino Politics: Identity, Mobilization and Representation*, edited by Roldfo Espino, David L. Leal, and Kenneth J. Meier (Charlottesville, VA: University Press of Virginia, 2007), 180. 2004 and 2014 tables available on the NALEO webpage: http://www.naleo.org/at_a_glance.

41. Don T. Nkanishi and James Lai, eds., *National Asian Pacific Political Almanac*, 15th ed. (Los Angeles: UCLA Asian American Studies Center Press, 2014).

42. Anna Brown and Sara Atske, "Blacks have made gains in US political leadership, but gaps remain," Pew Research Center, June 28, 2016, http://www.pewresearch.org/fact-tank/2016/06/28/blacks-have-made-gains-in-u-s-political-leadership-but-gaps-remain/.

43. Republicans Susana Martinez in New Mexico, Brian Sandoval in Nevada, Nikki Halley in South Carolina (has since resigned), and Democrat David Ige in Hawaii.

44. The African Americans were Tim Scott, R-South Carolina (when he was first appointed to replace Jim DeMint he became the first African American senator in South Carolina history); William Cowan, D-Massachusetts, Cory Booker, D-New Jersey (first African American senator in the history of New Jersey); Kamala Harris, D-California (Harris could count as African American and Asian). The Asians were Mazie Hirono, D-Hawaii (first Asian American woman elected to the Senate); and Tammy Duckworth, D-Illinois (first Asian American congresswoman in the state's history). The Latinos were Robert Menendez, D-New Jersey; Marco Rubio, R-Flor-

ida; Ted Cruz, R-Texas; and Catherine Cortez Masto, D-Nevada (first Latina elected to serve in the US Senate).

45. Before the 2016 elections there were 2 African Americans, 1 Asian American, and 3 Latinos. That represents a 40 percent jump in one election cycle.

46. These figures include California Senator Kamala Harris as both Asian and African American and Representative Adriano Espaillat (D-NY) as both Latino and African American.

47. Kristen Bialik and Jens Manuel Krogstad, "115th Congress sets new high for racial, ethnic diversity," Pew Research Center, January 24, 2017, http://www.pewresearch.org/fact-tank/2017/01/24/115th-congress-sets-new-high-for-racial-ethnic-diversity/.

48. Cameron, Epstein, and O' Halloran, "Do Majority-Minority Districts"; Canon, *Race, Redistricting, and Representation.*

49. For a comparative approach see Bernard Grofman and Lisa Handley, eds., *Redistricting in Comparative Perspective* (Oxford University Press, 2008).

50. David Butler and Bruce E. Cain, *Congressional Redistricting: Comparative and Theoretical Perspectives* (New York: Macmillan, 1992), 118.

51. Lani Guinier, *The Tyranny of the Majority: Fundamental Fairness in Representative Democracy* (New York: Free Press, 1994); Douglas J. Amy, *Real Choices/New Voices: How Proportional Representation Elections Could Revitalize American Democracy*, 2nd ed. (New York: Columbia University Press, 2002); Mark Rush and Richard Engstrom, *Fair and Effective Representation: Debating Electoral Reform and Minority Rights* (Rowman & Littlefield, 2001); Shaun Bowler, Todd Donovan, and David Brockington, *Electoral Reform and Minority Representation: Local Experiments with Alternative Elections* (Columbus: Ohio State University Press, 2003).

52. This norm of ethno-racial proportionality can also be found in affirmative action jurisprudence and almost every time judges are asked to define what would be the proof of an absence of discrimination.

53. Morgan Kousser, "Redistricting Wars: Party, Race and Redistricting in California 1971–1992," in *Race and Redistricting in the 1990s*, edited by Bernard Grofman (New York: Agathon Press, 1998).

54. T. Alexander Aleinikoff and Samuel Issacharoff, "Race and Redistricting: Drawing Constitutional Lines after *Shaw v. Reno*," *Michigan Law Review* 92 (1993): 588.

55. Butler and Cain, *Congressional Redistricting*, 3.

56. In many countries there is no residence requirement to run locally or nationally. The residence requirement in the US accentuates the incumbent effect in redistricting. In other countries when a district changes dramatically, an elected official simply finds another district more suited to his positions to run in.

57. *Colgrove v. Green*, 328 US 549 (1946). In this case Illinois congressional district lines had not changed since 1901. Vote dilution is defined by Dick Engstrom as "the practice of reducing the potential effectiveness of a group's strength by limiting its ability to translate that strength into the control of (or at least influence with) elected public officials." Richard Engstrom, "Racial Discrimination in the Electoral Process: The Voting Rights Act and the Vote Dilution Issue," in *Party Politics in*

the South, edited by Robert Steed, Laurence Moreland, and Ted Baker (New York: Praeger, 1980), 197.

58. *Gomillion v. Lightfoot*, 364 US 339 (1960). The Alabama legislature transformed the squarish district of Tuskegee into a 28-sided polygon in order to remove most African Americans.

59. *Baker v. Carr*, 369 US 186 (1962). Like in *Colgrove* the Tennessee state legislature districts had not been redrawn since 1901.

60. For a more detailed account see for instance Stephen Ansolabehere, James M. Snyder, *The End of Inequality: One Person, One Vote and the Transformation of American Politics* (New York: W.W. Norton & Company, 2008).

61. Preclearance did not apply to redistricting at first. The Department of Justice became more proactive after the 1969 decision *Allen v. State Board of Elections*, 393 US 544 (1969). In *Beer v. United States* 425 US 130 (1976) the Supreme Court held that Section 5 prohibited only retrogression. As long as the new districts did not leave African Americans voters worse off than the status quo, the DOJ must approve the proposal. *Beer* established that Section 5 did not create an obligation to maximize the political influence of racial minorities.

62. Congress amended the VRA after a 1980 Supreme Court decision, *Mobile v. Bolden*, 446 US 55, in which the Court argued that electoral districts, in the case at-large districts in the city of Mobile, Alabama, were unconstitutional if they were drawn with racially discriminatory intent. Because Congress thought *intent* was too difficult to prove, it instead focused on *effect*.

63. For a more in-depth discussion of the vote dilution see Heather Gerken, "Understanding the Right to an Undiluted Vote," *Harvard Law Review* 114, no. 6 (2001): 1663–743.

64. Richard Hasen, *The Supreme Court and Election Law: Judging Equality from Baker v. Carr to Bush v. Gore* (New York: New York University Press, 2003). In this book, Rick Hasen criticizes the structuralist approach sometimes known as "politics as markets" in election law scholarship. He argues that judges are political and should not be trusted to be election regulators. For a discussion of the institutionalist approach to election law, see Heather K. Gerken and Michael S. Kang, "The Institutional Turn in Election Law Scholarship," in *Race, Reform, and Regulation of the Electoral Process*, edited by Guy-Uriel E. Charles, Heather K. Gerken, and Michael S. Kang (Cambridge: Cambridge University Press, 2011), 86–100.

65. In *Karcher v. Daggett*, 462 US 725 (1983) the Supreme Court rejected a New Jersey congressional redistricting plan that had a total population deviation of 0.7 percent.

66. In 1986, the Court held that partisan gerrymandering claims are justiciable under the Constitution, but the justices disagreed about how to identify unconstitutional partisan gerrymanders. *Davis v. Bandemer*, 478 US 109 (1986). Since then, a majority of the Court has repeatedly declined to overturn Bandemer yet it has rejected every allegation of unconstitutional partisan gerrymandering that has come before it. *Vieth v. Jubelirer*, 541 US 267 (2004); *League of United Latin American Citizens v. Perry*, 548 US 399 (2006).

67. Pamela S. Karlan and Daryl J. Levinson, "Why Voting Is Different," *California Law Review* 84, no. 4 (1996): 1202.

68. The *Shaw* jurisprudence and its progeny, with their emphasis on individual rights v. competing state interest doctrine, was instrumental in the creation of election law as a distinct field from constitutional law.

69. On the justiciability of partisan gerrymandering since *Vieth* see for example Anthony J. McGann, Charles Anthony Smith, Michael Latner, and Alex Keena, *Gerrymandering in America: The House of Representatives, the Supreme Court and the Future of Popular Sovereignty* (Cambridge: Cambridge University Press, 2016); Nicolas R. Seabrook, *Drawing the Lines: Constraints on Partisan Gerrymandering in US Politics* (Ithaca, NY: Cornell University Press, 2017).

70. Cain and Zhang, "Blurred Lines," 886.

71. At the time of the writing of this book the most recent examples were *Bethun-Hill v. Virginia Board of Election*, 580_US (2017) and *McCrory v. Harris*, 581 US (2017). Distinguishing race from partisanship in these two southern cases is close to impossible but since partisan gerrymandering has been allowed so far, race is a more viable alternative. In the case of North Carolina, Republicans even claimed that the redistricting of the now notorious NC-12 was not about race, but was drawn to maximize the number of Republicans in Congress.

72. Gary W. Cox, *Elbridge Gerry's Salamander: The Electoral Consequences of the Apportionment Revolution* (Cambridge: Cambridge University Press, 2002), 210–11.

73. What is striking about the equal population in the US is that it is much more rigorous than in any other nation. Usually other nation redistricting processes allow much greater deviation. US redistricting is at the same time stricter and more politicized. Redistricting in other countries is usually more relaxed statistically and less politicized. Butler and Cain, *Congressional Redistricting*, 128.

74. Richard Hasen, "Race or Party: How Courts Should Think about Republican Efforts to Make It Harder to Vote in North Carolina and Elsewhere," *Harvard Law Review Forum* 127 (2014): 58–75.

75. For a discussion of these different approaches and the tension between election law and constitutional law see for instance Guy-Uriel Charles, "Judging the Law of Politics," *Michigan Law Review* 103 (2005): 1099–141; Heather Gerken, "Keynote Address: What Election Law Has to Say to Constitutional Law," *Indiana Law Review* 44 (2010): 7–22; Joseph Fishkin, "Equal Citizenship and the Equal Right to Vote," *Indiana Law Journal* 86 (June 2011): 1289–360.

76. As Morgan Kousser argued in his seminal 1998 article "Reapportionment Wars: Race, Party and Redistricting in California 1971–1992," in *Race and Redistricting in the 1990s*, edited by Bernard Grofman (New York: Agathon Press), 134–90.

77. Samuel, Issacharoff, "Supreme Court Destabilization of Single-Member Districts," *University of Chicago Legal Forum* 1 (1995): 238–39.

78. Seth McKee ed., *Jigzaw Puzzle Politics in the Sunshine State* (Gainesville: University of Florida Press, 2015) is excellent but focuses on the 2011 round of redistricting. Jonathan Winburn's *The Realities of Redistricting: Following the Rules*

and Limiting Gerrymandering in State Legislatures (Lanham, MD: Lexington, 2009) focuses on several Midwest state legislatures and the technicality of the redistricting process.

79. Danny Hayes and Seth C. McKee, "The Intersection of Redistricting, Race, and Participation," *American Journal of Political Science* 56, no. 1 (January 2012): 115–30.

80. James Blacksher and LaniGuinier, "Free at Last: Rejecting Equal Sovereignty and Restoring the Constitutional Right to Vote *Shelby County v. Holder*," *Harvard Law and Policy Review* 8 (Winter 2014): 39; Daniel P. Tokaji, "Responding to Shelby County: A Grand Election Bargain," *Harvard Law and Policy Review* 8 (Winter 2014): 71; Jon Greenbaum, Alan Martinson, and Sonia Gill," *Shelby County v. Holder*: When the Rational Becomes Irrational," *Howard Law Journal* 57 (Spring 2014): 811; Richard L. Hasen, "Shelby County and the Illusion of Minimalism," *William and Mary Bill of Rights Journal* 22 (2014): 713.

81. For a book dealing specifically with redistricting in the West, see Gary F. Moncrief, *Reapportionment and Redistricting in the West* (Lanham, MD: Lexington, 2011).

82. And it has been for a long time as Bruce Cain already observed in 1991 "there has always been a constant measurable racial and ethnic component to political alignments in the US and California since the 1840s." Bruce Cain, "The Contemporary Context of Ethnic and Racial Politics in California," in *Racial and Ethnic Politics in California*, edited by Byran O. Jackson and Michael B. Preston (Berkeley, CA: IGS Press, 1991), 10.

83. The most famous counter example is probably the New Hampshire House of Representative that has 400 members (each representing about 3,000 people) with an annual salary for legislators of $100. But even in Texas, the second largest state in the Union where state senators represent almost 900,000 people, state legislators make $600 per month, or $7,200 per year, plus a per diem of $190 for every day the legislature is in session.

84. If one compares to other large states: Texas (27 million people) has 31 senators and 150 Assembly members; New York's Senate number varies but is currently at 63 with 150 Assembly members for a 20 million population; Florida (also about 20 million people) has 40 senators and 120 Assembly members.

85. In Texas, New York and Florida state senators and Assembly members are elected for two years.

86. Eric McGee and Jack Citrin, "Introduction: Democracy, California Style," *Journal of California Politics and Policy* 9, no. 2 (2017).

Chapter 1

"One Person, One Vote"

How Minorities Benefitted from the End of Malapportionment

Symbolically speaking 1965 is a convenient starting point for any study on redistricting and voting rights because of the passage of the Voting Rights Act. However, the law did not have a concrete impact on redistricting until 1971. Yet 1965 remains pertinent here for two reasons. First, the passage of the Civil Rights Act of 1964 and Voting Rights Act of 1965 changes the national partisan context as it precipitated party realignment. As the Democratic Party became the party of racial equality, the Republican Party became the party of social conservatives. This is still very much the paradigm of American politics today. Second, in 1965 the California legislature was forced by the courts to redraw district lines to abide by the new "equal population" standard set by the *Baker v. Carr* jurisprudence and its progeny. Before Section 2 or Section 5 could take effect, "equal population" had tremendous consequences for minorities in California (and in other states). The intervention of the courts put an end to malapportionment in California and started what can be considered as the modern era of redistricting. Malapportionment favored sparsely populated rural areas by giving them a number of representatives greater than their districts' share of the state's population. "Equal population" corrected this bias and gave metropolitan areas an electoral weight proportional to the number of their residents. The strict "equal population" standard directly limited the legislature's attempt to protect incumbents or gain partisan advantage. And as an indirect consequence it helped ethno-racial minorities get better political representation. Since minorities, especially African Americans, were concentrated in urban centers they finally were able to make their voice heard at the ballots box. Because of the high rate of residential segregation, some urban areas concentrated so many minorities that candidates had no choice but to take their vote into consideration. For the first time, some districts were able to elect minority candidates, mostly African Americans. As Latino populations increased in metropolitan areas, they also soon benefitted from this new redistricting legal standard. "Equal population" was therefore responsible for the first wave of post–civil rights movement minority elected officials in the legislature. This was key in increasing diversity in the legislature as minority elected officials later intended in the 1970s and 1980s to influence the redistricting process to protect minority communities' political representation.

UNCONSTITUTIONALITY OF THE "LITTLE FEDERAL PLAN"

The history of redistricting in California was never a simple one and the courts regularly had to intervene.[1] Between 1920 and 1965 the battle between the rural and urban parts of the state to obtain an equitable political representation led to many conflicts and in wasn't until the Supreme Court ventured into the "political thicket" that urban areas were finally in a position to receive political representation proportional to their population.[2] Before the Supreme Court's intervention the fight over agenda control in the legislature was first and foremost between legislators representing geographical interests: rural versus urban and northern versus southern.

Like most of the western states California has a water problem. But this problem is hardly new. The northern part of the state receives almost all of the rainfall but the southern part of the state is where a big part of the population lives. As Los Angeles grew so did the political divide between the north and the south. Northerners wanted protection against abuses form the ever insatiable south in the form of a veto power over any water plan. From statehood in 1849 to 1920, demography was on the side of northerners since the majority of people lived in the north. However, in 1920, the census indicated that almost half of the state population was now living in the south. The northern political hegemony was doomed. Rural Californians, northern farmers, and people in the Bay Area were not ready to abandon water policy to southern city bosses. Political forces of the north coalesced around the idea of redistricting one house of the legislature not according to population anymore but according to geography, as was the case in the Federal Senate. The rational was that California was therefore simply following the federal model and that this was a balanced solution between two conflicting interests as was the case with big states and small states representation in the United States Congress. Besides, it would guarantee that corrupt southern machine politics would not control the state. The Farm Bureau Federation and the *Los*

Angeles Times were quite vocal about their fear of concentrating more voting power in cities and their "labor bosses."[3] This argument seemed to resonate with voters since the measure was defeated. It was then decided that the California Senate would get redistricted according to counties, since 50 of the 58 counties were in the north, northerners would have control over one house no matter how much or how fast southern population grew. The Assembly would still be apportioned according to population and the governor would still be elected by popular vote but the Senate districts would be based on counties and the north would therefore have *de facto* a veto power over any water plan. This "Federal Plan" provided that no county should have more than one state senator and that no more than 3 counties could go into one senate district. Los Angeles, with a population of one million people at the time, received one senator and, at the same time, 3 small counties containing 11,000 people also received 1 senator. The majority of the population in the state lived in 3 counties (Los Angeles, Alameda, and San Francisco) but only elected 3 senators while the minority of the state population elected the other 37 state senators.[4] The constitutional provision was adopted in 1926. It employed a "little federal" plan under which the California Senate was apportioned geographically and the Assembly on a modified population basis and it survived a referendum as early as 1928. It went into effect in 1931. The result of this reform was very consequential especially when one takes into account the two-third budget vote requirement. The growth of the disparities over the years is one controversial aspect. In 1931 the ratio of disparity was 279 to 1, in 1941, 280 to 1; in 1951, 301 to 1; and by 1961, 423 to 1. The second controversial aspect is that with a two-third budget vote, technically, one-third of all senators, representing but 5 percent of the population, could potentially derail legislation entirely or at least leverage significant concessions.[5] Robert Dixon describes the political dynamic of the state thusly:

> Reapportionment matters moved slowly in California and the state was represented in neither the "big six" reapportionment cases of June 1964 nor in the additional package of cases from nine states decided contemporaneously with short per curiam orders. Loose party alignments contributed to the blurring of reapportionment a clear-cut partisan issue in California. The California Senate tended to be dominated by rural senators, but in significant numbers their allegiance was Democratic. The most instrumental issue in California politics year in and year out, on which so much else depended, was the position and power of Los Angeles. It was Democratic-dominated, not closely attuned to the northern Democrats either rural or urban, and adjacent to Republican or conservative Democratic suburbs.[6]

Another effort to do away with this egregious redistricting occurred in 1948 with Proposition 13.[7] Los Angeles counted several million people and still had only one senator. Nonetheless Californians seemed satisfied to have a Senate controlled by rural interests, more conservative and stable, and less partisan than the Assembly. Proposition 13 was sponsored by the state labor federation, but forcefully opposed by the Chamber of Commerce.[8] Proponents of the proposition called it crucial to democracy, but opponents said it was a power grab by the big cities and liberal special interests, Republican Governor Warren, an ally of business interest, sided with the Chamber of Commerce and urged the people to not vote for an urban-dominated Senate. On October 29, 1948, Governor Warren declared: "Any weakening of these laws would incite a return of boss rule which we are happily rid of. Our state has made almost unbelievable progress under our present system of legislative apportionment. I believe we should keep it. . . . It is for this reason I have never been in favor of redistricting their representation in the State Senate to a strictly population basis."[9] A total of 2.2 million people voted against Proposition 13 and only one million for it. Only one county voted for the measure. Ironically, the proposition was defeated even in Los Angeles County even though it had so much to gain. Carey McWilliams described the episode as "the amazing spectacle of a people approving their own disenfranchisement."[10] In 1960 and 1962 Los Angeles County Supervisor Franck Bonelli launched referendums to try to fix the disparities. Proposition 15, in 1960, intended to reform the senate redistricting system but lost, as did the rather moderate Proposition 23 in 1962 even though both gubernatorial candidates, Pat Brown and Richard Nixon, backed the referendum.[11] In March 1962, Assembly Speaker Jesse Unruh had also introduced a constitutional amendment to make modest changes to the federal plan by increasing Los Angeles County's senate delegation from one to four. Unruh was able to push his proposal through the assembly swiftly but it died in the Senate. It wasn't until the Supreme Court intervened, with Earl Warren as Chief Justice, that California would go through its redistricting reform.

Until then, the courts were reluctant to hear cases on apportionment because these were political questions. That is why Justice Frankfurter dissented so vehemently against entering the "political thicket." However, in 1960, the discrepancy in California was such that the smallest district was 422 times less populated than the largest one. Some were more legitimate than others since some were mandated by constitution provisions and some were more the result of political calculation on the part of map drawers who very often hid their partisan intentions behind these constitutional provisions.[12] Differentiating between the two requires intimate knowledge of state politics and the redistricting process.

This discrepancy between rural and urban areas was therefore also a source of racial inequalities since racial minorities lived largely in metropolitan areas. Many Mexicans lived in rural areas as farm workers until 1964 and the end of the bracero program.[13] After 1964 many had to move to major cities to find other types of jobs just as Anglo residents moved to the newly created suburbs. The intervention of the Court helped urban areas to increase their political representation and therefore indirectly helped racial minorities to be represented and to be elected.[14] In 1962, the Supreme Court of the United States held in *Baker v. Carr* that claims of malapportionment brought under the Equal Protection Clause of the Fourteenth Amendment were justiciable.[15] This led to a series of cases where courts began exercising judicial authority over legislative reapportionment. The most notable cases were *Gray v. Sanders*, which established the "one person, one vote" rule,[16] *Wesberry v. Sanders*, which held that "as nearly as is practicable, one person's vote in a Congressional election is to be worth as much as another's,"[17] and *Reynolds v. Sims*, which held that "the Equal Protection Clause requires that the seats in both houses of a bicameral state legislature must be apportioned on a population basis."[18] The California Senate would therefore require a reapportionment of unprecedented proportions.

1965: FOCUS ON THE SENATE

The senate's apportionment method became clearly unconstitutional after the *Reynolds* decision.[19] After *Baker v. Carr*, Los Angeles lawyer Phil Silver filed a lawsuit against Secretary of State Frank M. Jordan in 1962 to try and force redistricting of the State Senate but he was unsuccessful. The court denied any injunctive relief at that time, as there was then available to the plaintiff a state remedy, namely, the Initiative Measure on the 1962 General Election Ballot, Proposition 23, which, if passed, would have reapportioned the State Senate. Also, Los Angeles Mayor Yorty and Supervisor Bonelli filed a suit against Lieutenant Governor Glenn Anderson, chairman of the Reapportionment Commission. The Supreme Court, in 1963, in *Yorty v. Anderson*, declared that the legislature in 1961 had altered the Assembly but had chosen to retain the Senate districts.[20] The case was determined on a non-federal question, i.e., the plaintiff had misjoined the wrong party as defendant. The proper party defendant should have been the Secretary of State, not the members of the Reapportionment Commission, which had no jurisdiction to reapportion the legislature, unless the legislature failed to act, which it had not. As a consequence, there was no need for the Commission to act. Then, Yorty and Bonelli sought a writ of mandate from the Supreme Court of the

State of California to compel a reapportionment of the Senate of Legislature of the State of California on a population basis. The Supreme Court rejected their claim in 1964 for want of jurisdiction.[21] *Wesberry* and *Reynolds* opened another legal avenue to Silver, Bonelli, and Yorty in their quest to reapportion the California Senate.

The California legislature considered several ways to try and circumvent the court's decision, but in the end had to comply. The Court's decisions caused real political problems for the California legislatures and its members. The Senate was going to be forced to redistrict while some 27 senators represented districts that did not have enough inhabitants. Los Angeles County, as we mentioned before, only had one senator while its population required fifteen. This was akin to mass political suicide for Hugh Burn's Senate. And, all of a sudden, fourteen assembly members potentially would have a chance to move up to the Senate in an open seat. Democrat Governor Pat Brown hired a reapportionment consultant to help with the complex overhaul of the Senate districts. Jesse Unruh, the speaker of the Assembly who was from Los Angeles (D-Inglewood), wanted the Assembly to play an important role in the redistricting of the Senate. Senator Stephen Steal who was one of the rural senators (D-West Point) and chaired the Senate Reapportionment Committee responded that only Senators would redistrict the Senate but, of course, most of them hoped it could be avoided. However, on December 3, 1964, a federal district court ordered the legislature to reapportion the Senate on a population basis before July 1, 1965 (*Silver v. Jordan*, 241 F. Supp. 576, S.D. Cal. 1965).[22] Thus a forty-year controversy was coming to an end.[23] The Senate acquiesced after a two-day strategy session.[24] But members of the upper house still floated several ideas to try and avoid redistricting the Senate. The California County Supervisors Association and Senator Richard J. Dolwig (R-Redwood) came up with an alternative: splitting California in two at the Tehachapi Mountains![25] Some proposed creating two Senate districts of equal population with twenty senators in each elected at-large. Others, among which prominent Democrats such as state senator from Los Angeles Thomas M. Rees, Assembly Speaker Jesse Unruh (also from Los Angeles), or even Governor "Pat" Brown, wanted California to support Illinois Republican Senator Everett Dirken's effort in introducing a federal constitutional amendment allowing a state legislature to have districts based on geography.[26] The GOP senator was pushing his amendment just after the nation witnessed the election of ten African American candidates to the Georgia state legislature as a result of the Supreme Court redistricting ruling. Denying equal population representation meant denying minorities, especially African Americans at the time, not to mention urban residents of all ancestry, access to public office. California State Senator Paul Lunardi (D-Roseville), on the wrong side of history, introduced a joint resolution requesting Congress to impose a two-year moratorium on federal court orders requiring reapportionment of state legislatures.[27] Assemblymember Don A. Allen Sr., Chairman of the Elections and Reapportionment Committee in 1965, rationalized the State Senate refusal to compromise on apportionment because many senators felt that to do so would constitute a "stab in the back" for those working for the Dirksen Amendment in Washington.[28] But with the Congress unwilling to pass the Dirksen Amendment (it fell 7 votes short in the Federal Senate),[29] some state senators supported efforts to call a constitutional convention on the issue. They passed two resolutions in the Senate forcefully denounced by Assembly Speaker Jesse Unruh because they would "condone the racist-based" legislatures of the southern states.[30] However, as symbolically important as these proposals were, these desperate tactics only amounted to postponing the inevitable. Under court pressure and without a viable alternative, the Senate came up with his first redistricting plan, keeping a slight majority of seats in the north and giving Los Angeles County and its 7 million residents only 12 seats and not the 15 to which it was entitled. The twelve senators would have run at-large within the boundaries of the county.[31] Such an arrangement was unacceptable for the Assembly which introduced its own bill indicating it intended to play a role in shaping the Senate. According to Tony Quinn, the California and Senate Assembly in 1965 differed greatly in style of politics:

> Since the 1950s the Assembly had been a partisan body, and it had gone through two highly partisan reapportionments. Assemblymen were younger, more aggressive, and much more partisan than the more casual Senate, which viewed itself as something of a men's club (there had never been a woman senator), a collegial debating society where passions were restrained and where personal relationships determined legislative success. . . . The Senate had remained in Republican hands throughout most of the twentieth century, since the small northern counties generally returned Republican senators. Even during the state's swing to the Democrats in the late 1930s, the Senate stayed Republican. But it was hardly more than nominal partisan rule: the real division in the Senate was rural-urban and north-south. After 1958, however, the Democrats took control and the Senate became a bit more partisan. . . . But the leadership, although Democratic, remained essentially conservative.[32]

As Robert Dixon explained in the spring of 1965: "There was little friendship between the senate and the assembly even though both were Democrat-dominated. The rural Democrat senators who controlled the Senate had much more in common with their Republican counterparts than with their fellow partisans from Los Angeles who played a dominant role in the Assembly."[33] With partisan, personal, and constitutional factors to satisfy both chambers deadlocked on the Senate redistricting. The first Senate bill, SB 6, was passed on to the Assembly on May 10, 1965, and the lower chamber modified the bill to accommodate Los Angeles Assembly members aspirations to move up to the Senate while at the same time trying to turn the Senate Democratic. While partisan aspect is important, the question of overlap between the Assembly districts and the several new Senate districts was a major problem. Some Assembly members had envisioned moving up to the Senate but they feared "nesting" the Assembly districts inside the Senate districts would transform them into training ground for challengers of the new senators. But when the Republican Senate leader's seat was redrawn so a Democrat could prevail in it, State Senator Thomas M. Rees (D-Los Angeles) blasted the proposed changes to the Senate Plan as "crass political gerrymandering."[34] While the modification was the work of Allen's Reapportionment Committee, it was perceived as a reflection of Speaker Unruh's influence, and the amendment was rejected by the Senate.[35] Rees had the Senate's support in his fight over Los Angeles Senate boundaries in part because he had backed the Dirksen Amendment. But the problem was that the Assembly had a point when it ascertained that the Senate Plan did follow the "one person, on vote" mandate. The Senate decided to kill the Assembly amendments after a closed-door caucus, therefore requiring a conference committee. This conference committee was no more able to reach agreement than the legislature had been. Each house blamed the other for obstructionist tactics while the July 1 deadline approached rapidly. It appears that at the end of the 1965 session, the Assembly viewed the redistricting impasse as the result of Senator Rees' personal ambition, the Senate's hope of federal constitutional reprieve through the Dirksen Amendment, and the constitutional and technical deficiencies of the Senate plan. On June 17, the Assembly decided to pass its own bill, AB 1978, which gave Los Angeles 15.5 seats. But the upper house would not comply. It amended SB 6 into the Assembly's bill and sent it back to the Assembly where it died on file. The legislature adjourned with no bill and no redistricting plan.

THE CALIFORNIA SUPREME COURT'S THREAT

Because of the legislature's failure to follow a judicial decree, the three-judge federal court panel set a hearing for August 16 to consider the appointment of a special master to draft a Senate redistricting plan. This hearing was postponed when the State Supreme Court assumed jurisdiction over the apportionment controversy. On July 14, 1965, the highest tribunal of the state ordered the governor and the California Secretary of State to show cause as to why the 1966 elections should not be put off until both the Senate and the Assembly had been redistricted. Indeed, the petition showed statistics indicating that although Assembly seats were apportioned primarily on an equal population basis, 24 of the 80 varied by more than 15 percent from the ideal average and the largest was over four times as populous as the smallest.[36] As a reaction the legislature asked the Court to return the reapportionment obligation to the legislature. Senator Teale justified the stalemate by declaring that at the 1965 session the Senate "had a gun at its head. The Assembly sat there big, fat, dumb and happy and didn't have to worry about anything except getting Senate seats for its members. This time there will be a bona-fide trading situation."[37]

On September 1, 1965, only one month after the Dirksen Amendment failed in the US Senate, the California Supreme Court came up with a temporary redistricting of the California legislature that would have become effective by December 9 if the legislature had not redrawn the lines itself (*Silver v. Brown*, 63 Cal.2d 270 [1965]). Logically, the California Supreme Court turned to the Assembly redistricting. Following the "one person, one vote" standard, the Court concluded that the ideal population of each of the 80 Assembly districts would be 196,167. The largest (306,191) deviated from the target by 52 percent and the smallest (72,105) by 63 percent. The Court identified the Californian constitution requirement of keeping counties whole as the main source of discrepancy but remarked that "under the decisions of the United States Supreme Court, the policies underlying the requirements of compactness and contiguity and maintenance of the integrity of political subdivisions cannot justify such extensive departure from population-based representation as exist in the case of the assembly."[38] After advising the legislature to do away with some constitutional principles, the Court added that the districts should not depart from the ideal target by more than 15 percent and that a majority of the members of each house should be elected by voters in districts containing at least 48 percent of the total population of the state. And to increase the pressure on the legislature to act on its own the Court even produced its own map that pitted several incumbents against one another and created a number of open seats.[39] The goal was for the judicial branch to force the legislative branch to act, which only happened once the federal court, in an interesting example of federal cooperation, let the California Supreme Court assume jurisdiction and set forth remedial measures unacceptable for legislators. Until then, the consequences of the refusal to abide by the federal court order were apparently not specific enough to goad the legislature. So we see that, in this case, mathematical guidelines for redistricting by a reluctant legislature proved to be crucial. As Robert Dixon observed:

> If the rule be simply "substantial equality," with no fixed mathematical boundary, plans keep coming unstuck and votes keep slipping away. One incumbent after another suggests that his seat can be saved merely by nudging a line this way or that, and thereby increasing the population disparity by only a handful of percentage points. The reapportionment map remains perpetually fluid; compromises and adjustments have a way of evaporating almost as soon as they are made. By contrast, fixed mathematical guidelines sharply limit the kind of uncontrolled and uncontrollable "guesstimation," the range of permissible negotiable issues is revealed, and a basis for firm bargaining and decision-making emerges.[40]

Yet judicial deference has actually become the norm in redistricting cases. Judges will defer to the legislature as long as possible. This deference flows from the recognition that redistricting is first and foremost a political matter and appropriately entrusted to the political branches. As the Supreme Court explained in *Abrams v. Johnson*, "The task of redistricting is best left to state legislatures, elected by the people and as capable as the courts, if not more so, in balancing the myriad factors and traditions in legitimate districting policies."[41] Courts tend to draw their own plan only as a last resort. Also another form of deference is that of federal courts toward state courts. The general rule of federal court deference to state redistricting policies extends to any state body, including state courts that may be in charge of the process of redrawing districts. So federal courts traditionally defer to state courts. The Supreme Court declared that "absent evidence that these state branches will fail timely to perform that duty a federal court must neither affirmatively obstruct state reapportionment nor permit federal litigation to be used to impede it."[42] Therefore, the state court usually prevails if it constructs a legal plan in time for use in the upcoming election.

BACK-TO-THE-WALL REDISTRICTING

Faced with this prospect, legislative leaders asked Governor Brown to call in a special session which he did on September 20. Don Allen (D-Los Angeles), chairman of the Assembly Elections and Reapportionment Committee, had already asked Governor Brown for a special session in the spring to take care of the 38 congressional districts. Brown declared that even though he would have liked to see all three line-drawings take place at the same time, the court order was only aimed at the Senate and therefore put extra pressure to focus on the Senate first.[43] Besides, the legislature knew that both houses would have to redistrict sooner rather than later to abide by the "one man, one vote" principle.[44] But at every turn, California leaders opted to postpone redistricting until they were absolutely forced to do so by the courts. One of the reasons for Governor Brown's position stemmed from Unruh's ambition for the governorship. In 1964 and 1965 Unruh created obstacles with the hope of discouraging Brown from running for another term. Redistricting was merely another tool to weaken the reelection bid. To follow closely the redistricting process Governor Brown hired Leroy Hardy, who had assisted Unruh in 1961,[45] as special consultant to analyze the effects of redistricting proposals. Because of Unruh's dominance as Speaker of the Assembly, the Senate gave the governor more support than the lower house and Rees's election to the Senate consequently drew him further from the speaker as well. If Unruh moved up to the Senate he would challenge President Pro-Tempore Hugh Burns of Fresno. Leroy Hardy sums up the personal aspect of the failure of elected officials to act in 1965 thusly:

> Senate rejection of the Assembly reapportionment amendment thus meant a victory for Rees, implicit assistance for the Governor, deference to the possible passage of the Dirksen Amendment, an endorsement of city boundary integrity, and a silent vote of confidence for Senator Burns. Conversely, the Assembly's refusal to accept Senate districts represented a triumph for Unruh, dedication to the equal population principle, and a desire of several Assemblymen to advance to the upper house.[46]

So in the fall of 1965, the California legislature started in earnest to redistrict both houses following the new judicial standard albeit very reluctantly. One member of the Senate Reapportionment Committee, Senator Vernon L. Sturgeon (R-Paso Robles) declared to the *Los Angeles Times*: "There is nothing wrong with California's present Senate representation. . . . We all reject the authority of the US Supreme Court to order reapportionment purely by population but there is no higher place to which we can appeal."[47] So with seventeen or eighteen senators facing "sudden death" both houses began to work on a compromise that would save as many rural senators as possible and, at the same time, give Los Angeles Assembly members the seats they sought. Another factor was, of course, partisan advantage. The Democrats intended to keep the 2 majorities they enjoyed in 1965 with 26 Democrats and 14 Republicans in the Senate, and 49 Democrats and 41 Republicans in the Assembly. The Democrats were therefore satisfied with the status quo since they would benefit its preservation. Lost among these different interests was the voice of racial minorities. The Mexican American community intended to influence the Senate redistricting plan but their electoral numbers did not carry enough weight and they lacked the institutional tools provided later by the Voting Rights Act.[48] One more factor that needs mentioning is the advent of computers. The year 1965 represents the beginning of the modern era of redistricting not only because of the involvement of the three branches of the federal government in the election process of the states but also because of the progress of computer mapping.[49] Their capabilities and precision revolutionized political science and redistricting even though the democratization and widespread use of redistricting software did not occur until the 1990s.[50]

In 1965 the Democratic leadership was mostly concerned with keeping incumbents happy. Not only because their votes were needed to pass any redistricting bill but because incumbents are a known commodity. Majority party leadership usually assumes that known minority members, as well as majority members, are more predictable and therefore easier to work with than unknown people who might replace them in modified districts. An incumbent's habits and ambitions are rather well known. Besides, a Republican resurgence was not anticipated. Indeed, the GOP was not in good shape since the election 1964 had almost wiped out the Republicans nationally. In California, the Republicans appeared to be about to let the most right-wing faction lead the party by nominating Ronald Reagan, a retired actor with ties to Goldwater, for governor in 1966. Observers thought turning the party over to Reagan would put an end to the Earl Warren era, an era in which the Republican Party dominated politics in the Golden State. The redistricting plan was therefore not aggressive and only aimed at protecting as many incumbents as possible under the new standard.

In the Assembly, the bill proposed changes in 58 of the 80 districts, including 19 of the 31 districts in Los Angeles County. But only 24 districts in the state (and none in Los Angeles County) had exceeded the Supreme Court's limit of 15 percent deviation from average district population. The bill went beyond what the Court had asked for. Simply protecting incumbents did not require abiding so closely to the "equal population" principle. This due diligence shows how concerned the legislature was with the Court's threat.

To draw this compromise plan, map drawers started up north where they formed 8 rural districts where 24 incumbent senators had their residence. Three of these 8 districts counted 4 senators seats. The rest of Northern California counted 11 districts with 1 or no senator. Three northern counties each gained a district: San Francisco, Alameda, and Santa Clara. In San Francisco and Alameda county (or what was left of it since the GOP leaning parts were added to Santa Clara), the Democrats expected to carry all 4 seats but could not agree on county division. The state constitution stated that "each senatorial district shall choose one senator. . . . In the formation of senatorial districts no county . . . shall be divided." But because of the discrepancies in population in California's counties,[51] the Court recognized it was impossible to abide by the "one person, one vote" federal imperative without some judicial restraint.[52] The legislature decided to draw 38 senatorial districts. Thirty-six of them elected 1 senator each. San Francisco County and urban Alameda County each contained twice the population of other districts and elected 2 senators each. So in the end, two Senate seats in both counties were elected at-large. In order to maintain the appearance of 40 single-member districts the legislature numbered each dual-member district twice.[53] This was California's first and last experimentation with at-large representation in the legislature, in part because at-large districts were the first targets of voting rights litigation under the Voting Rights Act.[54] After all, these 2 counties contained San Francisco and Oakland, 2 metropolitan areas with a high concentration of minorities virtually disenfranchised by at-large representation. Since then, and on several occasions, the Supreme Court has emphasized that court-drawn plans should use single-member districts.[55] The preference for single-member districts comes from the history of courts adopting multimember district plans to remedy malapportionment only reluctantly and usually in a hurry,[56] along with a parallel line of cases that challenged multimember districts as diluting minority votes.[57]

The bill redistricting both houses of the state's legislature was passed on October 11, signed on October 27, and the California Supreme Court affirmed its constitutionality on January 11, 1966.[58]

CONSEQUENCES ON THE CALIFORNIA LEGISLATURE

Northern California now counted 19 senators while it used to have 24. The 8 most populous southern counties (Los Angeles, Orange, Santa Barbara, Ventura Riverside, Sans Bernardino, Imperial, and San Diego) had now more votes in the legislature than the 50 northern and central California counties combined. The southerners controlled 46 of the 80 seats in the Assembly and 22 of the 40 Senate seats. The drawing of 22 districts in Southern California where only 4 senators were looking for reelection proved to be politics on the high wire. "Lame duck" senators were offered judgeship as an escape plan which they could only be sure of while Democratic Governor Brown was in office in 1966. Rolling the dice until after the 1966 election meant running the risk of not holding public office anymore. Openings in Congress helped secure other senators' careers, among which was the pivotal Thomas Rees. Los

Angeles County received fourteen full districts and shared one with Orange County. That meant that only half of the 31 incumbent Assembly members would have a good opportunity to move up to the Senate. The most senior retired, freshmen were excluded, meaning that 16 or 17. Assembly members had real ambition for a Senate seat. Democratic mapmakers in charge of drawing the Los Angeles districts took no risks. They simply divided LA County into Democratic and Republican neighborhoods: 8 cautiously balanced Democratic seats were drawn in the center of the county, with one more in the San Fernando Valley. Even though Ronald Reagan received 57 percent of the votes in Los Angeles County, Democrats won nine of the 14 seats, all by a wide margin. This quite remarkable since all these Democratic districts had substantial minority population and minority populations have, on average, much lower turnout rates than the Anglo population. Population concentration allowed the drawing of safe Democratic districts with Democrat registration that needed to be fairly high to compensate for a depressed minority turn-out rate. Redistricting limited Reagan's coattail in LA and to some extent in the lower house since the Republicans received 53.7 percent of the popular vote but only 44.7 percent of the seats.[59] However, the rest of the state was more competitive.

In the fall of 1966, with popular Ronald Reagan on the ballot virtually every other Senate seat was up for grabs. As Gallagher and Weschler observed: "The most dramatic impact of the reapportionment was the turnover of legislators in the 1966 elections. Almost half of the 128 members of the 1967 legislature were new to their job."[60] Only 18 incumbents held on to their seats and 22 new members joined the Senate. Counting the senators elected in 1962 and 1964, 28 of the forty senators were in their first or second term when Governor Reagan took office. In 1966 the new Democratic class,[61] some of them called themselves "The Young Turks," ended up taking power away from the "old guard" even though institutional changes took some time as the "old guard" Democrats (helped by freshman Moscone who kept the "Young Turks" in line) and "old guard" Republicans stuck together, reelecting Democrat Burns as president pro tempore.[62] Maybe things would have been a bit different if the Assembly Speaker Unruh had tried to move to the Senate. Speaker Unruh had the intention of building a majority coalition and take it to the Senate to challenge the leadership.[63]

> When Unruh let it be known that he was considering running for one such seat, he provoked a scrambling to succeed him as Speaker with Robert Crown and Carlos Bee being the most prominent, but not the only contender. In a seeming agony of indecision, Unruh, having already been reelected Speaker, filed for both his existing Assembly seat and for the new Senate seat in his home district,

> causing both Crown and Bee, with their respective backers, to be angry with him. Finally, when forced to choose he decided to stay in the Assembly. Crown and Bee were probably as angry with Unruh for having dangled the seat in front of their eyes as Unruh was angry with Pat Brown for doing the same to him with the governorship. "It was well known that Unruh coveted the governorship more than a senate seat, the speaker's office, or probably anything else in the world.[64]

Unruh decided to stay in his Speakership post in the Assembly until 1968 when the Democrats lost the majority. Jesse Unruh ran for governor in 1970 but, as most people forgot, really challenged Reagan while being in a relatively weak position as minority leader.[65] He lost by 7 percent, doing much better than Brown who lost by 15 percent in 1966 and his well-organized get-out-the-vote organization helped his party retake the Assembly and the Senate. One can't help but wonder if he could have won the governorship at some point had he run from the Senate or possibly as the Senate pro temp later on in the decade.[66]

Unruh who had been behind the controversial 1961 redistricting of the Assembly was once again in charge in 1965. In 1961, Democratic San Francisco was overrepresented with 5 seats and Republican Orange County underrepresented with 3 seats. After the *Silver v. Brown* decision and its 15 percent variation standard between districts the legislature was forced to correct this. Unruh kept the partisan balance by collapsing the last San Francisco Republican seat (Marina and Richmond) and sending it south to Orange County.[67] In quite a contrast with the Senate, the Assembly reapportionment required the legislative demise of only one member, Republican Milton Marks of San Francisco, and he had been assured of a Municipal Court appointment by Governor Brown. Even if Unruh and Allen had not collapsed the district, the writing was on the wall for Republicans seats in the Bay area and it would have turned Democrat at some point. The rest of the changes were minor ones except two that turned out to be crucial in retrospect. Democrats were forced to separate Santa Cruz County, then largely Republican, from Monterey, and Unruh pushed for Santa Cruz to join Merced County in an oddly shaped coastal to Central Valley district. This prevented the reelection of Merced Democrat Gordon Winton who, in 1966, lost to Republican Franck Murphy of Santa Cruz. Winston probably paid the price for having challenged Unruh for Speakership. Another Unruh antagonist was San Jose Democrat William Stanton, who attacked Unruh from the Democratic Party's left wing. His San Jose district was redrawn to give him more Republican neighborhoods, but no one seemed to think it would cost him his seat. But in 1966 the Reagan coattails reached all the way to Stanton's seat. Unruh had in effect redistricted 2 Democratic seats out of his 49 majority. The 1965 incumbent protection plan worked through the primaries at least: all 51 Assembly members who ran for reelection were renominated. However, in the general election Democrats lost 7 Assembly seats despite the 1965 reapportionment. After 1966, that majority fell to 42 seats. With 3 more losses in 1968, the Democrats lost the Assembly. Had Unruh left Winton and Stanton's districts safe he might have avoided the Republican takeover in 1968.[68]

It is very difficult to evaluate the impact of the mid-decade redistricting revolution and the "one person, one vote" in terms of policy changes. But one thing it did is give urban voters a fair share of representation and indirectly benefitted a few minority candidates. The Senate had never elected any African Americans. Assemblyman Byron Rumford of Berkeley, who in 1949 became the third African American ever elected to the California legislature, won the Democratic nomination in a district with a Democratic registration of 65.4 percent but lost to Republican Lewis S. Sherman.[69] Assemblyman Mervyn M. Dymally won the Twenty-ninth Senatorial District in south-central Los Angeles that had the heaviest Democratic registration in the state with 82.1 percent.[70] In the 1961 redistricting, Unruh induced a rapprochement of sorts with Black Assemblyman Augustus Hawkins when he enabled him to become congressman. At that time "Gus" Hawkins was the only elected official representing a Los Angeles constituency. Augustus Hawkins was a figure of civil rights and labor fights. He served in the California Assembly from 1935 to 1963 where he ran unsuccessfully for the Speakership in 1958. He became the first African American in California to be elected to Congress in 1963 with John F. Kennedy's endorsement. He served in the Twenty-ninth and then Twenty-first District covering southern Los Angeles County until 1991. He was one of the founders of the Congressional Black Caucus and famously authored Title VII of the 1964 Civil Rights Act. Five days after the passage of the 1965 Voting Rights Act the Watts riots occurred in his district.

In 1962 Unruh created 2 Black Assembly districts and 1 Black congressional district in Los Angeles, an important gain in comparison to one Black Assembly district prior to the 1961 redistricting. Indeed, in 1951 the Republicans had concentrated African Americans in a small number of districts even though their large number was not enough to prevent a "White primary," much less the election of a minority candidate. In Los Angeles the Black population was divided to prevent the election of an African American congressman. The Republican plan was accused of working against integration. But Unruh's offer in 1961 was much less than what the African American community had asked for.[71] It had asked for the "two-four" plan: 2 congressional seats and 4 assembly seats. However, this plan may not have been realistic. For one this plan would have cut Hawkins district (AD 65). His main goal was to carve a heavily Black congressional district for himself.

Therefore Hawkins's career priority entailed concentrating a large number of Black voters in one district rather than several districts. In a classic redistricting conundrum of race versus partisanship, the Democratic Party's best interest was to divide the heavily Democratic Black community among several Democratic districts in order to maximize the Democratic vote. Majority minority districts notoriously help the Republicans by making the adjacent districts more conservative and White. In the 1960s the Black community started to realize that its interests were not necessarily aligned with those of the Democratic Party's leadership. In the case of Los Angeles, the Black community's interest was not even aligned with that of Hawkins'.[72]

In 1962, Unruh supported the election of Black assembly candidate Dymally and made him an ally, a move that helped to eventually add other African Americans to Unruh's Assembly coalition:

> With its ties to organized labor, the Unruh-Dymally combine slated candidates, shared funds, and managed campaigns, using direct mail, slate cards, and sample ballots marked with favorite candidates. The Unruh-Dymally style in the Black community was Black oriented and directed toward traditional Democratic goals. Over time, Dymally was able to build a group of Black assembly members and state senators who owed their election to him.[73]

However, Unruh's relationship with the African American community was complicated. Unruh was the chief sponsor of California's basic civil rights law that bears his name and was passed in 1959 (California Civil Code Section 51). Yet his opposition to the California Democratic Council (CDC)[74] pitted him against future Los Angeles Mayor Tom Bradley but also, in 1965, he found himself on a collision course with Willie Brown when the latter started his career in the Assembly by refusing to vote for Unruh's reelection as Speaker.[75] The Democratic Party was divided along the Unruh-Dymally coalition of "moderates" in opposition to the mostly White liberal "reformers" of the CDC.

Another African American, Bill Greene (D-Los Angeles), was elected in Dymally's old district. Along with John J. Miller, Yvonne Brathwaite Burke (D-Los Angeles), the first African American woman elected to the Assembly, Leon D. Ralph (D-Los Angeles), and Willie L. Brown Jr. (D-San Francisco) who had been elected in 1964, they formed the Assembly's Black caucus.[76] Alfred H. Song (D-Monterey Park), Assemblyman of Korean origin, became the first Asian American elected to the California Senate.[77] The California legislature in 1966 looked a bit more like the rest of the state's population thanks to minority Democratic candidates.[78]

Besides this modest but real influx of diversity the real news was the Republican foray in the upper chamber. Nineteen Republican senators were

Figure 1.1 1966 Assembly Districts
Source: California Legislature at Sacramento Handbook, 1972.

elected thanks to the 1966 Reagan landslide while Democrats expected 15 or 16 Republican victories since so many seats were in the suburbs.[79] The Democratic majority was reduced to a 2-seat edge. And the GOP ended up controlling the Senate by 1969 thanks to 2 special elections after the death of 2 Democrat senators (Eugene McAteer and George Miller Jr.).[80] The shift of the center of political gravity to southern California completed the transfer of popular voting strength in the region. The 8 southern counties from Santa

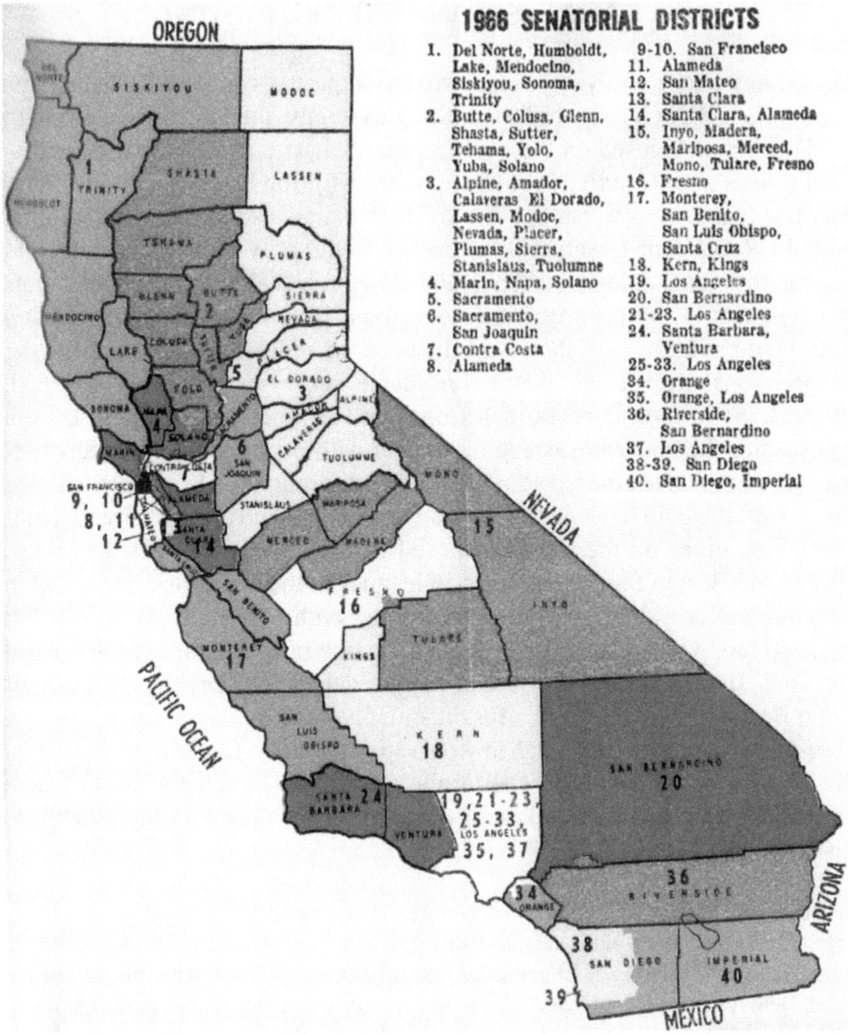

Figure 1.2 1966 Senatorial Districts
Source: California Legislature at Sacramento Handbook, 1972.

Barbara to San Diego now controlled more Senate and Assembly seats than the 50 remaining counties in the state. Moreover, 4 of the 6 statewide elected officers were now Republicans from the southland (Governor, Lieutenant Governor, Controller, and Treasurer). Besides, the new political balance between the north and the south did not simplify negotiations around water projects or gasoline tax revenues to fund freeway construction as the 2 regional faction fought over control of key committees.

1967 CONGRESSIONAL REDISTRICTING

The "one person, one vote" standard also impacted congressional districts. However, without a court order requiring to redraw the 38 districts and with the Democrats focused on the controversial Senate and congressional redistricting was put off until 1967. Unfortunately for the Democrats it was after they had lost the governorship. The Democrats now had to share redistricting with the Republican governor, his Republican minority in the legislature, and the congressional delegation. The 1966 election had also cost the Democrats several seats in the congressional delegation, including that of Democratic Rep. Harlan Hagan of Tulare, who had led the redistricting process for the congressional delegation. But a formidable successor was soon revealed. In 1967, a two-term congressman from San Francisco named Philip Burton emerged as the man in Washington to deal with on congressional redistricting. As soon as the courts had ruled on redistricting, the Democrats realized the impact it would have on California politics. Harlan Hagan chaired Democratic committee on the topic composed of Phil Burton and Thomas Rees. Hagan and Burton tried to get their colleagues in the legislature interested in the congressional delegation redistricting but without a court decision it fell on deaf ears. Once Hagan lost, Burton was the next natural member to fill the void. Burton hired a consultant for the delegation, Dr. Leroy Hardy of Long Beach, Hardy described Burton's involvement in reapportionment as a "crusade-like furor."[81] Burton had won a special election to Congress in 1964. As an Assembly member in California, Burton had developed a real knack for redistricting and electoral numbers trying to win his own San Francisco district:

> He began formulating a series of research-based political strategies that were nothing short of revolutionary in San Francisco. No one had done this sort of political spade work . . . he compiled voluminous charts comparing the number of Democrats to Republicans in the district for every six month period since 1948—adjusted for new precincts added after the 1951 reapportionment. He charted census tracts by race. He listed every Catholic church in the precinct number. He noted the number of voters who registered and voted in each of the district's 180 precincts in each of the primaries and general election since June 1952. . . . He went over precincts lists with colored pencils, underlining all Asian and Jewish names. These groups got specially targeted mail . . . Burton also noticed—and recorded—the fact in red and blue ink—that the number of blacks in San Francisco had increased by nearly 900 percent in ten years, from 4,800 in 1940, or 0.8 percent of the population, to 43,500 in 1950 and was still growing. By 1960, he projected there would be nearly 75,000 blacks, 10 percent of the population. His data showed that whites had a higher death rate and lower

birth rate than non-whites, which told him that the demographic trends would continue.[82]

Burton's task was quite complicated. In the Assembly he had butted heads with Unruh, who rebuffed him in 1965 when he first tried to redistrict the congressional delegation to abide early by the Supreme Court's "one person, one vote" principle, and many Republicans in the House did not trust him because of his strong partisanship. According to Republican consultant Anthony Quinn, the 1951 and 1961 congressional redistricting had been gerrymanders in which the party in charge had tried to "bury the opposite party."[83] In 1951, Republicans drew very effective districts that gave them a legislative majority as late as 1957, in effect postponing the Democratic domination of California politics. In 1954, for example, the Democrats managed to win 49 percent of the statewide vote for the Assembly but received only 40 percent of the seats.[84] More Assembly and congressional districts departed from population norms in the 1951 than in the 1961 apportionments.[85] In 1961, the Democratic gerrymandering increased their number in the California House delegation by 8 in the 1962 elections, while Republicans had increased their margin by only 5 in 1951. In all logic, so close to a new census and with a Republican governor, 1967 should have been a bipartisan affair.

The 1965 California Court decision that forced the redistricting of the Senate and the Assembly had been silent on congressional districts, yet decisions in other states suggested the population variation in California districts was too large to permit them to stay untouched for the rest of the decade. Besides, there were changes taking place in California's electorate that endangered Democratic incumbents. Reagan had carried many working-class neighborhoods that used to be the Democrats' bread and butter. The 1961 redistricting had spread the Democratic vote to increase the number of opportunities and their cushion was running thin. Another round of redistricting might be a good opportunity to save several incumbents. The most vocal incumbents were those in marginal districts or those facing adverse minority population concentrations.[86]

Although some Democrats had wanted to proceed with congressional reapportionment from the start of the 1967 session, others, such as Speaker Unruh, were not anxious to wade back into the quagmire that had consumed so much time in the 1965 session. Unruh was right to anticipate a difficult session with Ronald Reagan in the governor's mansion and increased Republican numbers in both houses. He saw no reason to add to his difficulties by putting redistricting on the agenda. But as the year wore on, the pressure for a new congressional plan increased. Democrats looking forward to the 1968 election liked less and less what they saw nationally. As the Vietnam War dragged on, Lyndon Johnson's popularity continued to plunge and the

Democratic Party began to split internally over the war issue. Moreover, the malaise generated by the lack of change in minorities' everyday life following the race riots in Los Angeles and San Francisco[87] was accentuated by the invalidation of the Rumford Act mandating the sale of property to Whites or Blacks alike. In November 1964 Californian voted for Proposition 14 that nullified the California Fair Housing Act of 1963. The Law protected the rights of minorities to purchase housing without being subjected to discrimination. It was enacted in response to weaknesses in earlier fair housing legislation in California. Upon its passage the California Real Estate Association launched a repeal campaign that won with a 2 to 1 margin. However, the California Supreme Court deemed Proposition 14 unconstitutional in 1966 (*Mulkey v. Reitman*, 64 Cal.2nd 529). The decision was affirmed by the US Supreme Court in 1967 in *Reitman v. Mulkey*, 387 US 369.

In this context of racial tension, Democratic Congress members who could see the potential for more losses became more stressed as election season approached. On the other side of the aisle, the GOP also had an interest in moving forward. The sudden shift of the state back in the Republican direction had allowed them to win 6 formerly Democratic seats, including 3 Democratic incumbents in the 1966 election. For instance, in 1961 the Twenty-fifth and Thirty-third Congressional Districts were created to satisfy the personal ambitions of state legislators for congressional careers (respectively Ronald B. Cameron and Kenneth W. Dyal). Both districts were marginally Democratic and fell to Republicans in the 1966 landslide (along with Hagan's who, as mentioned, was also replaced by a Republican). Republicans increased their number from 13 out of 38 in 1962 to 17 in 1966. Redistricting would help secure their gain by protecting their new incumbents.

The possibility of a bipartisan districting plan seemed enticing for both parties. Midway through the 1967 session, freshman Democratic Senator James Mills (D-San Diego), who had never been involved in redistricting, developed a plan and took it to DC where Republicans swiftly denounced his proposal as a plan that helped Democrats gain seats.[88] And soon after, a special Senate election in San Francisco (after the death of Eugene McAteer) gave the Republicans their twentieth member in the Senate, therefore evenly dividing the chamber between the two parties. Without a Senate Democratic majority, the Mills plan (Senate Bill 130) was no longer a possibility. Republicans then proposed their own plan. Its author, Assemblyman Charles Conrad, a redistricting veteran from the 1950s, called it the "minimum change plan" since he would have only redrawn 19 of the 38 districts. Democrats of course disagreed. They contended that the GOP engaged in subtle attempts to weaken marginal Democratic congressmen, and made it clear the plan would never pass the still-Democratic Assembly.

Two more events further complicated the situation. First, Leroy Hardy left the employment of the congressional delegation and developed a plan for a private client, Los Angeles Labor leader Abe Vicker, showing that it was possible to redistrict the congressional seats with a 1 percent population variation which had never been done before.[89] But his plan disturbed Congress members of both parties, for it had been drawn without congressional or legislative input. Second, the California Supreme Court returned to the political thicket. The Court responded to a lawsuit filed by Los Angeles attorney Phil Silver, a persistent litigant (the same plaintiff as in 1965) but not a spokesperson for any political interest, and as in 1965 set a deadline for the legislature to act by December 7, 1967.[90] Although the court had not required redistricting of Congress in 1965, similar cases in other states convinced the justices that reapportionment was necessary in 1967. Technically only 9 districts exceeded the 15 percent variance set by the court but the discrepancies were huge. For instance one Republican district in Los Angeles County was 41 percent above the average population and one San Francisco Democratic district was 27 percent below average.

Therefore Congress members faced two dangerous alternatives: either the court was going to draw its own plan or adopt the low variation Hardy plan. Some legislators, such as Deukmejian or State Senator John G. Schmitz (R-Tustin), openly accused the Court of making a mockery of checks and balances and of invading the legislature's jurisdiction which would set a terrible precedent if judges were allowed to legislate.[91] A legitimate criticism anticipated by Justice Frankfurter. Moreover, there were also some practical reasons to oppose a redistricting eight years after the last census only two years away from much more accurate numbers which led Ronald Reagan to call it initially an "exercise in futility."[92] But backed to the wall, elected officials united for the right to control their political destiny. Governor Reagan called a special session for November 7, and the Congressmen rehired Leroy Hardy.

Throughout October, in a series of private meetings, the congressional delegation tried to work out a plan all 38 Representatives could endorse. A bill was drafted, sponsored by Assemblyman Jack R. Fenton (D-Montebello), Chairman of the Assembly Elections and Reapportionment Committee and a close Unruh ally. Not surprisingly, the first version of the bill assisted those congressmen allied with Jesse Unruh and damaged several who had opposed him. In the meantime, Republican legislators worked on their own bill with Assemblyman Conrad's "minimum change plan" as its basis. But in Washington their colleagues, approached by Phil Burton, were negotiating with the Democrats. Set to protect their seats, Republicans and Democrats started to exchange constituents to respect the "one person, one vote" and remain in office.

Some Republican Assembly members, led by Assemblyman Conrad, complained that the bipartisan gerrymander would keep their party from making additional congressional gains, and insisted that the GOP should hold out for more. Indeed the Republicans picked up only one more seat in the rest of the decade when Democrat John Tunney ran successfully for the Senate in 1970 and abandoned his marginal district. But others wanted to settle the disputes before the Court stepped in and drew its own plan. The Fenton bill, that Assemblyman Kenneth Corey of Westminster characterized as "a totally incumbents" bill,[93] created a variation within 5 percent of the ideal population of 413, 610 and was approved very reluctantly by the California legislature.[94] The Senate voted 21 to 15, that is to say the exact number needed to send the bill to the Assembly for concurrence in minor technical amendments. The Assembly also voted for it very narrowly 42–35 (32 Democrats and 10 Republicans voted for the bill), one more than needed for final passage. So on December 6, one day before the Supreme Court deadline, the bill was sent to acting Governor Robert Finch for his approval.

In the end, the 1967 Congressional redistricting of California ended up being an example of incumbent gerrymandering. The *Wall Street Journal*, pretending to discover that redistricting is an incumbent sports, analyzed that the 38 incumbent Congress members "agreed on more than 50 shrewdly calculated transfers of territory among districts in order to cement themselves into office."[95] All incumbents in toss-up districts received a sizable influx of favorable constituents.[96] For example,

> Two Los Angeles County Republicans, Reps. Charles Wiggins and Craig Hosner, agreed to take over pieces of neighboring Orange County to help save Democrat Richard Hanna from creeping Republicanism. . . . Mr. Hanna gladly surrendered about 60,000 Orange Countians of Republican persuasion to Mr. Wiggins and about 25,000 to Mr. Hosner; in return the Democrat agreed to accept about 60,000 of Mr. Hosner's Los Angeles County constituents in the Democratic oriented community of Lakewood.[97]

Since the first goal of any politician is to be reelected, it is not surprising that partisan tensions could be left aside. One Democrat was quoted in the press explaining the circumstances behind the strategy: "Earlier in the year it was hard to think of the undercutting the comeback chances of Democratic colleagues who'd gone down last November. But as the 1966 election got more distant and Democratic prospects for 1968 kept looking worse, we all decided that the first law of politics is survival."[98] As a consequence, as Nixon narrowly won the 40 Electoral College votes of the state on his way to the presidency, all 37 congressional incumbents who ran in 1968 were reelected and all but 3 received at least 55 percent of the vote. Despite losing two percentage points (from 46.8 to 44.8) of the congressional vote between 1966 and 1968, the Democrats increased their delegation share by one seat with a 21–17 advantage in the congressional delegation.[99] No incumbent Representative lost in either of the two elections held under this plan. In fact, no incumbent House members lost in California's general election between 1968 and 1972, and only one open seat changed parties. One noticeable Democrat, Jeffrey Cohelan (Berkeley-Oakland Seventh District), lost his bid for reelection in the primary to Berkeley City Councilman Ronald V. Dellums. Dellums joined Hawkins to become the second Black congressman from California in modern times.[100] In 1970, the number of African Americans in the House of Representatives reached 12, or about 3 percent of the seats, for a national share of the American population of 11 percent.[101]

Incumbent protection usually means no new gains for minorities unless they can beat an incumbent during the primaries which is very difficult. Dellums was able to unseat Cohelan because of the exceptionally strong opposition to the Vietnam War inside the Democratic Party. In 1968, African Americans had a good chance of picking up a second congressional seat but map drawers delayed the inevitable. In 1967 the most notable exchange of territory involved African Americans when Democratic Congressman Hawkins absorbed Black sections from Democratic incumbent Wilson, Republican incumbents Clawson's districts and Democrat Latino incumbent Roybal. There were only 3 Latinos in the House at that time and Roybal was the only one from California.[102] Roybal served on Los Angeles City Council for thirteen years (from 1949 to 1962) after running unsuccessfully for Lieutenant governor of California in 1954 and losing a bitterly contested for a Los Angeles County Board of Supervisors seat in 1958, Roybal started in 1963 a thirty-year career in the House of Representatives.[103] A staple of Latino political life Roybal founded in 1976 the Congressional Hispanic Caucus and then co-founded the National Association of Latino Elected Officials (NALEO).

The Thirty-first District was designed in 1961 to go from the Harbor Freeway westward through Morningside Heights and Inglewood to West Chester and Sepulveda Boulevard, with Exposition Boulevard as northern border and El Segundo as southern border. But the population of the heavily Black Twenty-first District began to spread into the Thirty-first. So much so that White incumbent Representative Charles Wilson contemplated running in another district altogether.[104] Two years after the Watts riots and the passage of the Voting Rights Act, efforts were made by legislators to cut off substantial portions of the Black area on the east and add more blue-collar area on the southwest to prevent the election of an African American candidate. The district was still heavily Black but the African American community split its vote among two Black candidates (Ben Wyatt and Raymond Johnson) during the Democratic primary election.[105] Charles Wilson was reelected in 1968 and until 1981 when he was defeated in the primaries by Mervyn Dymally in large part because Wilson was censured by the House of Representatives, for financial misconduct stemming from the Koreagate scandal.[106]

The 1967 congressional redistricting seems to have ushered in a new phase in California's redistricting history in several ways. It was the first time the congressional delegation itself had drawn a plan. In both 1951 and 1961 most

Figure 1.3 1968 Congressional Disctricts
Source: California Legislature at Sacramento Handbook, 1972.

of the work was done by the legislature which presented a finished product to the congressional delegation. This time around the delegation got together to solve the problem with relatively limited input from the legislature and none from the courts. This was in no small part due to the talent of Representative Phil Burton.

By 1967, Burton became the delegation's spokesperson on redistricting, the one man other members would allow to draw the lines and negotiate the deals. And the key to his success is that he protected both parties. Burton saw his role as protector of the state's seniority in Congress. His job was to guarantee safe seats to senior members of the delegation. This meant they would rise on the committee ladders and be able to protect the state's interests in DC without having to worry about losing their district. Senior Democrats were undoubtedly helped in 1967, but since no Republican was harmed Republican Representatives were inclined to pressure their colleagues in Sacramento to accept the delegation plan. Some Republicans complained that the party could win more seats if the Republican base was more spread out, but Burton was able to use Republican Congress members to sell his plan and quiet his critics. Burton, a strong liberal, managed to build a relationship with Congressman H. Allen Smith, a conservative Republican from Pasadena, and Smith helped convince Republicans.

The year 1965 and 1967 mark the first redistricting in which county lines were abandoned as a factor, not only in redrawing the Senate, but also in drawing many congressional districts. Leroy Hardy, Burton's technical expert, admitted that the decline of the county line as a redistricting guide could open the doors to gerrymandering, but also reasoned that they were a relic of nineteenth-century divisions of the state that didn't reflect the metropolitan nature of modern California: "The congressional districts in many cases became true metropolitan areas, eliminating the parochialism inherent in districts following county lines. The new districts have the potential to become instrumentalities of the twenty-first century if congressmen respond to their broader responsibility and if the legislature recognizes their common problems that make county lines superfluous."[107]

Indeed, in many areas of the state county lines don't make sense. The "one person, one vote" revolution began with *Baker v. Carr* culminated in a way in 1969 in a case called *Kirkpatrick v. Preisler* in which the US Supreme Court held that congressional districts should attempt to achieve "precise mathematical equality."[108] This led to an almost complete abandonment of county lines as a redistricting factor, especially when the new standard was extended to legislative districts. In Los Angeles for instance this meant that Republican districts that needed more population were prolonged into Orange County and the only Democratic district in Orange County was moved to

Los Angeles County. In the Los Angeles metropolitan area even cities were not kept whole.[109] Court decisions at the federal level and at the state level in effect negated the constitutional rules relative to the grouping of whole counties and the grouping of whole assembly districts. Such negation was the only means by which equality of population could be achieved. With so many competing factors something had to give. In the hierarchy of redistricting factors incumbent protection has always been high, supplanted only by equal population. And soon, by race.

Race will become one of the most important factors in redistricting because of the strengthening of the Voting Rights Act and the emphasis put by the civil rights movement on the illegitimacy of the entire American democratic process if legislatures all remained White. But as we saw in California the first minority elected officials belonged to the Democratic Party. As the Donkey Party became the party of racial equality, protecting African American incumbents meant protecting Democrats. Very early on racial and partisan interests started to be correlated. But because this is California this correlation was not a White-Black affair for very long. Soon Latinos demanded representation and they needed to figure out the best strategy to get Latinos elected which they viewed as key to their political existence.

NOTES

1. John F. Gallagher, and Louis F. Weschler, "California," in *Impact ofReapportionment in the Thirteen Western States*, edited by Eleonore Bushnell (Salt Lake City: University of Utah Press, 1970), 71–90.

2. Gordon E. Baker, "The California Senate: Sectional Conflict and *Vox Populi*," in *The Politics of Reapportionment*, edited by Malcom E. Jewell (New York: Atherton Press, 1962), 51.

3. "Why the Bosses Favor Proposition 13," *Los Angeles Times*, September 30, 1948, A4.

4. Anthony Quinn, *Carving Up California: A History of Redistricting 1951–1983* (PhD diss., Rose Institute of State and Local Government, Claremont, CA, 1984), 108.

5. Leroy Hardy and Charles P. Sohner, "Constitutional Challenge and Political Response: California Reapportionment, 1965," *The Western Political Quarterly* 23, no. 4 (1970): 733.

6. Robert G. Dixon Jr., *Democratic Representation: Reapportionment in Law and Politics* (New York: Oxford University Press, 1968), 371.

7. California is 1 of 24 states that have adopted one form of popular initiatives. In states that allow initiative constitutional amendments citizens can simply short-circuit representative government. The multiplication and the professionalization of such initiatives in California ended up raising questions about the benefits of direct de-

mocracy as opposed to representative government. These states are sometimes called "hybrid" states: "But the deeper question is whether the merging of a separation of powers arrangement with a higher plebiscitary authority is a workable hybrid." Bruce Cain, *Democracy More of Less: America's Political Reform Quandary* (Cambridge: Cambridge University Press, 2015), 85.

8. "The Money behind Proposition 13," *Los Angeles Times*, October 22, 1948, A4.

9. "Old Words Have Bearing on New Issue," *Los Angeles Times*, March 7, 1965, K6.

10. Carey McWilliams, *California: The Great Exception* (Santa Barbara, CA: Peregrine Smith and Co., 1976), 212.

11. In 1961 Governor Edmund G. Brown even appointed a "blue ribbon" committee to study the issue.

12. The California constitution required no more than 3 counties to be grouped together to form a state senatorial district and no county could have more than one state senator. In the lower house, assembly districts could not cross county lines. In relation to congressional districts, whole Assembly districts had to be the building blocks in the creation of federal legislative districts.

13. The terms "Latino" or "Hispanic" were not used in state or federal statistics at the time. In 1960, according to the census bureau, the Hispanic population (defined by Spanish surnames) is estimated to have reached 9 percent of the state population.

14. John R.Owens, Edmond Costantini, and Louis F. Weschler, *California Politics and Parties* (New York: Collier-MacMillan, 1970), 285.

15. Before *Baker v. Carr*, federal courts would not decide lawsuits raising the issue of the constitutionality of malapportionment no matter the degree of discrimination allegation. The Court rational was that the question was political and therefore nonjusticiable, not the lack of jurisdiction on the part of the federal courts.

16. "If a State, in a statewide election, weighted the male vote more heavily than the female vote or the White vote more heavily than the Negro vote, none could successfully contend that that discrimination was allowable. See *Terry v. Adams*, 345 US 461 (1953). How then can one person be given twice or ten times the voting power of another person in a statewide election merely because he lives in a rural area, or because he lives in the smallest rural county? Once the geographical unit for which a representative is to be chosen is designated, all who participate in the election are to have an equal vote—whatever their race, whatever their sex, whatever their occupation, whatever their income, and wherever their home may be in that geographical unit. This is required by the Equal Protection Clause of the Fourteenth Amendment. The concept of 'we the people' under the Constitution visualizes no preferred class of voters, but equality among those who meet the basic qualifications. The idea that every voter is equal to every other voter in his state when he casts his ballot in favor of one of several competing candidates underlies many of our decisions." *Gray v. Sanders*, 372 US 368, 379 (1963).

17. *Wesberry v. Sanders*, 376 US 1, 2 (1964).

18. *Reynolds v. Sims*, 377 US 533, 568 (1964).

19. That same year, Silver filed a similar case in a federal district suit against Jordan, Governor Brown, and Attorney General Stanley Mosk, again unsuccesfully.

20. In *Yorty v. Anderson*, 60 Cal. 2d 312, 33 Cal. Rptr. 97, 384 P.2d 417 (1963).

21. *Yorty v. Jordan*, Sac. No. 7543 (appealed to the US Supreme Court, October 1964 Term, Case No. 250, and dismissed for want of jurisdiction on October 12, 1964, 379 US 8, 85 S. Ct. 68, 13 L.Ed.2d 22); and *Yorty v. Jordan*, Sac. No. 7582. In denying a writ in this case, the Supreme Court of California declared: "The petition to intervene and the petition for the writ of mandate are denied for the reason that any determination by this court on the question of legislative reapportionment would be premature until such time as the legislature has had an opportunity to consider the matter and to take such action as it may deem to be required pursuant to the expression of the United States Supreme Court in *Reynolds v. Sims*, 377 US 533, 84 S. Ct. 1362, 12 L. Ed. 2d 506, and companion cases."

22. Although hearings had been suspended it's the case started by Phil Silver that ultimately served as vehicle for Senate redistricting case.

23. In a surprisingly split vote decision the three-judge panel declared: "the Twenty-Eighth Senatorial District, Inyo, Mono and Alpine Counties, had a population of 14,294 according to the 1960 Federal Census, contrasted with the Thirty-eighth Senatorial District, Los Angeles County, with a population of 6,380,771. The disparity here is almost 450 to 1. It is invidious discrimination . . . and is debasement of the right to vote and deprives of the Equal Protection of the laws as guaranteed by the Fourteenth Amendment." *Yorty v. Jordan,* 309.

24. After the conference, State Senator Stephen P. Teale, chairman of the state reapportionment subcommittee, announce that the senators had agreed to (1) Exhaust all possible remedies to allow us to keep the bicameral legislative system as we know it; (2) That the senate must comply with court orders on reapportionment "without plying any games"; (3) That attorneys for the senate must determine if they can appeal the federal court order. They were instructed to file an appeal if legally possible; and (4) Finally the Senate determined to press for a constitutional convention of the states, as well as congressional action on a constitutional amendment to overturn the Supreme Court decision. Cited by Dixon, *Democratic Representation*, 374.

25. Robert M. Blanchard, "Redistricting Battle Lines Taking Shape," *Los Angeles Times*, February 4, 1965, A4. Dolwig introduced SB 109 and SCA 5 with 24 other senators co-authoring the legislation. The Senate passed the legislation but it died in the Assembly Committee in Interstate Cooperation.

26. Dixon, *Democratic Representation*, 373. The Dirksen Amendment was supported by the Farm Bureau Federation, the US Chamber of Commerce, National Farmers Union, and National Grange and State legislatures.

27. Staff writer, "Two-Year Moratorium on Redistricting Asked," *Los Angeles Times*, January 20, 1965, 10. In 1965 the California legislature passed SJR 3 which requested Congress to propose an amendment to the US Constitution to permit state legislatures to be apportioned according to the federal plan.

28. Hardy and Sohner, "Constitutional Challenge," 736.

29. Carl Greenberg, "State Reapportion Foes See Last Hopes Fade," *Los Angeles Times*, August 5, 1965, 13. The final vote was 57 to 39 because at the time a filibuster proof majority was two-thirds of the US Senate. In 1966 Dirksen amended his bill but It fell short by 9 votes.

30. Jerry Gillam, "Break Seen in Senate Redistricting Dilemma," *Los Angeles Times*, February 10, 1965, 10.

31. Jerry Gillam, "Redistricting Plan Unveiled," *Los Angeles Times*, April 7, 1965, 1.

32. Anthony Quinn, "*Carving Up*," 111–12.

33. Dixon, *Democratic Representation*, 374.

34. Robert M. Blanchard, "Assembly Unit Delays Vote on Redistricting," *Los Angeles Times*, June 11, 1965, 3.

35. It was assumed that the Assembly version of Los Angeles County Senate boundaries was drawn to elevate to the upper house Assemblymen who had worked with Unruh: Carroll, Dymally, Harvey Johnson, and Cusanovich, plus Assembly Reapportionment Committee staff chief Steven Smith.

36. Dary E. Lembke, "Supreme Court Issues Orders," *Los Angeles Times*, July 15, 1965, 3, 9.

37. Robert Blanchard, "Senators Seek Second Chance of Reapportion," *Los Angeles Times*, July 27, 1965, 3.

38. *Silver v. Brown*, 63 Cal. 2d 276–277 (Cal. 1965).

39. The judges knew what buttons to push to get action and at the same time rid themselves of the task. Drafting the judicial proposals was assigned to the most experienced judge in the field of redistricting. The creation of at-large districts would have required substantial election costs and other campaign difficulties. The proposed version created 7 multimember Senate seats and 9 multimember Assembly seats.

40. Dixon, *Democratic Representation*, 377.

41. *Abrams v. Johnson*, 521 US 74, 100 (1997).

42. *Growe v. Emison*, 507 US 25, 34 (1993).

43. Robert M. Blanchard, "Brown Puts Off Decision on Redistricting Session," *Los Angeles Times*, June 4, 1965, B.

44. "Assembly Warned about Full Reapportionment," *Los Angeles Times*, May 4, 1965, 3.

45. Along with William Campell Below and Steven E. Smith.

46. Hardy and Sohner, "Constitutional Challenge," 743.

47. Ray Zeman, "Battle on Reapportionment Reopens Today in Assembly," *Los Angeles Times*, October 11, 1965, 3.

48. "Latin Group to Push Redistricting Plan," *Los Angeles Times*, May 17, 1965, 3.

49. Richard Bergholz, "Computer Maps Senate Redistricting: Draws Lines That Eluded Legislators," *Los Angeles Times*, July 20, 1965, A1.

50. The oldest experimental work I found using computer technology to attempt to produce equal population districts in California but serving different political purposes, using 4 parameters to "gerrymander" Los Angeles and Santa Clara counties, is from a PhD student Stephen Slingsby, *The Gerrymander: Its Rise, Use, and Potential* (Claremont Graduate School, 1967). Also see Stuart S. Nagel, "Simplified Bipartisan Computer Redistricting," *Stanford Law Review* 17, no. 5 (1965): 863–99.

51. In 1960, Los Angeles County contained 6 million people while Alpine County contained 397 people. California, Population of Counties by decennial Census: 1900-90, compiled by Richard L. Forstall, US Bureau of the Census, http://www.census.gov/population/www/censusdata/cencounts/files/ca190090.txt.

52. "[Ww]e believe that it is for the Legislature and the people in the exercise of the legislative power of the state vested in them . . . to determine which provision or provisions . . . should be subordinated to comply with the equal protection clause of the United States Constitution. The makeup and apportionment of the Legislature involves peculiarly political questions that are not appropriate for this court to decide," *Silver v. Brown*, 63 Cal. 2d 280 (Cal. 1965).

53. Alameda County contained the 8th and 11th district, while San Francisco contained the Ninth and the Tenth Senatorial Districts. In the US the main electoral system is single-member plurality district. However, at the state level and moreover at the city and county government level a variety of systems are used: multimember, at-large, weighed voting. After all, US senators are actually elected in 2-member districts, a fact that is obscured by the staggering of senatorial terms.

54. Starting with *City of Petersburg v. United States*, 93 S. Ct. 1441 (1973), summarily affirming a district court decision that at-large elections for city council violated the Voting Rights Act because the city's expansion created a White population majority. Culminating in *Thornburg v. Gingles*, 478 US 30 (1986) and the Court's expression "vote dilution through submergence" to qualify at-large or multimember districts. Political scientists have demonstrated for a long time that single-member districts help racial minorities obtain political representation see for example, Bernard Grofman, "Alternatives to Single-Member Plurality Districts: Legal and Empirical Issues," in *Representation and Redistricting Issues*, edited by Bernard Grofman, Arend Lijphart, Robert B. McKay, and Howard A. Scarrow (Lanham, MD: Lexington Books, 1982), chap. 12; Richard Engstrom and Michael D. MacDonald, "The Effect of At-Large versus District Elections on Racial Representation in US Municipalities," in *Electoral Laws and Their Political Consequences*, edited by Bernard Grofman and Arend Lijphart (New York: Agathon Press, 1986), 203–25.

55. *Wise v. Lipscomb*, 437 US 535, 540 (1978) ("[A] court-drawn plan should prefer single-member districts over multimember districts, absent persuasive justification to the contrary"); *E. Carroll Parish Sch. Bd. v. Marshall*, 424 US 636, 639 (1976); *Connor v. Johnson*, 402 US 690, 692 (1971).

56. *Mahan v. Howell*, 410 US 315, 332-33 (1973); *Lucas v. Colo. Gen. Assembly*, 377 US 713, 731 (1964) suggesting in the context of a one person, one vote dispute that voters might not like multimember districts.

57. *Whitcomb v. Chavis*, 403 US 124 (1971), at 158–59 ("Criticism [of multimember districts] is rooted in their winner-take-all aspects, their tendency to submerge minorities and to over-represent the winning party as compared with the party's statewide electoral position, a general preference for legislatures reflecting community interests as closely as possible and disenchantment with political parties and elections as devices to settle policy differences between contending interests").

58. The whole story is a bit more complicated as it usually is in redistricting. As soon as the bill was signed by the governor, errors were discovered because of haste. A corrective measure was vetoed because it was attached to a special pension plan designed to help legislators negatively impacted by redistricting. The governor and both houses had to petition the Supreme Court to correctively "construe" the enacted

measure and the petition was honored. Oakland's district was 87 percent larger than average so the whole city had to be moved from one district to two others. Dixon, *Democratic Representation*, 378.

59. Leroy C. Hardy, "Considering the Gerrymander," *Pepperdine Law Review* 4, no. 2 (1977), 12. The total Republican vote for the Assembly election was 53.7 percent and for Congress was 53.1 percent. They received 47.5 percent of the Assembly seats and 44.7 percent of the House of Representatives' delegation.

60. Gallagher and Weschler, "California," 87.

61. Among these new senators was a not very well-known Assemblyman, George Deukmejian, in the Thirty-seventh District, who included a phonetic spelling of his name in his official stationery.

62. Robert Fairbanks, "Redistricting Aids Moscone: Freshman S.F. Democrat New Force in State Senate," *Los Angeles Times*, January 29, 1968, 3.

63. Lou Cannon, *Ronnie and Jesse: A Political Odyssey* (New York: Doubleday, 1969), 283.

64. Jackson K. Putnam, *Jess: The Political Career of Jesse Marvin Unruh* (Lanham, MD: University Press of America, 2005), 68.

65. For more on Unruh *cf.* the excellent Boyarsky Bill, *Big Daddy Jesse Unruh: The Art of Power Politics* (Los Angeles: University of California Press, 2007). And for more details on the 1970 election *cf.* chap. 13, 191–206.

66. For a somewhat biased account of his difficult relationship with Governor Brown by a former aide *cf.* James R. Mills, *A Disorderly House: The Brown-Unruh Years in Sacramento* (Hey Day Books, 1987). Mills was elected President Pro Tempore of the California Senate in 1970.

67. Quinn, "Carving Up," 129.

68. Quinn, "Carving Up," 130.

69. The first two were Frederick M. Roberts (1918–1934) and Augustus F. Hawkins (1934–1962) and served the same district.

70. Dymally, who later became Lieutenant Governor (1975–1979) and Congressman (1981–1993), was actually born in Trinidad and moved to the US as an adult. He became a naturalized citizen in 1957. When he won a seat in the State Assembly in 1962, he became the first foreign-born Black lawmaker elected to the state's lower house. In 1974, Dymally and George L. Brown, former Lieutenant Governor of Colorado, became the first two Blacks elected to statewide office in the US since Oscar Dunn (Louisiana Lieutenant Governor 1869–1971). Dymally was also 1 of 3 African Americans to hold statewide office in California including Wilson Riles, who served as California Superintendent of Public Instruction from 1971 to 1983, and Kamala Harris who was elected California Attorney General in 2011.

Unknown, without funds, and facing the fact that no Black had ever been elected to statewide office, Riles' election is the stuff of legends. Starting with a polled statewide strength of 7 percent in May, he received 25.2 percent of the primary vote in June and won in the November run-off election with a 54.1 percent.

71. Leroy Clyde Hardy, *Golden Betrayal: The Erosion of Representation and the Loss of Legitimacy in California* (Rose Institute of State and Local Government, 1993), 87.

72. Raphael J. Sonenshein, *Politics in Black and White: Race and Power in Los Angeles* (Princeton, NJ: Princeton University Press, 1993), 37.

73. Sonenshein, *Politics in Black and White*, 56–57.

74. The CDC came up at the beginning of the 1950s, inspired by Adlai Stevenson's presidential campaign and vowed to pursue a liberal agenda within the fragmented Democratic Party. Other states had their equivalent under different names. In California, educated, middle-class liberals helped the CDC to emerge as a force in state politics that intended to take the party leftward and away from its main enemy Unruh.

75. The irony, of course, is that Brown (a Phil Burton protégé) sort of became the Unruh of his era. For more on Brown's career cf. James Richardson, *Willie Brown: A Biography* (Berkeley, CA: University of California Press, 1996).

76. As an indication that Unruh relationship with the Black caucus was complicated we can notice that Willie Brown, a Phil Burton ally, refused to vote for Unruh's reelection as speaker in 1965.

77. Ray Zeman, "The Results of Redistricting," *Los Angeles Times*, June 23, 1966, A4.

78. African American leaders suffered one notable defeat. Byron Rumford lost in his bid for a State Senate seat in Alameda County by the thinnest of margins: 801 votes out of 320,727 votes cast. Richardson, *Willie Brown*, 139.

79. To get a sense of the political landslide, in Congress, State Senate and Assembly the combined Republican vote was greater than the Democratic, the first time since 1952. From 1964 to 1966, the Republicans' registration surged by 170,000 while the Democrats' dropped by 17,000. Totton J. Anderson, and Eugene C. Lee, "The 1966 Election in California," *The Western Political Quarterly* 20, no. 2 (1967): 535.

80. George Miller ran for his father's seat (SD7) in the March 1969 special election but lost to Republican John Nejedly 57 percent to 42 percent. After McAteer's death and Milton Marks election in his seat the count was 20 Republicans and 20 Democrats with the Republican Lt. Governor Robert Finch holding the tiebreaker vote.

81. Leroy C. Hardy, "Congressional Redistricting in California, 1965–1967: The Quilting Bee and Crazy Quilts," *San Diego Law Review* (June 1973), 761. This part owes much to Leroy Hardy's work. He worked as chief assistant to Ivan Hinderaker, the major consultant to the California legislature in 1951 and Staff Director for the Assembly elections and reapportionment committee in 1961 and a special consultant to Governor Brown in 1965.

82. John Jacobs, *A Rage for Justice: The Passions and Politics of Philip Burton*, (Berkeley, CA: University of California Press, 1995, [1997]), 42–43.

83. Quinn, "Carving Up," chap.1, 13.

84. Quinn, "Carving Up," chap.1. All these figures need to be taken with a grain of salt in the "nonpartisan era" of California politics when cross-filling was common practice.

85. Franck H. Way, "Brutal Butchery in the Two-Party System," in *The Politics of Reapportionment*, edited by Jewell, 255.

86. Hardy, "Congressional Redistricting," 760.

87. Governor Brown called the National Guard to put out a racial uprising in San Francisco in September 1966 and then sponsored a "law and order" Riot Act.

88. Courts in some states had taken redistricting plans from one house when the legislature as a whole proved incapable of working out a deal. With Mills's proposal, the courts would have an alternative plan available. A close ally of the Speaker, Mills, with this move, would gain independence in the Senate.

89. Vicker's appeal to the Court was consolidated with Silver's in *Silver v. Reagan*, 67 Cal. 2d. 432; 62 Cal. Rptr. 424; 432 P.2d 26 (1967).

90. *Silver v. Reagan*, 67 Cal. 2d.432; 62 Cal. Rptr. 424; 432 P.2d 26 (1967).

91. Ray Zeman, "State's Redistricting Struggle Heads for Conference Session," *Los Angeles Times*, November 16, 1967, 3. They were by no means the only ones, for instance Caspar Weinberger's op-ed piece in the *LA Times* by Caspar W. Weinberger, "Redistricting Ruling Was Bad,"*Los Angeles Times*, October 16, 1967, A4.

92. "Congressional Redistricting," *Los Angeles Times*, October 10, 1967, A4.

93. "County Gains 2 Votes in Reapportionment: Congressional Incumbents Seen Helped by Registration Gains under Redistricting," *Los Angeles Times*, December 7, 1967, OC1.

94. All but one district respected this variation. The Second District which extended from the Oregon border all the way to the San Bernardino County line exceeded the average by 8.1 percent. James Mills admitted it was too difficult to approve the bill if the lines of the Second District, represented by Rep. Harold T. (Bizz) Johnson (D-Roseville), were changed. Jerry Gillam, "Redistricting Bill Clears Legislature: Reluctant Approval Given to Beat State Supreme Court Deadline," *Los Angeles Times*, December 6, 1967, 3.

95. Joseph W. Sullivan, "Massive Gerrymander Mapped in California by 38 Congressmen," *Wall Street Journal*, November 9, 1967, 1.

96. Wiggins district went from 63.1 percent Democratic registration in his 1966 upset to a much more manageable Democratic registration of 50 percent in 1968. "County Gains 2 Votes in Reapportionment: Congressional Incumbents Seen Helped by Registration Gains under Redistricting," *Los Angeles Times*, December 7, 1967, OC1.

97. Sullivan, "Massive Gerrymander," 1. This represented for Hanna more than a 20 percent switch in constituency.

98. Sullivan, "Massive Gerrymander," 1.

99. David R. Mayhew, "Congressional Representation: Theory and Practice in Drawing the Districts," in *Reapportionment in the 1970s*, edited by Nelson W. Polsby (Berkeley: University of California Press, 1971), 283.

100. Cohelan was a White liberal close to union labor who had established a good record on civil rights issues. He represented an Alameda County district containing a large Black (40 percent) and Mexican American constituency with over a 2 to 1 Democratic registration advantage. Dellums was close to the "new Left" and recruited by the anti-Vietnam war activists. A self-proclaimed socialist, he admitted supporting many of the Black Panther Party's goals. Many students of the University of

California at Berkeley worked in his campaign. He served in Congress for twenty-seven straight years and was Oakland's mayor from 2007 to 2011.

101. In 1971, they officially created the Congressional Black Caucus when they renamed the "Democratic Select Committee" that had been created in 1969.

102. The other 2 were Democrats from Texas: Henry B. Gonzalez first elected in 1961 and Kika de la Garza first elected in 1965. Roybal was the first Latino member of the California congressional delegation since Romualdo Pacheco in 1879.

103. When he stepped down as city council member for the Ninth District the Council, African American Gilbert Lindsay was appointed as his successor. Latinos would not regain a seat until 1985 when Assemblyman Alatorre was elected in the Fourteenth District.

104. Leroy Hardy sums up his redistricting experience in 1967 thusly: "Several Democrats were anxious about racial or ethnic balances within their districts, because it is generally thought that a 35 percent Negro population might create a primary fight for an incumbent. Some congressmen sought additional "red-neck" (lower income White with former Southern Democratic ties) territory to balance Negro concentrations. Other Congressmen desired ethnic are as favorably disposed to Democrats, or they relished the balancing of Mexican American, Jewish, or Italians against other groups. Republicans were seemingly not plagued by the ethnic and racial balances, a point that probably reflects that party's composition." Hardy, "Congressional Redistricting in California," 787.

105. Richard Bergholz, "A District Ripe for Picking . . .," *Los Angeles Times*, April 9, 1968, A4.

106. Dymally is said to have entered the congressional race when he learned there would be two White candidates, scandal-plagued Representatives Charles H. Wilson of Hawthorne and former Representative Mark Hannaford, to split the White vote. After having won a bruising primary Dymally sewed up African American, Asian, and Latino votes in the heavily Democratic district. Dymally won 6 terms and retired from Congress in 1992.

107. Hardy, "Congressional Redistricting in California," 784.

108. 394 US 526, at 530–31. In this case the Supreme Court invalidated a Missouri Congressional redistricting plan because it had deviated from the ideal population standard more than 3.1 percent.

109. Howard Seelye, "Redistricting Plan to Cross County Lines: Incumbents Gain in Party Registration; State Senate Vote Due Today or Tuesday," *Los Angeles Times*, December 4, 1967, OC8; "Incumbents Benefit in House Redistricting," *Los Angeles Times*, May 5, 1968, OC_B5.

Chapter 2

Gridlock over One (Latino) Seat in 1971

Governor Reagan and the Republicans made a special effort to bring about change in the partisan composition of the state Legislative Assembly because of Unruh's systematic opposition but also for redistricting purposes. Reagan personally campaigned and raised large sums of money for Republican candidates. Assisting the governor was the widely publicized political stratagem called "California Plan," an eight-year-old program of the Republican Party designed by State Chairman Gaylord Parkinson to deliver control of the state legislature to the party in the 1970 election.[1] This was in anticipation of reapportionment which would come in 1971. They were so confident that they would be in charge in 1971 that they contracted with a Southern California computer firm and began preliminary data gathering.[2] The common wisdom at the time was that because of population grows in Southern California suburbs Republicans would also, within two years, control the congressional delegation.[3] The demographic projections proved accurate. In 1970 California had a population of nearly 20 million people which represented an increase of 25 percent since 1960 according to the census bureau. The 8 southern-most states contained 57 percent of the state's population while the urban-suburban parts of the state represented a whopping 91 percent of Californians. Most of the population's growth was situated in Republican-dominated suburbs. The greatest increases were in Orange and Santa Clara Counties which grew by 100 percent and 64 percent, respectively.[4]

But in a shocking departure from early Republican successes, in 1970, the Democrats won control of the Senate with 2 new seats affording a 21 to 19 majority and 4 additional seats providing a 43 to 37 margin in the Assembly. The Assembly races provided the testing ground for the Reagan "coattail campaign" and it turned out to be a complete failure to the delight of Big Daddy Unruh who emphatically declared: "we cut off his coat-tails clear up to the lapels."[5] But the future wasn't so bright for the Democrats. In 1970, about 60 percent of the Democratic Assembly districts required added population to conform to court standards, while several small Democratic districts had to be consolidated to create new districts of standard size. The major growth counties were generally Republican-voting, the losing areas were generally Democratic. The major growth in California had occurred in Orange County, California's most Republican county, which doubled in size during the 1960s (700,000 to 1.4 million people). Maybe the biggest challenge for the Democrats was that the 3 smallest congressional districts were Democratic and populated with African Americans and Latinos. That very year featured a complicated equation: the first African American in modern history to be elected to a statewide office, 2 African Americans chairing key assembly committees, and Democratic districts in jeopardy that were Black majority districts. Additionally, in 1968, Alex Garcia (D-Los Angeles) was elected to the Assembly followed in 1970 by Peter Chacon (D-San Diego).[6] In 1972, 3 more Latinos were elected to the State Assembly: Joseph Montoya, Ray Gonzales, and Richard Alatorre. They officially created the Chicano Legislative Caucus in 1973. Alatorre's election proved to be pivotal to redistricting negotiations. 2 groups were particularly active in Sacramento, especially after the East Los Angeles riots in 1970,[7] they were inspired by the African American gains in 1960 and 1965 and were asking for Chicano districts: the Coalition for Fair Reapportionment, headed by Herman Sillas, Democratic Party Secretary for Southern California and Citizens for Improved Representation,[8] headed by Cal State Los Angeles instructor Henry Pacheco.[9]

At the end of the 1960s it became clear, even to the Democratic leadership, that the creation of majority-minority districts probably was a more realistic approach to their political aspirations than the old belief that minorities would vote for "the man" regardless of whether he was African American, Latino, or Anglo.[10] The demands put pressure on the Democratic Party whose coalition included minorities.[11] On the one hand, if minority strength was concentrated, the Democratic strength in other districts was weakened. Therefore the concentration had serious partisan implications. On the other hand, the concentration of minority strength had tremendous implications for minorities themselves. So the party was faced with an electoral dilemma. Did the election of a few minority candidates in the federal legislature, and the need to concentrate non-Anglo voters to accomplish that goal, outweigh the advantage of electing several Anglo congressmen whose partial minority constituency would require their attention to minority issues? Or to put it another way, would the party or the communities' interests be better served with the creation of a few majority-minority districts or a few more influence districts?[12]

Here the expression "community of interest" is central for redistricting purposes. Redistricting standards can be divided in two types: (1) formal criteria focuses largely on the shape, size, racial, and socioeconomic composition of the districts, and (2) fairness of outcome measured by proportionality and seats-to-vote proportion. The case for formal criteria has always been that they constrain efforts to draw lines that intentionally and unfairly favor one party or group over others. Some formal criteria are easily measured and have become relatively uncontroversial, for example, that district boundaries must be contiguous (connected at all points) and have equal populations.[13] By contrast the concept of "community of interest" (COI), that is the expectation that districts be composed of "cognizable" common interests, are much more difficult to identify because there is a subjective component to the interests and boundaries of a given community. Residents in a given area need to perceive and acknowledge that a social, cultural, or economic interest is politically relevant to them. The geography of this community is also subjective since the boundaries of such a community do not necessarily coincide with government jurisdictions. Perception matters with respect to identifying communities of interest. Besides, to complicate matters, because in the US race and ethnicity are such important components of a sense of community that race, ethnicity, and "community of interest" are often conflated.

From a practical standpoint, 1971 was the first year that computers played a large role in the redistricting process. In the past, map drawers had depended on hand calculators and limited sets of data. The computer development allowed views of political and census data at once. Tracts could be added and subtracted from any district, and the impact was available immediately. Software providing color-coded precincts for Democratic and Republican registration was revolutionary and the possibilities seemed endless. This was the first round of redistricting in which population equality was required for all districts. The new norm was that districts should not vary more than a single percentage point from the state average. But equal population meant that city and county boundaries were no longer relevant. The technical precision of software changed the approach to redistricting completely. A politician's intimate knowledge of a region became less important than the computer's behavioral model. Some were tempted to think of redistricting as a purely numerical zero-sum game. Of course, events proved this a-political approach quite wrong.

THE EARLY COMPROMISES

With a Republican at the head of the state (Governor Ronald Reagan), and a small majority for Democrats in both states houses, as well as in Congress, electoral boundaries in 1971 should have been a compromise: an incumbent gerrymander like the one proposed in 1968 or 2001. Newly elected Assembly Speaker Bob Moretti (D-North Hollywood) brought in San Francisco Assemblymen John Burton and Willie Brown that Jess Unruh had kept out of the party's leadership positions. Moretti also pushed for Assemblyman Henry Waxman (D-Santa Monica), a Burton loyalist, to head the powerful Assembly Elections and Reapportionment Committee. The Assembly Democratic effort was headed by Michael Berman, Howard's younger brother and therefore a close ally of Assemblyman Waxman.[14] Waxman, Howard, Michael Berman, Phil Burton, and Willie Brown would all play crucial roles in politics, public policy, leadership wars, and redistricting for decades. Michael Berman would be involved in California redistricting until the independent citizen commission took over in 2010.

Mervyn Dymally (the only African American senator) was selected by newly elected President Pro Tempore Jim Mills to oversee the Senate redistricting which bode well for minority interests. Democrats had also contracted for computer services with American Computer Resources of Los Angeles, which had political ties to Assemblyman Cory. Congressman Burton's congressional effort was also aligned with that of the Assembly Democrats, and he had once more retained Professor Leroy Hardy as his consultant. For the Republicans, the redistricting work would be supervised in the Assembly by minority leader (and former speaker) Bob Monagan of Tracy and Jerry Lewis of San Bernardino, and in the Senate by John Harmer of Glendale. The GOP hired Professor Alan Heslop of Claremont Men's College to oversee their effort, and Thomas Hofeller, also of Claremont, for the technical and computer work.[15]

In 1971, Mexican Americans really took part in the conversation on representation in California. The community made no secret of its goal to lobby the legislature to push for more representation. The Californians for Liberal Representation announced it in press conference in January 1971, before taking its message to the US Commission on Civil Rights gathered in Sacramento and to the meeting of the Democratic State Central Committee. After all in 1967 the California Advisory Committee to the US Commission on Civil Rights had already concluded:

> East Los Angeles, the nation's largest Mexican-American community, has been effectively sliced up so that it would be difficult for a Mexican American candidate to win a city, state, or federal election as a representative of the district. As an example, East Los Angeles is divided into six different State Assembly districts, none with more than 25 percent Mexican-American population. Elections for seats on the Los Angeles City board of education are district wide, making it

> nearly impossible for a Mexican-American candidate to win. There is no Mexican American in the California State Assembly or Senate. Edward Roybal is the lone Mexican-American from California in the US House of Representatives.[16]

The Californians for Liberal Representation's main argument was crystal clear: the census revealed that 15 percent of Californians had a Spanish last name while no state senators were of Latino origin, only 2 Assembly members out of 80 and only one Congress member. It is to me noted however that first of all the methodology of identifying Latinos using surnames is problematic in itself. And second of all, and crucial in this case, Latino population numbers are far different from being equal to percentage of Latinos who are citizens or percentage of Latinos who are voting-age citizens. These numbers were therefore misleading. At the hearings, 2 Latino professors, David Lopez-Lee and Henry Pacheco presented maps of Los Angeles County showing that East Los Angeles was sliced in several Assembly districts but the problem was that Latino activists had to rely on the Assembly for statistics they did not have the resources to draw districts themselves and did not have data for areas outside East Los Angeles. Besides, there was no powerful Latino inside the process, since there was no Latino state senator and there were only 2 Latino Assemblymen but none of them was part of the Reapportionment Committee.[17]

Richard Calderon who lost to George Danielson in his bid for a congressional seat in 1970 declared in the press: "With the . . . past pattern of gerrymandering, it is very difficult to achieve a base for representation at any level. . . . The Establishment, the Democratic Party, is doing a very good job of radicalizing our community."[18] Considering the spatial segregation of the Latino community in the state, its representatives believed it should have been able to elect more legislators. How many more? Proportional representation would require about 12 Assembly members, 6 senators, and 6 Congress members. However, even under the hypothesis that proportional representation was philosophically desirable, from a practical standpoint, the Democrats were in a bind. For instance, Latino population has a high number of minors and a high number of noncitizens, along with a low turnout rate. Using general population as a baseline is always unrealistic. Besides, Los Angeles County was due to lose 3 Assembly seats because of population shift towards Orange County and other suburban areas. Incumbents were fighting for their political life. Therefore Mexican Americans were for the Democrats only one pressure group among many. The writing was on the wall and Latinos were bound to be disappointed and they knew it. During the first hearing of the Assembly Committee on Election and Reapportionment, headed by Henry Waxman, Alex Garcia (D-Los Angeles) went so far as to predict that Latinos would withdraw from the Democratic Party and form a third party: "The time has come. . . . Don't take us and divide us as you have in the past. This is going to be the last chance to give us a break."[19] A memo for Democrat Bill Greene, dated May 10, 1971, stated: "It would appear from the 1970 census figures and the Chicanos' apparent and legitimate threat to bolt the Party to form an ethnic one that the legislators will have to create, if not another congressional seat, then at least a new Assembly seat."[20] This memo confirms that the Californians for Liberal Representation wishes were way out of reach.

In the 1970s the Latino community was up for grabs and Republicans could have taken advantage of their disappointment in the Democratic leadership. Some tried but the "southern strategy" and its anti-minority stance and, later, the instrumentalization of immigration ruined any hope of the GOP courting Latinos nationally or locally.

The decisive electoral role played by minorities in California, especially in the Democratic coalition, was already obvious in the early 1970s, even if it has kept growing ever since. In 1970, Chicanos were already the largest minority group in California and numerically the largest minority group in any state. Even the Assembly Republicans, who drew first blood in September 1971 by presenting their plan before anyone else and directly to the public, included 3 Latino districts—a smart maneuver since 2 of the 3 districts were those of Speaker Moretti's closest lieutenants, Jack Fenton and majority leader Walter Karabian. The Republicans astutely made theirs the requests of Latino activists knowing the Democrats could not accept it. The Coalition for Fair Representation headed by Herman Sillas, helped by Henry Pacheco, had been lobbying in Sacramento for the creation of 4 Assembly districts and 2 Senate districts. Lamenting that no district had more than 30 percent Spanish-surname population, they decided to draw districts, using their own data since parties were not sharing theirs, with Spanish-surname concentration of 75 percent to 85 percent in order to obtain a voting age population majority for Latinos.[21] The problem with their approach is that it completely ignored the other districts and the partisan consequences of their modifications. It took some time for minority groups to learn the complexities of redistricting and come up with complete maps that could be used as bargaining chips with legislators. The development of cheap software and personal computers in the 1990s was crucial for the involvement of minority groups and the public at large. But in 1971, proposing a handful of districts without any considerations for the others, and threatening to go to court if these changes were not implemented, was just unacceptable for Democrats who argued that if they lost their legislative majorities Latino interests would not be better served, even with a few token elected officials. Henry Waxman, chairman of the Assembly Election and Reapportionment Committee (and a member of the Californians for Liberal Representation), actually had to clarify the party's position in the newspapers: "We attempted to minimize fragmentation. There will be a larger number of districts in which Mexican Americans, though far short of being a majority, are so large a minority as to require the attention and concern of whoever represents that district. Though more subtle than the election of a Chicano representative this too will prove a major source of increased Chicano political leverage."[22] And he went on giving examples of Anglo legislators being responsive to Chicano interests and Mexican American officials being elected in Anglo districts. And for good measure, he reminded the reader that "Assemblyman Willie Brown, a Negro, represents a district less than 25 percent Black," implicitly suggesting that if African Americans were satisfied with influence districts so should Mexican Americans.[23] Sillas wasn't naïve about the hierarchy of factors during redistricting: "First, the need to protect the incumbents, preferably himself, and after that his friends. Second, the need to protect and increase his party's numbers by squeezing more of his own party into the legislature. And third, to use anything that's left over for a showpiece of 'model' redistricting such as the Blacks got in 1960 and 1965."[24] This sentence illustrates both the civil rights constraint that the Black community represented but also the nascent rivalry between two groups believing they were forced to fight over limited resources. Moreover, it took forty years, several referendums, and an Independent Redistricting Commission to dial down the incumbency protection factor. Actually, it could be argued that the main reason why California voters took redistricting out of the hands of the legislature (and adopted term limits) was to reduce an incumbent protection that appeared, to many, undemocratic. In 1971, the California State Advisory Committee to the US Civil Rights Commission, chaired by Herman Sillas, already recommended taking redistricting out of the hands of the legislature to prevent the "same racist patterns" from taking place.[25] The report highlighted the fact that out of 15,650 elected and appointed officials at municipal, county, state, and federal levels in California only 310, about 2 percent, were Mexican Americans.[26] The committee's report quoted Jesse Unruh saying "reapportionments are designed by incumbents, for incumbents, as a service for incumbents"[27] and Mervyn Dymally declared "no incumbent wants to preside over his own death."[28] In a move that certainly irked the legislature, the committee members called for the courts to intervene, reasoning that any court-supervised redistricting would be better than any plan drawn by the legislature. In the end Sillas got what he asked for, even though it wasn't because of pressure from the Latino community.

In the 1970s minorities had neither the legal tools nor the technical expertise to put a dent into incumbency protection. All they had was their electoral weight which was still marginal enough for both parties to use Latinos, or make them feel, like political pawns. The Latino community, the notorious "sleeping giant," had low rates of citizenship and half the registration rate of other minorities. Most important for party leaders and elected officials was the potential for civil unrest on the part of minorities and the necessity to mitigate it.

THE CONGRESSIONAL PLAN

As mentioned before because of population growth in Republican areas, Democrats in Los Angeles County and San Francisco and Alameda were threatened to be redrawn out of their Assembly or Senate seat, unless map drawers were especially creative.[29] And even if the Democratic seats were preserved in the inner cities, to save everyone would require moving some incumbents in the suburbs, a risky electoral move. It truly represented a lost opportunity for Republicans who, under these circumstances, would have had an easy time coming up with a GOP gerrymander respecting equal population. Congressional redistricting presented a different set of issues. Because California's population had grown by 25 percent during the previous decade, the state was entitled to 5 additional congressional seats. In 1971 California passed New York and received the largest congressional delegation with forty-three seats.[30] Only ten of the 38 congressional districts in 1967 were undersized, and none would have to be collapsed or moved. 5 new seats could be drawn without any electoral harm to incumbents.

Because of the seniority rule in Congress, it was very important for Phil Burton to protect incumbents of all parties. This was in California's best interest. Burton had earned credit among his congressional colleagues for his role in 1967 since every House member was reelected in 1968 and 1970. However, state Republicans that had been shut out of the process didn't trust him one bit.[31] Next on Burton's priorities was to identify what the leaders of the California legislature wanted and meet their demands. Who wants to move up? With five new congressional seats, Burton could be king maker and buy loyalty from both parties. For instance, Senator Dymally had interest in a Congressional seat and that fit two of Burton's goals. By drawing a second Black district in Los Angeles, he would win over minorities. And by creating a new district in central Los Angeles the Democrat districts could expand into suburban territory. Since inner-city districts were underpopulated and Republican district overpopulated, the Democrats needed to optimize their partisan edge. Expanding Democratic districts into the suburbs ate up GOP territory without menacing urban Democrats. Shrinking GOP territory meant limiting the creation of new Republican districts in spite of their population gains.

But that wasn't all. GOP Representative Alphonzo E. Bell wanted to get rid of the conservative Palos Verdes Peninsula because he had had primary difficulties there. So Burton put this conservative area into the new Black districts. Bell solved his primary problem. This Republican influx into the Black district was harmless since it wasn't enough to significantly change its partisan makeup. In essence Burton neutralized the Palos Verdes Peninsula. This allowed Bell's district to absorb Culver City, the area where the Howard Berman Assembly seat was drawn. When Bell retired Berman (or possibly Waxman) would have a shot at a congressional seat. So with one move Burton solved his partisan problem of limiting GOP seats increase, made Dymally and the African American community happy and helped his Assembly allies with the potential for a future congressional seat.[32]

Phil Burton's last task was to maximize Democratic gains without hurting Republican incumbents. Of the 5 new congressional seats, Burton had so far used 2 (one for Dymally and one for GOP Senator Clair Burgener of San Diego). For the last 3, Burton decided to carve Democratic territory out of GOP existing districts. Putting Republican incumbents in safer district was a way guaranteeing they would pressure their leadership into accepting a plan that would benefit the Democrats. By knowing the terrain and his colleagues' needs Burton was able to create three Democratic districts and guaranteed the reelection of adjacent Republicans. As often, partisan gains came at the cost of electoral competition.[33] Of course Burton, and Leroy Hardy, tried to sell their plan as less partisan, arguing the three new Democratic seats were actually toss-ups. But congressional redistricting is a national endeavor and because of their poor results in 1970 Republicans were not in a position to compensate the losses with gains in other large states. GOP officials needed to keep an eye on the partisan balance in Congress in order not to be gerrymandered out of the majority for a decade.[34]

As it turns out Dymally did not like the Burton Plan and forced him to remove the Republican territory of Palos Verdes out of his district. With this move Dymally reminded Burton, who was too close to the Assembly in his eyes, that it was the legislature that was in charge of drawing the lines and that the Senate would play a crucial role. After all Mervyn M. Dymally was chairman of the Senate Committee on Elections and Reapportionment. Dymally made a politically costly and successful effort to increase state senate representation for the Latino population in East Los Angeles, creating a new district entirely within East LA. He also pushed for the creation of a second State Senate district in which an African American could be elected. Eventually it was all for naught since the Bipartisan Senate Plan died when the Assembly gridlocked and so did the Burton plan.

One of the most fascinating political battles centered on the California Thirty-eighth District in western San Bernardino, Riverside, and eastern Los Angeles counties. The new Thirty-eighth District was 1 of 5 new congressional districts that California was entitled to in 1971. With a Democratic registration edge of 2 to 1 (63.7 percent), it had the potential of being 1 of the 2 Democratic districts in the bipartisan plan to split the gain of 5: 2 Democratic, 2 Republican, and 1 party-neutral. Among the many Democrats interested in the district were 4 prominent contenders (David A. Tunno, George Brown Jr., Ruben S. Ayala,[35] and Terry Goggin). As the redistricting bill wandered through the legislative process, the lines of the proposed district changed daily, and toward the end, hourly, according to Leroy Hardy.[36] Inside the complex Democratic coalition each contender had his supporters: liberals, labor leaders, Mexican Americans, and African Americans who sided with each group from time to time. With a very thin Democratic majority in the Senate and in the Assembly, each group had its veto power. In the final bill, all the contenders fought for the primary nomination.[37] Veteran liberal George E. Brown Jr. won the general election and returned to Congress (after having lost his US Senate bid in 1970) where he kept his seat until his death in 1999.

THE BIPARTISAN SENATE PLAN

Senator Dymally really wanted to create a new Latino district in Los Angeles which was the key feature, and the center of all the controversy, of the Senate redistricting bill. Dymally wanted to deliver for minorities because he was himself non-White but also because this would put him in the position of leadership of minority Democrats. The Republicans came up with their plan first and Dymally answered with his own plan on October 6, 1971. The north needed to lose one seat because of population drop, so his plan collapsed a Republican seat up north (and moved Senate Republican Floor Leader Fred W. Marler Jr. of Redding 546 miles from his home) and created a Latino seat in Los Angeles. The new district stretched almost from the Los Angeles City hall all the way to Whittier. Democrats calculated that more than 50 percent of registered Democrats had Spanish last names, a school census indicated that 82 percent of schoolchildren had Spanish last names, and the Democrats represented 68 percent of the district voters, giving any Latino candidate a real chance if he won the primary.[38] Dymally was accused of gerrymandering for the sole purpose of electing a Mexican American senator. He answered by pointing out that he was proud of what he did for the Latino community, that Governor Reagan had told him he would veto any bill not including a new Mexican American district and that the new district corrected "a long standing ethnic abuse which short-changed a major community of people in

California. . . . Yes, Blacks and Browns have always been gerrymandered out before."[39]

Republicans accused the Democrats of wanting to expand their majority and declared they would ask the governor to veto the bill. To maintain the 21–19 status quo Dymally decided to eliminate Senator Lawrence E. Walsh's (D-Commerce) Thirty-seventh District. Parties usually have one incumbent that is either a political liability or doesn't have the right friends in the caucus. Walsh went out kicking and screaming, accusing the leadership of sacrificing him for minorities: "They are gutting my district deliberately to create this proposed Chicano district. It's racial discrimination in reverse."[40]

With equal population, map drawing became a bit more complicated and where one starts to draw districts defines where the difficulties will arise. Because of the political importance and population concentration around the Bay Area and the LA area, map drawers started there. This means that the districts that need to be adjusted were the ones in the last part of the map, the San Joaquin Valley. With each draft, each valley district became a bit more distorted. Incumbents complained and lines were shuffled. So much so that Dymally and his homologue John L. Harmer (R-Glendale) came up with a fourth redistricting map that became known, in a joint press release, and in an effort to get the necessary votes, the Bipartisan Senate Reapportionment Plan. On November 11, the Senate passed the Bipartisan Plan with a 32 to 2 vote (Walsh was one of the "no" votes). But five days later an Assembly special election derailed the whole process.

ALATORRE'S UPSET AND THE ASSEMBLY DEADLOCK

The early 1970s was a period full of uncertainties as far as California politics is concerned. Civil unrest and student protest was the norm. The national Democratic Party had exploded in 1968 in Chicago over the Vietnam War issue. No party had a clear view of what the future held and the Democrats feared their 1970 gains could have been an accident. Speaker Moretti, to protect this Speakership and his majority for several election cycles, wanted to gain seats in the Assembly. Assemblyman Waxman wanted to create a seat in Los Angeles for Howard Berman, his close friend and campaign manager. Howard Berman was also Michael Berman's older brother, the Democrats redistricting expert. But the Republicans would not have it. They wanted 37 seats for their 37 elected officials. After several rounds of negotiations, both party leaders and redistricting players (among which was Ways and Means Committee Chairman Willie Brown), gathered on November 15, 1971, and a deal was struck. The Democrats agreed to draw 37 Republican seats and

43 Democratic seats if the Republicans promised to muster the two-third majority vote necessary to override a governor veto in case Ronald Reagan wanted to play hardball. The two parties had reached an agreement about the new redistricting plan, the first complete one since the passage of the 1965 Voting Rights Act. One Democratic leader was absent from the negotiation. Majority Leader Walter Karabian was in Los Angeles to supervise the election of his aide Richard Alatorre. One the reasons Chairman Waxman gave as a justification to not create a new Assembly seat was that Richard Alatorre would win for sure in the Forty-eighth Assembly District giving the community what it had asked for.[41]

Alatorre was of Mexican descent and his election would have added a second Latino in the Assembly and a new Latino-friendly district had been created in the Waxman plan. This election would have gone a long way for the Democrats to show that in spite of the lack of Latino seats in their plan, they were able to deliver Latino representation. In a heavily Democratic district that had never gone Republican, Alatorre's election was a foregone conclusion. But on the Sunday night before the election, someone shot at the front of the home Republican candidate and Anglo millionaire Brophy while he was in a back room. All the Monday headlines were about the failed attempt murder of the candidate. Alatorre was also accused of pretending to be of Italian descent during the primaries in order to lure the Anglo vote of this working-class district. On Monday the two parties had worked out a deal on redistricting in the Assembly. On Tuesday Alatorre lost the election by 1,500 votes. An independent Latino candidate, Raul Ruiz of La Raza Unidad, siphoned 2,800 votes with a surprisingly well-financed campaign raising suspicion that the Republicans had helped the enemy of the enemy. Ruiz received 7 percent of the votes and Alatorre lost by 4 percent.[42] Democrats tried to play down the role of the activist party and dismissed it as a "one-time fluke."[43] Both parties were shocked and Karabian lost his majority leader position. And then the Republicans got greedy. Brophy's election gave the Republicans 38 incumbents and GOP leaders wanted all incumbents protected, arguing this was the only way the Governor could sign it. The 37 to 43 deal was not to their liking anymore even though Democrats pleaded that his election was an aberration and could not be duplicated in a regular election. Republicans came up with a new map that did not include a real Republican district for Brophy (the area was just too Democratic) but Democrats refused to even consider it. Moretti was already worried about his majority because of the fast suburban growth in the state and the Alatorre debacle comforted him in his caution.

Assemblyman Jerry Lewis of the Elections and Constitutional Amendment Committee famously drafted a memo that was found by the Democrats when they took over. When Lewis sanctimoniously accused the Democrats of gerrymandering, Speaker Moretti read passages of the memo in chamber. In it Lewis declared:

> In my judgment, our number one criteria should be a program designed to establish districts in California that will elect the highest number of Republicans to the Senate Legislature and the House of Representatives. A second item for consideration is the include in the plan Democrat districts with sizable majority for those who are measured to be the "least effective members" of the minority party. . . . I believe we have an unusually good opportunity to develop a "balanced and representative plan" which in reality is totally designed for partisan purposes.[44]

The Republican camp was split, and the Democrats proposed their own bill for the Assembly, together with the old plans for the Senate and Congress. Ronald Reagan decided to veto all three. "Thus, the twenty-year partisan battle over reapportionment in California was set off when an attempt by Democrats to increase ethnic minority representation was blocked by Republicans. Partisan and ethnic factors in California Reapportionment are inseparably intertwined."[45] Governor Reagan had initially agreed to sign Burton's plan as long as it was a fair split: 2 new Democratic seats, 2 Republicans, and 1 toss-up. But Burton, in an attempt to please Charles Teague, a senior GOP Representative, removed students and Latino cities from his Santa Barbara district to include them in Barry Goldwater Jr.'s. Junior called his dad who complained to Reagan about his son's treatment. Burton later admitted he should not have infuriated "the old man."[46]

Of course, another lesson is if the two parties had taken care of redistricting before the Alatorre special election, none of this would have happened.

When the Assembly negotiation reached an impasse, Assembly Democratic leaders decided to try to pressure Governor Reagan into signing their redistricting bill by amending it with the Senate bill. Senator of both parties resented that move because a single bill risked being vetoed but also because the politics of the Assembly was unnecessarily brought into the Senate. So Senate Democrats refused to vote on the amended bill and on December 2, the legislature recessed without having passed any redistricting bill. In an interview with Anthony Quinn, Phil Burton called the whole episode "amateur politics."[47]

But procrastinating was not limited to redistricting and the Democrats still had leverage. On December 3, Democrat leaders went to the governor's office and demanded a special session on redistricting. The legislature had not voted on a tax bill the governor wanted so much that he was willing to call a special session. On December 6, a special session started for the tax bill and the redistricting bill. The tax bill vote was a formality and the legislature recessed for ten days while the leadership attempted a new round of negotiations on redistricting. The attempt was short-lived.[48]

SPECIAL SESSION AND REAPPORTIONMENT COMMISSION

During the first round of negotiations it was assumed that Governor Reagan would sign the redistricting bill once the Republican leadership had agreed on a plan. But the governor received complaints about another gerrymander with oddly shaped districts. Reagan wanted a bill that would not damage the image he had created for himself and his staff began passing down suggestions to the legislature to make changes to the maps. Both parties were irritated by the incursion of the executive into redistricting affairs.

Democrats concluded that it was in their best interest to vote their plan without any input from the Republicans, let the governor veto them, and take their chances before the State Supreme Court. They believed it was possible to impose their bill over the governor's veto through the Court.

One reason why the Democrats thought this was the only alternative was the Republican-dominated state Reapportionment Commission. In November 1971, Lieutenant Governor Ed Reinecke, the presumptive chairman of the commission, and presumptive candidate for the 1974 gubernatorial election, invoked the constitutional provision that the Reapportionment Commission be in charge of redistricting if the legislature failed to do so. In 1926, in order to enforce the "federal plan," one portion of the 1926 Farm Bureau Federation Amendment created a reapportionment commission composed of the Lieutenant Governor, Attorney General, Controller, Secretary of State, and Superintendent of Public Instruction to redistrict the state if the legislature failed to do so. Since its creation was directly linked to the "federal plan" it wasn't clear whether or not the commission had been struck down by the California Supreme Court in 1965 in *Silver v. Brown*. What was sure for Democrats is that the commission would be composed of 3 Republicans (Ed Reinecke, Houston Flournoy, and Evelle Younger) and 2 Democrats (Edmund Brown Jr. and Wilson Riles), in effect putting the GOP in charge of the redistricting process. The Democrats called for a special session because even though they thought the Court had struck down the commission, they were not positive that absent any map the Court may not turn to the commission to come up with some kind of redistricting plan. It would be more difficult to argue that the commission plan was invalid if they had not produced one. On December 15, Lieutenant Governor Reinecke convened the commission and announced it would begin statewide public hearings and invited "interested" parties to submit plans. He emphatically declared that the commission would produce "a fair, honest and nonpartisan reapportionment . . . that is not the captive of incumbents to public office."[49] Brown, a presumptive candidate for the governorship in 1974, did not shy away from the fight. He readily denounced the meeting, quickly pushed through a two-third vote rule that temporarily handcuffed the Republican majority, called for a court hearing on the commission's validity and filed a lawsuit against Governor Reagan to force action on the question of the legislature's bill legality. Democrats filed a lawsuit the next day, drafted in the name of the legislature generally and the chairmen of the reapportionment committees of the Senate and Assembly specifically.

Then, among the redistricting chaos, Thomas Hofeller, an employee of Compass Systems, the GOP's computer firm, presented a plan he called the CSI Plan. The commission had adopted the criteria that all districts be contiguous and compact. And CSI Plan was very pleasing to the eye. But the Democrats and some Republicans denounced its partisan and political effects. Many incumbents in both chambers were forced to run against one another. The Democrats would lose their majorities in both chambers.[50] To sum up, the CSI Plan was a great impetuous for the legislature to act.

But by now both sides had lost patience and tempers ran high as Christmas break approached. The equivocation of the governor did not help. On December 18, 1971, Moretti and Dymally brought their bills for a vote which passed on a strict partisan basis and with great difficulty for the Assembly plan three days later.[51] Republicans called for the governor to veto the bills and threatened to sue the state if the legislature bills went through and Latinos threatened to sue because the bill was discriminatory against them. South Gate Mayor Frank Gafkowski and other Southeast mayors were contemplating suing because their city was split among many districts infringing the right of their community of interest or their city charter's explicit wording to have only one representative.[52] The bills sat on the governor's desk from December 21 to 30 as the Republicans built their technical legal case against them. On December 30, Governor Reagan vetoed all three. In his lengthy formal veto message scorching the Democratic leadership, written in part by Alan Heslop, he accused them of drawing: "tortuous boundary line around artificial and bizarre-shaped districts aimed solely at perpetuating themselves in office." He added: "Far worse, however, was the unfair way in which these gerrymandered bills split communities throughout the state and minimized representation of minority groups who hoped that finally their particular concerns might be met."[53] He singled out the district created for Howard Berman as an example of racial gerrymandering, declaring that it ensured "the election of an Anglo at a time when responsible yet long-underrepresented minorities are struggling to find ways to work within our political system. It is astounding and completely indefensible. I am sure the great majority of

Californians will agree with me."[54] His message was replete with criticism, using expressions such as "unnecessary appendages," "random disregard for preservation of communities of interest," "arbitrarily divided," "major flaw," "no rational purpose," and "totally indefensible." And after his statement, during questioning, for good measure, he ventured whether letting the Legislature in charge of redistricting wasn't a "gigantic conflict of interest."[55] With these blistering remarks Reagan tried to score political points with the public and discourage any attempt at overriding his veto. It was now up to the Court to fix the electoral system as the June 6 presidential primary was fast approaching.

THE CALIFORNIA SUPREME COURT INTERVENTION

Three redistricting-related cases were before the state Supreme Court in early 1971. The Democratic leadership, on behalf of the legislature, sued Lieutenant Governor Reinecke and its Reapportionment Commission. Secretary of State Brown had sued Reagan arguing the Democratic redistricting bills represented the highest expression of legislative intent and that respect of the constitutional principle of separation of powers superseded the governor's veto. The third lawsuit had been filed by former Republican Senator Thomas Kuchel, on behalf of Phil Burton and 32 congressmen (19 Democrats and 13 Republicans), who asked the Court to set aside the gubernatorial veto in the case of Congress. And on January 13, 1972, for good measure, 4 groups (California Rural Legal Assistance, MALDEF, the Lawyers Committee for Civil Rights Under the Law, and the Beverly Hills Bar Association Law) filed a lawsuit on behalf of 7 Mexican American voters, challenging the constitutionality of the legislature's redistricting plans.

Briefs were filed by attorneys representing African American and Latino groups asking the Court to reject the redistricting plans because it protected Anglo incumbents and discriminated against minorities. The Democrats explained that their original plan increased opportunities to elect minority candidates and that the Republican plan endangered 4 of the 7 minority-held seats in the Assembly. The Republicans claimed having created more minority districts but these overlapped with Democratic incumbents forcing Democrats to choose between Anglo incumbents and minority challengers.[56] But the Court did not address any of these issues.

On January 18, 1972, Chief Justice Donald Wright, a Reagan appointee, unsurprisingly dismissed the Reapportionment Commission that had been attached to the "Federal Plan," stating that the former and therefore by extension the latter, had been declared unconstitutional in 1965.[57]

However in a more surprising and difficult attempt to thread the political needle, the Court reinstated the 1965 districts for the Assembly and the Senate in spite of the population discrepancies. Moreover, the Court decided to enforce, albeit regretfully and temporarily, Phil Burton's redistricting plan for Congress because of the addition of 5 new Congressional districts that could not be left unfilled. What helped Burton's plan was that even though the California legislature was ambivalent, the congressional delegation was not. The bipartisan support of the members of Congress went a long way with the judges. The Court also had to take into consideration that the filing deadline for the 1972 June primaries was February 23. Under these circumstances, the Court believed it did not have enough time to produce new maps.

Democrats were satisfied with the ruling because, first of all, they dodged the dreaded Hofeller plan but, second, most of their districts had lost population since 1965. The Republicans were satisfied the Court had refused to implement the 1971 Democrat maps but the 1965 maps clearly were in the Democrats' favor. But this was a one-time deal since the court merely postponed the redistricting battle until after the 1972 elections. For sure, in 1973 new districts would be drawn either by the legislature or the Court. Indeed, if the legislature proved incapable of coming up with new maps once again, the Court would appoint 3 retired Appeals Court judges—"special masters"—to produce a new plan. To avoid such outcome, Assemblyman Henry Waxman even proposed a constitutional amendment authorizing the creation of an independent special commission to redistrict California.[58] The 6 members of the commission would have been appointed by legislative leaders and the congressional delegation. His proposal was defeated on the Assembly floor but it indicated that some Assembly members were open to alternatives probably because they realized that the legislature could not produce plans that could satisfy Governor Reagan and the Supreme Court.

Governor Reagan, who understandably resented the Court for ignoring his veto, in a statement that defies any understanding of California politics, and not so far off from the Schwarzenegger rhetoric of the 2000s, declared: "There is only one way to do reapportionment—feed into the computer all of the factors except political registration. That should not be a part of it."[59] This statement also demonstrates a misunderstanding of the basic practical aspect of redistricting. No computer can draw a single best set of districts if you feed it more than two factors.

The political consequences of the Republicans refusal to give up Brophy's district and the Supreme Court decision to implement old maps had awful consequences for California Republicans who suffered also from the national context. The Watergate scandal and the Vietnam quagmire eliminated any hope of any political coattail to a Nixon reelection. In California, Republican registration dropped precipitously in 1972.[60] A Republican governor in his sixth year did not energize the base while the McGovern-Humphrey primary invigorated Democratic registration.

In Congress, all incumbents were reelected. Assembly woman Yvonne Braithwaite Burke won the new African American Thirty-seventh Congressional District that Dymally passed up on and became the first Black woman elected to the California congressional delegation where she served for three terms.[61] The Democratic delegation majority went from 20–18 to 23–20, a good result for both parties given the 1972 election context. Only twenty Senate seats were up for reelection. The 1972 created a 20–20 partisan balance between the two parties, setting the table nicely for the 1973 redistricting negotiations.[62] But it was in the Assembly that the Republican "debacle" took place.[63] The GOP ended up losing nine seats in one of its worst showing in its history. The Democrats now counted three more Latinos in the Assembly, one more African American in the Senate, and one more in Congress.[64] The Fortieth District is instructive as far as the evolution of Latino politics. Alex Garcia, a Democrat, who was partly financed by the newly created California Chicano Caucus, was the favorite after having survived a close call in the primaries when he won by 200 votes against Al Torres. But he faced in 1972 a Latino Republican candidate on his right (Bob Aguirre) and Raul Ruiz on his left representing the marginal and short-lived La Raza Unitad Party. Almost recreating the conditions under which Alatorre lost a year before, in a tight race, Ruiz presence could have been decisive.[65] But La Raza Unitad Party soon fell into oblivion and Republican Latino candidates remained the exception rather than the norm.

REAGAN'S SECOND VETO

In its 1972 decision, the Court had set a December deadline for the legislature to pass redistricting bills. But with the elections in the fall, it wasn't until February 1973 that both houses returned to the drawing board.

In the Senate Dymally's new plan was pitted against Harmer's new plan for which he teamed up with moderate Democrat George Zenovich of Fresno. Their plan moved Dymally's district east into Latino neighborhoods of East Los Angeles potentially forcing him to run against Latino candidates. The adjacent second Black district that Dymally had drawn (represented by Anglo Senator James Q. Wedworth) saw its African American population reduced from 52 percent to 27 percent, practically eliminating the possibility of seeing a second minority candidate to the Senate for a decade. Harmer and Zenovich finally attempted to produce a Latino district that the community denounced as having only a 47 percent Spanish-surname population and therefore very more likely to elect an Anglo candidate.[66] Dymally blocked the Harmer-Zenovich plan in Committee and Harmer and Zenovich made sure there weren't enough votes on the floor for Dymally's plan. Both bills stayed in limbo for two months. Then, on May 1, 1973, the Supreme Court appointed 3 retired judges, 2 Democrats Harold F. Collins of Los Angeles, Alvin E. Weinberger of San Francisco, and 1 Republican, Martin J. Coughlin of Los Angeles, to act as redistricting "masters." The Court asked them to start their work in June to produce a plan by August 31. The Court also announced it would not accept "at-large" State Senate districts anymore, such as those in San Francisco and Alameda counties.[67] These districts made it harder for minorities to run candidates because larger districts cost more to run and they gave incumbents an unfair advantage over any challenger.

In a last desperate attempt, the Republicans amended their bill to satisfy Democrats' partisan qualms and a status quo 20–20 Harmer-Zenovich plan was passed on the May 23. Reagan was believed to be prepared to sign this bill.

But things were more complicated in the Assembly where the Democrats had a 51 seat majority. Republicans were ready to abandon negotiations and let the Court draw what could only be more favorable districts. The Democrats preferred a compromise and since a two-third majority of 54 seats was unrealistic, they offered 3 districts to the Republicans to buy their vote. By drawing these Republican districts the Democrats protected the adjacent districts making it a win-win all around.[68] But the Democratic leadership was unable to sell the deal.[69] It was not until late May that the lower chamber finally passed a redistricting bill by a vote of 63–12. It added 4 solidly Republican districts and would return 31–33 Republicans in the 1974 election. This gain wasn't enough for governor Reagan who only saw the 47 safe Democratic districts. Latino community spokespersons urged the Governor to veto the plans, counting on court intervention. He also announced he would veto again the congressional bill since Phil Burton had simply resurrected his old plan. Reagan would only sign the Senate bill. So once more, as in 1971, the Senate bill was merged with the Assembly bill (as well as the congressional redistricting plan) to try and force the governor to sign both.[70] If Reagan vetoed the bill he would kill a Republican-oriented Senate plan, an Assembly plan giving his party more seats and a congressional plan that incumbent Republicans supported. With the Watergate scandal as Damocles sword above the Republicans' heads nationwide, 1974 did not look good for the GOP. Toss in Ford's pardon of Nixon and 20 senators, 20 congressmen, and 31 assemblymen would be a miracle under these circumstances. But Reagan could not come back on his word and sign a bill giving his party a permanent minority status in the Assembly. He vetoed the bill. On June 28, the legislature tried to override Reagan's veto but fell short. For the first time in the state's history the Court was going to be in charge of redistricting.

THE SPECIAL MASTERS' PLAN

Court Intervention in Redistricting Litigation

Before delving into the special masters' plan it could be helpful to quickly review difficulties raised by court intervention in redistricting cases. Since courts tend to draw their own plans only as a last resort, a court is necessarily rushed in drawing a plan if it gives the legislature until the last moment to draw its own. Besides, a court operates under a compressed time frame that limits the possible factors it can take into account. With more time it could mediate among the opposing forces that shape the line-drawing process. Theoretically, a court with enough time could also improve its plan after receiving input from interested parties. However, the judicial process does not allow such deliberation and compromise making. Court-drawn plans, contrary to legislative bills, are not more than emergency measures implemented temporarily to make sure that elections take place under some set of legally acceptable lines. Moreover, the process is far from uniform in spite of how many times courts have drawn their own redistricting plans in the last fifty years. Nathaniel Persily distinguishes three procedural models, but an infinite number of permutations and alternatives are also possible.[71]

Special Masters

Courts use special masters to supervise the production of court-drawn plans to place some distance between themselves and the plan. Because it is such a political task, appointing a retired judge or a redistricting expert allows the court to not bear the responsibility of said plan. The court's role is to set the principles, if any, and approve, reject or present objections to the plan. This model requires the employment of a legal team to help the special master to develop a report to accompany the plan, as well as the employment of one or more experts to assist in the production of the plan and the accompanying affidavits. In this case the special master usually becomes the advocate of his or her own plan and responds to objections. The degree of isolation of the special master and his or her distance from the court varies with the context of the litigation.

The other two models are the court-controlled model and the adopted-plan model.

The Court-Controlled Model

Courts will eliminate the middleman and simply hire an expert to help them draw their own plan or draw it themselves. This model can be effective and inexpensive for judges who are less afraid of the potential fallout, the Court cannot disclaim responsibility for its map. Also, for plans that are remedying limited, specific, and identifiable defects in the extant plan, this approach seems most appropriate.

The Adopted-Plan Model

The Court can decide to place the burden of proposing a remedy on the parties to the litigation or any interested party willing to come up with a redistricting plan. This process may or may not require the hiring of an expert depending on whether the Court feels confident it can assess the proposal with certain legal and other requirements. The Court has the luxury of choosing from several outsourced plans at very low cost. Yet the risk is that the Court might find all plans deficient either because they violate the law or because they arise from narrow and often partisan interests. This approach can be merged with either of the two previous models to produce a hybrid. If one outsourced plan is superior it can be adopted saving the Court time. If not the Court or special master can work off one or more of the plans to produce a better one.[72]

Consequences of the Special Masters' Plan

The masters held four hearings around the state during which representatives of Black, Latino, and women's groups, probably suspicious of an all-White, male panel, asked the Court to pay more attention to minority rights and less to incumbent protection. Counties and cities also voiced their opposition to plans dividing them among districts. Lieutenant Governor Reinecke submitted the Hofeller plan and its eye-pleasing compact districts. Latino groups presented plans redrawing central Los Angeles, once again ignoring the ripple effect, that is to say the consequences for the other districts around the state. After reviewing all the different plans presented to them, the masters decided they would draw their own.

The plans, unveiled in September 1973, were drawn by staffers hired by the Court: law professor (and former poverty lawyer) Paul McKaskle and political scientist Gordon Baker. They were given straightforward criteria: keep cities and counties intact, make congressional districts as equal in population as possible but allow 2 percent variation in the legislature, and form compact and contiguous districts. Congressional and Senate districts should coincide as much as possible and Senate districts should include 2 Assembly districts.[73] In redistricting parlance this is called "nesting."[74] Nothing was explicitly said about race as a criteria yet it was understood that minorities' opportunities could not decrease and, if possible, should increase especially in the Senate. The Court had noticed: "There is also evidence that the Senate plan dilutes the voting strength of Blacks and persons of Spanish surname by dividing homogeneous ethnic groups into a number of districts or by "packing" too many members of an ethnic group into a single district."[75] The upper chamber now contained 2 African American districts, in essence returning to Dymally's original plan, and 2 Latino districts. In the lower chamber and in Congress the new majority-minority districts helped secure minorities' gains in 1972. Of course, because minorities in California were already voting overwhelmingly for the Democratic Party, these minority districts were also safely Democratic. Mexican American group representatives were especially elated. Herman Sillas rejoiced to "potentially have a good shot at 2 State Senate seats and 4 Assembly seats . . . 1974 could be a heck of a year for Chicanos with this reapportionment plan. . . . A great door has been opened without hurting any other community's interest."[76] The increase in Chicano representation did not come at the expense of African Americans. Here we see the meaning that community of interest has taken where it is conflated with racial/ethnic minority. It has been defined as an area with certain common economic, social, or cultural interests, because, in the US, the rationale for community-based districts is derived from a delegate view of representation. The community of interest definition lends itself well to the shortcut of race and/or ethnic communities in a context of residential segregation. The masters' wording in this case reveals that community of interest was understood as a territorial concept:

> Social and economic interests common to the population of an area which are probable subjects of legislative action . . . should be considered in determining whether the area should be included within or excluded from a proposed district in order that all of the citizens of the district might be represented reasonably, fairly and effectively.[77]

Incumbents were the real losers of the McKaskle-Baker plan. So much so that Assembly Majority Leader Jack Fenton, who was now in the same district as Walter Karabian, dramatically asked his colleagues for "a moment's silence for the demise of some of us."[78] Even minority incumbents were not necessarily protected. Mervyn Dymally found himself in the new Thirty-third District with Lawrence Walsh in order to create a new Mexican American district. Dymally declared he was happy with the change (he eventually ran in the Twenty-ninth District) and announced he would run for Lieutenant Governor in 1974. In the Assembly, the creation of the Mexican American

Twenty-fourth District potentially pitted Richard Alatorre and Alex Garcia.[79] Congressional candidates were not too thrilled with the changes to a plan that had protected incumbents and therefore seniority in Congress. Chet Hollifield and Bill Milliard the 2 most senior Representatives from each party lost their districts. Congressman Charles Wiggins (R-West Covina) whose political future was in jeopardy declared: “This entire episode is a tragic exercise in misused judicial power.”[80] One Republican and one Democratic congressional district disappeared under the new plan, which was not so bad considering the fate of incumbents in the state legislature. The homes of 29 Assembly members (18 Democrats, 11 Republicans) and 18 senators (10 Democrats, 8 Republicans) were now located in districts that contained at least one incumbent.[81] It is not surprising that incumbent protection is the one factor that the Court did not implement. It is the hardest one to justify. The population usually expects competition and competitive seats and often sees the absence of such seats as proof that politicians choose their constituents and not the other way around. And the Supreme Court admitted this much: “While protection of incumbents may be desirable to assure a core of experienced legislators, the objective of reapportionment should not be the political survival or comfort of those already in office. It is best if an incumbent’s continuation in office depended upon effectiveness and responsiveness to constituents rather than upon the design of district boundaries.”[82]

Besides, with so many factors to take into consideration, something has to give. As mentioned, even if at the time the census figures used for redistricting did not include race and even if the “Hispanic” category had not been created yet by the Office of Management and Budget, everybody kept an eye on race. In the same way, even if the data included to draw the lines did not include partisanship, every participant in the redistricting process kept an eye on the potential partisan consequences of any proposed plan. Significantly reducing the representation of one party or one community of interest was politically impossible. Incumbent protection is only vital for elected officials and reducing it would not draw the ire of public opinion, quite the contrary. Gordon Baker recognized that “adhering to geographic guidelines made it virtually impossible to avoid placing more than one incumbent in the same district.”[83] And because the special master did not have to take into consideration the self-interest, partisan interest and ideological interests of politicians, the districts they drew were more pleasing to the eye. As Morgan Kousser observed:

> These images of squarish districts mechanically drawn by supposedly disinterested technicians who were insulated from the pressures of politics or publicity were to recur repeatedly over the next two decades—pristine technocracy, as opposed to the messy, imperfect compromises that characterized the legislative

process. It is one of the ironies of the late twentieth century that citizens of the world's foremost democratic country put so little trust in the officials they elect, have so little understanding of the process by which laws are made, and accept so readily the intervention of unknown and unaccountable "experts" in making fundamental policy.[84]

Some lawmakers have even internalized this distrust in the redistricting process. In August 1973, Arlen Gregorio (D-San Mateo) introduced a bill in the Senate proposing a ballot measure creating a nonpartisan redistricting commission to draw congressional and legislative district lines.[85] Pundits chimed in. Bill Boyarsky of the *Los Angeles Times* explained to the reader that Court "guidelines are consistent with the thinking expressed by Gov. Reagan earlier this year when he vetoed a legislative reapportionment bill and cited at least dozen of instances of 'outright gerrymandering.' They are consonant also with language in the California Constitution. And they meet the common-sense test of fairness. . . . The result may be fewer 'safe' seats and more 'competitive' seats—which is all to the good. . . . Californians should never again be subjected to the type of flagrant gerrymandering that has followed each decennial census in past years, regardless of the party in power."[86]

In spite of the negative effect they had on incumbents, few spoke ill of the plans. First of all, it was very difficult to criticize a plan for keeping together cities, counties, or nesting Assembly seats inside Senate seats. These are all sensible factors for the electorate. Some elected officials even felt compelled to pander to public opinion: "I hope never again to return to old way of drawing political district lines just to accommodate incumbent politicians," declared Representative Alphonzo Bell (R-Pacific Palisade).[87] Second of all, politicians are pretty adept at the game of interparty musical chairs and many of them traded old constituents for more electorally favorable districts. For instance, in the new Twentieth and Twenty-first Congressional Districts, Republican Barry Goldwater (R-Tarzana) and Democrat James Corman (D-Van Nuys) just swapped sides of the Valley they previously represented to run in more friendly districts.[88] Assemblyman Howard Berman (D-Los Angeles) was not the only official to change residence to qualify for a new district (in his case AD 43).[89] In other words, politicians and parties adapted to the new map to minimize the risks and maximize incumbent protection.

And third of all, the new plan created so many marginal districts that nobody could predict the outcome of the 1974 elections. Party leaders on both sides declared they were confident they would be able to control the Senate. However, in 1980, State Treasurer, and former Democratic Assembly Speaker, Jesse Unruh declared at a redistricting conference in Claremont College that "there was a hell of a lot more flagrant Democratic Gerrymandering (in the court plan) than I would ever have had the guts to do in my most arrogant moment."[90] Whether the special masters' plan was a Democratic gerrymander was a topic of debate for political scientists for many years. With hindsight, it is difficult to argue that the masters' plan was very different in their prospective effects from the legislature's proposed plans.[91] Much more important external factors were the oil price shock that upended the economy and the political fate of President Nixon which damaged the Republican brand.

In the Senate, the Supreme Court did Republicans a favor when it declared that only senators whose terms expired in 1974 had to run in the new districts. 12 of the 20 seats expiring in 1976 were Republican-held. In 1966, the court had required all senators to run in new districts, even though some had two years remaining on their terms.[92] Yet, 1974 was a terrible year for Republicans nationally as the Watergate tsunami decimated the GOP. Even before the masters' districts became effective, Senate Republicans had lost two of their 20 districts in special elections. Democrat Ruben Ayala won a Republican seat in San Bernardino County, becoming the state's first Latino senator. In Ventura County, Senator Lagomarsino's Republican Senate seat was won by a Democrat in another special election. So the Republicans entered the 1974 elections holding 18 districts, and with only 6 of their incumbents at risk. And yet, they did not do well. Republicans won only 3 of the 20 Senate seats at stake. Democrats won the other 17 seats, and turned the 20–20 split of 1972 into a 25–15 edge as the 1975 session opened. If all 40 seats been up for election, the GOP might have lost as many as 4 or 5 more seats. One possible victim might have been Long Beach Senator George Deukmejian. In the masters' plan Deukmejian's district had been combined with the Long Beach seat of popular Democrat Joseph Kennick. If he had had to run in 1974, Deukmejian could have chosen to move to Whittier, which he also represented, and run for reelection in an open district there. But, according to Anthony Quinn, neither running in Whittier nor facing off with Kennick in Long Beach would have been attractive for any Republican in 1974.[93] Deukmejian's career might have ended in 1974, another collateral victim of the Watergate scandal. As it was, however, Kennick retired in 1976 and Deukmejian held off a Democratic challenge in the Long Beach district. In 1976, the Republicans number fell to 14 out of 40 Senators.[94] But the GOP somewhat recovered in 1978, the year of Proposition 13 and 1980, the year of Reagan's landslide. The GOP won 17 Senate seats in 1980, the last election under the masters' plan. That is one less than they had going into the 1974 election.

Before the 1974 elections, Assembly Republicans controlled 31 districts, 2 more than they had won in 1972, because of special election wins in 1973. In 1974, Republicans suffered a net loss of 7 seats and the Assembly welcomed a staggering 23 new members. In 1976, the Republicans lost 2 more seats. These two election cycles were notoriously awful for Republicans throughout the nation as the GOP paid a heavy electoral price for Nixon's resignation and pardon. In the 1977 session, Democrats held 57 of the 80 districts, their best mark since 1877. For four years during the middle 1970s, the Democrats controlled more than two-thirds of the Assembly, making the Republicans practically powerless in the legislative process. This led many Democrats to look very kindly on the court intervention, which was quite consequential in the early 1990s when legislators faced again the prospect of court intervention. Besides, this super-majority helped Jerry Brown's administration control legislation during Brown's first term. In that sense, Reagan's vetoes were terrible for his party. However, the Republicans made a real comeback in 1978, with a net gain of 7 seats. 4 of these districts had been lost in 1974. The GOP won 2 more seats in 1980 and, after 4 elections under the masters' plan, they controlled 32 districts. That is 1 more seat than they had when the plan went into effect.

The 1972 congressional elections had produced 23 Democrats and 20 Republicans under Congressman Burton's plan. But by 1974, because of the Watergate scandal electoral consequences, it became apparent that these numbers would not hold up. When the masters' Plan first came out, GOP Congressman Mailliard of San Francisco saw the writing on the wall and took a position with the Nixon administration. His seat was won in a special election by Democratic Assemblyman John Burton, Phil's younger brother, and Republicans entered the 1974 election with only 19 incumbents. They lost four seats in the 1974 Democratic landslide. These districts had been made more competitive by the masters' plan. In 1976 the GOP lost a fifth seat, giving Democrats a 29–14 advantage in the congressional delegation. But the GOP again recovered their losses. In 1978 and 1980 Republicans retook three of the 4 Watergate losses, capturing 5 Democratic seats while losing only one of their own. After the 1980 election the GOP held 21 congressional seats to 22 for the Democrats. That is one more seat than in 1972.

The stars aligned for Assemblyman Henry Waxman who won a congressional seat due to the masters' redistricting. In drawing the two Latino districts in central Los Angeles, a new district was formed in the Hollywood area to replace Holifield. This new district had a Democrat registration of 58.1 percent and overlapped one-third of Waxman's Assembly district. He easily won in 1974 raising suspicion among Republicans about this rapid ascension.[95]

In spite of the Democratic wave, minority gains were not as spectacular in the 1974 elections in part because 1972 had brought in new non-Anglo elected officials. Latinos now controlled 2 seats in the Senate (previously

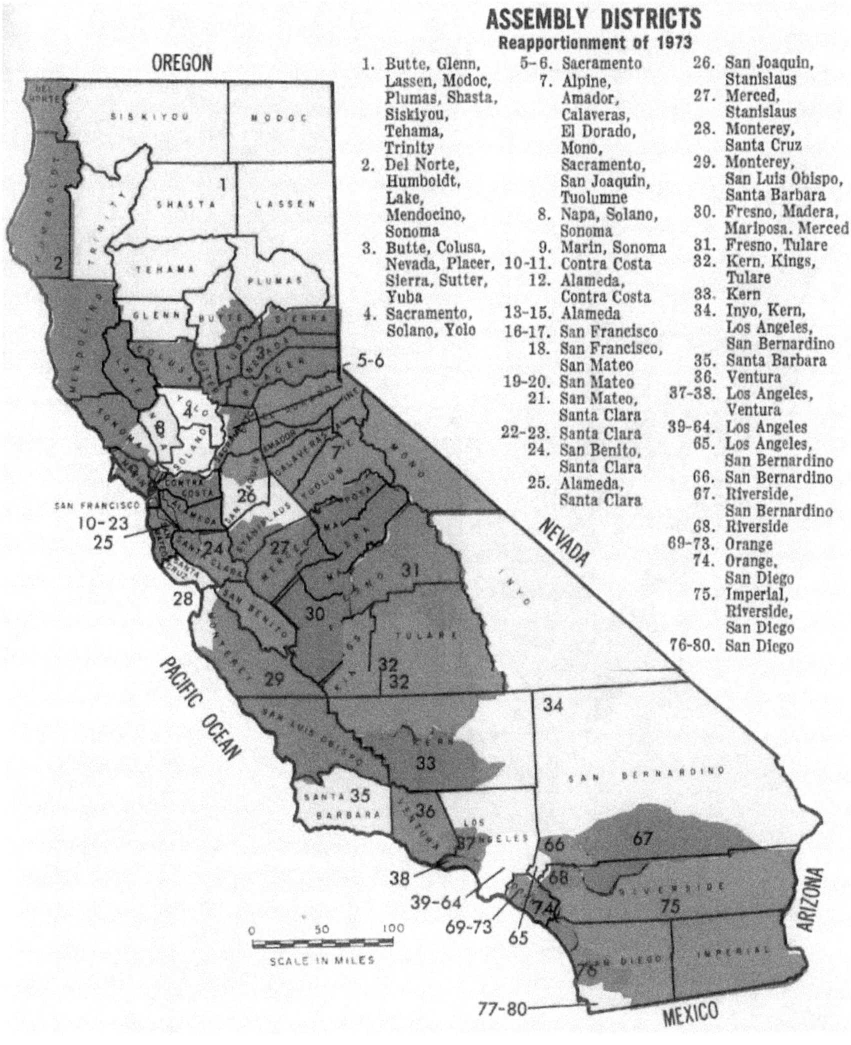

Figure 2.1 Assembly Districts: Reapportionment of 1973
Source: California Legislature at Sacramento Handbook, 1978

only had one) but lost one seat in the Assembly after having won three two years prior. African Americans gained one seat in the Senate and one seat in Congress, thus doubling their delegation in DC. Latinos and African Americans elected officials belonged to the Democratic as did the sole Asian State Senator Alfred Song. March Eu, former Assemblywoman elected in 1966 in AD 15 was elected in 1974 Secretary of State, the first and only Asian woman

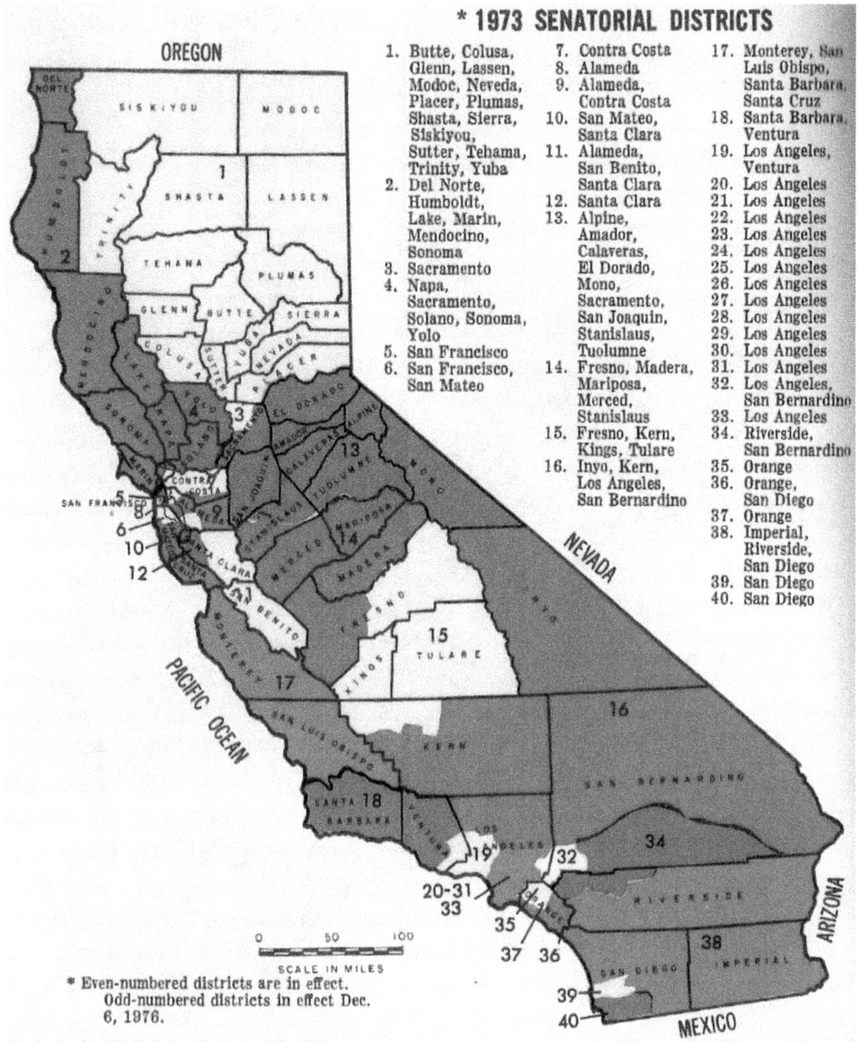

Figure 2.2 1973 Senatorial Districts
Source: California Legislature at Sacramento Handbook, 1978

elected to that post. She, too, was a Democrat. She was succeeded in her district by Floyd Mori, another Asian American Democrat. Paul Bannai elected in 1972 in the Assembly (AD 53) was the only Asian American Republican.[96] In 1974, California also elected one Japanese American to Congress, Norman Mineta. He was a Democrat. As more minorities were elected in California

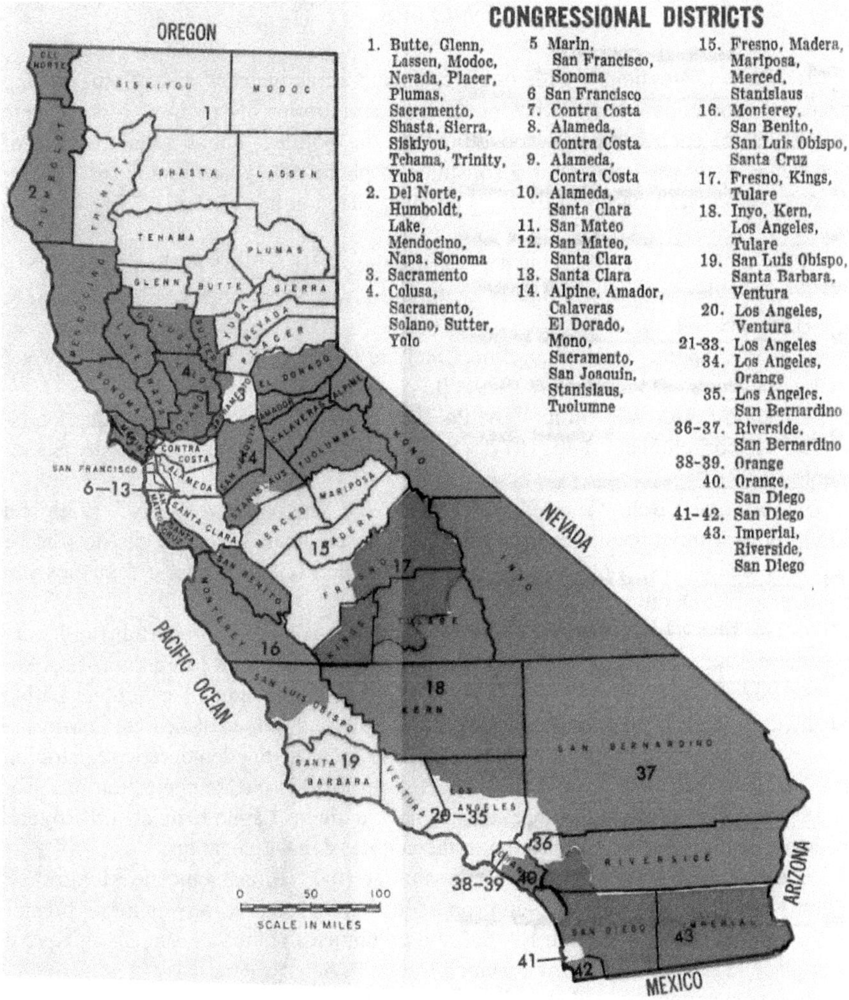

Figure 2.3 Congressional Districts
Source: California Legislature at Sacramento Handbook, 1978

and worked their way up the political food chain it became all too obvious that the Democratic Party's coalition was becoming more diverse. Race and partisanship seemed correlated to some extent but Latinos, a fast-growing population, were not quite sold on any of the two major parties yet. The 1980s solidified their inclusion into what will later be called the "rainbow coalition."

NOTES

1. "Party professionals with ample financing attractive candidates, issue-polling resources, computer voting behavior analysis and armies of precinct workers were marshaled for each campaign and ultimately the political public relations firm of Spencer-Roberts was retained in a consultant capacity on a year-round basis." J. Anderson Totton and Charles G. Bell, "The 1970 Election in California," *The Western Political Quarterly* 24, no. 2 (June 1971), 262.

2. Anthony Quinn, "Carving Up California: A History of Redistricting 1951–1983" (PhD diss., Rose Institute of State and Local Government, Claremont, CA, 1984), chaps. 3, 4.

3. R. W. Apple, "Population Shift Likely to Give California GOP New Power," *New York Times*, September 27, 1970, 30.

4. David Lester Wilkening, "The Political History of the California State Legislative Reapportionment, 1849–1977" (MA thesis California State University Sacramento, 1977), 233.

5. Totton and Bell, "The 1970 Election," 252. The party won only 2 (75th and 32nd), both without incumbents, of the 12 key Republican Assembly districts in the general election, lost 5 (16, 25, 30, 41, and 79) and failed to unseat 5 supposedly vulnerable Democratic targets (37, 45, 58, 67, 69).

6. The first 2 Latinos in the California State Legislature in modern history were elected in 1962: Phil Soto (D-La Puente, 1962–1966) and John Moreno (D-Los Angeles, 1962–1964). Moreno was defeated for his 1964 reelection when another Latino candidate, Dionicio Morales, split the Latino vote and helped Jack Fenton win the seat. Phil Soto's district was changed in 1965 to increase the democratic registration to 64 percent, but most were Anglo voters. Soto lost his bid for reelection in 1966. In 1967 the California legislature did not have a single Latino official. Ed Roybal, elected in 1962, was the only Latino in the congressional delegation.

7. Of the four dead during the demonstration (the National Chicano Moratorium March) that turned into a police-confrontation riot, Rubén Salazar was news director of the local Spanish television KMEX and columnist for the *Los Angeles Times*. It took place at Laguna Park, now renamed Ruben F. Salazar Park.

8. It was previously called Chicanos for Fair Reapportionment.

9. Sillas was also a member of the California State Advisory Committee to the United States Civil Rights Commission. Other organizations helped the involvement of the community: Congress of MexicanAmerican Unity, MALDEF, The Center for Law and Justice, California Rural Legal Assistance, Lawyers for Civil Rights Under the Law, various Chicano student associations.

10. By conventional wisdom, Republican districts are "safe" when about 50 percent of the eligible voters are Republican; similarly, 55 percent Democratic districts are "safe," as are minority districts that are about 65 percent minority in total population.

11. They not only demanded elected officials but also appointed ones. In 1970, out of 15,650 elected and appointed officials at the municipal, county, state, and federal levels, only 310 (barely 2 percent) were of Spanish origin. At the same time the

Latino population represented 20 percent of the state population. Richard Santillan, *California Reapportionment and the Chicano Community: An Historical Overview 1960–1980* (The Rose Institute, 1981), 13.

12. On the difficulty of defining what constitute an influence district, see for instance, Richard Engstrom, "Influence Districts and the Court: A Concept in Need of Clarity," in *The Most Fundamental Right: Contrasting Perspective on the Voting Rights Act*, ed. Daniel McKool (Bloomington: Indiana University Press, 2012).

13. For a discussion over the merits of formal criteria in the 1980s see Bruce E. Cain, "Simple vs. Complex Criteria for Partisan Gerrymandering: A Comment on Niemi and Grofman," *UCLA Law Review* 33, no.1 (1985), 214–16; Bernard Grofman, "Criteria for Districting: A Social Science Perspective," *UCLA Law Review* 33, no.1 (1985), 79–93; Daniel H. Lowenstein and Jonathan Steinberg, "The Quest for Legislative Districting in the Public Interest: Elusive or Illusory?" *UCLA Law Review* 33, no. 1 (1985), 12–35.

14. Michael Berman became a political organizer at sixteen and managed his first successful Assembly campaign, that of Henry Waxman, before he turned twenty-one. He was the core of what came to be known nationally as the "Berman-Waxman Machine." Shane Goldmacher, "The Waxman-Berman Machine Finally Shuts Down," *The National Journal*, January 26, 2013, http://www.nationaljournal.com/magazine/the-waxman-berman-machine-finally-shuts-down-20130124. Berman was especially close to Phil Burton whose biographer John Jacobs calls "the son he never had." For more on their relationship, see John Jacobs, *A Rage for Justice: The Passions and Politics of Philip Burton* (Berkeley: University of California Press, 1995, [1997]), 281–82.

15. Quinn, "Carving Up California," chap. 3, 7–8.

16. "California State Advisory Committee to the United States Commission on Civil Rights Report," 1967. Palo Alto, CA: Ernesto Galarza Collection, Department of Special Collections, Stanford University.

17. Morgan J. Kousser, *Colorblind Injustice: Minority Voting Rights and the Undoing of the Second Reconstruction* (Chapel Hill: University of North Carolina Press, 1999), 108.

18. Bill Boyarsky, "Mexican-Americans' Campaign for Legislative Power Begins; Chicano and Anglo Activists Join Forces to Gain Representation in Elective Offices through Redistricting," *Los Angeles Times*, January 21, 1967, C1.

19. Richard West, "Latins Threaten to Form 3rd Party Over Redistricting," *Los Angeles Times*, March 10, 1971, A1.

20. Memorandum prepared by A. J. Meyers for Assemblyman Bill Greene, May 10, 1971, 4, cited by Santillan, *California Reapportionment.*

21. Steven C. Smith, "Gains Sought by Mexican-Americans; Groups to Seek Strong Chicano Districts from Legislature during Reapportionment," *Los Angeles Times*, August 7, 1971, K1.

22. Henry A. Waxman, "Waxman Gives Views on Chicano Redistricting," *Los Angeles Times*, October 7, 1971, C7.

23. Waxman, "Waxman Gives Views on Chicano Redistricting," C7.

24. Richard Bergholtz, "New Unit Urged to Handle State Redistricting; Rights Advisory Group Calls Legislature Unfair to Mexican-Americans," *Los Angeles Times*, April 27, 1971, 3.

25. In a very vague statement: "That the power to reapportion be removed from the state legislature and placed in the hands of a body which is representative of all people in California." Or "that the power to reapportion at city and county levels be taken from the hands of the incumbents and placed with a commission representative of the people of the area in question."

26. "Putting Chicanos on the Political Map," *Los Angeles Times*, May 21, 1972, H1.

27. "Putting Chicano on the Political Map," H1.

28. Bergholtz, "New Unit Urged to Handle State Redistricting," 3.

29. "Major Redistricting Losers: LA and SF," *Los Angeles Times*, February 24, 1971, D4.

30. According to the formula used (in this case Hill's method), congressional reapportionment creates losers and winners. In the 1970 round of reapportionment, California with a population of 20,098,863 had a quota of 42.847 and therefore received 43 seats. One representative from California represented 467,415 people. On the opposite end of the spectrum, Delaware that had a quota of 1.177 only received one seat. One representative of Delaware represented 551,928 persons. M. L. Balinski and H. Peyton Young, *Fair Representation: Meeting the Ideal of One Man, One Vote*, 2nd ed., (Washington, DC: Brookings Institution Press, 2001), 72.

31. The Nixon administration held up census data for California, at the request of Governor Reagan, to make the task more difficult for Democrats. George Gould, Unruh's former aide from Southern California, became staff director of the Census and Statistics Subcommittee of the Post Office and Civil Service Committee. He had to put pressure on the deputy census director, a fellow Democrat, to obtain the early data and pass it on to Burton. Jacobs, *A Rage for Justice*, 282.

32. Quinn, "Carving Up California," chap. 3, 27.

33. For an estimation of the partisans gains in 1970, see Amihai Glazer, Bernard Grofman, and Marc Robbins, "Partisan and Incumbency Effects of 1970s Congressional Redistricting," *American Journal of Political Science* 30 (1987), 680–707.

34. "Politicians Preparing for Redistricting Fight: GOP Fears Being 'Gerrymandered' Out of House Control; Extra Seats at Stake," *Los Angeles Times*, November 27, 1970, K5.

35. Ayala, former chairman do the San Bernardino County Board of Supervisors, was a very close second in the crowded primary election. "Congress Races: Burgener, Ketchum Get GOP Bids; Brown Edges Ayala," *Los Angeles Times*, June 8, 1972, A 24.

36. Leroy C. Hardy, "Considering the Gerrymander," *Pepperdine Law Review* 4, no. 2 (1977), 262.

37. Richard Bergholz, "38th District: Myriad of Choices: Pros, Youth, Wealth Vie for Democratic Congressional Nod," *Los Angeles Times*, May 13, 1972, B1.

38. Jerry Gillam, "Democrats Unveil Redistricting Plan: Own Members, GOP Criticize Proposal for New Senate Lines," *Los Angeles Times*, October 7, 1971, A3.

39. Dymally is also quoted saying: "There is no question in my mind, we are in a spot. We've got to produce (more Chicano districts). And if we don't produce, I think you're going to see the rise and growth of La Raza Unidad Party. As a matter of fact, as it is now, we have concerns of their prolific growth in East Los Angeles," cited by Santillan, *California Reapportionment*, 23.

40. Gillam, "Democrats Unveil Redistricting Plan," A3.

41. Tom Goff, "Democrats Unveil Plan to Redistrict Assembly," *Los Angeles Times*, October 29, 1971, A3.

42. Frank Del Olmo, "Chicano Party Says It Defeated Alatorre in 48th District," *Los Angeles Times*, November 18, 1971, A3. Allan Hoffenblum also created fake "Democratic" committees that sent mail linking Alatorre to violent Latino gangs. Kousser, "Redistricting: California 1971–2001," in *Governing California: Politics, Government, and Public Policy in the Golden State,* eds. Gerald C. Lubenow and Bruce E. Cain (Berkeley, CA: Institute of Governmental Studies, 1997), 138–39.

43. Frank Del Olmo, "Raza Unidad: Barrio Power?: Chicanos, Other Factions Weigh Effects of 48th District Upset," *Los Angeles Times*, December 13, 1971, D1.

44. Daniel Hays Lowenstein, "Brief of Petitioner Edmund G. Brown Jr." in *Legislature v. Reinecke*, 6 Cal. 3d 595 (1972), vol. II, Exibit E (IGS Library, University of California Berkeley, 1972).

45. Morgan Kousser, "Reapportionment Wars: Race, Party, and Redistricting in California 1971–1992," in *Race and Redistricting in the 1990s*, edited by Bernard Grofman (New York: Agathon Press, 1998), 134–90.

46. Jacobs, *A Rage for Justice*, 284.

47. Quinn, "Carving Up California," chap. 3, 25.

48. Jerry Gillam, "Redistricting Compromise Bid Fails; Issue May Go to Court; Reconvening of Special Legislative Session May Be Idle Gesture; Reinecke Panel Meets, Makes No Progress," *Los Angeles Times*, December 16, 1971, A3.

49. Tom Goff, "Reinecke Calls Disputed State Redistricting Panel into Session," *Los Angeles Times*, December 15, 1971, A3.

50. William Endicott, "Reapportionment Plan Favoring GOP Studied," *Los Angeles Times*, January 5, 1972, I24.

51. Tom Goff, "Reagan Veto of Redistricting Bills Seen as Legislators Recess; Bitter Special Session Ends as Assembly and Senate Democrats Adopt Plans on Straight Party-Line Vote," *Los Angeles Times*, December 21, 1971, A1.

52. Steven C. Smith, "Redistricting Confusion Triggers Wide Concern; Southeast Leaders Express Worries about Splintered Representation in the Legislature," *Los Angeles Times*, December 30, 1971, H1.

53. Carl Greenberg, "Reagan Vetoes 3 Reapportioning Bills, Describes Them as Unfair," *Los Angeles Times*, December 30, 1971, 3.

54. Reagan's veto message, quoted in Quinn, "Carving Up California," chap. 3, 41.

55. Carl Greenberg, "Democrats' Remapping Bills Vetoes by Reagan: Proposals Branded as Totally Partisan; Court Ruling Likely," *Los Angeles Times*, December 31, 1971, 3B.

56. Lowenstein, "Brief of Petitioner Edmund G. Brown Jr."

57. *Legislature v. Reinecke I*, 6 Cal. 3d.595 (1972).

58. Tom Goff, "Legislature Still Faces Reapportionment Issue: Assembly Committee Moves Bill Setting Up Special Panel to Redraw District Lines," *Los Angeles Times*, June 18, 1972, B.

59. Tom Goff, "Governor Urges Redistricting Plan without Partisan Politics," *Los Angeles Times*, January 21, 1972, I14.

60. It lost 3 percentage points between 1970 and 1972 (39.8 to 36.7). Quinn, "Carving Up California," chap. 4, 45.

61. She was the third African American female elected to Congress but also became the first Congresswoman to have a child while in office and receiving maternity leave.

62. Tom Goff, "Divided Legislature: Passage of Key Bills May Be Tougher: Democrats Gain in Assembly but Lose Edge in Senate," *Los Angeles Times*, November 9, 1972, A1.

63. Carl Greenber, "Election a 'Debacle' for GOP, Flournoy Says," *Los Angeles Times*, November 11, 1972, 24.

64. In 1972, the number of Latino state legislators increased by 10 nationally: 2 in Texas, 5 in Arizona, and 3 in California. Frank Del Olmo, "Growing Latin Political Power Reflected in Election Results; Political Clout Shown by Mexican Americans," *Los Angeles Times*, November 14, 1972, B1.

65. Frank Del Olmo, "3 Mexican-Americans Seeking 40th Assembly District Seat," *Los Angeles Times*, November 2, 1972, B1.

66. Tom Goff, "'Bipartisan' Redistricting Plan OKd by State Senate 25 to 13: Harmer-Zenovich Bill Would Maintain 20–20 Party Balance; May Be Combined with Assembly Measure," *Los Angeles Times*, May 24, 1973, A3.

67. "State High Court Sets Up Redistricting Rules: But Decision Gives Legislature Third Chance to Do Job," *Los Angeles Times*, March 24, 1973, C1.

68. Quinn, "Carving Up California," chap. 4, 50–52.

69. Jerry Gillam, "Assembly Redistricting Shelved by Democrats; Some Republicans Broke Word to Back Bill, Moretti Claims," *Los Angeles, Times*, March 9, 1973, 3.

70. Jerry Gillam, "Reagan Veto Expected on Redistricting Law; Three Bills Merged into One Maneuver Designed to Enhance Override Chances," *Los Angeles Times*, June 15, 1973, 3.

71. Nathaniel Persily, "When Judges Carve Democracies: A Primer on Court-Drawn Redistricting Plans," *George Washington Law Review* 73 (August 2005), 1131.

72. Another caveat before 2013 and the *Shelby* jurisprudence was the difficulty of choosing a plan for jurisdictions covered by Section 5 of the Voting Rights Act since it needed to obtain preclearance from the Justice Department.

73. *Legislature v. Reinecke*, 110 Cal. Rptr. 718 (1973), 727–28.

74. The fact that California has exactly half as many State Senate seats as Assembly seats (i.e., 40 and 80 respectively) makes nesting a feasible option. But nesting is

usually considered negatively by most incumbent legislators because it automatically pits 2 Assembly members against one another for the next step up the political ladder.

75. *Legislature v. Reinecke*, 10 Cal. 3d 396 (1973), 416.

76. Bill Boyarsky, "Court Will Decide: Redistricting Plan: There Will Be Some New Faces in '74," *Los Angeles Times*, September 3, 1973, 1.

77. *Legislature v. Reinecke*, 516 P.2d 6 (Cal. 1973), 16.

78. *Legislature v. Reinecke*, 516 P.2d 6 (Cal. 1973), 16.

79. Richard Bergholz, "Little Effect Seen in Redistricting," *Los Angeles Times*, November 29, 1973, 3.

80. Mike Ward, "Six Incumbents Threatened by Redistricting Plan: Others in Valley in Good Reelection Position under Reapportionment Plan," *Los Angeles Times*, September 16, 1973, SG1.

81. Wilkening, "The Political History of the California State Legislative Reapportionment," 401–2.

82. *Legislature v. Reinecke*, 10 Cal. 3d 396 (1973), 417.

83. Gordon E. Baker, "Lessons from the 1973 California Master's Plan," in *Political Gerrymandering and the Court*, ed. Bernard Grofman (New York: Agathon Press, 1990), 306.

84. Kousser, "Reapportionment Wars," 145.

85. "Bill Proposes Nonpartisan Redistricting," *Los Angeles Times*, August 14, 1973, I4.

86. Bill Boyarsky, "The Death of Gerrymandering?" *Los Angeles Times*, September 5, 1973, B6. In this article, the author calls for more majority-minority districts and more competitive seats, ignoring that because of the high level of racial polarization these two goals are incompatible in practice.

87. "Office Holders Satisfied with Redistricting: Boundary Changes Bring New Representatives into Area, Other Major Shifts," *Los Angeles Times*, December 16, 1973, CS1.

88. Goldwater moved from a district with 51 percent Democrat registrants and 42 percent Republican to a district that was 47 percent Democrat and 46 percent Republican. Corman's new district figures were 59 percent Democrat and 34 percent Republican. The rule of thumb repeated in the literature for a competitive district at the time is 55 percent Democrat and/or 40 percent Republican.

89. Burton's new district had a Democrat registration of 53 percent and 37 percent Republican, a rather competitive district but the old Fifty-seventh District he had previously won was 53 percent Democrat and 40 percent Republican. Martha L. Willman, "Some Incumbents Get Edge under Redistricting: Redistricting Gives Incumbents Edge," *Los Angeles Times*, February 24, 1974, SF A1.

90. Richard Bergholz, "A Challenge: Fair Plan for Redistricting: College Group to Use Computer in Effort to Check the Legislature," *Los Angeles Times*, December 7, 1980, A3.

91. For a thorough discussion of how parties would have fared under various plans cf. Kousser, "Reapportionment Wars," 145–49.

92. The unavoidable consequence of these staggered terms is that, depending on where one lived, some voters had to wait six years to vote for a Senate representative

(1970 to 1976) while some others voted twice in two years for their Senate representative (1972 and 1974) and others waited four years.

93. Quinn, "Carving Up California," chap. 3, 66–67.

94. Senator Howard Way's retirement led to the election of California's first female senator, Rose Ann Vuich.

95. In an interview McKaskle explained that it was purely an unintended consequence of the creation of 2 minority districts but Anthony Quinn contends that "population patterns did not seem to justify the new district in west Los Angeles, even if it was replacing another district across town." Quinn, "Carving Up California," chap. 3, 64. Waxman served 20 terms in Congress in his safe Democratic seat until he retired in January 2015.

96. Republican Tom Hom had served on term between 1968 and 1970 (AD 79).

Chapter 3

The Battle for the Latino Vote and the Burton Plan of 1981

At the beginning of the 1980s, the political landscape in California had changed quite a bit. Both parties had lost 6 percent of their registrants between 1972 and 1980.[1] And while Governor Jerry Brown was Democrat, the Republican Party was rising from the ashes thanks, in part, to its victories in 1978 helped by Howard Jarvis' Proposition 13 phenomenon and then the landslide election of Ronald Reagan to the presidency. Between 1976 and 1980 the Democrats lost 20 seats in the Assembly, the Senate, and the House delegation, falling from respectively from a 57, 26, and 29 split to a 49, 21, and 22 split.

The Democrats could count though on a super majority (6–1) in the State Supreme Court. But in 1978 Republicans, led by State Senator H. L. Richardson, were almost successful in their attempt to oust Chief Justice Rose Bird. Jerry Brown appointed her as the first female justice in the state's history.[2] That same year the governor also appointed the first Black justice.[3] Rose Bird survived her reconfirmation by the thinnest of margins (51.7–48.3 percent).[4] Emboldened, the Republicans threatened to remove 3 of Jerry Brown's appointees in 1982. Republicans believed that threatened justices would likely veto Democrats' attempts at partisan gerrymandering.

In 1986 Bird became the only Chief Justice in the history of the state to be removed from office, along with Justices Cruz Reynoso, the first Latino to sit on the high court, and Joseph Grodin, a former labor lawyer, all 3 appointees of Governor Brown. In 1986, upon his reelection as governor, George Deukmejian appointed Associate Justice Malcolm Lucas as Chief Justice.[5] Deukmejian then appointed 3 new conservative associate justices, David Eagleson, John Arguelles, and Marcus Kaufman, thus creating the first conservative majority on the Court in several decades. This new conservative majority proved decisive for the 1990 round of redistricting.

The populist tax revolt and the Reagan revolution brought new young blood to a party that desperately needed it. These 13 freshmen Republicans in the Assembly caucus were so conservatives they called themselves the "Cavemen" a term they preferred to their other nickname the "Proposition 13 babies."[6] They quickly removed their minority leader, Assemblyman Paul Priolo of Malibu, who they believed was too accommodating with the Democrats, and replaced him with the first woman to hold major leadership position in the California Legislature: Caroll Hallett of Atascadero.

But Speaker Leo McCarthy's real challenge came from inside his own party. In 1974, McCarthy of San Francisco, with the help of the Berman brothers, had unseated Bob Moretti and beaten Willie Brown for the speaker position once Moretti had bowed out of the race. Howard Berman became majority leader with the promise of moving up to the speakership at some point, maybe in 1982 when McCarthy was expected to seek statewide office.[7] But the new electoral context pushed Berman and his supporters (mostly younger and more aggressive Assembly members) to hasten the process. In 1979, Berman called a caucus to assume speakership. However McCarthy would not step down and Republicans would not give their support to Berman to help him reach 41 votes. A year away from redistricting, Republicans were seriously concerned about the prospect of having Howard Berman his brother in charge of their political future. So the Assembly spent 1980 caught up in the Berman-McCarthy war with the minority party playing king maker. The GOP did not even capitalize on the split, with a mere gain of 2 seats during the 1980 elections, the Democrats keeping a solid 48-seat majority.

It was Willie Brown, the San Francisco African American Assemblyman who took advantage of the situation and announced his candidacy.[8] Brown had run for Speakership in 1974 against McCarthy and had lost. The stalemate gave him the opportunity he had been waiting for. Some Democrats switched to the "compromise candidate." Richard Alatorre, who thus far had been pledged to Berman, was one of them.[9] The Latino legislator from East Los Angeles became a pivotal vote and was therefore rewarded by Brown with the chairmanship of the Elections Reapportionment Committee. Because of the strange nature of the coalition that elected Brown to the Speakership many believed Alatorre would take care of the Republicans during redistricting. After all, with a bare plurality of the Democratic caucus and 28 Republican votes, he had received more votes from the minority party.[10] Brown had spoken about a redistricting compromise in 1971 and as far as the GOP was concerned anybody seemed more agreeable than Berman. By supporting Brown the Republicans hoped to create the conditions for a compromise, avoid the 1971 fiasco and protect most incumbents. With 48 seats, and then 49 when Assemblywoman Jean Moorhead switched parties, the Democrats could not gain much more. On the other hand, there was great pressure on Brown inside his party to draw partisan lines and prove himself to the party faithful who were suspicious of circumstances of his election. Brown's allies, Black Congressmen Ron Dellums and Augustus Hawkins, would have the ear of the speaker which other powerful Democrats resented. Racial politics and partisan politics are sometimes difficult to reconcile. Some also speculated that Altrorre wanted to carve a congressional seat for himself.[11] Why else would he have asked for the not glamorous Elections and Reapportionment Committee? Besides, Alatorre was a Latino and Latinos in the 1980s had let it known that their interest would come before the party's. And California Republicans were counting on it.

The national political landscape added pressure on the California Legislature. With a Republican landslide in 1980 during which they won the White House but also control of the Senate for the first time in a quarter century, the Republicans in several states took a very aggressive approach. They wanted to win the House in 1982 and redistricting would help them solidify gains in the suburban areas in the Sunbelt.[12] In early 1981, Republicans in Indiana, Colorado, and Washington had redistricted in such partisan ways that memos and letters rushed to California from other state assemblies, from the National Democratic Committee and from key political figures urging California legislators to adapt to the national Republican strategy.[13] In January 1981, a resolution was passed at the California Democratic Party convention stating that Republicans had only 33 percent of the state's registered voters but 42 percent of the Senate and 40 percent of the Assembly seats.[14] The implication was that this represented an advantage that redistricting should mitigate.

COURTING LATINOS IN THE ASSEMBLY

The first task of redistricting for Republicans and Democrats was to build technical capacities. The prolonged speakership fight had delayed the Democrats involvement. The 1970 reapportionment had introduced computer technology and the computer evolution of the 1970s had raised the stakes for both parties. Merging political data and census data is long and tedious especially with the level of accuracy now required for immediate analysis of redistricting plans. The Democrats needed to build their own set of data extremely rapidly or buy it from the Rose Institute at Claremont McKenna College. That second option was not really feasible as the links between the Institute and the Republican Party were too strong.

The Rose Institute had grown out of the 1970s redistricting and was headed by 2 consultants to the Assembly Republicans in the 1970 round of redistricting: Alan Heslop and Thomas Hofeller. The Rose Institute announced that it would make its state-of-the-art data (and its REDIS software) to minority groups in order for them to draw their own maps and compare them with that of the legislature.[15] Although part of Claremont McKenna College, the Rose Institute lacked an endowment and was dependent on grants and contracts. It was not your typical academic entity and it was linked with the Republican Party.[16] Heslop convinced the California Roundtable, mostly Republican businessmen, to provide a $688,000 grant to the institute to build its database and publicize the issue and for that purpose hired a public relations firm.[17] On November 16, 1979, and January 31, 1981, the institute sponsored conferences for members of the Latino community that were interested in the issue.[18] The conference attracted Latino community leaders from the entire state and from that meeting emerged a coalition called the Californios for Fair Reapportionment.[19] The idea was to coordinate a statewide campaign, paid mostly by MALDEF to push the legislature to draw lines favorable to the Latino community. The Rose Institute hired Dr. Richard Santillan of the California Polytechnic University at Pomona as the director of the "Latino Redistricting Project" to help with strategy, districts drawing and facilitate the free use of computers by CFR members.[20] The alliance with the Rose Institute made the Latino community, for the first time, a powerful lobby. The California Republicans had a plan to use its newfound partner to its electoral advantage. And for the first time, thanks to the Rose Institute computers, the Latino community was able to draw its own plans or see the impact of the various proposals by the Democrats and the Republicans. "You're dealing with a little more sophisticated community than in the past and we hope to utilize that in order to ensure our full suffrage," declared Rachel Murguia Wong during an Assembly Elections and Reapportionment Committee hearing in San Diego.[21]

At the national level, Republicans were sending mixed signals, to say the least, to the Latino community. On September 16, 1980, the US Senate Appropriation Committee endorsed a clearly unconstitutional Amendment introduced by Joseph M. McDade (R-PA) that had passed in the House of Representatives by a vote of 222–189. This bill would have forbidden counting aliens in the 1982 House reapportionment. Senator Walter D. Huddleson (D-KY) sponsored the Senate version and declared: "In effect, after the 1982 elections, there will be congressmen sitting in the House who owe their seats and to a certain extent, their political power to individuals who have no legal right in the United States and who have no allegiance to this country."[22]

But in California the demographic reality painted a different picture. Between 1970 and 1980, the Latino Community increased by 92 percent, from 2.37 million to 4.54 million, that is to say 20 percent of the state population at the time. In comparison Blacks increased by 30 percent to comprise 8 percent of the population with 1.8 million people. Asians and Pacific Islanders increased by 140 percent to reach 1.25 million people. The state, whose population represented 10 percent of the total population of the United States, accepted, in 1980, 20 percent of the legal immigrants which settle mostly in metropolitan areas. With higher birth rates, these immigrant groups were growing at a much faster rate than Anglos whose percentage of the population in California dropped from 89 percent in 1970 to 76 percent in 1980.[23]

Latino leaders were convinced that the masters' redistricting plan had not gone far enough in augmenting its political representation. They were determined to push for maximization or at least avoid the main errors of the past such as the division of Latino neighborhoods in three Assembly seats in San Jose or the Northeast Valley for example.[24] However, there was no consensus even in the Latino community as to what kind of plan could maximize Latino voting. Nor was there a consensus among political science experts of what constituted a Latino seat since the population was young, with a low rate of citizenship. But most importantly one can wonder if it was even reasonable to imagine, considering the political implications, that the Latino community could achieve proportional representation in any of the 2 chambers. People outside the Californios for Fair Reapportionment questioned corporate financing of the coalition with the Rose Institute and wondered if Latino interest was necessarily best served by placing Latino representation ahead of the interest of the Democratic Party. Was it a good calculation on the long run for the Latino community to help a party that would repeal the farm labor law (that Alatorre helped author) or end bilingual education?

Republicans knew that creating more Latino districts meant collapsing Anglo-Democrats' districts. And the GOP had no problem supporting more Latino representation as long as it was at the expense of the Democratic Party. Alatorre's job was therefore extremely complex since he had to satisfy Latino interest while protecting as many Democrat incumbents as possible. Los Angeles had 3 Latino Assemblymen in a county that was 27 percent Latino. Because of Alatorre's position it was a given that Latino incumbents would be well taken care of. But the question remained as to whether or not a new Latino district could be created. Because of the tense relations between the African American and the Latino communities in Los Angeles at the time, tampering with Black seats was not an option.[25] The only possibility was to take advantage of a retirement or collapse the seat of an unpopular Anglo incumbent. Los Angeles County needed to shed two Assembly seats. With no retirement in sight, two Assembly members would have to lose their district even if Speaker Brown had been reluctant at first.[26] When Californios met with Speaker Brown to discuss this possibility he gave them the names of one Democrat and one Republican who had not been part of the coalition that elected him. Californios worked on their maps thinking they could collapse those 2 seats. Unfortunately, Californios suffered from being outside legislative circles. When they presented their maps months later, the political conditions had changed.

Republicans refused a bipartisan proposal collapsing 2 Democratic seats and 2 Republican ones. The California GOP did not want to lose a single incumbent. Since they had helped the Speaker be elected they thought they had a claim to a better treatment. Especially since they felt they had never had the number of seats in the Assembly they deserved. A memo explained they had received only 40 percent of the seats while receiving 49 percent of the popular vote.[27] Besides, Republicans in the Assembly were restricted by the positioning of Republicans in the Senate and Congress. Working a deal with the Democrats would be treason to their colleagues. Another factor is the Reagan landslide election and the hope that a partisan realignment was imminent. It seemed to be in the party's interest to postpone redistricting until 1982 when the Republicans might control the Senate and the Governorship.[28] And finally, many Republican contemplated the possibility of financing a referendum on redistricting.[29] The qualification of a referendum against the redistricting bill would stay its implementation. If they portrayed the Democrats as "stealing" elections the issue might even help them win elections in 1982. With expected victories in the Senate and gubernatorial race they could star redistricting anew in position of strength. The Republicans had too many reasons to be inflexible. The problem is that the tension escalated. The Assembly Republican caucus went so far as to refuse to vote any bill requiring a two-third majority, killing legislation unrelated to redistricting and even Senate bills caught in the process.[30] In the end even if many Democrats were unsatisfied with their districts, the Republicans' attitude ended up uniting them.[31]

But the end of the bipartisan coalition and the reunification of the Democratic caucus changed the political dynamic of the legislature and the negotiating position of the Californios. The most promising opportunity to create a new Latino seat was a Jewish pro-Berman district vacated by a candidate who ran for Congress. However, Alatorre and Brown now that they had lost their Republican allies needed the Berman faction to pass any redistricting bill. Besides, the Bermans might have wanted to get back at the Republicans that they held responsible for Howard's defeat for the Speakership.[32] The Californios' coalition was based in Los Angeles, it was therefore crucial for them to make gains in Los Angeles County. Alatorre had no other option than to sell them more important gains in the rest of the state to compensate for his inability to deliver in Los Angeles County. Other areas of Latino population concentration had the advantage of being Republican territory. Alatorre had the opportunity of using the Republican strategy against them. Logically, Republicans were opposed to the creation of new Latino districts if it meant sacrificing one of their incumbents. Alatorre was very skilled at defusing Latino anger and making deals. When it was in the party's interest to increase Latino population he made good on his promise. When it was detrimental to the party he convinced the Latino community to accept a different outcome. The only exceptions were San Jose and San Diego.

In the 1973 Court masters' plan, the largely Latino East San Jose area had been divided among 3 Assembly districts held by Anglo Democrats. The Californios demanded that the San Jose neighborhoods be united into a single district, which caused problems for all three Democrats. Assemblyman McAlister was amenable to any changes, since he was planning to run for State Senate. But Democrat Dominic Cortese had barely won his race in 1980 and his victory margin depended on a big Latino vote. He refused to be pushed south in Republican area. Assemblyman John Vasconcellos, by all measures a real liberal who supported Latinos on most issues, bitterly resented the notion that he should give up his own seat to make room for a Latino. Vasconsellos had agreed to a Latino district in principle but it destabilized Cortese's district too much. Splitting the Latino vote in 2 districts with 24 percent Latino population was not an option for Californios who wanted a seat that was at least 34 percent Latino. There were no good solutions for Alatorre and Brown. If they sided with their incumbents they secured 2 votes but risked a lawsuit. If they satisfied the Californios, they might lose 2 votes. They gambled they could convince the 2 disgruntled Assemblymen to follow the party line and they were right.

In San Diego the situation was similar. The 1973 redistricting had split the Latinos into 2 districts. One of these seats already had a Latino Assemblyman and the Californios proposed to increase his district's Latino population. They also wanted to create a border district so border issues would have a voice in Sacramento. However, such a district would have to be narrow to stretch along the border and would include rural areas and urban areas. Assemblyman Waddie Deddeh did plan to run for reelection but insisted on keeping the district the way it was. Not only did Alatorre and Brown lose his vote but Deddeh became one of the strongest opponents of the redistricting plan.[33]

When negotiations with Republicans broke down, Alatorre became free to advance Democratic and Latino gains. In Bakersfield, Assemblyman Don Rogers' Republican district was turned Democratic with a large influx of Latino population. Republicans could not complain about the loss of that seat without appearing hypocritical toward the Latino population. Alatorre also united the Latino communities of Santa Barabara and Ventura County into one district which guaranteed a Democratic win in the Santa Barabara district. Miguel Garcia, head of the Californios for Fair Representation, declared in a press conference that the Assembly redistricting was a "major victory" for Latinos.[34]

In the end, under Alatorre's plan, the number of districts with at least 30 percent Latino increased from 10 to 16. A nice boost in influence that was not sufficient to elect Latino candidates but enough to help Democrats and hurt Republicans. Republican officials were displaced or threatened but had to be careful about the way they complained about it so as to not appear anti-Latino. They were not yet ready to cede the Latino electorate to the Democrats. That strategy came in the 1990s when a renewed nativism and anti-immigration rhetoric was perceived as electorally beneficial. In the 1970s Republicans had believed all along that if they had to go to court they would have gone with minority groups. Alatorre plan passed on a strict party-line vote 44–35 and it passed "preclearance" in December 1981.[35]

1983 Assembly Districts[36]

Figure 3.1 State of California 1980 Census Tracts: 1983 Assembly Districts
Source: Rose Insitute's California Political History Archive and Database.

IN THE SENATE

In 1981, the 23 Democrats senatorial majority was shaken by the defeat of their long-time colleague, Senator Al Rodda of Sacramento. This context helps explain why a partisan agreement was not an option.

Rodda was chairman of the Senate Finance Committee, an institution in the capital. But his home district in Sacramento had undergone subtle changes in the late 1970s, as white-collar workers moved into neighborhoods that were formerly populated by state employees. His upset made other senators wonder who could be next. Rodda was an "old-school" Democrat: a solid liberal vote on most issues, close to state workers. But like other Democrats he had come out against Proposition 13. Republicans saw a weakness and ran against him protégé of conservative Senator H. L. Richardson of Arcadia, unknown in Sacramento. The weekend before the election, Richardson's effective organization flooded the district with pamphlets denouncing Rodda's liberal voting record on taxes and crime. To the shock of the political establishment, Rodda fell on election day to thirty-year-old attorney John Doolittle.

In politics losing means a change of leadership. Long-time President Pro Tempore James Mills of San Diego was replaced by the more partisan Senator David Roberti of Los Angeles. Roberti was elected with the task of preventing another Rodda. The Democrats would protect their majority during redistricting and show Richardson and Doolittle the extent of their wrath over Al Rodda's defeat. To do so the Democrats would take advantage of a division in the Senate GOP caucus which was led by 2 moderates: Minority Leader William Campbell of Hacienda Heights, a former Assemblyman elected to the Senate in 1976, and GOP caucus chairman Ken Maddy of Fresno. Ten or 11 of the Senate's 17 Republicans supported Campbell, but six conservative senators were loyal to Richardson, who had tried on several occasions to remove Campbell from leadership. The Democrats decided to protect their own and then protect the Campbell-Maddy camp at the expense of Richardson and his allies. That way they could avenge Rodda but also create a caucus they would have an easier time working with in the future.

State Senator Daniel Boatwright of Concord, chairman of the Senate Reapportionment Committee, along with Alan Rosin the technical consultant that had been hired in 1971, protected Maddy and Campbell but added an incentive to go along with their plan. As mentioned before, Senate seats are elected on a staggered basis.[37] All the even-numbered seats are up one election cycle, the odd-numbered seats up in the next. Democratic leaders realized that if a senator representing an odd-numbered district were given an even number, he could not run for reelection when his seat came up, or may be forced to run for reelection before having finished his 4-year term. Switching district numbers was an unprecedented redistricting tactic. The drawback was obvious. The legislature would appear to temper with voters' representation. While it is inevitable with a staggered system that some constituents would have no senator for two years, it would appear that legislators were not trying to avoid such a situation but intrumentalize it for partisan gain. The State Supreme Court even validated the staggered system in 1973 in *Legislature v. Reinecke*.[38] But as the districts became public in late August, Boatwright let it be known that he was prepared to switch numbers to punish senators who would not support the Democratic plan. When Boatwright made his plan public in September 1981, it presented 40 unnumbered districts. The message was clear: any senators giving him trouble on redistricting would have his district number switched.[39]

Richardson was of course one the main targets of redistricting retaliation for the Rodda eviction. His compact San Gabriel Valley district was moved to the San Bernardino desert. His giant new district included Death Valley and Mount Whitney. Sending Richardson literally out in the desert meant keeping him so busy that he would not have the time to fundraise and campaign to unseat any more Democratic senators. The Democratic plan reduced the number of Republicans in the Senate from 17 to 14,[40] creating some openings for ambitious Assembly members such as Richard Robinson of Santa Ana.[41]

Boatwright tried to reassure the Latino community in the press early in the process. He talked about creating one new Latino district in the Senate, one new congressional Latino district, and 2 new Assembly districts. Boatwright realized he could not deliver a Senate Latino seat without significantly modifying David Roberti's district. Incumbents would not be eliminated to satisfy the Latino community but especially if that incumbent was president pro tempore. The price was too steep. Senator Boatwright's heavy-handed style and attitude made accommodations very difficult. Not only were Republicans mad at his plan, but Latino leaders, who were satisfied with the Assembly and congressional redistricting, attacked Boatwright's plan because it did not deliver the additional Latino seats Boatwright had promised in the spring. Boatwright responded that he had made the districts of two Los Angeles Latino senators more heavily Latino and had added Latino population to an African American district. Both communities were opposed to such a move because it would pit the two communities against each other for a decade. This was obviously not in the best interest of either the Latino or African American community. In the words of some of the Latino protagonists: "CFR developed cordial association with the Assembly Election Reapportionment Committee, which was in sharp contrast with CFR's relation with Senate committee staff. The relationship with the Senate committee became increasingly strained, and finally eroded to the point of confrontation."[42] One of the issues was the absence of Latino staff members on the Senate committee and the accusations that Californios for Fair Representation was a pawn of the Republican Party.

The plan was adopted 26–11 with the votes of 3 Republicans. Senator Milton Marks of San Francisco had been threatened with the loss of his committee chairmanship.[43] Senator Beverly (a former Assembly Minority Leader), Senator Craven, the GOP reapportionment vice-chairman, were both threatened with number switch. These three defections angered their fellow Republicans. The Democrats worked hard for these votes because they wanted a two-third majority for Boatwright's plan. Such a majority would have allowed the Democrats to pass the bill under an urgency statute which was immune from referendum.[44] They ended up passing the bill one vote short of a two-third majority.

1983 Senate Districts[45]

Figure 3.2 State of California 1980 Census Tracts: 1983 Senate Districts
Source: Rose Insitute's California Political History Archive and Database

PHIL BURTON'S "CONTRIBUTION TO MODERN ART"

The most talked about, and written about, redistricting plan of the 1980 round of redistricting is Phil Burton's congressional plan.[46,47] As opposed to 1971, Burton was not going to try to save all incumbents this time around. Burton's goal was to protect the Democratic coalition from the Republican tide that Reagan brought. Burton started preparing as soon as the 1978's gubernatorial victory results were in. There was no Republican Governor to veto his plan and Willie Brown, whom he had ushered into San Francisco politics, was a close ally.[48] Moreover, he was in a position to help the speaker. He could protect his friend's speakership by carving out seats for Brown's enemies in the Assembly: Howard Berman and his two lieutenants Richard Lehman of Fresno and Mel Levine of Santa Monica. A win-win for the party and a solution to its internal rivalries. Burton forged an alliance with fellow Congressman Henry Waxman, Howard Berman's ally, and hired Michael Berman to help with the redistricting.[49]

Phil Burton was elected to Congress in 1963 and John Burton succeeded him in the California Assembly. John became chairman of the Rules Committee and was respected by his peers, but was always, in a way, considered as Phil's little brother. His larger than life big brother did cast a big shadow. In 1974, John had a chance to join his brother in Congress when San Francisco Rep. William Mailliard unexpectedly stepped down. John had an important subcommittee chairmanship yet his entire career seems inseparable from that of his brother. In the late 1970s, because of what came to be later known as drug abuse, he almost lost his seat. Which did not seem to bother him that much since John Burton was not fond of DC. His marriage was over and he was a cocaine addict. In 1980, Republicans sensed political weakness and ran moderate Dennis McQuaid against John Burton. Burton lost Marin County but his strong San Francisco Bay numbers helped him win by 6 points. But the Republicans had made their point and held him to only 50 percent of the vote in a district that Jimmy Carter was able to carry. Phil took this as an offense against his family and swore to retaliate in kind. He knew his nemesis, ultra-conservative vice chairman of the Republican National Campaign Committee, John Rousselot had recruited McQuaid. Burton was so mad he cornered Rousselot and let him know he was high on his redistricting target list.[50] It is in this context that Phil Burton took on the redistricting process.

In 1980, California gained 2 new congressional seats. One seat had to be created in San Diego County but population growth was in a Republican area. Because the county contained already 3 Republicans, Burton let Representative Clair Burgener draw the new district knowing that he would protect the 3 Republican incumbents creating a Democratic seat in the leftover area. The opposition therefore had the illusion that they were part of the process and would support his plan. Another seat had to be created in the Central Valley where Assemblyman Richard Lehman lived. The problem was that Representative Tony Coelho of Merced, a power in the delegation, would be pushed northward into Stockton. Coelho had close ties to Fresno-area agricultural. Stockton residents were against the water delivery plans supported by Fresno farmers, so Coelho did not want Stockton in his district. He was one of Waxman's foe and had enough power in the Democratic delegation to block any redistricting proposal he did not want. Burton therefore drew a district that included both Fresno and Stockton connecting the two cities by a long strip that left Coelho's district untouched. Besides Stockton was cut in half, with one segment attached to Fresno and the other running through the mountains to the Oregon border. Stockton residents protested angrily to no avail. Republican incumbent Norman Shumway complained too but Burton assured him he would have a safe seat. The Lehman district had a very irregular shape and divided a city but such was the price to have another ally in Congress.

But these partisanship maneuvers are not what gave the Burton plan its controversial reputation. The first rule of redistricting is that the map drawer takes care of his own district and then protects his friends.[51] Well, nobody was better protected than John Burton. Phil made sure his brother, one of the most vulnerable in Congress prior to redistricting, had a district he could not lose. He even went so far as giving his brother some of his good Democratic precincts in San Francisco such as the predominantly Black Bayview and Hunters Point, along with parts of Telegraph Hill, North Beach, and Chinatown. And in doing so he put himself in jeopardy because he also absorbed some of John's difficult territory.[52] He took away from his brother the more conservative Richmond and Pacific Height districts of San Francisco and his own district dropped below a 60 percent Democrat registration rate.[53] Democratic Representatives Fazio and Lantos had to make room for the little brother by giving up respectively Vallejo and Daly City.[54] The incumbents protested but Burton reassured them by using his favorite sentence: "you're into your mothers' arms."[55] Actually, many Democrats were unhappy. Burton was trying to maximize the Democratic vote. And for that he had to spread Democratic voters for maximum results, which meant a tougher re-election for many incumbents.

Burton did not help his case when he declared unabashedly in the press that John Burton's district was his "contribution to modern art." And added for good measure: "It's gorgeous, its curls in and out like a snake."[56] A complete disregard to traditional redistricting purposes of compactness, contiguity and "community of interest" and an obvious violation of Proposition 6 freshly approved in 1980.[57] John's district jumped from 52 percent to 28 percent

Democratic edge to 57 percent to 25 percent and was 26 people short of the ideal 525,968-person district. Even Willie Brown had to admit that Phil Burton gave "arrogance a bad name."[58] The irony here is that John Burton decided not to run in 1982.[59]

Burton also reinforced all four Black incumbents (Augustus Hawkins, Mervyn Dymally, Julian Dixon, and Ron Dellum) by placing more African Americans and Democrats in their districts. About Dellum's new district, Burton declared: "It decreases his vulnerability from blatant, non-Black primary challenge." When asked to explain what he meant, he said: "He can't be beaten by a honky in the primary. He's in his brothers' arms."[60]

Republicans knew Burton would take care of his brother and protect other Democrats but they thought he would evenly divide the new 2 seats keeping the 1 seat difference in the delegation (22–21 Democrat Republican) and turn it into a 23–22 split. The Republican strategy, as in the Assembly, was to try and force the Democrats to create more Latino districts therefore concentrating Democrats in a few majority-minority districts to turn the adjacent districts safely Republican. In essence, they were trying to use the Voting Rights Act against the partisan foes.[61] This was the strategy already used in regards to the African American community, by far the most faithful group of the traditional Democratic coalition, at the national level.[62]

Burton kept extreme secrecy during the whole process, Michael Berman only saw John Burton's district when it was drawn. When the results of the Burton plan came to be known, Republicans were furious. They were on the verge of losing at least 5 seats.[63] Three GOP incumbents were collapsed into 3 southern districts. The districts of anti-busing Bobbi Fielder and Barry Goldwater Jr., who wanted to run for the US Senate, were collapsed.[64] Burton tore Representative Rousselot's district apart and only left his arch enemy with unwinnable districts. Rousselot had to run in a Democratic Latino district that had a 63 percent Democrat registration and a 53 percent Latino population, against a Latino candidate, Marty Martinez.[65] Or the Republican candidate would have to face another Republican incumbent Carlos Moorehead.[66] Rousselot chose Martinez and lost. To collapse Rousselot's district Burton also put Wayne Grisham and David Dreier in the same district (Pomona-Whittier).[67] As he had promised, he eliminated Dornan's district. Dornan's seat was marginal and became safely Democrat with an influx of west central Los Angeles African American neighborhoods.[68] Instead of trying to run against Mel Levine, Dornan decided to run for the US Senate (just like Goldwater) and lost in the primary to Pete Wilson. With these moves, along the 2 new seats, Burton created districts for Berman,[69] Levine, Lehman, San Diego Supervisor Jim Bates, and Marty Martinez. These 5 new districts along with John Burton's had at least a 27 percent registration advantage in 1982.[70] He also weakened Don Clausen's district (Santa Rosa), his long-time GOP colleague in the Interior Committee, because he felt he needed to satisfy the Brown faction of the Assembly.[71] All the spoil could not go to Waxman and his allies. Doug Bosco, a Brown supporter, ousted Clausen.

But Burton had one more stunner for the GOP. He managed to draw a third Latino seat. The first Latino seat belonged to incumbent Ed Roybal. The second Latino district was the new seat that Martinez eventually picked up.[72] George Danielson's district had been turning increasingly Latino and had barely survived Democratic primary challenges. Aware of the demographic evolution, Burton convinced Danielson to accept an appointment to the California Court of Appeal and increased the Latino population in his former district to 54 percent.[73] The third district was 48 percent Latino and Esteban Torres, another Waxman-Berman ally, was the candidate.[74] With this third Latino seat Burton gained the support of the Latino community and his Latino colleagues such as Alatorre. MALDEF was ready to sue until the third Latino district surprise. MALDEF director John Huerta called the redistricting "historic and unprecedented for Hispanics." At the national level in 1983 Latinos reached a historical 11 members in the Latino Caucus in the House of Representatives with 2 Latino pickups in California, 1 in Texas and 1 in New Mexico.[75]

But most importantly Burton's move was, once again, the perfect response to the Republicans' attacks. "The Republican Party has stated they have a deep and abiding interest in improving the Latino representation. Of course, in their congressional plan they don't have any. None at all."[76] And the partisan effects were long-lasting. As late as 1988, in the districts Burton drew for Congress, the winning candidate received more than 60 percent of the vote in 41 of the state's 45 House districts.[77] The Republicans blamed Burton for this partisan gerrymandering and Burton was more than happy to claim responsibility for this *tour de force*. But as Morgan Kousser's analysis suggest Burton's gerrymander might be an exaggeration as he wasted many Democratic votes to protect his allies. But in redistricting as in politics in general perception may be stronger than reality. To understand the Republican strategy in consecutive redistricting round one must bear in mind that the GOP was convinced that it had been maneuvered by Burton and an unfair gerrymander. That is one of the reasons why Republicans explored many avenues to undo the supposedly maximization of the Burton plan. With Democratic majorities the passage of the redistricting plan in both chambers was a formality. Yet, the partisan battle over redistricting was far from being over.

1984 Congressional Districts

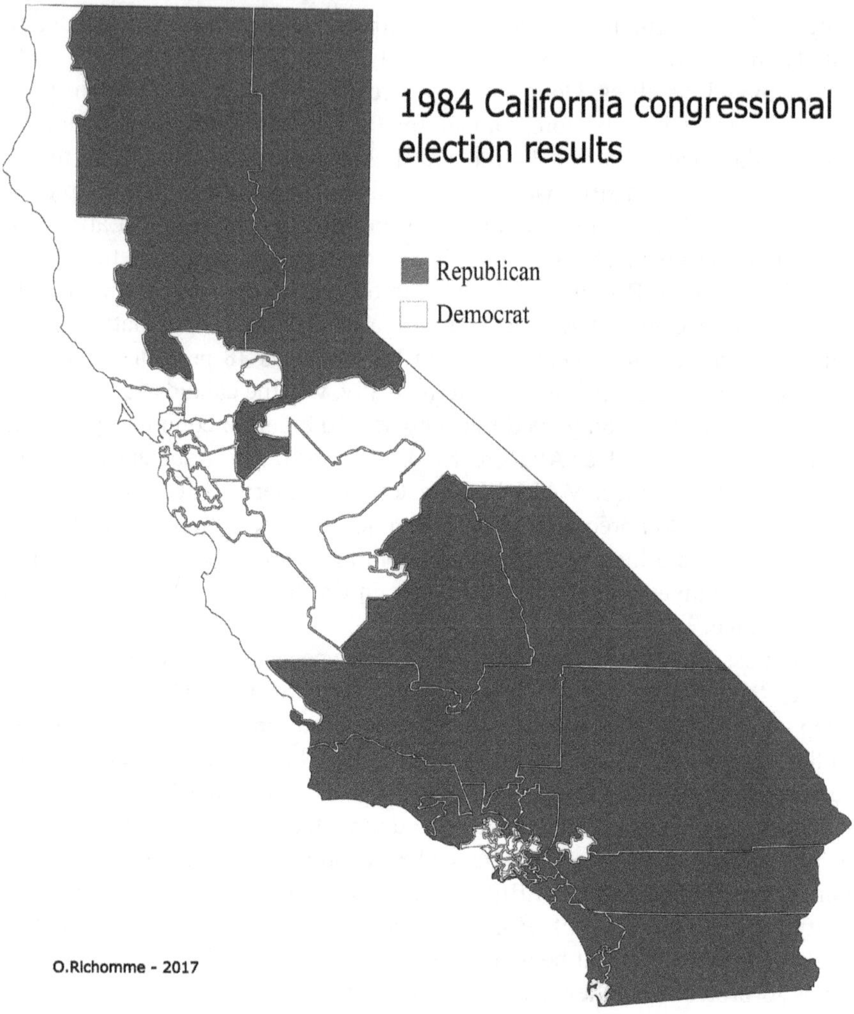

Figure 3.3 1984 California Congressional Election Results

THE REPUBLICAN REFERENDUM

Republican officials had warned during the redistricting process that if they lost the political battle they would take the matter directly to the people. A favorite complaint of the Republicans was that they had received 47 percent of the 1982 vote for Congress but only 37 percent of the seats. Republican

Assemblyman Robert Naylor summed up the mood in Sacramento in the closing day of the legislative session: "Reapportionment is the closest we come in this country to lining people up against the wall with a firing squad."[78] It was therefore no surprise to any of the people involved to see a ready-made referendum plan put into action by the GOP as soon as Governor Brown signed the redistricting bills into law.

The state Constitution provides two direct-democracy methods. The first one is the initiative process through which electors propose statutes and amendments to the Constitution to be adopted or rejected by the people. The second is the referendum through which electors approve or reject statutes or parts of statutes passed by the legislature, except urgency statutes, statutes calling elections and statutes providing for tax-levies or appropriations for usual current expenses of the state.[79] In the fall of 1981, the Republicans submitted three referendum petitions to overturn the legislature redistricting bill. The Republicans needed to get the signatures of 346,119 registered voters on petitions calling for a referendum in June 1982 on the Democrats' redistricting bill.[80] The strategy was to qualify for referendum and block the implementation of the redistricting plans until the people had a chance to vote on them. It was first perceived as a bargaining chip that could be pulled as soon as the Democrats made a reasonable offer. Such a referendum drive had to be done in 90 days and thus required a lot of money, which thankfully was not a problem for the GOP, even though in retrospect that money and energy might have been better spent on candidates during actual elections. The party ended up spending $600,000 just to qualify the measure but got a large portion of that money back later in fund solicitations.[81] For publicity on this obscure redistricting issue they even involved President Reagan who was the first one to sign the referendum petition in the White House Rose Garden for a splendid media operation.[82] Thanks to a well-funded mail-in operation the Republicans gathered close to 3 million signatures for their three referenda that became Propositions 9, 10, and 11.[83]

The Democrats responded in kind and various Assembly, Senate, and Congress members petitioned the California Supreme Court to issue a writ of mandamus which would have prohibited election officials from placing the referenda on the ballot and, therefore, requires them to use the lines voted on by the Democrats. The Democrats asked for an immediate hearing on their suit, a position backed by Secretary of State March Fong Eu who needed to know which district lines to use for the 1982 elections.

In *Assembly v. Deukmejian*, the Court held that the referendum petitions were valid and that reapportionment statutes were a proper subject for referenda.[84] But, as in 1971, the main problem was Congress and the fact that the California delegation was supposed to gain 2 seats. At-large elections for those two seats would have violated the federal law so the Court concluded that the 1981 redistricting lines had to be used for the 1982 congressional elections.[85] The only constitutional plan was the Burton plan with its almost perfect population equality.[86] The Republicans did not help themselves by going to court divided on the issue.[87] For the Senate and the Assembly the Court held that federal and equal protection concerns required using the plan that were the closest to the constitutional requirements. Therefore, and contrary to its finding in *Reinecke* a decade before, the Court concluded, in a 4–3 opinion authored by Chief Justice Rose Bird, that the 1981 plans had to be used temporarily for the 1982 primary and general elections.[88] The Republicans responded by threatening to join the ongoing recall effort of 4 Jerry Brown appointees on the Court. And they did oppose 3 of them in the November elections.[89]

In June 1982 the referenda were a success for the Republicans since both redistricting plans were rejected by more than 62 percent of voters. And yet, the Republican wave they hoped for never came and they suffered major losses in November at the polls. Ironically, in districts the people had rejected.

The Republicans knew they ran the risk of being without a majority or veto power after the 1982 elections and that if the Democrats were in charge of redistricting again, the results would be roughly the same. The California Roundtable, Common Cause,[90] Alan Heslop, and the Republicans hired attorney Vigo Nielsen Jr. to write a redistricting commission initiative. The proposed ballot initiative (Proposition 14) would strip the legislature of the power to reapportion legislative and congressional districts and give it instead to a 10-member appointed commission.[91] Four members of the commission were to be chosen by party caucuses in the Senate and the Assembly and 2 by the party chairmen.[92] Four independent members were to be selected by a two-third vote of the 7 most senior justices on the State Court of Appeals. But not more than 4 of the Justices could be of the same party. The 4 independent members were supposed to represent, according to the initiative, the state's "geographic, social and ethnic diversity."[93] The bipartisan nature of the plan was guaranteed by requiring 7 votes. But if the commission deadlocked the State Supreme Court had sixty days to draw its own plan. Which means that the party that did not have a majority on the Supreme Court had an incentive to compromise, so in the end the partisan makeup of the Court could be decisive.[94]

One of the main flaws in the writing of the proposition was its lack of mechanism guaranteeing the protection of racial minority rights. Various Democratic leaders and minority spokespersons criticized a commission composed of old, White middle-class men. Minority gains in the legislature could be rolled back according to critics.[95] The Democrats had a partisan interest in defeating the measure, however their criticisms were legitimate. No commission offered as much influence in the redistricting process as the Latino and African American communities had enjoyed in 1981, especially in the Assembly and in Congress. Minority groups had become such an integral part of the Democrats' coalition, electorally but also in legislative and congressional delegation, that the Democrats could not take the risk to not satisfy a large part of their demands during redistricting. Racial/ethnic affiliations were very much intertwined with partisan considerations.

Proposition 14 was defeated in November 1982 by an astonishing 55 percent to 45 percent vote on the same day that underdog Attorney General George Deukmejian won the closest gubernatorial race of the century.[96] The party used most of its money and energy defeating Tom Bradley, the first serious Black candidate for Governor. Deukmejian won by 50,000 votes out of 7.5 million cast[97] in a campaign in which race was such a central factor that it became known as the "Bradley effect."[98] The Republican National Committee did not back up Proposition 14 as it was probably too busy facing a tough national campaign. Besides, Proposition 14 was stuck between other propositions on the same ballot, Proposition 13, a water conservation initiative and Proposition 15, a handgun control initiative which logically attracted the attention of conservative activists and voters. Without much of a campaign by either party, the interest for the arcane question of redistricting never materialized and the proposition died quietly. So the November 1982 election delivered a new Republican governor and a defeat on Proposition 14. The Republicans also gained one seat in the Assembly and one seat in Congress and lost 2 seats in the State Senate.

The Democrats therefore hurried to pass a new redistricting plan before Deukmejian took office. The Democrats protected enough Republicans to obtain a two-thirds majority and the "urgency" status preventing another referendum. Governor Brown called a special session in December 1982. The lines, drawn with the help of Michael Berman, were quite similar to the ones that the voters had rejected in June. By that point, both parties had had enough of redistricting wars and the Republicans put up only a half-hearted opposition. Both sides seemed ready to move on. And yet, the exhaustive political wrangling lasted until the last minute.

Senator Roberti, who had nothing to gain in redistricting anymore, let the Republicans draw the 15 districts they had won as they pleased, in exchange for their support of a redistricting bill. But the Senate Republican leadership had a problem. When Senator John Doolittle was forced to run for reelection when his term was half over, he had lost to Democrat Leroy Greene. For some reason, maybe because he was simply "sick and tired of reapportionment,"[99] Senator Campbell tried to find a seat for Doolittle among the 15 Republican districts left. The only possible district was that of Senator Ray Johnson, a veteran Republican, ironically a supporter of Campbell's leadership. On the other hand, Doolittle had the support of the Richardson Senators faction. Doolittle wanted to draw the district to his liking. Campbell was accused of betraying a longtime allied in order to help his nemesis Doolittle and Richardson. The latter stayed quiet, plotting a leadership change that came fairly soon after.[100] One of the consequences of this redistricting battle was that, in the spring of 1983, Johnson announced he was quitting the Republican Party to run against Doolittle as an Independent. Senator Roberti immediately moved to protect Johnson's position on the Senate Rules Committee. From then on, the conservative Johnson became a Roberti supporter on key legislation, and Roberti managed to win himself another Democratic vote in all respects but party label. In 1984, however, Doolittle won the election despite "covert Democratic assistance to Senator Johnson."[101]

In the Assembly, to get the Republicans on board, Speaker Brown reluctantly agreed to a better district for Assemblyman Rogers and new Minority Leader Bob Naylor[102] and Richard Alatorre negotiated a package creating 32 Republican seats and 48 seats for the Democrats. But striking a deal was only one part of the equation, then the Republican and Democratic staffs needed to work together in drafting a bill. Rogers's district was to be one of the at-least 30 percent Latino districts that Alatorre had promised the Latino community. But the Republicans, to save Rogers, wanted the district to have a 37 percent Republican registration rate. Only a thorough dismemberment of the city of Bakersfield could achieve both goals. Bakersfield's other Republican Assemblyman, Phil Wyman, resisted the loss of some good neighborhoods, so in the end the electoral map of Bakersfield did not satisfy traditional redistricting factors because of race and partisanship. Bakersfield was by no means the only city to be affected. Assemblyman Nolan in the Forty-first District complained: "It's not fair for Burbank to be divided into two districts. Those people should only have to deal with one legislator. In addition Pasadena is now divided into two districts in this crazy-quilt pattern."[103] Nolan shared Pasadena with Latino Democrat Richard Alatorre of the Fifty-fifth District.

During this latest round of negotiation the polarizing Burton stayed away from Sacramento, and left the delicate negotiations on southern California to now freshman Congressman Howard Berman. But in the capital, Berman found himself in the middle of an intra-party fight involving again race and partisanship. African American Assemblywoman Maxine Waters accused the new Burton-Berman plan of having given veteran Representative Augustus Hawkins a bad district in order to protect adjacent districts, all allies of Berman. Hawkins, who had represented Watts in the Assembly and Congress since 1934, was probably not in real trouble. His district had been extended into the White enclave of Downey and might pose primary election problems for his successor. Maxine Waters happened to be the presumptive successor and she would not allow any congressional bill out of the Assembly until she was satisfied. Berman worked diligently for the unwanted parts of Downey to end up in Representative Glenn Anderson's district. So even though the new lines were in the end very similar the negotiations were still intense and boiled down to a few hours on Wednesday, December 29, 1982. For hours Berman patiently worked the Senate floor. Five of the 25 Senate Democrats were opposed to the bill and with no Republican senators in favor, there were too few votes to pass it. Berman had to satisfy Senator Henry Mello of Santa Cruz, and his heavy weight ally Leon Panetta, because his county was divided. Michael Berman prepared amendments shifting population. This move meant Panetta's district did not follow equal population standard anymore but it was too late to nit-pick.[104] "The Democrats had come so close to losing this bill that another reapportionment bill already on the Governor's desk had to be withdrawn and used as a vehicle for the Berman plan."[105] A referendum was briefly filed against this plan but no one had the energy left to try to qualify it and it died fairly quickly. All thought the 1980 round of redistricting had finally come to an end.

THE SEBASTIANI PLAN

In February 1983, thirty-year-old Assemblyman Don Sebastiani from the Napa-Sonoma area, heir to a wine fortune, and not a redistricting expert by any means, funded a statutory initiative to get redistricting on the ballot again.[106] A constitutional initiative would have been more likely to survive judicial scrutiny but it cost too much money because it required gathering more signatures than a statutory initiative.[107] Some California conservative leaders had asked, in vain, the Republican National Committee to commit $1 million to a new redistricting campaign.[108] At first, Sebastiani's only allies were political consultants whose livelihood relies on competitive elections.[109] He was convinced that if a good government map was presented to the voters they would prefer it to the gerrymander. The initiative, phrased as a statute and not an amendment to the Constitution, presented to the voters maps drawn at the Rose Institute by Republican consultants Allan Hoffenblum and Joseph Shumate.[110] Shumate was the principal line drawer and Hoffenblum was media coordinator. They were joined in their endeavor by Ronald Smith, as state chairman.[111]

Several powerful GOP legislators found themselves either living outside their districts or injured by the plan. Sebastiani tried to obtain the party's approval after having redrawn the lines as opposed to securing it before. Besides, most protected incumbents were satisfied with the existing lines.[112] However Sebastiani gathered signatures and gained momentum.[113] The Republican State Committee, under pressure from its base, pledged $300,000 of its 1.4 million bankroll to the Sebastaini Initiative.[114] Governor Deukmejian reluctantly called a special election which was estimated to cost between $8 million to $10 million. It was set for December 13, 1983, in a blatant effort to engineer a low turnout because of the holiday proximity.[115] Polls showed a low turnout would help the Sebastiani initiative.[116] The Democrats tried to bargain[117] and then sued in the State Supreme Court to prevent the initiative from going through.[118] They accused the Sebastiani plan of making no effort to protect minority or female incumbents. For instance the Democrats' lawyers pointed out that the Sebastiani plan reduced the Latino population percentage in Ed Roybal's congressional district from 63 percent to 16 percent and placed his home in the most Republican district in the state forcing him to face six-term incumbent Anglo Republican Carlos Moorhead. It merged the districts of freshmen Latinos Marty Martinez and Esteban Torres. Moreover, it pushed a conservative Anglo area into a second Latino-majority congressional district. It endangered at least one congressional seat held by an African American. Two congressional seats held by African Americans in LA County were merged with two Westside seats held by Anglo Democratic incumbents inevitably causing Black-Jewish conflicts. It packed African Americans in a Bay Area congressional seat they had been able to carry since 1968. The Sebastiani-Smith-Shumate-Hoffenblum plan cut the number of Assembly districts that were 35 percent or more Latino in population from 7 to 4. It removed the homes of newly elected State Senator Art Torres, Assemblyman Richard Alatorre and Speaker Willie Brown from their current districts and their new districts had minority population lower than in the previous districts.[119] Torres district Latino population percentage was reduced from 71 percent to 21 percent. Generally speaking it completely redrew Democratic districts all over the state. The Democrats also explained that the state constitution mandated one round of redistricting per decade. And this is the argument that was at the heart of the Court's 6–1 decision (*Legislature v. Deukmejian*, 34 Cal. 3d 658 [1983]).[120] The justices voted on a strictly partisan line, the Democrats prevailed and the Republicans looked bitter after yet another redistricting battle lost and threatened to qualify an initiative to force justices to run against candidates and not on their records.[121] They, in essence, threatened to modify the retention election system. A retention election is a periodic process whereby voters are asked whether an incumbent judge should remain in office for another term. The judge, who runs unopposed, is removed from the position if a percentage of voters (usually 50 percent) indicate that he or she should not be retained. Governor Deukmejian declared: "It's a sobering step for the highest court in the state to tamper with the people's right to determine how they should be represented."[122]

After Sebastiani's initiative was rejected by the Court, some conservatives looked for a compromise in the form of a commission in charge of the 1991 round of redistricting but without any attack on the current lines. The Republican Party was not on board, nor was Common Cause.[123] Sebastiani, convinced that presenting another initiative as a constitutional amendment was the solution to circumvent the Supreme Court decision, had to be dealt with by the Governor who did not appreciate being pressured by this maverick Assemblyman that the party did not seem to control.[124] He put his chief political operative, Sal Russo, in charge of a constitutional amendment campaign to create a redistricting commission.[125] The 1982 commission project proposed by Common Cause and the Republican Party was fairly balanced and bipartisan in comparison to Deukmejian's. His commission would have drawn new lines for all elections starting in 1986 and was comprised of current Appeals Court justices. Deukmejian substituted retired Appeals Court justices once the State Judicial Council objected that the task was too political for sitting judges.[126] The Republicans spent $4 million on qualifying and trying to pass the initiative that came to be known as Proposition 39.[127]

The Democrats matched the intensity of the Republican campaign with a heavy media coverage.[128] The avalanche of TV ads and billboards probably participated in the public's weariness of anything linked with redistricting.[129] The Democrats argued that 34 of the 38 current retired Appeals judges were Anglo males whose average age was seventy-three, whose current law practices would pose conflict of interest with their redistricting activities and whose actions would not be accountable to the voters. Former US Secretary of Education Shirley Hufstedler, the only female among the 38 retired Appeals justices, declared Proposition 39 would shut out of the reapportionment process such traditionally underrepresented groups as women and Hispanics. Latino activist Cezar Chavez also joined the fight against Proposition 39. In the end, Proposition 39 lost by the same margin as Proposition 14 (55–45 percent) two years before, except this time President Reagan was on the ballot and won reelection very easily.[130] In 1984, the GOP gained 1 seat in the legislature and 1 seat in Congress (Orange County's sole Democrat, Jerry Patterson). That was the only change in the California congressional delegation's party balance for the rest of the decade.

Some might have stopped there. Yet in February 1985, Sebastiani proposed a new two-pronged initiative that proposed new district maps and a constitutional amendment preventing the Supreme Court from overturning them. By then Sebastiani had become a sort of folk hero for conservative activists but the Republican leadership pushed him aside once again.[131] Deukmejian and other Republicans preferred to continue the legal challenge in federal court in the *Badham v. Eu* case.[132] Democratic attorneys argued that in opposition to racial gerrymandering Republican in California could not argue they had been shut out of the political process and that political parties did not deserve more protection from the courts in this regard than racial and ethnic minorities. A 3-judge panel sided with the Democrats on a partisan-line vote and in 1989 the US Supreme Court affirmed the district court's dismissal.[133] Only three justices wished to hear the case, the first to come before them since they had ruled political gerrymandering a justiciable issue in 1986.[134]

NOTES

1. Morgan J. Kousser, "Redistricting: California 1971–2001," in *Governing California: Politics, Government, and Public Policy in the Golden State,* eds. Gerald C. Lubenow and Bruce E. Cain (Berkeley, CA: Institute of Governmental Studies, 1997), 143. In 1980, the registration rates in California were 55 percent Democrats and 33 percent Republicans.

2. Why was Bird up for reelection so soon after her appointment? Supreme Court justices in California are usually reelected for twelve-year terms. Yet, when a justice replaces a retired or deceased justice, he or she must first go through reconfirmation by the electorate during the next gubernatorial election. For Bird, this was the 1978 election. Moreover, when a justice is appointed, it is to serve the balance of the term of the justice who previously held that seat. Consequently, Bird faced reelection in 1986, the end of Chief Justice Wright's term, her predecessor, giving the Republicans another opportunity to remove her from office.

3. Gene Blake, "Brown Picks Woman, Black for High Court," *Los Angeles Times,* February 13, 1977, A1.

4. Prior to Bird, no justice had received less than 62 percent of the vote for reelection. For more details, see Betty Medsger, *Framed: The New Right Attack on Chief Justice Rose Bird and the Courts* (New York: Pilgrim Press, 1983).

5. Deukmejian appointed his old friend and law partner; they had practiced law together many years earlier in Long Beach.

6. John Jacobs, *A Rage for Justice: The Passions and Politics of Philip Burton* (Berkeley, CA: University of California Press, 1995, [1997]), 403.

7. A move that Brown resented. Brown could never trust Berman after that episode.

8. For a more detailed account of this episode, see James Richardson, *Willie Brown: A Biography* (Berkeley, CA: University of California Press, 1996), 256–72.

9. Art Torres and Alatorre were close to Cesar Chavez, the head of the United Farm Workers union, and Chavez was close to Berman especially because of his work on the Agricultural Labor Relations Act.

10. And the first signs were not encouraging for Democrats. Brown gave 6 committee chairmanships and 19 vice chairmanships to the Republicans. He kept the promise he made Carol Hallett and the GOP that the Speaker would give up his biggest weapon: the power to assign legislation to committees. The new Assembly rules put that authority in the hands of the Rules Committee.

11. Anthony Quinn, *Carving Up California: A History of Redistricting 1951–1983* (PhD diss., Rose Institute of State and Local Government, Claremont, CA, 1984), chap. 4, 40.

12. Adam Clymer, "Democrats Warned of Districting Peril: Party Leaders Are Told of Efforts to Assist State Legislatures in Drawing Up New Lines," *New York Times*, February 14, 1981, 9.

13. Indiana's redistricting changed the House delegation split from a 6–5 Democratic advantage to a 7–3 Republican edge. In Washington, upon winning the legislature, the Republicans paid the Rose Institute $175,000 in consulting fees for a partisan result similar to that of Indiana.

14. Bruce Cain, a political scientist at Cal Tech at the time, and former lobbyist Jim Ticker were hired to head the Assembly redistricting over Michael Berman. Cain, *The Reapportionment Puzzle* (Berkeley: University of California Press, 1983), 83.

15. The institute's computer had been donated by former Nixon cabinet member David Packard.

16. The institute's main fundraiser, Dixon Arnett, was a former Republican state Assemblyman.

17. The American Medical Association gave $40,000, Fluor Corporation gave $25,000, and Hewlett-Packard donated a $90,000 computer. More PACs gave more money when the realized control of the House was at stake. Jacobs, *A Rage for Justice*, 431.

18. Richard Bergholz, "A Challenge: Fair Plan for Redistricting: College Group to Use Computer in Checking Efforts of Legislature," *Los Angeles Times*, December 7, 1980, A3.

19. The change from "Chicano" to "Californio" is instructive. "Chicano" comes from "Mexicano" and had overtone of political radicalism and ethnic nationalism. "Californios" on the other hand put the emphasis on tradition and integration. The switch showed CFR members were willing to compromise and negotiate. In 1981, this umbrella organization was a coalition of representatives of a number of Latino groups. Carlos Navarro and Richard Santillan, "The Latino Community and California Redistricing in the 1980s: Californios for Fair Representation," in *The Hispanic Community and Redistricting*, vol. 2, ed. Richard Santillan (Claremont, CA: The Rose Institute, 1984), 53–55.

20. Santillan, in his *Garza* testimony ten years later, confessed that he was so concerned about CFR losing its political independence that he accepted to take on the job only on the condition that no other Rose Institute employee would have any involvement in the Latino Redistricting Project. Santillan deposition quoted by Morgan J. Kousser, *Colorblind Injustice: Minority Voting Rights and the Undoing of the Second Reconstruction* (Chapel Hill: University of North Carolina Press, 1999), 110.

21. Claudia Luther, "Hispanics Demand a Slice of the Redistricting Pie," *Los Angeles Times*, March 7, 1981, A5.

22. Richard Santillan, *The Chicago Community and California Redistricting* (Claremont, CA: The Rose Institute, 1981), 9.

23. Robert Lyndsey, "California Becomes Melting Pot of 1980s," *New York Times*, August 23, 1981, 1.

24. Sandy Banks, "Latino Group to Press Redistricting Plan," *Los Angeles Times*, June 11, 1981, V18.

25. Cain, *The Reapportionment Puzzle*, 93.

26. Citing low registration rates, Brown declared in the press that Latinos would not get new Assembly districts at the expense of incumbent Democrats "just to achieve a racial minority district." Henry Mendoza, "Speaker Brown's Views about Redistricting Hit," *Los Angeles Times*, May 5, 1981, B3.

27. Memo to the Republican leadership from consultant Tony Quinn, titled "Realities of Reapportionment," July 2, 1981, cited by Cain, *The Reapportionment Puzzle*, 88–89.

28. Jerry Gillam, "Reapportionment Delay Supported: Sen. Richardson Says GOP Could Gain under Plan," *Los Angeles Times*, February 4, 1981, 3.

29. The Democrats missed an opportunity to challenge Don Sebastiani of Sonoma when they strengthened the freshman Assemblyman in 1981 when they removed heavily democratic Vallejo into Alatorre's district.

30. Claudia Lauther and Jerry Gillam, "GOP Bloc Threatens to Delay Bills in Rift Over Redistricting," *Los Angeles Times*, August 25, 1981, A 3.

31. Another possible factor explaining the end of the bipartisan agreement could be the rumors of the Republicans trying to remove Speaker Brown.

32. Quinn, "Carving Up California," chap. 4, 46. Quinn relates a conversation between Assemblyman Bob Naylor and Micheal Berman in which the latter admitted to this strategy. Naylor, as a response, allegedly compared Brown to Ayatollah Khomeini (53).

33. Cain, *The Reapportionment Puzzle,* 96

34. Richard Bergholz, "Redistricting Damned, Applauded by Critics," *Los Angeles Times*, September 10, 1981, A3.

35. Until 2013, under Section 5 of the Voting Rights Act, jurisdiction had to seek federal authorization to implement electoral changes. The Assembly plan was reviewed by the Department of Justice but the Senate opted to file suit of approval with the US District Court in Washington to avoid the possibility of a conflict of interest with Attorney General William French Smith, longtime friend of President Reagan, openly opposed the Democrats redistricting plans. Claudia Luther and Ronald J. Ostrow, "Redistricting Clears US Legal Hurdle," *Los Angeles Times*, December 2, 1981, B3.

36. Source: UC Berkeley *IGS: California Redistricting Resources*.

37. Cal. Const. art. 4, § 2(a). Therefore, since electors are shifted between senate districts, it is unavoidable that some become disenfranchised for a period of time.

38. "To obviate the inequality [between the voters] would substantially interfere with the orderly operation of the four-year staggered terms system after each reapportionment" (*Legislature v. Reinecke*, 516 P. 2d 6, 12 [Cal. 1973]).

39. Quinn, "Carving Up California," chap. 3, 34.

40. Doolitle's district was made more Democratic and he received an even number making sure he would not serve an entire term. Ollie Speraw and Dan O'Keefe's districts were much made Democratic. Another Richardson ally, John Schmitz of Orange County planned a US Senate race in 1982 that was cut short by scandals.

41. Jeffrey Perlman, "State Redistricting Taking Shape: Tentative New Districts Protect Incumbents, Anger GOP," *Los Angeles Times*, August 22, 1981, OC_A1.

42. Navarro and Santillan, "The Latino Community," 60. Carlos Navarro was co-founder and Research Chairman of Californios for Fair Representation.

43. In 1960, in the Assembly, Marks had voted for the Unruh redistricting while his party was opposed to it, in 1970, at one point, his district was supposed to be collapsed under Dymally.

44. Cal. Const. art. IV, §8(d).

45. Source: UC Berkeley *IGS: California Redistricting Resources*.

46. Always a good quote, Phil Burton's famous declaration about his brother's district appears in countless newspaper articles, cf. for instance, Wallace Turner, "Rep. Philippe Burton, Democratic Liberal, Dies on Visit to California," *New York Times*, April 11, 1983, B6.

47. Cf. for example, George L. Clark, *Stealing Our Votes: How Politicians Conspire to Control Elections and How to Stop Them* (Pittsburgh, PA: Dorance, 2004),\ 44–48; Charles S. Bullock III, *Redistricting: The Most Political Activity in America* (Lanham, MD: Rowman & Littlefield, 2010). For a deconstruction of the legendary Burton Gerrymander, see David Butler and Bruce E. Cain *Congressional Redistricting: Comparative and Theoretical Perspectives* (New York: McMillan, 1992); See also, Morgan Kousser, "Reapportionment Wars: Race, Party and Redistricting in California 1971–1992," in *Race and Redistricting in the 1990s*, edited by Bernard Grofman (New York: Agathon Press, 1998), 134–90.

48. "From Philip Burton, Willie Brown learned the white world of politics." Richardson, *Willie Brown*, 57.

49. Burton also hired Leroy Hardy again. Michael Berman wanted a more partisan approach and was a bit suspicious of Hardy's more neutral stance.

50. For a colorful description of the encounter cf. for instance Jacobs, *A Rage for Justice*, 425.

51. Burton is quoted by Gordon E. Baker as saying: "The most important thing you do, before anything else, is you get yourself in a position to draw the lines for your own district. Then you draw them for all your friends before anyone else's." Gordon E. Baker, "Judicial Determination of Political Gerrymandering: A 'Totality of Circumstances' Approach," *Journal of Law and Politics* 3 (1989), 13.

52. In a close 1982 race, State Senator Milton Marks challenged Burton in what was emphatically dubbed a "giant-killer" election. Adam Clymer, "Would-be 'Giant-Killer' on Coast Focusing on Burton's Personality," *New York Times*, October 23, 1982, 34.

53. Asian and Blacks constituted only 8 percent of his new districts and Latinos 6 percent.

54. Dennis McQuaid declared he did not mind the addition of Vallejo. What weakened him was the addition of Daly City and the removal of Richmond and Pacific

Heights where he campaigned hard in 1980, an investment now wasted. Jacobs, *A Rage for Justice*, 435.

55. Ellen Hume, "Phil Burton Is Key Redistricting Figure," *Los Angeles Times*, July 23, 1981, A3. See also Quinn and Jacobs that have each titled one of their chapters with this expression.

56. Jacobs, *A Rage for Justice*, 435.

57. This measure even asked for cities and counties to be kept whole. Alan Heslop of the Rose Institute released redistricting maps of Orange County keeping cities whole and under 2 percent population variations. Jeffrey Perlman, "A Redistricting Plan GOP Can Love, Democrats Hate," *Los Angeles Times*, May 6, 1981, OC_A1. Of course these maps did not take into account "communities of interest," such as Latino communities, which was also a requirement of Proposition 6.

58. Ellen Hume, "'Godfather of California Politics' May Be Mortal," *Los Angeles Times*, May 3, 1982, B1.

59. Wallace Turner, "California Lawmaker Resigning 'to Come Home'," *New York Times*, March 14, 1982, 29.

60. Jacobs, *A Rage for Justice*, 435.

61. Kings, Merced, Monterey, and Yuba counties came under the provisions of the Voting Rights Act that prevented the dilution of minority voting strength. Counties came under the Act if 5 percent of their populations were members of a single-language minority group on November 1, 1972, if registration and election materials had been provided only in English and if less than 50 percent of their voting age population voted in the 1972 presidential election.

62. Adam Clymer, "Blacks Seen Retaining 17 Seats in the House Despite Census Losses," *New York Times*, June 21, 1981, 1.

63. Claudia Luther and Jerry Gillam, "Democrats Could Gain Congress Seats in Redistricting Plan," *Los Angeles Times*, September 10, 1981, B3.

64. Rousselot had persuaded Bobbi Fiedler, a Jewish Republican on the Los Angeles School Board, to run against 10-term incumbent Jim Corman, the ranking Democrat on the Ways and Means Committee. Her victory (by a mere 800 votes) had tremendous consequences for the House. Corman lost in 1980 along with chairman Ullman. Tip O'Neil gave Ways and Means to Dan Rotenkowski. California legislators did not want to support Phil Burton's redistricting plan. Or rather, in return the state legislators wanted a congressional bill exempting their per diem living allowance of $75 a day from federal income taxes. Many faced thousands of dollars of back taxes because of a new IRS ruling. Burton's only solution was the Ways and Means Committee. Burton helped get 1-term Representative Bob Matsui into the Committee into Corman's slot. Burton struck a deal with the Texans who wanted the next opening in the Energy and Commerce Committee. Matsui wrote the amendment in the 1981 Reagan Tax Bill. Other states had to do the same. Jacobs, *A Rage for Justice*, 432. Interestingly, Rousselot sat on the Ways and Means Committee and probably could have saved his seat had he used his position as leverage.

65. However it was estimated that only 30 to 35 percent of the eligible Latino residents were registered to vote. Judit Cummings, "Rousselot in Tight Race for New Seat," *New York Times*, October 31, 1982, 38.

66. Mike Ward and Alan Maltun, "Redistricting Forces Hard Choices of GOP Congressmen: Rousselot, Moorhead May Have to Vie in Primary," *Los Angeles Times*, September 27, 1981, SG1.

67. Dreier, a product of the Rose Institute, defeated Grisham in the 1982 primary.

68. Quinn, "Carving Up California," chap. 4, 22.

69. To make room for Berman and for the good of the party former State Senator Bielenson, after resisting for a while, had to accept a district he wasn't satisfied with. Bielenson's first vote in the House of Representatives was a vote against Phil Burton for Majority Leader.

70. Kousser, "Reapportionment Wars," 164.

71. Burton was fond of him and had protected him in the previous 2 rounds of redistricting. Actually Clausen was so close to Burton that some of his colleagues wondered if he was divulging their strategy secrets to the enemy.

72. He ran in a special July primary election. He won with only 51 percent of the vote. In November, against Rousselot, he won only 54 percent of the vote.

73. And Burton harrassed Governor Brown until he appointed Danielson.

74. Torres had run in 1974 and lost against Danielson.

75. For more details, Maurilio E. Vigil, "Hispanics Gain Seats in the 98th Congress after Reapportionment," *International Social Science Review* 59, no. 1 (winter 1984), 20–30; for an even wider view of elected Latinos in the first half of the 1980s see Maurilio E. Vigil, *Hispanics in American Politics: The Search for Political Power* (Lanham, MD: University Press of America, 1987).

76. Jacobs, *A Rage for Justice*, 437.

77. Dan Balz, "California GOP Backs Redistricting Initiative," *Washington Post*, September 23, 1989, http://www.washingtonpost.com/archive/politics/1989/09/23/california-gop-backs-redistricting-initiative/53a95c3a-b3d5-494c-8167-0f4a68d7d263/.

78. Wayne King, "California GOP Plans Fight to Balk Redistricting: Petitions Due in a Week," *New York Times*, September 17, 1981, A17.

79. California Constitution, article II, § 8 (a) and 9 (a)

80. To get those signatures the party sent out 2.6 million referendum petitions. Richard Bergholz, "GOP's Ballot Drive on Redistricting to Face Legal Challenge," *Los Angeles Times*, October 9, 1981, B3.

81. Richard Bergholz, "GOP Will Take Aim at Ruling on Redistricting," *Los Angeles Times*, February 1, 1982, A12.

82. Richard Bergholz, "Reform Doesn't Mean 'Fair': Where Redistricting Is Concerned," *Los Angeles Times*, October 12, 1981, B3.

83. Quinn, "Carving Up," chap. 4, 60. Soon after the signature gathering business became a real industry in California.

84. *Assembly v. Deukmejian,* 30 Cal. 3d 638, 645 (1982).

85. *Assembly v. Deukmejian,* 664.

86. The Republican emergency request to the Supreme Court was denied. "Justice Denies GOP Plea on Redistricting," *Los Angeles Times*, March 11, 1982, A1.

87. Former Representative Charles Wiggins filed suit in federal court asking for the district court to impose his own plan (the one drawn by Tom Hofeller). But the Republican National Committee had hired a Los Angeles firm: Gibson, Dunn and

Crutcher, former firm of US Attorney General William French Smith. This firm filed a brief asking for at-large, statewide congressional election for the two new districts. The RNC lawyer argued against the Wiggins position. In final attempt, Wiggins asked the Court to postpone the primary election until the fall so people could first vote on the referendum. Quinn, "Carving Up," chap. 4, 73.

88. *Assembly v. Deukmejian,* 678. Justice Tamara was the deciding vote.

89. Wallace Turner, "GOP Favoring California Vote to Recall Judge," *New York Times*, February 1, 1982, A8; Philip Hager, "GOP-Backed Group Begins Drive to Unseat Justices Named by Brown," *Los Angeles Times*, October 11, 1982, C8. It is therefore less surprising to note that the Court also asked the parties to pay for their own court cost. The state picked up the tab for the Senate and Assembly, the Republicans had to pay to defend their referenda.

90. Interestingly Common Cause had joined the Democrats and Jerry Brown to pass the Political Reform Act in 1974.

91. Claudia Luther, "New Redistricting Initiative Submitted: Would Strip the Legislature of Its Role, Create Commission," *Los Angeles Times*, December 17, 1981, B3; "Initiative to Create Redistricting Commission Qualifies for Ballot," *Los Angeles Times*, June 22, 1982, B3.

92. Reapportionment by Districting Commission or Supreme Court. California Proposition 14 (1982), http://repository.uchastings.edu/cgi/viewcontent.cgi?article=1914&context=ca_ballot_props.

93. Bill Billiter, "Election Reform or Trojan Horse?: Partisan Storm Swirls about Plan to Revise Reapportionment Procedure," *Los Angeles Times*, October 14, E1.

94. Kousser, "Reapportionment Wars," 155.

95. Claudia Luther and Richard Bergholz, "Campaign Launched for Remap Initiative," *Los Angeles Times*, February 3, 1982, A3; "Civil Rights Panel Opposes Redistricting Commission," *Los Angeles Times*, October 15, 1982, B11; Franck Del Olmo, "Prop. 14 Endangers Latinos' Gains," *Los Angeles Times*, October 28, 1982, F11.

96. The proposition attracted only 79 percent of the votes cast for the gubernatorial election.

97. The state Republican Party, learning from its success in qualifying the referendum and Proposition 14, decided to send absentee ballot applications to every Republican household. About a hundred thousand critical extra votes were gained this way. Robert Lindsey, "Bradley Loses Close Contest on Coast," *New York Times*, November 4, 1982, A22.

98. The "Bradley effect" is the tendency of Anglo respondents to polls to overstate their support for an African American candidate supposedly out of fear of being perceived as racist. J. Payne Gregory and Scott Ratzan, *Tom Bradley: The Impossible Dream* (Minneapolis, MN: Roundtable, 1986).

99. Tracy Wood, "Senate Quiet Fears, Passes Its Reapportionment Plan," *Los Angeles Times*, December 24, 1982, I3.

100. Senator Richardson managed to put together a coup and ousted both Campbell and Maddy in mid-1983. Senator Jim Nielsen of Woodland became minority leader and Senator John Seymour of Anaheim became caucus chairman. They were both former Campbell-Maddy allies.

101. Quinn, "Carving Up California," chap. 4, 92.

102. Naylor was famous in Sacramento Capitol lore for having kept a prized memento from his own horse-trading days: the tablecloth on which Phil Burton, during a 1981 meeting in Washington, DC, offered him a tailor-made Silicon Valley congressional district in exchange for his agreement to support the Democratic congressional plan.

103. Greg Baxton, "41st Altered Most in Redistricting Plan," *Los Angeles Times*, January 2, 1981, GB1.

104. Michael Berman fixed this discrepancy, along with some other technical errors, after the plan was signed by the governor. But the Republican National Committee filed a lawsuit over this issue but in 1984 modified their suit into a general attack on partisan gerrymandering, arguing that it was in violation of the Fourteenth Amendment. The suit worked its way to the Supreme Court.

105. Quinn, "Carving Up California," chap. 4, 97.

106. Sebastiani was extremely conservative and voted regularly against social legislation. He also did not help his cause with his insensitive, sometimes misogynistic, remarks, and radicalism. He was, for instance, the only Assembly member to vote against Martin Luther King Jr.'s birthday as a state holiday.

107. To propose a statute, the California Constitution required that the number of electors signing the petition must equal 5 percent of the votes cast in the last gubernatorial election and for a constitutional amendment, the number of electors signing the petition must equal 8 percent of such votes.

108. Edward Rollins, President Reagan's political affairs assistant, declared a plan to draft an initiative "is definitely a back-burner thing now; it is definitely not a go." Richard Bergholz, "New GOP Strategy on Redistricting Develops," *Los Angeles Times*, February 4, 1983, B3.

109. Quinn, "Carving Up California," chap. 4, 99.

110. Allan Hoffenblum was a political analyst who was involved in California politics since 1968, when he served on the staff of the Los Angeles County Republican Party. In 1972, he served as field director in Los Angeles County for the California Committee to Re-elect President Nixon. He launched his own consulting firm in 1979 and later served as staff director for the GOP Caucus in the State Assembly. He co-founded the California Target Book in 1994 with Al Pross, providing detailed analyses that, at the time, were available nowhere else. Shumate became a household name in Sacramento. Shumate and Associates had a list of clients ranging from ballot initiatives to spotlight candidates like John McCain, Steve Poizner, Carly Fiorina, and Arnold Schwarzenegger. His name gained some international recognition when he became one of three American advisors who helped Russian President Boris Yeltsin win his reelection race in 1996.

111. Ronald Smith assisted in the state Republican redistricting effort in 1971. In 1973, he formed a political consulting firm in San Francisco with two other Republican activists, Joseph Shumate and former San Francisco Republican Central Committee Chairwoman Emily Pike. He managed several northern California campaigns and since he was a social liberal he even worked for some Democrats; for instance he worked for Diane Feinstein in her unsuccessful bid as San Francisco mayor in 1975.

But it's his last minute victory over Burke that made Smith his reputation. Cf. supra, chap. 4.

112. Richard Bergholz, "GOP Assemblyman Announces Petition Drive to Get Redistricting Plan on Ballot," *Los Angeles Times*, April 6, 1983, 22.

113. Among the legislators supporting Sebastiani's effort was GOP Senator Ollie Speraw, who had lost his district under the Senate plans. He was a client of Allan Hoffenblum and a wealthy man. The Sebastiani Senate plan had a seat he could run for, and Speraw decided to ride to the rescue by loaning Sebastiani a quarter of a million dollars to send out mail asking for signatures. The bulk of the signatures, 312,472, were gathered in Orange and San Diego counties. The $1 million campaign gathered over 570,000 signatures. Philip Hager, "Court Urged to OK Vote on Redistricting," *Los Angeles Times*, July 26, 1983, A3.

114. Luther and Bergholz, "Campaign Launched for Remap Initiative," A12.

115. There had not been an election in December in California in fifty years. Democrats were so afraid of a December low turnout that they tried to move the presidential election primaries to December 13 in a trailer bill to the budget. Deukmejian's first budget was embroiled in the Sebastiani fight and the national party was irate. Robert Lindsey, "California Breaks Budget Deadlock as Redistricting Fight Shapes up," *New York Times*, July 20, 1983, A20.

116. William Schneider, "Voter Turnout Is Key to Sebastiani's Hopes," *Los Angeles Times*, August 21, 1983, E1.

117. Senator Lockyer offered to support a slightly revised Proposition 14 reapportionment commission initiative to be effective for the 1988 elections if the special election was not called. Discussions were held between Democratic Assemblyman Davis and GOP Assemblyman Ross Johnson and a draft was prepared. However it is not sure the Democrats had the votes. When Lockyer in 1984 introduced a bill establishing a commission, he was pushed to resign his Senate Reapportionment Committee chairmanship.

118. Philip Hager, "Democrats Ask State Supreme Court to Stop Redistricting Vote," *Los Angeles Times*, July 20, 1983, A3; "Redistricting Row in High Court Lap: Panel's Decision Could Affect Control of State Legislature for Years to Come," *Los Angeles Times*, August 28, 1983, A3.

119. Keith Love, "Sebastiani Sets Political Bomb Ticking," *Los Angeles Times*, July 10, 1983, 1.

120. For a legal analysis of the Court's opinion, cf. for example, Frederick Lowell and Teresa A. Craigie, "California's Reapportionment Struggle: A Classic Clash between Law and Politics," *Journal of Law and Politics* 2 (1985), 250. The two authors were counsel to Sebastiani. Or also to a lesser extent Greg M. Salvato, "New Limits on the California Initiative: An Analysis and Critique," *Loyola of Los Angeles Law Review* 19 (1986), 1045–96.

121. Wallace Turner, "Coast Democrats Spurn GOP Deal," *New York Times*, September 15, 1983, A23.

122. John Balzar, "Sebastiani Left Reeling but Won't Give Up," *Los Angeles Times*, September 16, 1983, B1.

123. Walter Zelman, executive director of Common Cause, even declared "Nothing could be more harmful to the health of state politics or for the long-term goals of political competition and reapportionment reform that Sebastiani claims to support." Walter A. Zelman, "Time's Up on Sacramento's Game-Playing," *Los Angeles Times*, September 19 1983, C5.

124. John Balzar, "Sebastiani to Work for New Remap Effort," *Los Angeles Times*, October 3, 1983, B3.

125. GOP members of the legislature and of the congressional delegation were in support of another commission drive.

126. Common Cause was (already) pushing for a commission composed of citizens.

127. Reapportionment. California Proposition 39 (1984). http://repository.uchastings.edu/ca_ballot_props/929.

128. They matched the money raised by Deukmejian and hired BAD campaigns, the campaign firm headed by Michael Berman and Carl D'Agostino to lead the effort. The Republicans hired Russo-Watts, Inc., that had rescued Deukmejian's campaign. Doug Watts was media director for the Reagan-Bush reelection campaign.

129. The presence of other losing measures on the ballots, such as the fiercely contested Jarvis IV tax reduction plan, and two Ross Johnson initiatives on campaign contribution limitations and public aid and medical assistance programs (Propositions 40 and 41, respectively), might have contributed to Proposition 39's poor numbers. Robert Lindsey, "California Ballot Questions Dim Presidential Race," *New York Times*, October 8, 1984, B8.

130. It even lost in heavily Republican counties such as Orange and San Diego.

131. John Balzar, "Sebastiani Revives Reapportionment: This Time He's Finding GOP Leaders Decidedly Cool to the Issue," *Los Angeles Times*, February 13, 1985, OC3.

132. In March 1983 Republican Congressmen had already attacked the new congressional district lines in court and used the financial backing of the Republican National Congressional Campaign Committee to file a suit in a federal court.

133. *Badham v. Eu*, 694 F. Supp. 664 (N.D. Cal., 1988), aff'd mem. 109 S. Ct. 829 (1989). Bernard Grofman, Gordon E. Baker, and Bruce Cain (among others) were called upon as expert witnesses, extracts from their testimonies can be found in the 1985 summer edition of *PS* (18, no. 3).

134. *Davis v. Bandemer*, 478 U.S. 109 (1986).

Chapter 4

Race and Redistricting in Los Angeles County

Garza v. County of Los Angeles

LOCAL DOESN'T MEAN LOW STAKES

Political science research on redistricting usually focuses on the United States Congress and state legislatures where the stakes are high.[1] However, such a narrow focus ignores the vast majority of redistricting activity taking place in cities, counties, or special districts. Redistricting is a political exercise not really known by the general public because of its complexity and the lack of interest for its technicality. Besides it is also regarded by politicians as a prerogative of the legislature. Often used strategically to punish an enemy or an ally popular too, to reward or launch a career, the drawing of electoral districts is considered a very personal matter, where secret last-minute negotiations are a tradition. It is no surprise then that the most neglected by the press, redistricting at the local level, were the last to open their doors to minorities.

But the sheer size of California and the diversity of its population make for an interesting case study. There is a county in the United States where the stakes are higher than in any state legislature seat and most congressional seats. With more than 10 million residents, in 2014, LA County was more populated than 43 American states.[2] Even the second largest most populated county in the nation Cook County, Illinois, with its 5 million inhabitants, is dwarfed in comparison. Especially if one considers that the Cook County Board of Commissioners is composed of 17 members and had an annual budget, in 2014, of $3 billion and employed 22,000 people. LA County has no equivalent.[3] It is larger than the combined areas of Rhode Island and Delaware. The county is home to 88 incorporated cities and many unincorporated areas. That is why Deborah Seiler, Assembly Election Committee consultant in 1990, called it "the largest electoral district in the free world."[4]

The county's voters elect Los Angeles County Board of Supervisors a nominally nonpartisan governing body that is composed of five members that are sometimes called "the five little kings" and whose power before 1978 was described as follow by Bill Boyarsky:

> The lavish construction spending generated political patronage that flowed as steadily as the water in the fountain at the county Music Center. Building, architectural and engineering contracts went to friends and political supporters.
>
> Such patronage built political machines. With their vast network of contractors, donors, friends, staff members and other associates, supervisors were big men when it came time to choose candidates for city councils, the state Legislature or even Congress. The supervisors could kill bills in Sacramento or get them passed.[5]

The small size of the board means each supervisor represents over 2 million people, about three times the number of constituents for a member of the House of Representatives.[6] The board operates in a legislative, executive, and quasi-judicial capacity. As a legislative authority, it can pass ordinances for the unincorporated areas. As an executive body, it can tell the county departments what to do, and how to do it. As a quasi-judicial body, the board is the final venue of appeal in the local planning process, and holds public hearings on various agenda items. The board presides over health, fire, police, park library, street repair, and many other services. As of 2015/2016, the board of Supervisors oversaw a $28 billion annual budget and approximately 100,000 employees. LA County is one of the rare local jurisdictions that attracts national figures. In 2014, Hilda Solis a former member of the House of Representatives and former Secretary of Labor was elected in the First District. She replaced Gloria Molina and was in 2015 the only Latina on the board for a county that is 48 percent Latino.[7]

Elections for the First and Third Districts coincide with California's gubernatorial elections, while those for the Second, Fourth, and Fifth Districts coincide with the United States presidential election. There is a nonpartisan primary election in the spring or early summer. If no candidate receives a majority, a run-off election takes place between the top-two vote candidates in November. To curb the powers of the 5 supervisors, Los Angeles County voters passed Measure B in March 2002 with a majority of 64 percent, to limit the supervisors to 3 consecutive four-year terms.[8]

A HISTORY OF DISCRIMINATION

In the 1980s, LA County was already a political heavy weight. With 7.5 million in 1980, it grew to almost 9 million by 1990. In spite of being one of the most ethnically diverse areas in the world, until 1992 the board was an all-White male club. Between 1875 to 1991, no person with a Spanish last name was elected to the board. Before 1992, almost no woman, Black person, or Asian person had ever served on the board. The only exception was Yvonne Burke who briefly served when she was appointed in 1978 and was quickly voted out of office in 1980. One of the reasons is that incumbents' turnover is quite low on the board. Between 1945 and 1990 only 18 different persons had been part of the board. From 1970 to 1990, only 3 incumbents were defeated for reelection since incumbents were rarely challenged. Over this period, incumbents averaged a very comfortable 65 percent of the votes.[9] The two main reasons that explain this lack of renewal of supervisors are, as is often the case in high stakes politics, incumbent advantage and redistricting. Most Los Angeles County elections have been characterized by massive incumbent fundraising from employees' associations and favor-seeking businesses such as construction firms, developers, and lobbyists. Incumbents raise so much money that they often scare the competition away. The second means of incumbent protection is redistricting. Morgan Kousser in his thoroughly researched paper (and his testimony in the *Garza* case) demonstrated the pattern of White male incumbent protection over time.[10]

One particularly example is that of the 1959 redistricting. In 1958, John Anson Ford, retired from the Third District that he had held since 1934. Four candidates jumped into the open race, among them was Edward R. Roybal, a liberal Mexican American. In the run-off election he faced another Democrat, Ernest E. Debs. On Election Day, many of Roybal's Latino supporters were challenged at the polls (irregularly according to him). The election was so close that no less than 4 recounts were needed. After Roybal finished "393 votes ahead on election night, the county registrar discovered a 12,000-vote counting error."[11] After his victory over Roybal, Debs negotiated a deal with Republican Burton Chace of the Fourth District. Chace wanted to avoid a contest with well-connected Los Angeles City Council woman Rosalind Wyman. Debs could not strike a deal with another supervisor because he wanted to lower the Latino population in his district. He needed to annex Anglo areas and dump Latino areas. "After the election, Debs and his four supervisorial colleagues began a series of boundary changes that radically altered the Third District and swung it in his favor."[12] With each move, Debs' district became more Anglo, reducing the proportion of Latinos who had backed Roybal. "The Third District, which almost elected a Latino in 1958, had become a constituency where Latinos had dwindled."[13] The fast-growing Latino population in the San Gabriel Valley could have gone to the Third District, which would have strengthened its Latino population. But they went to the neighboring First District, Frank Bonelli's district, therefore splitting the community.[14] And every round of redistricting tells the same story. Before

1981, redistricting was used to strengthen incumbents, and evidence suggests that the supervisors kept the Latino core area split in order to prevent potential challenges from candidates especially the type who could appeal to Latino voters. "Specifically repeated treks of Supervisor Ernest Debs' Third District in western and northern directions, begun almost as soon as Debs barely vanquished the first major Latino politician in modern California history, Edward Roybal, diluted the Hispanic percentage of the population in the Third District markedly."[15]

Another interesting case study is that of the city council of Los Angeles in 1971 because it demonstrates a general pattern of discrimination but also because it involved later County Supervisor Edelman and many of the Latino activists that participated in the 1981 county redistricting.[16] Before 1971, Los Angeles City Council had been redistricted based on the number of registered voters. However, in 1971, the California Supreme Court, in *Calderon v. City of Los Angeles*, that redistricting had to rely on population and that it could take "group interest" into account.[17] Chicanos for Fair Representation decided to get involved in the redistricting process as the council's Charter and Administrative Code Committee, headed by Edmund D. Edelman, was studying two different plans.[18] CFR wanted the council to increase Latino population in two districts and disregard incumbent protection. Edelman who wanted to run for mayor in 1973 faced a dilemma. He needed 10 votes on the council to pass any plan and incumbents would not vote for a plan that was not favorable to them. Yet, Latino activists were pressuring him into increasing Latino population in a few districts. And to be elected Mayor Edelman would need votes from the fast-growing Latino community. Arthur Snyder, a Yorty ally and another potential candidate for mayor, provided Edelman with an opportunity. Snyder and his Fourteenth District had the second largest Latino community. By increasing the Latino community in the Fourteenth District Edelman thought he could satisfy Latinos and neutralize a threat.[19] Edelman increased the Latino population in Snyder's district from 38 percent to 68 percent and, for good measure, created a district with a 30 percent Latino population and one with a 23 percent Latino population. At the same time he maintained the status quo in the three districts presented by African Americans (Gilbert Lindsay, Billy Mills, and Tom Bradley). CFR and Snyder denounced the redistricting plan, arguing it did go far enough, still split Latino communities and had the support of the *Los Angeles Times*.[20] A report by the California State Committee of the US Commission on Civil Rights blasted the plan and MALDEF also proposed an alternative plan potentially electing 2 Latinos.[21] The council adopted the plan overwhelmingly. While vetoing the "Edelman Plan" Mayor Yorty declared that "incumbency was the highest priority of the council's decision. . . . There is some claim that fair representation for Mexican Americans influenced the City Council. Such a claim is illusory."[22] The council easily overrode his veto.

MALDEF and other groups sued in state court and lost.[23] They argued that the redistricting plan unconstitutionally diluted the Latino political power. Snyder was challenged in recall elections and regular elections by many Latino candidates but survived until 1985 and scandals caught up with him.[24] What the Snyder story illustrates is that a Latino population majority does not guarantee the election of a Latino candidate against a well-connected, good fundraising incumbent. However, Snyder made a real effort to connect with the Latino population and deliver for his district. Another lesson, useful to understand the 1981 county redistricting, is that when a majority of elected officials agrees that one colleague is expandable, redistricting can work in favor of minorities.

One other way the number of minority elected officials could increase would be through the expansion of the number of seats on the city council from 15 to 17. Such an effort failed in 1970 and it wasn't until 1985 that the first Latino was elected on the city council since Ed Roybal left for Congress in 1962. Esteban Torres, then president of the Congress of Mexican American Unity, that same year, pushed for the expansion of the number of seats on the LA County Board of Supervisors from 5 to 7. But the Los Angeles County Citizens' Economy and Efficiency Commission did not recommend the expansion. The Board voted 3–2 not to put a seven-member proposal on the ballot.[25] Again in 1974, the Economy and Efficiency Commission debated the seven-member expansion but refused to take a position and recommended that the issue be presented to the public via referendum.[26] In 1976, the Public Commission on Los Angeles County Governance recommended increasing the number of member to 9 in order help minorities get elected.[27] Supervisors James Hayes, Peter F. Schabarum, and Baxter Ward publicly denounced Proposition B using cost as the main reason for opposition.[28] Proponents progressively downplayed the minority election argument realizing it had no traction with the majority Anglo population and opponents avoided taking any anti-minority stand. Proposition B lost by a 65–35 margin.[29] In September 2015, the California Senate failed to muster the two-third vote to put a constitutional amendment on the ballot requiring large California counties, including Los Angeles, to expand their five-member Board of Supervisors to at least seven members.[30]

These recurring attempts stem from the problematic fact that Los Angeles County's unusually large districts and its campaign finance laws exacerbate existing current structural and socioeconomic barriers to participation in the democratic process by minorities. After all, the Senate Judiciary Committee Report on the 1982 amendments to the Voting Rights Act in which Congress clarified the Act's application regarding procedures with the effect of diluting minority voting power states as factor 3: "The extent to which the state or political subdivision has used unusually large election districts, majority vote requirements, anti-single shot provisions, or other voting practices or procedures that may enhance the opportunity for discrimination against the minority group."[31]

SETTING THE STAGE: THE 1980 ELECTION

Before the 1980 elections, Democrats enjoyed a 4–1 majority on the LA County Board of Supervisors. The lone Republican was Peter F. Schabarum who had been elected in the First District in 1972. The Democrats were Kenneth Hahn who was first elected in 1952 in the Second District, Baxter Ward was elected in 1972 in the Fifth District and Edmund Edelman succeeded Ernst Debs in 1974 in the Third District. When Republican James Hayes resigned in 1979, Governor Brown appointed Yvonne B. Burke as the first Black and the first woman in the board's history.[32] Burke had been elected to Congress in 1972 from non-Black majority district. She became known nationally when she became the vice-chair of the 1972 Democratic National Convention. In 1978, she gave up her congressional seat to challenge Deukmejian in the open race for California's Attorney General Election. Deukmejian ran ads centered on busing[33] and Burke's position on death penalty.[34] She lost by 3 percent.

Burke was appointed to the Fourth District that was two-thirds Anglo and less than 10 percent African American but 62 percent of registered voters were Democrats. Jerry Brown had carried the district in 1978 by a 59–41 margin.[35] Burke who had been born and raised in South Central Los Angeles was well known, used to campaigning in White districts, and her "crossover" brand of politics attracted positive media coverage. By January 1980, most serious political opponents had bowed out of the race. State Senator Robert Beverly candidly explained one of his reasons for not running: "There are those who want to beat Yvonne who are racists or close to it. That's one thing that bothers me. What to do with their support? I don't know how to handle that."[36] Then out of the blue, Deane Dana, a low-key telephone company engineer that had never run for public office jumped into the race. Although Dana worked as an engineer, his heart had always been in politics. Behind the scenes, he and his family were well known in Republican circles in the South Bay and on the Palos Verdes Peninsula. Dana worked on every campaign of his longtime friend Deukmejian, beginning in 1962 with his run for the Assembly.[37] Deukmejian's endorsement went a long way into forcing a runoff against Burke. His campaign manager, Ron Smith, knew Dana had to run an aggressive campaign to make a name for himself and differentiate his message from that of the other not well-known candidates. Dana received 21 percent of the votes to Burke's 42 percent and forced a runoff. The campaign reminded voters at every turn that Burke was African American, characterized her as extremely liberal and appealed to racial sentiments in its commercial.[38] The race took place as the city wrestled with the controversial issue of busing and the implications of school integration which Dana instrumentalized even though the Board of Supervisor had no influence over this issue since busing is administered by the Los Angeles Board of Education, a point made many times by Burke.[39] To counter her soft-on-crime image created by her race and her anti-death penalty that Deukmejian had exploited effectively in 1978, Burke used her endorsement by Republican Los Angeles Sheriff Peter Pitchess who was involved in a personal feud with Supervisor Schabarum.[40] With the polls tightening, Schabarum who could sense that the partisan control of the board was at stake, decided to contribute to Dana's campaign finance in hope of pushing him over the finish line.[41] This last-minute influx of money was used to send flyers in White conservative areas. The flyer displayed a picture of Burke. In most races it would be a counterproductive move when trying to be elected to display a photograph of your opponent especially when this one was a former model. Except this time the candidate was African American and the flyer explained that Dana was against "forced" busing of schoolchildren and accused Burke of being against "mandatory prison for rape." Burke later testified that only once had her photograph appeared in the literature of an opponent, that of a leader of the John Birch society.[42] Many Anglo male politicians denounced these tactics as "racist" yet Dana prevailed in the fall, winning 53 percent to 47 percent.[43]

Dana served on the board until 1996. Before announcing his retirement in 1996, Dana encouraged Don Knabe, his chief of staff for many years, to run for his seat. Knabe ran with Dana's moral and financial support[44] and served until 2016 when he was term-limited.

The election in the Fifth District between incumbent Baxter Ward, a former television newsman, and Mike Antonovich, a right-wing Assemblyman, did not attract as much media attention but was key in the loss of the Democrats' majority. Ward, who did not hire a professional campaign manager and refused contributions over $50, lost 45 percent to 55 percent.[45] In the Second District, Kenneth Hahn, a seven-term Anglo incumbent in a district that was at the time 42 percent African American, won handily with 88 percent of the votes. After such elections, the newly led Schabarum majority did not feel very secure. Schabarum had avoided a runoff in 1978 by only 6 percent against minor opposition.[46] Antonovich, Dana, and Schabarum's districts were not tailor-made for them. For instance, the Latino and Asian population in Schabarum's district were growing rapidly and already represented 40 percent of the district's population in 1980. But Republicans were not the only ones worried about their future elections. Edelman's district was 42 percent Latino and almost 9 percent Asian in 1980.[47] However, the 1980 round of redistricting was around the corner and would offer the opportunity to optimize their districts.

THE 1981 LOS ANGELES COUNTY REDISTRICTING PROCESS

Introduction

To determine the type of discrimination that can occur during redistricting, one needs to bear in mind that the Latino community in Los Angeles in the 1980s and early 1990s had particular demographic and partisan traits. By 1960, people identified with a Spanish last name had become the largest minority group in the county (9.6 percent of the population). In 1970, 15 percent of the county's population considered themselves Mexican Americans and another 3 percent non-Mexican Latinos. In the 1970s the Latino population increased by 68 percent and the African American population by 21 percent while the Anglo population decreased by 21 percent. In 1980 Latinos represented 27.6 percent of the county's population. In 1990, 37.8 percent of the county's population identified as Latinos. By 1995, Latinos surpassed Anglos as the largest group in the county, comprising 43.5 percent of the population compared to 35.1 percent for Anglos, 11.4 percent for Asians, and 9.9 percent for African Americans.

The Latinos community had a smaller proportion of registered voters than the African American or Anglo population in part because the Latino population contains a greater proportion of noncitizens and minors.[48] Moreover they were slightly less segregated than these two communities.[49] The Los Angeles Community Development Department identified housing clusters as Anglo, Black, Spanish, Mixed, and Asian between 1950 and 1980. On average, Anglo clusters were 87.5 percent Anglo, Black clusters were 81.2 percent Black, but "Spanish" clusters were 61.2 percent Spanish and Asians clusters were 36 percent Asian.[50] It is therefore easier to draw safe Anglo districts yet the level of segregation of the Latino community is still high enough that it's fairly easy to cluster them politically.[51] So splitting or concentrating the Latino community was as likely to produce discrimination. Latinos also voted disproportionately for the Democratic Party. According to one study, in 1988, 70.4 percent of Latinos registered in LA County were Democrats, 20.4

percent Republicans, and 9.2 percent declined to state or were affiliated with another party.[52] They represented 13.1 percent of registered voters.

In *Thornburg v. Gingles* (478 U.S. 30 [1986]), the Supreme Court interpreted Section 2 of the recently amended Voting Rights Act (1965), making the existence of polarized voting one of three elements necessary to prove the dilution of minority voting. In *Gingles*, the now familiar definition of racially polarized voting was framed as occurring when there is a "consistent relationship between race of a voter and the way in which the voter votes." That means that racially polarized voting occurs when minority and non-minority voters, considered separately, would have elected different candidates to office. A second element contained within the *Gingles* standard is whether or not the minority group in question constitutes a "politically cohesive unit." If Latinos did not behave as a cohesive unit at the polls, evidence of racially polarized voting on the part of non-Latinos would be difficult to find.[53] The irony of Garza is that evidence of "intent," supposedly more difficult to prove, was more prominent than the statistical evidence of racial polarization of the vote.[54] The reason why intent was so crucial in this case is that, on the one hand, there were harsh battles between experts on the issues of whether elections were racially polarized and whether it was possible to draw a district in which the Latino CVAP was equal or superior to 50 percent. On the other hand, there was no contradicting testimony on intent, an issue on which the defendants were not prepared for and on which the evidence was overwhelming. However subsequent studies have demonstrated the high level of racial polarization or racial bloc voting in Los Angeles County.[55]

Drawing the Lines

State and county laws and guidelines affected the county redistricting process. The most significant in 1981 was the necessity for the final plan to be accepted by four of the five supervisors. This was crucial in 1981 since the board had a Republican majority of 3 votes to 2 and was therefore precluded from imposing their preferred plan.[56] September 24, 1981, was set as a deadline to turn in a redistricting plan by the county's counsel office. After this date, the process would be taken out of the supervisors' hands and given to a three-person committee consisting of the District Attorney, the County Assessor, and the Sheriff. The first two, John Van De Kamp and Alexander Pope, were liberal Democrats. The third, Republican Peter Pitchess, was involved in a bitter feud with Supervisor Schabarum.

The necessity to obtain at least four votes from the five supervisors, the deadline, and the alternative authority meant that the two Democrats were in position of power if they stuck together. The population growth in the county was fairly even during the 1970s so there was no need to equalize the districts and therefore no need for major changes in the district boundaries. An incumbent gerrymander was therefore a logical conclusion. Republicans tried to instrumentalize the Latino population to weaken the Democrats as they had tried to do at the state level. Except the drive for more Republican seats and more Latino seats were complementary at the state level because the Democrats controlled the legislature. At the county level the interests of the controlling Republicans and the Latino community representatives were potentially conflicting. Criticism of the redistricting process in Sacramento was a criticism of the Democrats. In LA County it was a criticism of the Republicans. The Republicans, led by Schabarum and the two main political consultants Ron Smith and Allan Hoffenblum, could not ask organizations such as CFR to limit their demands to the two Democrat seats held by Hahn and Edelman. The Republican dream of solidifying their partisan hold on the board, weakening their political foes and building goodwill Latinos never materialized.

Hahn and Edelman had just been reelected with respectively 88 percent and 74 percent of the votes. They could have afforded changes to their districts. But now that they face a 3–2 Republican majority, they adopted a strictly defensive posture and from the beginning never seriously considered any redistricting that would deviate from the status quo.

In March 1981, Supervisor Dean Anna filed a motion for the board to appoint a boundary commission. One of the commission's goals was to ensure that ethnic minorities were "equitably represented." Yet right away it became obvious that incumbent protection would trump any other consideration.[57] That should not come as a surprise since the 5 members on the commission had links with one of the candidates. Two of the Republican members were none other than Ron Smith and Allan Hoffenblum. Quite telling is the fact that during the first meeting the commission was criticized by Latino activists because it did not contain any member of a minority group. Edelman moved to double the size of the commission to allow minority representation. Supervisors ignored the names suggested by groups such as Californios for Fair Representation and appointed either loyal insiders or outsiders irrelevant to the redistricting process.[58]

CFR knew too well that the supervisors would not accept a plan that would seriously threaten their careers. Some CFR members argued for the creation of two seats with Latino population of 65 percent and 52 percent. But Santillan and MALDEF attorney John Huerta pushed for a more acceptable compromise. The CFR plan, drawn with the Rose Institute data, therefore proposed a plan that increased the Latino population in the Third District to 50 percent and in the First District to 42 percent. But even that plan was never considered by the supervisors.[59]

The incorporated and unincorporated communities of East Los Angeles were mostly located in the Third District (Edelman) which in 1981 was 42 percent Latino. But in 1981, as well as 1971, the Latino communities of the greater East Los Angeles were united with Anglo communities of the San Fernando Valley (Panorama City, Van Nuys, Sherman Oaks, Studio City) as well as the county's west side upper-class cities of Beverly Hills, Bel-Air, and Westwood.

District One (Shubarum) was 36 percent Latino after the 1980 census and contained much the San Gabriel Valley Latino communities such as Lynwood, South Gate, Pico Rivera, El Monte, and La Puente. But again these areas were combined with White conservative communities (Paramount, Bellflower, La Miranda, Whittier, La Habra Heights, Walnut and Temple city, San Dimas, La Verne, Claremont, Glendora, Monrovia, and Bradbury).[60]

CFR decided early on to disrupt District Two (Hahn) as little as possible to cooperate with Black leaders. The district was 26 percent Latino, 43 percent African American in the 1981 plan. African American leaders wanted to unite predominantly Black (and Latino) Compton and Northern Long Beach into the Second District in the hope that if Hahn retired they might have an opportunity to elect a Black candidate. CFR, MALDEF, and the NAACP agreed on that move.[61] Instead the Supervisors decided to keep Anglo communities of Culver City, Hawthorne, and Lawndale in the district, effectively diluting the Black vote. Dana would have been more than happy with this move since he lost Compton in his election against Burke by a landslide (16,118 to 711).[62]

Districts Four (Dana) and Five (Antonovich) presented the least opportunities for minorities since they were the most homogenous and least diverse districts. They were both 16 percent Latino and 10 percent and 5 percent African American respectively. District Four was mostly composed of coastal communities and District Five was comprised primarily of San Fernando Valley communities, northern rural communities, and some communities north of the San Gabriel Valley.

The only alternative to CFR's plan were the plans proposed by Smith and Hoffenblum. These two plans increased the number of Latinos and African Americans in the two Democratic districts. Smith increased the proportion of Edelman's district that was either African American or Latino from 45.2 percent to 54.8 percent. Hoffenblum's increased it to 53.6 percent.[63] Smith and Hoffenblum's intent was clear: solidify the 3–2 Republican majority while making it easier for Edelman and Hahn to be challenged by a minority candidate. According to Morgan Kousser these two plans never had a chance: "In fact, both Republican plans, by reducing the Hispanic percentage in the district with the fastest-growing Hispanic population, Schabarum's, were unattractive to Latinos and the four rule prevented their adoption anyway, since Edelman and Hahn had no reason to accept the plan that made their partisan opponent more secure."[64] The Democrats logically refused and the board deadlocked. In an anti-climactic decision on September 24, 1981, the board adopted a status quo plan that left minority population percentages pretty much unchanged. It slightly reduced the Latino population in the Third District from 42.4 percent to 41.8 percent, therefore perpetuating a trend since redistricting systematically increased the share of the Anglo population in the Third District from 1959 to 1981.[65] Elected officials of both parties wanted to keep their seats and make trouble for their enemies. And for both parties the means to achieve these goals was through minority vote dilution.

> The type of racial/ethnic and class gerrymandering emanating from LA county's redistricting plans of 1971 and 1981 so divided, fractured, and diluted Latino communities that fair and equal chances to participate in the electoral process and be represented by someone of their choosing on the county board were effectively denied.[66]

Class gerrymandering has never been declared unconstitutional but the author's remark illustrates how race and class are often perceived by political activist as two sides of the same coin. The concept of "community of interest" has not been used in the jurisprudence to protect the political interest of the poor or what Julius Wilson calls the underclass.[67] However, in 1990, Richard Simon, observed that the conservative majority on the Board of Supervisors neglected public services and systematically favored financial investors, especially those in construction, using companies outside of the county.[68] And the economic situation of some LA County neighborhood is such that it is hard to disagree with this journalist. As a consequence it is difficult to isolate race and redistricting as a political issue and not make any link with socioeconomic conditions. For instance, in 2011, Gary Segura expressly linked the voting-related discrimination and general societal discrimination to the lower socioeconomic status and political mobilization of the Latino community in the US. Using 2008 general election data, which involved comparatively extensive minority mobilization, and should therefore yield a conservative estimate of the gap between Latino and non-Latino turnout, he found a Latino citizen voter registration within Los Angeles County of 68.9 percent, compared to 78.2 percent registration among Anglos; in 2010, he found 59.0 percent Latino citizen voter registration (consistent with overall diminished registration in midterm election years), compared to 65.8 percent registration among Anglos. Similarly, he found that 65 percent of the Latino electorate in Los Angeles County turned out to vote in 2008 compared to 73 percent of Anglos; in 2010, 41.6 percent of the Latino electorate turned out to vote, compared to 53.4 percent voting among Anglos.[69]

THE SUIT

The discrimination in redistricting between 1959 and 1971 could have been challenged in court under Section 2 and the Fourteenth Amendment. However in 1975 Latinos were included as a protected group under the Voting Rights Act giving the community more legal tools. And the 1982 Section 2 amendments and extension of the Voting Rights Act made the 1981 plan more easily challengeable.

In August 1988, the Mexican American Legal Defense Fund and the American Civil Liberties Union filed *Yolanda Garza v. County of Los Angeles*,[70] a voting rights suit in the US District Court for the Central District of California. It sought a redrawing of the districts for the Los Angeles County Board of Supervisors. Soon after, the US department followed with its own suit against the county. Plaintiffs alleged violation of the Voting Rights Act and the Equal Protection Clause by the county which they contended had intentionally discriminated against Latinos in drawing district lines in 1981. They also alleged that the 1981 districting plan had diluted the voting strength of Latinos in Los Angeles County. Plaintiffs sought the creation of a district with a majority of Latinos for the 1990 elections.

Before the case went to trial in January 1990, the County Board began settlement discussion with the DOJ and MALDEF which came as a surprise since it had thus far refused any negotiation. Political survival instinct kicked in and Deane Dana proposed sacrificing the one member that had a history of conflict with other board members. Latino population would be increased in Schabarum's First District. But when MALDEF and the DOJ were presented with the alternate plan, MALDEF countered with its own plan that the board rejected. MALDEF felt the 60 percent Latino population proposed by the board was too low because it only produced a 35 percent Latino voter registration rate. MALDEF pushed for a 75 percent Latino population district that produced a 45 percent Latino registration voter rate. Faced with irreconcilable parties the trial went on and Latinos obtained the district they had argued for.

After a three-month trial, the United States District Court found intentional discrimination in the 1981 reapportionment, and deliberate dilution of the Latino vote. The 1981 plan was found to be in violation of the Voting Rights Act, and the county was ordered to propose a redistricting plan containing a district with a Latino voting majority. The district court made detailed findings regarding the history of the Los Angeles County Board of Supervisors, including the fact that the Board of Supervisors had engaged in intentional discrimination in the redistricting that occurred in 1959, 1965, and 1971. The *Garza* court also found that

> the enormous size and population of each supervisorial district and the fragmentation of the Hispanic population core under the 1981 redistricting plan have impeded the ability of Hispanic persons to participate in the political process,

> deterred viable Hispanic candidates from running for the Board, and impaired the ability of Hispanics to elect Supervisors of their choice.[71]

The court also found that the 1981 redistricting was calculated in part to keep the effects of the prior discriminatory reapportionments in place, and to prevent Latinos from attaining a majority in any district in the future. On June 4, 1990, Federal District Court Judge David V. Kenyon found that,

> The Supervisors appear to have acted primarily on the political instinct of self-preservation. The court found, however, that the Supervisors also intended what they know to be the likely result of their actions and a prerequisite to self-preservation—the continued fragmentation of the Hispanic core and the dilution of Hispanic voting strength.[72]

The county created a redistricting plan in response to the district court's order that was presented to the Court on June 27. The plan increased the Latino population in Edelman's Third District to 74 percent and the percentage of Latino registered voters to 45.5 percent.[73] The Republicans could not move the Third District east to strengthen Republican hold on the First District, which would have been the easiest move, because it threatened Dana.[74] So the consultant convoluted solution was to extend tentacles, often not wider than one precinct, to pick up the desired areas, from Watts to Beverly Hills.[75] Besides the strange shape of the district, the NAACP and the SCLC objected to its consequences in the Second District. While maintaining African American population numbers it actually lowered the proportion of African American voters.

The Court rejected the plan as being "less than a good faith effort to remedy the existing violations."[76] Instead, the Court accepted, on August 3, a plan initially submitted by MALDEF and the ACLU, that created a district in which the majority of the voting age citizens was Latino. The new First District had a Latino population of 71 percent (where it used to be 49 percent), with Latinos representing 51 percent of the registered voters. And because racial affiliation is closely linked to partisan affiliation the district's percentage of voters registered with the Democratic Party jumped from 50 percent to 66.5 percent. Judge Kenyon ordered a primary in the new district for November.[77] The new court-ordered plan was delayed when the county appealed to the 9th Circuit Court of Appeals.

The county argued that in 1981 it was impossible to draw a district map with equal population in each district that contained a district with a majority of Latino voters. Plaintiffs argued that no such majority requirement should be imposed where there has been intentional dilution of minority voting strength. The county, therefore, also challenged the sufficiency of the District Court's findings regarding discriminatory intent.

On November 2, 1990, the 9th Circuit Court of Appeals issued its opinion in *Garza v. County of Los Angeles*, affirming in part the District Court's ruling against the County of Los Angeles. The District Court found the county liable for its intentional vote dilution on two theories. First, it found that Section 2 of the Voting Rights Act had been violated because the 1981 redistricting plan resulted in a dilution of Latino voting power. Second, the district court found that the county had violated Section 2 of the Voting Rights Act and the Equal Protection Clause because of its intentional discrimination in establishing and maintaining the redistricting plan.[78] The Court of Appeals found that the detailed findings by the District Court of intentional discrimination by the County Board of Supervisors were "amply supported by the evidence in the record."[79] Judge Alex Kozinski of the US 9th Circuit Court of Appeals, a conservative Reagan appointee, eloquently stated:

> The lay reader may wonder if there can be intentional discrimination without an invidious motive. Indeed, there can. A simple example may help illustrate the point. Assume you are an Anglo homeowner who lives in an all-white neighborhood. Suppose also that you harbor no ill feelings toward minorities. Suppose further, however, that some of your neighbors persuade you that having an integrated neighborhood would lower property values and that you stand to lose a lot of money on your home. On the basis of that belief, you join a pact not to sell your house to minorities to keep the status quo. Have you engaged in intentional racial and ethnic discrimination? Of course you have. Your personal feelings toward minorities don't matter; what matters is that you intentionally took actions calculated to keep them out of your neighborhood.[80]

The Court therefore found that holding animus toward a particular racial or language minority group is not necessary in order to intentionally discriminate against them. The Court of Appeals also found evidence of injury in the intentional splitting of the Latino vote, resulting in diminished opportunity for Latinos to participate in the political process. The Court concluded that the intentional discrimination violated both the Voting Rights Act and the Equal Protection Clause in intentionally gerrymandering districts to minimize Latino voting strength.

The main point of disagreement between the majority opinion and Judge Kozinski's dissent was over the proper remedy. In constructing its remedial plan, the District Court drew districts of equal population, as was required by state law. In so doing, the Court formed two districts where numbers of voting age citizens were much lower than those in the other three districts. This difference in voting age population created a disparity in voting power between citizens in a district with a low number of voting age citizens and a district with a high number of eligible voters.[81] The majority held that the District

Court acted correctly in redistricting according to total population, despite its effect on relative voting power,[82] whereas Judge Kozinski argued the "one person, one vote" principle announced by the Supreme Court in *Reynolds v. Sims* was violated by this redistricting plan.[83] In his lengthy dissent, he made a persuasive argument that other figures, such as the number of eligible voters, should be used to revise legislative districts in some instances.[84]

The county appealed the decision of the District Court, based on the Supreme Court's decision in *Thornburg v. Gingles*,[85] arguing that the districts drawn in 1981 were lawful since the challengers could not show that a district with a majority of Latino voters could be drawn in 1981. This last appeal increased the spending of taxpayers' money for the lawsuit to $4.5 million, a move that the *Los Angeles Times* called "cynical, secretive ruthlessly self-interested raid on public funds that is without precedent" and added for good measure: "Recall would not be too strong of a step against those who carried it out."[86] On January 7, 1991, the United States Supreme Court denied certiorari,[87] upholding a redistricting plan designed to allow Latinos to equally participate in the election of members to the Los Angeles Board of Supervisors.

As a result of the *Garza* litigation, Los Angeles County held a special run-off election for the newly created First District on January 22, 1991, for which Schabarum did not run.[88] Four major candidates emerged: Republican Sarah Flores backed by Dana and Antonovich; Los Angeles City Councilwoman Gloria Molina, a former CFR activist who as such had spent time at the Rose Institute drawing district lines in 1981; Art Torres, a liberal state senator with strong links to organized labor and Charles Calderon, a moderate state senator. These four candidates were all Latinos. Gloria Molina topped the 9-candidate field and Art Torres finished second. On February 19, 1991, Gloria Molina, by receiving 55 percent of the vote to 45 percent for Art Torres, became the first Hispanic to serve on the Board of Supervisors in over 100 years and the first woman ever elected to the board.[89]

Yet Alan Rosin, who served as staff director of the State Senate Committee on Elections and Reapportionment in the early 1970s and 1980s, keenly observed: "This is a one-shot, very limited reform. It creates a Latino district, but it doesn't address the issues of district size and entrenchment. Incumbents don't have any opposition. And the nonpartisan nature of the board prevents effective challenges because there's no base, no political party, around which the opposition can be organized."[90]

In 1991, Supervisor Hahn retired and two African American women ran for the open seat. Dianne Watson was the first Black woman elected to the Los Angeles School Board in 1975 and to the State Senate. She lost in 1992 to Yvonne Brathwaite Burke who, after being appointed in 1979, returned to the board where she served until 2008. *Garza* settled the fate of the board for the next three decades. The racial and partisan makeup of the board has remained the same ever since: one Latino Democrat, one African American Democrat, one Anglo Democrat, and two Anglo Republicans.

Beyond its local consequences *Garza* also had much broader consequences. First, it represents one of the rare occurrences of the use of Section 3 of the Voting Rights Act, also called the "bail-in" procedure or "Pocket Trigger." This procedure has been utilized sparingly since the Voting Rights Act's adoption. One of the reasons is that the Court must first find that the jurisdiction engaged in intentional discrimination, which is a very difficult standard to meet. However, with Section 4 eliminated in 2013 by the Supreme Court decision *Shelby County, Alabama v. Holder*, Section 3 has been viewed as an alternative.[91] The bail-in procedure's primary advantage is that it provides a nearly identical structure to the previous preclearance model under Section 5,[92] and at the same time is likely to pass constitutional scrutiny. The Section 3 bail-in provision does not rely on the Section 4 formula, or any other legislative calculation. Rather, jurisdictions become subject to preclearance under Section 3 upon an individualized determination by a court, and only after the jurisdiction has been found in violation of the Fourteenth or Fifteenth Amendment. If intentional discrimination is found, the Court not only has discretion to submit the jurisdiction to preclearance, but also retains discretion to determine how long the jurisdiction will be subject to preclearance. Moreover, courts have the flexibility to tailor the preclearance requirement to specific types of voting laws that the jurisdiction may attempt to change or amend.

In 1991, in connection with the *Garza* litigation, the Board of Supervisors entered into a binding stipulation for the county to be covered under section 3(c) of the Voting Rights Act (42 U.S.C. 1973a[c]),[93] which required preclearance of changes relating to County Board of Supervisors for a period of eleven years.[94] Though the decision to enter the stipulation was voluntary, as most "bail-in" procedures are, this preclearance involved the same process and the same substantive standards that are used to evaluate other jurisdictions displaying a record of discrimination against racial and ethnic minorities in the country. This coverage expired on December 31, 2002. This means that during the 2001 round of redistricting the board was still under the supervision of the Justice Department. After holding a series of public meetings, the Supervisorial Boundary Review Committee approved a recommended plan and the board approved it. On September 13, 2001, the DOJ validated a redistricting plan that kept the status quo.[95]

So after the court victory in the 1990s the status quo settled in once again. And in LA County things evolve slowly. In 2011 Latino activists were still pushing for the county to create a second Latino-majority district, saying demographic shifts required it. Latinos in 2011 made up 48 percent of the county population, up from 45 percent in 2000. And Latinos constituted a third of the county's potential voters, up from a little more than a fourth in 2000. Democrat Yaroslavsky was termed out in 2014 which provided an opportunity to redraw the line in a manner more favorable for Latinos. Yaroslavsky was a Jewish Supervisor who had been elected to the board in 1994 when Edelman did not seek reelection and had run unopposed in 2010. He had previously been a member of the Los Angeles City Council since 1975 where he was elected at the tender age of twenty-six. His district had a 46 percent Anglo population but also nearly 38 percent Latino.[96] In 2011 representatives of Supervisors Molina and Mark Ridley-Thomas, who is African American, supported creating a second Latino-majority district in a plan supported by the Los Angeles County Chicanos Employees Association. Delegates of the Anglo supervisors, Yaroslavsky, Knabe, and Republican Supervisor Michael D. Antonovich, backed district boundaries largely preserving, once again, the status quo.[97] Yet studies keep finding a significant level of racial polarization in LA County.[98] In the end, term limits and time helped deliver Democratic and female victories on the board. In 2016, with the victory of Democrat Janice Hahn[99] in the Fourth District and Republican Kathryn Barger in the Fifth, the two women joined Latina Democrat Hilda Solis who was elected in the first District 2014 after her stint in the Obama administration and fellow Democrat Sheila Kuehl[100] who was elected in the Third District in 2014 to form the first female majority in the history of the board. With African American Ridley-Thomas who was elected in 2008 in the Second District, Democrats reached a 4–1 partisan majority on the board. Yet, as of 2016 there was still only one Latino representative on the Los Angeles County Board of Supervisors. In 2014 Governor Brown vetoed a bill (SB 1365) amending the California Voting Rights Act to allow challenges to district lines that would have directly led to a lawsuit against the County Board of Supervisors (experts had already been approached).[101] In September 2016, in spite of the supervisors' opposition to it, Governor Brown signed a bill creating an independent commission to redraw the board's districts.[102]

So in many ways, the battle over LA County redistricting seems to have been, in retrospect, a dressed rehearsal for politicians and minority organizations before the redistricting battle of the 1990s but also the subsequent ones.[103] The Republican conundrum is that LA County was becoming more diverse and more Democrat and Republican counted on redistricting to keep their majority on the Board of Supervisors. But federal courts intervened to protect minorities' interests. In the 1990s Republicans in the legislature, realizing the power of the judiciary, decided to take advantage of their conservative majority on the state Supreme Court to control the outcome of redistricting or at least to prevent having another Phil Burton in charge of the process.

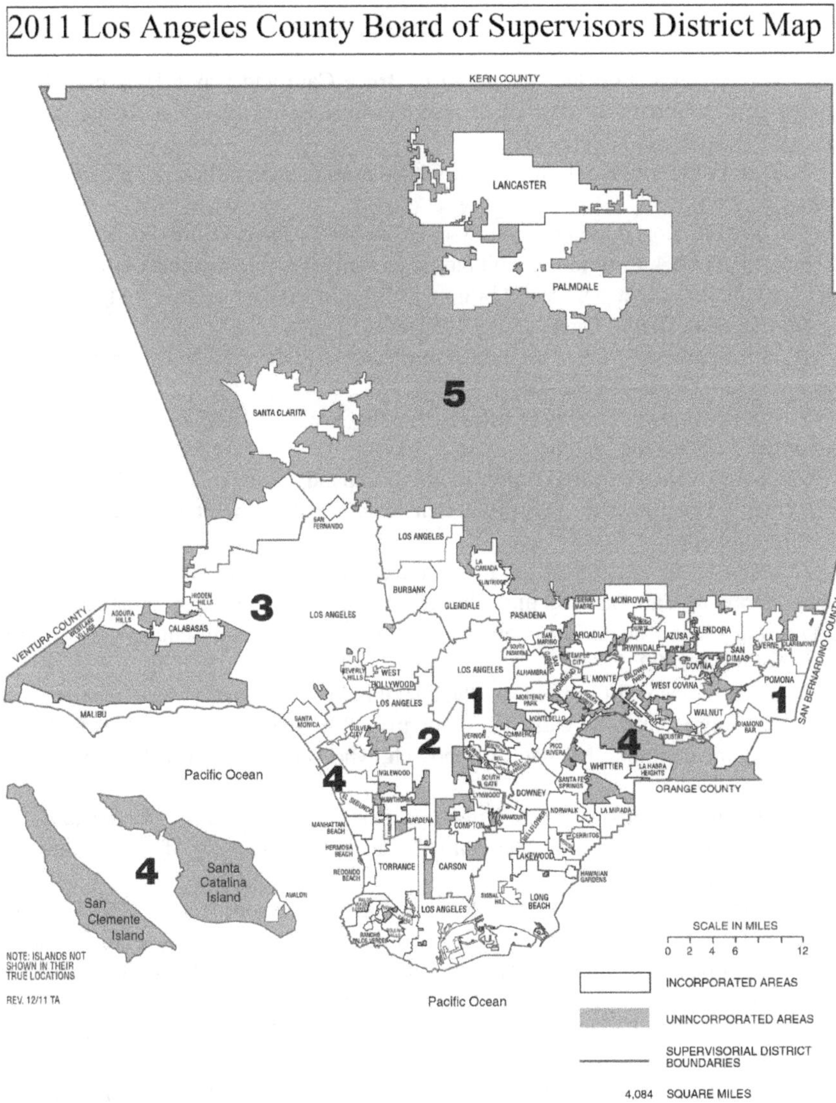

Figure 4.1 Los Angeles County Board of Supervisors District Map
Source: http://file.lacounty.gov/SDSInter/lac/1043452_BasicColorMap.pdf

NOTES

1. For one exception see, for instance, Bruce Cain and David Hopkins, "Mapmaking at the Grassroots: The Legal and Political Issues of Local Redistricting," *Journal of Election Law* 1 (2002), 515.

2. The five boroughs of New York City represented 8 million people that same year.

3. The third most populated county in the nation is Harris County in Texas (home of Houston), with 4.4 million inhabitants; it too only has five members in its governing board but its budget is under $2 billion. California has four counties in the nation's top ten (LA, San Diego, Orange, and Riverside).

4. Tim Schreiner, "LA Bias Trial Foreshadows Statewide Redistricting Fight," *San Francisco Chronicle*, January 29, 1990, A2.

5. Bill Boyarsky, "The Five Little Kings Who Are No More," *Los Angeles Times*, December 7, 1990, B2.

6. County voters rejected propositions to expand the board's size in 1962 and 1976, mainly because of the perception that "bigger" government would cost taxpayers more money.

7. Much to the chagrin of the Los Angeles branch of the ACLU: Mark Rosenbaum, "Drawing Fair Redistricting Lines," *Los Angeles Times*, September 27, 2011, http://articles.latimes.com/2011/sep/27/opinion/la-oe-rosenbaum-county-supervisors-redistricting-20110927.

8. If a supervisor fills a vacancy, the unexpired term counts toward the term limit if there are more than two years (half the term) left to serve. The provisions were not retroactive, meaning that Michael Antonovich, who was elected in 1980 served until 2016.

9. Morgan J. Kousser, *Colorblind Injustice: Minority Voting Rights and the Undoing of the Second Reconstruction* (Chapel Hill: University of North Carolina Press, 1999), 72.

10. Morgan J. Kousser, "How to Determine Intent: Lessons from LA," *Journal of Law and Politics* 7 (1991), 591–732. This chapter owes much to this seminal work.

11. Bill Boyarsky, "Crossover Dreams: Richard Alatorre Calls the Shots in East LA, But to Succeed Citywide He'll Have to Woo the Westside," *Los Angeles Times*, October 22, 1989, http://articles.latimes.com/1989-10-22/magazine/tm-616_1_east-los-angeles/6.

12. Bill Boyarsky, "Lost Drama in Voting Rights Suit," *Los Angeles Times*, March 7, 1990, B2.

13. Boyarsky, "Lost Drama in Voting Rights Suit," B2.

14. Equalization was not a factor since the districts had to be redrawn in 1965 after *Miller v. Santa Clara County* (1965) extended (or confirming) equal population standards to county redistricting.

15. Kousser, *Colorblind Injustice*, 85.

16. Richard Santillan, "The Chicano Community and the Redistricting of the Los Angeles County Council," *Chicano Law Review* 6, no. 0 (1983), 122–43.

17. "Racial or ethnic minorities often have distinct political interests, not shared by the general public, for which they seek political redress through their elected representatives" (*Calderon v. City of Los Angeles*, 4 Cal.3d 251 [1971], at 260).

18. Santillan, "The Chicano Community," 122, 127–28.

19. Santillan, "The Chicano Community," 133–34.

20. "Wanted: A Better Reapportionment Plan," *Los Angeles Times*, September 19, 1972, B6.

21. Erwin Baker, "LA Council's Plan for Redistricting Assailed," *Los Angeles Times*, September 7, 1972, OC6.

22. John Kendall, "Yorty Kills Council Redistricting Plan," *Los Angeles Times*, September 16, 1972, 1.

23. *Castorena v. City of Los Angeles*, 34 Cal. App. 3d 902 (1973).

24. Frank del Olmo, "Snyder Syndrome Even Gets Snyder," *Los Angeles Times*, August 30, 1984, D5; Rich Connel, "Art Snyder Again Beset by Political Turmoil," *Los Angeles Times*, December 14, 1992, OCA3.

25. Kousser, *Colorblind Injustice*, 91.

26. Report of the Economy and Efficiency Commission, December 1974, http://eec.lacounty.gov/Portals/EEC/Reports/48_7412RepEEC.pdf.

27. Bruce Keppel, "Voters Can Overhaul County's Government," *Los Angeles Times*, October 4, 1976, C1.

28. Bruce Keppel, "$6.5 million for Props A, B Seen," *Los Angeles Times*, October 29, 1976, B30.

29. Bruce Keppel, "County Mayor Plan Defeated," *Los Angeles Times*, November 4, 1976, 2.

30. The measure would have applied to all five counties with populations of 2 million people or more: Los Angeles, Orange, San Bernardino, Riverside, and San Diego. Patrick McGreevy, "Lawmakers Reject Measure Expanding County Boards of Supervisors," *Los Angeles Times*, September 10, 2015. http://www.latimes.com/local/political/la-me-pc-lawmakers-reject-supervisors-expansion-20150910-story.html.

31. The Seven "Senate Factors" are:

1. The extent of any history of official discrimination in the state or political subdivision that touched the right of the members of the minority group to register, to vote, or otherwise to participate in the democratic process;
2. The extent to which voting in the elections of the state or political subdivision is racially polarized;
3. The extent to which the state or political subdivision has used unusually large election districts, majority vote requirements, anti-single shot provisions, or other voting practices or procedures that may enhance the opportunity for discrimination against the minority group;
4. If there is a candidate slating process, whether the members of the minority group have been denied access to that process;
5. The extent to which members of the minority group in the state or political subdivision bear the effects of discrimination in such areas as education, employment and health, which hinder their ability to participate effectively in the political process;
6. Whether political campaigns have been characterized by overt or subtle racial appeals; [and]

7. The extent to which members of the minority group have been elected to public office in the jurisdiction.

(S. Rep. No. 97-417 [1982], 29)

32. Bill Boyarsky, "Mrs. Burke Becomes First Black, Woman Supervisor: Liberal Record May Make it Hard for Her to Hold Seat in Conservative, Largely White District," *Los Angeles Times*, June 15, 1979, B1; Kenneth Reich, "Yvonne Burk's Success Story: A Long Record of Being First," *Los Angeles Times*, June 15, 1979, B3.

33. Busing was a very racially charged issue in California in the late 1970s. W. B. Rood, "Brown Approves Nov. 6 Vote on Busing, Spending," *Los Angeles Times*, July 3, 1979, B1. Proposition 1, regarding the School Assignment and Transportation of Pupils, was on the November 6, 1979, statewide special election ballot in California as a legislatively referred constitutional amendment, where it was approved.

34. Larry Stammer, "Deukmejian-Burke Race Issues Battle," *Los Angeles Times*, October 16, 1978, A3.

35. Kenneth Reich, "Yvonne Burk's Success Story: A Long Record of Being First," *Los Angeles Times*, June 15, 1979, B3.

36. Victor Merina, "Yvonne Burke—No Opposition in Sight," *Los Angeles Times*, December 9, 1979, B1.

37. Jocelyn Y. Stewart, "Deane Dana, 78; Former LA County Supervisor Had Pro Busisness Stand," *Los Angeles Times*, April 22, 2005, http://articles.latimes.com/2005/apr/22/local/me-dana22.

38. Victor Merina, "Racism Issue Marks Burke, Dana Contest," *Los Angeles Times*, October 31, 1979, D1; Gerald Francis, "Old Political Hands Adds New Face in the Race of Supervisor," *Los Angeles Times*, October 5, 1980, WS1.

39. Victor Merina, "Burke Aide Calls Dana's Busing Charge Racist," *Los Angeles Times*, September 13, 1980, D14; "Burke Dana Clash on Busing in Final Debate," *Los Angeles Times*, October 29, 1980, D1

40. Kousser, *Colorblind Injustice*, 94.

41. Bill Boyarsky and Victor Merina, "Schabarum Raises $50,000 for Dana Attack on Burke," *Los Angeles Times*, October 30, 1980, D1.

42. Richard Simon, "Campaign Racial Overtones Raised in County Remapping Suit," *Los Angeles Times*, January 11, 1990, B3.

43. Bill Boyarsky, "Conservatives Win Control of Supervisors," *Los Angeles Times*, November 5, 1980, 1.

44. In 1996, Knabe raised more than $2.2 million. Jeffrey Rabin, "Funds Flow for Knabe, Trickle in for Swanson," *Los Angeles Times*, October 13, 1996, http://articles.latimes.com/1996-10-13/local/me-53566_1_don-knabe.

45. "Words and Dollars for Baxter Wards," *Los Angeles Times*, June 27, 1980, C6; Richard Simon, "Ward Antonovitch Race Heats Up, Brings out Personal Attacks," *Los Angeles Times*, October 5, 1980, GB1.

46. Sid Bernstein, "3 Challenge Schabarum in Reelection Bid," *Los Angeles Times*, May 30, 1978, C1.

47. Kousser, *Colorblind Injustice*, 96.

48. The 1980 Census estimated that the Spanish origin population under the age of eighteen was close to 40 percent.

49. Armando Navarro and Emilio Lazarin, *The People of California: A Atlas of Latino Communities* (Claremont, CA: The Rose Institute, 1990).

50. Carlos Navarro, "A Report on California Redistricting and Representation for the Los Angeles Chicano Community," in *The Chicano Community and California Redistricting*, vol. 1, ed. Richard Santillan (Claremont, CA: The Rose Institute, 1981), 141.

51. Bruce Cain, *The Reapportionment Puzzle* (Berkeley: University of California Press, 1983), 40.

52. *Facts and Figures about California's Latino Voters: 1988* (Claremont, CA: The Rose Institute, 1988), table 1. Also cited by Kousser, *Colorblind Injustice*, as exhibits in the *Garza* case.

53. The three-prong approach in *Gingles* was derived from James U. Blacksher and Larry T. Menefee, "From *Reynolds v. Sims* to *City of Mobile v. Bolden*: Have the White Suburbs Commandeered the Fifteenth Amendment?," *Hastings Law Journal* 34, 1 (1982), 1–64.

54. Kousser, *Colorblind Injustice*, 133.

55. For such a study between 1994 and 2010, Matt A. Barreto and Loren Colinwood, "A Review of Racially Polarized Voting For and Against Latino Candidates in Los Angeles County 1994–2010," Report 1 of 2, in *Report on Legal Standard Pertaining to the Los Angeles County Redistricting Process*, Justin Levitt (2011), 82–165.

56. The county charter only mentions a two-thirds vote.

57. Kousser, "How to Determine Intent," 652. Morgan Kousser was an expert witness during the *Garza* trial.

58. Kousser, *Colorblind Injustice*, 106.

59. Edelman never took a public position on CFR's plan but the 50 percent Latino population had the effect of removing part of the Jewish population of his district, his fund raising base that he had built over the years. That move, in itself, would have been enough to make him think twice about the change. The fact that he never voiced his concern is probably proof that he never took the plan seriously. Henry Weinstein, "Latinos Pushing Redistricting Plan: But LA Supervisors Are Expected to Oppose Major Changes,"*Los Angeles Times*, August 4, 1981, C1.

60. James Regalado, "Conflicts over Redistricting in Los Angeles County: Who Wins, Who Loses," in *Racial and Ethnic Politics in California*, vol. 2, eds. Michael B. Preston, Bruce E. Cain and Sandra Bass (Berkeley, CA: Institute of Governmental Studies Press, 1998), 381.

61. Some Compton officials opposed the move. They thought if they remained in Dana's district they might be able to influence his vote on some health and welfare measures and get a bigger share of construction and other funds. Joining Hahn's district meant they would have to compete with other poor minority communities for limited funds.

62. Dana, according to the *LA Times*, stalking out of Hahn's office, allegedly declared: "If I don't get rid of Compton, I won't vote for anything." Sid Bernstein, "Supervisors' Dispute Delays Redistricting Vote," *Los Angeles Times*, September 23, 1981, D1.

63. Kousser, "How to Determine Intent," 675.

64. Kousser, *Colorblind Injustice*, 125.

65. Kousser, *Colorblind Injustice*, 127, table 2.1.

66. Regalado, "Conflicts Over Redistricting," 374.

67. William J. Wilson, *The Truly Disadvantaged: The Inner City, The Underclass and Public Policy* (Chicago, IL: Chicago University Press, 1986).

68. Richard Simon, "County Board Ideology Yields to Politics," *Los Angeles Times*, March 18, 1990, B1.

69. Gary M. Segura, "An Evaluation of Hispanic Socio-Economic Conditions and Voter Registration and Turnout," in *Report on the Legal Standards Pertaining to the Los Angeles Redistricting Process*, Levitt (2011), Exhibit J, 391–401. http://file.lacounty.gov/bos/supdocs/62832.pdf.

70. 918 F.2d 763 (9th Cir. 1990).

71. *Garza v. County of Los Angeles*, 756 F. Supp. 1298, 1341, at 1342 (C.D. Cal. 1990).

72. *Garza,* 918 F.2d 763 (9th Cir. 1990), 768.

73. Richard Simon, "LA County Remap Plan Gives Edelan Latino District," *Los Angeles Times*, June 28, 1990, SDA31.

74. Dana's district was the least populated in 1990 and inheriting Edelman's district western liberal section might have made his reelection difficult. Besides, Edelman was living in this area and he had to run in the district which contained his home. He would have been formidable opponent for Dana. Kousser, *Colorblind Injustice*, 130.

75. Richard Simon and James Rainey, "Edelman Put in Latino District by Board Plan," *Los Angeles Times*, June 28, 1990, A1.

76. *Garza,* 918 F.2d (9th Cir. 1990), 768.

77. James Rainey, "Judge's Ruling on Remap Puts First District Race for Supervisor in Limbo," *Los Angeles Times*, July 1, 1990, SE_AJ5; Frederick M. Muir, "It's a New Race for Supervisors after Judge OKs Changes in First District," *Los Angeles Times*, August 4, 1990, SDA30.

78. *Garza,* 918 F.2d (9th Cir. 1990), 769.

79. *Garza,* 771.

80. *Garza,* 778, n1.

81. Dennis, L. Murphy, "Garza v. County of Los Angeles: The Dilemma over Using Elector Population as Opposed to Total Population in Legislative Apportionment," *Case Western Reserve Law Review*, 41 (1991), 1013.

82. *Garza*, 773–76.

83. Garza, 779 (Kozinski, J., concurring in part and dissenting in part.)

84. Garza, 780–85.

85. In *City of Mobile v. Bolden* (446 U.S. 55 [1980]), the case concerned whether at-large systems of voting were adopted or maintained with a racially discriminatory intent or whether they had discriminatory effects, a plurality of the Supreme Court held that the 1965 Voting Rights Act prohibited only intentional discrimination, not practices which diluted minority votes without invidious intent. *Bolden*, 765–66. In 1982, in response to the *Bolden* decision, Congress amended the Voting Rights Act so that it would also forbid any practice shown to have a disparate impact on minority

voting strength. *Bolden*, 766; See 42 U.S.C. § 1973(b) (1988). After this amendment, the Voting Rights Act forbade both intentional discrimination in reapportionment and facially neutral apportionment had the effect of minority vote dilution.

In 1986, the Supreme Court decided *Thornburg v. Gingles* (478 U.S. 30 [1986]), which discussed the meaning of the 1982 amendment to the Voting Rights Act. In *Gingles,* there was no claim of intentional discrimination (80). Rather, the claim was that the districting scheme had the effect of diluting the vote of black voters (46). *Gingles* established three threshold preconditions for determining when a jurisdiction must draw districts specifically designed to ensure that a particular minority has the effective opportunity to elect representatives candidates of their choice. The first *Gingles* condition is that the minority group is "sufficiently large and geographically compact to constitute a majority in a single-member district" (50). The second *Gingles* threshold condition is that the minority group is politically cohesive; the third is that the majority votes sufficiently as a bloc to enable it "usually to defeat the minority's preferred candidate" (51).

86. "Outrageous Back-Room Deal," *Los Angeles Times*, June 29, 1990, SDB6.

87. 59 U.S.L.W. 3421, 1991 WL 793. The unanimous three-judge decision on the liability issue discouraged other judges on the Ninth Circuit Court of Appeals from ordering an en banc rehearing and the Supreme Court from granting certiorari.

88. Tom Waldman, "Luring the Latino Vote—The Scramble for LA County's New Supervisorial Seat," *California Journal* 22, no.1 (1991): 20–21; Page E. Bucy, "Sidebar to the New LA County Supervisorial Seat—Redistricting by Lawsuit," *California Journal* 22, no.1 (1991): 22–28.

89. Richard Simon, "Molina Wins Historic Contest for Supervisor," *Los Angeles Times*, February 20, 1991, A1; "Molina Elected to LA Supervisor's Seat," *Los Angeles Times*, February 20, 1991, SDA18.

90. Bucy, "Sidebar to the New LA County Supervisorial Seat."

91. On Section 3, see Travis Crum, "The Voting Rights Act Secret Weapon: Pocket Trigger Litigation and Dynamic Preclearance," *Yale Law Journal* 119 (2010): 1992; Paul M. Wiley, "Shelby and Section 3: Pulling the Voting Rights Act's Pocket Trigger to Protect Voting Rights after *Shelby County v. Holder*," *Washington and Lee Law Review* 71 (2014): 2115.

92. Unlike Section 5 preclearance language, Section 3 provides the Attorney General or a local Federal District Court with jurisdiction to hear preclearance requests—not the District Court for the District of Columbia.

93. *Garza & United States v. County of LA*, Nos. CV88-5143 KN, CV88-5435 KN, slip op. at 2 (C.D. Cal. Apr. 26, 1991), provided by Levitt, *Report on the Legal Standards*, exhibit F.

94. M. David Gelfand, "Voting Rights Developments: Academic Reflections and Practical Projections for the 1990s," *Stetson Law Review* 21 (1992): 715.

95. Nicholas Riccardi, "New Supervisorial Districts Just Like the Old," *Los Angeles Times*, June 27, 2001, BA.

96. John Hoeffel and Rong-Gong Lin, "Taking a Risky Stand on Plans for Latino District," *Los Angeles Times*, September 15, 2011, A1.

97. Lin Rong-Gong, "Bid for More Latinos on Board Sets up Fight," *Los Angeles Times*, August 6, 2011, A1. Because of the four-vote requirement one Democrat had to join the Republicans for their plan to be adopted: Ridley-Thomas provided that vote, arguing that he was hoping courts would strike it down.

98. Matt Barreto for instance demonstrated the degree of polarized voting in three of the Los Angeles County Supervisorial Districts the 2010 June primary. Matt A. Barreto, "Latino Candidates and Racial Block Voting in the 2010 Primary and Judicial Elections." Report Commissioned by The Los Angeles County Chicano Employees Association (Alhambra, CA, December 3, 2010); For a study of RPV in 2008 elections, see Matt A. Barreto and Loren Collingwood, "Latino Candidates and Racial Block Voting in Primary and Judicial Elections," Report Commissioned by: The Los Angeles County Chicano Employees Association (Alhambra, CA, October 31, 2009).

99. A former Los Angeles City Council member, who is the sister of former Los Angeles mayor James Hahn.

100. Khuel, a former child actress, was a member of the State Assembly from 1994 to 2000. She was the first openly gay California legislator and in 1997, she was the first woman to be named Speaker Pro Tempore in California. She was a state senator from 2000 to 2008.

101. Abby Sewel, "Governor Jerry Brown Vetoes Expansion of State Voting Rights Act," *Los Angeles Times*, October 4, 2014, http://www.latimes.com/local/lanow/la-me-pc-governor-veto-voting-rights-20141001-story.html; For more on the California Voting Rights Act, see chapter 7.

102. Patrick McGreevy, "Brown OKs Redistricting Commission," *Los Angeles Times*, October 1, 2016, B3. SB 958 requires district lines to be drawn by bipartisan groups and diverse representatives of the county. The members of the commission would be randomly selected in 2020 by the county Auditor-Controller from a pool of applicants whose eligibility will be determined by the Los Angeles County Registrar-Recorder/County Clerk. However, it's not exactly patterned after the California redistricting commission because the political party preferences of the 14 commission members, as shown on the members' most recent registration affidavits, will be proportional to the total number registered voters. This commission will therefore be much more partisan than the CRC. For more on the CRC, see chapter 8.

103. Robert B.Gunnison, "Patchwork Power," *San Francisco Chronicle*, February 23, 1991, A14.

Chapter 5

Strategic Gridlock of 1991

Republicans Bet on the Judiciary

THE DEMOGRAPHIC POWER OF MINORITIES

During the 1980s the population of the state of California increased by 26 percent to reach 30 million people in 1990. The Anglo population grew by 8 percent to reach 17 million people, the Black population grew by 17 percent to reach 2.1 million people, the Latino population grew by 69 percent to reach 7.7 million people, and the Asian population grew by 127 percent to reach 2.7 million people.[1] In the early 1990s many minority political activists made the election of non-Whites a priority. They argued it was more important for minority voters to elect representatives from their racial/ethnic group than to elect representatives of a particular party because incumbents who are different from their constituents cannot serve them as well even when they share a common partisan affiliation. In the debate between "effective" and "substantial" representation they clearly chose the former. This meant that their strategy relied heavily on nonpolitical, and especially legal, tactics to achieve political gains. As discussed earlier, California minorities made significant gains in officeholding in the 1960s, 1970s, and 1980s. This holds true at all political levels.[2] Not all African American or Latino officeholders had been elected in minority-majority districts but most did. This fact seemed to suggest that the nature of the electoral system and the composition of districts could be critical to electoral success. Therefore the attention of minorities in 1991 was closely focused on redistricting. African Americans and Anglos were faced with a decreasing share of the population and tried to resist any loss of representation. On the other hand, Latinos and Asians face a strong increase of their populations and, logically, sought to increase their political power. Nevertheless, in the early 1990s, the California electorate was disproportionally White and middle class at all levels. Latinos and Asians had a citizenship rate lower than the rest of the population along with lower turnout rates. Yet, low income non-Whites are the most likely beneficiaries of redistributive programs and social services. Therefore, the clash over taxation and government services comes down, at least in the implicit discourse of many politicians, to the White middle class sharing resources with disadvantaged non-White populations.

California minorities in the 1990s did not form a united coalition, the prophesied "rainbow" scenario of the 1984 campaign, to further the representational interests of all racial or ethnic minorities. One reason is that the diversity in the California population forms the basis of political division. There is a sharp diversity among the different groups and, within those groups, differences between generations and income levels which results in fluid alliances rather than permanent minority coalitions. For instance, African Americans and Latinos, overall, shared important partisan and socioeconomic similarities that made them share views that were statistically distinguishable from Anglos and Asians and even many Democratic Anglos and Asians.[3] However, one of the most important distinctions between the two groups was that one was mostly native born and the other was composed of immigrant. Latinos had very important language and cultural concerns not shared by the African American community such as bilingual education or immigration reform.[4] The competition between the two groups was not perceived as being only political but also economical. Besides, inter-group diversity is much deeper than usually acknowledge. That is because of the performative power of racial and ethnic statistics, and especially the Census and the Office of Budget and Management Directive 15 that created what David Hollinger called the "ethno-racial pentagon," tends to make this intra-group diversity invisible.[5] The age, the nationality and the number of years an immigrant has lived in the US are essential factors. A fifth generation family of Japanese Americans has almost nothing in common with a recently immigrated family from Vietnam. Diversity of religion, language, along with histories of antagonism, prevent meaningful lasting political alliances. Some immigrants are even divided by political divisions from their country of origin. For all these demographic divisions, building coalitions is extremely difficult.[6] In the case of Asian Americans, weighing on redistricting was particularly difficult because of the lack of spatial concentration. First, nationality groups have to be put together to form an Asian coalition. Second, the manner in which the population is concentrated may not favor district drawing. Third, because they may not be numerous enough Asian American communities may have to coalesce with other minority groups and run the risk of seeing their specific interests unheard.[7]

Another factor to take into consideration is the structural political changes of the early 1990s in California. The percentage of registered Democrats and registered Republicans had been on steady decline since the 1960s. In 1990 voters who registered with the Democratic Party represented 50 percent, those who registered with the Republican Party 39 percent, down from a 54 percent to 35 percent edge in 1980.[8] Complementary, the number of independent (decline to state) had steadily increased. In 1990 it reached 11 percent.[9] Of course, partisan affiliation's meaning varies across the country and being Democrat or a Republican in California needs to be understood in the context of the political spectrum of the state.[10]

REPUBLICAN VICTORIES

At the end of the 1980s, the Republican strategy rested on two key ideas. Redistricting is essential to achieve political domination and Republicans had been taken advantage of in 1981. This second assertion, that Burton single-handedly hindered the Reagan revolution, was exaggerated. Yet it cannot be denied that the Burton redistricting had a negative impact on the Republican Party.[11] However, the GOP's obsession with undoing the Democrats' redistricting plans probably led the party astray. The feeling in Sacramento was that by concentrating their energy and resources on redistricting initiatives or the removal of Rose Bird as Chief Justice of the state's Supreme Court, the Republicans probably neglected one of the most fundamental aspects of winning elections: candidate quality. By not investing enough in their candidates the Republican Party may have depressed the field by discouraging better candidates from running or supporters from investing their time and money. There was some truth to Speaker Willie Brown's statement in 1991 when he said the Republicans only had 31 seats in the Assembly because they had fielded inferior candidates and had run poor campaigns.[12] For instance the Thirty-fifth Assembly District was up for grabs in 1982 when Republican Brooks Firestone was defeated by 1990 votes by Democrat Jack O'Connell.[13] In 1984, the GOP ran County Sheriff John Carpenter, instead of a more polished politician, and lost a seat that was there for the taking. Another example is the Sixty-eighth Assembly District in Riverside where Democrat Steve Clute was considered vulnerable by the Republican Party in 1984. But they ran Police Lieutenant Gil Olivarria who lost by 6,000 votes out of the 113,290 cast.[14] In the Senate the GOP also had opportunities to pick up seats throughout the decade.[15] For example, in the Thirty-third District in Orange County, when Democrat Paul Carpenter was elected to the State Board of Equalization in 1987 (and subsequently stepped down and went to prison for corruption) Democrat Cecil Green picked up the seat. Senate President Pro Tempore David Roberti, Green's chief financial supporter, ecstatically declared in 1987: "We have broken the backs of the Republicans. . . . It's going to be very hard for the Republicans to take control now."[16] And again, in 1988, when incumbent Cecil Green (breaking state history for campaign spending) won against Don Knabe by 3,500 votes in a tough fight to keep a Democrat majority in the Senate prior to the 1990 redistricting.[17]

The political battle to control redistricting never really ebbed throughout the 1980s. It could be argued that the fight began in earnest as early as 1986. That year 16 of the 20 seats at stakes were held by Democrats with 2 open seats because of retirement. With a 26–14 advantage the Democrats were one seat short of a two-third majority. But even without a super-majority that would have allowed the dominant party to override gubernatorial veto, pass spending and tax bills, and enact urgency legislation, the sheer number of Democrats in the upper chamber was a problem for Governor Deukmejian.[18] The Republicans naturally intended to seize this electoral opportunity and John Seymour, chairman of the Republican Caucus, probably betting the GOP opposition to Chief Justice Rose Bird would help them make inroads, speculated the Republicans could win 5 seats.[19] In the end the Republicans gained 2 Senate seats and 3 Assembly seats, all open seats, in a year when the Democratic voter registration reached its lowest point since 1934.[20]

Winning the Senate majority before the 1990 round of redistricting was so crucial for the methodical John Seymour that he lobbied President Reagan to appoint Democratic State Senator Wadie P. Deddeh to an ambassadorship in the Middle East in order to create an open seat in San Diego.[21] However, in spite of the conviction for political corruption of two Democratic senators (Montoya and Carpenter) the Republicans could not win a majority of seats in either chamber before the 1991 round of redistricting. When the 1991 session started the Democrat majorities were of 26–13 (plus independent) in the Senate and 47–31 in the Assembly.[22]

But no matter, the GOP had other weapons at its disposal. First, it was successful in its campaign to replace the Democratic majority on the State Supreme Court with a Republican one. Using death penalty as a wedge issue, the GOP was able to replace the first female chief justice, the first Latino liberal Associate Justice and another liberal Associate Justice. After leading the fight against Rose Bird, Governor Deukmejian appointed his former law partner Malcolm Lucas, an Anglo male, as chief justice.[23] In all, the governor appointed five justices. For many observers it was difficult not to see this entire episode as a blatant form of nepotism and also a blow to diversity. This new conservative majority proved decisive in the 1991 redistricting war. Yet, controlling the judiciary is only a third of the equation. Controlling the governorship would be key. Republican National Chairman Lee Atwater declared in 1989 that California's gubernatorial campaign would be the number one race in the country because of its potential impact on the nationwide struggle for reapportionment because the GOP had not controlled the House of Representatives since 1954.[24] The California congressional delegation was composed in 1991 of 26 Democrats, 19 Republicans, and gained 5 seats after the 1990 census. Winning the governorship was therefore crucial for the GOP and the nationally ambitious Senator Pete Wilson was the obvious nominee. His election was the Republicans' second success in controlling redistricting outcome. He won a close gubernatorial election against San Francisco Mayor Diane Feinstein (49.3 percent to 45.8 percent) who two years later won Wilson's seat in the US Senate. One of the reasons was because the Democratic Party had had a hard time mobilizing its party faithful. According to one observer from the Center for Politics and Policy at the Claremont Graduate School: "the party took its constituencies for granted, slighting organization and get-out-the-vote efforts and failing to tame the absentee-ballot monster."[25] But what might have helped Wilson the most is his timing. The Democratic apparatus might have been in disarray but the party's legislative leadership was preoccupied with two referendums on term limits. Coming off a multimillion-dollar campaign against two redistricting initiatives in the June 1990 ballot, their time, money, and energy were spent trying to beat Proposition 131 and 140. Proposition 131 was defeated (62 percent to 38 percent) but Proposition 140, despite being massively outspent,[26] passed with 52 percent of the votes and started a political revolution in Sacramento.[27]

Proposition 140, sometimes called the Schabarum initiative because it was backed by controversial Los Angeles County Supervisor Peter F. Schabarum, limited the number of terms that California State senators and assembly members could stay in office.[28] Members of the California State Assembly were limited by its provisions to three two-year terms and members of the California State Senate to two four-year terms.[29] It also imposed a lifelong ban against seeking the same office once the limits were reached. Proposition 140 also limited the total amount of the California State Legislature's expenditures on staff salaries and operating expenses which means that elected officials had to cut legislative staff by a third.[30] Proposition 140 was very consequential for redistricting in 1991. In effect it killed two birds with one stone. This law forced Democrats with the most experience to retire later on in the decade among which was Speaker Willie Brown who was the Republicans' archenemy. Besides, Proposition 140 ended up limiting political dialogue during the 1991 redistricting round. According to Tim Hodson, who was, in 1991, staff director of the Senate Elections and Reapportionment Committee, in spite of the Democratic majority each individual Republican had less of an incentive to look for a compromise that would protect him, or her, long term in a given district. The Democratic majority's leverage was therefore weakened because it did not have the power to impact the careers of colleagues, positively or negatively, for as many years as it used to.[31]

Wilson's support for Proposition 140 may have earned him the enmity of nearly every sitting legislator but the GOP now controlled the governorship and the Supreme Court. But because the GOP victory in the gubernatorial election had not been a foregone conclusion, Republicans had made plans to use another weapon at their disposal: direct democracy.[32] As mentioned, the Republicans sponsored two redistricting initiatives in June 1990. Proposition 118 that would have imposed a two-third majority in both houses, signed by the governor and ratified by voters.[33] If the legislature did not act by July 15 in the year after the census, a difficult threshold for any legislature, the Supreme Court, controlled by the conservatives, would take over. Another proposition on the same ballot, proposed by other Republicans, would have taken effect if it had received a larger majority than Proposition 118. Proposition 119 tried to establish a judge-appointed commission that would have considered plans proposed by interested groups.[34] This commission would have been composed of 5 Democrats, 5 Republicans, and 2 independents, all chosen by the judiciary,[35] while taking into consideration racial, ethnic, gender, and geographic diversity of its members. Proposition 118 was written by top Republican activists and had strong support from GOP incumbents. Proposition 119 was more of a grassroots product, sponsored by San Mateo County Republican Supervisor Tom Huening and the League of Women Voters.[36]

Both initiatives placed detailed new restrictions such as prohibiting districts from jumping certain county boundaries and limiting the number of times that cities and counties could be divided. And they both included provisions designed to make districts more compact and competitive. "Competitive" was defined here as districts containing Democrats and Republicans in proportions that were within 2 percent of the parties' statewide share of registered voters.[37] From a practical standpoint the initiatives never mentioned if all those factors were compatible or even feasible. Since in 1990 the Democrats had a 50 percent to 39 percent advantage in voter registration, the competitive clause seemed to not hurt Republicans. Indeed at the time Republicans believed, and data suggested, that they could win almost any district in California in which Democrats accounted for less than 50 percent of the registered voters.[38] This implied that the gap between Democrats and Republicans wasn't too wide. This rule of thumb changed over time with the emergence of unaffiliated voters which changed the two-party dynamic.

Proposition 118 did not mention the protection of minorities. Proposition 119 required the redistricting plans to meet the standards of the federal Voting Rights Act before being considered by the commission. It also required that minority communities be neither diluted nor concentrated in a way that diminished their representation. But as both initiatives appeared together on the ballot, both sponsored by Republicans, as a consequence both were easily lumped together and attacked for being against minorities interests by the Democrats and minority organizations such as California Common Cause, the National Organization for Women, and MALDEF but also the Sierra Club and the League of Conservation Voters.[39] Supporters of the initiatives mentioned that minorities had not fared well under the Democrats since in 1975 there were 7 African Americans, 6 Latinos, and 2 Asian Americans in the legislature and in 1990 there were 9 African Americans, 6 Latinos, and no Asians. Supervisor Huening defended his initiative by stating that it provided opportunities for challengers and that minorities could take advantage of it but that argument seems to have failed to convince the public. Supporters of the initiatives also complained that only 9 incumbents had been defeated in California in the 580 elections between 1982 and 1990. Yet it seems logical to any observer that a two-third majority requirement would only result in more incumbent protection for both parties. However such majority requirement along with voter validation through referendum and a tight schedule would almost guarantee that redistricting would be performed by the Supreme Court.

In the end the fact that major corporations such as Chevron and Hewlett Packard contributed to the propositions gave the Democrats, labor unions, and other liberal interest groups the narrative they needed. They ran a series of TV ads featuring James Garner, Jack Lemon, and Bea Arthur attacking the initiatives as plots by "big business" to seize control of the state legislature. Of course these corporations had also contributed to the campaigns of many Democratic members of the legislature. But none were on the ballot.[40] Besides, it reinforced the perception by pro-environment voters along the coast that they would be concentrated in the smallest number of "compact districts." Both sides fighting for or against the redistricting initiatives in 1990 combined to spend more than $6 million.[41] And once again, the Democrats surprisingly defeated both redistricting propositions. Proposition 118 and 119 received respectively 33 percent and 36 percent of the positive votes, with nearly 50 percent of self-identified Republicans joining 80 percent of Democrats in voting no.[42]

COCHISE, GERONIMO, AND THE ART OF COMPROMISE

In 1990, on the eve of redistricting, fractures of recent reapportionment wars lingered like political fault lines, especially in the congressional delegation. The Republicans intended to take over the House of Representatives and no delegation was larger than California's, especially with its 5 additional seats for a grand total of 52. Representative Howard Berman of Panorama City, in charge for redistricting for the congressional delegation, accused the GOP of wanting to eliminate 12 Democratic seats. Representative William Thomas of Bakersfield who was initially the GOP's congressional point man on redistricting summed up the state of mind of his party thusly: "The contest is to wear down the enemy. . . . We're Geronimo, we're Cochise. You fire and you fall back."[43] The new Assembly Minority Leader Bill Jones of Fresno sang to the same tune: "Reapportionment is the whole ballgame. . . . This is what it's all about. The political landscape of California will be shaped in no small part by that for the next ten to twenty years."[44] The political setting was that of another knockdown, drag-out confrontation. Freshly elected Representative Doolittle was quickly propelled into a leadership position in the California Republican delegation in the House. His California GOP colleagues even elected him chairman of their crucial Committee on Reapportionment, hoping to make the best of his connections in Sacramento. Even more audaciously, Doolittle took the post as part of a "coup de caucus" by hardline conservatives who ousted more moderate veterans Jerry Lewis of Redlands and Bill Thomas of Bakersfield from leadership posts in the delegation. But one of Doolittle's first moves created more discord. He proposed hiring Jerry Zanelli, the former top aide to Senate President Pro Tempore David Roberti, to serve as redistricting consultant for the California House Republicans. The move was abandoned after it drew outrage from state Republicans, including those close to Governor Pete Wilson. Doolittle's critics dreaded the idea of incumbent Republican House members negotiating a cozy incumbent protection deal with Democratic leaders.[45] 1991 was a time of confrontation not deal making. Republican Party professionals in Washington and the Wilson-led GOP in California believed they would be in better position to challenge a Democratic-drawn redistricting in the courts if they avoided any effort at compromise that could be cited as a sign of bipartisan cooperation. At the same the national party supported efforts to help racial minorities win new congressional districts. The strategy was designed to drive a wedge between minorities and their normal Democratic allies and also to make Anglo Democratic incumbents more vulnerable to challengers by draining off many of the reliably Democratic minority voters from their districts. Racial affiliation and partisan affiliation were, once more, a double-edged sword.

The Democrats enjoyed majorities in the Assembly, the Senate, and the congressional delegation but the Republican veto power along with the growing importance of the Voting Rights Act did not leave the Democrats with many options: they had to appease minority groups and make a deal with either moderate or conservative Republicans. After all, the 1990 census showed that Latinos constituted 26 percent of the state population but numbered only 10 among the 165 members of the legislature and Congress. And as we mentioned earlier, *Garza* had an immediate impact on California redistricting. Redistricters in 1991 viewed the Voting Rights Act as "a nuclear weapon in the hands of the federal Department of Justice and voting rights group like MALDEF, the NAACP, and CAPIFR (California Asian-Pacific Islanders for Fair Redistricting)."[46]

To ensure minority input, the Democrats placed Latinos in strategic redistricting positions. Peter Chacon of San Diego was named chairman of the Assembly Elections and Reapportionment Committee and Art Torres was selected to head the Senate Elections and Reapportionment Committee. Latinos were appointed as counsels to each committee and technicians were instructed to group together areas of minority concentration.[47] In order to negotiate with Republicans, the Democrats came up with a three-plan strategy. Three plans were presented to the public as proof of the Democrats willingness to strike a compromise with any Republican. All three plans were designed to appeal to a faction of the Republican Party.

Plan A, the Democrats' favorite plan, was a very long shot and was mostly a negotiating document to help Democrats bargain with Republicans or to present in court in case the negotiations failed. Plan A protected all 45 incumbents. Of the seven new seats, one, a heavily Latino district in Los Angeles County, would be solidly Democratic. Two others would almost certainly go to Republicans. Three seats, one along the coast in Santa Barbara and Ventura, would be competitive but leaning Democrat. If the Democrats held all their seats and won the new ones leaning their way, they would control 31 of the delegation's 52 seats.

Plan B had some bipartisan support and its congressional map proposal was even endorsed by Georgia Congressman Newt Gingrich. It concentrated Republican seats in areas believed to be strongly anti-abortion and pro-gun. This was supposed to be the conservative plan. Plan B was designed to seek a veto override in the legislature if Wilson vetoed. It transformed the district of Democratic Representative Glenn Anderson of San Pedro into one favoring Republicans, and was drawn in a way that could be attractive to Assemblyman Tom Mays of Huntington Beach. Of the seven new seats, one was a Republican-leaning district in which Assemblyman William P. Baker of Danville could have run. Another was a district in the eastern San Joaquin Valley and Sierra foothills that could have been attractive to either Dean Andal or David Knowles, two freshman Republicans in the Assembly. Another new, solid Republican district would have included areas represented at the time by Assemblyman Pat Nolan of Glendale. Plan B also created a new seat in Orange County that could have made it easier for Assemblyman Ross Johnson

(R-La Habra) to be elected to Congress. Finally, Plan B included three seats favoring Democrats in Los Angeles, along the Santa Barbara-Ventura coast and in San Diego. Democrats were expected to have a 28–24 advantage.

Plan C, the supposedly moderate third plan, created seats in areas where Republicans were believed to be more likely to be pro-choice and pro-environment. Plan C was also designed to appeal to Republicans. Like Plan B, it would have transformed the seat of Representative Anderson into a Republican-leaning district, reducing the Democratic margin in the existing seats to 25–20. One of the new seats, the Los Angeles Latino seat, would have been solidly Democratic. Three seats would have been solidly Republican. Three others would have been competitive. The final makeup of the delegation was expected to be 28–24 in favor of the Democrats. But in a good Republican year the delegation could be split down the middle.[48]

THE SENATE AND THE VOTING RIGHTS ACT

The Senate plan was the easiest to negotiate. The less partisan chamber passed a bipartisan plan on a 37–0 vote. What factors can explain this unanimous vote? Of course, the upper chamber has been historically less partisan and designed institutionally to be so. But the Senate also entered the 1991 redistricting cycle convinced the Voting Rights Act would be the dominant issue for redistricting in the 1990s. Due to a 1982 congressional amendment to the Voting Rights Act, in response to a 1980 decision in which the Supreme Court established that a discriminatory intent was needed to prove a Section 2 violation,[49] Congress redefined the discrimination standard as requiring only the proof of discriminatory effect, regardless of whether the practice was enacted or operated for a discriminatory purpose. Besides, Section 5 preclearance requirement prohibited certain jurisdictions from implementing any change affecting voting without receiving preapproval from the US Attorney General or the US District Court for DC.[50] to prove that the change did not discriminate against protected minorities or did not have any retrogressive effect.[51] Five counties in California were covered by Section 5[52] and redistricters in 1991 were afraid the Justice Department was going to implement the congressional mandate. This fear was confirmed early in the process when the DOJ, under President Bush, invalidated plans in New York and Mississippi because they infringed African Americans' and Latinos' right to representation by an official of their choice.[53]

So the Voting Rights Act in 1991 impacted the Senate redistricting in three areas:

> the intended impact of the number of minority-majority districts; the intended impact on the public access requirement, which also had unintended effects on

the openness of the entire process; and the unintended consequence of providing the Senate leadership with an effective means of rejecting the unreasonable demands of individual members.[54]

The importance of the Voting Rights Act is clear when one looks at President Pro Tempore David Roberti's evolution on the question of Los Angeles redistricting. In late 1990, staffers were informed that the Democrats' leadership would not consider any plan that would impact adversely the party or its incumbents in Los Angeles. By July 1991, Roberti was engaged in convincing his colleagues to vote for a plan that would collapse an Anglo Democrat's district in LA and turn another one, held also by an Anglo Democrat, into a Latino majority district. The Senate plan, eventually passed by the legislature and later vetoed by the governor, created 4 Latino-majority districts, 10 Latino-influence districts, 3 African American districts, and 2 Asian-Pacific Islander influence districts. Yet it doesn't mean minority organizations were entirely satisfied with the plan. The notorious sixteenth Senate seat was the target of their ire.[55] Even though Blacks were the only minority with political representation almost proportional to their percentage of the population,[56] the California NCAAP partnered with the Congress of Racial Equality (CORE), whose vice-chairman Steve Hamilton was Republican at the time, to draw some partial maps that packed more African Americans in districts that were already represented by Black representatives. Their influence was therefore reduced in adjacent districts. Their proposal didn't seem to help Black representation all that much but sure seemed to help Anglo Republicans. However the African American community was actually far from being unanimous about this diagnosis and this alliance. Alice Huffman of the California NAACP has been a controversial player in Sacramento politics. Her motives in 1991 were questioned and her position may not have represented the position of the association as a whole.[57]

As mentioned before, in 1981, Phil Burton's attitude was extremely secretive. The Senate and the Assembly redistricting process was not as opaque as that of Congress in part because Willie Brown and David Roberti were too new on the job to imitate their congressional colleague. In 1991, the political culture in Sacramento was still one that was suspicious of transparency when it came to redistricting. Public disclosure was an especially contentious issue. For instance, when the Senate announced it intended to make the congressional maps public, the entire congressional delegation, Republicans and Democrats, took issue with the very idea. The suspicion ran so deep that the congressional plans, which had been drawn by the Assembly and therefore incorporated in the Assembly bill, were given to the Senate without maps. It wasn't until Senator Roberti refused to take the congressional and Assembly bills on the Senate floor that the figures were sent to the Senate staff. At the time, the Senate's redistricting process was the most public in the state's history and was lauded by various voting rights groups. The Senate held more public hearings than in 1981 (19 in total), made sure that the hearings were more substantive, and were more open to public influence.[58] For instance, minority groups expressed criticism of the Senate maps, citing areas in Sacramento, San Francisco, Oakland, and the Central and San Fernando valleys where traditionally Democratic African American, Asian American, and Latino populations were split among several districts to bolster Democratic chances. After a series of hearings, Senate map-makers altered the lines. In San Francisco, the Asian American community was consolidated into the district represented by independent Quentin Kopp. It had been split between Kopp's district and that of Democrat Milton Marks. In the Sacramento area, a large chunk of African American voters in the city's south area, originally sliced off to increase Democratic registration in a neighboring district, was reattached, thus increasing the number of African American voters in the district represented by Democrat Leroy Greene.[59] So, the two full days of hearings held after the final plan and maps were made public and resulted in significant changes in several districts. The reason for the new level of transparency was that the Senate leadership, both Democrat and Republican, was mindful of the power of the Voting Rights Act and paid close attention to the Federal Justice Department's regulations pertaining to public access to the redistricting process.[60] Because California was a pre-clearance state, the Senate leadership thought the Bush administration would submit any plan proposed by the legislature to a rigorous review. The Senate therefore made sure it completely abided by federal regulations.[61]

Another consequence of this full compliance with the Voting Rights Act is that DC could be used as the "bad cop" in forcing individual lawmakers to accept painful changes. The Voting Rights Act was so feared that, according to Tim Hodson, staffers and the leadership were sometimes able to use it to fend off senators' unreasonable demands that were not even related to voting rights issues.[62] The Voting Rights Act therefore helped create a bipartisan, viable plan without damaging the consensual nature of the leadership relationship with the senators.

AT WITS' END: THE ASSEMBLY AND CONGRESS PLANS

On September 10, the Assembly released two sets of plans. However, the nuts-and-bolts data for districts was given out on a regional basis, making it tough for groups to analyze the state as a whole. In addition, maps for some districts were not included in either plan, and several district maps that were included were incomplete, with boundary lines extending off the page. Critics grumbled that the maps were too vague and that there was not enough time to adequately review them. Minority groups complained that their communities were split up, thus diluting their power and potentially violating provisions of the federal Voting Rights Act. Republicans complained that the two Democratic plans created only 32 and 33 districts where GOP registration reached 40 percent which was the threshold generally considered necessary for a Republican-leaning seat. To complicate matters, the Assembly issued two sets of maps because several lawmakers had yet to decide whether to run for reelection to the Assembly or for Congress. Should they opt for reelection, one set of maps would be used; should they opt for Congress, another set would be used. This, of course, reinforced the suspicion that redistricting was meant to protect incumbent politicians rather than the interest of the public.

In response to the Assembly's effort, several odd coalitions began to emerge. First, Republican leaders joined with traditionally Democratic Latinos. A Latino coalition had presented its own set of Assembly maps, which it declared were non-negotiable. The Latino plan seemed to guarantee Republicans a better than ever chance to control the lower house, because by concentrating Latino voters it created 40 other districts with GOP registration of at least 40 percent. But not all Republicans were so inclined, thus sowing the seeds for another odd coalition, that of Democrats and conservative Republicans. This coalition grew out of rifts inside the Republican Party itself and pitted conservatives against moderates both in Washington and in Sacramento. Essentially, conservatives, led by Congressman John Doolittle of Carmichael, supported a plan that protected GOP incumbents but left the majority of the delegation firmly in Democratic hands. Moderates, led by Governor Wilson and Assembly Minority Leader Bill Jones, wanted a plan that could enhance the number of congressional and legislative districts favorable to Republicans but not necessarily protecting incumbents. Even the Bush administration chimed in, with White House Chief of Staff John Sununu supporting Wilson and calling for a redistricting plan that maximized Republican opportunities.[63] At one point, Senate Minority Leader Ken Maddy complained that as many as five separate cliques of Republicans were trying to draw up acceptable congressional plans. Outside groups, like Common Cause, complained that the public hearings were a sham and that the real work was being done behind closed doors.

But the real nitty-gritty work in those last few days, as the Assembly rushed to complete a plan, was not the drawing of districts. It was the search for enough votes to override what promised to be a certain gubernatorial veto. A two-thirds Assembly vote (54) was required to pass a redistricting plan over Wilson's objection, and Democrats could gather only 47. That meant 7

Republicans had to buck their party and their governor to side with Democrats. Finally, on September 19, Democrats jammed through not two but three bills containing three alternative redistricting plans for the Assembly and the congressional delegation.

The same Senate plan was attached to all three of the Assembly Democrats' plans (A, B, and C). Once again the reasonable upper chamber fell hostage to the lower chamber's strategy. Speaker Brown forced both bills to be presented together to Governor Wilson in hope that a bipartisan Senate plan might convince him to accept a more partisan Assembly plan but also because he hoped a unanimously passed plan would play well in front of the Supreme Court and might therefore force Governor Wilson to think twice about using his veto power. The Assembly Speaker declared in front of his house: "This is drop-dead day. There is no other opportunity. This is it."[64] But no Republican voted for any of the three bills. Senator Bill Leonard of Big Bear, chairman of the Senate Republican Caucus, in a bombastic metaphor declared about the different plans: "Drawing a distinction between them is like drawing a distinction between rape and date-rape."[65] Without any Republican vote, overriding a gubernatorial veto was impossible. And Speaker Brown to declare: "I'm at wits end. I'm at the breaking point. I do better letting the courts rip me off."

Minority organizations sincerely had thought the Republicans would hear their grievances.[66] African Americans relied mostly on Speaker Brown and the Black Legislative Caucus to deliver for them. The Mexican American Legal Defense and Educational Fund (MALDEF), the Asian Pacific Legal Center (APLC), and the League of United Latin American Citizens decided to remain independent from both parties, worked on their maps, and even proposed, for the first time in the state's history, a common redistricting plan.[67] Of all the interest groups,[68] only MALDEF, with more than $200,000 to spend on its redistricting effort, attempted to draw a statewide plan. MALDEF proved an interesting exception to the exclusionary logic of the redistricting process in 1991. As a representative of the minority group with a voting base too large to be ignored, MALDEF became a player. The deal makers had little choice but to cut the Latino organization in on the redistricting negotiations. Its experts worked closely with the legislature's reapportionment committees, mostly behind the scene, sharing political information and receiving technical assistance. One measure of MALDEF's clout was that the plan it finally presented to the legislature drew two largely Latino congressional districts as well as matching Assembly and Senate seats through the Central Valley. That configuration threatened the Anglo incumbents in the area.

On the other hand Asian Pacific Americans for Fair Reapportionment did not fare as well. After months of waiting for the state to untangle California census data, the group purchased the information only to learn that it was not in a form that could be easily integrated with political data that identify race and ethnicity. Without melding the two data sets, it was impossible to draw boundaries for districts that would concentrate Asian voters, let alone a statewide map. Moreover, if the actual drawing of lines is comparatively simple, collecting political data such as registration figures or voting histories from past elections remained very expensive. Finally, because of the extreme diversity of the community and the lack of statewide organization with advocacy experience, it proved to be quite a challenge for Asian Pacific Island Americans (APIA) to develop a unified front, even with conscientious efforts to maintain substantive outreach. Indeed, there were actually two California Asian Pacific Americans for Fair Reapportionment groups, one in San Francisco, one in Los Angeles with limited coordination. And when individuals emerged who lobbied their legislators about their own district agenda it created confusion as to which group "truly" represented the voice of the APIA community.[69]

But the main problem was that because of their lack of experience, and lack of access to data, minority groups only provided partial maps.[70] These maps did not take into consideration the ripple effect throughout the state and especially on Anglo incumbents.[71] A good example would be new Assembly district proposed by Armando Navarro of the Coalition for Fair Representation during hearings by the Senate and Reapportionment committee. Navarro proposed a new Latino majority district that sliced more than 100 miles north to south through the heart of Riverside and Imperial counties. Navarro was trying to link the Latino population in Coachella and Imperial valleys because since 1983 the Coachella valley was split into three Assembly districts which, allegedly, made it difficult for people to participate in the political process. However, the new district did not take into consideration political geography since Riverside County was split by the San Bernardino mountains creating *de facto* two different communities.[72] But more importantly the new district did not take into account the effects on other districts.[73]

Republicans saw a partisan advantage and supported the minority groups partial maps.[74] But, to the Democrats, these maps appeared amateurish and these missteps limited considerably minority groups' influence on the process.[75] Besides, MALDEF was walking a tight-rope by trying to advance the interest of Latinos without diminishing Black representation.[76] The ultimate result might have been more Republican districts and Democratic leadership was quick to argue that minorities would not be better off without the Democratic majorities that brought them their powerful committee positions.[77] As a rule of thumb, in the 1990s in California a district was considered safely Democratic if its registered population was at least 56 percent but considered safely Republican if its registered population was at least 43 percent Republican because the GOP is traditionally more assiduous in getting out the vote. Because of racial polarization, that is the tendency for people of one racial group to vote for a candidate of the same racial group, minority registration rate is not the only information that needs to be taken into consideration. It must be balanced with partisan consideration because most minority candidates register with the Democratic Party or vote for it. It must also be balanced with the history of the populations in a given district to crossover, that is the voters' willingness to vote for a candidate of another racial group.[78] And above all, redistricting is a zero-sum game; one district cannot be drawn in a vacuum.

In the end, all these debates were for naught since Governor Wilson rejected any type of negotiation.[79] Governor Wilson's strategy turned out to be the simplest of all. He plainly refused to negotiate or let any other Republican negotiate seriously with the opposite party in the Assembly, the Senate, or Congress.[80] Instead, he envisioned to appoint a redistricting commission, without consulting any Democratic or minority group leaders, use his veto power over any proposed redistricting plan, force the Supreme Court to take over redistricting altogether and propose that the masters use the special commission's plan as blueprint.[81] This willingness to run the dice and let the Court carve out the districts is directly linked to the confidence the conservatives had in the new majority on the Court that was privately nicknamed "Pete's law firm" by Wilson's aides around the Capitol.[82] In addition, federal courts would likely follow the dictates of the federal Voting Rights Act that pushed in 1991 for the creation of a maximum number of minority-leaning districts, a move that Republicans believed worked to their advantage.[83] Some scholars have tried to debunk this theory and shown that the VRA actually hinders Republican gains.[84] But the truth is probably in between. Scholarly work seems to show some partisan advantage for Republicans when majority-minority districts are drawn. Yet Democrats have been creative enough to counterbalance this disadvantage with imaginative maps that led to unusually-shaped districts in the 1990s that, in turn, the Supreme Court struck down in its *Shaw* line of jurisprudence. Besides, no matter the case, it doesn't change the fact that political operatives in the 1990s were convinced that majority-minority districts, because of the ripple effect, helped the Republicans' electoral chances overall. The only problem with this strategy was that it could have been unhinged by incumbent Republicans who figured it was in their interest to cut a deal for secure seats with Democratic lawmakers rather than rely on Supreme Court justices. All Wilson had to do was convince them that they would be taken care of or that anything was better than a Democrat redistricting plan.

WILSON'S REDISTRICTING COMMISSION

In July 1991, Governor Pete Wilson appointed his 6-member reapportionment panel. At first glance it appeared rather balanced as far as gender, race, and partisanship were concerned: two retired Republican judges, one of whom was Asian-American, a thirty-six-year-old Condoleezza Rice, fresh off her stint at the National Security Council under President Bush, and three Democrats, among whom one was Latino. The commission was headed by eighty-three-year-old Democrat, Dewitt Higgs, a former chair of the California University Board of Regents.[85] However, none of its members had any redistricting experience.[86] When Wilson announced the appointments at a news conference he encouraged the commission to hold public hearings but conceded it was not required to do so, right away drawing the ire of Common Cause and the League of Women Voters. Wilson also declared that the commission's recommendations would be submitted to the judiciary if the legislature failed to pass a redistricting plan he deemed "fair."[87] The commission in turn hired expert Professor Peter Gordon, a political scientist at the University of California Santa Barabara and former court expert in the 1973 redistricting episode. The other experts were Professor Richard Morill, a geographer at the University of Washington, who had drawn plans for the Rose Institute in 1981,[88] Professor Charles Hampton, a mathematician from the College of Wooster in Wooster, Ohio. Robert Post, professor of Constitutional Law at the University of California at Berkeley, was selected as legal counsel.

Unfortunately the commission took too long to draft its redistricting plans and Governor Wilson wasn't able to use it as a negotiation tool with the legislature. On the contrary David Roberti was able to use the commission tardiness as proof that the governor's deadline was unreasonable.[89] And, to make matters worse, when the commission finally presented its plans it seemed to have neglected minority representation. For instance its congressional plan reduced the number of African American Representatives from 3 to 1, the number of Latino Representatives from 10 to 5. In the Assembly the commission members had packed African American voters in one district and had probably pitted a Latino incumbent against an African American one in another.[90] The commission's districts were pleasing to the eye but blatantly diluted minority groups vote and therefore were clearly in violation of the Federal Voting Rights Act.[91] That did not prevent Wilson from endorsing the plans proposed by his commissions.[92] Yet Governor Wilson had no choice but to hire redistricting consultant Joe Shumate, the author of the 1983 Sebastiani Plan, to fix the plans which, this time, were kept away from the public eye.[93] The commission proved that a supposedly independent commission is no guarantee that an impartial process would result in acceptable districts because of its consequences on partisanship or minority representation.[94]

The legislature passed its plans on a strictly partisan base and as anticipated Governor Wilson vetoed the bills.[95] The Supreme Court chose three special masters, 3 retired Anglo judges, 2 Republicans (George A. Brown and Rafael H. Galceran), and 1 Democrat (Thomas Kongsgaard) who had been appointed by a Republican. The masters relied mostly on redistricting consultant Paul L. McKaskle, professor of law at the University of San Francisco, who had already drawn lines for the court in 1973.[96] The new plans were scheduled to be released by November 29 and interested parties had until December 29 to file court briefs commenting on the proposal. County clerks were supposed to receive the information about the districts by February 20, that is, 104 days before the June 2 primaries. In the meantime, the legislature and the governor could find a compromise but it was very unlikely since the relationship between Democrat leadership and the governor was so strained. In September 1991 Wilson was quoted in the press as saying: "Speaker Brown can take those threats and stick them in the same drawer as his vetoed gerrymander."[97]

Wilson v. Eu

Two of the most distinguished political science professors and redistricting consultants testified in the fall of 1991.[98] During the November hearings Professor Bernard Grofman indicated without any ambiguity that in taking into account all the different criteria congressional Plan C proposed by the legislature was the best plan:

> If we look at the three criteria that are the ones which must govern, one person one vote, avoiding minority vote dilution and the state constitutional criteria, particularly those aspects of the state constitutional criteria that can be most clearly defined, which is significant city and county splits, then with respect to the one person one vote grounds, plan "C" easily is the best, no ifs and buts or maybes.[99]

The Democrats' favorite, Plan A, created 2–3 more districts than any of the Republican plans (the masters' plans, the commission's, Shumate and Jones's) in which the Latino registration was above 20 percent. Moreover, the Republican plans had a tendency to dilute minorities' influence by scattering minority voters into heavily Republican districts.[100]

In October, Bruce Cain concluded that Assembly Plan A produced 7 districts in which a Latino candidate had a meaningful opportunity to win the general election (Districts Fifty-five, Fifty-six, Fifty-nine, Sixty, Sixty-three, and Eighty). In addition, it provided 5 districts in which Latinos had a meaningful opportunity of electing the candidate of their choice (districts 39, 46, 47, 48, and 72). Moreover, it contained 4 districts in which the Democratic registration was such that Latinos could dominate the party's primary and win the general election (Districts Twenty-three, Twenty-five, Sixty-six, and Seven-nine). Unlike Plan A, Plan B and C created an open seat where there was the possibility of electing a Latino candidate. According to Cain, all three plans contained 7 districts in which an African American candidate could be elected (Thirteen, Forty-seven, Forty-eight, Forty-nine, Fifty, and Fifty-four all presented African-American population of 30 percent and Democratic registration of 60 percent or more; District Seventeen had a proven history of electing African American candidates).[101] And as mentioned before, the Senate plan was a bipartisan affair and never a point of contention.

Figures 5.1 and 5.2 sum up the African American and Latino percentages in the 45 districts of the Burton-Berman plan of 1990 and the seven alternative plans for the 52 congressional districts for 1991. What transpires here is that few plans produced districts in which a minority group could dominate by itself and the contrast lies in the minorities' capacity to influence the result of the elections. The Democratic-leaning plans (1990, A, B, C, and MALDEF) tended to concentrate minority populations while the Republican-leaning plans (the masters', the commission's, Shumate, and Jones's)[102] tended to scatter them. That is logical since it's in the Democrats' electoral interest to concentrate minorities in influence districts and it's in the Republicans' electoral interest to pack Democrats in a small number of districts and disperse the rest in as many Republican-dominated districts as possible. So to get the full picture one needs partisan registration number to complete racial numbers. When minority percentages are coupled with registration numbers we see that Plan A produced 11 districts where Latino population was between 30 percent to 60 percent and Democratic registration advantage over Republican was 15 percent or more.[103] 30 percent to 60 percent Latino

Table 5.1 Black Population District Breakdown for 1990 and 1991 Congressional Proposed Plans

	1990	*Masters'*	*A*	*B*	*C*	*Gov. Com.*	*Shumate*	*MALDEF*
0–9.9	29	43	41	43	41	43	44	42
10–19.9	11	5	7	5	7	5	4	6
20–29.9	1	0	0	0	1	2	0	1
30–39.9	1	2	3	2	1	1	3	2
40–49.9	2	2	1	2	2	0	1	1
50–59.9	1	0	0	0	0	1	0	0

Source: Kousser, "Reapportionment Wars," 175.

Table 5.2 Latino Population District Breakdown for 1990 and 1991 Congressional Proposed Plans

	1990	*Masters'*	*A*	*B*	*C*	*Gov. Com.*	*Shumate*	*Jones*	*MALDEF*
0–9.9	6	4	7	6	3	6	6	5	4
10–19.9	17	20	23	21	26	20	19	21	25
20–29.9	6	12	4	10	7	11	13	12	8
30–39.9	9	6	8	6	7	5	5	6	4
40–49.9	3	4	4	3	3	4	3	0	4
50–59.9	1	3	2	2	2	4	4	5	5
60–69.9	3	2	3	3	3	1	1	2	1
70–79.9	0	0	0	0	0	1	0	1	0
80–89.9	0	1	1	1	1	0	1	0	1

Source: Kousser, "Reapportionment Wars," 175.

is not enough to produce Latino registration rates high enough to secure the election of the preferred minority candidate. And a 15 percent registration margin advantage is what was needed in 1992 to make sure that a Democrat was elected. Minorities (especially African Americans) vote overwhelmingly for Democrats and therefore, to elect their candidate of choice, minorities need to be in Democratic districts. By contrast the masters' plans contained 9 such districts, the governor's Commission 8 and the Jones's, plan only 7. Therefore Republican plans produced less Latino influence districts and even less of those were winnable by a Democrat. This demonstrates again that if one wants to predict the impact of a redistricting plan race and/or ethnicity needs to be cross-referenced with partisanship.

Discussions over the different alternative plans was short though since the special masters rejected all outside proposals and used Article XXI of the state constitution and the *Reinecke* precedent, that is to say criteria that are the most open to interpretation and therefore the most controversial, as the main reason to propose their own plan. For the Assembly they declared: "Whatever the case, we do not believe the plans submitted comply with article XXI and Reinecke IV requirements of the integrity of the geographic regions or contiguity as we interpret them." For Congress they continued: "the violations of Article XXI are even more egregious than those of the Assembly plan." For the Senate: "We ultimately rejected the plan for several reasons, including but not limited to problems with whether the configurations were suitable for "nesting." As for the MALDEF plan: "We disagree, ultimately, as to the extent to which Article XXI could be ignored in the quest to build minority districts."[104] The masters concluded their report by declaring: "we did not use political data in the drawing of district lines. Nor have drawn boundaries on the basis of their impact on incumbents."[105] However, when one takes into consideration the non-retrogression standard set forth by the Supreme Court jurisprudence on the Voting Rights Act which prevents the reduction of the number of majority-minority districts, and when one considers that those minority elected officials are mostly Democrats and that, for instance, African Americans vote Democrat at a rate close to 90 percent, any consideration of race has important partisan implications. Democrats have an electoral incentive to concentrate minorities in "influence districts" to maximize the partisan effect. Republicans, on the other hand, have an incentive to disperse and effectively waste those minorities that cannot be packed into a minimum number of districts. In 1991, the Voting Rights Act's job was to prevent the Republicans from packing minorities and prevent the Democrats from spreading them into only influence districts. To blind oneself to partisanship during redistricting, as the masters pretended, would guarantee to endanger minority representation. The plan the special masters presented in December 1991 was considered by practically all observers as a victory for the Republicans.[106] Yet Judge Brown echoed the masters' statement and disingenuously declared in the press: "We had no agenda, no political purpose and we did not consider any political consequences."[107] If that was true it would have been completely irresponsible on the part of the judges. Declaring that other factors need to be taken into consideration and declaring that redistricting can be an apolitical endeavor are two different things. Pretending that politics can be taken out of redistricting is a disservice to the public in its comprehension of the mechanism of representative democracy. Besides, by examining the record it is obvious political consequences were taken into consideration by the masters.[108] As expected, Governor Wilson praised the redistricting plan, stating that the competitive districts set up in many areas of the state gave the Republican Party an "infinitely better" chance of winning a majority in the Assembly and in the congressional delegation: "Their plan will provide the basis for the first truly competitive elections California has seen in a decade."[109] But delivering more seats to the GOP and creating more competitive districts are two different things. The Court's plan actually ended up creating less competitive seats than previous plans.[110] To be fair, while analyzing a redistricting plan can help decipher the author's intention, estimating the partisan bias of a redistricting plan is extremely difficult since it inevitably requires establishing an arbitrary range of what constitutes a competitive district.[111]

Nonetheless, the new redistricting plan did seem to especially target Democrats. Sacramento's two Democratic Assemblymen, Phillip Isenberg, and Lloyd Connelly, two longtime allies, were placed in the same Ninth District that included the bulk of the city.[112] Likewise, Ted Lempert (San Mateo) and

Jackie Speier (South San Francisco) were tossed in the same district.[113] Tom Bates of Berkeley[114] and Bob Campbell of Richmond were also placed in the same district.[115] Assemblyman John Burton, termed out in 1996, had to move from District Thirteen to District Twelve, a district with an Asian population of 36.7 percent.[116] In the Senate, President Pro Tempore David Roberti ended up with no district to run in and had to rely on the forced resignation of one of his colleagues on corruption charges to be reelected. Congressman Vic Fazio of Yolo County, and author of the unpopular congressional pay raise, now in the Third Congressional District, saw his district's Democratic registration rate lose 4 percentage points with an already high Republican registration.[117] In Westside Los Angeles, Henry Waxman and Anthony Beilenson were put in the same Twenty-ninth Congressional District.[118] Thomas Hofeller, redistricting director for the Republican Congressional Committee, said the new plan produced 25 districts in which Republicans had a good chance of being elected, 24 in which the Democrats had the edge and 4 toss-ups.[119]

Some Republican incumbents also had to play musical chairs much to the delight of Governor Wilson. Indeed Wilson had made entrenched Democrats and ultra-conservative Republicans the villains in his budget and policy fights. He bet that a more moderate new group of legislators would help him advance his agenda and build a record to run for higher office.[120] He wasn't the first nor the last governor to (mistakenly) believe that "independent" redistricting held the key to his political future.

Minority organizations reacted negatively to the masters' plans. The African American community in Los Angeles County was upset about Representative Julian Dixon's district because a much safer seat could have been drawn. Instead the special master moved in affluent Jewish Democrats and removed Anglo Republicans which set the table for an inter-group battle the day Dixon would retire.[121] The Latino community was not satisfied with the new district that did not reflect their population growth.[122] MALDEF had proposed a plan creating 6 Assembly and 3 State Senate districts with Latino population of 40 percent or more of the estimated registered voters. The masters' plan only included 4 Assembly and 2 Senate districts that met those criteria.[123] MALDEF pushed for 4 Congressional Latino Districts (Thirty-one, Thirty-two, Thirty-seven, and Thirty-nine in the MALDEF plan) while the consensus was 3. The governor's independent panel proposed 2 Latino districts which was a clear case of retrogression and would have therefore been declared unconstitutional if the plan had been adopted. Latino candidates ended up winning 4 congressional districts in 1992.[124] MALDEF also objected to lines in the Oxnard area, San Bernardino County, San Jose, San Bernardino and San Joaquin valley. SD3 was also harshly criticized because it linked heavily Black and Latino neighborhoods in San Francisco with mostly Anglo Marin. One of the points of contention is that the master only used population statistics and did not take into consideration the fact that Latinos or Asian Americans were much more likely to not be citizens and that these communities are very young with low registration rates. As a result, for example, Representative Don Edwards' seat that stretched from San Jose to Fremont was 30 percent Latino in population but in November 1988 Latinos represented only 15 percent of the electorate. The district was 25 percent Asian in population but they represented 4 percent of the electorate.[125] Minority groups advocated for population percentages closer to 70 percent in order to ensure 40 percent of the electorate. Larry Shinigawa of the California Coalition of Asian Pacific Americans for Fair Reapportionment criticized the new maps because the Assembly plan split San Francisco at Tween Peaks dividing the Asian American community. The new Twelfth Congressional District, which included Southwest San Francisco, only contained 25 percent of Asian Americans while his group had advocated for a 41.5 percent district that could have been drawn in this area.[126] The only change recommended by the Asian community that was incorporated by the Special Master was a unified city of Torrance were Asian Pacific Islander Americans comprised over 20 percent of the city population and had doubled between 1980 to 1990.[127] In 1998, the Fifty-third Assembly District elected George Nakano, a Japanese American and the only APIA Assemblyman from Southern California at the time.

Democrats and minority groups (MALDEF and the NAACP) challenged the masters' plans in the State Supreme Court and appealed to federal judges in hope of overturning the new redistricting maps but to no avail. Their claims were rejected, without a full hearing, on straight party-line votes.[128] Chief Justice Malcolm Lucas quickly dismissed any claims of partisan effect without much justification which, in his case, raised the issue of the independence of justices because of Lucas's history of partisan behavior (after all he was Deukmejian former law partner)[129] but more importantly frustrated all parties involved since partisan gerrymandering while justiciable in theory is practically unassailable for lack of standard.[130] Justice Stanley Mosk in his dissent declared:

> One need not be a cynic to detect the hypocrisy in the political gamesmanship known as reapportionment. Whichever party is in power immediately following the decennial census inevitably undertakes the task with a view to its self-preservation, and the opposition cries foul. The reality is that neither party has a monopoly on virtue. . . . At present the courts can do little to prevent this decennial debacle.[131]

However this wasn't the end of the judicial challenges to the masters'plan. Partisanship isn't the only point of contention in the jurisprudence over redistricting. Race is highly controversial since it raises questions about the very nature of representation and, while the standard is far from being clear, race is justiciable and sometimes even used as a proxy for partisanship. If a partisan gerrymander cannot be proven the next best hope to have the lines redrawn is to claim racial gerrymander. And vice versa, a racial gerrymander can be defended as partisan in nature.[132] After the US Supreme Court decision in *Shaw v. Reno* (509 U.S. 630 [1993]), which applied strict scrutiny to racial gerrymandering, two Anglo lawyers apparently not linked to any partisan group, filed a court challenge to the new California redistricting plans.[133] Because the masters' report openly admitted taking race into consideration to abide by the Voting Rights Act the plaintiffs argued that they, as well as other Anglos in the state, had been discriminated against.[134] According to their reasoning race-conscious redistricting diluted White voters' strength in violation of the Equal Protection Clause of the Fourteenth and in violation of the Fifteenth Amendment. The three-judge panel concluded that: "the masters' redistricting plan, as approved by the California Supreme Court, is not racial gerrymandering, but rather a thoughtful and fair example of applying traditional redistricting principles, while being conscious of race. . . . We conclude that in the context of redistricting, where race is considered only in applying traditional redistricting principles along with the requirements of the Voting Rights Act, that strict scrutiny is not required. However, if it were required, we conclude that this California redistricting plan has been narrowly tailored to meet a compelling state interest."[135] This statement was consistent with *Miller v. Johnson* (515 U.S. 900 [1995]) that was decided the same day and applied strict scrutiny only when race was the "predominant factor" and legislators had disregarded "traditional race-neutral districting principles." It was also consistent with Sandra Day O'Connor upcoming pivotal opinion in *Bush v. Vera* (517 U.S. 952 [1996]): "The districts at issue fail this test, since all three are bizarrely shaped and far from compact, and those characteristics are predominantly attributable to gerrymandering that was racially motivated and/or achieved by the use of race as a proxy."[136] None of these decisions defined precisely what type of test could determine the "bizarre" shape of a district.[137] Redistricters were not much better off after such jurisprudence: partisan gerrymandering was justiciable but without standard and the standard under which strict scrutiny would be applied to racial gerrymandering involved some sort of esthetic notion about the acceptable shape of districts.

PARTISAN CONSEQUENCES OF REDISTRICTING

The year 1992 was an electoral catastrophe for the Republicans. The very strong 75 percent turnout rate did not favor the GOP. The Democratic presidential candidate carried the state for the first time since 1964[138] even though

Governor Wilson chaired George Bush's California campaign. George H. W. Bush was not necessarily popular with minorities as he had vetoed the Civil Rights Act of 1990 (sometimes called the Hawkins-Kennedy Act). It would have reversed several Supreme Court decisions that had shifted the burden of proof of discriminating hiring practices of women and minorities from the employer to the employee. Because of the presidential veto Congress had to pass a less comprehensive 1991 Civil Rights Act. In 1992, the Democrats won 2 Senate races electing the first 2 California female Senators Diane Feinstein and Barbara Boxer.[139] In the House delegation the Democrats reached 31 seats and the Republicans 21, with two very narrow victories.[140] Republicans won 4 of the 7 newly created districts but lost 6 of the 8 seats vacated by incumbents who either retired or ran for the Senate.[141] The one-term Republican Frank Riggs was the only incumbent of either party to lose.[142] In the Senate the Democrats maintained their majority with 23 seats to the Republicans 15. And in the Assembly the Democrats net gained one seat reaching 48, winning 60 percent of the seats for only 50.7 percent of the votes, the Republicans dropped to 32 seats. There are many reasons why the Democrats were able to overcome the new Republican-drawn districts. First and foremost was the recession which, at the time, was the deepest and longest since the Second World War and made the incumbent president's party unpopular. Second, the Democrats nominated more experienced and moderate candidates who often outperformed their opponent in the oh-so crucial fundraising race.[143] Third, Democrats registered more than twice as many voters as the GOP in the six months preceding the election and ended up out-registering the Republican Party during a presidential election year for the first time since 1976. As a consequence, the Republican registration rate declined in 17 of the 18 most competitive Assembly districts prior to the 1992 election.[144] In 44 of the 52 congressional districts Republican registration dropped at least one percentage point between February and October 1992.[145] Overall, in 1992, the Democrats still enjoyed a 7.2 percent lead in registration (46.8 percent to 39.6 percent and 9.7 percent "decline to state"), down from 10.5 percent lead in 1990 (with a 9 percent "decline to state").[146] The masters' plan did not produce the GOP victories that some had anticipated but it doesn't mean that the plan wasn't biased toward the Republicans. There is strong evidence that such bias existed and that this bias was even much stronger in other Republican plans.[147] But redistricting is not the only factor to take into consideration and in 1992 external forces played a major role.

Latinos were also the winners of the 1992 elections. Xavier Becerra ran in what was supposed to be Ed Roybal's new district after his old seat had been split between CD 30 (downtown and northeast Los Angeles) and CD 33 (southeast Los Angeles). Roybal retired and endorsed his longtime chief of staff who eventually dropped out and supported Becerra. This was the only competitive election for Congress among Latinos.[148] Roybal's daughter, Assemblywoman Lucille Roybal-Allard ran in the 33rd and won. The two incumbents Matthew Martínez and Esteban Torres won reelection in CD 31 (lower San Gabriel Valley) and CD 34 (east of CD 33). Before 1992, Latinos held only 4 of the 80 Assembly seats. After 1992 they held 7: Six from Los Angeles County and one from San Bernardino County. Redistricting and vacancies created these opportunities. Becerra and Roybal-Allard ran for Congress and Polanco sought reelection. That left 5 vacant seats with Latinos representing at least a third of registered voters and Democrats representing at least half of the registered voters.[149] Again, Latino elected officials made clear to Anglo candidates that there would be repercussions if they tried to run in these districts. So the 5 races opposed 10 Latinos that belonged to two factions of the Latino coalition. "The two networks, one led by Supervisor Molina and retiring US Representative Roybal and the other by Assemblyperson Polanco, Council member Alatorre, and State Senator Torres went head to head in the 5 vacant assembly districts and the congressional district vacated by Roybal. The Molina-supported candidate won the congressional seat and one assembly seat and the Polanco, Alatorre, Torres-supported candidates won the other 4 assembly seats."[150] All of these candidates were, needless to say, Democrats.

Of course 1994 told a totally different story as external factors played the opposite role they had played in 1992. The Republican wave swept California, as it did almost everywhere else in the nation,[151] in spite of stable registration figures in the state between 1992 and 1994. The Democrats lost 9 seats in the Assembly, 2 in the State Senate, and 3 in Congress, with several contests being extremely close. In Congress Frank Riggs regained his Congressional District One in a rematch against one-term Democratic incumbent and future Green Party candidate Dan Hamburg. In CD 19 (northern San Joaquin Valley) George Radanovich easily unseated incumbent Richard Lehman. Lehman's district had been made considerably more Republican after the 1991 round of redistricting. His district incorporating some more rural territory in the Sierra Nevada as well as the more conservative eastern portion of Fresno. At the same time, he lost his share of Stockton to the new Eleventh District, and lost most of his Latino constituents to the neighboring Twentieth District. Lehman had barely held onto his seat in 1992, winning by only 1,100 votes. Finally in marginal CD 49 (San Diego County) then-Imperial Beach mayor Brian Bilbray won a plurality of the votes (48.5 percent) with a margin victory of 2.5 percent against one-term incumbent Lynn Schenk. A libertarian candidate and a Peace and Freedom Party candidate each received 5 percent of the votes. In 1994 the fate of Democrats in the California delegation could have been worse. For instance, longtime California politics veteran George Brown Jr. barely survived reelection in CD 42 (San Bernardino County) as he managed to squeeze a 1.3 percent margin victory.[152] In CD36, that ran along the Santa Monica Bay, freshman incumbent Jane Harman won by a margin of 0.4 percent. In CD 24, Southwestern San Fernando Valley, along Highway 101 corridor, 8-term incumbent Anthony B. Beilenson won by less than 2 percentage points. And in CD 3 (Sutter and Yolo Counties), as was already the case in 1992, Vic Fazio had a tough reelection campaign where he won by 3 percentage points. It is to be noted that Republicans also had a very close call in CD 22 (San Luis Obispo County) where Andrea Seastrand, Assembly member Eric Seastrand's widow, barely defeated Walter Capps with a 0.8 percent margin. Capps ended up winning the seat in 1996.

In the State Senate the Democrats managed to only lose 2 seats maintaining a 21–17 majority. In Senate District Twelve, north of the San Joaquin Valley, Dick Monteith unseated three-term Democratic incumbent Dan McCorquodale by a 2 percent margin. After redistricting, the Twelfth District which was formerly based in eastern Santa Clara County was shifted entirely into the more conservative Central Valley. In SD 36 (Riverside County) Ray Haynes won easily, as did Bob Hurtt who had won a special election in 1993 in SD 32 (San Bernardino County) when Ed Royce ran for Congress. In SD 16 (Kings County) Democrat Jim Costa unseated Republican incumbent Phil Wyman by a 3 percent victory margin.

It's in the Assembly that the Democrats suffered their worst defeats. The Republicans regained the majority in the Assembly, 41–39, for the first time in twenty-five years.

Democrats thin victories included: in Assembly District Seventeen (Stockton) Michael Machado gave the Democrats a rare win albeit by the thinnest of margins 50.7 percent to 49.3 percent. In AD 20 (Fremont) Liz Figueroa, a San Francisco Latina of San Salvador origin, won by less than one percentage point.

Republican gains: In AD 25, which included parts of Modesto in the north and parts of Fresno in the south, Republican George House easily beat Democratic incumbent Margaret Snyder. In AD 28, which included the Latino parts of Monterey, San Benito, and San Cruz counties, Republican Peter Frusetta picked up a seat and won against Lilly Cervantes by less than 0.5 percent. In AD 30 (centered on Kings County), Brian Setencich gave Republicans another pickup with a 1.5 percent victory margin. Brook Firestone, a two-term Assembly member, easily picked up AD 35 (Santa Barabara and Ventura counties). In AD 54 (Palos Verdes Peninsula), Steven T. Kuykendall defeated Democratic incumbent Betty Karnette by a margin of 0.5 percent. In AD 56 (Downey) Republican Phil Hawkins defeated Democratic incumbent Bob

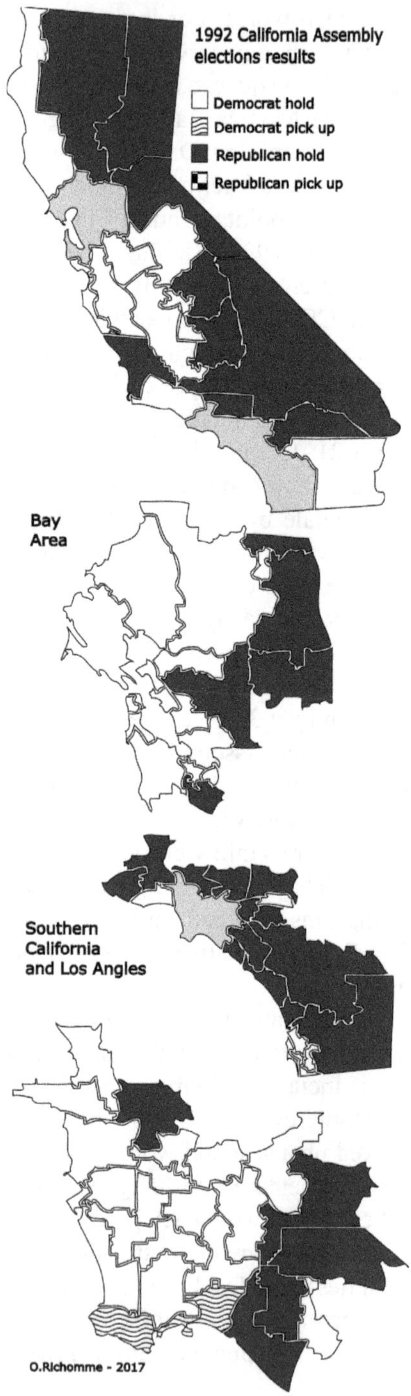

Figure 5.1
1992 California Assembly Elections Results

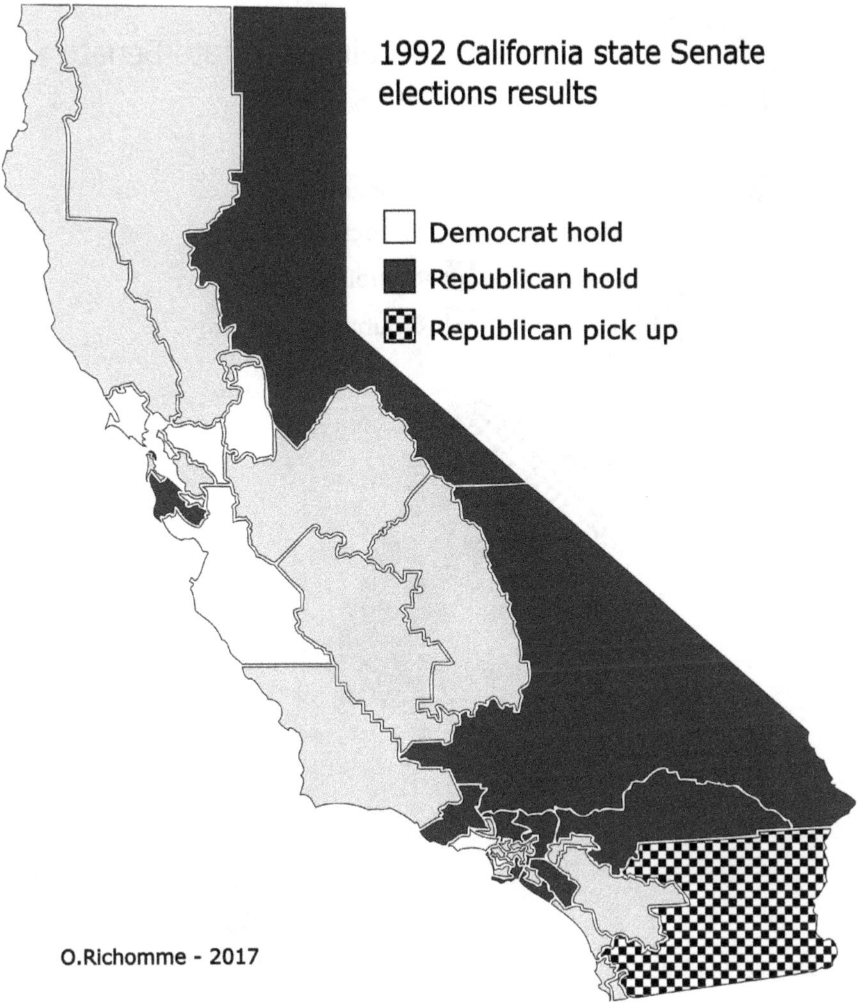

Figure 5.2 1992 California State Senate Elections Results

Epple by 10 percentage points. Jim Morrissey won District Sixty-nine (Santa Ana) by a 7 percent margin to give the Republicans another seat. In AD 77 (Sand Diego County) Republican Steve Baldwin won by 11 points against incumbent Tom Connolly.

Republican holds: In AD 24 (Cupertino) Jim Cunneen kept the district under Republican control with a 1.3 percent margin victory. In AD 27 (Santa Cruz), Republican incumbent Bruce McPherson survived by a 2 percent margin.

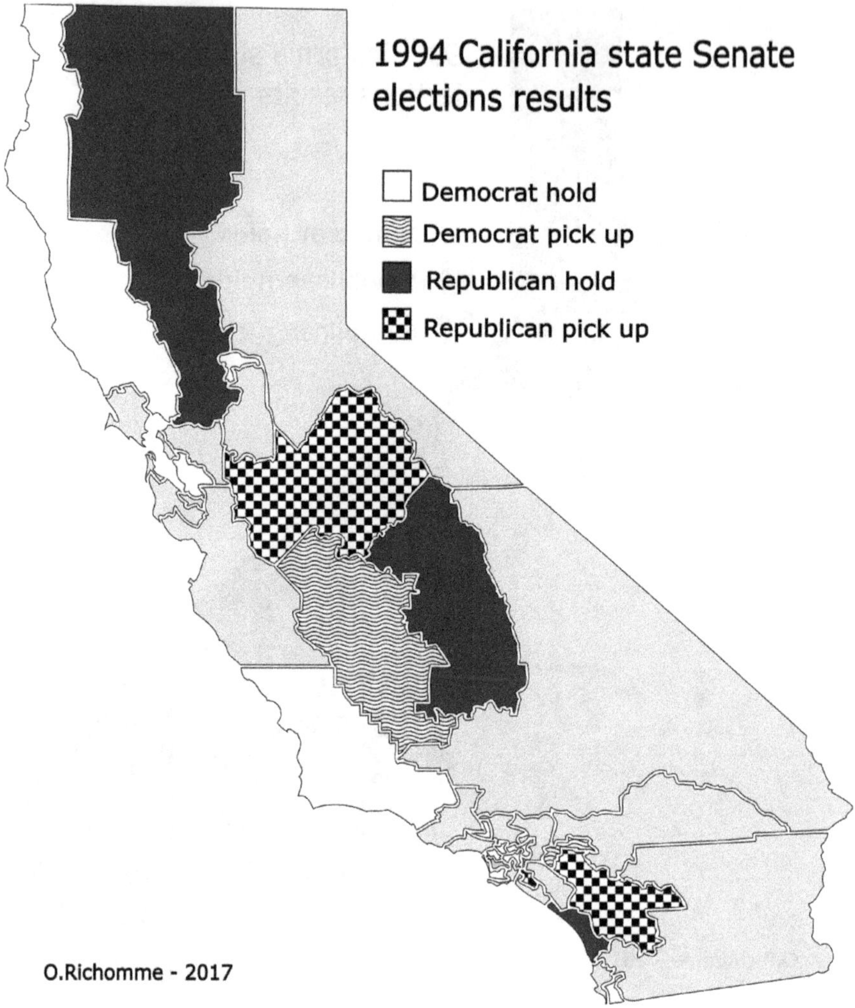

Figure 5.3 1994 California State Senate Elections Results

In 1994 incumbent Governor Wilson won reelection yet, surprisingly, former Jerry Brown Chief of Staff Gray Davis, a Democrat, was easily elected Lieutenant Governor.[153] Wilson ran on an anti-immigration platform backing the notoriously divisive Proposition 187.[154] But before we analyze the effects of the Republican strategy toward the Latino community we need to take a detour to discuss the turmoil inside the Assembly after the 1994 elections when the lower house elected its first female speaker.

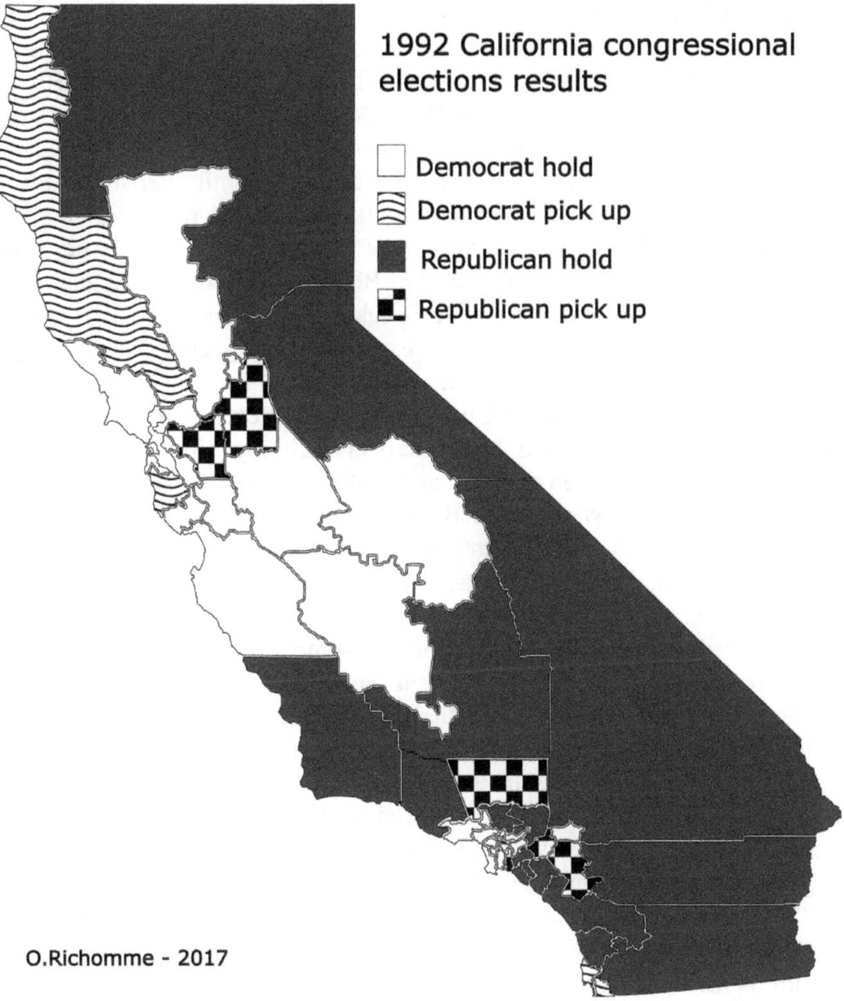

Figure 5.4 1992 California Congressional Elections Results

Republicans gained a one-vote majority the Assembly (40–39) in a special 1995 Spring election and were ready to put then-assemblyman Curt Pringle of Garden Grove in the leadership slot. This threatened longtime Democratic Speaker Willie Brown's fifteen-year hold on power. Brown at first persuaded moderate Republican-turned-Independent Paul Horcher to keep him in power.

Meanwhile, Doris Allen (R-Cypress) was running in a special election for her State Senate seat. She became enraged when GOP party leaders officially endorsed a fellow assemblyman Ross Johnson (R-Irvine) in a hotly contested three-way primary. Allen lost the election challenge. When Horcher was recalled from office and replaced by a more loyal Republican, Speaker Brown skillfully convinced a still-fuming Doris Allen to vote with the Democrats and become Speaker herself, although Brown would continue to lead the legislative body as head of the Democratic Caucus until after the result of the mayoral election of San Francisco he had decided to run in.[155]Allen was elected on a 40–38 vote, receiving all 39 Democratic votes plus her own. The other 38 Republicans voted for Jim Brulte of Rancho Cucamanga. She became the Assembly's first female Speaker for a mere 102 days. Allen's defection outraged her Republican colleagues and it triggered a political fight inside the GOP ranks. A fight that was full of gender politics and caught national attention. Republican Curt Pringle led a recall effort with the support of Governor Wilson and Allen lost overwhelmingly in November 1995. Before her removal, Allen resigned as Speaker and handed the gavel over to another Republican who backed Brown, Brian Setencich. However, when Brown resigned his seat in the State Assembly to be sworn in as mayor of San Francisco, Setencich lost that vote, restoring the Republicans' majority and allowing them to elect Pringle as Speaker in January 1996. Setencich himself was defeated for reelection in that June's GOP primary. Following her recall, Allen turned her back on politics, even though she did try one last time to regain her old seat in 1998. Allen died of cancer in 1999.[156]

In the mid-1990s Republicans across the United States started to realize immigration was a wedge issue that could help them electorally if used properly. However, Proposition 187 backfired for the Republicans in California. After the passage of the referendum the Latino community mobilized to help eligible people to ask for citizenship[157] and their turnout increased in 1996.[158] In 1996, more than 1.5 million undocumented immigrants in California who had qualified for amnesties in the late 1980s and had fulfilled their citizenship requirements were eligible to vote for the first time. More than half of these new citizens were Latinos.[159]

Much of Proposition 187 was eventually declared unconstitutional by federal judge Mariana Pfaelzer.[160] In 1998 newly elected Governor Gray Davis at first offered to put the matter of the remaining part of Proposition 187 in the hands of a federal mediator, infuriating his lieutenant Governor Cruz Bustamante.[161] When Gray Davis finally refused to appeal the decision he put an end to the controversy five years after the passage of the referendum.[162] But while the controversy was put to rest the political impact of Proposition 187 could still be felt many years later.[163] Once again, Proposition 187 shows how difficult it is to differentiate racial politics from partisan politics. Especially when one considers that in the 1990s there seemed to be a racially divisive initiative every election cycle. In 1996, Californians voted for Proposition 2009, which put an end to affirmative action policies in California the public sector, with a 54 percent majority. It was supported by Governor Wilson and the Republican Party. And in 1998, Proposition 227, also supported by Wilson and the state's Republican Party passed with 61 percent of the votes.[164] The initiative limited bilingual education for non-English speakers to one year, triggering long and inconclusive debates and studies about the benefits and drawbacks of bilingual education. These propositions maintained the sentiment that minorities were the targets of ballot measures and helped motivate communities to mobilize and register to vote. In the 1990s more than one million new Latinos registered and they did either as Democrats or as "decline-to-state" voters. The Latino electorate almost doubled during the 1990s in part as a result of these initiatives and the anti-minority image it gave to the GOP.[165]

The Republican victory of 1994 was short-lived as in 1996 the Democrats regained the majority in the Assembly in 1996 with a 4 seat gain (43–37). In 1996 term limits, for the first time, there were and every member who was serving when voters passed the initiative in November 1990 was barred from seeking reelection. That created opportunities in the form of 32 open seats but not necessarily for new blood. Seven former Assembly members, who had left the house for some time, sought to win back their seat. Five of the former members ran in districts where the incumbent was termed-out and one challenged a freshman. The first Democratic gain occurred in Assembly District Twenty-seven left open when McPherson ran for Senate District Fifteen. In AD 27 (Santa Cruz) Fred Keeley easily won by more than 20 percent. In the Forty-third District (Glendale) left open when Republican James Rogan ran for Congress, Democrat underdog Scott Wildman won by a 0.2 percent margin (192 votes). Democrat Jack Scott easily unseated vulnerable Republican incumbent Bill Hoge in Assembly District Forty-four (Pasadena).[166] Finally, in AD 56 (Downey) Sally M. Havice won by a 2 percent margin for a fourth Democratic gain. The losses could have been worse for Republicans if Peter Frusetta in AD 28 had not thwarted off Lilly Cervantes one more time with a 1.6 percent victory margin. In 1996 minorities also made gains in the Republican ranks. Most notably Rod Pacheco ran for the California State Assembly in the Sixty-fourth District (Riverside). With his victory, he became the first Latino Republican elected in more than a century. He was elected leader of the Republican caucus, marking the first time in the state's history that a Latino served in that capacity.

The Democrats kept their majority in the Senate (22–16) with a net gain of two seats. Adam Schiff easily won the open SD 21, which included the wealthy suburbs north of downtown Los Angeles; Betty Karnette won the open SD 27 by 3 percent of the votes; Dede Alpert won in SD 39, in San Diego County, previously held by an Independent. Democrats only gained two seats because Republican McPherson won in SD 15 (Monterey, Santa Cruz, Benito counties) by a 1.5 percent margin and fellow Assembly member Richard Rainey won the Seventh District, Boatwright's former district in Contra Costa County, by 0.4 percent.

In the congressional delegation the Democrats picked up 3 seats (29–23) among which was that of Loretta Sanchez when she barely defeated 6-term GOP Representative Bob Dorman in the Forty-sixth District (a 64 percent minority district in Orange County) by a thin margin of 1 percent of the votes, making her the sole Latina of the delegation. Also, in the East Bay, Democrat Ellen Tauscher defeated Republican incumbent Bill Baker in CD 10 by 1.4 percent. In CD 22 (San Luis Obispo County) Walter Capps defeated Republican incumbent Andrea Seastrand by 4 percent. When African American Walter R. Tucker III resigned from Congress in December 1995, due to scandals involving accepting and demanding bribes while mayor of Compton, it opened the heavily Democratic seat (CD 37) for African American female Juanita Millender-McDonald who won a tough 9 candidate primary but then sailed through a general election with a whopping 85 percent of the votes.[167] A number that is not uncommon in naturally occurring heavily Democratic, majority-minority districts in Los Angeles. With these additions the California delegation now counted a grand total 9 women (out of 52), all Democrats.[168] Bill Clinton easily carried the state for reelection as president even as Proposition 209 put an end to affirmative action in the public sector.

In 1998 Gray Davis won the gubernatorial election by 20 percentage points, at the same time as Proposition 227 ended bilingual education in the state.[169] Democrats increased their Assembly majority (48–32) and their Senate majority (25–15). In the Assembly the Democrats continued to make up for the 1994 losses and picked up 5 seats. In AD 30, a 60 percent minority district, Latino Dean Florez, who later became President Pro Tempore of the California Senate, defeated freshman Republican incumbent Robert M. Prenter. Hannah Beth-Jackson picked up AD 35 (Santa Barbara), a seat she held until she was termed out in 2004. In 2012, she won election to the State Senate when she defeated Republican incumbent Tony Strickland in SD 19.[170] Alan Lowenthal won the open AD 54 by less than 3 percent. He was later elected to the State Senate and then the US House of Representatives. Latina Nell Soto picked up AD 61[171] before moving on the State Senate in 2000 when she won Congressman Joe Baca's former seat SD 32. Latino Lou Correa picked up AD 69 after losing that seat in 1996 by 93 votes.[172] He later served in the State Senate (SD 34) and won election to the House of Representatives in 2016 (CD 46 became open when Loretta Sanchez ran for the US Senate).

The Assembly added another Latina when, in AD 31 (which included the Latino portions of Fresno, Visalia, and Tulare), Sarah L. Reyes easily kept Cruz Bustamante's seat under Democratic control. George Nakano was also elected in 1998 (AD 53) and served until 2004.[173] During his time in the Assembly he served as the chairman of the Democratic caucus, he was the first Asian American to hold that leadership position. The year 1998 really is an interesting year for minorities in California politics as many prominent politicians were elected that year. We mentioned Dean Florez, Lou Correa, or Hannah Beth-Jackson but 1998 is also the year African American Herb Wesson was elected in AD 47 (Culver City). He was then elected Speaker of the Assembly in 2002, the second African American to be elected to that post.[174] Gloria Romero was also elected in 1998 in AD 49 (Monterey Park). She became the first female elected majority leader of the State Senate from 2001 to 2008. Marco Antonio Firebaugh was elected in AD 50 (a heavily Latino seat east of downtown Los Angeles) and during his final term in the Assembly he served as majority leader and chairman of the California Latino Legislative Caucus. The Republicans also managed to hold on to AD 60, in LA County, by running another Latino named Pacheco, this time Bob Pacheco, who won against Ben Wong. Charlene Zettel the lone Republican Latina won in CD 75, a San Diego GOP stronghold at the time.

In the Senate the Democrats picked up two extra seats when former Assemblywoman Jackie Speier won in the open SD 8 (west and south of San Francisco) and when Joe Dunn defeated Republican incumbent Bob Hurtt by 3 percent in SD 34 (Orange County). Another female Debra Bowen was elected in safely Democratic SD 20 (Van Nuys). In 1998, Assemblywoman Deborah Ortiz, former Chief of Staff of Richard Polanco and former leader at the Latino Coalition for Fair Sacramento Redistricting, moved to the Senate when she won in SD 6 (Sacramento County). She was joined by Liz Figueroa, who won in SD 10 (southeastern shore of San Francisco Bay), and Martha Escutia in SD 30 (San Jose). Two more Latinos joined the Senate. Richard Alarcón was elected in District Twenty, a 60 percent minority district, where he served as majority whip for eight years; and Joe Baca was elected in SD 32, which combined two San Bernardino County Assembly Districts (Sixty-one and Sixty-two) with large minority populations.[175] With the reelection of Richard Polanco and Hilda Solis the Senate became much more Latino and female. In 1998, John Burton was elected president pro tempore of the Senate until he was termed out in 2004.

In the congressional delegation the Republicans finally won Vic Fazio's seat when he retired and Doug Ose was elected in the northern, agricultural Third District. They also temporally picked up one more seat in the congressional delegation in the Thirty-sixth District (Santa Monica Bay) when Jane

Harman unsuccessfully ran for governor. Steven Kuykendall barely beat Janice Hahn. But, in 2000, Harman won her seat right back.[176] Other notable changes worth mentioning are, for instance, when Esteban "Ed" Torres retired in CD 35, the most democratic congressional district in the state, he was replaced by Assemblywoman Graciela Flores "Grace" Napolitano. When Representative Dellums retired from Congress, he endorsed longtime aide Barbara Lee. In April 1998, during a special election with an abysmal 16 percent turnout, the California delegation gained one more female African American Representative. Dellums's retiring led to a series of special elections. Lee's victory meant she resigned from the State Senate. Democrats Don Perada, Dion Aroner, and Keit Carson did not receive a majority of the votes in a September 1998 15 percent–turnout special election with a 900-vote difference between the top two candidates (Perada and Aroner). They were therefore forced to a run-off but it was not to be a run-off between the top two finishers because both were Democrats. Under California election law at that time, if no candidate received a majority in a special election for a partisan office, there had to be a run-off among the top finishers of each political party, not the top two vote-getters overall. Therefore, Aroner and Carson were eliminated because, like Perata, they were Democrats. The special election was consolidated with the November general election and Perada won easily in this heavily Democratic Bay Area district. But Perada had remained on the Assembly ballot where he also won. He could not possibly serve in both chambers and he therefore resigned his Assembly seat right away triggering a special election in February 1999. Oakland Mayor Elihu Harris should have won that seat easily yet that election was the stage of one of the greatest political upsets in the state's history. On February 2, with a 19.5 percent voter turnout, Harris finished first with 49 percent of the vote. But 49 percent of the vote is short of the simple majority to avoid a run-off election. Democratic Oakland lawyer Frank Russo came in second place with 37 percent, and Green Party candidate Audie Bock received 8.7 percent of the vote. Again, as in the State Senate election, California law required a run-off election between the top finishers of each political party. As a consequence, because Russo was a Democrat, like Harris, he was eliminated. A special run-off election was called for March 30, 1999, between Elihu Harris as the Democratic Party candidate, and Audie Bock as the Green Party candidate. In an effort to boost voter turnout in Black-majority, heavily Democratic precincts in Oakland, the Harris campaign, working for an African American, sent targeted mailers to households in selected precincts, urging voters to vote for him and receive a fried chicken meal if they presented a voting stub at selected supermarkets. Because of the perception of vote buying and the racist undertone voter backlash was massive.[177] On March 30, in a special run-off election with 15 percent turnout, Harris lost by less than 1,000 votes to Audie Bock who became the first Green Party candidate in the country to be elected to a state legislative body.

That seat was easily regained in 2000 when Chinese-American Wilma Chan won CD 16 (east of San Jose). Her victory was 1 of 3 for the Democratic Party which increased its majority in the Assembly to 50 seats with two more pickups: one by Rebecca Cohn in AD 24, in the heart of the Silicon Valley, and one by Simon Salinas in AD 28, a majority minority district south of the Bay Area. Other minorities elected to the Assembly for the first time where Democrats Joe Canciamilla in AD 11 (San Pablo Bay), Manolo Diaz in AD 23 (Willie Brown's former district in east San Francisco), Carol Liu in AD 44 (Pasadena), Jenny Oropeza in AD 55 (an 80 percent minority district in LA County), Edward Chavez in AD 57 (a 64 percent Latino district in eastern San Gabriel Valley), Gloria Negrete McLeod in AD 61, Juan Vargas in AD 79 (a 76 percent minority district in San Diego County) and openly gays Jackie Goldberg in AD 45[178] and Christine Kehoe in AD 76 (San Diego).[179]

In 2000, in the Senate, where odd-numbered districts were up for reelection, the Democratic Party gained one seat and increased its majority to a 26–14 advantage. In the Fifth District, Assembly member Michael Machado barely won access to the Senate against Republican Alan Nakanishi with a razor-thin 0.6 percent margin.[180] Republican Assemblyman Bob Margett won his ticket to the Senate in SD 29 against Richard Melendez by 1 percent of the votes. No other race was very close. Even Democratic Assembly member Tom Torlakson's victory against Republican incumbent Richard Rainey in District Seven (mostly Contra Costa County) was a blow-out, confirming how difficult it had become for Republicans to win in the Bay Area.

In 2000 the Democrats increased their majority in the California congressional delegation. As mentioned, Harman won her seat back. But Japanese-American Mike Honda won CD 15 (Santa Clara County) when Republican Tom Campbell retired. Adam Schiff beat Jim Rogan in CD 27 (Pasadena) and Hilda Solis won CD 31, in the lower San Gabriel Valley, when NRA member and partial-birth abortion opponent Democratic incumbent Matthew Martinez lost renommination.[181] Martinez switched to the Republican Party when he lost the primary. Finally, Susan Davis beat Republican incumbent Brian Bilbray in CD 49 (San Diego County) increasing the number of women in the delegation to 16.[182]

We see that the lower house, at the end of the 1990s, was getting more diverse as the Democrats increased their majority. The Assembly, therefore, played its role of incubator of young lawmakers who used their elections as a springboard for longer careers. This is especially flagrant in 1998. We also see that, by the end of the decade, the effects of redistricting had worn out, minority registration was up and the Democratic Party maintained its solid registration lead.[183] By 1999, the Democrats still had an 11 percent lead in party registration, with 46 percent compared to 35 percent for Republicans (13 percent declined to state). With such a built-in advantage, combined with important residential segregation and other redistricting constraints, the most creative remapping can only generate limited electoral gains. Despite claims by scholars and journalists alike, redistricting plans in California have not produced partisan miracles. However, it led to vast increases in minority representation that we will now analyze more thoroughly.

MINORITY DESCRIPTIVE REPRESENTATION INCREASE

Thanks to the constraints imposed by the Voting Rights Act, the 1990s saw some increase in minority representation in California politics, especially Latinos, at least in the Assembly. While there were 11 minority elected officials in the Assembly in 1990 (7 African Americans and 4 Latinos), their number reached 29 by the end of the decade (4 African Americans, 22 Latinos, and 3 Asian Americans). State Senator Richard G. Polanco, the Los Angeles Democrat who headed the legislature's Latino caucus, was credited with playing a key role in recruiting candidates, gaining endorsements, raising funds and coordinating campaigns.[184] With Polanco's help, the numbers of Latinos elected to the California Assembly increased from 4 in 1990 to 22 in 2000.

In the Senate, the gains were more modest. The number of Latinos increased from 2 in 1990 to 6 in 2000 (with no Asian Americans). In the congressional delegation, the gains were a bit better. 9 minority officials were sent to Washington in 1990 as compared to 12 in 2000. Again, the main gain was among Latinos which increased their number from 3 to 9 in a decade.[185]

As we can see in figures 5.5 and 5.6, the demographic changes in California led to a dramatic increase in minority representation even though its broader political implications were postponed because the bulk of the growth came from immigration. Foreign-born immigrants had to become naturalized citizens and, then, become involved in California politics for their presence to be felt. In 1991, the special master was very aware of the Voting Rights Act constraints and, therefore, augmented the number of majority-minority districts, especially those in which Latinos were a majority of the voting-age eligible population. As figures 5.3 and 5.4 show, between 1990 and 1995, 4 new state senators and 17 new Assembly members that belonged to a racial/ethnic minority group were elected.

According to Cain and Kousser, when term limits took effect, minority gains rose to 33 new members in the Assembly and 9 in the Senate between

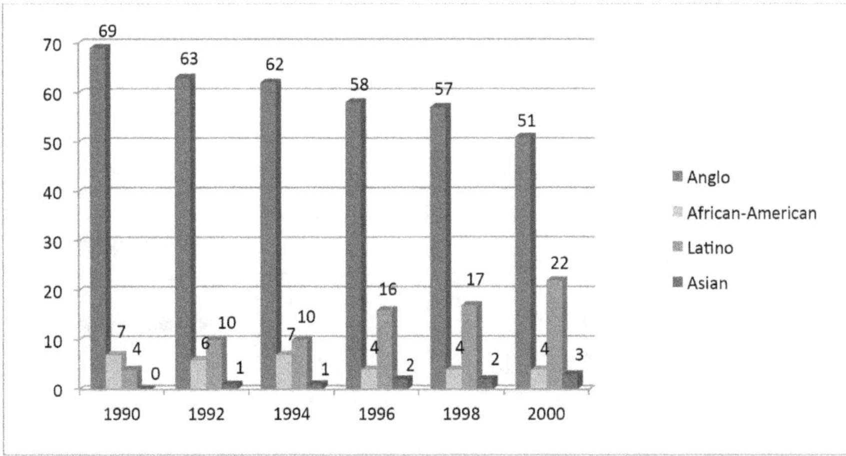

Figure 5.5 Assembly Members by Race/Ethnicity
Source: Compiled from the histories of the California African American Caucus, the California Latino Caucus, and the California Asian and Pacifi0lander Caucus along with elected officials personal website biographies and the press.

1996 and 2001. The authors estimate that, between 1990 and 1995, 11 of the 17 newly elected minority members won for reasons not attributed to term limits. "However term limits removed minority legislators at the same time that they opened up seats. During the 1990s, 10 women and 19 minority legislators were termed out, and the loss of such members as Willie Brown was costly for the influence and expertise of minority legislators. The net effect of

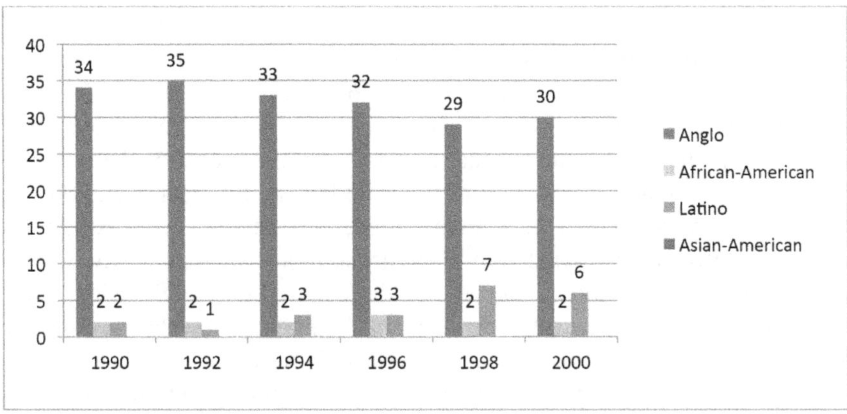

Figure 5.6 State Senate Members by Race/Ethnicity
Source: Compiled from the histories of the California African American Caucus, the California Latino Caucus, and the California Asian and Pacific Islander Caucus along with elected officials personal website biographies and the press.

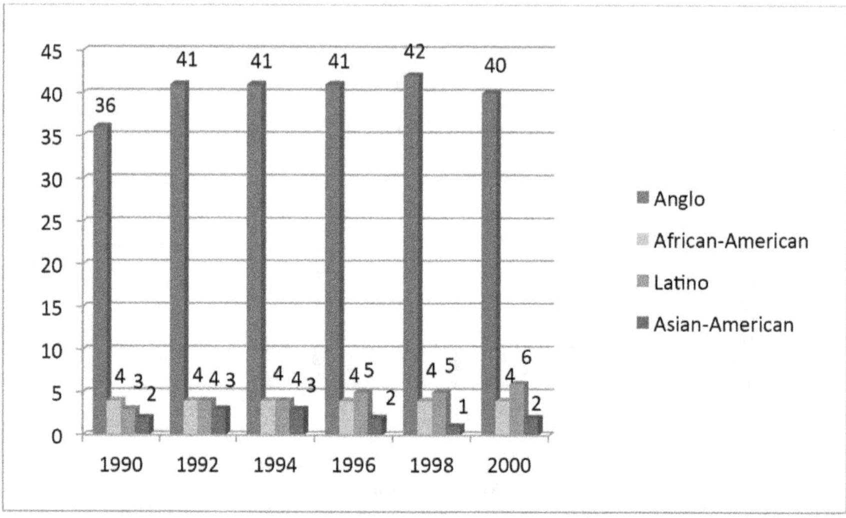

Figure 5.7 Members of the House of Representatives by Race/Ethnicity
Source: Compiled from the histories of the California African American Caucus, the California Latino Caucus, and the California Asian and Pacific Islander Caucus along with elected officials personal website biographies and the press.

Proposition 140 can be seen more clearly by looking at the total numbers of minorities in the legislature rather than by focusing on newly elected members."[186] In Congress, where there were no term limits, the gains by minority officeholders were more modest, going from 9 in 1990 to 12 in 2000.

To put these figures in perspective one can compare them to the demographics of the state. According to the 1990 census, 26 percent of the state population was Latino, yet 6.7 percent of the congressional delegation and 5 state legislators were Latinos. Asian Americans (and Pacific Islanders) represented 9.3 percent of the state population but 4.4 percent of the US House seats and none was elected in the state legislature. African Americans comprised 7 percent of the state population and held 8.9 percent of the congressional delegation and 7.5 percent of the state legislature seats. By 2000, the California population was 32 percent Latino, 11.2 percent Asian American, and 6.4 percent African American. Each group represented respectively 11.5 percent, 3.8 percent, and 7.7 percent of the congressional delegation. They also represented 23.3 percent, 5 percent, and 5 percent of the state legislature. Therefore, we can see that for Latinos and Asian Americans whose demographic groups increased rapidly in the 1990s, term limits seem to have made seats in Sacramento more attainable than seats in DC. For African Americans, whose share of the population was reduced over the same period, term limits made them vulnerable in the state legislature and the absence of term limits made their congressional seats safer.[187] In essence, term limits in California seem to have accelerated an inevitable occurrence due to demographic evolution and the Voting Rights Act imperative.

What can explain this increase in the number of minority elected officials in the 1990s in California? As mentioned before, the Proposition 187 effect shows that the Latino population not only grew but also became more politicized. Between 1994 and 2000, the Latino proportion of Democratic registration augmented from 16.1 percent to 22.1 percent, a 37.3 percent jump.[188] The increase was especially pronounced between 1994 and 1996 which lead to the creation of many districts in which 20 to 30 percent of the Democrats here Latinos. Therefore, this increase in Latino population but also in registration changed the calculus in many Assembly races where many Latino candidates ran as soon as the Latino population was large enough. In his analysis of Assembly races in the 1990s Morgan Kousser draws a direct line between Latino registration rates and electoral success. The new Latino lawmakers were almost all elected in district where Latinos comprised 40 percent or more of the Democratic registration.[189] The author concludes that "the increasing number of Latinos elected was a function of the increased number of Latino voters, not increasing ethnic crossover voting."[190] Because of racial polarization rates the perfect recipe for Latino electoral success in California in the 1990s was in heavily Democratic districts where Latinos enjoyed at least a 10 percent advantage over Anglo Democrats. The number of Anglos should not be too high so a Latino candidate can win in the primaries but the number of Latinos should not be too high either in order to not waste Latino votes and maintain Democratic and Latino opportunities in other districts. That subtle balance may therefore vary from one district to the next.

During the following decade though, the number of Latinos elected stagnated because of an incumbent protection redistricting plan and the only representation gains came from the Asian community whose numbers were extremely low in 2000.

We just saw that the 1990s were a crucial turning point in California as the Republican Party abandoned all efforts to court the largest growing minorities: Latinos. As the state was becoming more diverse, and racial minorities' political interest aligned with that of the Democratic Party, the GOP decided to instead double-down on its Anglo base and tried to boost Anglo mobilization around racially divisive issues such as affirmative action and immigration. In a way the Republican Party pushed its "Southern Strategy" to its logical continuation. However, demographic evolution in California shows that this strategy has obvious limits in such a diverse state and it can backfire. Also, one should not assume that because the Republican Party brand became unpopular among minorities that Latinos or Asians were welcome with open arms under the Democratic coalition. As the 2001 redistricting demonstrates, the Democrats, and especially Anglo incumbents, only reluctantly made room for newly elected officials. The calculation was simple: in a two-party system if the GOP is openly hostile to minorities they had no other alternative than to side with the Democrats. The party did not have to go above and beyond to satisfy their grievances.

NOTES

1. Richard Paddock, "Big Population Gains drive Legislators in Redistricting State," *Los Angeles Times*, March 25, 1991, OCA3.

2. Fernando J. Guerra, "The Emergence of Ethnic Officeholders in California," in *Racial and Ethnic California*, eds., Byran O. Jackson and Michael B. Preston (Berkeley, CA: IGS Press, 1991), 117–31. For some prominent examples: Los Angeles City Councilman Richard Alatorre, the first Latino elected to that body in two decades (and a veteran of thirteen years in the State Assembly); Michael Woo, the first Asian American member of the Los Angeles City Council; and Lionel Wilson, the first Black mayor of Oakland.

3. Cain, "The Contemporary Context," 17.

4. The attitude towards illegal immigration varies inside the Latino population among native-born and foreign born and among citizens and foreigners. Zoltan Hajnal and Mark Baldassare, "Finding Common Ground: Racial and Ethnic Attitudes in California," *Public Policy Institute of California* (2001), 17.

5. Hollinger, *Postethnic America.*

6. For more detailed figures, Jack Citrin and Benjamin Highton, "How Race, Ethnicity and Immigration Shape the California Electorate," Public Policy Institute of California, 2002.

7. The case of San Diego, for instance, in 1990 demonstrates that point. After the city of San Diego abandoned at-large elections in 1988, Asians who represented 12 percent of city's population and 8 percent of the county's population, had a hard time finding a suitable coalition partner. When the Chicano Federation filed a lawsuit against the County Board of Supervisor in September 1991, minority coalitions presented several redistricting plans. Linda Trinh Võ, *Mobilizing an Asian American Community* (Philadelphia, PA: Temple University Press, 2004), chap. 6.

8. For 2014 these figures were 44 percent and 29 percent. http://www.ppic.org/main/publication_show.asp?i=1090.

9. In 2014 it reached 21 percent, with 7 percent choosing another minor party. Ibid.

10. For an attempt to measure public opinion and compare all 50 states, see Robert S. Erickson, Gerald C. Wright, and John P. McIver, *Statehouse Democracy: Public Opinion and Policy in American States* (Cambridge, MA: Cambridge University Press, 1993). According to this national study from 1976 to 1988, California Democrats were more liberal than Democrats in every other state except Connecticut. And

California Independents were more liberal than those of all other states. Erickson, Wright and McIver, *Statehouse Democracy*, 40.

11. See for example, Bruce E. Cain, "Assessing the Partisan Effects of Redistricting," *The American Political Science Review* 79, no. 2 (1985): 320–33.

12. Daniel Weintraub, "'Incumbents Come First in Redistricting,' Speaker Says," *Los Angeles Times*, August 30, 1991, A3.

13. Douglas Shuit, "Close Race Fought in Santa Barbara Area," *Los Angeles Times*, October 14, 1984, OC_A17.

14. Louis Sahagun, "Newcomer in Challenge for Assembly Seat," *Los Angeles Times*, October 3, 1986, OC_A10.

15. Steven Churn, "Late Donations Boost Green's Senate Drive," *Los Angeles Times*, November 4, 1988, OC_A3.

16. Mark Gladstone, "Democrats Win Senate Seat in Key Election," *Los Angeles Times*, May 13, 1987, 10.

17. One of the reasons why 1988 was not a good year for Republicans in the Assembly might be when Karin Watson, a former agribusiness representative, pleaded guilty to extorting money for Assembly Republican leadership. Minority leader Pat Nolan of Glenndale became politically radioactive, lost his position, and the Democrats, while also targeted by the FBI investigation, were quick to link some candidates to their leadership. Richard Paddock and Mark Gladstone, "GOP Leader Nolan, Target in FBI Capitol Sting, Urged Colleagues to Keep Silent," *Los Angeles Times*, August 28, 1988, A3.

18. Democrats controlled 20 of the 22 standing committees allowing them broad control over the legislative process but also helped them in such matters as the confirmation of the governor's appointees.

19. Douglas Shuit, "State GOP Betting on 1986 as Its Year to Gain Senate Seats," *Los Angeles Times*, March 23, 1986, SD3.

20. Douglas Shuit and Jerry Gillam, "GOP Gains 2 Senate, 3 Assembly Seats to Bolster Its Position," *Los Angeles Times*, November 6, 1986, A3. One of the seats vacated was that of longtime Assembly Rules Committee and top Brown lieutenant, Lou "The Enforcer" Papan, one of the most colorful legislators in the history of the state. For example, he received his nickname after he knocked a colleague unconscious and sent him to the hospital over an Assembly leadership dispute.

21. Shuit and Gilliam, "GOP Gains," SD 3.

22. Many Republicans blame redistricting for their electoral woes. But some of the blame must fall on members of the legislature. During the 1980s, Californians voters as a group became more Republican and elected a Republican governor and voted for a Republican presidential candidate in every election. They elected a Republican US senator and barely reelected Democratic US Senator Alan Cranston. Daniel Weintraub, "Infighting Dooms GOP Power Play," *Los Angeles Times*, April 10, 1990, OCA3.

23. Harriet Chiang and Robert B.Gunnison, "Wilson Picks Conservative as Supreme Court Justice. LA Judge Would Replace Retiring Liberal," *San Francisco Chronicle*, July 30, 1991, A1; Harriet Chiang and Robert B. Gunnison, "How Wil-

son's Appointee May Affect Court. Appointment Surprised the Legal Experts," *San Francisco Chronicle*, July 31, 1991, A11.

24. Robert Shogan, "90 California Governor Race Seen as Key to Redistricting," *Los Angeles Times*, October 26, 1989, A3.

25. Sherry Bebitch Jeffe, "After Election, Comes the Dawn of Reality for Pete Wilson," *Los Angeles Times*, November 18, 1990, M5.

26. Precise estimates are difficult because the spending for both initiatives overlap (around $3 million were spent for both initiatives and $5 million against). John M. Allswang, *The Initiative and Referendum in California 1898–1998* (Berkeley, CA: Stanford University Press, 2000), 169.

27. For an analysis of Proposition 140's consequences see, for instance, Bruce E. Cain and Thad Kousser, *Adapting to Term Limits: Recent Experiences and New Direction* (Berkeley, CA: Public Policy Institute of California, 2004).

28. Proposition 140 was intended to apply to California's Congressional delegation but the US Supreme Court in 1995 ruled in the case *US Term Limits, Inc. v. Thornton* (514 U.S. 779), that states could not limit terms of their federal representatives.

29. Harriet Chiang and Robert B. Gunnison, "State High Court OKs Term Limits For Legislators," *San Francisco Chronicle*, October 11, 1991, A1.

30. It also stopped the practice of state legislators earning state retirement benefits from their service in the state legislature.

31. At the time of our conversations, Tim Hodson was Director of the Center for California Studies at California State University, Sacramento.

32. At least four competing measures were being prepared by California conservatives in 1989. GOP consultant Joe Shumate was quoted as saying: "Come hell or high water there is going to be something on the ballot in 1990 and it will be another donnybrook because the Democrats in the Legislature cannot let it pass." John Balzar, "Stunned State GOP Looks to Voters for Rescue on Redistricting in '90," *Los Angeles Times*, January 18, 1989, LF21.

33. Legislature Reapportionment Ethics Proposition 118 (1990). http://repository.uchastings.edu/ca_ballot_props/1023/.

34. Reapportionment by Commission. Initiative Constitutional Amendment and Statute. Proposition 119 (1990). http://repository.uchastings.edu/ca_ballot_props/1024/.

35. Among a panel of members from nonpartisan and nonprofit organizations.

36. Daniel Weinstraub, "Voters May Redesign Redistricting," *Los Angeles Times*, May 27, 1990, OCA38.

37. This was part of the reapportionment initiative sponsored by Republican State Senate Bill Leonard of Redlands that failed to qualify.

38. Democrats tend to be poorer and move more often than Republicans. So each district actually has fewer Democratic voters than the registration rolls suggest.

39. Greg Lucas, "Jackson in Redistricting Fight. He Says That Propositions 118 and 119 Would Hurt minorities," *San Francisco Chronicle*, May 22, 1990, A7.

40. Editorial, "Dishonest Ads Again Sink Reapportionment," *San Francisco Chronicle*, June 7, 1990, A24. This efficient ad and mail-in campaign was led by none other than Michael Berman.

41. Daniel Weintraub, "Redistricting Measures Costliest on the Ballot," *Los Angeles Times*, June 2, 1990, A29.

42. Daniel Hays Lowenstein, "The Message That Voters Sent in Rejecting Propositions 118 and 119," *Los Angeles Times*, June 17, 1990, M5.

43. Alan C. Miller, "Parties Dig In for Redistricting War," *Los Angeles Times*, September 3, 1990, OCA3.

44. Daniel Weintraub, "Lawmakers' Fall Session Is Sure to Be Divisive," *Los Angeles Times*, August 18, 1991, SBA3.

45. Larry Liebert, "Doolittle in Washington," *California Journal* 22, no. 6 (1991).

46. Tim Hodson, "Disappearing Constraints: Voting Rights and Gerrymandering in 1991 and 2001," *Politics and Policy: A Journal of the Pat Brown Institute of Public Affairs* (1998), 75

47. Kousser, "Reapportionment Wars," 167. When MALDEF experienced technical difficulties the Democrats offered assistance without any intention of distorting MALDEF's intentions. Ibid.

48. Daniel M. Weintraub, "Democrats Pass Redistricting Plans," *Los Angeles Times*, September 20, 1991, A3. Morgan Kousser compiled data for all the 9 different congressional plans with ethnic percentages estimates for every district. Kousser, "Reapportionment Wars," 175.

49. *City of Mobile v. Bolden*, 446 U.S. 55 (1980).

50. For many reasons, including expense and time, it is much easier to seek preclearance through the DOJ process than through the court system.

51. Section 5 of the VRA applies only to those jurisdictions where the US Department of Justice has found a history of discrimination in voting toward minority groups. The coverage formula, Section 4(b), was originally designed to encompass jurisdictions that engaged in egregious voting discrimination in 1965, and Congress updated the formula in 1970 and 1975.

52. In California, Section 5 applies to Kings, Merced, Monterey, and Yuba counties. As a practical consequence the racial statistics for these counties (citizen voting age population, racial polarized voting, etc.) are extremely precise. The Berman/D'Agostino archives at Berkeley's IGS show that those districts were set aside with a level of statistical details far superior to the rest of the state. Another consequence is that, from a practical standpoint, any redistricting of the state probably needed to start with those 5 counties.

53. The results were impressive for minority descriptive representation gains. In the congressional redistricting, after 1990, the number of African American and Latino majority-minority districts doubled from 26 to 52. Consequently, the number for African American Representatives increased by 50 percent and that of Latinos by 38 percent, the largest increase in minority representation in absolute terms in US history. Bruce E. Cain and Kenneth Miller, "Voting Rights Mismatch: The Challenge of Applying the Voting Rights Act to 'Other Minorities,' in *Voting Rights and Redistricting in the United States*, ed. Mark E. Rush (Westport, CT: Greenwood Press, 1998), 141.

54. Hodson, "Disappearing Constraints," 76.

55. In 1982, the Sixteenth Senate District was built around Bakersfield but jumped the Tehachapi Mountains to grab a mostly Black portion of Pasadena to add more

Democrats to the district of Walter Stiern who was reelected but the district elected a Republican when Stiern retired.

56. Latinos numbered 7.7 million in 1990, about 26 percent of the state's population but of the 165 legislative and congressional seats, only 10, or 6 percent, were filled by Latinos. Asian Americans made up about 9 percent of the state's population but only had two members in Congress and none in the legislature. Blacks, with 13 representatives in Congress and the legislature, were the only minority with proportional representation (7.9 percent of all representatives for a 7.4 percent share of the state's population).

57. Huffman has been accused over the years of leveraging her position in the NAACP to line her pockets through her consulting firm. LunaTaryn, "How a High School Dropout Fought Her Way to the Pinnacle of California Politics," *Sacramento Bee*, November 1, 2016, http://www.sacbee.com/news/politics-government/capitol-alert/article111682772.html.

58. Allan Heslop conceded: "I would love to be able to criticize the Senate plan, but they produced a decent one with reasonable maps. Anyone who has a basic knowledge of California political geography could find their way around. They held open hearings in different parts of the state throughout the process and they came out with an acceptable bipartisan plan." Lisa Foster, state executive director of Common Cause, agreed: "The Senate, she says, provided historical voting data and basic demographic breakdowns by district and then presented maps that adhered to census tract lines so that outside groups could more easily compute how the new lines affected specific minority communities." Still, Foster complained about the end result: "The problem with the Senate was that the process was good, but they still produced an incumbent protection plan." Eric Auchard, "Carving California with a Computer: The High-Tech Drawing of Districts,"*California Journal* 22, no. 10 (1991).

59. A. G. Block, "The Reapportionment Failure: Legislature's Plans Fall to Wilson's Veto," *California Journal* 22, no. 10 (1991).

60. Hodson, "Disappearing Constraints," 77. Preclearance states were asked to show, among other things, evidence of "opportunities for the public to be heard, and of opportunities for interested parties to participate in the decision to adopt the proposed change and an account of the extent to which such participation, especially by minority group members, in fat took place." 28 C.F.R. Sec. 51.28f, https://www.law.cornell.edu/cfr/text/28/51.28.

61. It went so far as to produce a thirty-minute video, available in four languages, explaining redistricting and how to affect the process. In this pre-internet era, the video was distributed widely in the state.

62. Hodson, "Disappearing Constraints," 77.

63. Block, "The Reapportionment Failure."

64. Weinstraub, "Democrats Pass Redistricting," A3.

65. Weinstraub, "Democrats Pass Redistricting," A3.

66. Democrats made promises about an open process. Republicans made promises too. Early on, they offered free software and political data to minority groups. But Larry Shinigawa, who directed computer operations for the Asian-Pacific Americans for Fair Reapportionment, declared in the press having submitted a request for

software and data from the Republicans and never heard back from them. Auchard, "Carving California."

67. Irene Chang, "Asians, Latino Join in Proposal for Remapping," *Los Angeles Times*, August 31, 1991, B2. The proposed plan tried to create an Assembly district in the West San Gabriel Valley with cities containing large Asian populations (Alhambra, Monterey Park, Rosemead, and San Gabriel) to reach 28 percent Asian population while retaining a 55 percent Latino majority.

68. In 1991, an alliance of gay and lesbian political-action committees did not actually propose districts. But using demographic and electoral data, including AIDS mortality statistics plotted by census tract from the Centers for Disease Control, the group produced color maps showing concentrations of gays and lesbians around the state. That data was transmitted to the legislature, some of it personally to Brown and Senate President Pro Tempore David Roberti in hopes of the creation of a "gay" Assembly seat.

69. On the difficulty of organizing the APIA community see April Chung, "Non-citizen Voting Rights and Alternatives: A Path toward Greater Asian Pacific American and Latino Political Participation," *UCLA Asian Pacific American Law Journal* 4 (1996), 163.

70. And even when they did, the result was not acceptable. The special masters in their report admitted that they "felt that the treatment of the non-minority areas in their plans was not well thought out," and added in a footnote, "We do not mean this as a criticism of the motive of MALDEF in submitting complete statewide plans. Since the entire focus of the MALDEF effort was on creation of Latino districts, it is not surprising that the districting in non-minority areas has the flavor of being an afterthought." Report and Recommendations of the special masters on Reapportionment to the Supreme Court of California, No. S0228355, 1992, 46.

71. It wasn't until 2001, with cheaper and more powerful softwares and with more data available to the public, that minority organizations started to master the entire technical redistricting process and were able to produce their own complete maps.

72. Bill Stall, "Political, Legal Battle over Redistricting Looms," *Los Angeles Times*, August 22, 1991, VCA3.

73. Another example would be when Richard Farjado of MALDEF during a Senate hearing proposed to join the Latino community around Santa Fe Springs in Los Angeles County with the Latino communities in Orange County to form a Latino Senate district. However, to do so meant splitting cities. And again Farjado's proposal did not take into consideration the ripple effect through the state.

74. Daniel M. Weintraub, "Minorities Get GOP Support in Remap Battle," *Los Angeles Times*, August 26, 1991, A3. "Latinos Offer Own Plan for Redistricting," *Los Angeles Times*, September 6, 1991, A3. This was not a California phenomenon. The Republican National Committee vigorously allied itself to minorities seeking to win the maximum number of seats in Congress or in state legislatures. Former Education Secretary William J. Bennett accused the RNC of embracing quotas that President Bush had denounced in employment. Ronald Brownstein, "Quotas in Elections," *Los Angeles Times*, August 28, 1991, OCA1.

75. Interview with Tim Hodson. For a discussion of Asian Americans' involvement in the 1990 redistricting, see Leland Saito, *Race and Politics: Asian-Americans, Latinos and Whites in a Los Angeles Suburb* (Urbana: University of Illinois Press, 1998), 158–80.

76. Professor Bernard Grofman remarked in a public hearing: "Even plans that are drawn with the best of motives, the MALDEF plan for example, which affects to the open area inadvertently splits some of Oakland Black in such a fashion that arguably to would be retrogression even though the particular black population numbers are not that high." Special Masters on Reapportionment, Public Hearings, November 1, 1991, 276.

77. Daniel M. Weintraub, "Chance Fading for Bipartisan Deal on Reapportionment," *Los Angeles Times*, September 17, 1991, VYA3.

78. Some authors such as Michael Kang have argued that majority-minority districts actually reduce racial polarization. Michael S. Kang, "Race and Democratic Contestation," *Yale Law Journal* 117(2008): 778–84, 787.

79. Vlae Kershner, "Legislature Sends Wilson 3 Remap Plans. He Promises 3 Vetoes,"*San Francisco Chronicle*, September 20, 1991, A1.

80. There were many reasons why Democrats believed Wilson was negotiating in bad faith. One of them was the governor sought legislative approval for $300,000 to develop his own district mapping system. In May 1991 his office was in the process of retaining lawyers to intervene in the lawsuit they believed was inevitable. Richard, Zeiger, "The Reapportionment Puzzle—Carving Up California," *California Journal* 22, no. 4 (1991).

81. Kousser, "Redistricting," 150.

82. Kousser, "Reapportionment Wars," 168.

83. David Lublin, "The Election of African-Americans and Latinos to the U.S. House of Representatives 1972–1994," *American Politics Quarterly* 25 (July 1997): 792–810; Bernard Grofman and Lisa Handley, "Estimating the impact of voting-rights-act-related districting on Democratic strength in the U.S. House of Representatives," in *Race and Redistricting in the 1990s*, ed. Bernard Grofman (New York: Agathon Press, 1998), 51–67.

84. Adam B. Cox and Richard T. Holden, "Reconsidering Racial and Partisan Gerrymandering," *The University of Chicago Law Review* 78, no. 2 (Spring 2011), 553–604.

85. The other members were Donald Franson (vice-chairman), Betty Barry-Deal, Elwood Lui, Carlos Mendoza Teran.

86. Daniel M. Weintraub, "Wilson Outlines Redistricting Strategy," *Los Angeles Times*, July 19, 1991, A3.

87. Jerry Gillam, "Wilson Picks Redistricting Panel," *Los Angeles Times*, July 27, 1991, VCA 21.

88. On Morill's plan in 1981, Bruce Cain observed: "Indeed, the press and the legislators had to spend several days puzzling over the maps before they could figure out how the old seats matched with the new ones and what would be the fate of various legislators. When the confusion was finally cleared up, the press discovered that the plan had abolished the districts of seven incumbents (6 Democrats and 1 Republican),

including that of the newly elected Speaker of the Assembly, the first Black ever to hold that office. In short the bind impartiality of Morill's plan would have effectively wiped out one of the most significant racial achievement in the history of California politics!" Cain, *The Reapportionment Puzzle*, 14.

89. Daniel M.Weintraub, "Wilson Asks Court to Takeover Redistricting," *Los Angeles Times*, September 7, 1991, A1.

90. Under the commission's congressional plan, in Los Angeles County, the three most heavily Black districts had African American population percentages of 57.3, 20.7, 14.7. This means that one district was heavily packed and the Black incumbents in the other two would probably lose their seat. The Democratic plan, by contrast, spread the Black population in the three seats (respectively 40.5 percent, 38.3 percent and 30.1 percent). The masters' plan did roughly the same (40.3 percent, 42.7 percent, 33.6 percent). Under those two plans, given the degree of racial polarization in that region at the time, the African American incumbents would have likely retained their seats. Kousser, "Reapportionmpent Wars," 170.

91. Arturo Vargas declared on behalf of MALDEF in a public hearing: "To our knowledge, the plans developed by the Governor's redistricting panel is the only one that has been proposed that would decrease the number of congressional districts in which Latinos could elect representatives of their choice." Special Masters on Reapportionment, Public Hearings, November 1, 1991, 166.

92. Daniel Weintraub, "Wilson Panel Remap Would Help Republicans," *Los Angeles Times*, October 12, 1991, A31.

93. Vlae Kershner, "Wilson Keeping Secret His Panel's Remap Plan. He Won't Reveal It until Issue Goes to Court," *San Francisco Chronicle*, September 25, 1991, A1.

94. Even special masters had to conclude: "We would have been tempted to accept the plans submitted by the commission if we did not feel that the plans were inadequate in the treatment of minority communities. This aspect of the commission plan was the subject of substantial criticism by minority groups and by the representatives of both the Democratic and Republican parties. The Governor's amendments attempted to correct these problems (and constituted in our view a tacit admission of the problem), but fell short of what we thought was appropriate." "Report and Recommendations of Special Masters on Reapportionment in the Supreme Court of California," No S0228355, 1992, 46.

95. Jim Doyle, "Wilson to Go to Court in Remap Fight," *San Francisco Chronicle*, October 3, 1991, A23.

96. Eugene C. Lee, professor emeritus of political science at UC Berkeley, Rich Langree, a Supreme Court staff attorney, Guy B. Colbur, a retired court staff attorney, and staff members Rebecca Sullivan, Gang Morozumi, and Erica Drewes assisted McKasckle.

97. Philipp Hager and Daniel M.Weintraub, "Redistricting Task Goes to State Justices," *Los Angeles Times*, September 26, 1991, A3.

98. 54 Cal. 3d 471; 816 P. 2d 1306 (1991).

99. Grofman, Public Hearing, 293.

100. Kousser, "Reapportionment War," 173.

101. Bruce Cain declaration in *Wilson v. Eu*, October 20, 1991.

102. The Shumate plan was the modification of the governor's commission plan by Governor Wilson's consultant Joe Shumate. The Jones plan was the one offered by the Republicans in the legislature.

103. Kousser, "Reapportionment Wars," 173–74.

104. "Report and Recommendation," 42–46. However, Cain and Mac Donald have shown that "nested districts, no matter whether they are constructed through aggregation or division, impede the creation of majority-minority districts and lead to more city and county splits than non-nested districts do." Bruce Cain and Karin Mac Donald, "The Implications of Nesting in California Redistricting," IGS Study, August 2007. In 1981, when the California legislature controlled the line-drawing process, it has opted against nesting (same in 2001). In 1973 and 1991, when the courts have done the redistricting, they have nested.

105. Masters Report, 98.

106. Vlae Kershner, "Court's Panel Reveals Its Plan for Redistricting. Republicans Expected to Gain Seats," *San Francisco Chronicle*, December 3, 1991, A1; Daniel Borenstein, "Political Winds in Big Shift," *Contra Costa Times*, December 3, 1991, 10F4; Carl Irving, "Latinos, GOP Gain in Remap Plan," *San Francisco Examiner*, December 3, 1991, 10F3; Jon Matthews, "Panel Remaps Puts Incumbents at Risk," *Sacramento Bee*, December 3, 1991, A1; Daniel M. Weintraub, "Remap Could Bring Major Gains for GOP," *Los Angeles Times*, December 4, 1991, A1; Lara Mecoy, "House Remap Plan Boosts GOP," *Sacramento Bee*, December 4, 1991, A1; Jon Matthews and Llana DeBare, "GOP Could Seize Legislature," *Sacramento Bee*, December 4, 1991, A16; Dan Walters, "New Redistricting Plan Whacks the Democrats," *San Jose Mercury News*, December 4, 1991, B11; Daniel Weintraub, "Wilson Got His Wish in Remap Plan," *Los Angeles Times*, December 5, 1991, A3; Dan Walters, "New Era for State Politics," *San Francisco Daily Journal*, December 6, 1991, A4.

107. Philip Hager, "How Panel Redrew Political Maps," *Los Angeles Times*, December 8, 1991, VYA3.

108. To take only one example when Arturo Vargas of MALDEF during his presentation to the masters proposed the creation of a new Latino district in Los Angeles, here is presiding Master Brown's response: "Has the incumbent congressman looked at and approved it or not, or do you know, like Dymally." Vargas explains that the most impacted incumbent was Maxine Waters. Brown's response: "The other, Dymally, do you know if Dymally. . . ." Public Hearings, 170.

109. Kathleen Z. McKenna, "Governor Supports Remapping," *Oakland Tribune*, December 4, 1991, A1.

110. A study by Ed Constantini, political science professor at UC Davis, is cited by Daniel Weintraub, "When the Course of Reapportionment," *Sacramento Bee*, December 16, 1991, B 15.

111. A spread between the winning and losing major party candidates of 10 percent of the vote or less (45–55 percent) has become the conventional standard of a marginal race post-election. Before the votes are cast it is obviously a trickier matter. Would a hypothetical plan be more competitive (and more fair) if it contained 5 districts of registration margins between 0 and 5 percent and 6 districts with registration margins between 5 percent and 15 percent than a plan that contained 9 districts with

registration between 5 percent and 10 percent and 3 districts between 11 percent and 13 percent?

112. Lloyd Connelly was appointed to the Sacramento County Superior Court. Isenberg won reelection with 66 percent of the votes.

113. Ted Lempert unsuccessfully ran for a US Senate seat primary in 1992 and came back to the Assembly in 1996 for one term. Jackie Speier won AD 19 with 75 percent of the votes in the general election.

114. Tom Bates won AD 14 in 1992 with 82 percent of the votes.

115. Robert Campbell ran unopposed in the Eleventh District.

116. He won reelection with 65 percent of the votes in the general election.

117. His district was 52 percent Democratic and 37 percent Republican, post-redistricting those figures were 48 percent and 39 percent. Fazio won reelection and became chair of the House Democratic Caucus until he retired in 1998.

118. "Remap Wars: Court Plan Is Out and GOP Is All Smiles but Demos See Silver Lining," *Calpeek* 13, no. 45 (1991). "Gas Tax Tony" won reelection in the Twenty-fourth District in 1992, barely won reelection in 1994, and retired in 1996.

119. Laura Mecoy, "House Remap Plan Boosts GOP," *Sacramento Bee*, December 4, 1991, A1.

120. Sherry Bebitch Jeffe, "Why Republicans May Rue Their Heartfelt Support for Term Limits," *Los Angeles Times*, December 8, 1991, M6.

121. Dixon died in office in 2000 and was replaced in the Thirty-second District by African American Dianne Watson.

122. One of the reasons MALDEF was frustrated is because of the comparison with Texas where more Latinos seemed to have found success in the 1970s and 1980s. Ronald Brownstein, "2 States of Progress for Latinos," *Los Angeles Times*, August 1, 1990, OCA1.

123. Daniel Weintraub, "Latino Group Seeks to Alter Remap Plan," *Los Angeles Times*, December 17, 1991, A3.

124. CD 30, which was won by Becerra, had a Latino population of 61 percent, a Latino voting age population of 57 percent, and a Latino registration rate of 34 percent. CD 31 which was won by Martinez had a LP of 59 percent, a LVAP of 54 percent, and a LR of 42 percent. CD 33 which was won by Roybal-Allard had a LP of 84 percent, a LVAP of 79 percent, and a LR of 48 percent. CD 34 which was won by Torres had a LP of 62 percent, a LVAP of 58 percent, and a LR of 43 percent.

125. Bert Robinson and Stephen Robitaille, "Minorities May Not Gain Quickly from Newly Drawn District Lines," *San Jose Mercury News*, December 8, 1991, 1A.

126. Carl Irving, "Remap to Uproot Politicians," *San Francisco Examiner*, December 17, 1991, A6.

127. Torrance's APIA community included a large Japanese American population that was well established and had a consistent voting record that made it a cognizable "community of interest." Additionally, the city of Torrance was a large South Bay interest, with a fully functioning independent City Council and school system. Kathay Feng, Keith Oaki, and Bryan Ikegami, "Voting Matters: APIAs, Latino/a and Post-2000 Redistricting in California," *Oregon Law Review* 81 (2002): 882n140.

128. Associated Press, "Hispanic Group Fights Remap," *San Francisco Chronicle*, December 18, 1991, A17; Jim Doyle, "US Judges Refuse to Block Remap. Challenge to California's plan fails," *San Francisco Chronicle*, January 29, 1992, A11. *Members of the California Democratic Congressional Delegation v. Eu* (790 F Supp 125 [N.D. CA 1992]) and *Wilson v. Eu* (1 Cal. 4th 707 [1992]). The NAACP joined the suit in front of the federal court but not the State Supreme Court.

129. Lucas famously and publically endorsed State Attorney General Dan Lungren for Governor. Lungren argued *Wilson v. Eu* and often argued before the Supreme Court. Maura Dolan, "Justice Says He's Sorry about Endorsement," *Los Angeles Times*, August 10, 1995, A3.

130. *Davis v. Bandemer* (478 U.S. 109 [1986]); *Vieth v. Jubelirer* (541 U.S. 267 [2004]); *Gill v. Whitford* (585 US [2018]).

131. 1 Cal. 4th 740.

132. For instance in Texas in 2006 *LULAC v. Perry* (548 U.S. 399 [2006]) the Supreme Court ruled that only District Twenty-three of the 2003 Texas redistricting violated the Voting Rights Act for racial reasons. The Court refused to throw out the entire plan, ruling that the plaintiffs failed to state a sufficient claim of partisan gerrymandering. Here some members of the Court were responsive to the theory of "partisan symmetry" developed in an amicus brief submitted by professors Andrew Gelman, Bernard Grofman, Jonathan Katz, and Gary King.

133. *DeWitt v. Wilson*, 856 F.Supp. 1409 (1994).

134. They also challenged the constitutionality of California Election Code, section 25003, a term limitation statute, and section 6402(b), a statute permitting candidates to run for only one congressional seat. These claims were considered nonjusticiable.

135. *DeWitt v. Wilson*.

136. *Bush v. Vera*, 517 U.S. 952 (1996), at 954. It is to be noted that the Court's jurisprudence was influenced here by the work of Richard H. Pildes and Richard G. Niemi, "Expressive Harms, 'Bizarre Districts,' and Voting Rights: Evaluating Election-District Appearances after *Shaw v. Reno*," *Michigan Law Review* 92, no. 2 (1993), 483–587.

137. This opaque jurisprudence reminds us of other cases involving the use of race in affirmative action policies. Race can be taken into consideration if it is one factor among many and not the predominant factor. What makes a factor "predominant" is often in the eye of the beholder. To be effective race-conscious processes must not be too obvious: "The Court demands that social integration be visible so as to send a message of inclusion, but it insists on deliberately obscurantist processes of individualized consideration so as to prevent inclusion from modulating into a regime of group entitlements." Robert Post, "Affirmative Action and Higher Education: The View from Somewhere," *Yale Law and Policy Review* 23, no. 25 (2005), 31.

138. He even won San Diego County for the first time since 1944.

139. Adding to the governor's woes, Barbara Boxer soundly beat John Seymour, Wilson's hand-picked candidate.

140. Nationally the Democrats only lost 9 seats and kept 259 seats in the House of Representatives during the 103rd Congress. Before the election California Republican

Party Chairman Jim Dignan predicted that his party would win 29 seats in the House of Representatives. Pat Morrison, "Congress Races Being Run on Road Full of Potholes," *Los Angeles Times*, October 13, 1992, A1.

141. The Democratic congressional delegation also added 5 women for a grand total of 7.

142. Glenn F. Buntin, "Democrats Win 10-Seat Edge in Congressional Delegation," *Los Angeles Times*, November 5, 1992, SD A3.

143. Vic Fazio, for instance, spent 1.6 million, the fourth largest amount for a congressional candidate in the country. Democratic Rep. George E. Brown Jr. outspent his opponent 2 to 1 to win his sixteenth term.

144. Daniel Weintraub, "GOP Bid for Assembly Control Becomes a Long Shot," *Los Angeles Times*, October 5, 1992, A1. Almost a quarter of Republican primaries for the Assembly featured a contest between a "real" conservative and a moderate. The conservative candidates won 11 of those races but lost 5 general elections.

145. Pat Morrison, "Congress Races Being Run on Road Full of Potholes," *Los Angeles Times*, October 13, 1992, A1.

146. "Report of Registration," September 8, 2000, http://elections.cdn.sos.ca.gov/ror/ror-pages/60day-presgen-00/historical-registration-stats-60-day-close.pdf.

147. Kousser, "Reapportionment Wars," 177–83.

148. Becerra faced School Board Member Leticia Quezada. Latinos used their leverage to prevent an Anglo candidate from running. In previous races, such a scenario led to the splitting of the Latino vote and the election of the Anglo candidate. So when rumors started floating that Assemblywoman Friedman, an ally of Representatives Berman and Waxman, was a potential candidate, Latino organization passed the word that Latino elected officials would not support any statewide candidate that had links to Friedman, Berman, or Howard. Latino-elected elites prevented an Anglo challenge by leveraging their electoral weight in a crowded US Senate primary race.

149. AD 46 (Orange County) which was won by Caldera had a Latino Population of 70 percent, Latino Voting Age Population of 65 percent, and Latino Registration rate of 35 percent. AD 49 (San Diego County) won by Martínez had a LP of 55 percent, a LVAP of 51 percent and a LR of 44 percent. Brand new AD 50 (San Diego County) which was won by Escutia had a LP of 89 percent, a LVAP of 86 percent and a LR of 55 percent. AD 57 which was won by Solís had a LP of 64 percent, a LVAP of 59 percent and a LR of 40 percent. AD 58 which was won by Napolitano had a LP of 62 percent, a LVAP of 58 percent, and a LR of 44 percent.

150. Fernando Guerra and Luis Ricardo Fraga, "Theory, Reality and Perpetual Potential: Latinos in the 1992 California Elections," in *Ethnic Ironies: Latino Politics in the 1992 Elections*, eds. Rodolfo O. de la Garza and Louis DeSipio (Boulder, CO: Westview Press, 1996), 143.

151. Rhodes Cook, "Do the Math, and the Result Is: Not Much of a Contest," *Washington Post*, October 6, 2002, B3. The Republicans won a whopping 54 seats in the House of Representatives to regain the majority for the first time since 1952, 8 US Senate seats (for a 52–48 majority), and 10 governorships (from 20 to 30) along with many state legislatures.

152. He had some very close calls in the 1990s even if he managed to pull off victories. In 1990 he received a meager 52.7 percent of the votes against San Bernardino County Supervisor Rob Hammock. In 1992 famous pilot Dick Rutan limited him to 50.7 percent. The 1996 race was even tighter as he barely defeated San Bernardino County Superior Court Judge Linda Wilde with 50.5 percent, winning by only 996 votes.

153. In 1998 President Bill Clinton had so little confidence in Davis's chances of being elected governor that he pleaded with Feinstein to enter the gubernatorial race.

154. Maria Puente and Gale Holland, "'Deep Vein of Anger in California / Proposition 187 Reinforcing Divisions," *USA Today*, November 11, 1994, 8A; Gale Holland, "Proposition 187's Effects Ripple across California,"*USA Today*, November 21, 1994, 2A. For an analysis of the discriminatory nature of the initiative campaign see, for example, Kevin R. Johnson, "An Essay on Immigration Politics, Popular Democracy, and California's Proposition 187: The Political Relevance and Legal Irrelevance of Race," *Washington Law Review* 70 (1995), 629.

155. B. Drumond Ayres Jr., "California Speaker Frustrates G.O.P. One Last Time," *New York Times*, June 6, 1995, http://www.nytimes.com/1995/06/06/us/california-speaker-frustrates-gop-one-last-time.html.

156. Nancy Hill-Holzman and Jean O. Pasco, "California and the West: Doris Allen First Female Speaker of Assembly, Dies," *Los Angeles Times*, September 23, 1999, http://articles.latimes.com/1999/sep/23/news/mn-13311.

157. Lydia Chávez, *The Color Bind: California's Campaign to End Affirmative Action* (Oakland: University of California Press, 1998), 253.

158. More than two-thirds of newly registered Latino voters went to the polls in 1996. Ted Rohrlich, "Latino Voting in State Surged in 1996 Elections," *Los Angeles Times*, December 31, 1997, http://articles.latimes.com/1997/dec/31/news/mn-3813. Generally speaking, naturalized citizens tend to vote less than born-citizens. Louis DeSipio, "From Naturalized Citizen to Voter: The Context of Naturalization and Electoral Participation in Latino Communities," in *Immigration and the Border Politics and Policy in the New Latino Century*, eds., David L. Leal and José E. Limón (Notre Dame, IN: University of Notre Dame Press, 2013), 149–81.

159. For instance, locally, labor unions and immigrant rights groups showed they could channel the anger of these new voters in a Democratic primary for a seat in the Assembly in inner-city Los Angeles. These organizations organized a campaign for Gil Cedillo and identified nearly 9,000 newly registered Latino voters in a district in which there were fewer than 14,000 votes cast. They presented Cedillo as the candidate best qualified to fight Wilson, the campaign claimed to have turned out 45 percent of the new citizens on Election Day to help put Cedillo in office. Rohrlich, "Latino Voting."

160. In *League of United Latin Am. Citizens v. Wilson*, 908 F. Supp. 755, 769 (C.D. Cal. 1995) the Circuit Court struck down the initiative for intruding on the federal power to regulate immigration.

161. This created an early chasm between the two and it haunted Davis in 2003 during the recall election. Larry N. Gerston and Terry Christensen, *Recall! California's Political Earthquake* (Armonk, NY: M.E. Sharp Publisher, 2004), 41.

162. Rene Sanchez, "Divisive Proposition 187 Is Voided; Ruling Stands against Calif. Anti-Alien Law,"*Washington Post*, July 30, 1999, A03; Aurelio Rojas, "Federal Judge Rules against Proposition 187. State Cannot Regulate Immigration," *San Francisco Chronicle*, March 19, 1998, A17; Haya El Nasser, "Judge Puts Proposition 187 on Hold / Immigration Measure May Be Headed for Supreme Court," *USA Today*, November 17, 1994, A3.

163. George Skelton, "GOP's Prop. 187 Wounds Healing, But Dems Are Bleeding," *Los Angeles Times*, May 11, 2006, B3; Ed Mendel, "Group Seeks Prop. 187-Like Ballot Measure," *San Diego Union-Tribune*, December 3, 2003, A6; John Wildermuth, "Wilson Would Carry Plenty of Baggage in a Bid for Senate; Support for Prop. 187, Utility Deregulation Could Cost Him Votes," *San Francisco Chronicle*, April 20, 2003, A25.

164. In 1998 Latino and Asian Pacific children represented 40 percent and 11 percent of the California school population respectively and many of them did not speak English or did not speak English at home. That represented quite a challenge for an educational system ill-equipped to deal with what could be perceived as an opportunity in the age of globalization.

165. Terry Christensen and Larry N. Gerston, "Initiative as Catalysts for Racial Politics," in *Racial and Ethnic California: Continuity and Change*, eds., Sandra Bass and Bruce E. Cain (Berkeley, CA: Public Policy Press, 2008), 121–37.

166. In 2000, Scott beat Wildman in a race for the Senate seat vacated by Adam Schiff.

167. Tucker was sentenced to 27 months in prison in 1996 for extortion and tax evasion.

168. They were Lynn Woolsey, Nancy Pelosi, Ellen Tauscher, Anna Eshoo, Zoe Lofgren, Lucille Roybal-Allard, Maxine Waters, Jane Harman, Juanita Millender-McDonald, Loretta Sanchez, and Barbara Lee.

169. This successful initiative, which he self-financed, was opposed by all 4 gubernatorial candidates and made Ron K. Unz, the darling of the national conservative media, the new incarnation of Howard Jarvis.

170. In 2013, Jackson introduced a bill to pre-register fifteen-year-olds to vote. Now sixteen- and seventeen-year-olds in California can pre-register to vote online. She also authored the California Fair Pay Act, one of the toughest pay equity laws in the country.

171. AD 61 was designed as a minority district by the Supreme Court masters which took the Latino portion of Pomona in Los Angeles County, then swung east into San Bernardino County to pick up Ontario and Chino. Consequently, the Sixty-first is 55 percent minority, with a Latino population of 42 percent. However, Latinos accounted for only 20 percent of registered voters in 1991. That is why the district did not change parties until the end of the decade.

172. In 1991, AD 69 had a 65 percent Latino population but only 9 percent of the district's Latinos were registered to vote. The district as a whole had only 80,685 registered voters out of nearly 380,000 residents.

173. Nakano was born in the US but his family and him spent four years in internment camps during World War II.

174. Wesson ran for the Tenth District council of the city of Los Angeles in a special election in 2005. When he ran for a full term in 2007 he was elected with a comical 99.7 percent of the votes. In 2012, he became president of the City Council.

175. When Alarcón was termed out in 2006, he ran unopposed for the Thirty-ninth State Assembly District representing the San Fernando Valley area. Shortly after winning office, Alarcón expressed his intention to seek a third term in 2007 as Los Angeles City Councilman in the Seventh District, replacing Alex Padilla, who was resigning after being elected to the State Senate. He resigned from the Assembly after tenure of 102 days.

176. During the 1998 gubernatorial race she was called "the best Republican in the Democratic Party." George Skelton, "In the Ring with Contenders for Governor," *Los Angeles Times*, March 23, 1998, http://articles.latimes.com/1998/mar/23/news/mn-31902.

177. Debra J. Saunders, "The Chicken Dinners Come Home to Roots," *San Francisco Chronicle*, April 2, 1999, http://www.sfgate.com/opinion/saunders/article/Chicken-Dinners-Come-Home-to-Roost-3318760.php.

178. AD 45 was one of 6 districts drawn by the Supreme Court's master with the intent of sending a Latino candidate to the legislature. Located in East Los Angeles, the district's population is more than 63 percent Latino, although they accounted in 1991 for only about 35 percent of the registered voters. The district was also 18 percent Asian.

179. In 2000, Republican Janice C. Leja agreed not to assume her Assembly seat as part of a settlement with the Attorney General's office, in addition to pleading guilty to misdemeanor violations in relation to campaign finance reporting.

180. Japanese-American Nakanishi represented AD 10 between 2002 and 2008.

181. CD 31 was created to capture the minority communities in the area, including Alhambra and Monterey Park on the west through El Monte and Azusa on the east. The Latino population was at 58 percent but the Latino percentage of registered voters reached 41 percent.

182. Thanks to the sole female Republican Mary Bono who replaced her late husband in office, as did Democrat Lois Capps when her husband passed away also in 1998.

183. In 1998 Democratic registration rate reached 46.7 percent, Republican rate was 35.6 percent and decline to state 12.5 percent.

184. Among his election success stories are Democratic State Senators Deborah Ortiz, Liz Figueroa, and Richard Alarcón as well as Democratic Assemblyman Tony Cardenas. To try to increase the number of elected Latinos at the local level Polanco teamed up with the Los Angeles City/County Latino Redistricting Coalition, headed by Marshall Diaz, and introduced in 1998 a bill to expand the Los Angeles County Board of Supervisors. Ted Rohrlich, "Coalition Attempts to Boost Latino Election Wins," *Los Angeles Times*, December 24, 1998, B1.

185. Because ethno-racial affiliation is a personal matter, identifying someone's sense of identity is tricky. Researchers must rely on caucus membership, official biographies, ethnic organization membership or press coverage. Relying solely on last names for Latinos especially is not enough.

186. Cain and Kousser, *Adapting to Term Limits*, 11. The same figures are also available in a wider discussion of term-limits effects in California: Bruce Cain, Thad Kousser, and Karl T. Kurtz, "Institutional Imbalance: The Effects of Six-Year Term Limits in California," in *Legislating without Experience: Case Studies in Legislative Term Limits*, eds., Rick Farmer, Christopher Z. Mooney, Richard J. Powell, and John C. Green (Lanham, MD: Lexington Books, 2007), 17–42.

187. Farmer, Mooney, Powell, and Green, *Legislating*, 14. For another comparison of term-limits effects on minority in other states, see for example Stanley M. Caress, Charles Elder, Richard Elling, Jean-Philippe Faletta, Shannon K. Orr, Eric Rader, Marjorie Sarbaugh-Thompson, John Strate, and Lyke Thompson, "Effect of Term Limits on the Election of Minority State Legislators," *State and Local Government Review* 35, no. 3 (2003), 183–95. For a broader approach, see for example, Thad Kousser, *Term Limits and the Dismantling of State Legislative Professionalism* (Cambridge, MA: Cambridge University Press, 2005); Stanley M. Caress and Todd T. Kunioka, *Term Limits and Their Consequences: Aftermath of Legislative Reform* (Albany, NY: SUNY Press, 2012).

188. J. Morgan Kousser, "Has California Gone Colorblind?," in *The New Political Geography of California*, eds., Frederick Douzet, Thad Kousser, and Kenneth P. Miller (Berkeley, CA: Berkeley Public Policy Press, 2008), 282.

189. One needs to notice that inferring election success varies according to the measuring method. In California in the 1990s Latinos won almost every Assembly seat in which they represented either 70 percent of the general population or the voting population, 50 percent of citizen voting age population or Democratic registration, or 40 percent of the general registration.

190. Kousser, "Has California," 282.

Chapter 6

The Status Quo Gerrymander of 2001

MALDEF Sues the Democrats

THE POLITICAL CONTEXT OF 2001

Following the 2000 census the legislature of California found a compromise fairly quickly. After thirty years of open warfare between Democrats and Republicans, and after 6 new Democrats were elected to Congress between 1996 and 2002, most experts expected a confrontation like the ones that took place in Colorado, Pennsylvania, and Texas.[1] With a razor-thin Republican majority of 221 in the House of Representatives in 2000, all eyes would be on redistricting. The National Democratic Redistricting Project had put together a nonfederal committee called "Impact 2000." Its pamphlet stated: "2001 Redistricting is the KEY to Winning a Democratic House Majority in 2002."[2] It briefly described the population shifts by state and the legal redistricting landscape along with a breakdown of the partisan control of each state. While the document acknowledged that redistricting would probably result in partisan parity,[3] it implied that because the Republican majority was so thin that the slightest advantage especially in a large state such as California could be the difference maker and welcomed financial contribution to that end.[4] However, there was no partisan confrontation over redistricting in 2000 in California. One reason for this unexpected compromise is certainly that no party had a broad enough majority to try to maximize its number of Representatives without the risk of creating a national scandal as it was the case in other states. The Republicans, in the states where they were in charge of redistricting, were so aggressive that the controversies lasted for years. In Texas, a second round of redistricting in 2003 helped President Bush keep his bare majority in the House but eventually led to Tom Delay's downfall.[5] The tremendously Democratic strength in California increased pressure on Democrats in Sacramento to contemplate drawing favorable congressional lines to offset a loss of seats in other states but the risk of a backlash for being too greedy was great.[6]

In California, with the defeat of 4 GOP incumbents in the fall of 2000,[7] the Democrats enjoyed a 32–20 majority in the congressional delegation, which meant they could not realistically increase the number of their Representatives without the risk of producing an extremely complex electoral map that could potentially lead to two politically risky situations: a lawsuit from the Republican Party or a new referendum on redistricting reform if the redistricting bill wasn't passed with a 2–3 majority.[8] In addition, the party would have run the risk of over-diluting the Democratic vote and potentially lose some seats on the long haul because of the demographic changes not anticipated between 2001 and 2011 in some districts or because those changes are sometimes difficult to forecast as economic uncertainties shuffle populations. In short, the Democrats did not want to reach a point of diminishing returns. At least that was the rationale. The logic was sound but it set in stone the status quo. However the Republican Party became very unpopular under the Bush administration, especially with the ill-advised decision to intervene militarily in Iraq, and the Democratic turnout was exceptionally high in 2008 with a historic Barack Obama victory—so much so that the California Republican Party's registration rate decreased during the decade. Michael Berman's redistricting turned out to be as risk-averse as Phil Burton'. Contrary to state Capitol lore, Phil Burton's 1981 redistricting aimed first and foremost at protecting his allies. The most flagrant example was, of course, the protection John Burton at the expense of Phil's own district. This set the stage for 2001 when Berman proved to be as risk-averse. Consultants and elected officials wanted a two-third majority, referendum-proof bill but in the end that plan postponed Democratic and minority gains during a decade in which the Republican brand became very unpopular at the national level and especially in California.

The November 2000 victories of Democrats Jane Harman in Long Beach, Adam Schiff in Glendale and Mike Honda[9] in San Jose provided three more votes for Democrats in Congress but they also created headaches for Democratic mapmakers who needed to figure out how to strengthen and protect a trio of Anglo or Jewish incumbents in marginal districts while Latinos wanted one or two more seats in Los Angeles. If Republicans had maintained control of those districts, Democrats could have carved them up to help neighboring Democrats. Protecting Harman and Schiff might happen at the expense of Latinos. As for Honda, he captured the only district in the Bay Area held by a Republican. Any loss of population in that region would have led to the collapse of a district resulting in intraparty squabbles.[10]

If Democrats wanted to expand their number, they had to expand outside Los Angeles and the San Francisco Bay Area into places that were more competitive. That is because much of the state's growth in the 1990s came in the Central Valley, the Inland Empire, and the region between Orange County and San Diego, all more conservative than the two big metropolises. Orange County saw largely White communities transformed by large influxes of Asians and Latinos, potentially setting the stage for political changes in the Republican Party bastion.

But, with only one extra seat in 2000, their options were limited, especially since the Fifty-third District had to be created somewhere in Southern California. Party strategists looked into carving out a safe Democratic seat stretching north from the Central Valley, put the one new seat in friendly territory covering parts of the Inland Empire and Imperial Valley, and collapse the districts of two or three Republican incumbents. The potentially vulnerable candidates were David Dreier of San Dimas, Elton Gallegly of Simi Valley, Gary Miller of Diamond Bar, and Steve Horn of Long Beach.[11] After all, Representative Horn, R-Long Beach, was reelected in the fall of 2001 by less than 1,800 votes, making him a perfect redistricting target.[12] The other option consisted in parceling out new Democratic populations to strengthen existing Democratic districts that needed it, such as those of Representatives Ellen O. Tauscher in the Bay Area, Lois Capps in Santa Barbara, and Jane Harman of Rolling Hills. That second scenario had the advantage of leaving previous districts generally intact and leading to the creation of the new Fifty-third District in a major growth region such as the Inland Empire, Riverside, and San Bernardino counties.

However, to complicate matters partisan calculations cannot be separated from racial considerations. Democrats had intra-party issues as Latino groups pushed again for greater representation. Creating new districts with Latino majorities would have come at the expense of incumbents in such places as the San Fernando Valley and elsewhere around Los Angeles. Many of the areas in which the Latino population had burgeoned in the 1990s were traditionally represented by African American or Anglo leaders. There was concern in the African American community about seeing political power diluted by demographic shifts, such as in the Thirty-seventh Congressional District in southern Los Angeles County. There, African American Democratic Congresswoman Juanita Millender-McDonald represented increasingly Latino neighborhoods in Compton, Wilmington, and north Long Beach. Her district, which was 34 percent Black in 1990, had been inundated with new Latino residents.[13] However, the increase in Latino representation could not happen at the expense of African American representation.

In the legislature, the changes considered were never as dramatic because there were few places left in California with significant Democratic registration that were not already represented by Democrats. Their dominance was even more salient in the legislature where the Democrats increased their gains in 1998 and 2000. With a 50 to 30 seat majority in the Assembly and a 26–14 majority in the Senate, the Democrats were a few seats shy of a two-third majority, a tantalizing target but a difficult one to reach. In 2001, the two main political factors were term limits because of their impact on incumbents' strategies and California's new designation as a state without a racial majority. The traditional power contests between north and south, central valley and coast, urban and rural areas were not forgotten but dwarfed by most pressing issues. While in 1991, term limits had just been approved by voters and the impact was still several years off, in 2001 most state elected official were impacted by term limits. That meant that while congressional redistricting was left to DC members, California legislators were now much more interested in moving on up to a congressional seat, which has no term limits. With term limits legislators were less worried about the long-term evolution of their district and more interested in the future of the congressional seat they coveted. As a consequence, incumbent Representatives did not only want redistricting to protect them from Republican threats but also from ambitious Democrats. Assemblyman John Longville (D-Rialto), chairman of the Assembly Redistricting Committee, acknowledged this much when he declared in the press: "Understandably, members of Congress are looking over their shoulders. If I were in Congress, I'd be a little nervous."[14]

One wrinkle at the time of redistricting negotiations was the state's electricity crisis.[15] The governor had to decide if he really wanted to pick a fight over redistricting at the very same time he needed Republican support to solve the energy crisis turned into a budget crisis. Davis needed a two-third majority to pass a budget, a fact that gave badly outnumbered Republicans what little leverage they had. Besides, Gray Davis's personality or strategy was not a confrontational one. Davis could not risk bearing the brunt of voters' anger for not delivering on his vows to hold electricity prices down, ensure adequate power supplies or punish energy producers that had manipulated the markets. The prospect of skyrocketing energy prices, rolling blackouts, and the potential threat of higher taxes or budget cuts in popular programs had every member of the legislature nervous about the electorate's reaction in 2002.[16]

CREATING STATISTICS

Every ten years, before the political battle can take place, participants need to agree and the statistical data to be used. Dear to minority organizations was the census undercount.[17] The stakes are high for states such as California, Texas, and Florida, places with hard-to-count masses of new immigrants and urban poor. Studies suggest that a sampling-enhanced census, yielding higher population figures for those states, could channel hundreds of millions of dollars in federal funding to them over the next decade. Such aid would benefit programs including indigent health care, child care block grants, and vocational education. However Republicans in Congress, and among them California Republicans, opposed the Clinton administration plan to use sampling to adjust the census estimation.[18] Once again the racial/ethnic argument is inseparable from the partisan one because the plain political reality that the people who are easiest to miss in a traditional census are usually judged more likely to vote for Democrats at a time when Republicans are aiming to hold on to their tenuous majority in the House. In 1999, the Supreme Court barred the use of census sampling for the purpose of dividing congressional seats among the fifty states, yet, the ruling allowed sampling for such purposes as redrawing legislative boundaries within states and calculating how to distribute yearly federal aid to the states.

In 1980, the US Census Bureau had decided not to adjust the census because too many data were missing. In 1990, the bureau sought to adjust, but the administration overruled the bureau, finding that adjustment was unlikely to improve accuracy.[19] California's undercount in 1990 was estimated at more than 800,000, the largest in the nation. In 1992, a cross-section of the state delegation, including such influential Republicans as Representatives Dreier and Thomas petitioned, to no avail, the federal government to adjust California's 1990 census total of 29.7 million residents upward by using the results from a survey that was a de facto population sample.[20] The bureau planned to adjust the 2000 census but in the end decided not to because it turned out to be much more accurate than the one in 1990 and the two methods, the Post-Enumeration Survey (PES)[21] and demographic analysis (DA), showed conflicting estimates.[22] A 2001 study by the US Census Monitoring Board[23] found that minorities in California lost voter representation in 8 legislative districts and 1 US Congressional district when corrected census data was not released from the 1990 census. California is among the most affected states because of the systemic undercounting of minorities.[24] While generally speaking the census is fairly accurate, local differences can be very important especially in poor communities.[25] Minority group advocates explained that the use of corrected data would have enhanced minority voter opportunities by increasing the baseline of majority-minority districts. That particular fight over the type of data to be used was lost by minority groups. Although there has been a vigorous debate over using adjusted versus unadjusted census data after the 2000 census, the issues has taken a back seat as of late. The major population-related issue in the last two redistricting cycles centered more on whether to use Voting Age Population (VAP) or Citizen Voting Age Population

(CVAP) numbers when accounting for minority populations under the VRA which in California is so crucial because of the low citizenship rate in the Latino community.[26]

Another political fight in 2000 revolved around the multiracial responses. The 2000 census had a major change with a tremendous potential effect on redistricting.[27] For the first time, respondents could check more than one box in the category for race. This created up to 126 racial and ethnic categories, a significant increase from the nine categories possible in the 1990 census. As a consequence, the PL 94-171 data used in the 1990 census differed significantly from that of the 2000 census. The decision to allow people to check multiple boxes made the 1990 census data incompatible with the 2000 data. The ability to compare data over time being critical to the enforcement of civil rights laws, the Office of Management and Budget which oversees the census devised a method for allocating each of the multiple race responses back into a single race category. Any respondent checking both a minority race box and a White race box was assigned to the minority racial category. Therefore, the numbers for African American, Asian, American Indian/ Alaska Native, Native Hawaiian, or Other Pacific Islander, and some "other race" reflected single race responses and multiple race responses in which the minority race box and the white race box were checked. That way minority groups did not see any drop in their numbers because of this new racial classification method. All respondents choosing more than one minority race box comprised the "Other Multiple-Race" category which is much smaller and therefore more manageable. As in the past, the DOJ analyzed Latinos as a separate group for purposes of enforcement of the Voting Rights Act even though the census continues to call it an "ethnic" group.[28]

MINORITY INPUT

The task of processing census data into political geography used to be so daunting that in 1981, when Professor Bruce Cain was hired as a consultant by the California Assembly he sought assistance from Pasadena's Jet Propulsion Laboratory. The NASA center had one of the few computers in the country with GIS (geographic information systems) technology. In 2001, for the first time, the census data were available online to anyone with a computer, and the legislature had to draw plans for the required public hearings even though much of the work of the arcane art of redistricting was still done behind closed doors, for the first time, minority groups were able to generate their full comprehensive maps and answer every criticism from the legislature with statistical accuracy.[29] In California, thanks to the work of Bruce Cain, all the data necessary to draw districts such as electoral boundaries, census figures and past election results could be downloaded from the statewide database from the Institute for Governmental Studies' website.[30] Minority groups intended to take full advantage of this technological evolution, especially the two groups that felt they had not been treated fairly in the past: Asian Americans and Latinos. Their disappointment in 2001 was commensurate to the level of hope they had built up prior to redistricting.

As we mentioned before, the position of racial groups was weakened because the Voting Rights Act, which was such an important source of leverage in 1991, no longer wielded the same force. The US Supreme Court ruled that race could not be the "predominant" factor during redistricting in cases such as *Shaw v. Reno* (1993) and *Miller v. Johnson* (1995).[31] As the California state legislature began its public hearings in 2001 another Supreme Court decision *Hunt v. Cromartie* (532 U.S. 234 [2001]) declared that race could be taken into consideration as long as it was not the "dominant and controlling" factor which cleared some confusion as to whether race could be used at all. And as the courts reduced the importance of race as a redistricting factor they elevated "traditional" districting principles such as compactness, contiguity, respect of political subdivision and, of course, the very vague but essential "community of interest."[32]

Moreover, racial/ethnic groups in California had to worry about conflicts among themselves. Changing demographics, especially in the Los Angeles Basin, created enclaves where incumbents of one race/ethnicity represented population centers dominated by another.[33] Lynwood, for instance, was represented in the Assembly by Democrat Carl Washington, an African American. But Latinos now made up the majority of the district residents and were fast becoming a majority of the voting population as well.[34] The 1997 mayoral election in Los Angeles is probably a turning point in that regard because for the first time the Latino vote surpassed the African American vote.[35]

Jewish-Latino tensions surfaced during a brutal 1998 State Senate primary in the San Fernando Valley between two Democrats: former minority leader in the Assembly Richard Katz and Los Angeles City Councilman Richard Alarcón.[36] Alarcón won by a razor-thin margin,[37] but the resentments spawned by that campaign were barely beginning to fade. Deeper conflicts could surface when Latinos, Jews, African Americans, Anglos, and Asians try to sort out contested territories. To head off these potential conflicts, several groups started to coordinate their efforts at the national level. Ahead of the 2000 round of redistricting the MALDEF, the NAACP Legal Defense Fund and the National Asian Pacific American Legal Consortium released an almost 100-page free redistricting guide, the first of its kind, aimed at educating non-Anglo communities about the importance of redistricting and participation in that process.[38] It was distributed widely at redistricting workshops across the state.[39] The three organizations also put together a one-day conference in May 2001 on the UCLA campus. There are probably many reasons why these communities decided in 2000 to unite. Leland Saito proposed a few: "the new legal framework that made race subordinate to traditional criteria; the complexity of the redistricting process, given the multiple ways that urban space can be divided up into communities of interests; an understanding that the state legislature controls redistricting; and gerrymandering which has historically fragmented minority communities."[40]

Since in the 1990s, the Latino population had soared by 43 percent. California's 11 million Latinos represented in 2000 31 percent of its population. MALDEF and the William C. Velasquez Institute pushed to draw a new House district into the San Joaquin Valley that could help elect another Latino House Member. Latino groups wanted to create a new Fifty-third Congressional District that would include most of Tulare County and the city of Fresno in the agriculture-rich Central Valley.[41] Those areas represented at the time by Republican Representatives Cal Dooley, Bill Thomas, and George Radanovich. The region fell just south of the Modesto-based district of Democrat Representative Gary Condit, whose political and legal woes assured he would play the role of the proverbial sacrificial lamb.[42] The new proposed district would have been nearly 47 percent Latino. The groups also wanted to amass large Latino bases in the Long Beach–based district of Representative Steve Horn and the Palm Springs–based district of Representative Mary Bono, another Republican. Horn's Thirty-eighth District would have changed dramatically under the groups' plan. The Thirty-eighth would have shifted the primarily Latino cities of Huntington Park, Cudahy, South Gate, Lynwood, Paramount, Bellflower and parts of other nearby cities into one district. The new district would have been about 69 percent Latino. The plan for Bono's Forty-Fourth District would have joined Imperial County with parts of Riverside County to unite Latino communities in the southeast part of the state. That district would have been nearly 50 percent Latino.

In 2001, Asian Americans played a bigger role in electoral politics in California. They had obtained more rights with extension of Section 203 in 1992 and had dabbled in redistricting in 1990.[43] Now the Asian community also had allies in the legislature. George Nakano, one of four APIAs in the Assembly (representing the Fifty-third District in the South Bay) served on the Assembly Election and Reapportionment Committee. The presence of Nakano and three other APIA Assembly members, especially during behind the scenes redistricting negotiations, proved vital in enhancing the strength and voice of the APIA community.[44] The Coalition of Asian Pacific Americans for Fair Redistricting[45] (led among others by Kathay Feng of the Asian

Pacific American Legal Center of Southern California) caught the attention of legislators when the organization proposed a carefully sculpted Assembly plan that its drafters said could help elect up to 10 candidates of its growing communities.[46] The proposed districts would have a plurality of Asian Pacific Americans, but not a majority. The group rationale was that in efforts to elect candidates of their choice those voters would form coalitions with like-minded organizations, perhaps African American or Latino community activists.[47]

> Groups like MALDEF and NAACP-LDF had much more experience in the redistricting process than CAPAFR, and much could be learned from working with these groups. Also, a unified proposal presenting the interests of all three groups would eliminate the possibility that individual group interests would be pitted against each other by the legislature. More importantly, a cross racial coalition strategy would embody the larger goal of achieving voting rights through adherence to larger social justice principles. In the 2001 round of redistricting, grass-roots work addressing both intra-group and inter-group unity proved beneficial for APIA interests in the redistricting process.[48]

Assembly and Senate redistricting committee hearings around the state drew sparse crowds, and proposed maps were introduced by only two groups: MALDEF and CAPAFR.[49] Latinos and Asian Americans proved that they could work together as they agreed for instance on the Forty-ninth Assembly District boundaries in the western San Gabriel Valley. The district of Assembly woman Judy Chu (D-Monterey Park) shed 6 percent of its Latino population to reach 46 percent and increased its Asian American population by 3 percent to reach 39 percent. The Anglo population increased by 3 percent and reached 12 percent.[50] MALDEF supported the new district boundaries even though it reduced its population because it understood that this area was crucial for its Asian American redistricting partners. The Latino population in this area did not grow very fast while the Asian American population was booming. Instead MALDEF wanted to focus on fast-growing Latino population areas such as southeastern Los Angeles. And since the MALDEF proposal also split the Asian American population in the San Gabriel Valley in 2 congressional districts it can be seen as case of give and take.[51] Besides, research has shown that Asians (and for that matter African Americans) and Latinos in California can vote cohesively as a group.[52]

In the end minority input was neglected, as it was anticipated by most observers, even before the process had started in earnest. A. G. Block, editor-in-chief of the *California Journal*, observed:

> Some observers think the Legislature will respond by closing the door to outside groups. Its relevant committees may hold public hearings, but they'll merely

> serve as a front for the real work done in private. In the Assembly, the Elections and Reapportionment Committee bears the mandate for redistricting, and chairman John Longville (D-Rialto) believes his panel will play a substantial role in fashioning the new seats. Few insiders believe Longville's committee will do anything but put a public face on the process, with the real work done behind the scenes by, among others, Cavala in the Speaker's Office of Majority Services. The situation is even murkier in the upper house. As of February, Senate President pro Tempore Burton had yet to name a chairman of the Senate Elections and Reapportionment Committee nor assign any members to it, fueling speculation that the committee itself will be virtually irrelevant to the process.[53]

The only minority group that seemed to obtain concession from the legislature were African Americans who were in a different situation than Latinos and Asian Americans because their demographic relative strength was dwindling and they were not trying to gain seats but to only keep the ones they held. For instance, African American groups complained the revised redistricting plan called for Meadowview to remain in Sacramento's Ninth Assembly District. Critics had charged that moving about 36,000 minority voters out of south Sacramento into the more rural Seventeenth Assembly District, represented by Barbara Matthews (D-Tracy), would reduce the chances for an African American candidate to succeed Darrell Steinberg (D-Sacramento), who faced term limits in 2004. Under the revised plan, Matthews' district picked up the Democratic voters it needed by extending farther south to include all of Merced County.

THE GREAT COMPROMISE OF 2001

The Republicans appeared, at first, to be divided on the strategy to adopt toward redistricting. Representative Jerry Lewis resigned in May 2001 as head of the state's GOP House delegation after a series of flare-ups over how Republicans should deal with the state's Democratic-controlled redistricting process. Representative Bill Thomas, the soon-to-be chair of Ways and Means in the House of Representatives, had sought to take the lead on plotting their party's remap strategy. Thomas had some background in redistricting. In 1999, he co-sponsored an unsuccessful effort to place a voter initiative on the 2000 ballot that would have shifted control of redistricting from the state legislature to the courts.[54] Bill Thomas maintained his position throughout the process that the "incumbent protection" plan was "not in the public's interest." "I have always said it is wrong for incumbents to draw districts to protect incumbents of either party," Thomas said. "There will be no opportunity for the voters in California to defeat or elect a candidate of the party opposite to the one for which the seat was drawn. That is wrong."[55] Thomas believed that uncompetitive congressional races gave voters no real opportunity to be heard, and that by locking themselves into a minority status this way, Republicans were compromising their own chances of making a comeback in California. Moreover, Thomas also thought that, at some point, Republicans would need to attract significant Latino votes and that, by agreeing to place most of the state's Latino voters in uncompetitive Democratic districts, Republicans risked distancing themselves from these voters therefore making it that much harder to make inroads in the community in the future. His reasoning was sound but Thomas made no headway in his own party and short-term pragmatism prevailed.

By August 2001 legislative leaders of both parties officially declared they sought to adopt plans that preserved the bipartisan status quo that would tighten the Democratic lock, but also allowed Republicans to keep their relatively few seats without the prospect of further weakening. Senator Don Perata (D-Alameda), chief architect of the Senate plan declared: "Our goal is for a status quo reapportionment, I think if we do it right, we will have a bipartisan plan that will not be challenged" by a statewide referendum or in front of the Republican-dominated Supreme Court.[56] His counterpart Senate GOP Leader Jim Brulte of Rancho Cucamonga acknowledged that bipartisan cooperation was dictated by political pragmatism: "We Republicans have an incentive to work with Democrats because we know they can do the redistricting without us. They have an incentive to work with us because they know we can do a referendum and throw it into the court."[57] Assembly Speaker Bob Hertzberg (D-Sherman Oaks) concurred: "If we can pass a bipartisan plan, it takes the whole edge off."[58] Democrats would avoid an all-out conflict and Republicans were guaranteed to not lose seats.

Political consultant Michael Berman, Representative Howard Berman's brother, was hired both by Senate President Pro Tempore John Burton, to do the Senate redistricting, and by Democrats in the California congressional delegation all chipped in $20,000 each to pay for his services on their behalf.[59] The secretive Berman was now the veteran of four redistricting cycles.

When the new plans were unveiled unsurprisingly most incumbents were protected.[60] In the House Ellen Tauscher's seat was turned solidly Democratic but as expanded in a very smart way to include more liberal, labor-oriented areas in order to force her to walk the party line more closely.[61] The Central Valley district of Representative Richard Pombo (R-Tracy) now stretched into Alameda and Contra Costa counties, giving the Bay Area its only GOP member of Congress even if his presence was short-lived. The only contested primary battles would take place because of term limits in the Assembly:

Dion Aroner (D-Berkeley) and Lynne Leach (R-Walnut Creek) were term limited.

The strongest opposition in passing the bipartisan redistricting plan came in the Assembly, where backers narrowly rounded up the two-thirds support needed for the Senate and congressional plan. A majority of Latino Assembly members only backed the plan once mapmakers had made last-minute changes to the congressional plan to increase Latino voting strength in Southern California districts. However, MALDEF was angered by the San Fernando Valley district drawn for Representative Howard Berman by his brother. Latino redistricting advocates cheered creation of the proposed Fifty-third Congressional District. Some, however, were angered by what they said was the arbitrary splitting up of Latino communities in the San Fernando Valley between districts now held by Democrats Howard L. Berman of Mission Hills and Brad Sherman of Sherman Oaks. The United Farm Workers had a good relationship with Berman who championed farm issues but keeping him in DC came at a steep price. The Democrats replaced the district's largely Latino neighborhoods in Pacoima, San Fernando, and Arleta (some 170,000 people) with mainly non-Latino communities in Sherman Oaks, Studio City, Toluca Lake, and Burbank.[62] The Latino population in Berman's Twenty-sixth District was reduced from 66 percent to 40 percent and the Latino Voting Age population from 60 percent to 35 percent when heavily Latino communities were moved into Sherman's Twenty-seventh District.[63] The share of registered voters in the district who are Latino fell from about 40 percent to 18 percent.[64] With a click of a mouse the Democrats managed to turn the Latino registration efforts back ten years in this area which was understandably unacceptable for MALDEF.[65] Those objections drew support from State Senator Richard Polanco (D-Los Angeles), the dean of the Latino caucus in the legislature, who said the redistricting proposal would need to be modified before it could be approved by the legislature.[66]

The MALDEF threatened to sue if the plan was signed into law and it wasn't the only minority organization unhappy with the legislature's proposals. Because of their limited resources, APALC and CAPAFR concentrated their efforts on Assembly districts which cover smaller areas and therefore gave Asian Americans a better chance to form districts in which they would have an influential vote. They especially complained that the San Jose neighborhood of Berryessa was split among four state Assembly districts, even though over half of Berryessa's population was Asian American or Pacific Islander and, according to activists, were sharing common interests and needs.[67] Another example of APIA vote dilution would be San Francisco, which had an Asian American population of 31 percent and was divided between two newly redrawn districts, the Twelfth and the Thirteenth. The Thirteenth Assembly District, located entirely within the city, was only 23 percent Asian American. The Twelfth Assembly District, which took in the western half of San Francisco and half of Daly City, was 42 percent Asian American. The number of Asian Americans in the Twelfth was boosted by the inclusion of half of Daly City, which was itself 50 percent Asian Americans. But since they had only analyzed Assembly districts, APALC and CAPAFR did not consider filing a lawsuit regarding the Senate and congressional districts. However they also believed that the Asian American population in the San Gabriel Valley was split. The 4 cities with the largest Asian American populations (Monterey Park, Rosemead, Alhambra, San Gabriel) were split into 3 Senate districts (Twenty-one, Twenty-two, and Twenty-four) and 2 congressional districts (Twenty-nine and Thirty-two).[68] Monterey Park was split between two congressional districts.[69] During hearings Kathey Feng asked the legislature to reconsider: "We do ask that you revisit the Senate and congressional configurations which have carved this west San Gabriel Valley area up into so many pieces as to create a virtual glass ceiling for our community's representation at these higher levels of government."[70]

Map makers usually have too many factors to take into account when redrawing district lines. As is always the case in redistricting, it is virtually impossible to satisfy all interests especially when partisan stakes are so high. For instance, environmentalists found themselves battling some of their closest allies in the Legislature, including Senate President Pro Tem John Burton (D-San Francisco), when they protested against the Senate redistricting plan.[71]Burton also played a key role in changing the lines of his own San Francisco-based district to help his old ally, San Francisco Mayor Willie Brown, returned to the Legislature after his term as mayor ended. The new Senate lines split the heart of San Francisco's gay community, the Castro district, and thus eroded the base that Assemblywoman Carole Migden or some other gay or lesbian candidate would have needed to run for the Senate. Another group was women elected officials. Democratic Assemblywomen complained that they were drawn into Republican State Senate districts, blocking their path to higher office.[72]

Democrats in 2001 limited the increase of Latino districts, because of the Republican Party's weak standing with the Latino community Democrats knew Latinos had nowhere else to go and Democrats decided to protect all incumbents and the status quo. The Senate validated the bills by a 38–2 vote and the Assembly by a 65–8 vote.[73] On September 17, 2001, Governor Gray Davis signed the redistricting bills into law, four days later MALDEF filed a lawsuit on behalf of 24 registered voters.[74]

BERMAN BROTHERS V. MALDEF

As in previous decades, it was on the familiar terrain of political representation of minorities that the California redistricting was attacked.[75] However, using the same arguments as in the 1990s, as its population continued to increase, the Latino community did not win its case. One of the reasons for this loss was national: the Supreme Court jurisprudence reduced the power of the Voting Rights Act in the 1990s and early 2000s, and limited in its impact on the round of redistricting 2001. The other factor was that incumbent protection has always been considered a "traditional" redistricting principal. In *Cano v. Davis* the Court decided to see partisanship at work while MALDEF thought it was race/ethnicity. Howard Berman declared in the press that he was "terribly disappointed" that MALDEF had filed its suit. "For thirty years in public office, I have not merely voted for, but have led the legislative battles to enact issues of importance to the Latino community," he said. "I guess for MALDEF, it's more about skin color and ethnicity than the philosophy and the quality of representation." Michael Berman, breaking his usual silence in such matters, said that overall his plan "massively protected Latino voting power" statewide.[76]

Once again Los Angeles County is a fascinating case study since it illustrates all the paradoxes of redistricting in general but in California in particular. LA County offers the perfect political climate to exacerbate the tensions of political power distribution that is the art of redistricting. The fights for the distribution of political power to control public spending and the allocation of tax burden have taken place almost entirely among Democratic constituencies competing for resources, revenues and services. In this context, redistricting is more urgent than it might otherwise be. The San Fernando Valley is especially fascinating. It was an Anglos stronghold in the 1970s. It became the epitome of defensive White conservative middle class opposed to court-ordered school busing and rising property tax. It became a center (some would argue the birth place) of the tax revolt that produced Proposition 13 in 1978 that helped Reagan win the White House. In 1980, Bobbi Fiedler, a leader of a valley anti-busing group, won an upset election to Congress as a Republican.[77] But in two decades, Latinos, Asian Americans, and liberal Anglos crossed the mountains to the north and west and replaced the aggrieved conservative electorate that had dominated the valley transforming it into one of the most racially diverse areas in the US.

The California population increased by 4.1 million in the 1990s, an increase that was mainly due to the growth of the Latino population. In Los Angeles as a whole, the proportion of Latinos in the population almost tripled, from 18.5 percent in 1970 to 46.5 percent in 2000, and the percentage of Asians has grown from 3.7 to 9.9 percent. African-Americans declined from 17.3 percent of the population to 10.9 percent, but the falloff was sharpest for Anglos, who went from 60.1 percent to 29.7 percent. Moreover, the 2000 census contained a big surprise for Democrats since areas controlled by the Democrats and composed primarily of minority groups saw their population decline. This was particularly true in the Los Angeles County. To maintain the same number of Democrats Michael Berman had to increase the population in each of the 10 congressional districts in the county by 45,000 people on average.[78] Equal population is not a problem in itself. Capturing voters in neighboring districts is not necessarily very complicated, even if history has proven that a trial or a referendum is always a possibility. But the type of people who moved from the county and the type of people needed to replace them was the major issue here. Indeed, the percentage of Anglo and African American voters had decreased in the county. Latino groups wanted the number of Latino-majority districts to increase to reflect this demographic change. But, practically, it meant reducing the number of Anglo and/or African American elected officials. Of the 16 districts that composed (fully or partially) Los Angeles County in 2001, four had a Latino representative, while Latinos accounted for 45 percent of the county population. The governor could not sign a redistricting bill reducing the number of African American Congressmen for obvious political reasons. And MALDEF never asked for another minority group to lose representation. The loss would have to be carried exclusively by Anglo Congressmen. But Anglo incumbents were untouchable. Starting with Howard Berman, Michael's brother, who had the ultimate protection.[79] When the Berman plan became public Sherman, realizing his district's Latino population had gone from 20 percent to 52 percent, forced a redraft of the map to equalize the Latino population between Howard Berman's district, now with a 55.6 percent Latino population and his, with a more manageable 36.5 percent Latino population.[80] The move appeased Sherman but not Latino organizations.[81] Eight Anglo and African American Democrats were protected at the expense, in some way, of the Latino population which was ultimately perceived as a threat to non-Latino incumbents. The Democrats were willing to provoke the wrath of Latinos to ensure the reelection of incumbent candidates of both parties and maintain the status quo to reach a two-third veto-proof vote. They tried to convince in vain many Latino organizations that their gains would be achieved at the expense of the Republicans, but the demographic and political realities were telling a different story. According to MALDEF, despite the fact that 80 percent of the population growth in the state in the 1990s was due to the Latino population because of racial polarization, Latinos only had an opportunity to elect a candidate of their choice in nine of the state's 53 congressional districts and seven of the State Senate's

40 districts. Ultimately MALDEF pitted itself against Democratic incumbent Representatives Berman and Filner and lost.MALDEF, with its experience from the 1990s, attacked the redistricting plans for the Congress and Senate, arguing that they violated Section 2 of the Voting Rights Act (preventing vote dilution) and the Equal Protection Clause of the Fourteenth Amendment (preventing racial gerrymandering).[82]

The Latino community unevenly supported MALDEF in its suit. Elected officials tend to question the legitimacy of organizations such as MALDEF when they do not go in their direction. Some wanted to maximize the number of elected officials of their group, because the census showed that the Latino population represented 32 percent of the state population in 2000. Others argued that the Latino community represented only 16 percent of voters, while Latinos elected officials represented 22.5 percent and 23.7 percent of the Senate of the Assembly, indicating that political representation of Latinos was satisfactory. Thirteen State Senate or congressional seats were kept or strengthened by the plans of 2001 and a new Latino seat was created in Congress. After all, MALDEF only challenged 3 of the 93 districts of the two plans. Many politicians, perhaps satisfied with their assured reelection, and aware of the difficulty of finding a compromise on a sensitive subject, did not hesitate to criticize the MALDEF lawsuit. State Senator Don Perata (D-Alameda), who as chairman of the Senate redistricting committee conducted the congressional maps through the legislature, called the suit "ridiculous" and noted that 23 of the 26 Latino legislators voted for the redistricting plans (all 7 Senators and 16 out of 19 Assembly members). In a sworn declaration to the court in support of the plan he stated: "It is a dishonor to the Latino representatives who serve in Sacramento [the state capital] for MALDEF to say they participated in intentional racial discrimination . . . [that] California's Latino elected officials participated in a plan to cancel out Latino votes, or that they are somehow less capable than unelected private groups like MALDEF of protecting the interests of their Latino constituents."[83]AB 632 was carried in the Assembly by Assemblyman Gil Cedillo (D-Los Angeles). Referring to the breadth of Latino legislative support, Cedillo declared:

> This is significant and very positive, because it is distinguished from our recent past, when our communities have had to depend on the courts or advocacy groups outside the legislative process to . . . protect the rights of groups in our society. And so today things are different. We, the voting representatives—the representatives of the communities who have sent us here—can speak directly for our communities to safeguard their democratic rights through the representative process. This direct power and participation marks a new era of openness and democracy for us, one in which we need not insist that we are so powerless that we must take our grievances to other non-representative institutions.[84]

Advocating for a multiracial coalition, Martha Escutia and Gloria Romero, representing the Thirtieth and the Twenty-fourth Senate Districts, in their letter to the *Los Angeles Times*, called the trial "frivolous and racially divided." They added:

> MALDEF claims that Berman's 55.6 percent Latino district is not "Latino enough." But the voters in the new Berman district have demonstrated a willingness to support progressive candidates of any race. Residents in the areas that comprise the new district voted for Antonio Villaraigosa for mayor and for Rocky Delgadillo for city attorney in the recent Los Angeles city election and voted overwhelmingly for Cruz Bustamante for Lieutenant Governor . . . The elections of State Sens. Deborah Ortiz (D-Sacramento) and Liz Figueroa (D-Fremont) in non-Latino areas demonstrate that a strong Latino candidate need not have a district packed with Latino votes. . . . Latinos need not limit themselves to only seeking office in "safe" Latino districts. We should not relegate ourselves to only a few court-imposed barrios. Our success lies in proclaiming that the Latino agenda is (and should be) the American agenda.[85]

MALDEF lawyers argued, first, that the Latino community of the San Fernando Valley was divided in two which prevented the election of a Latino Congressman (CD28).[86] The ulterior motive was to protect Representative Howard Berman. Second, they argued that four neighborhoods of San Diego (Barrio Logan, Logan Heights, Golden Hills, and City Heights) had been excluded from the Fifty-first District to protect Representative Bob Filner. Third, they argued the Latino population concentration in the Thirtieth Senate District was too high (75 percent) which deprived its neighbor, the Twenty-seventh Senate District (southeast of Los Angles), of Latino population. With this extra Latino population the Twenty-seventh Senate District could have been a majority-minority district. Ten year earlier these claims might have had more weight. For example, the Fifty-First Congressional District did have an unorthodox shape. But in ten years the jurisprudence on racial gerrymandering had evolved. MALDEF requested that the Court block temporarily the four primaries from taking place as scheduled in March to which Senate's lawyer, Jonathan Steinberg, replied that "it would make Bush versus Gore look like child's play."[87] Again the national context did not play in MALDEF's favor.

The three-judge court, composed of Margaret Morrow, Christina Snyder and Stephen Reinhardt, all Democratic appointees, in *Cano v. Davis* (211 F.Supp.2d 1208 [C.D. Cal. 2002]), examined racial polarization in the 2000 cycle within two relevant areas of Los Angeles County: the area comprising Senate District Twenty-seven, and the area comprising Congressional District Twenty-eight.[88] The court found that Latino voters in this area voted cohesively; indeed, it found "overwhelming" evidence in the record that Latinos throughout Los Angeles County voted monolithically for Latino candidates.[89] The court found that Latino voters in this area also "unquestionably" voted cohesively.[90] But under Gingles condition 3, it found that in significant relevant portions of Senate District Twenty-seven (Cerritos, Bellflower, Lynwood, and Bell), non-Latino voters in 2000 sufficiently supported Latino-favored candidates that the Latino community was not deprived of the effective opportunity to elect its candidates of choice.[91] And the Court noted that plaintiffs in this case had not identified for the record any Latino-preferred candidate defeated in the areas of that district. Therefore the Court declared that what the plaintiffs were looking for was "a redistricting plan that contains the maximum number of majority-Latino districts possible. This is not a requirement of constitutional districting."[92] As with Senate District Twenty-seven, however, the Court found that under Gingles condition 3, non-Latino voters in 2001 and 2002 in the district showed sufficient support for Latino-preferred candidates that a single defeated Latino candidate in 1998 did not demonstrate that the Latino community in the district was usually deprived of the effective opportunity to elect its candidates of choice.[93] Without "White Bloc Voting" or with some evidence of "racial cross-over" the Court dismissed the claim that voting was as polarized as MALDEF pretended even though the *Garza* case had found a decade earlier that Los Angeles County was racially polarized.[94] As for discrimination the Court found that: "The evidence in the record is also uncontroverted that Latino legislators and interest groups played a significant role in the 2001 redistricting process with respect to both CD 28 and CD 51."[95] According to the Court the plan did not try to influence one group over the other because of the districts' diversity:

> They cannot, under any fair reading, be characterized as "White districts" or "Caucasian districts." Nor are they districts that can only be reasonably understood to "belong" to one ethnic or racial group. To the contrary, the districts at issue here are diverse and multiethnic: each contains a variety of racial and ethnic groups; none unites any single group of individuals within its boundaries for the purpose of permitting that group to exercise hegemony. In fact, Latinos are the largest number of persons in any single racial or ethnic group in each district, and the number of whites in each case is substantially lower. In CD 28, for example, the voting-age population is 49.2 percent Latino, 37.2 percent White, 6.9 percent Asian, and 4.3 percent Black. Congressional District 51 is even more diverse: in that district the voting-age population is 49 percent Latino, 25.1 percent white, 13.8 percent Asian, and 9.7 percent black. There is no evidence that the legislature sought to ensure that voters of any particular race would dominate either district.[96]

Morgan Kousser in his testimony stated that "the Assembly plan seems largely unobjectionable"[97] but concluded that as far as Congressional District

Twenty-eight and Senate District Twenty-seven were concerned: "The blatant numerical patterns and the demonstrable foreknowledge of discrimination in these districts by themselves create a strong prima facie case that they were adopted with a discriminatory intent. Abundant qualitative evidence . . . supports this conclusion."[98] Kousser breaks down the population move from Berman to Sherman's district to conclude: "But it is possible that one could defend the shift of Latinos from Berman's to Sherman's district on partisan ground. . . . The only difficulty with this plausible explanation is that the facts do not support it. . . . A partisan motive in the case cannot substitute for a racial one."[99] The Court responded: "While he focuses heavily on evidence of intent, Dr. Kousser does not squarely address whether the legislature neglected traditional districting principles." The Court concluded: "The legislature's adherence to such [traditional] principles is fatal to plaintiffs' Shaw claim."[100] As previously mentioned these principals are compactness, contiguity, preservation of county lines or subdivisions, preservation of communities of interest, preservation of core or prior district and, of course, last but not least, protection of incumbents. The outside observer can be surprised by the idea that these other redistricting principles would be considered to not have any racial effects. Accepting that traditional principals are race neutral seems at best naïve and at worst a misconception of the central role that race plays in American history and politics.

However, MALDEF thought it had the proverbial smoking gun to prove intent. In a declaration filed in US District Court in Los Angeles as part of the MALDEF lawsuit, Assemblyman Juan Vargas, a San Diego Democrat and one of Assembly Speaker Robert Hertzberg's lieutenants who had twice run against the Democratic Congressman Bob Filner, said that consultant Michael Berman told him he had "to divide Hispanics; Filner won't survive otherwise. And you just want to see him die a slow death."[101] Because federal voting rights laws prohibit mapmakers from "deliberately choosing to exclude or include voters based on their ethnicity" to influence election outcomes, MALDEF thought they had good case of blatant intentional discrimination.[102] Vargas also declared that Berman told him "that every Democratic member of Congress was supposed to pay him $20,000" and those who did not "might not like their districts." While Berman's fees had been disclosed and were no secret, Vargas' declaration provided a rare behind-the-scenes account of personal, ethnic, and legal disputes that are often part of the secretive process of redistricting. Perata said legislators redrew Filner's new district to make it more heavily Latino at Vargas' request.[103] Latinos still accounted for 53 percent of the VAP in Filner's new Fifty-first Congressional District. They did so by giving Filner heavily Latino Imperial County. Filner could handle 53 percent because he had a twenty-year history of winning elections in majority Latino districts, including his two races against Vargas which made Vargas's declaration look like that of a sore loser. But Vargas, in his declaration, said the Assembly came up with an alternative plan that included Imperial County and the four Latino neighborhoods in San Diego. Vargas declared Berman told him Filner wouldn't accept the Assembly alternative because it had too many Latinos. "Michael Berman told me, 'I have a fiduciary responsibility to Filner to draw a district where he won't lose to you or a Hispanic in the primary,' Vargas said. Furthermore, Vargas said Berman told him, "I'd have to give (Filner) his money back." The 600,000 dollars to redraw the congressional district lines seems like a lot of money for most Californians and raises question about the public's interest and potential conflict of interest. In spite of all this, the Court saw a personal partisan bitter fight where MALDEF saw anti-Latino discrimination. The Court found no discriminatory intent because other factors could supposedly explain the districts: "Plaintiffs contend that, having put forward some evidence of intent, they have no burden other than to meet any non-racial explanations for the district proffered by defendants."[104] And the Court concluded: "Assuming plaintiffs' proffered evidence to be true, we seriously question whether it raises a genuine issue of fact with respect to the type of invidious intent required under Bolden."[105] Some lawyers involved in the case wondered what more evidence a court might need to actually prove intent. And the Court brought the lawsuit to a close by stating: "The legislature lawfully chose to exercise its considerable discretion in redistricting to create three districts in which Latinos are the largest single ethnic or racial group, in which Latinos will inevitably play a significant role in the election of representatives, and in which Latino candidates may well be elected to office when the current incumbents leave their posts if not before. Moreover, Latinos participated fully in the redistricting process and elected Latino representatives, many of whom hold important positions in the state legislature, overwhelmingly approved the redistricting plan."[106] With a Supreme Court jurisprudence that never precisely defined what constitutes an influence district or a minority-majority district, and for good reason because it varies over time and regions, judges have ample room to defer to the legislatures: "The crux of plaintiffs' argument, and the crux of the debate surrounding CD 28 during the redistricting process, is the fact that the legislature's plan reduced the percentage of Latinos in the district. Latino advocacy groups wanted another majority-Latino district created, while the legislature originally proposed creating two Latino influence districts. The legislature, as previously noted, had no obligation to maximize the number of majority-Latino districts drawn."[107] MALDEF appealed the decision to the more conservative Supreme Court which unanimously affirmed the lower court's summary judgment. The verdict proved to be as divisive as redistricting itself.[108] What the Cano case illustrates is the political tension between minority activists who try to increase the number of representatives from their community and their historic allies in the Democratic Party, may they be the leaders who try to increase their majority or incumbents who seek personal security and reelection. This case illustrates what Bruce Cain already observed in 1991:

> Minority officeholders tend to pursue a more party-oriented strategy (especially once elected to office) while community activists and organizations (e.g., LULAC, NAACP, MALDEF) tend to adopt a more special interest approach. A second trend in American electoral politics, which constrains minority political strategies is the growing importance of the incumbency advantage. . . . First it places the elected incumbent in a powerful position within minority political communities. . . . A second implication of the incumbency advantage for California's minorities is that it places an even greater focus on redistricting and litigation as a means of enhancing the prospect of minority representation.[109]

PARTISAN AND RACIAL RESULTS

The 2001 redistricting bipartisan deal meant most competitive seats occurred in the primaries. As exit polls from the *Los Angeles Times* confirmed, the midterm primary, with its historically low turnout, brought conservative Republicans into the booth (57 percent of the Republicans who voted in the primary considered themselves conservatives, as opposed to 38 percent who described themselves as liberal/moderate). That dynamic played havoc with the ambitions of moderate GOP candidates, mostly for the legislature, nearly all of whom lost when confronted with a conservative opponent. On the Democratic side, moderates, the so-called "new Democrats," also suffered at the hands of liberals, who voted in greater numbers than did moderates. The legislature that convened in December featured a more conservative Republican caucus and a more liberal Democratic one, with less centrist legislators even though they are crucial for any deal making and therefore governing.[110] For this reason, partisan gerrymandering protecting incumbents is often thought of as being the source, or at least responsible in part, of partisan polarization.[111]

Overall, in 2002 Democrats gained a congressional district to give them 33 of the state's 52-seat delegation. They won the only seat that was considered competitive formerly held by Democrat Gary Condit (CD 18 in Merced County). Democrats lost ground in the legislature, however. Their edge in the State Senate fell to 25–15 with the loss of SD 12 (Merced). Assembly

Democrats lost two seats (AD 78[112] and AD 80[113]) and nearly dropped a third (AD 30[114]), although they still enjoyed a 48–32 margin in the lower house.

Turnout, especially among Latinos, was the main reason why Democrats lost legislative seats. According to a *Los Angeles Times* exit poll, Latino turnout plunged to 10 percent, –4 points below 1998 and back to pre-Proposition. 187 levels. The upward trend in Latino voting, which has been a boon to Democrats since 1996, seemed, in 2002, to have lurched into reverse. In 2002, Latinos absence seems to have made a difference. A case in point is Imperial County, which was 60 percent Latino and where Democrats outnumbered Republicans nearly 2 to 1. Turnout in Imperial County was 35 percent, helping Republican Bonnie Garcia carry the county en route to victory in AD 80.[115] Another interesting case helps put turnout in perspective. In this mostly White, affluent LA district, Republican Tony Goss won only 30 percent of the vote against incumbent Democrat Henry Waxman. That translated into more than 53,000 votes. But Goss received more total votes than Democratic winners in 6 other districts (Cal Dooley, Xavier Becerra, Lucille Roybal-Allard, Linda Sanchez, Joe Baca, and Loretta Sanchez), most of whom captured two-thirds of the vote in districts where more than 60 percent of the population is Latino. These figures need to be put in perspective with scholarly works that suggest that majority-minority district increase voter participation.[116] In a sense Democrats by striking a bipartisan deal may not have served their long-term electoral interest.

In the congressional delegation minority representation numbers stagnated. In 2002, right after redistricting, the number of Latinos was 7, the number of African Americans was 4, and the number of Asian Americans was 2. By 2010, the number of African Americans was 4, the number of Latinos was 6 and the number of Asian Americans was 3. In 2000, prior to redistricting these figures were 4, 6, and 2. So a net gain of descriptive representation of one Asian American representative, which was not such a strong gain because the delegation already had 3 Asian American representatives in 1992, with 4 African Americans, and 4 Latinos. Latinos number increase to 9 in 2002 and peaked at 10 in 2008, a very good year for the democrats nationally, but was back to 6 on the eve of the new round of redistricting.

In the 2011–2012 legislative session, the last one before redistricting, there were 33 ethno-racial minorities in the California legislature, 29 in the Assembly, and 14 in the Senate.[117]

After the 2010 elections, in the Assembly there were 8 APIA, 6 African Americans, and 15 Latinos.[118] In the Senate there were 3 APIA, 2 African Americans, and 7 Latinos.[119] As a point of comparison in 2002, there were 26 minorities in the Assembly: 6 Asian Americans, 4 African Americans, and 16

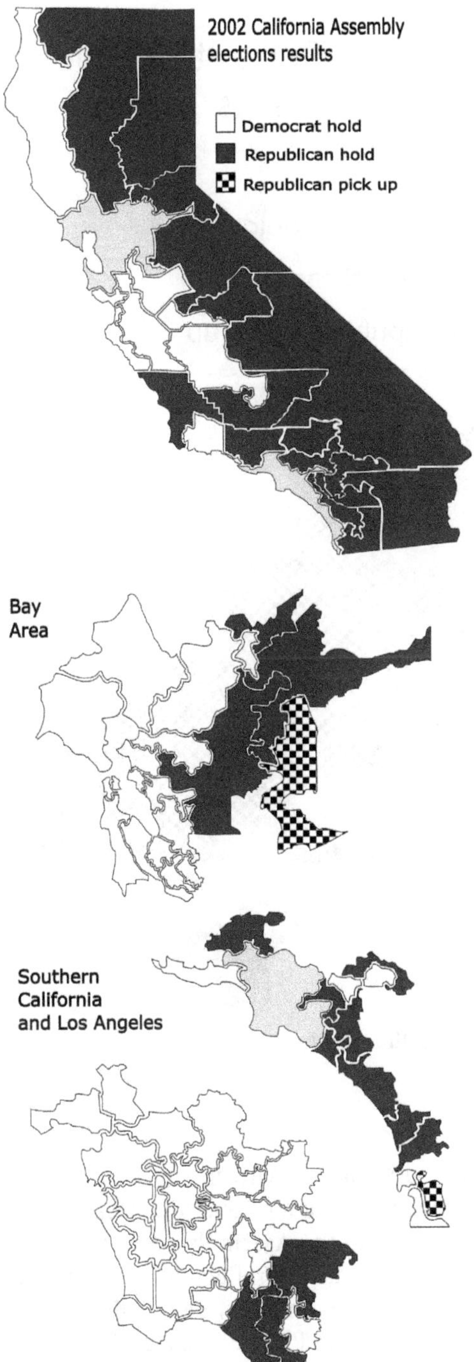

Figure 6.1
2002 California Assembly Election Results

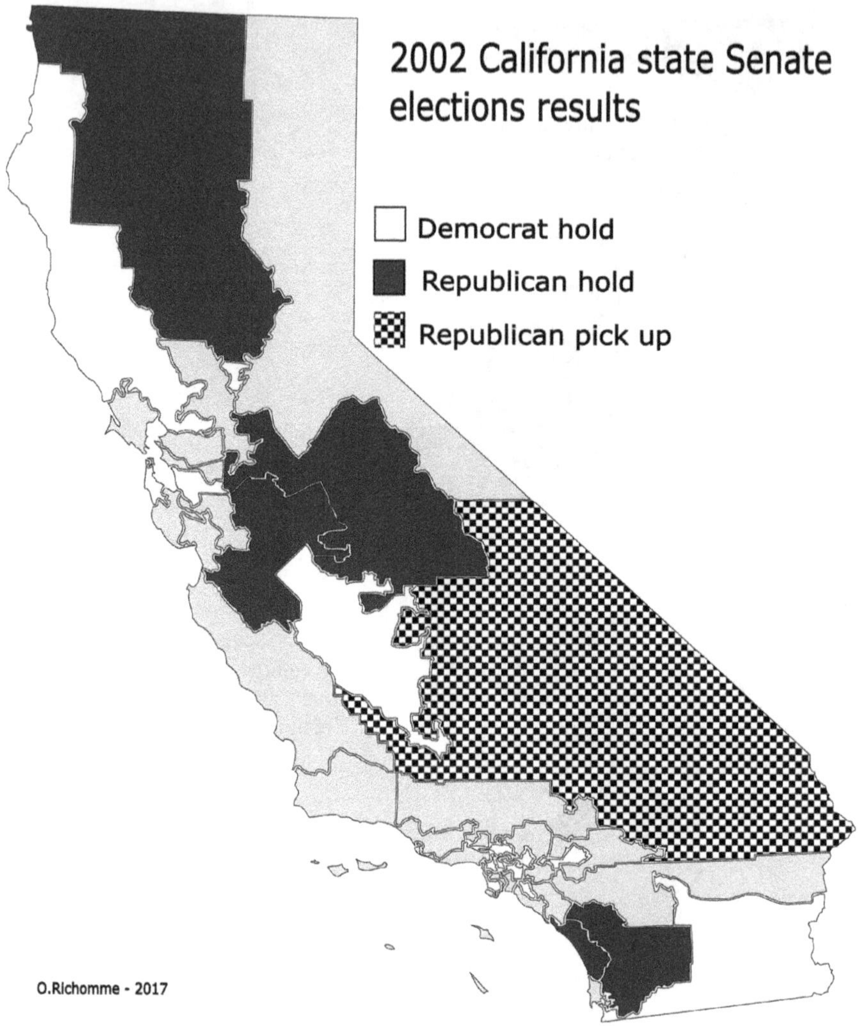

Figure 6.2 2002 California State Senate Election Results

Latinos. There were 11 minorities in the Senate: 2 African Americans and 9 Latinos. So a net loss of 3 elected officials for Latinos over the decade. And as mentioned before the number of Latinos in the Assembly peaked at 22 in 2000, so from their perspective their numbers did not reflect the demographic evolution of the state by a wide margin. The only minority gain in descriptive representation in a decade came from Asian and Pacific Islander Americans who had nowhere to go but up since they had no state senators to begin with.

Another factor that is inherent to incumbent protection and that seemed to irk the electorate was the game of musical chairs among allies or even family member. An example of such practice in 2002 could be AD 14 (Berkeley). In this Democratic district (58 percent Democratic registration, 18 percent Republican, and 16 percent Decline to State), Loni Hancock's husband, Democrat Tom Bates, held this seat for twenty years before he was term-limited in 1996. Bates' chief of staff, Democrat Dion Aroner, held it for the next six years before she, too, was termed out. In 2002, it was Hancock's turn. That

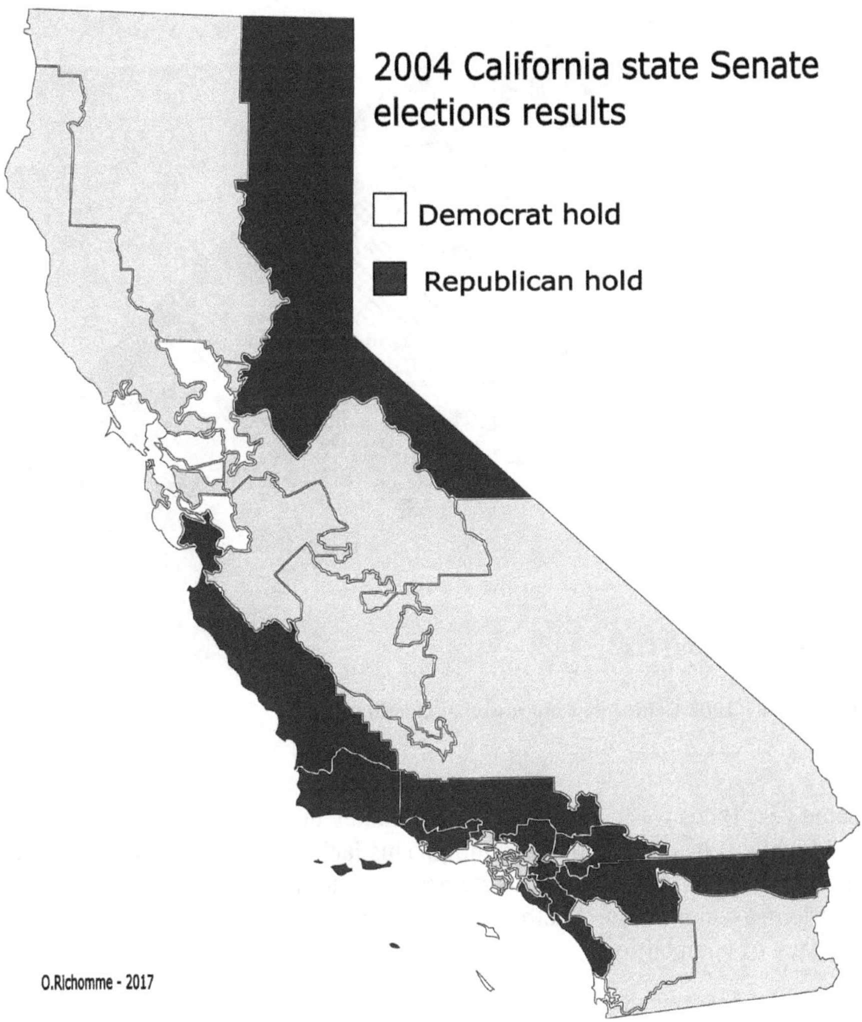

Figure 6.3 2004 California State Senate Election Results

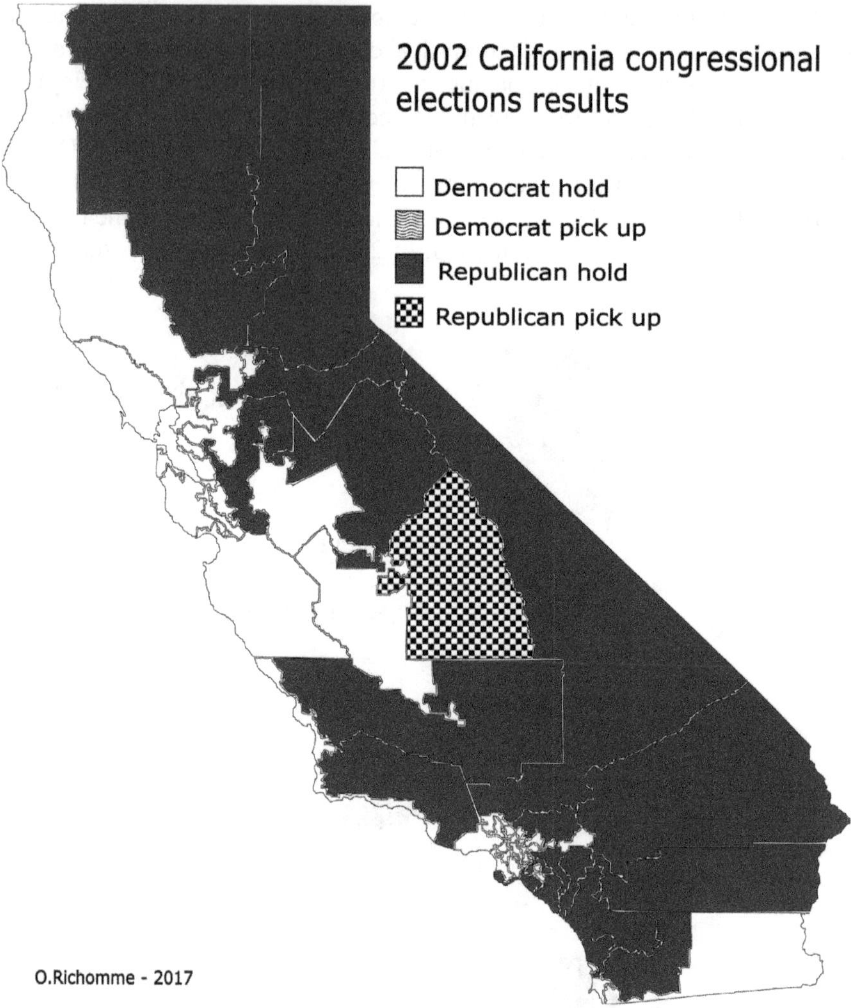

Figure 6.4 2002 California Congressional Election Results

same year Bates was elected mayor of Berkeley in November, a job Hancock held while Bates was in the Assembly. This lack of turnover was often cited in opinion polls about the electorate desire for term limits or independent redistricting commission. Another factor often cited especially after 2002 was the lack of competition.

CONSEQUENCES ON COMPETITION

The plan proposed by the Democrats protected most incumbents of both parties and thus greatly reduced electoral competition. The two parties were satisfied with the status quo even though the national Democratic Party wasn't.[120] Michael Berman is said to have met with President Bush's aide Karl Rove to make sure the Republicans approved the plan. Rove's strategy was to keep the president's majority in the House and establishing a floor for the number of Republicans out of California helped in that regard.[121] Rove was still haunted by Bush's dismal performance in California in 2000, he agreed Republicans should cut their losses and take Berman's deal.[122] RNC communications director Steven Schmidt declared the map was "a victory for the national Republican Party, California is the only state in the country where the maps are being redrawn where one party has complete control of the process and we didn't lose any seats."[123] Or as Senate GOP leader Jim Brulte put in: "Our redistricting was designed to protect the Republican majority in Congress, and it has. I did my job, and I'm proud I did."[124]

Gerrymandering has always served to protect incumbents but in 2001 this technique was pushed to its limits in California, illustrating the national trend. Out of the 53-seat House delegation only one was considered competitive in 2002: that of Representative Gary Condit who lost during the primary elections because of his legal troubles and significant population changes in his district.[125] Except for Condit, all the incumbents were reelected, and 50 of them obtained at least 60 percent of the vote.[126] Only one Republican seat was not protected, that of Representative Stephen Horn who, at the age of seventy, decided to retire. While 9 of the 52 congressional seats were considered very competitive in 2000, that is the two parties' registration figure less than 6 percentage points apart (between 47 percent and 53 percent), only one met this criteria in 2002.[127] Additionally, the six incumbent Democrats in the most competitive districts saw the number of their supporters increase on average by 4.8 percent and the 9 most vulnerable Republican incumbents benefitted from the same protection.[128] Overall, incumbent Republicans in a difficult position received an average boost of 6.3 percent of Republican voters in their district, which made their reelection a formality especially when one takes into consideration the built-in advantage of incumbency.[129] According to Lublin and McDonald, the percentage of congressional districts won by less than a 20 points decrease from 27 percent in 2000 to 6 percent in 2002 to 4 percent in 2004.[130]

However, the fate of Congress is primarily a national issue, and redistricting strategies in each state inevitably depend on the party's national orientation. Democrats sought to maintain the status quo in the states they controlled. Republicans abandoned the fight in those states to better focus their resources in states where they had the majority. For example, in California, in December 2001, Tom Davis, who was head of the Congressional Campaign Committee for the GOP, already suggested he would not invest money in the California in 2002 cycle.[131] This means that 8 representatives in Congress had no real opposition from the GOP. This phenomenon can also be measured by the steep drop in campaign spending in 2002 in California. In the end, only 2 of the 50 incumbents of both parties in 2002 had to face an opponent who had already been elected.[132] 2 out of 50, represents an opposition of 4 percent while in 1972, 1982, and 1992 this "quality" opposition reached 18 percent. Therefore the 2002 congressional election produced the smallest number of incumbent defeat, the smallest number of new members, and the highest number of incumbents reelected since the Second World War.[133] Because these figures were the result of a bipartisan compromise there wasn't much accusation of a Democratic gerrymander. However, the Democrats received 62.3 percent of the House delegation seats while the Democratic candidates received 53.7 percent of the votes. These figures are very close to those of the supposed Burton gerrymander in 1982 when the Democrats won 62.2 percent of the seats but received only 50.9 percent of the votes. What observers and the public focused on was the fact that competition seemed to have vanished from elections. The Assembly plan reduced the number of potentially competitive districts by two-thirds (from 18 to 6) and the Senate map included on one competitive district.[134] Because there were no real opportunities in congress, none of the 38 Assembly and Senate members that were term-limited in 2002 decided to challenge a House member. Only Condit's seat and the newly created district attracted new blood.

In 2004, only a handful of federal congressional races were competitive nationwide.[135] This 2002 and 2004 dip of competition is attributed at least in part to sophisticated bipartisan redistricting in large states.[136] So in that sense California was just an extreme example of a national trend. In the Golden State, not one seat of 153 changed party affiliation even if some new faces arrived in Sacramento courtesy of term limits.[137] Between 2002 and 2010, the partisan composition of California's US House delegation changed by only one when the Democrats picked up one seat in 2006 to increase their majority to 34–19. During the same period, only a stunning two of 253 incumbent representatives (0.8 percent) lost their bids for reelection, while just 14 of 265 contests (5.3 percent) were won by less than ten percentage points; 233 of these 265 (87.9 percent) races were either blowouts (20 percent+ margin of victory) or uncontested. In the Senate, the Democrats lost one seat in 2002 to hold on to 25 seats, a number that they maintained until 2012 thanks to a very small number of competitive districts.[138] In the Assembly, the share of seats won by less than 10 points fell from 10 percent 11 percent in 2000 to 5 percent in 2002 and 6 percent in 2004.[139] The Democratic majority did not evolve much either over the decade, increasing from 48 in 2002 to 51, in 2008 and 52 in 2010.[140] In the Assembly, for instance, in 2010 so nine years removed from redistricting, only 3 districts (Five, Fifteen, and Thirty-five) were won by less than 10 points.[141] In the Senate, that same year, only one seat was won by less than 10 points.[142]

This kind of gerrymandering raises fundamental theoretical and practical questions. Most journalists, and the public at large, probably consider that electoral competition is the essence of any democratic system. And many political scientists would concur.[143] It is interesting to observe the reaction of the Supreme Court when confronted with this issue. Its reasoning in *Davis v. Bandemer* (4478 U.S. 109 [1986]),[144] which was delivered on the same day as *Gingles*, can be quite surprising. The Court focused on what it considers to be partisan gerrymandering, thus establishing a theoretical separation between racial and partisan gerrymandering. However, to use Justice Stevens's expression "racial and political gerrymandering are two species of the same constitutional concern." That is why Justice Kennedy is open to find a manageable standard even though he does not seem to have found so far a satisfying quantitative index. Furthermore, as mentioned before, because of the high level of racial polarization in the US, racial and partisan affiliations have become "two sides of the same coin."[145] From a practical standpoint it is very difficult to distinguish one from the other. In the US partisanship and race are both political by nature. Partisan considerations have racial implication and vice-versa. African Americans have been voting for the Democratic Party at a rate equal or superior to 90 percent. Consequently any discriminatory procedure against this community has a strong partisan effect. For the court it seems that race as a redistricting principle was always a more "constitutionally suspect motive" while partisanship seemed to belong to more "ordinary and lawful" motives. In 2004, the Court revisited the issue in *Vieth v. Jubilirer* the plurality opinion determined that partisan gerrymandering claims were non-justiciable because there was no discernible and manageable standard for "adjudicating political gerrymandering claims."[146] The court did not explicitly overturn its Bandemer ruling, in which five justices were unwilling to determine that partisan gerrymandering claims were non-justiciable. In *Vieth*, Justice Anthony Kennedy concurred with the ruling of the Court to uphold the District Court's decision maintaining that cases of political gerrymandering were not justiciable. He did not, however, foreclose the possibility that judicially manageable standards for gerrymandering could be developed in future cases before the Court.[147] In 2018, the issue of partisan gerrymandering and the lack of standards are again addressed by the Court in *Gill v. Witford*. Scholars are split on whether the Court should even try to come up with partisan gerrymandering standard.[148]

This lack of competition may also have had another consequence. The argument goes that it may have changed the attitude of elected officials who were, as a consequence, less inclined to compromise which, in turn, makes governance that much harder.[149] In 2004, about one-third of the population in the US identified as Democrat, one-third as Republican, and one-third as Independent. About half of the voters was registered with one party (one-sixth of the state population) and they elected the party's candidate in the primary elections. However, only a quarter of them participated in these elections. Therefore, one-twenty-fourth of the country's population chose the candidate to be elected. But these voters represent a minority of party members. They are the most active and are the true followers. A candidate in a district must, first and foremost, convince activists, and it is not in its interest to campaign toward the center in the primaries. Incumbents lose more often the primary elections than the general elections. Primaries pushing them toward the party extremes and do not encourage them to seek compromises once elected. Political negotiations become harder in the House of Representatives and gridlock becomes the norm as real possibility of finding common ground between the two parties gets elusive.[150] Blaming partisan polarization on redistricting alone is of course simplistic as polarization is just as entrenched in the Senate, yet the argument is easy to follow and it can't be denied that gerrymandering probably is not conducive of political compromises and good governance. Bipartisan redistricting deals have lost the appeal they had in the past.[151]

Again, California supposedly illustrated this national trend narrative. The *Wall Street Journal* took the example of the supposed "ideological spin" of the representative Ellen Tauscher in order to highlight the "bipartisan scandal known as gerrymandering."[152] Tauscher was elected in 2002 with no real opposition (no Republican candidate and a Libertarian candidate) while she received only 4,000 votes more than her rival in 1996.[153] She was in 2000 the most endangered Democrat in the state (her district was split 42 percent Democrat, 40 percent Republican before redistricting). Tauscher was part of the so-called "New Democrats" and was the Vice President of Organizational Leadership Democratic Council. She was open to free trade and repudiated her party on protectionist issues. The business world saw her rise positively and financially participated to her reelection. Yet during the conflict on trade in 2001, she refused to vote with the Republican camp. The *Wall Street Journal* traced this change of positioning to the fact that this "New Democrat" was now in a safer more liberal district:

> As Ms. Tauscher's trade vote shows, all of this has real-world political consequences. Though Ms. Tauscher no longer need worry about losing to a Re-

publican, what she does have to worry about now is the Democratic primary, where the new challenge will come from a labor-left far less amenable to her pro-trade views. Her local paper, the *Contra Costa Times*, calls this "punitive redistricting."[154]

Redistricting gets blamed for the polarization of House of Representatives even though the empirical proof is very thin at best[155] but also in state legislatures.[156] For some commentators, the historic budget crisis in California, which was one of the factors participating in Governor Gray Davis's recall in 2003, was more or less directly linked to redistricting.[157] In view of the partisan compromise and the unlikely possibility of reshuffling the partisan balance in the California legislature, experts had anticipated the political impasse on subjects as sensitive as the budget for example.[158] Uncompetitive districts, as we just explained, don't help elected officials open up to compromise and make it difficult to find, in the case of California, some Republicans get the necessary two-third majority to levy taxes.[159] In contrast, another factor that is at least as important in this regard is term limits. Indeed, term limits led to the election of politicians inexperienced in the art of negotiation. Term limits are just as important a factor in explaining why California became in the early 2000s "virtually ungovernable."[160] But some issues get more traction than others and redistricting became the scapegoat of California woes. Term limits was immune to criticism by the public because it was chosen through direct democracy. The public perceived career politicians who stay in office for decades as individuals holding power rather than experienced politicians more knowledgeable than their younger counterparts. Redistricting played in that narrative of a legislature undermining the democratic process because, as the saying goes, the people did not elect its representatives anymore but it was actually politicians that chose their constituents. That is the narrative that helps explain, in part, why so many propositions dealing with redistricting made their way to the ballot after the 2001 round of redistricting.[161] But before we can talk about the genesis of the Independent Citizens Commission, we need to discuss the mini-revolution that took place in local redistricting with the often neglected yet consequential California Voting Rights Act of 2001. The law as authored by a Latino civil rights lawyer who grew frustrated with the limitation of the Federal Voting Rights Act. It was sponsored by a Latino Senate Majority leader. It helps illustrate how minorities are pushing for electoral reform to change the political landscape of California. But ending at-large elections the CVRA is providing representation at the local level for minorities and at the same time it also creates a diverse pool of experienced local candidates that the Democratic Party will be able to tap into in the future. Race and partisanship are intertwined even when elections are supposedly nonpartisan.

NOTES

1. Associated Press, "G.O.P. Effort in Texas Fails in Bid to Redraw Districts," *New York Times*, July 26, 2003, A9; "Texas Tries Anew on Redistricting," *New York Times*, September 9, 2003, A14; "Texas Senate Approves Redistricting Plan," *New York Times*, September 24, 2003, A25; Ralph Blumenthal, "Texas Republicans Report a Deal on Hotly Disputed Redistricting," *New York Times*, October 9, 2003, A24; "After Bitter Fight, Texas Senate Redraws Congressional Districts," *New York Times*, October 13, 2003, A1; Carl Hulse, "Colorado Court Rejects Redistricting Plan," *New York Times*, December 2, 2003, A26; Scott Gold, "Judges Uphold Texas' Contested Election Maps," *Los Angeles Times*, January 7, 2004, A10.

2. "Impact 2000," Dotti Mavramattis (executive director), Peter Cari (Targeting/Analysis), Gerry Hebert (Legal Counsel), and Mark Gersh (NCEC). On file with author.

3. 49 House members, 25 Democrats, and 24 Republicans, carried their districts with 55 percent of the votes or less in 1998, with 4 Republicans and 3 Democrats winning less than 50 percent.

4. This short-lived committee had nothing to do with the sweeping National Democratic Redistricting Committee headed by Eric Holder.

5. Steve Bickerstaff, *Drawing Lines in the Sand: Congressional Redistricting in Texas and the Downfall of Tom DeLay* (Austin: University of Texas Press, 2007).

6. House Minority Leader Richard Gephardt was introduced at the national party convention in the summer of 2000 as "the next speaker of the House." It didn't work out that way then since Republicans retained control of the House in November 2001. In 2001, the Democrats were in control of the governorship and both houses of the legislature in 21 states.

7. Essentially, in 2000, the Democrats picked off all the marginal seats available. Representative Brian Bilbray (R-San Diego) was defeated by Assemblywoman Susan Davis (D-San Diego). In Glendale, Republican incumbent James Rogan lost to Democratic State Senator Adam Schiff, while Palos Verdes Democrat Jane Harman ousted Republican incumbent Steven Kuykendall. In the Silicon Valley, another Democratic Assemblyman, Mike Honda, defeated GOP Assemblyman James Cunneen in an open seat that had been held by Republican Tom Campbell.

8. Moreover, under a two-thirds urgency vote, the new lines take effect immediately, rather than in January, reducing candidates' uncertainty about where they would file.

9. In 1996 Japanese-American Democrat Mike Honda beat out three Democratic rivals to win a safe San Jose Assembly district that was 50 percent Latino and 23 percent Asian. Honda's campaign slogan was "Si Se Puede."

10. A. G. Block, "Putting the Puzzle Back Together," *California Journal* 32, no. 3 (2001), 10.

11. Mark Z. Barabak, "California to Gain Only One congressional Seat," *Los Angeles Times*, February 26, 2001, A14; "Democrats Rule the Redistricting Roost in California Politics," *Los Angeles Times*, July 25, 2001, A15.

12. Democrats ended up eliminated his district (Thirty-eighth). They moved his home and the bulk of Long Beach into the Thirty-seventh District represented by Rep. Juanita Millender-McDonald (D-Carson). At the same time, the Orange County Forty-fifth District of Representative Dana Rohrabacher (R-Huntington Beach) stretched up the coast to take in the ports of Long Beach and Los Angeles and parts of the Palos Verdes Peninsula. Other areas represented by Rohrabacher were split between the Thirty-third District of Representative Lucille Roybal-Allard (D-Los Angeles) and the newly created Latino-majority Fifty-third District. Horn retired in 2001 and Linda Sanchez won the democratic leaning Thirty-ninth District. Simon Richard and Merl Jean, "Rep. Horn to Retire," *Los Angeles Times*, September 5, 2001, B3.

13. Mighuel Bustillo and Nicholas Riccardi, "Parties Rush to Overhaul Political Maps," *Los Angeles Times*, March 31, 2001, B1.

14. Carl Ingram, "Democrats Have Luck of Draw in Redistricting," *Los Angeles Times*, August 19, 2001, B7.

15. For more details on this complex issue, see, for example, James L. Sweeney, *The California Electricity Crisis* (Stanford, CA: Hoover Institution Press, 2002).

16. Susan F. Rasky, "Redistricting Defanged by Energy Crisis," *Los Angeles Times,* April 22, 2001, M1. At the time of the redistricting negotiations Davis was struggling to win legislative approval of a deal he struck with Edison to rescue the utility from bankruptcy. Several lawmakers opposed the deal, contending that it is too rich for Edison. Dan Morain and Mark Z. Barabak, "Davis Sharpens Attack on Bush Energy Plan," *Los Angeles Times*, May 19, 2001, A1.

17. For a more general discussion Harvey M. Choldin, *Looking for the Last Percent: The Controversy over Census Undercount* (New Brunswick, NJ: Rutgers University Press, 1994); Margo J. Anderson and Stephen E. Fienberg, *Who Counts?: The Politics of Census Taking in Contemporary America* (Russell Sage Foundation, 1999); Peter Skerry, *Counting on the Census: Race, Group Identity and the Evasion of Politics* (Washington, DC: Brookings Institution Press, 2000).

18. Nick Anderson, "Census Touchy Subject for State's GOP House Members," *Los Angeles Times*, March 31, 1999, 3. Only one, Tom Campbell of San Jose, of the 24 Republican Representatives from California openly supported using sampling for the 2000 census.

19. The state of California and the city of Los Angeles were plaintiffs in a case after a 1991 decision by then-US Secretary of Commerce Robert Mosbacher to ignore statistical data documenting the undercount, when he ordered states and cities to use only raw census numbers as the basis for redrawing political district lines. The lower courts had sided with Mosbacher, but the appellate court ruled he hadn't justified the decision, given its disproportionate impact on minority communities. In *Wisconsin v. City of New York* (517 U.S. 1 [1996]) the Supreme Court upheld the constitutionality of Secretary Mossbacher's decision.

20. Studies showed that under adjusted numbers Southern California and Arizona would have gained in 1990 one new congressional seat apiece, at the expense of Pennsylvania and Wisconsin, and that Los Angeles would be entitled to $150 million more a year in state and federal funds. Shawn Hubler, "Low Count of Minorities Nnot Justified, Court Says," *Los Angeles Times*, August 10, 1994, A1.

21. The post-enumeration survey is also called "Census Coverage Measurement." It measures the coverage of the US household population (excluding people in "group quarters," such as nursing homes or college dorms). It surveys a sample of the US housing units and then matches the responses to the census, resulting in estimates of error.

22. The estimated loss in federal funding for the state of California for the period from 2002 to 2012: $1.5 billion. US Census Monitoring Board, Presidential Members, Final Report to Congress, September 1, 2001, http://govinfo.library.unt.edu/cmb/cmbp/reports/final_report/FinalReport.pdf.

23. The US Census Monitoring Board, established by Congress in 1997, was a bipartisan board that monitored the Census Bureau's conduct of the 2000 census. At the time California Lt. Governor Cruz M. Bustamante was a member of the board. This is one of the reasons why he sponsored the legislation that launched California's large census outreach campaign in California as he served on the California Complete Count Committee. The state spent $24.7 million to increase the Census 2000 response rate among California's population.

24. In 2000, the undercount rate in California was 1.5 percent while for African Americans it was 2.7 percent and for Latinos it was 2.6 percent. Paul M. Ong and Doug Houston, "The 2000 Census Undercount in Los Angeles County," Working Paper #42, December 2002, http://164.67.121.27/files/Lewis_Center/Publications/LACensusUndercount.pdf.

25. The LA County undercount was 300,000 in 1990 and 170,000 in 2000.

26. Nathaniel Persily, "The Law of the Census: How to Count, What to Count, Whom to Count, and Where to Count Them," *Cardozo Law Review* 32 (2011), 755.

27. Another change was the splitting of the Asian/Pacific Islander into two groups. "Native Hawaiians" have not been able to obtain the status "Native Americans" they have been lobbying for but they obtained a Pacific Islander category in which they are, by far, the largest group.

28. Kenneth Prewitt, "The Census Counts, the Census Classifies," in *Not Just Black and White: Historical and Contemporary Perspectives on Immigration, Race and Ethnicity in the United States*, eds., Nancy Foner and George M. Frederickson (New York: Russell Sage, 2004), 145–64. For a comparative perspective, David I. Kertzer and Dominique Arel, eds., *Census and Identity: the Politics of Race, Ethnicity, and Language in National Censuses* (Cambridge, MA: Cambridge University Press, 2002). On the consequences for redistricting in 2000, see Nathaniel Persily, ed., *The Real Y2K Problem: Census 2000 Data and Redistricting Technology* (New York: The Brennan Center for Justice, New York University School of Law, 2000).

29. Daniel Yi, "Political Mapping Process Is Redrawn," *Los Angeles Times*, August 11, 2001, B1; For a review of the history of computer use in redistricting, see Micah Altman, Karin Mac Donald, and Michael McDonald, "From Crayons to Computers: The Evolution of Computer Use in Redistricting," *Sociological Science Computer Review* 23 (2005), 334–46.

30. http://statewidedatabase.org/. According to one observer "Financed by the State of California, but run as an independent database hosted by UC Berkeley, the SWDB is exemplary in the quality of the data it provides and the access that it gives

to the public." Michael Halberstam, "Process Failure and Transparency Reform in Local Redistricting," *Election Law Journal* 11 (2012), 455.

31. Pamela Karlan, "The Fire Next Times: Reapportionment after the 2000 Census," *Stanford Law Review* 50, no. 3 (1998), 731–63.

32. In *Cromartie II* the Court reversed the three-judge district court's finding of a *Shaw* violation as clearly erroneous, because there was insufficient evidence to show that the district was unexplainable on a basis other than race.

33. For more details about African American migration in LA in the 1990s, see David M. Grant, Melvin L. Oliver, and Angela D. James, "African-Americans: Social and Economic Bifurcation," in *Ethnic Los Angeles*, eds., Roger Waldinger and Mehdi Bozorgmehr (New York: Russell Sage Foundation, 1996), 379–411.

34. In 2002, when Carl Washington's legislative career was ended by term limits, former Lt. Gov. and Congressman Mervyn Dymally returned to the Assembly at age 76. He won the Compton-area seat (Fifty-second Assembly District) he had first won in 1962 to keep it in African American hands. Latinos outnumbered African Americans by over 2–1 in the district, and Dymally faced labor union official Alexandra Gallardo-Rooker. Termed out of the Assembly in 2008, Dymally lost a grueling Democratic primary election for a State Senate seat to Rod Wright and retired at age eighty-two.

35. Studies showed that the electorate was 65 percent Anglo, 15 percent Latino, 13 percent African American, and 4 percent Asian American. "Profile of the City Electorate," *Los Angeles Times*, April 10, 1997, A27.

36. Republican Los Angeles Mayor Riordan's endorsement of Alarcón in the Senate race helped the councilman among Anglo voters. Senator Richard Polanco led virtually every Latino political leader to line up behind Alarcón except for Democratic Latino Assembly Speaker Villaraigosa whose "non-endorsement" in that race was motivated, in part, by a similar need to reach out beyond his Latino base in preparation for his run for mayor of Los Angeles in 2001.

37. 38,577 votes for Alarcón against 38,546 for Katz in SD 20 (Los Angeles County).

38. MALDEF, NAACPLDF, NAPALC, *The Impact of Redistricting in Your Community: A Guide to Redistricting*. On file with author.

39. This is essential. A publication in 1989 attempted to raise awareness about African American and Latino representation through redistricting but without any link with local community information and empowerment efforts it remained a scholarly exercise. O'Hare William, ed., *Redistricting in the 1990s: A Guide to Minority Groups* (Washington, DC: Population Reference Bureau, 1989).

40. Leland Saito, "The Politics of Race and Redistricting in California, 2000–2002," in *Remapping Asian American History*, ed. Sucheng Chan (Walnut Creek, CA: Alta Mira Press, 2003), 226.

41. The proposal and all the maps are available on the WCVI's website: https://wcvi.org/redistricting.html.

42. Condit's Central Valley Eighteenth District was ripe for a GOP takeover (President Bush carried it by 9 points) and it bordered two Democrats desperately in need of help, Ellen Tauscher and Cal Dooley, who faced competitive challengers in

2000. Condit lost by 18 points in the primary against Assemblyman Dennis Cardoza (D-Merced). Matea Gold and Bettina Boxall, "Condit's Loss Brings Sense of Relief to Central Valley," *Los Angeles Times*, March 7, 2002, B1.

43. Section 203 of the VRA requires certain jurisdictions to provide bilingual oral and written assistance in the languages of limited-English proficient communities. In 1975, Congress enacted VRA Section 203, "recognizing the link between language barriers and low voter turnout." However, Asian Pacific Island American communities found the 5 percent threshold to be too high. Thus, outside of Hawaii, in 1990 no APIA language community could qualify. However, due to extensive advocacy on the part of civil rights groups, in 1992, Congress amended and reauthorized section 203. The amendments kept the old 5 percent threshold, but added a numerical benchmark that could be attained, along with the illiteracy requirement. As a result, APIAs, American-Indians, Alaska Natives, and additional Latina/o voters were able to receive the benefits of Section 203. James Thomas Tucker, *The Battle over Bilingual Ballots: Language Minorities and Political Access under the Voting Rights Act* (Burlington, VT: Ashgate, 2009).

44. Feng, Oaki, and Ikemagi, "Voting Matters," 898.

45. CAPAFR was born from the efforts of the Asian Pacific Legal Center in Los Angeles to organize redistricting groups in 1998 building on their 1990 redistricting experience and the 2000 census outreach campaign.

46. At the time there were four Asian Americans: three women of Chinese descent and a man of Japanese heritage in the Assembly and none in the Senate.

47. Their goal for the Assembly was to keep minority communities whole. AD 16 (Alameda), North Oakland, and its African American community were made whole and joined with Oakland; AD 22 (Silicon Valley), Cupertino, Sunnyvale, and Mountain View were unified and made whole; AD 45 (Los Angeles), Philippine Town and Chinatown, each split in two by the 1990 lines, were made whole; AD 49 (Los Angeles), Monterey Park, Alhambra, El Monte, Rosemead, San Gabriel, San Marino, and South El Monte in the west San Gabriel Valley were unified in one assembly district; AD 68 (Orange County), Little Saigon and Koreatown, each split in two by the 1990 lines, were made largely whole; AD 75 (San Diego), Mira Mesa, split in two by the 1990 lines, was made whole; AD 78 (San Diego), Paradise Hills, the eastern portion of Chula Vista, and Bonita were united in one district. Feng, Oaki, Ikemagi, "Voting Matters," 898–99.

48. Feng, Oaki, and Ikemagi, "Voting Matters," 883.

49. The plan presented by the CAPAFR did not include congressional districts.

50. The African American population represented less than 1 percent. The registered democratic population was 50 percent and the Republican registered population 27 percent. Mexican American Legal Defense Fund, *Proposed Legislative Districts United States Congress, Senate, State Assembly*, submitted on September 4, 2001.

51. Michael Finnegan, "Latinos May Gain Few Seats in Redistricting," *Los Angeles Times*, August 26, 2001, B1. The Twenty-ninth was 9 percent Asian American and the Thirty-second was 10 percent Asian American. MALDEF, *Proposed Legislative Districts*.

52. An analysis of the vote in 2010 in AD 49 suggested "that significant majorities of Asian and Latino voters supported Eng's 2010 election. Over 90 percent of Latinos supported Eng, and more than 70 percent of Asian Americans supported him. In contrast, more than 70 percent of Whites supported Taylor, Eng's White opponent. These voting patterns indicate political cohesion between Asian and Latino voters, satisfying the second *Gingles* precondition that minority voters usually vote together as a group." Matt Barreto, Christian R. Grose and Ana Henderson, "Redistricting: Coalition District and the Voting Rights Act," Research Brief, (The Chief Justice Earl Warren Institute on Law and Social Policy, UC Berkeley Law School, May 2011), 7.

53. A. G. Block, "Putting the Puzzle Pieces Together," *California Journal* 32, no. 3 (2001), 10

54. Nearly two years before, Thomas berated then-Republican National Committee Chairman Jim Nicholson for refusing to endorse or help finance his redistricting plan for California. The Supreme Court took the unusual step of pulling Proposition 24 off the 2000 primary ballot for breaking single-subject rule. It would have slashed state legislators' pay and transferred redistricting responsibility to the Supreme Court. Maura Dolan and Mark Gladstone, "State High Court Pull Initiative off March Ballot," *Los Angeles Times*, December 14, 1999, A1. The proposal was originally drafted by Republican anti-government activist Ted Costa and presented to Republicans by maverick initiative activist Ron Unz.

55. John Mercurio and Ethan Wallison, "No Gold Rush in California: Democrats May Look for Gains Elsewhere," *Roll Call*, September 10, 2001.

56. Ingram, "Democrats Have Luck," B7.

57. Jim Brulte later admitted that the referendum threat was a bluff because his party did not have the funds for it. Peter Schrag, "Politicians Settled for 'Draw' in Redistricting," *Sacramento Bee*, February 17, 2002. http://statewidedatabase.org/resources/Redistricting_News/california/2002/february/politicians_settled_02_17_02.html.

58. Shrag, "Politicians Settled."

59. Representatives Loretta and Sanchez were famously quoted in the press saying: "Twenty thousand is nothing to keep your seat. . . . I spend $2 million (campaigning) every election. If my colleagues are smart, they'll pay their $20,000, and Michael will draw the district they can win in. Those who have refused to pay? God help them." Hanh Kim Quach and Dena Bunis, "All bow to redistrict architect Politics Secretive, single-minded Michael Berman holds all the crucial cards," *Orange County Register*, January 21, 2001, 1.

60. Margaret Talev, "New Districts to Solidify Position for Incumbents," *Los Angeles Times*, September 1, 2001, B3; Carl Ingram,"Redistricting Plan Unveiled by Assembly," *Los Angeles Times*, August 30, 2001, B9.

61. David S. Broder, "Calif. Democrats Seek Stability in Redistricting Plan," *Washington Post*, August 30, 2001, A2. Tauscher's new district still expanded from its former Contra Costa County base to take in parts of three other counties, including Solano and Sacramento. But state legislators ultimately kept Orinda, Moraga, and Lafayette in her district.

62. Michael Finnegan,"Latinos Blast Rep. Berman in Map Fight," *Los Angeles Times*, September 7, 2001, B3

63. MALDEF's proposal maintained it at 60 percent with a 25 percent Anglo Voting Age Population with a deviation of 0.02 percent.

64. The percentage of registered Democrats fell from 58 percent in the previous district and 57 percent in the MALDEF proposal to 51 percent in the legislature's proposal. With a Republican registration increase to 28 percent, Berman still had enough of a margin to be easily reelected without facing a Latino opponent in the primary. Mexican American Legal Defense Fund, *Proposed Legislative Districts*.

65. By contrast the three returning Latino Republicans were given ideal districts: Assemblyman Abel Maldonado of Santa Maria got a new Senate seat drawn for him, Assemblyman Bob Pacheco of Walnut got an excellent district, and GOP Assemblywoman Charlene Zettel found an open Senate seat in her San Diego neighborhood.

66. Carl Ingram, "LA Area Gets State's New Congressional Seat," *Los Angeles Times*, September 1, 2001, A1.

67. Behind the scene the Asian Pacific American Legal Center really thought veteran Assembly Staffer Bill Cavala (and his counterpart Joe Shumate) disrespected them. During our interview Kathay Feng, now the executive director of California Common Cause, remembered the sense of injustice she felt as a young lawyer and how formative this experience with the legislature was. Kathay Feng interview, November 2016.

68. Carl Ingram, "Revised Districts Hinder Minorities, Critics Say," *Los Angeles Times*, September 6, 2001, B8.

69. In 2000, in Monterey Park, Asian Americans represented 61 percent of the city population, Latinos 29 percent.

70. Kathay Feng, cited by Saito, "The Politics of Race," 231.

71. Carl Ingram, "Activists Upset by Central Coast Remap," *Los Angeles Times* September 9, 2001, B6.

72. Assemblywoman Helen Thomson of Davis saw her hopes for a Senate seat vanish when Democratic line-drawers made the seat she wanted safely Republican (for a male Republican colleague) and put her hometown in the district of a fellow Democrat, Senator Mike Machado. Democratic Assemblywoman Hannah-Beth Jackson of Santa Barbara was eyeing the safe Senate seat occupied by retiring Democratic Senator Jack. The seat had been held by Democrats for twenty-five years. Instead, they went to great lengths to make sure Jackson did not have a Senate seat, cutting the old O'Connell district in two, and giving its number to a new Republican seat in the Central Valley. Jackson served out the remaining two years of her Assembly term and then was termed out. She had to wait until 2012 to win the Nineteenth Senate District. Fresno Democratic Assemblywoman Sarah Reyes had hoped for a Senate seat but the leadership drew the district for Assemblyman Dean Florez.

73. Carl Ingram, "State Redistricting Bill Passes Senate," *Los Angeles Times*, September 13, 2001, B6; Senate also passed 40 to 0 a bill rewriting state Assembly districts. Carl Ingram, "Plan to Redraw Districts Passes," *Los Angeles Times*, September 14, 2001, B8.

74. The California Latino Redistricting Coalition, a group that included the Los Angeles County Employees Association and the Latino Coalition for Fair Reapportionment, petitioned the US Department of Justice to challenge the design of several legislative and congressional districts. The Senate seats contested in the petition were the Fifteenth, represented by Bruce McPherson (R-Santa Cruz) and the Twenty-seventh represented by Betty Karnette (D-Long Beach) and the Twelfth District seat held by Dick Monteith (R-Modesto). The Congressional districts contested were the Twenty-eighth, represented by Howard Berman (D-Mission Hills), the Forty-second, held by Gary Miller (R-Diamond Bar), the Fifty-first District represented by Bob Filner, (D-San Diego) and the Twenty-second by Bill Thomas (R-Bakersfield).

75. Another suit was filed in September 2001 in the Sacramento County Superior Court. A bipartisan group of San Joaquin County officials filed a lawsuit charging that new legislative and congressional districts illegally cut up the county and its biggest city, Stockton. Another suit claimed that the plan unconstitutionally divides an Asian American community in San Jose into two Assembly districts, possibly diluting their influence. And another suit in that same Santa Clara County demanded that the Morgan Hill area did not contain more than one Assembly, Senate, and congressional district. The Supreme Court declined to hear any of those lawsuits. The San Joaquin County case is *Andal v. Davis* (S101573). The Santa Clara County cases are *Kennedy v. Davis*, S101719 and *Nadler v. Davis* (S101651).

76. Kenneth Reich, "Latino Group Sues over Redistricting," *Los Angeles Times*, October 2, 2001, B1.

77. Richard Simon and Dade Hayes, "Pro-Busing Stand Halted 20-Year Tenure," *Los Angeles Times,* August 31, 1997, 3. Fiedler won in 1980 by 752 votes out of 153,770 cast.

78. Hanh Kim and Bunis, Dena, "All bow to redistrict architect Politics Secretive, single-minded Michael Berman holds all the crucial cards," *Orange County Register*, January 21, 2001, 1.

79. Finnegan, Michael, "Latinos May Gain Few Seats in Redistricting," *Los Angeles Times*, August 26, 2001, B1.

80. "Howard stabbed me in the back" could be heard by journalists on a plane. Sherman also declared to the press: "I do not feel that Michael Berman did as well for all his clients as he did for his brother." Michael Finnegan, "Neighboring LA Democrats Trade Barbs over Redistricting," *Los Angeles Times*, September 8, 2001, B3.

81. Michael Finnegan, "Remapping Plan Fails to Appease Latinos," *Los Angeles Times*, September 11, 2001, B3.

82. The bipartisan redistricting plan was sued unsuccessfully by three other "communities of interest": *Andal v. Davis* (S101573), *Kennedy v. Davis* (S101719), and *Nadler v. Davis* (S101651).

83. Declaration of State Senator Don Perata cited in Thomas B. Edsall, "A Political Fight to Define the Future: Latinos at Odds over California's Two New Democratic Congressional Districts," *Washington Post*, October 31, 2001, A8.

84. Cited in "Point/Counterpoint: Redistricting challenge," *California Journal* 32, no. 1 (2002), 38.

85. Martha Escutia and Gloria Romero, "MALDEF's lawsuit is racially divisive," *Los Angeles Times*, November 1, 2001, B13. It is to be noted that some observers have suggested that Escutia and Romero's article was a self-serving publicity stunt, helping them tremendously with the Latino community, but was in the end quite hypocritical because their districts seemed to waste Latino votes.

86. The Latinos in the valley grew from 11.6 percent in 1970 to 38 percent in 2000; the percentage of Asian Americans went from 1 percent to 9.7 percent. African Americans increased their share of the valley population from 1.7 percent to 4.9 percent. But the valley's Anglo population dropped from 85.3 percent to 47 percent. It was no longer the numerical majority.

87. David Rosenzweig,"Judges Asked to Postpone Voting in 4 House Districts," *Los Angeles Times,* November 1, 2001, B7.

88. In 2000, Senate District Twenty-seven contained 846,792 people (8.9 percent of the county's 9,519,338 people), and Congressional District Twenty-eight contained 639,087 people (6.7 percent of the county's population). Senate District Twenty-seven ran north from Long Beach (which is south of the Latino communities assessed above, and with a substantially different socioeconomic composition), includes Cerritos and Bellflower (along the San Gabriel River and the 605 freeway), Lynwood (along the Los Angeles River and the 710 freeway), and Downey (which bridges both). Congressional District Twenty-eight ran west along the Hollywood Hills (south of the Latino communities assessed, and with a substantially different socioeconomic composition), up into some of the San Fernando Valley neighborhoods lining the 101 freeway and north along the 170 freeway into Panorama City, Pacoima, and San Fernando itself.

89. *Cano v. Davis*, 211 F.Supp.2d 1208 (C.D. Cal. 2002), 1235.

90. *Cano v. Davis*, 1242.

91. *Cano v. Davis*, 1236–37. In 1988 the 9th Circuit Court that covers the state of California in the case *Romero v. Pomona* applied the 50 percent CVAP standard. In 2003 in *Georgia v. Ashcroft* (539 U.S. 461), a majority of the Supreme Court endorsed a softening of the majority-minority requirement. In 2006 in *LULAC v. Perry* (548 U.S. 399), another majority of the Supreme Court treated registration data as superior to population data when determining political opportunity. In *Bartlett v. Strickland* (556 U.S. 1 [2009]) a plurality of the United States Supreme Court found that the first step in determining whether the VRA might require the drawing of a majority-minority district (the first *Gingles* precondition) is to determine if the minority population is sufficiently large and compact to constitute a majority in a single member district. That is, minorities had to constitute 50 percent or more of the voting population of a given district. The Court rejected a claim that the VRA required a state to disregard state redistricting criteria in order to draw a district where African American voters constituted less than 50 percent of the voting age population, but along with some support from White "crossover" voters, were able to elect a candidate of choice. The Court specified that it was expressing no judgment on the issue of coalition districts, such as whether a combined minority population over 50 percent satisfies the first *Gingles* precondition.

92. *Cano v. Davis*, 1221.

93. *Cano v. Davis*, 1243–44. Berman defeated Godinez in the 1998 primaries while receiving 22 percent of the Latino vote and 91 percent of the non-Latino votes according to estimates cited in the case.

94. Scholarly articles seem to contradict the Court's findings in *Cano*. "These results demonstrate that not only Latinos are politically cohesive in their support of Latino candidates in Los Angeles County, but also that non-Latinos vote consistently against Latino candidates and issues." Yishaiya Absoch, Matt A. Barreto, Nathan D. Woods, "An Assessment of Racially Polarized Voting For and Against Latino Candidates in California," in *Voting Rights Act Reauthorization of 2006: Perspectives on Democracy, Participation, and Power*, ed., Ana Henderson (Berkeley, CA: UC Berkeley Public Policy Press, 2007), 127; Kousser, "Reapportionment Wars."

95. *Cano v. Davis*, 1246.

96. *Cano v. Davis*, 1217–18.

97. Declaration of Expert Witness Morgan Kousser, *Cano v. Davis*, May 13, 2002, 6.

98. Declaration of Expert Witness Kousser, 7.

99. Declaration of Expert Witness Kousser, 18–20.

100. *Cano v. Davis*, 1230.

101. Deposition of Juan Vargas, April 4, 2002, *Cano v. Davis*, No.CV 01-08477 MMM (RCx). This declaration was echoed by Xavier Flores, the executive director of the San Fernando Valley organization Pueblo y Salud, who declared Sherman expressed his anger about the new boundaries in two phone conversations with Flores. Antonio Gonzalez, president of the William C. Velasquez Institute, declared Michael Berman told him that he wanted to ensure his brother's reelection by limiting the number of Latinos in Howard Berman's new district. Gonzalez said in his declaration to the Court that Michael Berman told him: "We don't want Howard working on district maintenance at home when he could be frying better fish in DC." Laura Mecoy, "Charges Mount in Remap Lawsuit," *Sacramento Bee,* October 31, 2001, http://archive.fairvote.org/redistricting/reports/remanual/canews6.htm#charges.

102. Denise Hulett, a San Francisco lawyer from MALDEF who worked on *Davis v. Cano*, recalled fifteen years later in our interview being very surprised at the court's decision. Even years later her disappointment was palpable.

103. The leadership thought linking Imperial County to Filner's territory was a more natural fit than tying the agricultural and desert county to the San Diego coast. Vargas finally ousted Filner in 2012 after another round of redistricting this time by an independent redistricting commission.

104. *Cano v. Davis*, 1225.

105. *Cano v. Davis*, 1246.

106. *Cano v. Davis*, 1251–52.

107. *Cano v. Davis*, 1230.

108. Matea Gold and Michael Finnegan, "No Consensus on Latino Vote Ruling; Politics: Some See Court Redistricting Decision as Sign of Progress. Others Fear It Will Halt Gains," *Los Angeles Times*, June 14, 2002, B1.

109. Cain, "The Contemporary Context," 20–21.

110. "Primary Election Results:Congress and Legislature," *California Journal* 34, no. 4 (2002), 29.

111. Micah Altman and Michael McDonald, "Redistricting and Polarization," in *American Gridlock: The Sources, Character and Impact of Political Polarization*, eds. James A. Thurber and Antoine Yoshinaka (Cambridge, MA: Cambridge University Press, 2015), 45–63.

112. At long last, the Republican Party captured AD 78 after more than a decade of trying to pry it out of the hands of Democrats. In years past, Lucy Killea, Dede Alpert, and Howard Wayne kept the Seventy-Eighth firmly in Democratic hands, despite voter-registration numbers that often favored Republicans. But that was the old, pre-redistricting AD 78. The new one resembles the previous version in number only; not one precinct of the old Seventy-eighth was included when map-makers created this district in 2001. Ostensibly, they made it friendlier for Democrats, and it was counted as a Democratic district in the status quo reapportionment plan. But Chula Vista Republican Mayor Shirley Horton won it thanks to lots of resources and low voter turnout.

113. Democrat Joey Acuna Jr. district turnout was 41 percent, a good distance below statewide turnout, which was a good distance below the worst turnout in California history. Republican Bonnie Garcia ran a campaign that cost nearly $1 million resulting in a GOP pickup in a district (with registration rates of 46 percent Democrat and 38 percent Republican) that was supposed to produce a Democrat. The only fulfilled promise is that with it its 60 percent Latino population it would produce a Latino elected official.

114. In AD 30, Democrat Nicole Parra squeaked past Republican Dean Gardner by fewer than 200 votes out of 52,000 cast. Democrats held a 13-point registration edge and outspent their Republican challenger roughly 10 to 1. In addition, their candidate was the daughter of a popular supervisor from Kern Co., which supplied the district's largest chunk of registered voters. And, their candidate was Hispanic in a district where 61 percent of the population and 40 percent of registered voters are Latino. Parra was the number-one priority for the United Farm Workers, which has long and deep roots in the district and owned a network of radio stations that broadcast into every corner of the region. Parra had government experience as district aide to the area's popular Democratic congressman, Cal Dooley. Republicans, on the other hand, were represented by a White businessman from Bakersfield with no elective base and little government experience.

115. California Journal's Editors, "CJ's District-by-District Analysis—Congress," *California Journal* 40, no. 11 (2002), 20.

116. Claudine Gay, "The Effect of Minority Districts and Minority Representation on Political Participation in California," Public Policy Institute of California, 2001; Matt A. Barretto, Gary M. Segura, and Nathan D. Woods, "The Mobilizing Effect of Majority-Minority Districts on Latino Turnout," *American Political Science Review* 98, no. 1 (2004), 65–75; Hayes and McKee have also shown that redistricting in itself influences voter participation Danny Hayes and Seth C. McKee, "The Participatory Effects of Redistricting," *American Journal of Political Science* 53, no. 4 (2009), 1006–23.

117. 35 if one counts Lebanese-American Republican Katcho Achadjian in the Assembly and Armenian American Democrat Joe Simitan in the Senate.

118. Richard Pan (AD 5), Mariko Yamada (AD 8), Fiona Ma (AD 12), Mary Hayashi (AD 18), Paul Fong (AD 22), Das Williams APIA (AD 35), Mike Eng APIA (AD 49), Warren Furutani (AD 55); Sandré Swanson (AD 16), Holly Michell (AD 47), Mike Davis (AD 48), Steven Bradford (AD 51), Isadore Hall III (AD 52), Wilmer Carter (AD 62); Michael Allen (AD 7) lost reelection in 2012 in AD 10, Nora Campos (AD 23), Luis Alejo (AD 28), Henry Perea (AD 31), Felipe Fuentes (AD 39), Gil Cedillo (AD 45), John Pérez (AD 46), Ricardo Lara (AD 50), Tony Mendoza (AD 56), Roger Hernandez (AD 57), Charles Calderon (AD 58), Norma Torres (AD 61), Jose Solorio (AD 69), Ben Hueso (AD 79), Manuel Perez (AD 80).

119. Leland Yee (SD 8), Carol Liu (SD 21), Ted Lieu (SD 28); Roderick Wright (SD 25), Curren Price (SD 26); Michael Rubio (SD 16), Alex Padilla (SD 20), Kevin de León (SD 22), Edward P. Hernández, Ronald Calderon (SD 30), Gloria Negrete McLeod (SD 32), Lou Correa (SD 34), Juan Vargas (SD 40).

120. Jim Ellis, director of House Majority Whip Tom DeLay's (R-Texas) leadership PAC, Americans for a Republican Majority, or ARMPAC, declared that House Minority Leader Richard Gephardt (D-Mo.) had to be "extremely disappointed by this California map. For 20 Republican seats to be protected is a very good place for us to start." John Mercurio, "Horn Retires After Losing District; Incumbents Protected by Redistricting Map," *Roll Call* (DC), September 6, 2001, http://archive.fairvote.org/redistricting/reports/remanual/canews5.htm#rchorn.

121. Eric McGhee, "Redistricting and Legislative Leadership," Public Policy Institute of California, 2008, 9.

122. At the same time, Howard Berman and Nancy Pelosi were "selling the Berman plan to Gephardt and the Democrat Congressional Campaign Committee Chairman, Representative Martin Frost of Texas, on similar, tactical grounds." Carl M. Cannon, "California Divided," *California Journal* 32, no. 1 (2002), 8.

123. Cannon, "California divided," 8.

124. George Skelton, "Bush's Bumbling Won't Benefit State's Democrats," *Los Angeles Times*, August 14, 2006, B3.

125. Alison Mitchell, "Redistricting 2002 Produces No Great Shake-Ups," *New York Times*, May 13, 2002, A20.

126. Gary Jacobson, "All Quiet on the Western Front: Redistricting and Party Competition in California House Elections," in *Redistricting in the New Millennium*, ed. Peter F. Galderisi (Lanham, MD: Lexington Books, 2005), 233.

127. Partisan registration is a strong predictor even as a declined state has risen. According to Jacobson between 1966 and 2000 the proportion of variance in the House vote explained by district registration grew from 55 percent to 88 percent. Gary C. Jacobson, "Partisan and Ideological Polarization in the California Electorate," *State Politics and Policy Quarterly* 4 (2004), 121.

128. Jacobson, "All Quiet," 226 and 228.

129. From 1992 to 2000, Republicans in districts containing less than 47.7 percent Democrat electors were all reelected. Democrats won all elections in districts containing at least 56 percent Democrats. One way one can estimate if a district is

competitive is to consider that a district containing less than 47 percent or more than 56 percent Democratic voters is not competitive.

130. David Lublin and Michael McDonald, "Is It Time to Draw the Line?: The Impact of Redistricting on Competition in State House Elections," *Election Law Journal* 5, no. 2 (2006), 146.

131. Editorial Staff, "Cheating Seating," *Wall Street Journal*, December 27, 2001, http://archive.fairvote.org/redistricting/reports/remanual/canews6.htm#cheating.

132. These two opponents' experience was very limited since they had won elections in school board districts.

133. Jacobson, "All Quiet," 231–32.

134. Lisa Plendl, "Are Voters Dissed by Redistricting?" *California Journal* 32, no. 1 (2002), 12.

135. Gary C. Jacobson, "Competition in US Congressional Elections," in *The Marketplace of Democracy: Electoral Competition and American Politics*, eds. Michael P. McDonald and John Samples (Washington, DC: Brookings Institute Press, 2006), 27–52.

136. In 2001, 233 seats were drawn under such bipartisan plans as opposed to 147 seats in 1991. Michael McDonald, "Redistricting and Competitive Districts," in *The Marketplace*, 234; Richard Pildes, "The Constitution and Political Competition," *Nova Law Review* 30 (2006), 269–94.

137. Term limits in California did not seem to foster more competition. Cain, Bruce, John Hanley, and Thad Kousser, "*Term Limits: A Recipe for More Competition?*" in *The Marketplace*, 199–221.

138. In 2002 the Democrats conceded SD 18 when incumbent Roy Ashburn ran unopposed.

139. Lublin and McDonald, "Is It Time,"146. The number of unopposed candidates increased. In 2000, 98 percent of State House Elections features two major-party candidates, in 2004 only 93 percent. Lublin and McDonald, "Is It Time," 150.

140. In 2008, 5 seats changed parties: 1 to the Republican Party and 4 to the Democratic Party. In 2010, the Democratic Party gained 2 seats: the Fifth District from the Republicans and the Thirty-first District from a termed-out Independent. (The number of Democrats was back to 50 Assemblyman Bill Emmerson (D-63) wins the special election for the Thirty-seventh Senate District seat to replace John J. Benoit, therefore their net gain was only one seat).

141. And AD 35 (Santa Barbara) was won by 9.8 percent by Das Williams.

142. In SD 12 (Merced) Republican Anthony held on to his seat by 2 points.

143. For an example of an exception, cf. Thomas Brunell, *Redistricting and Representation: Why competitive Elections are Bad for America* (New York: Routledge, 2008).

144. In *Bandemer*, Indiana Democrats challenged a 1981 Republican gerrymander on equal protection grounds as "political discrimination." They asserted that the redrawing of legislative district lines were deliberately designed to disadvantage Democratic candidates for the General Assembly. A three-judge district court found that the redistricting plan constituted political gerrymandering in violation of the equal protection clause of the Fourteenth Amendment. The Court rejected the racial

discrimination claims of a second group of plaintiffs, finding instead that because of their tendency to vote Democratic, Blacks were victims of political discrimination, the same charge leveled by the first plaintiffs.

145. Cain, "Moving Past Section 5."

146. *Vieth v. Jubelirer* (541 U.S. 267 [2004]), Justice Scalia opinion, joined by Rehnquist, O'Connor, and Thomas.

147. "If workable standards do emerge to measure these burdens, however, courts should be prepared to order relief," *Vieth v. Jubelirer*, Justice Kennedy concurring opinion. For such an attempt, see for instance Nicholas O. Stephanopoulos and Eric M. McGhee, "Partisan Gerrymandering and the Efficiency Gap," *University of Chicago Law Review* 82 (2015), 831.

148. "The Supreme Court almost exclusively focuses on equal population and racial gerrymandering has liberated as much as it constrained the self-interested behavior of politicians and parties, yet a judicial plunge into the political thicket or partisan or bipartisan gerrymandering might be even more problematic." Thomas Mann, "Redistricting Reform: What Is Desirable? Possible?," in *Party Line: Competition, Partisanship and Congressional Redistricting*, eds. Thomas Mann and Bruce Cain (Washington, DC: Brookings Institution, 2005), 93.

149. For an article arguing that redistricting is not responsible for the decline in the number of competitive districts, defined as a district with a near balance of partisanship see for instance Alan Abramowitz, Brad Alexander, and Matthew Gunning, "Don't Blame Redistricting for Uncompetitive Elections," *PS: Political Science and Politics* 39 (2006), 87–90. For scholars concluding the opposite, see for instance John W. Swain, Stephen A. Borrelli, and Brian C. Reed, "Partisan Consequences of the Post-1990 Redistricting for the US House of Representatives," *Political Research Quarterly* 51, no. 4 (1998), 945–67; Bruce E. Cain, Karin Mac Donald, and Michael McDonald, "From Equality to Fairness: the Path of Political Reform Since *Baker v. Carr*," in *Party Lines: Competition Partisanship and Congressional Redistricting*, eds. Bruce Cain and Thomas Mann (Washington, DC: Brookings Institution, 2005).

150. JeffreyToobin, "The Great election Grab: When does gerrymandering become a threat to democracy?, " *The New Yorker* 79, no. 38 (2003), 63.

151. There was a time when bipartisan fairness seemed a desirable reform goal almost endorsed by the Supreme Court. In *Gaffney v. Cummings* (412 U.S 735 [1973]), 751–54, the Court held that a "political fairness principle" that achieves a rough approximation of the statewide political strengths of the two major parties does not violate the Equal Protection Clause.

152. Editorial Staff, "Cheating Seating."

153. Alison Mitchell, "Redistricting 2002 Produces No Great Shake-Ups," *New York Times*, May 13, 2002, A20.

154. Mitchell, "Redistricting 2002," A20. Actually Tauscher did not only refuse to support Pelosi but supported her opponent Stanley Hoyer. Pelosi a close ally of Senate President Pro Tempore John Burton was first elected in 1987 in the district formerly held by Philip Burton and later by the late congressman's widow, Sala Burton.

155. Nolan McCarty, Keith T. Poole, and Howard Rosenthal, *Polarized America: The Dance of Ideology and Unequal Riches* (Cambridge, MA: MIT Press, 2006);

Stephen Ansolabehere, James M. Snyder Jr., and Charles Stewart III, "Candidate Positioning in US House Elections," *American Journal of Political Science* 45, no.1 (2001), 136–59.

156. Eric McGhee, "Redistricting and Legislative Partisanship," Public Policy Institute, 2008, http://web.ppic.org/content/pubs/report/R_908EMR.pdf.

157. Franck del Olmo, "Redistricting Plays a Part in Budget Crisis," *Los Angeles Times*, July 6, 2003, M5; Mark Martin, "Politics Intensify Budget Troubles. Redrawn Districts, Term Limits Decrease Compromise Incentive," *San Francisco Chronicle*, July 6, 2003, A1.

158. Matthew G., Jarvis "Redistricting Reform Could Save California from Itself," *California Journal of Politics and Policy* 1, no.1 (2009); Justin Buchler, "Redistricting Reform Will Not Solve California's Budget Crisis," *California Journal of Politics and Policy* 1, no.1 (2009).

159. California passed its two-thirds majority requirement in 1933. In 2004, Democrats and their labor allies qualified Proposition 56 to lower the two-thirds vote to 55 percent. Despite huge spending for the measure, it only received 34 percent.

160. John M. Broder and Dean E. Murphy, "A Recall Vote Seems Certain for California," *New York Times*, July 24, 2003, A1.

161. For an analysis of public opinion on redistricting, see Joshua Fougere, Stephen Ansolabehere, and Nathaniel Persily, "Partisanship, Public Opinion, and Redistricting," *Election Law Journal* 9, no. 4 (2010), 325–47.

Chapter 7

The California Voting Rights Act

Latinos End at-Large Districts

JOAQUIN AVILA'S LEGACY

The California Voting Rights Act has had a tremendous impact on local politics in California and like most influential pieces of legislation it almost never came about. If it wasn't for the tenacity of one visionary voting rights attorney, the situation of minorities' voting rights in California would be quite different.[1]

Joaquin Avila worked for MALDEF from 1974 to 1985, first as a staff attorney, then as a regional associate counsel and from 1982 to 1985 as president and general counsel. In 1985, he opened a private practice solely dedicated to voting rights cases, the only one of its kind at the time. At MALDEF he had acquired great experience fighting voting rights cases under equal protection standard and when the Supreme Court rendered its decision in *Mobile v. Bolden*, Avila testified before Congress in 1981 to reauthorize and amend the Voting Rights Act. His testimony focused on the state of Texas and put the emphasis on local jurisdiction and especially the problem that at-large schemes represented for Latinos.[2] While the new amended Section 2 voted by Congress was a great victory for voting rights advocates because it eliminated intent as part of the evidentiary process to establish discrimination, the new interpretation of the Section 2 introduced "geographical compactness" as first precondition. Indeed, federal voting rights cases under Section 2 require that a successful plaintiff show that (1) the minority group be sufficiently large and geographically compact to form a majority of the eligible voters in a single-member district, (2) there is racially polarized voting, and (3) there is White bloc voting sufficient usually to prevent minority voters from electing candidates of their choice.[3] Only if all three of these "preconditions" are proven, the court then proceeds to consider whether, under the "totality of circumstances" the votes of minority voters are diluted.[4]

An ethnic or racial minority had to be geographically compact enough to create a majority-minority district in which the said minority could amount to 50 percent of eligible voters and then 50 percent of the Citizen Voting Age Population after the *Romero* jurisprudence. Much to the chagrin of Avila, many preliminary studies done before challenges showed that this threshold was too high in many cases. While potential clients came to his office he had to turn them down and explain to them that he could not file the case in spite of a high racial polarized voting and a history of no minority electoral success. So as early as 1984, Joaquin Avila recognized that a state law eliminating the geographical compactness criteria would help fight voting rights cases especially since no court has agreed on a standard to measure "compactness." From 1989 to 1992, he worked with Assemblyman Peter Chacon to try and pass bills eliminating at-large elections only to see those bills vetoed by Republican Governors once they were accepted by the legislature.[5] He tried to work with MALDEF on this issue but the Latino organization made a strategic decision of not focusing on the local level.

Avila especially worked on passing a bill after the seminal Section 2 case in California *Gomez v. Watsonville* that was successful on appeal to the US Court of Appeals for the 9th Circuit.[6] The *Gomez* decision helped to renew efforts at the community level to eliminate discriminatory at-large elections and therefore at-large election challenges were filed in other parts of California.[7] The *Gomez* case was a legal success that reverberated throughout the state and the switch to districts led to the election of Latino Oscar Rios in 1989, the community's preferred candidate,[8] who was then elected mayor.[9] However, the period of successful Section 2 enforcement in California did not last. This was part of a national trend observed by Cain and Miller where Section 2 violations were harder to prove for "other minorities," meaning other than African Americans.[10] According to Joaquin Avila two major unsuccessful at-large election challenges discouraged any further litigation by private parties.[11] The two cases involved challenges to the at-large method of election in the El Centro School District and the City of Santa Maria.[12]

> These cases consumed substantial resources, and, in the case of the Santa Maria litigation, a final decision was not rendered until ten years after the case had been filed. Perhaps the most chilling aspect of these losses were the efforts by the defendants to collect on their Bill of Costs filed pursuant to federal law. In the El Centro School District litigation, the ultimate Bill of Costs was pared down to $19,462.01. The district court denied the plaintiffs request to re-tax the costs, but did provide for a ten-day stay to permit the plaintiffs to seek a stay before the US Court of Appeals for the Ninth Circuit. The School District suc-

> cessfully applied pressure on the plaintiffs to dismiss their appeal in exchange for the School District to withdraw its Bill of Costs. A similar litigation strategy was pursued in the Santa Maria litigation. As a result of the El Centro and Santa Maria litigation experiences, since 1992, no private litigants have filed at-large election challenges under the VRA.[13]

Since the private bar had been thus far largely responsible for enforcement of minority voting rights, Avila was convinced that this activity needed to be incentivized. Any new state law should accomplish two goals: remove the compactness factor and help private lawyers with their cost.

For several years Avila doubled his effort to have a bill passed in the legislature with no success. It wasn't until 2000 when NALEO invited Avila to do a presentation on redistricting before the legislative caucus of minority officials that Avila mentioned to them that while legislative redistricting was important, local at-large districts were the single most important hurdle to minorities' elections. At the time most cities and school or other districts in California elected their governing boards using at-large election systems.[14] The exceptions (those that elected by district) tended to be the very large cities and school districts. Getting people elected at the local level was crucial to have a pool of experienced candidates that could then be viable candidates for the legislature. This argument probably struck a chord with Richard Polanco who was at the time the Senate majority leader because he approached Avila about sponsoring a bill that became SB 976. His Chief of Staff Saeed Ali took Avila's proposal to the legislative council which came back with a document that Avila described as "completely off-base."[15] He therefore decided to write his own bill, with advice from Robert Rubin, former legal director for the Lawyers' Committee for Civil Rights (LCCR) of the San Francisco Bay Area, convinced that it would not become law. But Richard Polanco really believed in Avila's bill and his position as majority leader meant he was owed many favors in the legislature. The bill died once in the Senate but Polanco resuscitated it. It worked its way to the Assembly which tweaked it marginally and was back in the Senate for concurrence. It was adopted in the Senate by a vote of 24 to 10 and in the Assembly by a vote of 47 to 25. In July 2002, Governor Gray Davis pondered vetoing the bill. When Davis representatives contacted Avila, he immediately called Senator Polanco who apparently found the words to convince the governor to sign the bill into law. The California Voting Rights Act of 2001 became law in 2002, with an effective start date of January 1, 2003, "with little fanfare, indeed practically unnoticed by the public or the media."[16]

However this was only the first part of the battle, because a law is only as useful as the extent to which it is enforced. It took Avila more than two years to put the organization together to take on their first case with Robert Rubin.

They filed their first suit in 2003 against the Hanfort Unified School District[17] and it was immediately settled and the attorney's fees to the plaintiffs were part of the settlement.[18] So the case was a success but the law wasn't really tested.

The real test for the new law came in 2004 when the city of Modesto was sued and fought back. Avila and Rubin contacted George H. Brown since they needed a major law firm (Heller Ehrman) for such a big case. The team filed a suit under the CVRA on behalf of some Latino residents of the city of Modesto. The plaintiffs claimed that racially polarized voting was preventing Latinos from being elected. Moreover, the city had only elected one Latino council member since 1911 even though the city Latino population exceeded 25 percent, therefore demonstrating an absence of electoral success. They initially lost the case in 2005 when the Stanislaus County Superior Court Judge, Roger M. Beauchesne, sided with Modesto and declared the law unconstitutional. Judge Beauchesne argued that the law showed preference to minorities without requiring them to demonstrate need and also ruled that the requirement for the city to pay attorney's fees was an unconstitutional gift of public funds. But they appealed and the constitutionality of the CVRA was finally confirmed by the Fifth District Court of Appeal in December 2006.[19] When the California Supreme Court refused to review the case in 2007, Avila breathed a sigh of relief. His vision had come to fruition. *Sanchez v. Modesto* ended in settlement after the city voted on a ballot measure to use district voting by 2009. But the city still had to pay $3 million in fees for the defendants' lawyers. In the middle of the Great Recession all city halls and school boards in California paid close attention to such a settlement. And many lawyers did too as voting rights litigation appeared more appealing. Avila had told lawmakers when he testified for the bill in 2002 that he expected other attorneys would take on cases because of favorable incentives written into the measure.[20] Some might argue that it was self-serving for lawyers to write a law that helps them get paid.[21] Yet it is precisely the cost that is the real deterrent for municipalities and makes it not worth it to fight. The cost of switching to district elections is very minimal in comparison and that is why so many cities are nowadays doing it voluntarily. The CVRA is such a deterrent that in many cases it is not even used. In essence it has become, for the local level, what the VRA was in the 1990s.

THE CALIFORNIA VOTING RIGHTS ACT: A QUIET REVOLUTION?

The California Voting Rights Act addresses the problem of at-large elections within the context of racially polarized voting. At-large districts were a product of the Progressive movement in the early twentieth century to try and weaken neighborhood parochialism and machine politics and to implement a jurisdiction-wide perspective. During the Progressive era the lack of competition in local elections was also perceived as a big issue. Progressives therefore pushed for nonpartisan elections as a solution to the problem of one-party rule in the cities. Their idea was to promote more business-like administration of cities. But business efficiency was also designed to discourage participation by the masses as it had a racial and class component.[22] They were successful in the sense that nonpartisan elections are a feature of most American cities. Even though in nonpartisan elections the party name does not appear on the ballot and parties do not play a formal role it does not mean that, as a matter of constitutional law, parties are barred from participating in the election.[23] So national parties are weakened by nonpartisan elections but when they get involved in local elections they do bring organizational power. Besides, academic work has shown that voters rely on party affiliation even in non-partisan elections. A study of down-ballot, nonpartisan statewide elections in California showed that voters had difficulty choosing whom to support in the absence of partisan identification. Moreover, a large percentage of voters changed their candidate preference when they discovered their party affiliations.[24] And yet electoral competition at the local level is almost non-existent.[25] This is particularly problematic for under-resourced minority challengers of local political machines.

The California Voting Rights Act applies to all levels of governments: cities, school districts, and special election districts. It applies only to at-large and from-district electoral systems, or combination systems.[26] Indeed, there are more than two possible redistricting systems. At one extreme are single-member districts and at the other is at-large election of all members of a city council or other legislators in a given jurisdiction. At-large systems are those in which each member of the governing board is elected by all the voters in the jurisdiction. In between single-member and at-large systems there are different alternative systems. "From-district" elections require each member of the governing board to live within a particular district. However, elections are still by all the voters in the jurisdiction, rather than being limited to the voters within a district. There are also combination systems in which, for example, a primary election may be conducted "by-district," but the general election is conducted "from" those same districts: the top two vote winners in the primary election in each district run for election "at-large" in the general election. All these variations can be challenged if the minority plaintiffs can show that racially polarized voting (RPV) limits their ability to elect or influence the election of minority-preferred candidates.[27]

Unlike with the federal VRA there is no requirement of proving geographic compactness, and no necessity to create a hypothetical single-member district consisting of over a 50 percent Latino eligible voter population. In a way, the CVRA remedies the loophole in *Bartlett* which allows for crossover districts to be drawn in the redistricting process, but does not allow valid crossover claims under Section 2.[28] The CVRA reads:

> An at-large method of election may not be imposed or applied in a manner that impairs the ability of a protected class to elect candidates of its choice or its ability to influence the outcome of an election, as a result of the dilution or the abridgment of the rights of voters who are members of a protected class.[29]

The major requirement is that plaintiffs must prove racially polarized voting that prevents the ability of a protected class to elect candidates of their choice or to influence the outcome of an election.[30] The term "protected class" as used in the CVRA, has been recognized as race-neutral in identifying those plaintiffs who have standing to bring a claim and seek remedial action under the statute.[31] A protected class is defined by the CVRA as "a class of voters who are members of a race, color or language minority group, as this class is referenced and defined in the federal Voting Rights Act."[32] Subdivision (b) of California Election Code Section 14028[33] also lays out the framework for the plaintiffs' burden of proof, borrowing from some VRA case law such as *LULAC v. Clements*, where racially polarized voting may be determined through an examination of election results in which at least one candidate is a member of a protected class, elections involving ballot measures, or any other electoral choices that impact the rights and privileges of members of a protected class.[34]

In addition, there is no need to prove the other Senate Report factors as required under the Federal Voting Rights Act. These Senate Report factors are probative and can be introduced, but they are not necessary.[35] What the federal and CVRA have in common is that there is no requirement to prove an intent to discriminate against minority voting strength. Once a court finds that the elements previously mentioned have been met and a violation of the CVRA has taken place, the Court must implement appropriate remedies, including district-based elections tailored to remedy the violation.[36]

And as mentioned before, maybe the most important innovation of the CVRA is that it mandates the award of costs, attorney fees, and expert expenses to prevailing plaintiffs.[37] On the other hand, prevailing party defendants are not entitled to costs unless the court finds the action to be "frivolous, unreasonable or without foundation," a very high standard. Or as Morgan Kousser puts it:

> Unlike in federal litigation, plaintiffs may be held to be "prevailing parties" (and thus collect fees and costs) if there is a "causal connection" between their lawsuit and a change in the defendants' behavior—for example, if a defendant jurisdiction switches from at-large to district elections once a lawsuit is announced, even if only minimal legal paperwork is ever filed. This last provision encourages lawyers to file numerous lawsuits without the fear of having to carry them through complicated hearings, depositions, and trials, and it encourages local jurisdictions to settle well before they begin to run up large bills.[38]

So the CVRA has been very successful in responding to one of the main gaps in Section 2 of the VRA that is the difficulty in bringing Section 2 claims at the local level and in rural communities. However, some issues remain as Paige Epstein noted:

> Thus, while coalition, crossover, and influence districts clearly seem to be *allowed* under the CVRA, it remains unclear to what extent such districts are desired, required, or implemented, and what shape such districts are required to take. Relatedly, the CVRA does not appear to allow for vote dilution claims to be brought against jurisdictions with district-based election systems.[39]

What is clear however its that at-large elections are disappearing in California but slowly because it's done exclusively through litigation or the threat of litigation. The CVRA puts redistricting litigant at the heart of the redistricting process making them the main agent of electoral reform.[40] The CVRA pushes a bit further the procedural regime ushered in by the Supreme Court some fifty years ago when it made litigants agents of redistricting.

THE SLOW DEATH OF AT-LARGE ELECTIONS THROUGH LITIGATION

The question raised by at-large elections in the context of the minority rights revolution is not new. In 1968 Paul A. Freund wrote that "while the major outlines of the reapportionment doctrine may be settled, there remain a host of questions still unresolved: its application to local government, the legal status of gerrymandering, the limits on multimember districts, the use of weighted or fractional voting in the legislature."[41] In 1982 Malcolm E. Jewell was still wondering: "As we enter the period of post-1980 reapportionment, one of the questions that remain is whether the trend toward single-member districts in state legislatures and city councils will continue."[42] In California, in 2017, the process is underway through litigation. First came Modesto, then Compton, Anaheim, Escondido, Whittier, Palmdale and others.[43] Ethnically

Table 7.1. California Voting Rights Challenges to Cities with Population over 50,000

City Population 2010	*Charter*[1]	*Electoral System*	*Minority %*[2]	*Lawsuit Filed*	*Settlement Terms*	*Attorney Fee to Plaintiff*
Anaheim 336,265	Yes	At-large	53% Latino	Yes	Ballot measure for SMD and increase the size of council; keep separate mayor	$1.2 million
Bellflower 76,616	No	At-large	54% Latino; 14% Af.Am	Yes	N/A	N/A
Compton 94,455	Yes	From-districts with separately elected mayor	66% Latino; 30% Af. Am	Yes	Ballot measure for single-member Districts successful; keep at-large mayor	Confidential but subject to PRA request
Escondido 143,911	No	At-large	48% Latino	Yes	SMD established by Comm'n; keep at-large mayor	$385,000
Fullerton 135,161	No	At-large	34% Latino	Yes	N/A	N/A
Highland 53,161	No	At-large	49% Latino	Yes	Ballot measure for SMD	N/A
Merced 78,958	Yes	At-large with separately elected mayor	49% Latino	No	Ballot measure for SMD and change GME to Nov. even[3]; keep separate mayor	N/A
Modesto 201,165	Yes	Numbered posts with at-large voting	36.5% Latino	Yes	Ballot measure for SMD with separate mayor	$3 million

Palmdale 152,750	Yes	At-large with separately elected mayor	55% Latino; 13% Af.Am	Yes	Settlement to switch to SMD and GME Nov. even	$4.5 million
Santa Barbara 88,410	Yes	At-large with separately elected mayor	40% Latino	Yes	Settled before trial, switched to SMD	N/A
Santa Clarita 176,320	No	At-large	30% Latino	Yes	Change GME to Nov. Even; Cumulative voting if approved by court[4]	$600,000 less if contribution of cum. vot.
Tulare 59,278	Yes	At-large	56% Latino	Yes	Ballot measure for SMD passed	$225,000
Tulare 68,548	Yes	At-large	35% Latino	No	Ballot measure for SMD with separate mayor	N/A
Visalia 124,442	Yes	At-large	45% Latino	Yes, after ballot measure for SMD failed	Court-ordered process for SMD	$125,000
Whittier 85,331	Yes	At-large	66% Latino	Yes	Ballot measure for SMD with separate mayor	N/A

Source: Some of this information was summarized in Kimberly Hall Barlow and Marguerite Mary Leoni, "The California Voting Rights Act—an Update," League of California Cities Annual Conference, September 4, 2014. On file with author.

1. Most cities are without the ability to address the potential of CVRA liability except through the ballot box.
2. Percents are of total population based on 2006–2012 American Community Survey.
3. The goal is to change municipal balloting dates to coincide with state and national general elections to encourage better turnout.
4. A cumulative voting system was blocked when Secretary of State Alex Padilla said that there was no definition of a cumulative voting system in state law that would allow the Secretary of State to certify it. The proposed OPTO-MARK system had not been tested for use in a cumulative voting election environment by the Secretary of State's office.

diverse cities that hold at-large elections and have few minority officeholders have proved vulnerable to lawsuits under the California Voting Rights Act. All a plaintiff has to do is demonstrate that racially polarized voting exists[44] and sometimes that can be done with election results that reveal contrasting outcomes between predominantly minority precincts and Anglo ones. Roughly 75 percent of California school boards use at-large voting, as do many city councils and other local boards. Many jurisdictions fear a lawsuit have switched to single-member district elections, usually after receiving the "demand letter" from lawyers. No local government has won a state voting rights lawsuit, and jurisdictions that can't demonstrate fair treatment of minorities in at-large election systems must pay plaintiffs' legal fees. So across California, community college and school districts are eliminating at-large elections.[45] Cities have been reluctant, leading to a series of legal actions.

The 50,000 threshold is arbitrary here but it stems from the observation that city sizes matter as far as districts are concerned. Indeed one could argue that the need for districts is linked to the size of the city. In a small city where campaign is cheap and a candidate can visit most households herself, the need for district is harder to justify, or it might actually be counterproductive in the case of a small city with a majority Latino population.[46] This hypothesis seems to be confirmed by Latino successes for mayoral elections. Latino mayor numbers are driven by small cities. More than half of Latino local elected come from cities with less than 40,000 inhabitants. Also, 72 percent of all Latino elected officials sit on council seats in cities with a population of under 75,000. Only 19 percent of Latinos are elected to city council seats in cities with populations over 100,000.[47]

BROWN V. BLACK IN A SEA OF BLUE?: *GONZALEZ V. CITY OF COMPTON*

One of the interesting developments of the CVRA is that it provides us with an insight into the tension inside the Democratic coalition. At the legislative level Latinos have usually had to convince the Democratic leadership to push Anglo incumbents out of office to gain seats. Latinos have tried to work with African American and Asian American elected officials to avoid open conflict. At the local and supposedly non-partisan level, minority tensions occurred because of the CVRA. The city of Compton had been a bastion of African American community in South Central Los Angeles but demographic changes pushed Latinos to ask for more representation.

In 1980, the city of Compton, a heavily Democratic city, had a population composed of 73.9 percent African American and 21.1 percent Latino.

By 2000, it was 40.3 percent African American and 56.8 percent Latino. By 2010, it was 66 percent Latino and 30 percent African American but Latinos never comprised more than 30 percent of registered voters.[48] The city council has not reflected that demographic evolution since no Latino candidate has been elected to city office in the recent past. No Latino candidate even won the primary elections.

A group of Latino voters sued the city under the California Voting Rights Act of 2001. Plaintiffs Felicitas González, Flora Ruiz, and Enelida Alvarez sued the City of Compton in December 2010, claiming that the city's mixed at-large method of elections violated CVRA the because it prevented Latino voters from electing candidates of their choice in this city of almost 100,000. The plaintiffs were represented by Joaquin Avila, Director of the National Voting Rights Advocacy Initiative at Seattle University School of Law, and by Rosen, Bien, & Galvan, LLP of San Francisco.[49] During our interview Joaquin Avila explained that MALDEF was reluctant to take on the case because the City Council was controlled by African Americans. It had never been done. And this is why this case resonates so strongly because it was presented as Latinos using the CVRA to fight African Americans for local representation. Since MALDEF refused, Joaquin Avila having been born in the city of Compton felt compelled to take on the case.[50]

The city denied the plaintiffs' allegation and maintained that its electoral system was equally open to all voters and could only be changed by voters. The trial started in May 2012 in Los Angeles Superior Court.[51]

Morgan Kousser was hired as an expert witness and he attempted to measure racial polarization in a city with a notoriously low turnout.[52] His testimony showed prevalent racial polarization in the city of Compton suggesting low Latino turnout does not fully account for Latino losses in the city because African Americans, who form a substantial majority of the electorate, would turn out at sufficiently high levels to assure victory in an at-large system. He concluded by stating:

> Every statistical model of the Compton elections produces roughly similar results, and all show racial polarization in the same patterns. From Proposition 187 in 1994, through four municipal elections from 2001 to 2011, Latino candidates never drew enough non-Latino support to progress from primaries to runoff elections, much less actually to gain election. In only one of eleven contests did non-Latinos cast more than 10 percent of their votes for a Latino candidate, and in only four of the eleven did more than 1 percent of non-Latino registered voters support Latino candidates. In all but two of the eleven elections, Latino candidates captured pluralities of the Latino vote, and in four of them, more than two-thirds. In sum, voting patterns in precincts with different percentages of Latino registrants or voters differed systematically and starkly.[53]

In other words, in an at-large election in an electorate in which Latinos comprise only at best 30 percent of the potential voters, they can only elect the candidate of their choice if they turn out at more than twice the level of all other voters.

After denial of preliminary injunction, the case and attorney's fees ultimately were settled. In the settlement, the city agreed to provide two opportunities for Compton voters to decide whether to establish district-based elections for City Council by placing charter amendments on the June 2012 ballot and, if the measure failed to pass in June, to place it on the ballot for the November 2012 elections. The city also agreed to provide voter education on the proposed charter amendments. If the charter amendments were passed, the city agreed to draw electoral districts according to the 2010 census. Plaintiffs were also given the opportunity to review the proposed electoral districts. The next City Council election was slated for April 2013.

In 2013, the newly redistricted majority-Latino Second District of the city of Compton elected its first Latino and the youngest councilman in its history.[54] Isaac Galvan defeated incumbent Lillie Dobson in an election with a total abysmal turnout of 16 percent (9 percent in precinct and 7 percent by mail).[55] This case proves that the idea behind the CVRA is sound. It can help to create a pool of minority (Latino) candidates at the local level that would then have an opportunity to move on to higher office. Issac Galvan ran in 2016 for a State Senate seat in the Thirty-fifth District even though he did not win the top-two primary as the minority vote was split three ways between three non-Anglo candidates (one Asian, one Latino, one African American) proving again how crucial racial affiliations are.[56]

GEOGRAPHICAL DISTRICTING AND WINNER-TAKE-ALL

It is difficult to evaluate the real impact of the CVRA because the shifts to districts have been so recent that they may not have led to the election of minority candidates. Yet if one were to try to assess the first lesson of the CVRA is that, in itself, switching to districts is no guarantee of electoral success. In the Third District of the city of Anaheim in 2016, Jose F. Moreno defeated incumbent Jordan Brandman by 41 votes.[57] In 2016, in the city of Palmdale, while having two majority-minority districts only elected one Latino councilman.[58] In Whittier instead of responding to the voting rights lawsuit by establishing a pure district system, as other municipalities have done, officials reached a compromise. They created a new structure for the City Council in which four members would be elected by district and the fifth would be elected at-large. The fifth council member would also serve as mayor but would have no more power than the other council members and would vote with them as well.[59] In 2016 Whittier elected its second Latino council member in its history but that did not change the balance of power in the city which was to be expected.[60] The main problem is that once litigation is over the bulk of the work in terms of community empowerment, outreach, and get-out-the-vote operation remains to be made. If activists limit their tasks to hiring lawyers to change the election system but don't follow through with on-the-ground political outreach then the CVRA can't live up to its expectation.

And the expectation is quite high because it clearly is to achieve levels of representation in proportion to the political weight of a given community. For instance the Leadership California Institute California Latino Legislative Caucus and NALEO present figures in a way that is very explicit: according to the census Latinos represented in 2014, 38.6 percent of the California population but 19.6 percent of voter registration on average between 2002 and 2012. During the same period, Latino represented, on average, only 16.5 percent of the California electorate. These figures are directly compared with Latinos' descriptive representation at different levels of responsibility. In 2015 they represented 12.5 percent of state senators, 23.8 percent assembly members, 9.8 percent of county supervisors, and 14.6 percent of City Council members.[61] Pointing out the discrepancy in this manner implies that the ultimate goal is some sort of proportional representation. While being a crucial reform for the emergence of minority elected officials at the local level, single-member plurality districts may not be the most adequate way to reach proportional representation. Yet, there does not seem to be a real impetuous, to say the least, in the US and in California in particular to push for some form of proportional representation.

What strikes the outside observer is that, for all the reform efforts and political experiments taking place in California in the last half-century, the issue of proportional representation has made little headway, which confirms the expression that Bruce Cain used to describe it: "the last taboo in American politics." Nevertheless, the CVRA begs the question of alternative electoral system. Joaquin Avila, in our conversation, only expressed his preference for district elections but this preference was not based on any political theory or empirical justification. As the genesis of the law summed-up in this chapter we can see that Avila, a Latino civil rights attorney, operated only in the frame provided by the federal VRA and was only looking for a way to tweak it to make litigation more efficient at the local level and increase Latino representation in rural areas. The impetus behind his effort was not to come up with a new way to look at elections and minority representation. At-large elections have a bad reputation among minority groups, for good reasons, because they have been used in the context of a "winner-take-all" system designed to frustrate minority groups. This is a paradoxical trend because most activists seem to advocate for single-member plurality districts while at the same time wishing that elections would yield proportional results understood as the only way for minorities to be "fairly" represented. Here lies the paradox: "if one's highest priority is to achieve proportionality one has to opt for proportional representation; conversely, if one is unwilling to abandon plurality and geographical districting, one can try to minimize extreme disproportionalities . . . but one has to reconcile oneself to not getting proportional or near proportional results."[62] One of the main criticisms of proportional representation is that in the US most local elections are nonpartisan and *in fine* PR, in whatever its form, is a call for partisan politics undermining primaries and often making party leaders "king makers." Yet SMDs in a "winner-take-all" context still raises many questions.

The CVRA by omitting the requirement that the racial minority be geographically compact seems to have opened the door to alternative voting systems, at least when there is no such geographic compactness. The CVRA suggests the use of single-member districts as remedies but does not foreclose the use of modified, at-large remedies.[63] However, California courts have not yet imposed a non-winner-take-all voting systems, while the *Sanchez* decision has noted the possibility without criticism.[64] Yet, the CVRA only allows liability for at-large systems while leaving single-member district systems unaddressed.[65] Therefore, jurisdictions in California often adopt single-member district elections, not because they necessarily see them as better, but because doing so prevents litigation under the CVRA.

While the promises of the VRA and court intervention in the regulation of elections led many minority groups and activists frustrated about the modest results in increased descriptive representation, the most successful reforms passed in California over the past twenty years have been the CVRA that forces switching to single-member districts and the Independent Redistricting Commissions that took redistricting out of the hands of the legislature.[66] However, both of these reforms by themselves are no guarantee that minorities will reach descriptive representation proportional to their electoral weight.

NOTES

1. For instance his fight to eliminate at-large elections in school districts goes back to the 1970s. "At-Large Elections Can Keep Chicanos Off School Boards," *Un Nuevo Dia* 2, no. 4 (1976), 13.

2. Testimony of The Mexican American Legal Defense and Educational Fund on the Voting Rights Act, Presented By Joaquin G. Avila, Associate Counsel, Before

The Subcommittee on Civil Constitutional Fights of the Judiciary Committee US House of Representatives, June 5, 1981. On file with author.

3. *Thornburg v. Gingles* (478 U.S. 30 [1986]), 50–51

4. 42 U.S.C. § 1973(b) (prescribing the totality of the circumstances standard).

5. For example, Assembly Bill No. 2, California Legislature, 1989–1990 Regular Session. A.B. No. 2 mandated district elections for school districts meeting certain criteria. The bill passed both the Assembly and the Senate, but was vetoed by the governor; Assembly Bill No. 343, California Legislature, 1989–1990 Regular Session. Initially A.B. No. 343 provided for changes in election procedures relating to schools and community college districts. These changes facilitated the ability of local communities to establish district elections. On August 7, 1990, the State Senate amended A.B. No. 343. The Senate amendment changed the focus of the bill to the retention of certain election records. These election records consisted of information relating to voter registration and voter turnout. The bill did not go beyond the Senate Appropriations Committee; Assembly Bill No. 845, California Legislature, 1989–1990 Regular Session. A.B. No. 845 permitted municipalities in response to litigation based upon the federal Voting Rights Act, the Fourteenth and Fifteenth Amendments to the United States Constitution, a federal civil rights act, 42 U.S.C. § 1983, and Article I or Article II of the California Constitution, to adopt an ordinance which incorporated district elections as a proposed remedy without the necessity of first securing public approval in an election. The bill passed both the Assembly and the Senate, but was vetoed by the governor; Assembly Bill No. 1002, California Legislature, 1991–1992 Regular Session. A.B. No. 1002 would require school districts meeting certain criteria to adopt a district based election system for electing members to the school board. The bill passed both the Assembly and the Senate, but was vetoed by the governor; Assembly Bill No. 1107, California Legislature, 1991–1992 Regular Session. A.B. No. 1107 facilitated the procedures for permitting community residents to petition their school districts for establishing district-elections. The bill passed both the Assembly and the Senate, but was vetoed by the governor; Assembly Bill No. 2949, California Legislature, 1991–1992 Regular Session. A.B. No. 2949 followed basically the same language as A.B. 1107 which affected the procedures for petitioning school districts for establishing district elections. Became Law: Chapter 350, Statutes of 1992.

6. *Gomez v. City of Watsonville* (863 F.2d 1407 [9th Cir. 1988]). In 1960, the city of Watsonville had a population of 11,572 including 1,000 Latinos. By 1980, the city's population reached 25,543 with 11,509 Latinos. Latino residents made up 40 percent of the city's voting age population, yet only 37 percent of the city's citizens. Although the District Court found evidence of racially polarized voting, it concluded that the Latino population was not sufficiently cohesive politically and geographically compact to satisfy Section 2 requirements. The District Court recognized that 95 percent of Latinos had voted for the same candidate but focused on low voter registration and turnout among Latinos as the main reason. The Circuit Court disagreed with this assessment, considering instead that "low voter registration evidences the lingering socioeconomic effects of past discrimination." *Gomez v. City of Watsonville*, 1416, footnote 4.

7. The first direct consequence that the neighboring city of Salinas settled right after *Gomez* to avoid such an expensive trial. It switched to districts for city council but maintained at-large election for mayor. Simon Salinas became the city's first Latino councilman and was elected in a district in which turnout was higher than in Anglo districts. For more details, especially about the city of Pomona for which she was a redistricting consultant, see Florence Adams, *Latinos and Local Representation: Changing Realities, Emerging Theories* (New York: Garland, 2000), chap. 3.

8. Another candidate, Anthony Campos was elected in 1987 but he was perceived by local Latino activists as too close to Anglo interests. For more details on the local political context surrounding the Gomez case, see Paule Cruz Takash and Joaquin Avila, "Latino Political Participation in Rural California," Working Group on Farm Labor and Rural Poverty, Working Paper #8, February 1989.

9. Mark Stein, "One Latino Wins, 3 Others Lose in Watsonville Vote," *Los Angeles Times*, December 6, 1989, A3. An anecdote can help understand how consequential method of election can be. Denise Hulett, National Senior council for MALDEF, recalled in an interview that she talked to the head of the EEOC that was conducting an investigation about sexual assault. In all the cities he investigated, Latina women told him law enforcement was absent. Only in Watsonville did they say the police cared about their sexual assault claims. That is because after the *Gomez* case a Latino mayor was elected and he selected a Latino Chief of Police. Method of elections can have consequences on criminal law enforcement. Interview with Denise Hulett, 2016.

10. "Even before the retrenchment of *Shaw* and its progeny, 'other minority' plaintiffs lost more often than they won. The failure to meet one or more of the *Gingles* criteria could often be traced to the problems of group heterogeneity and multiracial context. The circumstances of Asians and Latinos differ from those of African Americans in important ways, a situation we have called group heterogeneity." Cain and Miller, "Voting Rights Mismatch," 161.

11. So much so that in 1999 it's the US Justice Department that threatened to sue the city Santa Paula if it did not switch to a district system, not Latino activists. The city of Santa Paula had a population of 59 percent Latino but only had one Latino city council member. Margaret Talev, "Santa Paula Not Alone in Voting Issue," *Los Angeles Times*, September 26, 1999,1.

12. *Aldasoro v. El Centro School District* (922 F. Supp. 339 [S.D. Cal. 1995]), *Ruiz v. City of Santa Maria* (160 F.3d 543 [9th Cir. 1998]).

13. Joaquin Avila, Eugene Lee, and Terry M. Ao, "Report: Voting Rights in California: 1982–2006," *Southern California Review of Law & Social Justice* 17, no. 131 (2007), 149.

14. At the time, there were a total of 478 municipalities: 108 chartered cities, and 370 general law cities. Out of the total number of cities, only twenty-seven, or 5.6 percent, conducted elections by districts. Based upon a 1995 survey, it was estimated that 65 percent of public school districts conducted at-large elections, 20 percent had candidate residency districts and at-large voting, and 15 percent had district elections.

15. Joaquin Avila interview, 2016.

16. Florence Adams, "Minorities and Representation in the New Millennium," in *Redistricting in the New Millennium*, ed. Peter F. Galderisi (Lanham, MD: Lexington Books, 2005), 177.

17. *Gomez v. Hanford Joint Union School District*. There had not been any Latino on the district board of trustees in twenty years, despite a population that was 38 percent Latino.

18. It wasn't the first time that Hanfort (population of 33,000 in 1990) made the news because of at-large elections.In 1993, the at-large City Council election was switched to district after the Department of Justice found that, in the context of racially polarized voting, this method diluted minority votes. Hanforf is the largest city in Kings County, a jurisdiction that is covered by Section 5 of the Voting Rights Act. The DOJ refuse preclearance because the city's annexations diluted Latino populations and at-large election systems had prevented of Latino voters to elect a candidate of their choice. Adams, *Latinos and Local Representation*, chap. 5.

19. *Sanchez v. City of Modesto* (51 Cal. Rptr. 3d 821 [2006], 145 Cal. App. 4th 660).

20. Michael R. Blood, "Jackpot: Lawyers Earn Fees from Law They Wrote," *The Associated Press*, http://www.newsday.com/news/nation/jackpot-lawyers-earn-fees-from-law-they-wrote-1.1590856.

21. Greg Lucas, "Voting Rights Act: A Free Generator for Lawyers?," *Calweekly*, May 5, 2011, http://capitolweekly.net/voting-rights-act-a-fee-generator-for-lawyers/; The controversy surrounding the Dinuba case over J. Avila's fees did not help in this regard. Adams, *Latinos and Local Representation*, 72–73. Even though on need to admit that big settlements, or the threat of an expensive trial, are the only things that seem to get the jurisdictions' attentions and force reform.

22. For a study of partisan bias in California, see for instance Eugene C. Lee, *The Politics of Nonpartisan Elections in California Cities* (Los Angeles: University of California Press, 1957). For an overview of the literature, see Carol A. Cassey, "The Nonpartisan Ballot in the US," in *Electoral Laws and Their Political Consequences*, eds., Grofman Bernard and Arend Lijphart (New York: Algora Publishing, 2003), 226–41. For a discussion of race, see for instance, William P. Collins, "Race as a Salient Factor in Nonpartisan Elections," *The Western Political Quarterly* 33, no. 3 (1980), 330–35.

23. *Cal. Democratic Party v. Lungren* (919 F. Supp. 1397, 1399 [N.D. Cal. 1996]) (California constitutional amendment barring parties from endorsing candidates in nonpartisan elections violates the First Amendment).

24. Brian F. Schaffner and Matthew J. Streb, "The Partisan Heuristic in Low-Information Elections," *Public Opinion Quarterly* 66, no. 4 (2002), 569–70. Since this article deals with statewide contests it is not certain that party endorsement, which only recently became possible in California, has the same effect at the local level.

25. Voter turnout is substantially lower, incumbents are safer, and scholars have found no indication that candidates engage in any substantial policy competition. Brian Schaffner, Matthew Streb, and Gerald Wright, "Teams without Uniforms: The Nonpartisan Ballot in State and Local Elections," *Political Research Quarterly* 54, no. 7 (2001), 19–22. For a study investigating why this is the case see David

Schleicher, "Why Is There No Partisan Competition in City Council Elections? The Role of Election Law," *Journal of Law and Politics* 23, no 4 (2007), 419–73.

26. Elec. Code § 14026(a), 14027.

27. Suspect features under the CVRA include a history of electoral losses by minority candidates or a history of unresolved issues disproportionately impacting the minority community (affordable housing, street and sidewalk maintenance, juvenile crime, etc.), while the said minority represents an important part the of the general population.

28. *Bartlett v. Strickland* (556 U.S. 1[2009]), Justice Kennedy's opinion: "States that wish to draw crossover districts are free to do so where no other prohibition exists. Majority-minority districts are only required if all three *Gingles* factors are met and if §2 applies based on a totality of the circumstances. In areas with substantial crossover voting it is unlikely that the plaintiffs would be able to establish the third *Gingles* precondition—bloc voting by majority voters." For a larger discussion on potential claims by coalition plaintiffs under the CVRA Joanna E. Cuevas Ingram, "The Color of Change: Voting Rights in the Twenty-First Century and the California voting Rights Act," *Harvard Latino Law Review* 15 (2012), 183–231. http://harvardllr.com/wp-content/uploads/2012/09/HBK104.pdf.

29. Cal. Elec. Code § 14027.

30. Elec. Code § 14028.

31. *Sanchez v. City of Modesto* (145 Cal. App. 4th 660, 681–86 [Cal. Ct. App. 2007]) cert. denied (552 U.S. 974 [2007]), holding that CVRA is race-neutral, that the city failed to show that CVRA was facially invalid and that all persons, regardless of race, have standing under CVRA to sue for race-based vote dilution, such that CVRA is not subject to strict scrutiny under equal protection jurisprudence.

32. Cal. Elec. Code § 14026(d), referring to 42 U.S.C. § 1973, et seq.

33. Elec. Code § 14028(b).

34. *League of United Latin Am. Citizens, Council No. 4434 v. Clements* (999 F.2d 831, 865, 876 [5th Cir. 1993]) (en banc) (LULAC II) ("Section 2 and the Senate Report instruct us to consider the number of minority candidates elected to office." One of the Senate Report factors for a Section 2 claim that goes toward the totality of circumstances analysis of vote dilution "is the willingness of the racial or ethnic majority-in this case, White voters-to give their votes to minority candidates.")

35. The Senate report included the following factors: The extent of any history of discrimination in the jurisdiction that touched the right of the members of the minority group to participate in the democratic process; the extent to which the jurisdiction uses devices that may enhance the opportunity for discrimination, such as majority vote requirements or anti-single shot provisions; whether the members of the minority group bear the effects of discrimination in such areas as education, employment, and health, which hinder their ability to participate effectively in the political process; whether political campaigns have been characterized by overt or subtle racial appeals; and, the extent to which members of the minority group have been elected to public office in the jurisdiction.

36. Cal. Elec. Code § 14029.

37. See id. § 14030. Moreover, the state court is authorized to grant upward adjustment or a fees multiplier.

38. Morgan J. Kousser, "Do the Facts of Voting Right Support Justice Roberts's Opinion in Shelby County?," *Transatlantica* 1 (2015), https://transatlantica.revues.org/7462.

39. Paige Epstein, "Addressing Minority Vote Dilution through State Voting Rights Acts" (University of Chicago Public Law & Legal Theory Working Paper No. 474, 2014).

40. Lisa Marshall Manheim, "Redistricting Litigation and the Delegation of Democratic Design," *Boston University Law Review* 93 (2013), 563.

41. Paul A. Freund, *Democratic Representation: Reapportionment in Law and Politics* (New York: Oxford University Press, 1968), 6.

42. Malcolm E. Jewell, "The Consequences of Single and Multi-Member Districts," in *Representation and Redistricting Issues*, eds. Bernard Grofman, Arend Lijphart, Robert B. McKay, and Howard A. Scarrow (Lanham, MD: Lexington Books, 1982), 129.

43. Jean Merl, "Officials in City Agree to District Voting," *Los Angeles Times*, May 7, 2015, B1.

44. The trial court in *Jauregui v. City of Palmdale* (Los Angeles County Super. Ct. No. BC483039) held that it was sufficient if plaintiffs proved that polarized voting occurred in an at-large electoral system. Upheld on appeal, B253713 (Cal. Ct. App. June 10, 2015).

45. Mitchell Landsberg, "Making Sure Minorities' Vote Counts," *Los Angeles Times*, January 4, 2009, B1. National Demographics, Douglas Johnson's company, identified in 2016 195 jurisdictions that had switched to district elections: 131 school districts, 28 cities, 1 county, 27 community college districts, and 8 other special districts. http://www.ndcresearch.com/updated-counts-cvra-driven-changes/.

46. An example would be the city of Corcoran, with a population a bit superior to 8,000 in 1990 that switched to districts in 1993 for a gain that is not obvious. Adams, *Latino and Local Representation*, chap. 6.

47. Leadership California Institute California Latino Legislative Caucus National Association of Latino Elected and Appointed Officials (NALEO), "The Status of Latinos in California: An analysis of the growing Latino population, voting trends and elected representation, 2015", http://leadershipcaliforniainstitute.org/sites/all/files/Status percent20of percent20Latinos percent20Report percent20Preview.pdf.

48. Using Spanish-surname estimates.

49. The City of Compton is represented by City Attorney Craig Cornwell and his deputy, Jose Paz, and by the Marin County office of Nielsen, Merksamer, Parrinello, Gross & Leoni LLP.

50. Interview with Joaquin Avila, 2016.

51. *Gonzalez et al. v. City of Compton*, Case No. C45094 (Los Angeles County Superior Court Cal. 2010).

52. This racial polarization study is the only one available because the city or their expert witness Prof. Michael Herron did not do election analysis.

53. Morgan Kousser, "Racial Polarization in Compton Elections, 1994–2011," A Report for *Gonzalez v. City of Compton*, 44, on file with author. We are indebted with Professor Kousser in many different ways; one of them is for sharing his numerous court reports and expert testimonies in California and other states.

54. Jennings Angel and Sewell Abby, "Aja Brown Elected Compton's Mayor," *Los Angeles Times*, June 6, 2013, AA1.

55. City of Compton, General Municipal Election, June 4, 2013, Summary Report, June 10, 2013. http://www.comptoncity.org/civicax/filebank/blobdload.aspx?BlobID=25793. Galvan received 767 votes against 458 for his opponent.

56. He received 32,000 compared to 35,000 for Japanese American former Assembly member Warren Furutani (AD 51). African American Assembly member Steven Bradford (AD 62) received 50,000 votes in the primaries and won the general 54 percent to 46 percent.

57. Ballotpedia, Municipal Elections in Anaheim, California 2016. https://ballotpedia.org/Municipal_elections_in_Anaheim,_California_(2016).

58. African American Councilman, Frederik Thompson lost reelection against Anglo Steven Hofbauer.

59. Previously, the council members were all elected at-large and they choose one of themselves to be mayor for a short term.

60. Editorial, "Voting Rights in Whittier," *Los Angeles Times*, December 29, 2013, A25.

61. Leadership California Institute, California Latino Legislative Caucus, National Association of Latino Elected and Appointed Officials (NALEO), The Status of Latinos in California.

62. Arend Lijphart, "Introduction to Part II," in *Representation and Redistricting Issues*, eds. Bernard Grofman, Arend Lijphart, Robert B. McKay, and Howard A. Scarrow (Lanham, MD: Lexington Books, 1982), 105.

63. Cal. Elec. Code § 14029 ("The court shall implement appropriate remedies, including the imposition of district-based elections, that are tailored to remedy the violation").

64. *Sanchez v. City of Modesto* (51 Cal. Rptr. 3d 821, 828 [Cal. Ct. App. 2006]).

65. Cal. Elec. Code § 14027 ("An at-large method of election may not be imposed or applied in a manner that impairs the ability of a protected class to elect candidates of its choice").

66. The only two exceptions are San Francisco in 2002 and Oakland in 2006 adopted "instant runoff" voting (IRV) also called "ranked choice" voting, but the measures were implemented mainly to ensure majority rule and increase turnout.

Chapter 8

Tenth Time Is a Charm

The Citizens Redistricting Commission

THE FAILURE OF PROPOSITION 77

After the bi-partisan gerrymander of 2001, the controversies over line drawing were far from being over.[1] In 2003 a new Republican governor was elected in California after the recall election of Democratic Governor Gray Davis only 10 months after his own reelection. This recall election, which was very exceptional in many aspects, was criticized for being an attack on minorities.[2] Arnold Schwarzenegger was an ambitious politician in spite of the exceptional conditions under which he was elected and, as the 2006 reelection campaign loomed, he was determined to make inroads on a few reforms he felt strongly about. Redistricting was one of them.[3]

Schwarzenegger took the decision, against the wishes of the RNC,[4] to launch the debate on redistricting reform in California, explaining to elected officials that he was seeking a compromise to remove the hegemonic power of the legislature and create more competitive districts, without defining what constituted for him a competitive district.[5] However, he also declared, preemptively, that he would not hesitate to launch an initiative campaign if the elected officials refused to cooperate.[6] He even gave them an ultimatum.[7] Schwarzenegger wanted to succeed where his predecessors had failed, and it is clear that for a time, things looked bright since there was a consensus among both majorities that redistricting was in need of reform. The nature of which remained to be defined. Both parties had reasons to be dissatisfied with the 2000 compromise and both parties thought they might find something to gain. However, in the spring of 2005, even though an agreement could have been reached, the situation deadlocked.

First, the governor's insistence that the new lines be applied immediately in 2005, that is in time for the 2006 elections, was politically unrealistic.

Republicans blamed their 2004 defeat on the 2000 redistricting compromise and Schwarzenegger was counting on redistricting to make the Democrat-controlled legislature more open to compromise with him. But because redistricting is based on census estimates, the new lines of 2005 would have to take into consideration the 3.5 million people that had moved to the state since 2000, otherwise the new redistricting plan was sure to end up in court and would probably be thrown out because it would violate the equal population principle. Moreover, as it was pointed out at the time in the press by Tim Hodson, the geography, the demography and the self-sorting of electors in the Golden State were such that it was impossible to make elections really competitive. According to his estimation, only 6 extra Assembly districts could be more competitive (for a grand total of 18 out of 80) and only 8 Senate districts out of 40 could possibly be competitive. While this increase in competition might be considered an improvement it hardly could revolutionize California politics.[8] Besides, by February polls started to show that the governor's popularity was dropping which considerably lowered his chances of forcing a deal.

A second factor helps explain why the Democrats were unlikely to strike a deal with the governor. Democrat legislators resented his ordering of an early election.[9] As a response they proposed a bill (SCA 3) that would have created a redistricting commission, knowing that the two-third majority required to have the constitutional amendment project submitted to voters was a long shot. This bill felt more like a rhetorical device used by the Democrats to accuse the Republicans of refusing the possibility of a compromise.[10]

Finally, a third factor needs to be mentioned. The Republicans had not anticipated enough the putting together of an alternative referendum. When they realized their initiative proposal was nowhere near ready, they improvised urgently and decided their best option was to adopt Ted Costa's. Costa is this unique figure in California politics who always seems to have an initiative plan up his sleeves. The problem is Costa's referendum proposal was of poor quality. The initiative project gathered the 900,000 signatures necessary to present the constitutional amendment referendum to California voters and it appeared as Proposition 77 on the ballot.[11] Proposition 77 proposed the creation of a commission composed of former judges, called special masters, who would be in charge of drawing congressional districts, Assembly and Senate districts, and districts for the Board of Equalization.[12] The setting of this commission was quite convoluted: the California Judicial Council was supposed to select 24 volunteer retired judges. The 4 leaders of the Republican and Democrat parties (2 per party and per chamber) would choose 3 judges each from the opposite party.[13] Then each legislator could knock off one judge. Finally, 3 judges out of the 8 left had to be selected. Out of those 3, one had to be a Republican and one had to be a Democrat.

The referendum also stipulated that the new districts should apply for the 2006 primary elections which meant that the state had until December 30 to choose the three judges, hold two public hearings, and draw the new district lines. An impossible task in such a small amount of time especially if one considered the state also needed to obtain preclearance from the Justice Department for the counties covered by Section 5 of the federal Voting Rights Act. Moreover, this initiative would have put a lot or pressure on local jurisdictions that would have had to put together elections in a hurry. Finally, the most improbable section of the proposition stated that judges should not take into consideration people's political affiliation while drawing the lines. Once the new lines were drawn, they were supposed to be submitted to the people via referendum. If voters rejected the new plan, the commission would have to start the process again for the next round of election, so in this case 2008.[14] With this initiative, California would have become the only state in the Union to choose commissioners randomly in a pool of candidates, to let retired judges draw electoral district lines and the only state, along with Arkansas, to have a commission composed of only three members.[15] The author of the proposition justified this exceptional measure by the need to learn from other states commissions' mistakes but his opponents easily denounced an "irresponsible experiment."[16]

However flawed Proposition 77 was it had the advantage of raising awareness about redistricting and the absence of competition after the bi-partisan plan of 2001. As we already mentioned, for instance in 2004, out of 153 state and congressional elections races that year, no district switched from one party to the other.[17] In spite of this favorable context, the measure was so poorly written that it was easily attacked. Lawmakers, in a surely self-serving fashion but nonetheless justified reasoning, objected that taking politics out of redistricting was an illusion. Redistricting remains a highly political business even in the states that have adopted supposedly independent commissions. Commissions don't fundamentally change the partisan nature of redistricting, they provide at best a different political buffer.[18] The supposedly partisan neutrality of judges was attacked in the press by prominent Republican consultant Tony Quinn, highlighting the divide between the governor and the base of his party.[19] Choosing judges on a voluntary basis all but guaranteed that only the judges most interested in the issue would participate.[20] Many judges are reluctant to step into the political thicket or the media circus that redistricting has become.[21] Moreover, one can easily imagine that party leaders would not be inclined to select judges that would make their reelection difficult. Proposition 77 foresaw this possibility and envisioned that the chief clerk would step in. However, the chief clerk being selected by the legislature, that person would risk losing his or her job by coming between the commission and the legislature, an untenable position.

The second set of criticism came from minority organizations. Since the districts had to be drawn extremely rapidly after the 2005 November elections, minority groups such as the Asian Pacific American Legal Center argued that they would be hurt by an accelerate process. Asian Americans tend to live in Anglo neighborhoods and therefore have a harder time using the federal Voting Rights Act to protect their interest. For instance, Little Saigon is a Vietnamese neighborhood in the northern part of very conservative Orange County.[22] For the first time in 2004 they elected a Vietnamese American Van Tran, to the Assembly (AD 68), and because the community is quite conservative they elected a Republican. Under Proposition 77 such districts, and therefore such results, would have been more unlikely because the address of the candidates would not have been taken into consideration anymore. Minority organizations mobilized against Proposition 77 to save the 2 Asian Americans, 4 African Americans, and 8 Latinos representing California in DC, along with the 7 Asian Americans, 6 African Americans, and 28 Latinos serving in the state legislature in 2005. The NAACP reminded people of the situation before the 1965 Voting Rights Act. Ernest Smith of the Los Angeles branch of the NAACP recalled that during the 1950s African American neighborhoods in South Central were represented by James Roosevelt, a politician living in Beverly Hills.[23] Proposition 77 was openly accused of being a Republican scheme to reduce the number of minority officials and increase GOP numbers.[24] Of course, Republicans pointed to Howard Berman's district and his protection by his brother as evidence minorities were not necessarily well served by the Democrats and the current redistricting process.[25] That point struck a chord with some minority members.

John Trasviña, vice president of MALDEF, chimed in that the new districts would hurt Latino interests and that retired judges did not represent the diversity of the state.[26] Retired judges were old, Anglo wealthy men out of touch with the rest of the state's population plight. According to the Assembly Committee Election 89.8 percent of retired judges were men over 70 years old whose pension was on average 94,000 dollars a year while the average income in California was 53,000 dollars per year. Racial statistics did not exist for the state magistrates but existed at the federal level. 74 percent of federal judges were Anglo males.[27] A 1997 report by the California Judicial Council declared that 90 percent of California judges were Anglo.[28] To leave out any mention of diversity during the committee selection process was a major blunder on the part of the authors of Proposition 77. As early as 1982, Proposition 14 stressed the importance of ethnic or racial composition the redistricting commissions. Even in 2000, the last time a referendum tried to create an independent redistricting commission using retired judges, the authors explicitly mentioned the importance for the commission to reflect the ethnic and cultural diversity of the state of California.[29] This is one of the reasons why Proposition 77 was so easily criticized and defeated.

Yet, this oversight wasn't the only one. As it turns out the third factor that explains the defeat of Proposition 77 came from the courts. Governor Schwarzenegger's decision to hop on the Ted Costa train, and his association "The People's Advocate," at the last minute ended up costing him dearly. In a twist that even a Hollywood script writer would not have anticipated, the Schwarzenegger administration learned that the text submitted to the state to become Proposition 77 was not the same as the text that was presented to voters who signed the petition.[30] According to the law, and in all logic, the two texts have to be identical. Attorney General Bill Lockyer sued and the Court sided with him.[31] A political, judicial, and media full-on battle ensued until the different appeals ended up in front of the State Supreme Court.[32] The Court decided it did not have the time to examine the details of the case before the election and that its final decision had to be postponed but that the differences between the two documents seemed to be benign. In the meantime, Proposition 77 would be submitted to the voters, letting the people decide. Since the people rejected it,[33] the Court, relieved of any political pressure, confirmed its temporary ruling.[34]

Democrats but also Republicans raised funds against Governor Schwarzenegger's proposal.[35] About $30 million were spent for and against Proposition 77. Proponents spent a bit more than $11 million and opponents more than $18 million.[36] The Republican Party officially supported Proposition 77 but some strange bedfellows, such as Berman and Doolittle for instance, found a common enemy. The governor bet big on direct democracy and lost big since all four of the propositions he supported were defeated at the polls––a signal that wasn't lost on his fellow Republicans, to the point that the incumbent governor had a very hard time obtaining the party's support for his reelection bid.[37] Too add insult to injury Governor Schwarzenegger even unsuccessfully supported another redistricting commission, Issue 4, in Ohio.[38]

PROPOSITIONS 11 AND 20 CAMPAIGNS

While Proposition 77 was a failure at the polls it demonstrated that public opinion was disturbed by the lack of competition. And who could blame them. At the time of the 2008 election, only four seats had changed parties in 495 California legislative and congressional races. But redistricting also irked the California electorate and its populist tradition because of the "conflict of interest" inherent to the legislature drawing its own electoral lines. Moreover, Proposition 77 flushed out of the bushes people in favor of such reform. Good government organizations realized there were many people dissatisfied with redistricting and started putting pressure on the legislature to pass redistricting reform. California Common Cause believed that redistricting reform could be achieved by developing a version of the initiative that would attract other groups. This effort was reinforced by poll results in the spring of 2006, which showed California's electorate was supportive of moving redistricting away from the legislature to an independent commission. By the summer of 2006, even though the odds were against them, a group of 70 advocates was working on a proposal that later became Proposition 11.[39] Several of these good government organizations shared many interests with the Democratic Party, their natural ally and they took Democratic leadership at their word when they said they would pass redistricting reform.[40] Democratic state Assembly member Alan Lowenthal had been developing bills to reform redistricting. Senate President Pro Temp Don Perata and Assembly Speaker Fabian Nuñez also made proposals without much success in the legislature. Indeed, it was probably too much to ask the legislative branch to reduce its own power voluntarily. Besides with the electoral gains acquired by Latinos and successes in leadership positions they were poised to dominate the redistricting process which made many Republicans and Democrats uneasy. Several bills were introduced in the legislature but after two years of lobbying, after a bill was mysteriously lost in 2007, and missed a deadline for a vote in the Senate, Kathay Feng had enough. The former director of the Asian Pacific American Legal Center who had recently moved up the political food chain when she became the director of California Common Cause, in concert with other organizations, decided their window to launch a referendum campaign to take redistricting out of the hands of the legislature was closing and they had to act quickly. After giving up on the legislature's ever surrendering the power to shape districts, despite its leaders' promises to do so, the reform groups collected signatures and placed Proposition 11, also known as Voters First Act, on the November 2008 ballot. In retrospect, alienating Kathay Feng and her organization (APALC) during the 2001 redistricting cycle might have been long-term miscalculations. The repercussions were that Democrats ended up fighting Common Cause and other good government organizations over the creation of an independent redistricting commission. They lost that fight by the thinnest of margins (50.7–49.1 percent),[41] and in spite of historical Democratic turnout, because the authors of Proposition 11 were able get together an unusual coalition of good government organizations, some minority leaders, some prominent Democrats and members of the state's Republican Party. Besides, even when minority organizations came out against Proposition 11, their message was muddled by seemingly somewhat contradictory positions: The California State conference supported the proposition while the NAACP Legal Defense Fund opposed it; the Asian American Legal Center came out against it but, as mentioned before, Kathay Feng, one of the coauthor of Proposition 11, used to be its director and it's precisely because of her experience in 2001 dealing with redistricting that she decided to take the matter to the people; MALDEF, and its new leadership, came out against Proposition 11 but Steve Reyes, the other proposition co-author used to be a lawyer for MALDEF. Besides, MALDEF was the only organization that sued against the bi-partisan redistricting in 2002 and felt they, once again, received the short end of the stick. It was therefore difficult under those circumstances for their followers to really believe that the status quo should prevail. And this apathy of the movement against Proposition 11 is visible in its mobilization and fundraising.[42]

After all, it wasn't even obvious that the bipartisan gerrymander of 2001 had been beneficial for the Democratic Party. It had allowed Democrats to get a referendum-proof two-thirds majority which was its main goal but it had also prevented the party from obtaining a larger majority as the national Republican Party became less popular under George W. Bush and as the state Republican Party registration kept shrinking. The sentiment in 2008, with the full-on strength of the Obama coalition and after the 2006 mid-term elections that had been very favorable to the Democrats, was that redistricting hindered the Democratic Party in California. As *Los Angeles Times* political columnist George Skelton put in an op-ed: "If there'd been even a fair redistricting in 2001—let alone a Democratic gerrymander—Democrats could be cleaning up in legislative and congressional races this fall."[43] The real winners of 2001 seemed to have been incumbents of both parties who did not have to worry as much about reelection.

So the reasons for discontent over the 2001 round of redistricting was real and deep but it took a lot of political skills on the part of the authors of the proposition to create this diverse coalition of interests. One of the first difficulties is that California, as we have seen, had a long history of referendums aiming at creating independent redistricting commissions and these attempts had all been by Republicans or people tied to Republican interests. In a state dominated by the Democratic Party this was the first obstacle. The second is that most of these attempts had failed because the previous propositions all failed to adequately and explicitly protect minority representation. Proposition 11 authors learned from those mistakes in part because their professional background was that of minority voting-rights protection. So the Voters First Act is a reaction to both the 2001 round of redistricting and Proposition 77's shortcomings.

While Proposition 77 would have moved the redistricting authority for the Assembly, Senate, Congress, and Board of Equalization Districts away from the legislature, Proposition 11 did not include Congress. This deliberate decision was made by the drafters to ensure that members of Congress would not use their considerable funds and influence to defeat the proposition as they had done against Proposition 77. In contrast with some other forms of redistricting commission, the California Independent Citizens Commission would give no say to the Legislature on plan approval. Due to the intense criticism of the racial and ethnic makeup of the pool of retired judges, Proposition 11 substituted them with registered citizens. The mid-decade redistricting was taken out in part because of the costs involved and the unavailability of current census data. Finally, competition as a criterion was eliminated from Proposition 11 for many reasons. First, research had shown that only a few seats in California could be drawn to be competitive because of its self-sorting electorate that had most Democrats concentrated along the coast and most Republicans living inland.[44] Second, competition as a criterion is "muddled in its application by definitional issues, including which data are most appropriate to use. Furthermore, a potentially competitive district is vulnerable to campaign finance discrepancies, candidate quality, the national political climate, and the sheer fact that electoral mobility changes partisan support in districts over time."[45] Third, as mentioned before, research showed competition criteria to be in conflict with some traditional redistricting criteria and aspects of the federal Voting Rights Act. Again, with too many criteria, something's got to give.

Proposition 11 set up a commissioner selection process that was very complex. It was designed to eliminate candidates with conflicts of interest and strong partisan affiliation and to find qualified citizens. The problem with this approach was that while redistricting is an arcane difficult technical task, the selection process excluded anyone who had, in the preceding 10 years, worked for a campaign or a candidate for federal or state office, or a political party, been elected to a party central committee, or served as a paid consultant to any of these entities. In addition, candidates could not have contributed more than $2,000 to certain campaigns. These restrictions extended to a potential applicant's immediate family.[46] Virtually all the people in the state with any experience in redistricting were ineligible due to these restrictions by virtue of having worked for either a candidate or a party.[47] Even potential candidates who had only been involved at the local level often had partisan ties that excluded them. This implied, and it was probably not evident to the voters, that the commissioners would have to rely on a redistricting consulting firm to complete such a daunting task in such a short amount of time.

Proposition 11 ensured that the commissioners reflected the diversity of the state, implying a representational model, and appeared as politically neutral as can be through a strict process analogous to a trial jury selection. Three state auditors would narrow the applicant pool to 60. Proposition 11 allowed legislative leaders the right to strike two nominees each from three sub-pools of twenty each chosen by the State Auditor.[48] From the remaining applicants, state auditors randomly drew eight to serve on the commission. These 8 selected from the other remaining applicants the final six who would serve with them. Proposition 11 mandated that the 14 commissioners be composed of 5 Republicans, 5 Democrats, and 4 members from neither party. Moreover, it put in place voting rules that required bipartisan agreement.[49] The idea was to create a centrist bloc, which for the most part happened in 2011 in California, to give the CRC as much legitimacy as possible. Republicans loved this bipartisan balance because it gave them a political weight during redistricting that was disproportionate to their dwindling registration figures in the state.[50]

Proposition 11 also mandated a process that used ranked criteria in the following order: (1) Equal Population, (2) Compliance with the Voting Rights Act, (3) Contiguity, (4) Respect for City and County Boundaries, Neighborhoods, and Communities of Interest (if possible without violating preceding criteria), (5) Compactness, and (6) Nesting.[51] The presence of traditional redistricting criteria was not surprising. What was more surprising was Proposition 11 ranked these criteria and, even more so, that they ranked subdivision and community preservation fairly high.[52] The fourth more important criteria read that "the geographic integrity of any city, county, city and county, local neighborhood, or local community of interest shall be respected in a manner that minimizes [its] division."[53] The idea being that preserving these "geographical communities of interest" would make districts more coherent and thus improve voter participation and, in the end, the quality of representation.[54] Most importantly, as Kathay Feng recalled her experience of 2001, the goal of reform was to put every criterion above incumbent self-interest.[55] In a way, it was her response to Democratic consultant Bill Cavala and Republican consultant Joe Shumate. And it was Steve Reyes's response to Howard and Michael Berman.

But listing criteria in order of importance meant that the constraint would be greater to use formal or informal criteria for a different use. California now clearly prioritizes this vague criterion over, for instance, competition that is not mentioned. For instance, much of the justification in the press for supporting Proposition 11 was about restoring competition, even though that criterion doesn't appear in the referendum. Making community of interest input so high on the list of criteria implied that the ability of mapmakers to create competitive districts would be limited. Quite the opposite actually since stressing communities of interest actually results in homogenous districts. From a practical standpoint, as we have seen before, the vagueness of the concept of community of interest invites map drawers to pursue other goals and cloak them as community of interest. Competitiveness depends very much on the hierarchy of redistricting criteria and that, in the end, is a political decision. One had to be a bit naïve to believe it only took a bipartisan panel of citizens, unconnected to incumbent legislators and relying on neutral criteria, to create competitive district boundaries without explicit instructions to do so and without using political data. Partisan fairness and competition cannot be the indirect effect of the commission's composition and compliance with supposedly "neutral" formal criteria. The one rule of redistricting, in California or anywhere else, is that in the end everybody finds racial or partisan bias in the lines.

So why was competition so central to the passage of the referendum even though it is never mentioned in text of the law? That is because in the 2000s lack of competitive districts became the scapegoat for all the ills of the state's governance. Proponents of the referendum argued that independent redistricting would help make the legislature more capable of solving health care, water supply, budget and other intractable troubles. In 2008, Schwarzenegger signed a state budget that was a record-breaking eighty-five days late because Republican and Democratic legislators couldn't compromise. Afterward, the governor immediately touted Proposition 11.[56]

Opponents of Proposition 11 made some good points. For instance they argued that the Democratic Party, which held a strong majority in Sacramento, should not unilaterally disarm. Because conservative states such as Texas have gerrymandered in favor of congressional Republicans, they argued, California had to keep gerrymandering in favor of Democrats. Proposition 11 anticipated these criticisms. The drafters of Proposition 11 excluded congressional districts to avoid triggering a well-funded opposition campaign by House Speaker Nancy Pelosi (D-San Francisco). Minority groups responded that they could not afford to participate in two simultaneous redistricting processes. They did not see how this double process could help them in any way. Also, because many commercials and comments implied that the redistricting commission would lead to more competition; opponents of the measure had an easy line of attack.[57] They simply noted that this claim was false and that nothing in the initiative required mapmakers to try to balance Republican and Democratic voters evenly so that district races are more competitive. Opponents also called the selection of the redistricting panel convoluted and many predicted deadlock. Furthermore, some goals Proposition 11 imposed on mapmakers, especially nesting two Assembly districts in each State Senate district and that cities be kept intact, would eliminate the flexibility necessary for line-drawers to give Latino, Asian, and African American neighborhoods enough voting power to sway elections. Another reason for opposition by minorities was that many minority elected officials had reached positions of power and felt threatened by reform. Putting redistricting in the hands an unknown entity meant risking losing the power and leverage they had finally acquired. Latinos were poised to dominate redistricting so this measure appeared to go against their political interest.

Last but not least, the ballot measure was sponsored by a long list of nonpartisan good government groups: Common Cause, AARP, the League of Women Voters, and the newly created coalition California Forward.[58] The *Los Angeles Times* and *San Francisco Chronicle* supported Proposition 11. Prominent Democrats, such as former Governor Gray Davis, former Treasurer Steve Westly, and former Assembly Speaker Robert Hertzberg, came out in favor of the initiative. In contrast to 2005, when most of California's Republican Congressmen opposed Proposition 77, no high-profile conservatives voiced any objections. However the proposition was also backed by Governor Arnold Schwarzenegger, who gave $2.5 million of his political money, and the Los Angeles Area Chamber of Commerce. Florida businessmen were even invited by Governor Schwarzenegger who persuaded them to write checks of $2,500 to $250,000 to support Proposition 11. The $16 million raised by Schwarzenegger and other proponents of the measure fueled opponents' claims that it was "a GOP power grab."[59]

Proposition 11 was in essence asking the Democrats to move from a position of control which they could not accept. California's Democratic establishment lined up to oppose the initiative, as did interest groups such as the California Federation of Teachers, California Correctional Peace Officers Association, California Labor Federation and NAACP Legal Defense Fund. Though the California Democratic Party and some of its traditional supporters decried Proposition 11, they did not invest much in its defeat. The campaign against the measure only raised $1.5 million, most of it from the party and unions for prison guards and government employees.

Two years later, voters expanded the scope of the commission by approving Proposition 20 (61 to 39 percent) which added the drawing of congressional districts to the commission's purview. By a wide margin (57 to 43 percent), voters defeated a measure on the same ballot to eliminate the commission entirely (Proposition 27).[60] The independent citizen commission model had been approved by a narrow margin in 2008 but the electorate in mid-term elections is traditionally more conservative. In 2010 turnout was especially low and was a Republican wave election as the Democrats lost 63 seats in the House, the highest loss by a party in a midterm election since 1938. Not surprisingly, election results show increasing support for redistricting from 2008 to 2010.[61] This two-step, two year approach proved decisive for reformers as their coalition strengthened and the second part of the reform fell in the midterm Republican wave. Proposition 20 enhanced the importance of "communities of interests" in the redistricting process beyond what was included in Proposition 11, adding more details and included wording, absent from Proposition 11, that suggested keeping similar income groups together as much as possible.[62] It also shortened the commission's deadlines by one month while augmenting its workload by adding the drawing of congressional districts. This new time constraint was added to allow more time to defend the maps in court. However, it shortened an already tight schedule putting more pressure on the consulting firm and the commissioners who now had to create 4 statewide maps containing a total of 177 districts.[63]

SELECTING COMMISSIONERS

The framers of Proposition 11 believed in the process and put the emphasis on a rigorous screening process for the members on the commission but also, later on, for the counsel and consultants. For such a convoluted process to go as smoothly as it did, it needed some luck along the way. The first stroke of luck was choosing the state auditor that oversees the Bureau of State Audits (BSA) to facilitate the commission's selection process. In all logic it should have been the Secretary of State. But this partisan office can be a bit too close to the legislature, and polled very poorly in opinion surveys, so the authors of Proposition 11 opted for the less-known state auditor. It operates with relative independence from the legislature and the governor's office, aside from relying on funding from them. The BSA usually conducts audits, and this task was completely outside their usual scope of activities.[64] Little did Feng and Reyes know that the Secretary of State's Office at time, Debra Bowen, was going through a rough patch and would probably not have been as diligent in the handling of the process.[65] The BSA took the entire endeavor very seriously and began by drafting regulations to clarify the many issues on which the proposition was silent and created a timeline that set target dates. One of the first challenges was to get regular citizens to volunteer for a less than glamorous task. In the early stage of what turned out to be a two-year procedure,[66] the first batch of people that seemed interested in redistricting were mostly older Anglo voters. The pool of volunteers needed to be much more diverse in order to attract enough qualified minorities. The auditor concluded they should conduct an active outreach campaign to motivate applicants. Yet, the entire budget that Proposition 11 allowed for the redistricting process was $3 million over three years. The BSA took advantage of California's *Voter Information Guide*, which is sent to every registered voter in the state for each election. A half-page advertisement was placed in it in hope that voters would see it and apply. The BSA then proceeded to hire a national public relations firm[67] to conduct its outreach campaign and had to be mindful of Proposition 209 in its effort to reach every voter and not target specifically minority communities.[68] The BSA asked the legislature for $2.24 million to fund these activities. This would have left the commission with a budget of only $760,000 to actually conduct the entire redistricting. It also put the BSA ino the position of having to compete for funding with the commission it was creating. The California legislature, which was dealing with a state budget crisis at the time, only agreed to fund $500,000 and instructed the auditor to finance the rest from the allotted budget.[69]

This is when the commission's second stroke of luck occurred. The James Irvine Foundation offered to help with the outreach program. The foundation had funded certain activities that participated in the passing of Proposition 11.[70] The James Irvine Foundation funded minority advocacy groups and voting rights groups to conduct outreach and education and to encourage their constituencies to apply to the commission. These groups also assisted in filling out applications and helping applicants prepare for the interview process.[71]

The proper selection process was a quite elaborate series of filters, featuring elements of a college admissions application, lottery selection, and diversity balancing.[72] The extensive outreach effort produced more than 36,000 positive responses. The State Auditor's Applicant Review Panel (ARP), which must be composed of one Democrat, one Republican, and one unaffiliated person, invited those who were formally qualified to fill out an extensive supplemental application that required four essays of 500 words or less, plus information about education, employment history, campaign finance contributions over $250, criminal history, and a listing of family members and related potential conflicts of interest.[73] All this information was made public on the internet, open for comments.[74] Moreover, applicants had to provide 3 letters of recommendation. A total of 4547 people successfully completed these supplemental forms. This group was reduced to 120 individuals (40 Democrats, Republicans, and Independents each) who were interviewed and then reduced again to 60, evenly divided by party affiliation.[75] At that point, legislative leaders of both parties from both houses, the Big Four, were each allowed to strike two persons from each of the three groups, leaving 36 people per group who, then, were subjected to a lottery.[76] Because with a lottery process there is a risk that the results might be skewed, the 8 who were thus randomly selected then picked the remaining 6 in order to reflect state diversity.[77] The first 8 commissioners only included one Latino, making that group 13 percent Latino in a state that had a Latino population of 37 percent. The first 8 were reminded of this fact by various groups that represent Latinos, including the National Association of Latino Elected and Appointed Officials

(NALEO), which urged them to "fulfill their responsibilities under Proposition 11 by remedying the inadequate representation of Latinos."[78]

In the end, the CRC was diverse with respect to race, gender, and ethnicity, but not with respect to education and class. The 8 randomly selected commissioners were: Vincent Barabba, a Republican Businessman from Capitola; Cynthia Dai, a Democrat CEO and professor from San Francisco; Stanley Forbes, an unaffiliated bookstore co-owner from Esparto; Connie Galambos Malloy, an unaffiliated urban planner and policy developer from Oakland; Elaine Kuo, a Democrat researcher from Mountain View who resigned; Jeanne Raya, a Democrat lawyer and risk manager from San Gabriel; Jodie Filkins Webber, a Republican self-employed attorney from Norco; Peter Yao, a Republican former mayor and engineer from Claremont. These 8 commissioners selected: Gabino Aguirre, a Democrat retired teacher and school principal from Santa Paula; Maria Blanco, a Democrat nonprofit executive from Los Angeles; Michelle R. DiGuilio, an unaffiliated community planner and homemaker from Stockton; Lilbert "Gil" R. Ontai, a Republican architect and lecturer from San Diego; M. Andre Parvenu, an unaffiliated geographer and urban planner from Culver City; Michael Ward, a Republican chiropractor and polygrapher from Anaheim; and Angelo Ancheta, a Democrat law professor from San Francisco selected to replace Elaine Kuo. On January 19, 2011, the commission chose as its executive director, Dan Claypool, the project manager of the BSA team that had organized the selection process.

SELECTING A CONSULTANT

The next crucial task was to hire a consulting firm to do the actual line drawing. Republicans already felt upset that the commission's executive director was a Democrat (although only minimally active) and that the commission had not hired a Republican firm as VRA counsel. The commission did not have the support of a majority of the Republican members to select the VRA counsel favored by the Democratic and nonaligned members, an issue that was resolved when the Republican-supported firm withdrew. On March 18, after the withdrawal of the competing firm, the commission voted unanimously to retain the law firm Gibson, Dunn & Crutcher as Voting Rights Act counsel, striking a sort of partisan balance with Daniel M. Kolkey, a Republican and principal drafter of Proposition 20,[79] and George Brown, a Democrat, as principal attorneys.[80] However, when the commission hired Q2, accusation of partisanship were all over the news.[81]

Only two small local firms had applied: Q2 and the Rose Institute. If the state had provided funding with a much larger sum, there would have been more bidders with potential interest from national firms. So because of the budget constraint the options in front of the commissioners were narrow: two firms that had ties to the partisan redistricting wars of the past. The commissioners were familiar with Q2's managing partner, Karin Mac Donald, who, as director the Statewide Database, had briefed the commission in some of its early meetings.[82] As mentioned in our previous chapters, the Statewide Database emerged from a database that was originally created for California's State Assembly, to be used in the redistricting of 1981 when Bruce Cain was their consultant. In 1993, the California Legislature voted to house the database permanently in a nonpartisan environment at the Institute of Governmental Studies (IGS) at UC Berkeley under Cain's supervision. In 2009, the Statewide Database moved to an off-campus building at Berkeley Law. The information in the Statewide Database is a public resource and available for free to anyone interested in the political and demographic makeup of the State of California. In that sense its mission fit the commission's desire for transparency and citizens' involvement. Q2 had been created as a partnership between Bruce Cain and Karin Mac Donald and even though Bruce Cain had not been involved in line drawing since 1982 and was the director of Berkeley DC program and living in DC. Mac Donald was perceived to be Bruce Cain's protégé and therefore accused of sharing Cain's partisan penchant even though she has never registered with the Democratic Party.

The other bidder was National Demographics president Doug Johnson, a research fellow at the Rose Institute whose strong ties with the Republican Party were described in our previous chapters. As a redistricting consultant Johnson had worked on the state of Florida's State Senate Committee on Reapportionment, and the state of Arizona's Independent Redistricting Commission for Congressional and Legislative Redistricting in 2001. Johnson is a Republican who worked as Legislative Director to US Representative Stephen Horn. Johnson is an academic but his publications were scarce[83] in comparison to Mac Donald's, who published extensively in prestigious publications[84] and developed over the years a great reputation in the field of redistricting. And two of the commissioners were very familiar with this academic field since vice chairperson Blanco was the director of the Warren Institute[85] and Commissioner Ancheta a law professor specialized in Voting Rights.[86] Their criticism of Johnson's bid carried some weight because they knew the academic field well. But as Democrats their remarks could be interpreted as partisan. Johnson's bid had two major flaws. First, it was badly presented and looked unprofessional. The author even admitted it when he remarked that document's paging was confusing: "the numbers get haywire."[87] The commission was also irked by the fact that Johnson's team was staffed with a lot of graduate students. Staff counsel Johnston observed: "By the way, if you look at the résumés of these 22 people, they're students, not surprisingly."[88] And these students were fellows or interns working for members of the legislature as part of the Fellowship ran through CSUS, which raised the question of potential conflict of interest.

The second flaw of the bid was precisely the question of conflict of interest. Doug Johnson did not file under his company National Demographics but as the Rose Institute because he believed the small size of his company would not have allowed him to carry out the task. The main problem was the absence of source of funding for the Rose Institute that is part of Claremont McKenna College and the fact that no details about other sources of funding were given in the bid. The CRC was about transparency and went to great length to avoid any, or the appearance of, conflict of interest. Republican Commissioner Barabba, former director of the US Census under Nixon and Carter, declared upon voting against Johnson's bid: "I'm having a hard time voting for this because I think there's other deviations in this proposal that I would like to have raised because I think it makes a stronger case."[89] Barabba's criticism was particularly damning because he could not be accused of partisan bias. Commissioners Yao, Ward, Filkins-Webber (all 3 registered Republicans), and Democratic Commissioner Ray voted to pursue the Rose Institute bidding.

In retrospect the commissioners are probably glad they did not hire anybody associated with the Rose Institute because in June 2014 David Alan Heslop, founding director of Claremont McKenna College's Rose Institute of State and Local Government, and former adviser to Presidents Ronald Reagan and George H. W. Bush, was sentenced to twenty-one months in federal prison and three years of supervised parole, and ordered to pay $300,000 in restitution for defrauding the Twenty-Nine Palms Band of Mission Indians.[90] Doug Johnson bailed Paul Bardos, one of the co-conspirators, out of custody in 2012 and commented on the case in the press: "Johnson described the lawsuits and indictment as merely a contract dispute problem. He said the federal government is prosecuting the case because it involves a sovereign Indian tribe."[91]

Although Q2 had extensive experience drawing district lines for cities and other local bodies, the firm did not have statewide redistricting experience, and some commissioners were concerned that Q2 could not handle the massive California task alone. Not many bidders could meet the needs of the massive map drawing job but Q2 came up with a well-organized method to tackle the task by dividing the state in four areas and assigning one person in charge of one region to avoid hand over and to save time. Each regional manager could attend meetings with local communities. The method required more management from Mac Donald but it made sense since no one can really be familiar with the complexity of an entire state map such as California.

Q2, a company entirely composed of women, benefitted from the presence of experienced members such as Nicole Boyle, Q2's only other full-time staffer along with Mac Donald, whose mapping expertise was widely recognized,[92] and Ana Henderson, who used to work at the Civil Rights Division of the Justice Department.[93] The commissioners seemed to be reassured by her Voting Rights Act experience both with Section 2 and Section 5.[94]

Commissioner Ward proposed to bring in another line-drawing consultant to review and examine Q2's work because he was concerned about partisan bias. While his position was understandable, adding a review process to an already tight schedule did not seem feasible. Q2 turned down a joint proposal from the Rose Institute because of "methodological" differences. In short, they did not think the Rose Institute students had the adequate training. Besides, Q2 team was at first reluctant to propose a bid and into dive into this political circus.[95] Most people familiar with redistricting were very skeptical this experiment could work, especially considering California's history. It was precisely because the Rose Institute turned out to be the only bidder that Mac Donald and her colleagues decided to jump in, almost at the last minute.[96] The commission unanimously selected Q2 Data and Research after having asked for a firewall for Bruce Cain. Ironically, being associated with Bruce Cain, one of the best redistricting experts in the country and a renowned scholar, turned out to be Mac Donald's greatest liability.

> These conflicts over hiring masked some underlying partisan and ideological differences in redistricting that do not simply disappear with the removal of incumbent elected officials from control of the process. The larger disagreements revolve around how to apply the VRA and the model of COIs. These are not technical issues but political and philosophical ones, and they did emerge in the process of mapping in 2011.[97]

As we can see, because redistricting is such a technical task, the hiring of consultants, lawyers, and staffers is particularly crucial. Citizens who lack the expertise and don't want to rely on experts risk making basic mistakes that can have important partisan or legal consequences. On the other hand relying too heavily on those experts can lead to being accused of letting the experts' political bias transpire in the final product. Expertise has therefore an unavoidable tradeoff. This almost derailed the California Redistricting Commission in 2011 but also the one in Arizona.

DRAWING THE LINES

The California Constitution contains specific language prohibiting the use of traditional political redistricting factors. As a consequence, incumbency protection and partisan districting are formally eliminated.[98] Yet, eliminating information about incumbency does not necessarily translate into anti-incumbent redistricting. Favoring an incumbent, a candidate, or a party *on purpose* is not allowed by the state constitution but neither is discriminating against incumbents, candidates, or parties. The prohibitions also have an important legal effect as Angelo Ancheta has observed: "they undermine federal constitutional claims against the Commission based on partisan gerrymandering, because such claims require proof of intentional discrimination against a party by the redistricting body."[99] However it does not mean that the commission was apolitical. It is fairly easy to use other demographic factors as a proxy for partisanship. Protecting a neighborhood or a socioeconomic community often will have the practical effect of protecting an incumbent or favoring a party. Because of the state's political geography and the tendency of electors to self-sort, many of these alignments occur "naturally," even when they are not intended.

Moreover the way a map is drawn will have consequences because of the ripple effect. From instance, as anybody who has ever tried to draw district or use GIS software knows, if you start drawing district at the Oregon border or at the Mexico border, your map will look quite different. Because of the preeminence of the federal Voting Rights Act and the fact that 5 counties in California were covered by Section 5, any map needed to start there. This compliance with Section 5 of the Voting Rights Act over the years meant that some of the districts containing counties subject to preclearance were similar in shape to the districts developed in previous decades. Section 5 jurisprudence prohibited the retrogression of minority voting power in the covered counties, which meant that some of the contortions previously necessary to maintain minority voting blocs were maintained in the post-2010 lines.

> The Commission treated these districts as largely fixed and immovable pieces of the puzzle, which of course affected the design of the surrounding districts. Given the constraints of the Voting Rights Act, it is highly unlikely that a different entity would have done it much differently; regardless of whether it was a commission or a legislative committee who drew the lines, they would have been bound by the law and would have drawn comparable districts to protect minority voters.[100]

One of the main differences between the CRC and the previous rounds of redistricting is the high level of transparency and the immense amount of input from all kinds of communities in the state.[101] However, there is such as thing as too much information. A major downside to the high level of public participation was that the Commission became overwhelmed with often repetitive information. Between April and July 2011, the Commission conducted 34 public hearings, located in 32 cities throughout the state, with a total of over 2,700 speakers (including many whose comments were translated from other languages). More than 20,000 individuals and groups submitted written comments or maps.[102] The commission underestimated the amount of time that it would take to process the public information and it overestimated the usability of that information, and then it simply ran out of time. This led to what commissioner Ancheta called "redistricting 'big data' problem": "The goal of maintaining communities of interest became a particular problem because of the subjectivity of public opinions regarding "communities. . . . And without strong guidelines for identifying communities of interest and for resolving conflicts, the Commissioners could pick and choose from several variations in district lines because there was usually *some* basis for a community of interest or neighborhood that could be found in the public testimony."[103]

But the democratic ideal rests on the ideal that information access and the desire or capacity to participate is high among all citizens. However, if the history of direct democracy in California taught us anything is that this is far from being the case. Information access is asymmetrical. Citizens are neither knowledgeable nor eager to learn about the arcane process of redistricting. A high level of public input alone does not guarantee a complete picture of what was needed to draw the lines. Some communities, particularly those in poor rural areas and those with smaller populations, such as Native Americans, are notoriously underrepresented in the political process.[104] Because these are voluntary activities, it is inevitable that some individuals and groups will be more eager to participate than others. Commissioners had to fill in the gaps to the best of their knowledge in a very short amount of time. The diversity of the commission helped in making sure that a lot of different perspectives were taken into consideration, yet there is no process that can guarantee that all points of view will be heard, especially given the time constraints. Besides, the commissioners had to "weigh the source of the information they receive as they evaluate the merits of a particular community of interest."[105]

A good example is the fact that even something as basic as race and ethnicity was forgotten in the initial process. In the rush to publish initial draft maps in early June, the commission drew fire from civil rights advocates and minority community groups, because it released maps that lacked racially polarized voting analysis. A racially polarized voting report requires in-depth statistical analyses in key areas of the state that contain sizable populations of African Americans, Latinos, or Asian Americans and is an essential element in determining whether a majority-minority district should be drawn to comply with the Voting Rights Act. Because racial polarization data is essential to determining compliance with the Voting Rights Act, they should have been incorporated into any map produced for public comment.

Hiring a consultant to prepare the report had been postponed, and a full report wasn't available until later in the summer much to the chagrin of Karin Mac Donald.[106] Consequently several potential majority-minority districts could not be drawn in time for the initial drafts.[107] The first maps released in June 2011, which completely upended the 2,000 maps, created 10 Latino assembly districts (as opposed to 8 in 2001) while MALDEF presented the commission with maps that showed 17 majority-minority Assembly districts! The first maps also presented 4 Latino Senate districts (the same as 2001), and 5 Latino congressional districts (as opposed to 6 in 2001).[108] This, of course, was unacceptable for Latino organizations while the community's population kept increasing to reach 37 percent of the state population in 2010, an increase of 5 percent since 2000. Census figures had shown that much of California's growth was fueled by Latinos who saw their numbers increase by nearly 28 percent to 14 million, and Asian Americans who saw a nearly 31 percent gain to nearly 4.8 million people. The 2 other major demographic groups were in retreat: Anglos declined more than many demographers had predicted, dropping 5.4 percent to just under 15 million while the number of African Americans declined by about 1 percent to nearly 2.2 million residents. Besides, California's minority population had grown most dramatically in the interior of the state implying political power would shift away from traditional strongholds such as Los Angeles and San Francisco and into the Inland Empire and Central Valley.[109] Minorities hoped these numbers would translate into opportunities to gain control of elected offices in those areas.

African American groups also were concerned by the first maps. LA County's black population dropped from 9.5 percent to 8.3 percent between 2000 and 2010. African American leaders formed the African American Redistricting Collaborative to monitor closely the impact the new demographics could have on the 3 African American Congress members in districts historically represented by African Americans: Democrats Karen Bass, Maxine Waters, and Laura Richardson. Under the 2000 boundaries, African American citizens of voting age accounted for 24.8 percent of the population in Bass' Thirty-third District, 30 percent in Waters' Thirty-fifth District and 22.1 percent in Richardson's Thirty-seventh District. In the first maps, released June 10, those percentages had dropped to 21.8 percent for Bass and 22.9 percent for Waters but increased to 23.5 percent for Richardson. In later versions the CRC corrected course and Bass' Thirty-seventh District went up to 25 percent and Waters' Forty-third District to 24.2 percent, but Richardson's now Forty-fourth District dropped to 18 percent, enough to make African American leaders nervous.[110] They were right. Most of Richardson's territory became the Forty-fourth District and in 2012 she ran against fellow Democratic

Congresswoman Janice Hahn who defeated her bid by a landslide 20 percentage points. When Hahn ran, and won, in the Fourth District of the Los Angeles Board of Supervisors, she was replace in CD 44 by Nanette Barragán.[111] Asians also complained about the first draft. An amateurish interest group had fostered a majority-Asian congressional district in LA County, wasting a huge percentage of Asian votes, ignoring the fact that Judy Chu could be (and was) elected in a district that was less than a third Asian American.

The harsh reaction to the first draft led to important changes. The rest of the process felt rushed. The CRC had initially promised to publish 2 more drafts and hold public meetings for comments but could not make good on those promises. Some observers could conclude that the procedure changes betrayed promises of transparency because of time constraints.

In the final plan announced in August 2011, the number of Latino districts jumped to 14 in the Assembly, 5 in the Senate, and 7 in Congress.[112] So in all, 2011 maps adopted by the commission resulted in the creation of eight new majority-Latino districts, with most of the gains coming from the Assembly plan. This did not necessarily satisfy Latino activists who had hoped for more but because of the large number of Latinos under eighteen years old, the low percentage of Latinos who are US citizens and especially their notoriously low voter turnout. Latinos traditionally get frustrated by the number of Latino districts or elected officials that are never proportional to their percentage in the state's population. MALDEF President and General Counsel Thomas A. Saenz expressed concern about the State Senate and congressional maps and pondered legal action. These changes, though, also allowed saving some incumbents that had been endangered in the first draft such as Democratic Representative Loretta Sanchez who initially was targeted for a Republican congressional district.[113]

The commission created the first state level district with an Asian American majority population in the San Gabriel Valley. This represented a great victory for Pacific and Asian Americans activists because, as we mentioned before, that area had been split up among several districts in 2001 and their recommendations had been disregarded. Moreover a number of state districts were drawn that recognized gay and lesbian neighborhoods for the first time, again showing that activists' demands from the past had been heard.[114] Community of interest analysis gets even more complicated when one crosses ethnic/racial data with statistics on sexual orientation.[115] This is especially important to notice in the light of the controversy surrounding the compactness criteria, the fourth ranked criteria in the state constitution. Tensions arose between good government groups and the commission over its VRA counsel's interpretation of the importance of compactness. In the end, compactness was subordinated to higher ranked criteria such as city boundaries and community of interest.[116]

The approval of the maps was almost unanimous: the commissioners voted 13–1 to approve the state legislative maps and the Board of Equalization map, and 12–2 to approve the congressional map. Commissioner Maria Blanco expressed reservations similar to MALDEF's before casting her vote to approve the plan.[117] She stated that the State Senate district represented at the time by Democrat Alex Padilla of Pacoima in the San Fernando Valley was changed into one with far fewer Latinos of voting age. Commissioner Michael Ward voted against all the new legislative maps. He was the only member of the panel to do so. He accused his colleagues of violating their legal mandate by making some decisions based on "political" considerations.[118] Ward's charge was disputed by Republican commission Chairman Vincent Barabba. He declared that decisions were made in open meetings, and there was "no basis" for the accusation that they were due to political considerations.[119]

To comply with Section 5 of the Voting Rights Act maps were then precleared by the US Department of Justice. However, it wouldn't be redistricting time if a plan did not end up in front of judges. The commission therefore had to defend its maps in court and two separate lawsuits were filed in the California Supreme Court. Republicans challenged both the state senate and the congressional maps.[120] Both lawsuits were unanimously dismissed. A parallel lawsuit filed in US District Court challenged the congressional maps. The plaintiffs alleged California's Thirty-seventh, Forty-third, and Forty-fourth Congressional Districts violated the Equal Protection Clause of the Fourteenth Amendment and the VRA, and requested the Court appoint special masters to redraw the lines. It was also dismissed.[121]

A fourth state court action attempted to put the senate map on hold while a Republican-sponsored referendum with signatures were gathered to qualify a referendum on the senate map for the ballot.[122] The referendum drive to overturn the state senate lines was led by State Senator Mimi Walters (R-Laguna Niguel) and Orange County businesswoman Julie Vandermost through a committee called Fairness and Accountability in Redistricting. Republican contemplated launching a referendum on the congressional map but they disagreed as to whether it would produce the expected result.[123] Funders of the initiative complained about partisan consequences, such as districts that placed two GOP incumbents in the same seat.[124] A redrawing of congressional districts would not necessarily have solved these issues because California's constitutional requirements prohibit the use of incumbency and candidate information. The State Supreme Court unanimously dismissed the postponing of the senate districts implementation. The court ruled on January 27, 2012, that the commission's plan would be used if the referendum qualified because it had been found to be constitutional and was the best option.[125] The Senate district plan was therefore used for the 2012 elections.[126] The referendum on the Senate plan did gather enough signatures to qualify for the ballot, and became Proposition 40 in the November 2012 election. However, since it had become clear that the commission's districts would be used in the 2012 elections, the effort to rescind the Senate plan lost momentum, and there was no active campaigning against the plan. Proposition 40 was rejected by the voters 28 percent to 72 percent.[127]

BE CAREFUL WHAT YOU WISH FOR

What did the CRC bring about? First, it was designed to exclude redistricting and political experts for a very complex task with real financial and time constraints. As a consequence, the commissioners relied heavily on consultants. In 2011 everything depended on Q2. One can speculate that if National Demographics had been chosen, the lines but also the processes would have been quite different. Second, it was designed to exclude the most relevant information, for example, party registration, from being used. This encouraged the use of proxies and made criticism of the plans either uninformed or surreptitiously informed, as parties or candidates, but not the media or the commissioners, could evaluate the political and racial effects of what they were doing. In that way, the CRC could be considered somewhat less transparent than the previous system. And finally, Section 5 constraints were key to keeping the lines fair. After *Shelby County*, the process will probably be very different, because advocates of minority rights won't be able to use preclearance as leverage against other interest groups.

In the end, the whole 2011 redistricting process cost over $13 million.[128] It only cost taxpayers about $10 million because, as mentioned earlier, the Irving Foundation grants covered more than $3 million in outreach programs.[129] The amount was far from the unrealistic $4 million estimate by the California legislative analyst.[130] The $10 million total includes selecting commissioners, the actual line drawing and the legal defense of the maps. As mentioned before, of this total, the commissioner selection process was the most expensive element, costing over $4 million. Direct line-drawing expenses, including establishing and running the agency, commissioner per diems and travel costs, fees for consultants and legal counsel, and the costs of meetings and hearings, added up to about $3 million. The bills for the legal defense of the maps were approximately $2 million. This cost was high because the California Attorney General declined to represent the commission and outside law firms had to be hired.[131]

An important part of the future success of the Independent Commission is whether or not it will be funded adequately. The commission's budget may not be sufficient to fully fund an outreach program that is at least as thorough as the one provided by outside groups in 2011. However, because the proposition based future funding on the expenditures of the previous redistricting, the California legislature may be forced to allocate significantly more funds. Budget fights are always a feature of California politics but since the legislature is dominated by the Democrats, the fund allocation might be a smoother process than previously anticipated.

Indeed one of the great ironies of the California Redistricting Commission is that it was originally a Republican idea, funded mostly by Republican funds. Yet, conservatives were not satisfied with the process when they realized they could not implement the redistricting procedure used in 1971 and 1991.[132] They fumed when their consultant was not selected. They raged when they understood that the commission would not take political data into account to draw more competitive districts.[133] First of all, there are more Democrats in California than there are Republicans nowadays and redistricting can't change that fact. Second, the way voters are sorted out in California with Democrats along the coast and Republicans inland, the only competitive districts that could be drown would have to be thin strips extending from the coast all the way to the valley. But, most importantly, the reason why the CRC's history is so ironic is that in 2012, the Democrats won a two-third majority in both houses of the legislature, a feat they had not achieved in thirty-four years, not even under the supposedly Democrats gerrymander of 1980. If it wasn't for direct democracy the California GOP would have been almost politically powerless. The Democratic leadership even came around on the CRC and ended up championing the idea of independent commissions in California but also in other states, convinced that it was in its partisan interest. The great losers of 2011 were individual politicians because the commission did not any vote from the legislature the main criteria the commission did away with was incumbent protection. The Democratic Party might have benefitted from the new maps but not individual politicians. While it is impossible to take politics out of redistricting, many voters thought of redistricting as an exercise in politicians selecting their constituents in behind closed door deals. Promises of more transparency and less incumbent protection are really what drove the success of Proposition 11 and the only factors that an independent commission could realistically have an impact on.

However there is no guarantee that what worked in 2011 might work in other states or might even work again as smoothly in California.[134] The CRC benefitted from the involvement and funding from outside groups but it also benefitted from a state auditor that really worked toward protecting the integrity of the selection process. The CRC was very lucky that the selection process produced commissioners so knowledgeable, such as a former director the Census Bureau who was a Republican while the hired consultant was accused of being a Democrat. The selection process that encourages race and ethnicity to be taken into consideration to select the final 6 commissioners has not been challenged successfully under Proposition 209 statutes[135] but the act could challenged on other grounds.[136] That is why Karin Mac Donald predicted this commission probably was the "purest" that California will experience.[137] Political actors have a tendency to adapt to constraints and find ways to circumvent them. There is no reason to believe that partisan actors will not try to rig the election process by anticipating the conflict of interest criteria. Changing on party's affiliation and refusing to work for an elected official in preparation for the selection process is not that high of a hurdle. Creating a redistricting firm without any visible conflict of interest is also easily doable. If the California experience with direct democracy has taught us anything it is that political actors have learned to use all the rules to maximize partisan advantage.

ELECTION RESULTS: HOW THE DEMOCRATS LEARNED TO STOP WORRYING AND LOVE THE CRC

The 2012 election was in many ways a perfect storm. The demographic evolution of the state combined with an older generation of congressional members, new districts maps that did not take incumbency into consideration and a new primary system upended California's elections at the same time as Democrat President Obama was running for a second term. The simultaneous presence of the new "top-two primary" in 2012 complicates the assessment of the independent impact of the citizen redistricting process. A "top-two" primary system lets voters choose any candidate, regardless of party, with the two candidates receiving the most votes advancing to the fall election. Therefore the general election can feature, for instance, two candidates of the same party. The top-two system produced some unusual change: 28 races in the 2012 election pitted two candidates of the same party against each other. Yet all but one of the 28 same-party races occurred in districts that were unlikely to have hosted competitive races in the past. The top-2 primary did not seem to have changed the political landscape as much as reformers had hoped.[138]

More competition occurred in 2012. Among races between candidates of opposing parties, 18 percent had a margin of victory of less than 10 points, up sharply from the 7 percent average of the last ten years.[139] The 2012 elections produced 38 new Assembly members, 9 new state senators, and 14 new members of Congress, compared to an average of 30, 10, and 3 over the previous decade. Three incumbents were defeated in the Assembly and a whopping 7 in Congress. Out of 10 losing incumbents, 7 were in districts that had been significantly redrawn.

In Congress, Democrats and Republicans battled for at least 10 of California's 53 seats as part of their fight for control of the House of Representatives. Democrats picked up 4 US House seats, a strong showing in a redistricting plan that already favored them. Inside the congressional delegation the Democrat majority grew to 38 members against 15 Republicans. There were unprecedented battles on the congressional Democratic delegation. Democratic Representative Brad Sherman defeated Berman 60 percent to 39 in a highly contentious, multimillion-dollar affair for the now famed San Fernando Valley seat.[140] At least $13 million poured into the bitter, widely watched contest between congressional veterans Berman and Sherman, whose similar voting records left little to set them apart.[141] The new political maps put both lawmakers' homes into the Thirtieth Congressional District, a new heavily Latino district. Some other lawmakers who found themselves in similar circumstances retired or sought office elsewhere. Sherman had a big advantage in the new district since more than half of his old district overlapped it. This was the only election loss for the seventy-one-year-old Berman, who won his first race, for state Assembly, by ousting a longtime Republican incumbent in 1972. Many factors explain his defeat and a revamped election system, that sends the top-2 primary finishers to the fall election regardless of party, is one of them. But with their proposition, Feng and Reyes were probably the most influential Californians in ending Howard Berman's career without his brother's help to carve a district for him. The writing had been on the wall because of the increase in Latino population in the San Fernando Valley but there is no denying that the CRC commission did what the legislature couldn't do, that is upending one of its most senior members' districts.

The same-party fight between Richardson and Hahn in the Forty-fourth District in southeast Los Angeles County drew special attention from California's African American congressional delegation. Members worried that their ranks would shrink to three with the probable defeat of African American Richardson who was badly weakened by an ethics committee inquiry into illegal use of staffers.[142] Richardson had previously represented portions of inland Los Angeles and inland Long Beach, all of Carson, Compton, and Signal Hill, as well as parts of other municipalities. Yet, her former district (CD 37) was split almost in half, with the bulk of her territory becoming the Forty-fourth District. Richardson's home in Long Beach was drawn into the new Forty-seventh District but, fighting for her political survival, she moved her residence into the Forty-fourth District because its demographics were more similar to her old district that is majority Black and Latino. Democrat Janice Hahn, who had represented the neighboring Thirty-sixth District (San Pedro) since July 2011, had her home drawn into the Forty-fourth as well, setting the stage for another intraparty contest. But Representative Janice Hahn, formally endorsed by the Democratic Party, easily beat Laura Richardson 60 percent to 39 percent in a newly drawn district that included many minority, working-class communities but Richardson's reputation was so irreversibly damaged that she never stood a chance.

Representative Lois Capps (D-Santa Barbara), a moderate who was in a safe Democratic district that was turned competitive, was viewed as one of the Democrats most vulnerable House members in California but she ended up defeating Republican former lieutenant governor and state lawmaker Abel Maldonado of Santa Maria.[143] In some of the closest races for Congress, Representative Brian P. Bilbray (R-Carlsbad) was defeated by Democrat Scott Peters, a San Diego environmental attorney, in the Fifty-second District. Democratic emergency room Latino physician Raul Ruiz narrowly won against Anglo Representative Mary Bono Mack (R-Palm Springs) in the Inland Empire Thirty-sixth District.[144] In a Democratic minority showdown state Senator Gloria Negrete McLeod defeated 7-term incumbent Joe Baca in the new Thirty-fifth District.[145]

The Democrats gained three seats in the State Senate and two in the Assembly. In both chambers these gains pushed the Democrats over the two-third threshold needed to pass tax increases without Republican support and without fear of a referendum. It was the first time either party had captured two-thirds of the seats in the Senate or Assembly in thirty-four years. And the first time in eight decades that a party held a supermajority in both houses.

One key race was the Seventeenth Senate District, where Democratic Assemblyman William Monning of Carmel easily beat Republican Larry Beaman. Democrats also picked up one of three other competitive seats to reach the crucial number of 27. In the new Fifth District Cathleen Galgiani defeated Republican Bill Berryhill by 2,500 votes. Richard Roth won the new Thirty-first District. In another critical battle, State Senator Fran Pavley (D-Agoura Hills) won the Twenty-seventh District against Republican Todd Zink, a deputy district attorney for Los Angeles County.

The lower house of the legislature also had its share of hard-fought intraparty contests. In Los Angeles, City Councilman Richard Alarcón, running for the Thirty-ninth Assembly District, while awaiting trial on felony charges of voter fraud and perjury, logically lost against fellow Democrat Raul Bocanegra, a former legislative aide.[146] In the Forty-seventh District (San Bernardino), African American Cheryl Brown won against fellow Democrat Joe Baca Jr., son of former Latino Congressman Joe Baca.[147] In the Fiftieth District (Santa Monica), Jewish Caucus member Richard Bloom beat incumbent Democrat Betsy Butler by 1,500 votes. In the Tenth District (Marin County), Chairman of the Jewish Caucus Marc Levine narrowly beat one-term incumbent Latino Michael Allen. In AD 59 (Los Angeles), African American Reggie Jones-Sawyer narrowly beat Rodney D. Robinson.

One needs to notice that a two-third majority is no guarantee that the Democrats could govern unopposed. Indeed, the supermajority of 2012 was short-lived. It lasted only eighty-one days, until a Central Valley Latino senator resigned his seat to take a government affairs job in the oil and gas industry and was replaced by a Republican. Even before this turn of events, differences had erupted among Democrats on a handful of legislative proposals. To make matters worse, no less than three Democratic senators got into legal trouble and were suspended.[148] However, the loss of the supermajority was not as damning as it once would have been. Ever since November 2010, when Proposition 25 was approved by 55 percent of the electorate, the two-third majority is not the Holy Grail it used to be. Proposition 25 lowered the threshold to enact the state budget to a simple majority solving some of the budget issues.[149] Yet, at the same time the sometimes schizophrenic California electorate passed Proposition 26, which imposes a new two-thirds mandate for imposing or raising a fee, one of the most important tools used to balance the budget since raising taxes requires a two-third majority. Since 2010, the California budget therefore needs to be approved by a simple majority but tax or fee increases by a supermajority.

2012 Assembly Districts and Election Results

In 2014 Democrats increased their majority in the congressional delegation to 39. Latino Democrat Paul Aguilar beat Republican military officer Paul Chabot by 2,500 votes in the Thirty-first District after barely surviving the top-2 primary. In the State legislature the Democratic Party's bid for a new supermajority in the state Senate failed, thanks to Republican victories in a few key races. State Senator. Andy Vidak (R-Hanford) defeated Democratic challenger Luis Chavez, a Fresno Unified School District trustee, in the Fourteenth District which has tilted Democratic among registered voters and includes all of Kings County and parts of Fresno, Kern, and Tulare counties. In the Thirty-fourth District, where Republicans have a slight edge in voter registration, Republican Janet Nguyen, an Orange County supervisor who became the first Vietnamese-American woman state legislator in the nation,

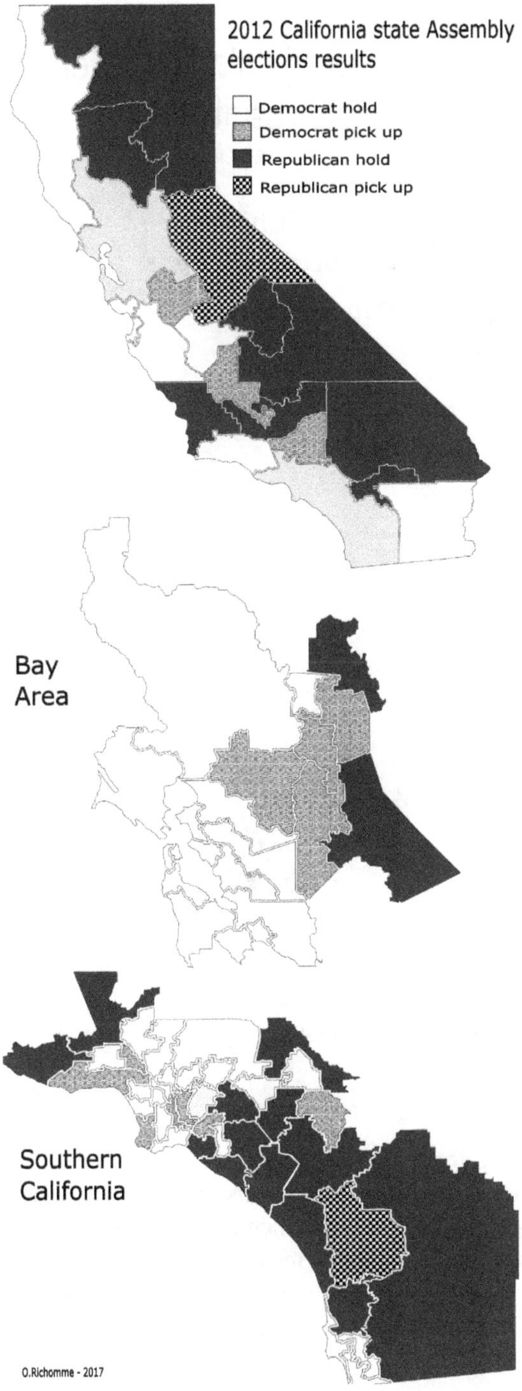

Figure 8.1
2012 California State Assembly Elections Results

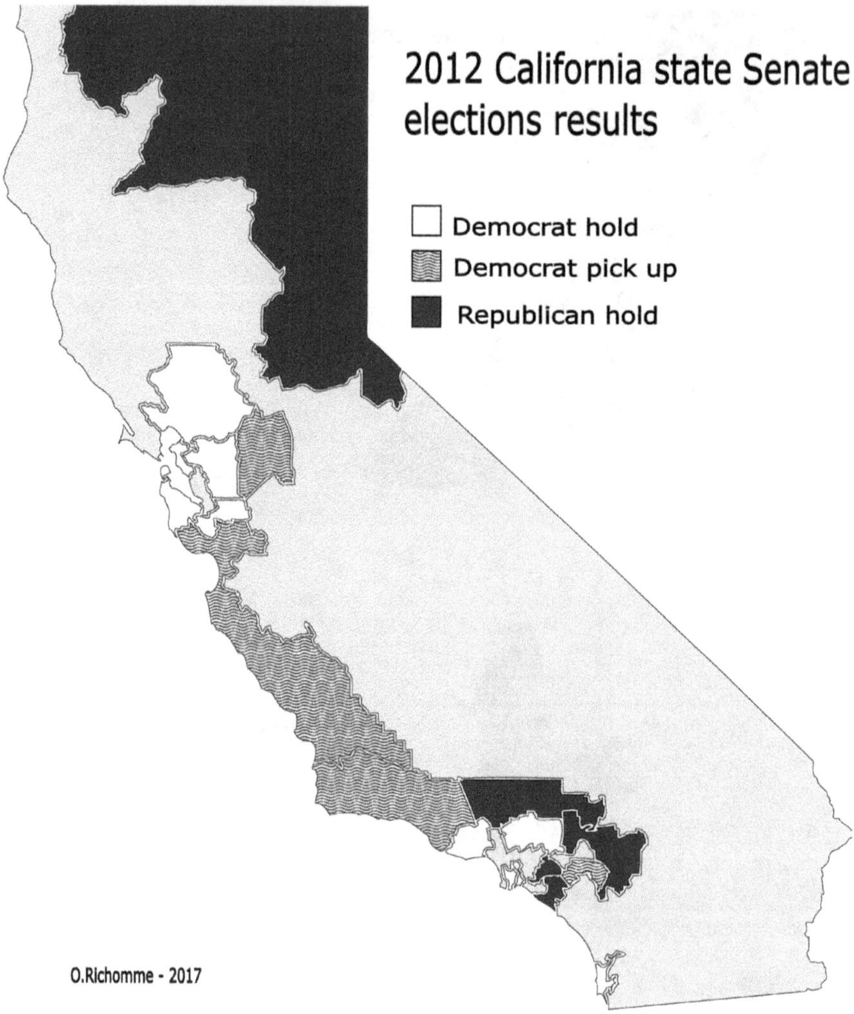

Figure 8.2 2012 California State Senate Elections Results

crushed Democrat Jose Solorio, a former Assemblyman and son of migrant farm workers.[150] The Democrats ended up with 25 seats in the upper house. The supermajority was a long-shot to begin with since the Democrats had to win 13 of the 20 seats up for election in 2014.[151] Besides the CRC eliminated a Bay area district to transfer it to Riverside County because of population growth in the Inland Empire. The newly created Twenty-eight District (won by Jeff Stone) was solidly Republican.

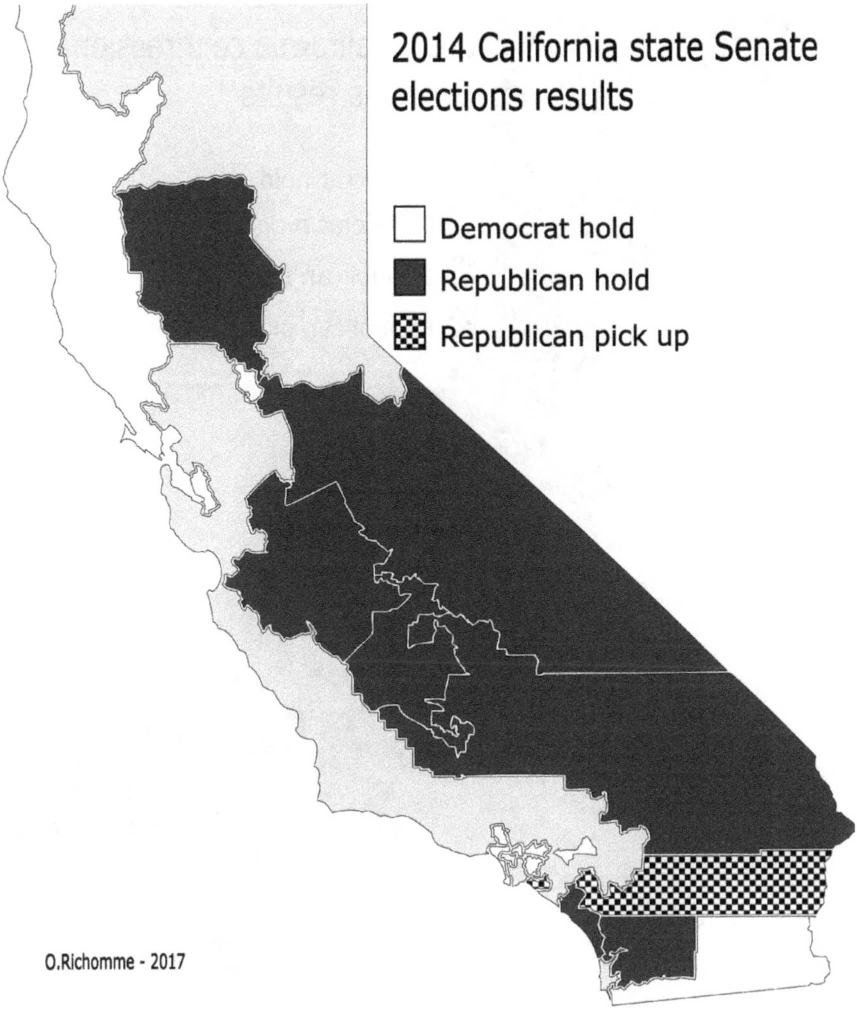

Figure 8.3 2014 California State Senate Elections Results

In the Assembly Republicans won several close races, including in Orange County Sixty-fifth Assembly District. In it Korea-American challenger Young Kim, a Republican but a former aide to Representative Ed Royce (D-Fullerton), took down the Democratic incumbent, Latina Assemblywoman Sharon Quirk-Silva in a district that was evenly split with registration rates of 37 percent of Democrats and 35 percent for Republicans.[152] That defeat, and another in Southern California's Thirty-sixth Assembly District where

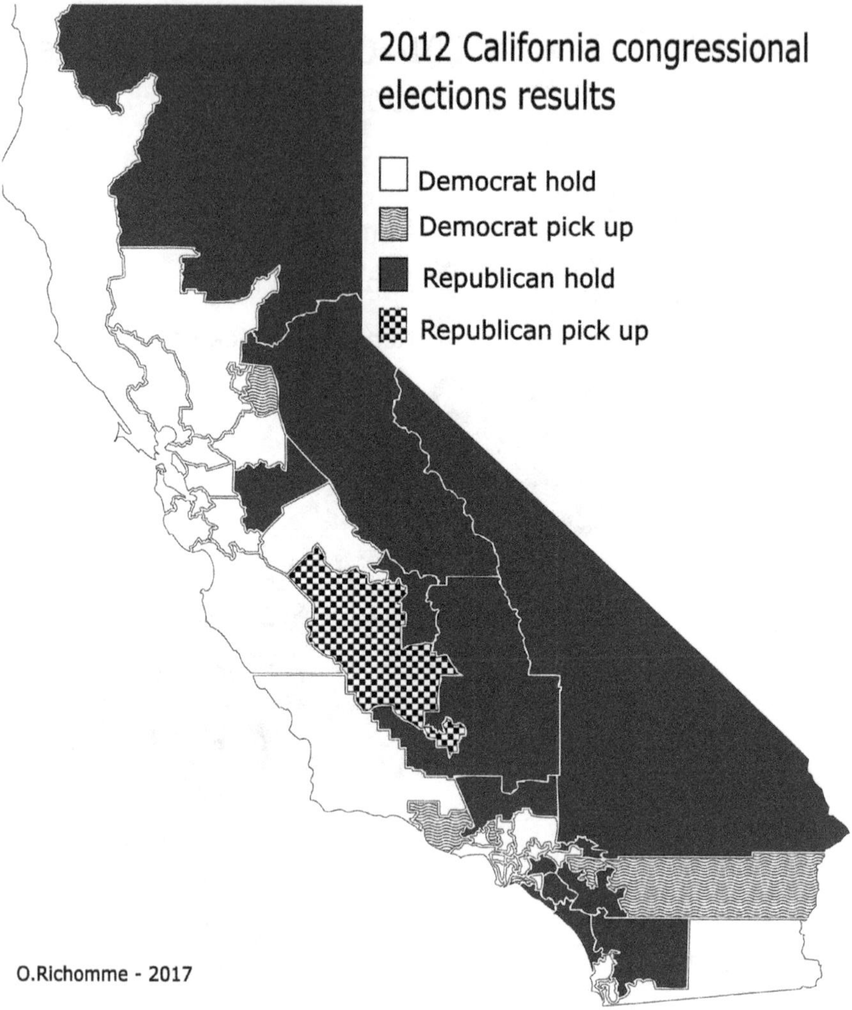

Figure 8.4 2012 California Congressional Elections Results

incumbent Steve Fox lost to Tom Lackey, left Democrats trailing in their attempt to retain their Assembly supermajority. Fox and Quirk-Silva won surprising victories in 2012 and couldn't repeat the feat in 2014. Republicans also picked up AD 16 and 66. Assemblyman Al Muratsuchi (D-Torrance) lost reelection in Los Angeles County's Sixty-sixth Assembly District to Republican challenger David Hadley. In the East Bay's Sixteenth District, Republican Catharine Baker scored a rare Bay Area victory for the GOP when she defeated Democrat Tim Sbranti. The Democrats ended up with a 52 seat majority in the lower house.[153]

With their 2014 victory GOP leaders touted the diverse backgrounds of their newly elected members. Three new Republican lawmakers came from Asian backgrounds: Senator Janet Nguyen (R-Santa Ana) was born in Vietnam; Assembly members Ling-Ling Chang of Chino Hills was born in Taiwan and Young Kim of Fullerton was born in South Korea. They helped increase the membership of the California Asian and Pacific Islander Legislative Caucus from 11 to a record 12 members.[154] The California Legislative Black Caucus reached a record 11 members for the first time in its forty-seven-year history and increased to a record 12 in December 2014 when Assemblyman Isadore Hall III (D-Inglewood) won the special State Senate election after Wright's resignation.

2016

Prior to the 2016 elections, the Democrats held every statewide office and the 2 US Senate seats. With the new top-two primary for the first time in a statewide contest, voters had only two Democrats to choose from in the open US Senate contest between California Attorney General Kamala Harris and Representative Loretta Sanchez (D-Orange).[155] In the November elections, with the election cycle dominated by Donald Trump's extremely close victory for the presidency, Democrats maintained their 39 seat majority in the congressional delegation and increased their legislative dominance. They picked up three state Assembly seats and regained a two-third majority. They also gained one seat in the State Senate and reclaimed a two-third majority there too. The congressional delegation partisan breakdown remained the same with 39 Democrats and 14 Republicans.

In a game of back and forth in the AD 65, Democrat Sharon Quirk-Silva recaptured her seat against one-term incumbent Republican Young Kim. In the Sixty-sixth District Japanese-American Al Marustuchi regained his seat after losing by 700 votes in 2014.[156] The third Democrat pick-up occurred in AD 60 where Latina Sabrina Cervantes defeated two-term incumbent Eric Linder.[157] In spite of these important victories in the Assembly, the Reyes-Brown race was perhaps the marquee legislative matchup for interest groups seeking to influence the final outcome. Some $70 million were spent by independent political action committees in 2016, a 44 percent increase from the record set just two years earlier.[158] In an Assembly district where 52 percent of the voters were Latino and only 5 percent were African American, Cheryl

Brown, a business-aligned Democrat who is African American, lost to a more liberal Latina Eloise Reyes.

In the State Senate, Democrats needed only a single pickup but had to do so in districts that have been historically friendlier to Republicans. In the end, only one seat changed hands. Democrats regained their two-third majority with the victory of Josh Newman, an advocate for veterans' programs, in a tightly contested race east of Los Angeles. Newman defeated Assemblywoman Ling Ling Chang (R-Diamond Bar) by less than 1 percent of the votes, giving the Democrats 27 seats in the 40-member Senate to complement their 55 seats in Assembly.

But 2012 should serve as a cautionary tale. It proved that winning is easier than governing. Yet a supermajority is an amazing tool to have at one's disposal. A supermajority prevents the GOP from blocking Governor Jerry Brown's appointments to boards and commissions. Taxes can be increased and laws put into effect immediately. It also takes a two-third majority of Senate and Assembly members to place an amendment to California's Constitution on the ballot. However, any tax increase would have to pass muster with Governor Jerry Brown, who has proven to be reluctant to embrace new taxes. So much so that he refused to endorse the extension of high earner income taxes, Proposition 55, which voters approved in 2016. Although a supermajority of legislators can override a governor's veto, no legislature has been able to do so since a Brown veto was overridden in 1979. Besides, as one-party majority expands, it become more heterogeneous. Enthusiasm on the left will probably be tempered by the continued strength of a group of business-aligned Democrats who belong to what is now known around the Capitol as the "moderate caucus." This group is composed of centrist politicians whose numbers and prominence have increased since the 2012 creation of new primary rules and longer term limits. These Democrats have pushed back on a number of proposals. Their most famous success was scaling back a sweeping 2015 climate change proposal that they saw as harmful to middle-class families. Members of "mod caucus" have often controlled enough votes to slow down or stop bills favored by more liberal lawmakers and requiring a simple majority in the Assembly. As long as the Republican Party's registration numbers remain as low as they are in contemporary California, the Democrats can afford two factions.

In 2016 the legislature hit a new record as far as diversity is concerned. Not on gender because the number of women actually was the smallest in nearly two decades. It dropped by 4 to reach 27 women in the legislature.[159] All demographic groups saw decreases in the number of women except Latinas, who doubled their ranks from five to 10 lawmakers. However racial and ethnic diversity reached an all-time high. The number of non-White lawmakers has increased from 47 to 53, with gains made among Asian/Pacific Islander, Latino, and multiracial lawmakers. Increases were strong among Asian Pacific Islander (from 12 to 13) and Latino members (from 23 to 27). However the number of African American lawmakers decreased by one. All 10 African American members are Democrats, 9 of 13 API members are Democrats and 25 of 27 Latino members are Democrats proving again that only one party is responsible for descriptive diversity of elected officials. In addition, Todd Gloria (AD 78, D) and Tony Thurmond (AD 15, D) consider themselves multiracial.[160] The rise in diversity is most pronounced in the Assembly, where the majority of legislators, 54 percent, are now ethno-racial minorities.[161] However CRC's impact on the diversity of the legislature should not be overstated. Demographic evolutions can only be contained for so long. Besides, term limits played a crucial role in ending White incumbents careers, especially before the switch allowing Assembly members to serve for twelve years. Fewer incumbents mean less incentive to protect them through redistricting. What the CRC seems to have produced is more opportunities in Congress for minorities.

While Democrat leadership in Washington used to be opposed to the idea of independent redistricting commissions, they have come around. Nancy

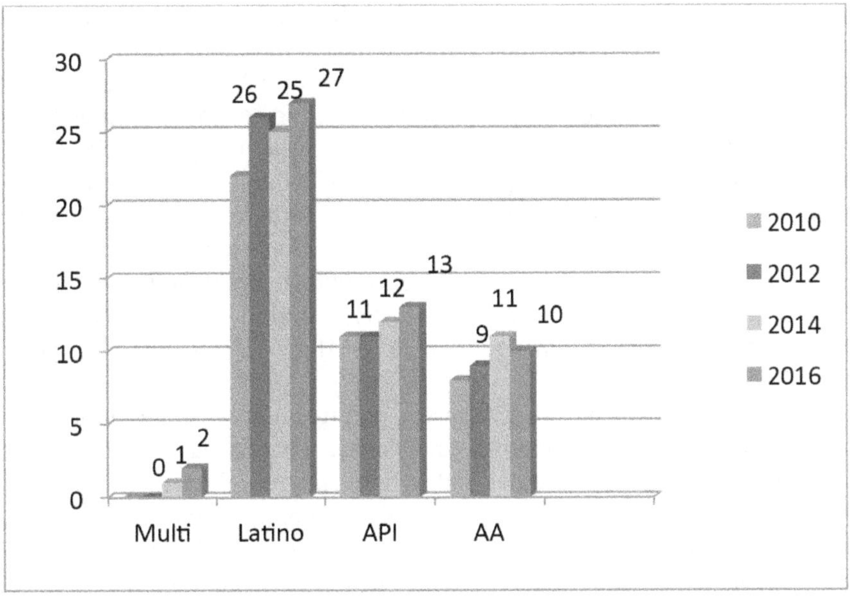

Figure 8.5 Ethno-racial Diversity in the California legislature 2010–2016
Source: Compiled from the histories of the California AfricanAmerican Caucus, the California Latino Caucus, and the California Asian and Pacific Islander Caucus along with elected officials personal website biographies and the press.

Pelosi co-sponsored a redistricting reform proposal in 2015 which needs to be noted, since it is a rare occurrence for party leaders who tend not to lend an official signature to bills.[162] This formal endorsement indicates that Democrats in DC have come to support non-partisan redistricting because they realized it might be in their partisan advantage and their only hope to rein in partisan gerrymandering in the House. Sponsored by Rep. Zoe Lofgren (D-Calif.), the legislation would require states to establish "an independent, multi-party redistricting commission" chosen randomly from a qualified pool. The group would be charged with drawing congressional districts that should be "geographically contiguous; have boundaries that minimize the division of any community of interest, municipality, county, or neighborhood; and be geographically compact."[163] Lofgren introduced various versions of her bill in each Congress since 2005, but support increased in 2015 with 37 co-sponsors, and Democratic leaders have played up the proposal by including it in the party's "good governance" package. This type of proposal has no chance of passing the House though. Everybody knows that a "non-partisan" commission can be used as a partisan tool. It all depends on how it's shaped. As a consequence the next battleground for the Democratic Party and good governance groups, such as Common Cause, is taking place at the state level where they are trying to push for independent redistricting commissions or put restrictions on the legislature in the redistricting process. At the time this book was written, new bills had been put forward in Colorado, Florida, Georgia, New Hampshire, Utah, Virginia, along with 2 referendums in South Dakota and Illinois. The South Dakota Redistricting commission amendment was rejected by voters in December 2016, 57 percent to 43 percent. In Illinois in 2016, the reform group Independent Maps, with the support of the Republican Party, gathered enough signatures to qualify its Independent Redistricting initiative patterned after the CRC for the fall election. However, the State Supreme Court struck the measure as unconstitutional and removed it from the ballot.[164] This failure illustrates the difficulty of crafting referendum that can pass constitutional muster in a given state and shows, again, how exceptional the CRC actually is.

What this last episode of California politics also illustrates is that the alignment of minorities' interests and the Democratic Party's interest did not occur organically. Minorities had to fight and push through electoral and institutional reform to reach levels of political representation commensurate with their electoral weight. The political and ideological realignment that occurred nationally after the passage of the VRA pushed minorities to favor the Democratic Party at higher rates. In California especially, over the past twenty years, since Governor Wilson all the way to Donald Trump, anti-immigration rhetoric reinforced the GOP's image of a party hostile to ethnic and racial minorities, in particular Latinos. However elected official never relinquish positions of power voluntarily and Democrats are no exception. Minority activists who were tired of waiting on the party to make room for them had to get creative and politically savvy to force reforms that could get them the numbers necessary to increase their political power. In a system based on single-member geographic districts and a winner-take-all electoral process in the context of racial polarization, minority groups need to find a way to weigh in on redistricting. The context has changed and conjoined polarization reshuffled the political bargaining calculation but redistricting remains central to exist as a political group.

NOTES

1. The number of failed redistricting initiatives is much larger if one counts the ones that even failed to qualify, were withdrawn or removed by courts. The previous redistricting initiatives in the history of the state of California that qualified but were not mentioned in this book were, in chronological order: 1926, Reapportionment Commission (Proposition 20; rejected by voters), Legislative Reapportionment (Proposition 28; approved by voters); 1948, Senate Reapportionment (Proposition 14; rejected by voters); 1960, Senate Reapportionment (Proposition 5; rejected by voters); 1962, Senate Reapportionment (Proposition 23; rejected by voters). California Secretary of State, Initiatives by Title and Year, http://elections.cdn.sos.ca.gov/ballot-measures/pdf/initiatives-by-title-and-summary-year.pdf.

2. Gray Davis, in a desperate attempt to attract Latino voters, signed a law allowing undocumented immigrants to apply for a driver's license. Franck del Olmo, "Now Latinos Are in the Driver's Seat," *Los Angeles Times*, July 27, 2003, M5; Vicky Haddock, "Politics and Race," *San Francisco Chronicle*, September 28, 2003, D3; Peter Schrag, "Race and Gubernatorial Recall: Can They Be Linked?," *Sacramento Bee*, July 30, 2003, B7. Minority organizations took the matter to court where they argued that the accelerated calendar of the recall election did not leave enough time for poor cities to change the electoral machines that were faulted for the debacle in Florida in 2000. Adam Liptak, "*Bush v. Gore* Outlives Its Limited Warranty for Use in California," *New York Times*, September 16, 2003, A21.

3. Some Republicans were surely emboldened by the success of the Texas mid-decade redistricting. Nancy Vogel, "Looking to Design a Fairer Map," *Los Angeles Times*, February 13, 2005, B1; Ronald Brownstein, "Redrawing Rules and Boundaries," *Los Angeles Times*, March 5, 2005, A18.

4. RNC Chairman Ken Melhman and other prominent Republican leaders urged the governor to leave Congress out of his initiative out of fear of losing political clout in DC. Peter Nicholas, "GOP Fears a Redistricting Backfire," *Los Angeles Times*, February 8, 2005, A1.

5. Peter Nicholas, "Government to Call for Special Session; Legislature Will Be Asked to Consider New Ways to Rein in Spending and Draw Political Districts," *Los Angeles Times*, January 1, 2005, A1.

6. Thomas Mann believes that since elected officials do not abandon power voluntarily the only way to create an independent redistricting mechanism is through direct democracy. Thomas Mann, "Redistricting Reform: What Is Desirable? Possible?," in *Party Line: Competition, Partisanship and Congressional Redistricting*, eds. Thomas Mann and Bruce Cain (Washington DC: Brookings Institution Press, 2005), 111.

7. This tactic had worked before in 2004 when the threat of an initiative campaign helped pass workers comp legislation.

8. Tim Hodson, "Is a Sacramento Mega-Deal in the Air?," *San Francisco Chronicle*, June 24, 2005, B9. Douglas Johnson, affiliated with Claremont-McKenna College and the Rose Institute, who had worked on redistricting plans for the Republican Party in the past estimated that Proposition 77 would create 7 competitive seats in the Assembly, 8 in the Senate, and 10 in Congress. Douglas Johnson, Elise Lampe, Justin Levitt, and Andrew Lee, "Restoring the Competitive Edge" (Claremont, CA: The Rose Institute, 2005).

9. Nancy Vogel, "Modest Changes Seen Under Proposition 77. Redistricting Would Create Some Closer Races, a Study Says, But as Power Shift Is Thought Unlikely," *Los Angeles Times*, September 27, 2005, B1

10. Christian Berthelsen, "Dems Offer Redistricting Plan to Counter Governor's Plan. GOP Says It Leaves Legislature with Too Much Power," *San Francisco Chronicle*, June 29, 2005, B2. This plan would have created a citizens independent commission in charge of redistricting. 7 of the members would have been selected by 2 Democratic legislators and 2 Republican legislators. The final three members would have been appointed by the governor, the judicial council and the president of UC.

11. For the official summary of Proposition 77, see California Legislative Analyst's Office, "Voters Empowerment Act," http://www.lao.ca.gov/ballot/2005/77_11_2005.htm.

12. The California Board of Equalization (created in 1879 by a constitutional amendment) is a public agency charged with tax administration and fee collection in the state. The authorities of the board fall into four broad areas: sales and use taxes, property taxes, special taxes, and acting as an appellate body for franchise and income tax appeals (which are collected by the Franchise Tax Board). The board is made up of 4 directly elected members, each representing a district for four-year terms, along with the State Controller, who is elected on a statewide basis, serving as the fifth member.

13. The judges running could not have been candidates for partisan elections before.

14. John Wildermuth, "'Nonpartisan' measure draws partisan debate. Redistricting plan hotly contested at legislative hearing," *San Francisco Chronicle*, September 27, 2005, B2.

15. At the time 12 states used different forms of commissions: Alaska, Arizona, Arkansas, Colorado, Hawaii, Idaho, Missouri, Montana, New Jersey, Ohio, Pennsylvania, and Washington. 2 states have consultative commission (Vermont and Maine). 5 states used alternative commissions when the legislature deadlocks on redistricting: Connecticut, Illinois, Mississippi, Oklahoma, and Texas. 7 states used commission to

draw congressional districts: Arizona, Hawaii, Idaho, Indiana, Montana, New Jersey, and Washington. Elizabeth Garret, *Redistricting: Another California Revolution?*, Initiative and Referendum Institute, University of Southern California, report 2005-1 (2005), 3; For more details on the creation and function of these commissions, cf. Nathaniel Persily and Melissa Cully Anderson, "Regulating Democracy through Democracy: The Use of Direct Legislation in Election Law Reform," *Faculty Scholarship at Penn Law* (2005), 58. https://scholarship.law.upenn.edu/faculty_scholarship/58.

16. John Wildermuth, "Redistricting Initiative Would Set State Apart. But Opponents Blast Proposition 77 as a 'Reckless Experiment,'" *San Francisco Chronicle*, October 7, 2005, B3.

17. Jill Stewart, "Terminator vs. Gerrymander," *New York Times*, November 7, 2005, A23.

18. Bruce Cain, "Redistricting Commissions: A Better Political Buffer ?," *Yale Law Journal* 121, no. 7 (2012), 1808–44.

19. Tony Quinn, "Leave Redistricting to These judges?Absurd!," *Sacramento Bee*, March 13, 2005, E5. Republicans are especially suspicious of judges from the Ninth Circuit Court that are often accused of taking liberal positions.

20. Jim Sanders, "Ex-Judges Drawing Districts under Proposition 77 Likely Would Be Older White Males," *Sacramento Bee*, October 27, 2005, A3.

21. This deference goes back at least to Justice Frankfurter's opinion in *Colegrove v. Green* (328 U.S. 549 [1946]).

22. Yet in 2016 Hillary Clinton won Orange County, it was the first time that a Democrat carried the county since the Great Depression.

23. Lisa Richardson, "Foes Say Governor Targets Minorities. Schwarzenegger's Ballot Measure Would Weaken the Power of Blacks and Latinos, Critics Contend," *Los Angeles Times*, October 27, 2005, B8.

24. Harrison Sheppard, "Proposition 77; Con: Measure Power Grab by GOP," *The Daily News of Los Angeles*, October 13, 2005, N1.

25. Harrison Sheppard, "Moving the Lines of Power. Study: Redistricting Could Favor Latino in Congress," *The Daily News of Los Angeles*, September 27, 2005, N3.

26. Wildermuth, "Redistricting initiative," B3.

27. Sanders, "Ex-judges Drawing," A3.

28. California Judicial Council, Advisory Committee on Racial and Ethnic Bias in the Courts, *Final Report of the California Judicial Council Advisory Committee on Racial and Ethnic Bias in the Courts* (San Francisco, CA: The Committee, 1997).

29. Proposition 24 was supported by Ron Ulz, a very wealthy Silicon Valley entrepreneur. However, the proposition did not make it to the ballot as the State Supreme Court deemed unconstitutional because it asked voters more than one question. *Senate of the State of California v. Jones* (21 Cal. 4th 1142 [1999]).

30. Jim Sanders, "Redistricting Revelations Spark Furor Letters Fly among Political Attorneys over Differences in Wording on Proposition 77," *Sacramento Bee*, July 16, 2005, A3; John Wildermuth, "Redistricting Measure Could Drop Off Ballot," *San Francisco Chronicle*, July 7, 2005, B2.

31. John Wildermuth, "Redistricting Plan Thrown Off State Ballot," *San Francisco Chronicle*, July 22, 2005, A1.

32. Peter Schrag, "Proposition 77: Off Again, On Again, Gone Again," *Sacramento Bee*, August 17, 2005, B7. On July 21, 2005, Judge Gail Ohanesian of the Superior Court invalidated the proposition (*Lockyer v. McPherson*, 2005 WL 1719252 [Cal. Super. Ct. July 21, 2005]). On July 25, the 3rd Circuit Court of Appeal suspended the Superior Court's decision. On August 9, the Appeal Court concluded that the difference between the two texts was too significant and the proposition should not appear on the ballot (*Costa v. Superior Court*, 32 Cal. Rptr. 3d 562 [Cal. App. 2005]). On August 12, the Supreme Court of California reintegrated Proposition 77 to the November election (*Costa v. Superior Court*, Case No. S136296 [Cal. Aug. 12, 2005]).

33. John Wildermuth, "Voters Reject Attempt to Take Boundary-Drawing from the Hands of State Legislators," *San Francisco Chronicle*, November 9, 2005, A14.

34. Jim Sanders, "Ruling Settles Ballot Dispute; Discrepancies in Wording Shouldn't Have Stopped Vote on Proposition 77, Top Court Says," *Sacramento Bee*, February 17, 2006, A3. Cf. *Costa v. Superior Court* (128 P.3d 675, 690 [Cal. 2006]).

35. John Wildermuth, "Redistricting: Incumbents Team Up to Oppose Schwarzenegger on Proposition 77," *San Francisco Chronicle*, August 26, 2005, B1. The Federal Election Commission lifted fundraising restrictions for Democrats and Republicans for the November 2005 referenda. Alexa H. Bluth, "Initiative Funding Limit Lifted for Lawmakers," *Sacramento Bee*, August 19, 2005, A1. In all, during that election some $300 million were raised over four propositions, among which Propositions 78 and 79, dealing with the price of prescription drugs for poor people concentrated most of the money with the astronomical sums spent by pharmaceutical lobbies. Alan Laguardia, "Ballot Watch: A weekly Update on Proposed State Ballot Measures for a Special Election," *Sacramento Bee*, October 29, 2005, A3.

36. National Institute on Money in State Politics, Proposition 77. Followthemoney.org, http://www.followthemoney.org/entity-details?eid=10246412.

37. Governor Schwarzenegger was always suspected of being a Republican in Name Only (RINO) because he was married to Maria Shriver, a member of the Kennedy family, and Schwarzenegger upon his election right away hired Susan Kennedy as his Chief of Staff while she had been Cabinet secretary under Gray Davis and chair of the California Democratic Party.

38. Joe Hallett, "Much Needed Redistricting Reform Isn't in the Cards for Ohio," *The Columbus Dispatch*, November 13, 2005, 5B; "Schwarzenegger Wants Ohio Issue 4 to Pass," *The Columbus Dispatch*, November 6, 2005, 4A; Jim Siegel, "Redistricting Amendment Proposal Could Means Less Black Legislators," *The Columbus Dispatch*, September 25, 2005, 1A. One of the reasons why the poorly written Ohio proposal did not pass is it contained a provision about the necessary number of competitive seats defined as "by a mathematical formula, that is the product of the number of balanced districts multiplied by two, plus the total number of other remaining competitive districts, minus the total number of unbalanced uncompetitive districts multiplied by two." Ohio Secretary of State, State Issue 4: Amended Certified Ballot Language, http://www.sos.state.oh.us/sos/elections/Research/electResultsMain/2005ElectionsResults/05-1108Issue4/State percent20Issue percent204 percent20Amended percent20Certified percent20Ballot percent20Language.aspx.

39. In the fall 2008, there had been 12 redistricting initiatives in US history, and only four had succeeded. In the previous thirty years, the record was even worse: just one in seven managed to pass in Arizona in 2000. Reforms often occur in states and localities where direct democracy allows voters to bypass the legislature via ballot propositions. Typically, state majority parties respond ferociously to efforts to change the redistricting process. They usually outspend and out-organize reformers.

40. The Irvine Foundation funded a working group through California Common Cause which brought together various stakeholder groups to reach a compromise that would lead to either legislation or a ballot initiative.

41. Proposition 11 passed by less than 200,000 votes out of 12 million votes cast.

42. Supporters of the Proposition 11 raised $14 million to promote its passage, versus the $1 million raised by opponents.

43. George Skelton, "Proposition 11 Foes Waging an Orwellian Campaign," *Los Angeles Times*, October 9, 2008, B1.

44. Bruce Cain, Karin Mac Donald, and Iris Hui, "Competition and Redistricting in California: Lesson for Reform" (Berkeley, CA: Institute for Governmental Studies, 2006); Frederick Douzet, Kenneth P. Miller, and Thad Kousser, eds., *The New Political Geography of California* (Berkeley, CA: Public Policy Institute Press, 2008).

45. Karin Mac Donald, "Adventures in Redistricting: A Look at the California Redistricting Commission," *Election Law Journal* 11, no. 4 (2012), 472.

46. So far this stringent commission's procedure represents the ultimate degree of separation from legislative conflict of interest.

47. In the early state process the Bureau of State Auditors proposed requiring analytical and mapping skills, but they are not widespread among Californians. The leadership of the three minority caucuses in the legislature asked BSA to reconsider in order to extend the pool of potential applicants.

48. The Speaker, the Assembly Minority Leader, the Senate President Pro Tem, and the Senate Minority Leader could strike two names from each party's sub-pool for a total of 24 strikes.

49. To approve a major matter, including approving the final maps, the Commission must obtain "yes" votes from at least three Democratic commissioners, three Republican commissioners, and three commissioners who are not affiliated with either major party.

50. In 1996 registration figures showed 47.4 percent Democrats, 36.8 percent Republicans, 5.2 percent Other Parties and 10.6 percent No Party Preference. In October 2016, these figures were 45 percent Democrats, 26 percent Republicans, 4.8 percent other parties, and 24.3 percent No Party Preference. http://elections.cdn.sos.ca.gov/ror/ror-pages/15day-gen-16/hist-reg-stats.pdf.

51. Criteria 5 and 6 are prefaced by the words "To the extent practicable, and where this does not conflict with the criteria above." California Constitution article XXI, § 2(d).

52. Cain, "Redistricting Commissions," 1826. "The geographic community of interest (GCOI) criterion was given much more emphasis [in the California initiatives] than in the past."

53. California Constitution §2 (d)(4).

54. For an attempt at measuring quantitatively if the redistricting plan of 2011 did respect communities of interest, see Nicholas O. Stephanopoulos, "Redistricting in the 2010s: Communities and the California Commission," *Stanford Law & Policy Review* 23, no. 281 (2012), 281–332; For a more qualitative approach that puts the emphasis on public testimony, see Karin Mac Donald and Bruce Cain, "Community of Interest Methodology and Public Testimony," *UC Irvine Law Review* 3, (2013), 609–36.

55. Kathay Feng interview, 2016.

56. Nancy Vogel, "Proposition 11 Aims to Redo Map," *Los Angeles Times*, October 14, 2008, B1.

57. The official voter pamphlet mailed to registered voters stated: "If legislators don't have to compete to get reelected, they have no accountability to voters. That means they don't to work together to solve problems such as education, health care, road, crime and state budget. Proposition 11 will keep politicians tuned in to voters needs." California Secretary of State, Voter Information guide, November 2008.

58. California Forward was created by four California civic organizations, including Common Cause. The other organizations included the Center for Government Studies, the New California Network, and the Commonwealth Club's Voices of Reform Project whose senior staff became the senior staff at California Forward. The Commonwealth Club's Voices of Reform Project was funded by the James Irvine Foundation that was instrumental in the outreach program to select commissioners.

59. Nancy Vogel, "Key Proposition 11 Donors Have GOP Ties," *Los Angeles Times*, October 24, 2008, B1. Major financial support for both Proposition 11 and the subsequent Proposition 20, which included congressional redistricting, came from moderate Republican activist Charles Munger; National Institute on Money in State Politics, Proposition 11: Changes Authority for Establishing Assembly, Senate and Board of Equalization District Boundaries from Elected Representatives to 14 Member Commission. Follow the money.org, https://www.followthemoney.org/entity-details?eid=10246632.

60. Billionaire entertainment mogul Haim Saban was the largest donor for Proposition 27 in part because the main endangered incumbent was Howard Berman who was the chairman of the House Foreign Affairs Committee and a strong supporter of Israel. Shane Goldmacher, "Battle Lines over Redistricting," *Los Angeles Times*, October 29, 2010, AA1. Both Proposition 20 and Proposition 27 contained so-called poison pill provisions. If they both received a majority vote, the proposition that received the highest majority vote would go into effect.

61. Raphael J. Sonenshein, When the People Draw the Lines: An Examination of the California Citizens Redistricting Commission (2013), 13–14. https://cavotes.org/sites/default/files/jobs/RedistrictingCommission percent20Report6122013.pdf.

62. "A community of interest is a contiguous population which shares common social and economic interests that should be included within a single district for purposes of its effective and fair representation. Examples of such shared interests are those common to an urban area, a rural area, an industrial area, or an agricultural area, and those common areas in which the people share similar living standards, use the same transportation facilities, have similar work opportunities, or have access to

the same media of communication relevant to the election process. Communities of interest shall not include relationships with political parties, incumbents, or political candidates." http://www.wedrawthelines.ca.gov/downloads/voters_first_act_for_congress.pdf.

63. 53 congressional districts, 40 Senate districts, 80 Assembly districts, and 4 Board of Equalization districts.

64. "It came out of the blue. We had no idea. . . . It wasn't necessarily considered the most desirable assignment to take on in the Sacramento world." Steven Russo, cited in Sonenshein, "When the People," 18.

65. Bowen, a former alcoholic who also battled pain killer addiction while in the State Senate, confessed in the press having suffered from depression for thirty years. When she was Secretary of State she was often away from the office. In 2014, as she was still in office, she lived in a trailer park. Patrick McGreevy, "Secretary of State Debra Bowen Tells her Struggle with Depression," *Los Angeles Times*, September 5, 2014, A1.

66. The total cost of the selection process was $4 million.

67. Ovilgy Public Relations Worldwide.

68. Proposition 209, also known as the California Civil Rights Initiative, was passed in 1996. It added Section 31 to Article 1 of the California Constitution which reads: "The state shall not discriminate against, or grant preferential treatment to, any individual or group on the basis of race, sex, color, ethnicity, or national origin in the operation of public employment, public education, or public contracting."

69. Mac Donald, "Adventures," 477–78.

70. For instance it helped launch California forward.

71. The Foundation awarded several grants: $50,000 to the Los Angeles Urban League; $65,000 to CAUSE (California Coast Alliance for a Sustainable Economy); $100,000 to NALEO Educational Fund; $100,000 to The Greenlining Institute; $165,000 to APALC; A larger grant awarded to California Common Cause, for $250,000, covered both the selection and the deliberation phases. Common Cause sub-granted a portion of its Irving grants totaling $92,500 to APALC, the Center for Governmental Studies, the Institute for Governmental Studies, the LWV, MALDEF, the NAACP, NALEO, and the Rose Institute. Sonenshein, "When the People," 20.

72. It is interesting to notice that the classical Athenian democracy principle of lottery is not completely random here. The series of strange candidates that volunteered in 2003 to succeed Governor Davis when he was recalled was probably a strong reminder to Californian reformers that some form of selection was indispensible.

73. And to prevent future conflicts of interest, Proposition 11 also prohibits commissioners from seeking office, working as paid staff or as a paid consultant to state or federal legislators, or registering as a lobbyist for a period of time after serving on the Redistricting Commission.

74. The whole redistricting process was quite transparent in part because the commission was required to conform to California's open meeting law, known as the Bagley-Keene Act. This law ensures transparency and accountability on state boards and commissions but not the legislature. Almost all meetings containing three or

more commissioners must occur in public, the meetings must be fully accessible to the members of the public, and the public must receive adequate and timely notice in advance of the meetings.

75. To prevent party switching, applicants must have voted in two of the past three statewide elections and must have been registered to vote as a member of the same party (or unaffiliated with any party) for at least five years.

76. In 2010 legislative leaders used all of their strikes. These eliminations don't have to be justified.

77. As the state Constitution puts it: "including, but not limited to, racial, ethnic, geographic, and gender diversity."

78. MacDonald, "Adventures," footnote 103.

79. He was also legal affairs secretary for Republican Governor Pete Wilson, served as GOP Governor Arnold Schwarzenegger's lead negotiator for tribal-state compacts.

80. The Commission's legal committee was originally split along party lines, with Republicans on the committee supporting a firm known for its defense work on the Voting Rights Act (Nielsen, Merksamer, Parrinello, Gross, and Leoni was also registered as a lobbying firm which many commissioners saw a source of conflict of interest) and Democrats supporting a firm that had experience with plaintiff-side work and had a year before successfully challenged California's ballot measure banning gay marriage. The impasse was only resolved because the Republican preferred firm withdrew its application after realizing it did not have sufficient support.

81. Redistricting expert Tony Quinn led the charge: "Over GOP opposition, the commission hired Berkeley demographers as their line drawers who had ties to the Democrats, and a staff made up almost entirely of Democrats." Tony Quinn, "Judging the Redistricting Commission," *The California Journal of State Politics and Policy* 3, no. 3 (2011); "Opinion: Redistricting Commission showing Political Bias," *Mercury News*, April 5, 2011, http://www.mercurynews.com/2011/04/05/opinion-redistricting-commission-showing-political-bias/; Dan Walters, "Redistricting Panel Shows True Colors of Ideologies," *Sacramento Bee*, March 25, 2011, https://wedrawthelines.ca.gov/wp-content/uploads/sites/64/2011/03/public_comment_20110325_walters.pdf; Meheta, Seema Meheta, "California's Redistricting Panel Can't Escape Political Pressure," *Los Angeles Times*, March 19, 2011, AA3.

82. Training on redistricting issues was also provided by Justin Levitt (Loyola Law School), Ana Henderson (Berkeley Law), and Hans Johnson (Public Policy Institute of California).

83. His 4 articles on redistricting were all published by the Rose Institute.

84. Often with Bruce Cain as a co-author.

85. Since 2014 Mari Blanco is executive director of the University of California's Undocumented Legal Services Center. Previously she served as executive director of the Chief Justice Earl Warren Institute at UC Berkeley School of Law, as executive director of the Lawyers' Committee for Civil Rights of the San Francisco Bay Area, as an Equal Rights Advocates attorney, as associate director and associate professor at Golden Gate University School of Law, and as National Senior Counsel for the Mexican American Legal Defense and Educational Fund.

86. In the post°1990 redistricting cycle, Ancheta was a staff attorney with the Asian Pacific American Legal Center of Southern California. He represented the Coalition of Asian Pacific Americans for Fair Reapportionment (CAPAFR) before the special masters and before the California Supreme Court.

87. California Redistricting Commission, *Before the California Citizens Redistricting Commission*, In the matter of Full Commission Business Meeting, State Capital Building, Room 447, March 19, 2011, 130 (hereafter: Transcript).

88. Transcript, 119.

89. Transcript, 201.

90. Heslop pleaded guilty to conspiracy to commit bribery and cheating the tribe out of millions of dollars related to construction and real estate transactions from 2006 to 2008. In a scathing pre-sentencing memo filed in US District Court in Los Angeles on June 16, 2012, federal prosecutors described Heslop as a man driven by greed and remorseless for his actions, a man who has denied and fought the allegations from the beginning until the end.

91. Heslop's co-conspirators and co-defendants were former Rose Institute senior research associate Gary Kovall, his wife Peggy Anne Shambaugh, and Paul Bardos, a former student of Heslop's. Joe Nelson, "Former Claremont McKenna Official Pleads Guilty to Bribery Case," *San Gabriel Valley Tribune*, April 8, 2014, https://www.sgvtribune.com/2014/04/08/former-claremont-mckenna-official-pleads-guilty-in-bribery-case/.

92. According to a *New York Times* article: "Nicole Boyle is known around the University of California at Berkeley's Institute of Governmental Studies as the 'G.I.S. queen.' Dean E. Murphy, "Who Should Draw the Lines," *New York Times*, October 23, 2005, http://www.nytimes.com/2005/10/23/magazine/who-should-redistrict.html.

93. Ana Henderson is the Director of Opportunity and Inclusion at the Chief Justice Earl Warren Institute on Race, Ethnicity, and Diversity and a Lecturer-in-Residence at the University of California, Berkeley, School of Law. Vice-chair Blanco was therefore very familiar with her work.

94. Transcript, 76–77 and 247.

95. Both Johnson and Mac Donald who were not used to being in the spotlight were taken aback by the political backlash. Johnson, whose wife is of Thai descent, was particularly hurt by criticism from the Asian community that he would discriminate against minorities. Mac Donald, who was used to being lauded for giving redistricting information for free at the Statewide Database, now had to face the reality that everything she did was analyzed through a partisan lens.

96. Mac Donald interview 2016. The transcript reflects the last-minute bid filing.

97. Sonenshein, "When the People," 30.

98. As mentioned before Proposition 11 specifically prohibits the use of certain types of political data in the definition of communities of interest, including relationships with political parties. However, voting on initiatives for example is often used as a proxy for party identification in California. The commission decided early on to broaden the letter of the law and not use any political data unless required for VRA assessment purposes.

99. Angelo N. Ancheta, "Redistricting Reform and the California Citizens Redistricting Commission," *Harvard Law and Policy Review* 8, no.1 (2014), 126.

100. Ancheta, "Redistricting Reform," 127.

101. Because census variables were of limited use for the assessment of communities of interest the commission asked Californians to provide information about what they considered to be their community of interest and neighborhood boundaries. As a guide, the commissioners used a "community of interest" explanatory handout developed by Berkeley Law's Redistricting Group. *California Redistricting Criterion: Communities of Interest (COI)*, The Redistricting Group at Berkeley Law, http://redistrictinggroup.org/wp-content/uploads/2011/04/Communities-of-Interest_2pagehandout_byTRGBL.pdf. (The Redistricting Group consists of staff of the Statewide Database and the Chief Justice Earl Warren Institute on Law and Social Policy at the University of California, Berkeley Law. This project was conceived in early 2009 and funded by the James Irvine Foundation.)

102. California Citizens Redistricting Commission, *Final Report on 2011 Redistricting* (2011), http://wedrawthelines.ca.gov/downloads/meeting_handouts_082011/crc_20110815_2final_report.pdf.

103. Ancheta, "Redistricting Reform," 130–31.

104. The Mexican American Legal Defense and Educational Fund (MALDEF) and the Asian Pacific American Legal Center (APALC) in collaboration with the Coalition of Asian Pacific Americans for Fair Redistricting (CAPAFR) were of course heard throughout the process. After all, MALDEF, APALC, and CAPAFR were among the groups that implemented outreach and training programs in the communities they serve.

105. Mac Donald and Cain, "Community of Interest," 616.

106. The commission ended up hiring UCLA Professor Matt Baretto to conduct RPV analysis.

107. Another important factor when drawing section 2 seats was that, since *Bartlett v. Strickland* (556 U.S. 1, 1 [2009]), these districts had to be drawn with a minimum of 50 percent of the Citizen Voting Age Population.

108. Vladimir Kogan and Eric McGhee, "Redistricting California: An Evaluation of the Citizens Redistricting Commission Final Plans," *Journal of California Politics and Policy* 4, no. 1 (2012), 7. The 2011 estimates are based on census block-level Citizens Voting Age Population. For 2001, they used district-level measures calculated using a special tabulation from the 2000 census data.

109. For example, Riverside County saw its Latino population increase by 78 percent. That could present problems for the region's elected officials, such as US Representative Ken Calvert (R-Corona), who represents parts of Orange and Riverside counties. The Latino population in his district increased 64 percent. Seema Mehta, "Census Augurs Inland Power Shift," *Los Angeles Times*, March 9, 2011, A1.

110. Jean Merl, "Minority Districts on Dividing Lines," *Los Angeles Times*, July 25, 2011, AA1. Waters district's population is also 46 percent Latino, 12 percent Asian, and 15 percent Anglo and a Cook PVI D+26. Bass' district is 39 percent Latino, 9 percent Asian, and 24 percent Anglo with a Cook PVI of D+34.

111. In 2016, she defeated Isadore Hall III in a district that is almost 70 Latino and 17 percent African American.

112. Kogan and McGhee, "Redistricting California."

113. Loretta Sanchez had left the Latino Caucus after accusing Rep. Joe Bata of sexism. The ripple effect benefitted Sen. Bill Emmerson, R-Hemet, who was no longer in the same Senate district as colleague Joel Anderson, R-Alpine. Assemblywoman Bonnie Lowenthal, D-Long Beach, who was no longer drawn into an Orange County Republican district.

114. The commission heard testimony from Equality California, a gay-rights groups that claims 700,000 members. In a dramatic cultural evolution, the Census Bureau now releases data on same sex couples in the US. https://www.census.gov/hhes/samesex/.

115. This minority voting rights evolution is exemplified by John Pérez (D-Los Angeles) who was the Assembly Speaker at the time and was the first openly gay Speaker and a Latino. He wasn't elected in a district with a large LGBT population.

116. One example of the VRA counsel's point of view prevailing was in the separation of Santa-Ana and Anaheim. The two areas had been combined in 1991 and 2001. In the end, the two areas were combined to form a Section 2 seat for the Assembly (AD 69) but were mostly separated in the Senate district (SD 34). Mac Donald and Cain, "Community of Interest," 634–35.

117. "We have a Senate 3 District in Northern California that received a lot of public comment that involves the areas of Martinez, Crockett, traditional areas of Contra Costa that are usually grouped together along a portion of the Highway 4 and that have a strong identity. We understand that this is not ideal, but I want to say that there are a lot of other issues around the state on Senate maps where we have less than ideal districts and that we weren't always able to balance all the things that we needed to balance population, communities of interest, Section 5, Section 132, geographic concerns, divisions like bridges that 14 people didn't want us to cross." California Citizens Redistricting Commission, *Before the California Citizens Redistricting Commission*, In the Matter of Full Commission Business Meeting, University of the Pacific, McGeorge School of Law, Classroom C 3200 Fifth Avenue Sacramento, California, July 29, 2011, full transcript, 15. http://wedrawthelines.ca.gov/downloads/transcripts/201107/transcripts_20110729_sacto.pdf.

118. "In my opinion, the Commission failed to fulfill its mandate to strictly apply the Constitutional criteria and consistently applied race and community of interest criteria, and sought to diminish dissenting viewpoints." *Before the California Citizens Redistricting Commission*, July 29, 2011, 35.

119. Patrick McGreevy and Richard Simon, "New Voting Maps Face Challenges," *Los Angeles Times*, August 15, 2011, AA1.

120. *Radanovich v. Bowen* (No.S196852 [Cal. Sept. 29, 2011]); *Radanovich v. Bowen* (No. S196852 [Cal. Oct. 26, 2011]).

121. Under the California Constitution, the Supreme Court has original jurisdiction in legal challenges to any of the commission's plans. California Constitution Article XXI, § 3(b)(1). Yet, a state constitutional limitation is not binding on the

jurisdiction of federal courts and claims under federal law could also be litigated against the commission in federal court. *Radanovich v. Bowen* (No. 2:11-cv-09786-SVW-PJW [C.D. Cal. Feb. 9, 2012])

122. McGreevy and Simon, "New Voting Maps," AA1.

123. Majority whip Kevin McCarthy (R-Bakersfield) among the Republicans who thought it wasn't a good use of campaign resources.

124. "Republicans Likely to Abandon Referendum on Congressional Maps," *Capitol Weekly*, September 20, 2011, https://capitolweekly.net/republicans-likely-to-abandon-referendum-on-congressional-maps/.

125. The two alternatives proposed by the plaintiffs were a court master drawn plan or use the previous 2001 plan. *Vandermost v. Bowen* (269 P.3d 446 [Cal. 2012]), at 483.

126. Jim Sanders, "GOP Ends Effort to Kill California Senate Districts, Won't Push Proposition 40," *Sacramento Bee*, July 13, 2012, 4A.

127. Proposition 40 would have invalidated the commission's State Senate plan and appointed special court masters to draw maps.

128. Sonenshein, "When the People," 66. As a point of comparison, the Arizona Commission's work in 2001 cost about the same amount while the state is much smaller.

129. The Irvine Foundation also funded "Redistricting Assistance Sites," technical assistance centers that were open to the public, equipped with multiple computers with redistricting mapping software, and staffed by a technical consultant from the Redistricting Group at UC Berkeley, in six locations throughout California. The Irvine Foundation, along with the Ford Foundation, also provided funding to the Advancement Project to develop an online mapping resource called ReDrawCA.

130. California Secretary of State, California's Official Voter Guide 2008, Budget Summary, http://voterguide.sos.ca.gov/past/2008/general/titlesum/prop11-title-sum.htm.

131. Ancheta, "Redistricting Reform," 135.

132. That was particularly strange in Tony Quinn's declaration in *Vandermost v. Bowen* because the context was quite different. Declaration of Dr. T. Anthony Quinn, PhD, in support of petition for writ of mandate or writ of mandate (on file with author). For instance the Voters First Act ranks redistricting criteria by which the special masters did not have to comply. Besides, the interpretation of the Voting Rights Act dramatically changed since in the 1990s after the *Shaw v. Reno* series of cases dealing with the use of race in redistricting. More recently *Bartlett v. Strickland* (556 U.S. 1 [2009]) had further defined majority-minority requirement under Section 2 of the VRA.

133. The website "fox and hounds" was especially active with longtime Republican consultant and member of the Rose Institute board of directors Tony Quinn leading the charge. Tony Quinn, "Excluding the Public: Redistricting Commission Goes Dark," *Fox and Hounds*, July 11, 2011, http://www.foxandhoundsdaily.com/2011/07/9186-excluding-the-public-the-redistricting-commission-goes-dark/; Steven Greenhut, "More Proof Dems Manipulated Redistricting," *Fox and Hounds*,

December 22, 2011, http://www.foxandhoundsdaily.com/2011/12/propublica-ignores-worst-redistricting-lines/.

134. Because other states in the Union are less populated, smaller in size and more homogenous than California it seems logical to think that such an independent commission could easily be implemented. Yet, had Californians known the final price tag it is doubtful Proposition 11 would have been successful, especially since the vote was so close.

135. *Connerly v. State of California* (229 Cal. App. 4th 457 [2014]).

136. In the case *Arizona State Legislature v. Arizona Independent Redistricting Commission* in 2015 the United States Supreme Court in a 5–4 vote upheld the right of Arizona voters to remove the authority to draw election districts from the Arizona State Legislature and vest it in an independent redistricting commission.

137. Mac Donald, "Adventures."

138. Douglas J. Ahler, Jack Citrin, and Gabriel S. Lenz, "Do Open Primaries Improve Representation? An Experimental Test of California's Top-Two Primaries," *Legislative Studies Quarterly* 41, no. 2 (2016), 237–68; Thad Kousser, "The Top-Two, Take-Two: Did Changing the Rules Change the Game in Statewide Contests?," *The Journal of California Politics and Policy* 7, no.1 (2015).

139. Eric McGhee and Daniel Krimm, *California's New Electoral Reforms: The Fall Election,* (Public Policy Institute of California, 2012), http://www.ppic.org/main/publication_show.asp?i=1039.

140. Jean Merl, "Berman Loses His First Election—and His Seat," *Los Angeles Times*, November 8, 2012, AA9.

141. Jean Merl and Patrick McGreevy, "Democrats Gain Big in the Legislature," *Los Angeles Times*, November 7, 2012, A1.

142. She was found guilty by the House Ethics Committee on seven counts of violating House rules by improperly pressuring her staff to campaign for her, destroying evidence and tampering with witness testimony. In August 2012, she was reprimanded by the full House. John H. Cushman Jr., "House Reprimands Richardson," *New York Times*, August 2, 2012, https://thecaucus.blogs.nytimes.com/2012/08/02/house-reprimands-richardson/.

143. Republicans set aside their differences with Maldonado over his 2009 vote, as a state Senator, to raise taxes in a budget deal and eventually rallied behind his bid to defeat Capps.

144. At the time, the spouse of late Sony Sono, who she replaced after his death in 1998, was the only Republican female of the California delegation. In 2014, Mimi Walters was the only Republican female in the delegation.

145. A few weeks leading up to the election McLeod's campaign benefitted from $3.2 million in independent expenditures from the Federal Super PAC of billionaire Michael Bloomberg, who was mayor of New York City at that time. Baca had not been supportive of Bloomberg's efforts for stronger federal laws for gun control. In 2015 Baca announced he switched his party affiliation to Republican. In Congress Baca was a member of the Latino and Native American caucuses.

146. Prosecutors alleged that Alarcón, who had pleaded not guilty, lied about where he lived so he could run for the City Council post.

147. When Baca was chairman of the Congressional Hispanic Caucus he was accused of using funds from his PAC (BOLDPAC) to finance his sons (Joe and Jeremy) unsuccessful campaigns. At the time, Loretta Sanchez and five other members resigned from the PAC in protest because they disagreed with the funds being used to run his sons against other Latino candidates.

148. The story sounded like a bad Hollywood movie. One senator, Leland Yee of San Francisco, a gun control advocate, was charged with conspiring to traffic in arms from the Philippines, and taking bribes from undercover FBI agents including one who posed as a marijuana dealer. He pleaded guilty and was sentenced to five years in prison. In 2004 Leland Yee became the first Asian American in state history to become Senate Pro Tempore. Another state senator, Ron Calderon of Los Angeles was accused of taking bribes from federal agents impersonating Hollywood film executives. And a third, Rod Wright from Inglewood, was convicted of perjury and voter fraud after lying about where he lived when he ran for office.

149. Proposition 25 also requires state legislators to forfeit their pay in years where they have failed to pass a budget in a timely fashion.

150. Nguyen replaced termed-out state Latino Senator Lou Correa (D-Santa Ana) who in 2016 was elected to the Forty-sixth District of the House of Representatives long held by Latina Democrat Loretta Sanchez.

151. Because of staggered State Senate terms only half of the state senators in uneven districts were up for reelection in 2012. Therefore for two years some 4 million Californians were represented by someone not elected by their community. California is not the only state to have kept staggered elections. Yet some states have addressed this issue by reassigning legislators whose terms continue past redistricting (they are called "holdover" legislators) to represent new districts. For more on this technical question, see for instance Margaret B. Weston, "One Person, One Vote: Staggered Elections, Redistricting and Disenfranchisement," *Yale Law Journal* 121, no. 7 (2012), 2013.

152. Democratic Party committees spent nearly $2 million in the last month of the campaign to protect Quirk-Silva. In October, the California Republican Party directed more than $650,000 to help Kim. Patrick McGreevy and Melanie Mason, "GOP Has Early Lead in Key Legislature Races," *Los Angeles Times*, November 5, 2014, A9.

153. That number could have been lower. First-term incumbent Ian Calderon barely survived in the Fifty-seventh District in spite of a 20-point democratic registration advantage. Calderon is the nephew of Senator Ronald Calderon (D-Montebello) and former Assemblyman Ron Calderon and he was probably plagued by his uncles legal woes. Patrick McGreevy and Melanie Mason, "Gains in Legislature Not So Easy for Democrats," *Los Angeles Times*, June 5, 2014, AA4.

154. Such a big APIA caucus had important consequences. For instance it put an end to Latino and African American hopes to roll back the state's ban on affirmative action in public colleges. Patrick McGreevy and Melanie Mason, "A Time of Give and Take?," *Los Angeles Times*, December 1, 2014, AA1.

155. The top-2 primary also had an interesting effect on noncompetitive parts of the state. In parts of LA County such as the San Fernando Valley and central Los Angeles, in 2016, the only Republican candidates to appear on the ballot were President

Donald Trump and Vice President Mike Pence. For the other down the ballot votes the 818,000 electors in the county had to choose among Democrats. Javier Panzar, "Ballot for Parts of LA County Has GOP 'Dead Zone,'" *Los Angeles Times*, October 27, 2016, A1.

156. Muratsuchi's campaign smartly set up a website called hadleytrump.com with audio and video of Hadley being confronted about whether he would support the presumptive Republican nominee. Christine Mai-Duc, "Legislative Races to Watch," *Los Angeles Times*, June 6, 2016, B4.

157. Previously Cervantes was the district director for Assembly member Jose Medina (AD 61). She was also the Director of the California Voter Registration Project. Eric Linder is an anti-tax son of a Mexican immigrant father. In 2012, at age thirty-three he won against seventy-year-old Democrat Jose Luis Perez. He ran unopposed in 2014. The district has a registration rate of 40 percent Republican and 35 percent Democrat but a 52 percent Latino population according to the 2010 census. It has a Voting Age Population that is 35 percent Latino, 7 percent Asian, and 7 percent African American. John S. Klemanski, David A. Dulio and Michael Switalski, *Campaigns form the Ground Up: State Elections in a National Context* (New York: Routledge, 2015), 131–41.

158. John Myers, "Democrats Wait to Reclaim Supermajority in Legislature," *Los Angeles Times*, November 10, 2016, B9.

159. Jazmine Ulloa, "Legislature Sees Rise in Diversity, Drop in Women," *Los Angeles Times*, November 26, 2016, B1.

160. Gloria has Latino, API, White and Native American ancestry (he is an enrolled member of the Tlingit Haida Indian Tribes of Alaska). Thurmond identifies as African American and Latino.

161. "Demographics in the Legislature, November 2016 Election Update," California State Library, California Research Bureau, December 15, 2016, https://www.library.ca.gov/Content/pdf/crb/reports/CRB_2017-2018_Legislature_Breakdown_-_Special_Update_2018-08-07.pdf.

162. Mike Lillis, "Deep in Minority, Dems Look for Redistricting for Hope," *The Hill*, August 29, 2015, http://thehill.com/homenews/house/252226-deep-in-minority-dems-look-to-redistricting-for-hope.

163. A similar bill, sponsored by Reps. Jim Cooper (D-Tenn.) and Reid Ribble (R-Wis.), mandated comparable commissions, but with members appointed directly by the state leaders from each party.

164. Kim Geiger, "Judge Knocks Redistricting Off Ballot in Loss for Rauner," *Chicago Tribune*, July 20, 2016, http://www.chicagotribune.com/news/local/politics/ct-illinois-redistricting-lawsuit-ruling-madigan-met-20160720-story.html.

Chapter 9

Conjoined Polarization in California and the Evolution of Redistricting

IS DEMOGRAPHY DESTINY?

A famous statement in political science is that demography is destiny, meaning a candidate's political fortune is dictated by the composition of the population electing him or her. Even though it may not always be the case, and redistricting is a good example of how demographic evolutions can be tempered, demography remains fundamental. As California became a minority-majority state in the twenty-first century, it was inevitable that minorities' capacity to elect minority candidates would increase and that, conversely, Anglos' influence on the ballot would decrease. No amount of redistricting shenanigans can completely offset that trend. The only question remaining was to what extent and at what pace would evolution in the demographic landscape produce changes in politics. What strategies would different interest groups adopt to try and influence redistricting?

Non-Hispanic Whites are no longer a majority in the state and have not been for a decade. But, as of 2016, for the first time Latinos have surpassed Whites to become the largest ethnic group in the state. Together with Asians Pacific Islanders and African Americans, they represent 60 percent of the state's population. Demographic trends also indicate that the Latino and Asian categories keep increasing while the White category decreases. The percentage of the African American population in the state has been declining slightly over time. While the state's demographic trajectory has tremendous political implications, it should not be mistaken as being equal to an inversion of electoral power. As we have seen, demographically dynamic populations such as Latinos have a large percentage of minors. Moreover, communities with large immigrant populations, such as Latinos and Asians, contain a significant amount of non-citizens. Besides, traditionally speaking, these two

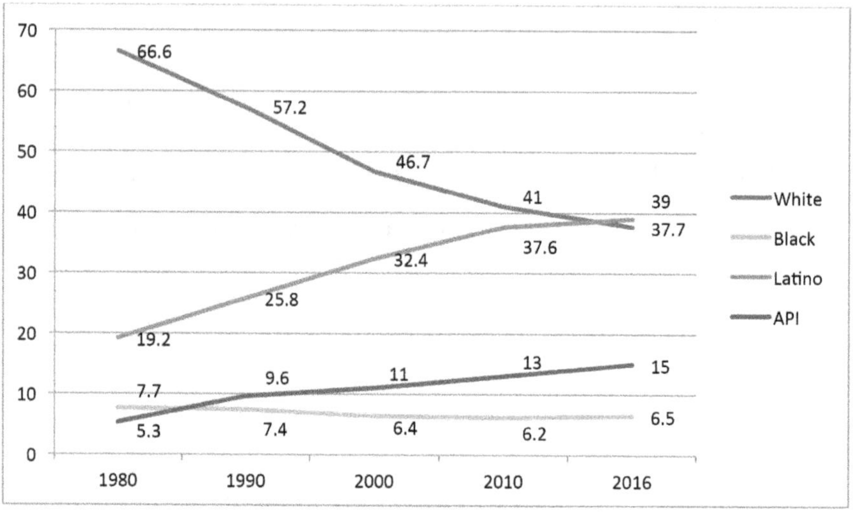

Figure 9.1 California Population by Race and Ethnicity since 1980 (all categories exclusive)
Source: US Census. 1980–1990: California—Race and Hispanic Origin: 1850 to 1990, https://www.census.gov/population/www/documentation/twps0029/tab08.html. 2000–2010: http://censusviewer.com/state/CA. 2016: US Census, Quick facts, California, 2016.

groups have a long history of registration rates that are significantly lower than that of Anglos or African Americans which means that even when they are US citizens they do not influence the vote in a manner that is commensurate with their demographic weight. As a consequence, figure 9.1 shows that while non-Hispanic Whites only represent 37 percent of the state's population, during the 2016 elections, they still represented 55 percent of the total turnout. That is the group's lowest point ever but it still represents a majority of the votes cast. This percentage is even higher during the mid-term elections when non-White turnout is notoriously low. In 2014, non-Hispanic Whites represented 62 percent of the total turnout while African Americans represented 6 percent (a 2 percent drop from 2012), and Latinos represented 19 percent (a 4 percent drop compared to 2012). In 2014, Latinos and Asians displayed registration rates under 50 percent (respectively 48 percent and 46 percent). In other words, the number of wasted minority votes, that is the number of actual votes compared to the number of adult citizens, reached an all-time high with more than 6 million non-Anglos eligible who did not vote. These figures highlight again that registration and turnout, and therefore outreach programs and mobilization, are key to the future of the California electorate.

Table 9.1 also shows that as early as 1982 Latino groups could claim that Latinos represented as many votes as African Americans and therefore were

Table 9.1 California Electorate Breakdown by Race and Ethnicity since 1980

Year	*Race/Ethnicity*	*VAP*	*CVAP*	*REG*	*REG%*	*TO*	*TO%*	*REG Share*	*TO Share*	*VR Potential*
2016	Total	29,894	24,89	16,096	64.67	14,416	89.56			8,794
	White	21,592	18,104	12,084	66.75	10,908	90.23	75.07	75.66	6,02
	N-H White	1,248	11,954	8,732	73	8,020	92	50	55.6	3,934
	AA	1,849	1,768	1,018	57.58	856	84.09	6.32	5.93	750
	Latino	10,221	7,092	3,882	54.73	3,345	86.17	24.11	23.2	321
	API	4,838	3,585	2,08	58.03	1,859	89.38	12.92	12.89	1,505
2014	Total	2,903	24,455	14,113	57.73	8,949	63.4			10,342
	White	21,429	1,806	10,753	59.55	7,093	65.96	76.19	79.26	7,307
	N-H White	12,326	11,907	7,83	65.75	5,551	70.1	55.5	62	4,077
	AA	1,846	1,787	1,043	58.37	535	51.29	73.9	5.97	744
	Latino	10,023	6,859	3,294	48.03	1,707	51.82	23.34	19.07	3,565
	API	4,409	3,486	1,628	46.70	933	57.3	11.53	10.42	1,858
2012	Total	28,357	23,419	15,356	65.6	13,462	87.7			8,063
	White	21,33	17,692	11,785	66.6	10,391	88.2	76.75	77.2	5,907
	N-H White	12,317	11,866	8,544	72	7,628	89.3	55.6	56.7	3322
	AA	181	1,714	1,192	69.5	1,063	89.2	7.76	7.90	522
	Latino	9,935	651	3,684	56.6	3,157	85.7	23.99	23.45	2,826
	API	3,915	2,839	1,645	57.9	1,38	83.9	10.71	10.25	1,194
2010	Total	27,381	22,767	13,864	60.9	10,725	77.36			8,903
	White	20,828	17,331	11,016	63.6	8,666	78.67	79.5	80.8	6,315
	N-H White	12,418	11,985	8,197	68.4	6,713	81.9	59.1	62.6	3,788
	AA	1,728	1,661	932	56.1	708	75.97	6.7	6.6	729
	Latino	9,004	5,816	3,025	52	2,058	68.03	21.8	19.2	2,791
	API	386	2,938	1,472	50.1	1,008	68.48	10.6	9.4	1,466
2008	Total	26,993	21,816	14,885	68.2	13,828	92.3			6,931
	White	20,823	16,837	11,775	69.9	10,982	93.3	79.1	79.4	5,062
	N-H White	12,581	12,048	8,783	72.46	8,255	94	59	59.7	3,265

(continued)

Table 9.1. *(continued)*

Year	*Race/Ethnicity*	*VAP*	*CVAP*	*REG*	*REG%*	*TO*	*TO%*	*REG Share*	*TO Share*	*VR Potential*
	AA	1,682	1,646	1,105	67.1	1,073	97.1	7.42	7.76	541
	Latino	8,859	5,193	3,263	62.8	2,961	90.7	21.92	21.41	193
	API	3,626	2,688	1,599	59.48	141	88.18	10.74	10.19	1,089
2006	Total	26,318	21,25	13,239	62.3	10,104	76.3			8,011
	White	20,284	16,349	10,756	65.79	8,336	77.5	81.2	82.5	5,593
	N-H White	1,254	11,977	8,461	70.6	6,739	79.6	63.91	66.7	3,516
	AA	1,665	16	847	52.9	608	71.8	6.40	6.02	743
	Latino	818	4,676	2,481	53.1	1,717	69.2	18.74	16.99	1,195
	API	3,656	2,745	1,336	48.7	948	70.95	10.09	9.38	1,409
2004	Total	26,085	20,693	14,193	68.6	12,807	90.2			6,5
	White	20,083	15,913	11,286	70.9	10,273	91	79.52	80.12	4,627
	N-H White	1,235	11,777	8,976	76.21	8,311	93	63.2	65	2,801
	AA	1,678	1,564	1,141	73	1,035	90.7	8.04	8.08	423
	Latino	8,127	4,433	2,455	55.4	2,081	84.8	17.3	16.25	1,957
	API	3,636	262	1,379	53	1,162	84.26	9.71	9.07	1,241
2002	Total	24,405	19,642	12,025	61.2	8,355	69.5			7,617
	White	19,185	15,668	993	63.4	7,011	70.6	82.58	83.9	5,738
	N-H White	12,484	11,891	7,994	67.72	5,844	73.1	66.5	70	3,897
	AA	1,503	144	801	55.6	549	68.5	6.66	6.6	639
	Latino	6,964	3,974	2,017	50.8	1,206	59.8	16.77	14.4	1,957
	API	3,306	2,172	1,122	51.65	727	64.79	9.33	8.7	105
2000	Total	24,749	19,837	13,061	65.8	11,489	88			6,776
	White	1,977	1,606	10,839	67.5	9,618	88.7	82.99	83.7	5,221
	N-H White	13,362	12,659	8,979	71	8,071	88.9	68.7	70.2	3,680
	AA	1,678	1,606	1,039	64.7	873	84	7.95	7.6	567

	Latino	6,514	3,489	1,919	55	1,597	83.2	14.69	13.9	157
	API	3,027	1,908	1,007	52.77	848	84.2	7.7	7.4	901
1998	Total	23,696	19,016	12,356	65	9,593	77.6			666
	White	19,121	15,582	10,383	66.6	8,225	79.2	84.03	85.74	5,199
	N-H White	1,295	12,492	8,675	69.4	6,925	79.8	70.2	72.2	3,817
	AA	1,579	1,505	962	63.9	669	69.5	7.79	6.97	543
	Latino	5,723	2,743	1,641	59.8	1,291	78.7	12.79	11.65	1,102
	API	2,706	1,657	854	51.5	587	68.7	6.9	6.2	267
1996	Total	22,871	18081	12,827	70.9	11,079	86.4			5,254
	White	1,849	14,981	10,892	72.7	9,445	86.7	84.91	85.25	4,089
	AA	1,363	1,328	904	68.1	773	85.5	7.05	6.98	424
	Latino	5,723	2,743	1,641	59.8	1,291	78.7	12.79	11.65	1,102
1994	Total	22,639	21,199	12,544	59.2	10,417	83			8,655
	White	18,799	1,758	10,978	62.4	9,223	84	87.52	88.54	6,602
	AA	1,237	1,214	742	61.1	540	72.8	5.92	5.18	472
	Latino	5,736	2,698	1,427	52.9	1,183	82.9	11.38	11.36	1,271
1992	Total	22,34	n/a	12,884	n/a	11,769	91.3			n/a
	White	18,759	n/a	11,349	n/a	10,482	92.4	88.09	89.06	n/a
	AA	1,268	n/a	812	n/a	712	87.7	6.3	6.05	n/a
	Latino	5,443	n/a	1,384	n/a	1,135	82	10.74	9.64	n/a
1990	Total	21,289	n/a	11,666	n/a	9,027	77.4			n/a
	White	17,998	n/a	10,259	n/a	8,063	78.6	87.94	89.32	n/a
	AA	1,173	n/a	732	n/a	493	67.3	6.27	5.46	n/a
	Latino	4,739	n/a	1,218	n/a	844	69.3	10.44	9.35	n/a
1988	Total	20,194	n/a	11,935	n/a	1,044	87.5			n/a
	White	17,084	n/a	10,370	n/a	9,123	88	86.89	87.39	n/a
	AA	1,252	n/a	870	n/a	731	84	7.29	7	n/a
	Latino	4,261	n/a	1,04	n/a	827	79.5	8.71	7.92	n/a

(continued)

Table 9.1. *(continued)*

Year	*Race/Ethnicity*	*VAP*	*CVAP*	*REG*	*REG%*	*TO*	*TO%*	*REG Share*	*TO Share*	*VR Potential*
1986	Total	19,421	n/a	11,128	n/a	8,798	79.1			n/a
	White	16,508	n/a	9,839	n/a	7,808	79.4	88.42	88.75	n/a
	AA	1,185	n/a	776	n/a	578	74.5	6.97	6.57	n/a
	Latino	369	n/a	993	n/a	731	73.6	8.92	8.31	n/a
1984	Total	19,063	n/a	11,724	n/a	10,618	90.6			n/a
	White	15,994	n/a	10,252	n/a	9,308	90.8	87.44	87.66	n/a
	AA	143	n/a	941	n/a	824	87.6	8.03	7.76	n/a
	Latino	3,164	n/a	978	n/a	826	84.5	8.34	7.78	n/a
1982	Total	1,784	n/a	10,276	n/a	8,670	84.4			n/a
	White	15,075	n/a	909	n/a	7,703	84.7	88.46	88.85	n/a
	AA	1,177	n/a	758	n/a	628	82.8	7.38	7.24	n/a
	Latino	2,944	n/a	860	n/a	659	76.6	8.37	7.6	n/a
1980	Total	16,503	n/a	9,902	n/a	8,879	89.7			n/a
	White	14,193	n/a	8,814	n/a	7,934	90	89.01	89.36	n/a
	AA	1,254	n/a	771	n/a	674	87.4	7.79	7.59	n/a
	Latino	2,574	n/a	695	n/a	587	84.5	7.02	6.61	n/a

VAP: Voting Age Population; CVAP: Citizen Voting Age Population; REG: Registered Voters; Reg. %: Registered Percentage (Reg./CVAP); TO: Turnout; TO%: Turnout Percentage (TO/REG); REG Share: Race/ethnicity Turnout/Registration; TO share: Race/ethnicity Turnout/Total Turnout; VR potential: unregistered Citizens (CVAP-REG). Source: census voting and registration for November elections in California since 1980.

legitimate in asking representational numbers on par with that of the African American community. Of course redistricting is more complex and residential patterns are crucial. At the time, such claims could not be satisfied in part because Latinos were more spread out and located in more conservative rural districts than African Americans. But for Latino activists, Latinos have been the most important minority in the Golden State from an electoral standpoint for decades.

Asian and Pacific Islanders passed African Americans in terms of voting number in 2002, as displayed in figure 9.1. This contributed to making the comparison with that community's representation right after the 2001 round of redistricting a source of frustration for API proponents. African Americans have a longer history of political involvement and grassroots organization and they do vote for the Democratic Party at a higher rate. Their residential concentration patterns also make majority-minority districts easier to create. However, while the VRA and redistricting in 1965 were perceived as a way to help African Americans get elected to office especially in the south, a state like California shows that in the West, but also in many parts of the country, redistricting already is, and will be in the future, as much if not more, about Latino and Asian representation.

PARTISANSHIP EVOLUTION

What characterizes California today is not only the diversity of its population but also the shrinking of the Republican Party. As the state was becoming less White it was also becoming bluer and the two trends seem inseparable.

In 2016 the Democratic Party registration rate was 44.9 percent, the Republican Party registration rate was 26 percent and the "Other/Decline to State" rate was 29.1 percent. "Decline to State" alone was 24.3 percent. In California, at present, Republican registration is lower than "Decline to State."[1] In order to get a sense of the scope of this electoral revolution, one only has to look at figures from two decades prior when Governor Wilson decided to instrumentalize race and immigration related anxiety for his reelection. In 1996, the Republican Party registration rate was 36 percent and the "Decline to State" rate was 11 percent (with the Democrats at 47 percent). So in twenty years, the Republican Party in California lost close to 30 percent of its registration rate while the "Decline to State" category more than doubled and the Democrats' registration rate remained stable. We can see in figure 9.2 that Democrats have had somewhat of a registration advantage in California since the 1950s, however that advantage has widened since the 1990s. In the 1980s, Democrat and Republican registration plateaued as "Decline to State"

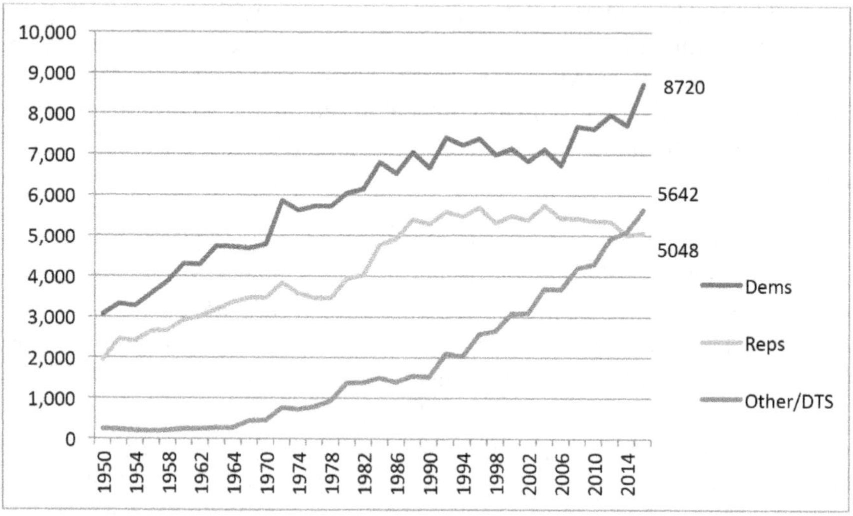

Figure 9.2 California Partisan Registration Statistics
Source: California Secretary of State, Historical voter registration and participation in statewide general elections 1910–2016, http://elections.cdn.sos.ca.gov/sov/2016-general/sov/04-historical-voter-reg-participation.pdf.

increased. But since the mid-2000s, the Republican Party rate has been free-falling and both the Democrat and "Decline to State" rates have increased. In 2004, the Republican registration total numbers were the same as 1996 with 5.7 million people. Since then it has lost 700,000 registrants. Since 2006, the Democratic Party's registration number augmented by 1 million people. The presidency of George W. Bush (and its unpopular war in Iraq) seems to have damaged the Republican brand. One can probably assume that the current Trump administration has done nothing to improve the GOP's image in California. Polls actually suggest Donald Trump is one of the least popular presidents ever.[2] This means that the mentioned California trends should continue.

These registration rates have a direct impact on the Republican share of the electorate. Today, in California, the GOP represents roughly a quarter of eligible voters (figure 9.3). They represented 40 percent of eligible voters up until the 1990s. The Democrats represented 45 percent of eligible voters in 2016 and "Decline to State" almost 30 percent. Since Democratic rate has remained stable since 2000, it looks like the Republican Party is transferring registration to the "Decline to State" category. A California Public Institute Survey from 2016 indicates that more likely-to-vote Independents leaned toward the Democratic Party rather than toward the GOP (41 percent to 32 percent), while 27 percent leaned toward neither party. Democratic leanings among Independents were similar in 2008 (44 percent) and 2012 (43 percent), as were Republican leanings (28 percent in 2008, 30 percent in 2012) and as was the share of likely voters leaning toward neither major party (28 percent in 2008, 27 percent in 2012).[3]

This registration advantage historically in favor of the Democrats helps explain in part why the GOP hardly ever won a majority of either houses of the legislature since the 1960s, and why it has not won a majority of the seats in the congressional delegation over that period. Table 9.2 shows that the Republicans only won a slim majority of the seats in the Assembly in 1968, the year of the infamous Democratic Chicago convention fiasco, and in 1994, the year of the congressional Republican wave led by Newt Gingrich. Even in 1980, the year former California Governor Ronald Reagan was elected President, the Assembly remained solidly Democrat. In 1980 though, the Republicans were close to winning a majority in the State Senate (21–19) as they had done in 1968. Similarly, in 1980, the Democrats only won one more seat than the Republicans in the congressional delegation (22–21). the years 1968, 1980 and 1994 represent the high points of Republican political victories in California as they either won a majority of the Assembly or reduced the Democratic majorities in the Senate or the congressional delegation. However, these trends also show that national waves usually have a tremendous impact on local politics and that redistricting never performed miracles in California. Over fifty years, the party breakdown of both chambers of the legislature and the congressional delegation roughly followed partisan registration rates.

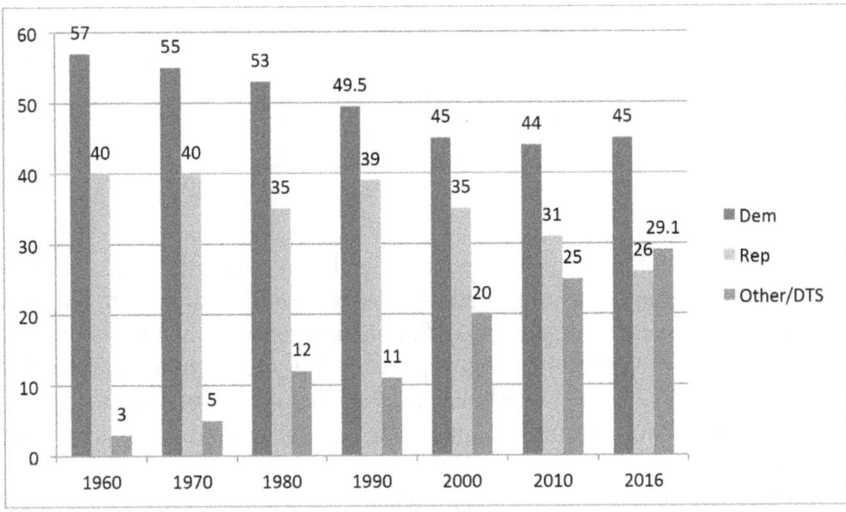

Figure 9.3 Party Registration Share of Eligible Voters in California 1960–2016
Source: Calculated from California Secretary of State, Historical voter registration and participation in statewide general elections 1910–2016, http://elections.cdn.sos.ca.gov/sov/2016-general/sov/04-historical-voter-reg-participation.pdf.

Table 9.2 Partisan Balance in California's Assembly, Senate, Congressional Delegation since 1964

	Assembly		*Senate*		*Congress*	
Year	*D*	*R*	*D*	*R*	*D*	*R*
1964	49	31	23	17	23	15
1966	42	38	21	19	21	17
1968	**39**	**41**	21	19	21	17
1970	43	37	21	19	20	18
1972	51	29	22	18	23	20
1974	55	25	25	15	28	15
1976	57	23	26	14	29	14
1978	50	30	26	14	26	17
1980	47	33	21	19	22	21
1982	48	32	23	17	28	17
1984	47	33	25	15	27	18
1986	44	36	24	15	27	18
1988	47	33	24	15	27	18
1990	48	32	24	13	27	19
1992	48	32	22	13	30	22
1994	**39**	**41**	21	17	27	25
1996	43	37	23	16	29	23
1998	48	32	25	15	28	24
2000	50	30	26	14	32	20
2002	48	32	25	15	33	20
2004	48	32	25	15	33	20
2006	48	32	25	15	34	19
2008	51	29	25	15	34	19
2010	52	28	25	15	34	19
2012	55	25	29	10	38	15
2014	52	28	25	14	39	14
2016	55	25	27	13	39	14

Now that Republican registration has fallen in California the state seems to be immune, or least not as impacted as other parts of the country, to national electoral waves such as the one in 2010. For each house of the legislature and the congressional delegation, 1994 represents the year Democrats recorded their lowest numbers. Democrats have either maintained or increased their numbers in the State Assembly, in the State Senate, and in the congressional delegation since that low point of 1994.

Another reason why the 2010 Republican wave did not have much of an impact in California is because the electorate of this majority-minority state is still racially polarized. Asian, Latinos, and African Americans represent half of the population of the state but voted for the Democratic Party at rates of 58 percent, 65 percent, and 80 percent, respectively for the senatorial election of 2010 according to the *New York Times* exit polls. Whites voted for the Democratic Party at a rate of 43 percent.[4] Demography may not be destiny but it sure helps. One of the reasons why the previous 2001 bipartisan redistricting cannot be credited for preventing the Republican wave from hitting the legislature and the congressional delegation is that all 6 statewide elections (US Senate, Governor, Lieutenant Governor, Secretary of State, Attorney General and Controller) were won by the Democrats in 2010, and most of them by a fairly wide margin. If anything, the bipartisan redistricting of 2001 prevented Democrats from winning larger majorities. The ever increasing minority population of the state, coupled with the registration advantage, operates as a buffer for national Republican waves. That is because race and partisanship go hand in hand in California politics and its redistricting history illustrates how deep the connection is.

CONJOINED POLARIZATION IN CALIFORNIA AND ITS IMPACT ON REDISTRICTING

The evolution of the number of minority elected officials in the Assembly shows that Latinos started benefitting from redistricting in the late 1960s, after the passage of the VRA, and won a record five Assembly seats in 1973 when Latino elected officials created the Hispanics legislative caucus. However, that number stagnated for another two decades. Actually, Latinos lost two seats in the 1970s showing that in spite of its promise the special master's plan did not increase their opportunities. In the 1980s, their representation flat-lined at 4 Assembly members throughout the decade until it shot up in the 1990s under the combination of term limits, demographic increases and citizenship rate increases leading to higher Latino turnout. What is probably the most striking in figure 9.4 is that the number of Latino elected officials in the Assembly actually decreased during the 2000s. It clearly shows why Latino organizations believed that the 2001 bipartisan redistricting was hindering their progress. That is because the redistricting conducted in 1981 and then in 2001 did not try to maximize majority-minority districts as Latino activists had hoped. The priority was, as it often is, incumbent protection. Redistricters did not want to take the risk of increasing Latino representation too much because they deemed it too risky, for the Democratic majority and its incumbents, to concentrate Democratic voters in too few districts. Besides, in 1980, the Latino population was still scattered in many rural areas with a large percentage of the population under eighteen, a low rate of citizenship and a low registration rate. In the Assembly, the strategy was not to create many

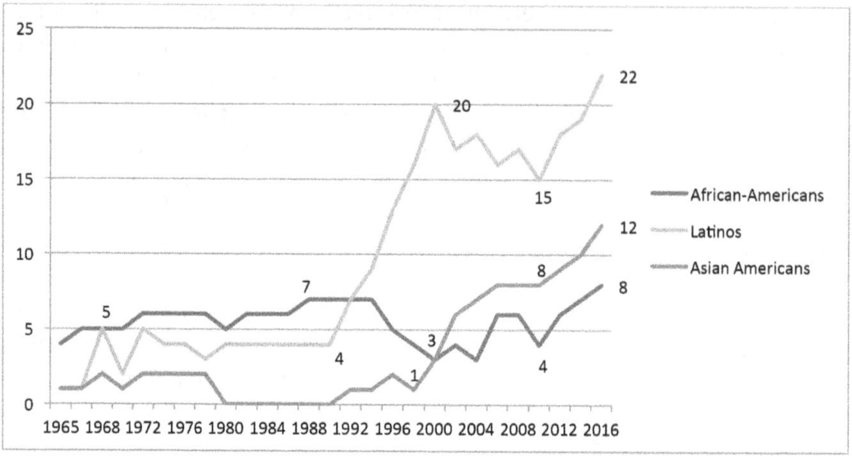

Figure 9.4 Minorities in the California Assembly since 1965
Source: Compiled from the histories of the California African American Caucus, the California Latino Caucus, and the California Asian and Pacific Islander Caucus along with elected officials personal website biographies and the press.

majority-minority districts. Instead, the Democrats decided it was best to increase the Latino population in many districts to give the community a chance to really influence the election. As Bruce Cain's seminal work explained it, the democratic leadership very cleverly used a Latino Assembly member to sell that strategy. The only problem was that by 1990 the number of Latino elected officials had not gone up at all and activists wondered if their interest was indeed aligned with that of the Democratic Party. Consultant Michael Berman was involved in both redistrictings and was the main villain in the MALDEF trial in 2001. The 1981 Democratic "tour de force" was actually much more risk-averse than the legend of Phil Burton would have us believe. The 2001 round of redistricting focused so much on keeping each party's seat numbers that it was detrimental to minorities, especially Latinos, even though it was authored by the Democrats.

The number of Asian American Assembly members fell to zero in 1980 and stayed that way for a decade. Their low registration numbers and their lack of political organization meant neither party really saw them as electoral players. African American interests on the other hand were not forgotten by the Democratic Party and their African American Speaker. They reached a then all-time high toward the end of the decade as their share of the Assembly (8.75 percent) surpassed their share of the electorate from 1988 to 1996 (around 7 percent during presidential cycles).[5] In 1992, the Latino elected officials line crossed the African American line for good as the Latino representation reached almost 10 percent of the California turnout. Latino representation reached its then-historical record in 2000 on the eve of redistricting. The 1991 redistricting offered more seat-winning opportunities first because the 1965 Voting Rights Act, as amended in 1982, was as its apex. And second because the Special Master's plan tended to pack and, therefore, waste Democratic voters in some districts and scatter the rest in Republican districts. The best proof that the 1991 masters' Plan was not minority friendly is the way it split the most Democratic-leaning community: African Americans. The community lost 4 of its Assembly members over the decade to reach 3, a number not seen since the 1960s.

Other factors explain the Latino spectacular increase. Term limits for instance helped to renew the pool of candidates and therefore weakened incumbent advantages. But the most important factor is demographical in nature. The number of Latinos over eighteen mushroomed in the 1990s and by the end of the decade the number of Latinos obtaining citizenship augmented in part as backlash against anti-immigration Republican measures. In many Democratic districts, Latino numbers reached the threshold where they could tilt the election in favor of their candidate of choice. This critical mass varied from district to district but a rule of thumb could be that, in the 1990s, unless Latinos represented 40 percent to 50 percent of the Citizens Voting Age Population in a given district their chances of electing a Latino candidate were slim.[6] This approximation only gives an idea of the critical mass needed to turn a district into an "influence" district, an "opportunity" district or a "crossover" district. For all these types of districts a critical mass is required, and in the 1990s the Latino population growth helped reach that threshold in many more districts than in the past.

The 2001 redistricting cycle stopped Latinos' progression in the lower house. Over the decade, as their population in the state increased from 32 percent to 37 percent and their percentage of the state's turnout increased by almost 50 percent (from 14 to 20 percent), Latinos lost 5 elected officials in the Assembly. The Latino community had to wait until 2014 to find again the same share of the lower house seats (25 percent) as they had in 2000. The bipartisan plan of 2001 protected incumbents and did not make Latino representation a priority.

In 2000, the African American and the Asian American lines crossed each other for good. During that decade, the number of African American Assembly members never reached its 1990s high of 7 seats. The number of seats they controlled actually dropped to 3 twice during the decade (representing 3.75 percent of the chamber's seats). They had to wait until 2014 to find their mid-nineties numbers again. Only in 2016 did they reach their new record-high of 8, which represents an even 10 percent of the Assembly's seats, which is superior to their share of the state's population and electorate.

During the 2000s, the number of Asian American elected officials augmented under the combined effects of demographic increases and term limits as it did for Latinos in the 1990s. Asian Americans elected to the State's Assembly increased from 3 to 8 in a decade (that is 3.75 percent to 8 percent of the Assembly's seats). Their percentage of the population went from 11 percent to 13 percent, and their turnout went from 7.5 percent to 9.5 percent of the total turnout. Prior to redistricting in 2010, the number of minorities in the Assembly was 15 Latinos, 8 Asian Americans, and 4 African Americans, totaling 27 out of 80. Three election cycles later those numbers reached 22, 12 and 8 respectively for a historical total of 32. These numbers give each minority group a political representation that was in 2016 proportional to their share of the general population. By not having to pass a legislature vote, the CRC redistricting plan did not have to take incumbency in consideration. This does not mean that CRC plan was not accused of having a partisan tilt. What the CRC cannot be accused of is having protected individual politicians as it pitted many incumbents against one another. One of the reasons why it is easier to create majority-minority districts in the lower house is because

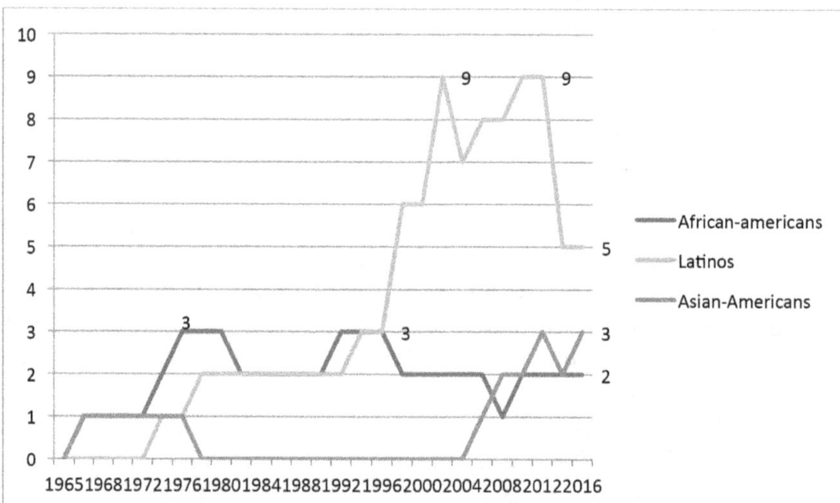

Figure 9.5 Minorities in the California State Senate since 1965
Source: Compiled from the histories of the California African American Caucus, the California Latino Caucus, and the California Asian and Pacific Islander Caucus along with elected officials personal website biographies and the press.

Assembly districts are smaller than in the Senate, therefore, the threshold to create majority-minority or influence districts is much lower.

In the Senate, the number of African American or Asian American senators has never exceeded 3, that is, 7.5 percent of the total number of seats. There are many reasons why Asians do not traditionally have many senators representing them. The most important one is their demographic distribution. Majority-minority districts rely on population concentration or residential segregation patterns. Asian Americans rarely form population clusters big enough to create the majority of a Senate district population. As a consequence, during Democratic primaries Asian Americans very often have to win against Latino and African American candidates as was the case in the SD 35 (South Bay of LA County) in 2016. Or, if they are nominated by the Republican Party, they face the task of winning against the Democratic candidate, who can be a Latino and benefits from minority votes as was the case for Republican Ling Ling Chang who barely lost in 2016 in SD 29, a district located at the intersection of LA, Orange, and San Bernadino counties.

The number of African American senators reached its peak in 1996 with 3 to equal the number of Latino senators. In the second half of the 1990s, Latino Assembly members benefitted from strong Latino voter numbers and term limits which opened up seats previously held by Anglos. Their number reached an all-time high in 2002 with 9 senators. They reached 9 again in 2010 and 2012 before losing 4 members in 2014 in part because of term limits. As previously mentioned, due to the combination of Proposition 140 in 1990 and Proposition 28 in 2012, members elected to the State Senate were restricted to two four-year terms (three terms of two years for the Assembly) if they had been elected before 2012. Those elected thereafter can now spend a maximum of 12 years in the legislature independent of term combination within the Senate or the Assembly. Democratic Latinos were especially impacted by this measure as many were elected in 2006 or 2008. Figure 9.5 shows that the California Redistricting Commission did not really create more minority opportunities in the Senate. In 2016, a total of 8 senators belonged to a racial or ethnic minority (20 percent of the seats). Asian Americans held 7.5 percent (3 senators) of the Senate seats, while they represented more than 10 percent of the electorate and 16 percent of the population; 5 percent were held by African Americans (2 senators almost on par with their share of the electorate); 12.5 percent for Latinos (5 senators) while they represented around 20 percent of the electorate and almost 40 percent of the state's population. One can easily see that Asian and Latino organizations may not be satisfied with these numbers and argue that they are not proportional to their share of the electorate. However, there is a silver lining for Latinos especially. As they were term-limited, the most prominent Latino senators looked for other jobs and the good news is some of them found outlets. Alex Padilla, in 2014, was elected Secretary of State for instance. The CRC did create new opportunities for minority candidates in Congress and the natural aspiration for a State Senator is to move up the political food chain and go to DC. For instance, former state senator Juan Vargas was elected to Congress in 2012 in CD 51 (along the Mexican border), the same year that Gloria Negrete McLeaod who was elected to Congress in CD 35 (Pomona). She then lost to former Latina State Senator Norma Torres in 2014. Former Latino State Senator Lou Correa was elected to Congress in 2016 in CD 46 (Santa Ana). Latinos have dramatically improved their representation in Congress since 2010 as they multiplied the number of their Representatives by 2 to reach a total of 12. Asian Americans also doubled the number of their Representatives (to reach 6) as we can see with figure 9.6.

The evolution of the number of minority elected officials in the California congressional delegation follows a familiar pattern. In the late 1960s and early 1970s, thanks in part to the equi-population ("one person, one vote") doctrine, African Americans were able to elect 3 Representatives, the same number of seats they hold today. In the meantime, in the 1980s and 1990s, their number plateaued at 4. That number is more or less proportional to their share of the population even though the US Supreme Court has always maintained that the VRA did not guarantee proportional representation for minorities. Asian Americans had to wait until 1980 to elect their first Representative

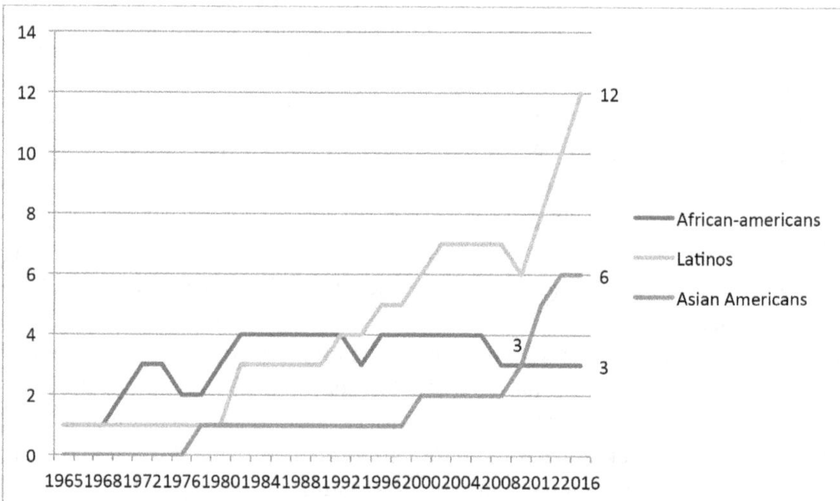

Figure 9.6 Minorities in the California Congressional Delegation since 1965
Source: Compiled from the histories of the California African American Caucus, the California Latino Caucus and the California Asian and Pacific Islander Caucus along with elected officials personal website biographies and the press.

and needed to wait another twenty years to increase that number to two. It was not until 2010 that the number of Asian American's elected officials really took off in part because the CRC lifted incumbent protection but also because the demographics and political participation of the Asian population reached a critical mass. As shown in figure 9.1, in 2016, Asians represented 15 percent of the state's population. And as table 9.1 shows, they reached in 2008 the symbolic threshold of 10 percent of the total voting turnout during an election cycle with a very high electoral participation.

Latinos only had one Representative until the 1981 redistricting. That number jumped to 3 but remained the same for a decade. The 1981 redistricting increased their number so they would have a number of seats closer to their share of the population; but, at the same time, it capped that number at 3. In 1992, the Latino line in figure 9.6 crosses the African American line. During the 1990s, Latinos doubled the number of their Representatives, from 3 to 6, that is about 12 percent of the state's delegation in 2000 while they represented 32 percent of the state's population but 14 percent of turnout. The masters' plan created more opportunities for Latinos as the VRA encouraged them to do so, but also wasted Latino votes by creating 24 congressional districts for which the Latino population was under 20 percent. The 2001 redistricting offered one new opportunity (Linda Sánchez was elected in CD 39, southeast of LA County) but capped the Latinos in the delegation at 7 throughout the 2000s except for 2010 when they lost Hilda Solis to the Obama administration and Asian American Judy Chu was elected in her district, CD 27 (Pasadena). During every following election cycle Latinos picked up two new seats as the CRC helped boost their number by removing incumbency protection and therefore confirming that the status quo gerrymander of 2001 had actually held them back.[7]

Table 9.3 gives an indication of the effect each congressional plan could potentially have in 1991, 2001, and 2011. But first, one needs to note that population is a notoriously bad indicator of the political strength of the Latino or Asian communities because of their large number of minors, their low rates of citizenship and their lower rate of registration as indicated in table 9.2. For instance, in 2001, Congressional District Sixteen (eastern part of the city of San Jose and southern part of Santa Clara County), which was represented by Zoe Lofgren, had a heavily Latino population (39 percent) but Latinos accounted for only 2 percent of registered voters. In that same district, Asian Americans accounted for 27 percent of the population but only 5 percent of registered voters. As a consequence, because of racial polarization, a district must be heavily Latino or Asian in population to obtain critical mass of Latino or Asian voters. Therefore, the threshold allowing the election of a minority candidate will vary depending on whether one uses general

Table 9.3 Minority population in California Congressional Districts 1991–2011

	1991 Masters' Plan[1]		2001 Bipartisan[2]			2011 CRC Plan		
Population	*Latinos*	*AA*	*Latinos*	*AA*	*API*	*Latinos*	*AA*	*API*
0–9.9%	4	43	1	46	24	0	46	24
10–19.9%	20	5	12	4	21	11	5	18
20–29.9%	12	0	10	3	5	12	2	7
30–39.9%	6	2	11	0	3	10	0	3
40–49.9%	4	2	7	0	0	7	0	0
50–59.9%	3	0	3	0	0	3	0	1
60–69.9%	2	0	7	0	0	8	0	0
70–79.9%	0	0	1	0	0	1	0	0
80–89.9%	1	0	1	0	0	1	0	0

1. Here the Asian American population was not added because in 1991 only one district in San Francisco had an API population over 20 percent. But while this district 27 percent API population its citizenship and registration rates were so low that it only represented 7 percent of the district's electorate. In other words Asian Americans were not a significant electoral factor. Figures are provided by the Statewide database.
2. Racial percentages are from 2007–2009 ACS 3-year estimates as displayed in the Statewide database website.

population, Voting Age Population, Citizen Voting Age Population, Share of Registration, or even share of Democratic Registration. Nonetheless, general population, and its breakdown by racial and ethnic groups, is crucial because at the time of redistricting it is the only data available. Minority vote dilution would be much easier to prevent if redistricters worked with data such as up-to-date Citizen Voting Age population.

The use of artificial threshold can also be problematic. At first glance it appears that in 2011 African Americans had one less district with a population over 20 percent than in 2001. But Congressional District Thirteen (centered on Oakland and Berkeley) had, in 2011, an African American population very close to 20 percent (19.92 percent). The district was also 20.84 percent Latino and 22.27 percent Asian with a Democratic registration of 63 percent (7 percent Republican and 18 percent No Party Preference). These numbers make it a majority-minority district with a long tradition of electing African American candidates and Barbara Lee has been easily reelected. So each district's minority population number should be measured against the percentage of other minorities and party registration because race and partisanship are closely intertwined especially when a few percentage points variation for either one can make all the difference. An African American population around 20 percent in a very diverse district with high Democratic registration gives the community the possibility to elect the candidate of their choice. That is why no software can replace an intimate knowledge of a state's political dynamics. In contrast, what table 9.3 shows is that in 1991 the special masters' plan created 4 districts where the African American population was packed: two with populations over 30 percent and 2 with populations over 40 percent. Therefore, in 1991, the Voting Rights Act was used as an excuse to pack minority voters in a few districts and scatter the others in Republican districts. If liberal Anglos and other minorities demonstrate a readiness to vote for a minority candidate of choice, a majority-minority district is, in that case, not necessary or even counterproductive. Packing minorities is rendered easier also because of strong trends of racial residential segregation among minorities and in the African American community in particular. The 1991 plan also contained 24 districts in which Latino population was under 20 percent. In such districts, Latino votes are wasted because Latinos can't really influence the vote, especially in districts heavily Anglo or with a Republican majority.

Table 9.3 also shows that in 2011, the last district with less than 10 percent Latino population was eliminated. The CRC also redrew lines of two districts with Latino population under 20 percent and changed them into districts with Latino population between 20 percent and 30 percent; thereby, giving Latinos a better chance of electing the candidate of their choice, especially if the district is a Democratic majority district and contains other minorities. Such a district is not ideal to elect a Latino, though, as table 9.4 demonstrates. A classic congressional Latino district looks more like that of Jimmy Gomez, CD 34 (city of Los Angeles), which is 65 percent Latino, 5 percent Black, 20 percent Asian, and has a 57 percent Democratic registration (with 12 percent Republican and 20 percent No Party Preference).[8] However, even high Latino population numbers are no guarantee of Latino election success. For instance, CD 21 (centered on Kings County) is 71 percent Latino (49 percent Latino CVAP) but it is 47 percent Democrat, 32 percent Republican, and 16 percent DST. A 15-point Democratic advantage in registration is quite a head-start but CD 21 was won in 2012 by former Assembly member David Valadao, a young, moderate Republican of Portuguese descent in favor of comprehensive immigration reform.[9] By contrast, CD 29 (Van Nuys) is 68 percent Latino (50 percent Latino CVAP) and was won by Latino Tony Cardenas because it is 55 percent Democrat, 19 percent Republican, and 19 percent DST.[10] A 26-point registration advantage almost guarantees a victory for the Democrats and a 50 percent Latino CVAP makes it very likely that Democrat would be a Latino. The CRC created, in 2011, one more district with a Latino population over 60 percent for a grand total of 8 while that number was 2 in 1991. While there are 13 congressional districts with a Latino population superior to 50 percent, only 7 districts have a Latino CVAP over 50 percent (CD 29 (Van Nuys): 50 percent; CD 32 (El Monte): 50 percent; CD 34 (Los Angeles):50 percent; CD 35 (Pomona): 52 percent; CD 38 (Lakewood): 51

percent; CD 40 (Downey): 73 percent; CD 51 (stretches from San Diego to Imperial County): 51 percent.

In 2011, the CRC also created, for the first time, one district with an Asian American population over 50 percent (CD 17 centered on Fremont) and 2 more congressional districts with an Asian population percentage in the 20s. Mike Honda and then Ro Khanna were elected in CD 17, a congressional district with the highest Asian population in California and a 38 percent Asian CVAP. However, minority candidates, especially Asian Americans, are not elected exclusively in majority-minority districts as shown in table 9.4. For instance, long-time incumbent Doris Matsui carries on her husband's legacy as she was reelected in CD 6 (Sacramento) with an Asian CVAP of 13 percent (53 percent Anglo CVAP). Ami Bara, a candidate of Indian descent, barely defeated Republican Dan Lungren in 2012 in CD 7 (Elk Grove), a district with an Asian CVAP of 10 percent (69 percent Anglo CVAP) and registration rates of 39 percent for the Democrats and 38 percent for the Republicans. Judy Chu was elected in CD 27, a district with an Asian CVAP of 32 percent (39 percent Anglo CVAP). Ted Lieu was elected in CD 33 (Torrance): 10 percent Asian CVAP and 76 percent Anglo CVAP. Mark Takano was elected in CD 41 (Riverside), a district with an Asian CVAP of 6 percent and an Anglo CVAP of 43 percent. Racial polarization being much lower for Asian American candidates they manage to get elected in Anglo-majority Democratic districts. In CD 39 (Fullerton), Republican incumbent Ed Royce had a hard time being reelected in 2016 in a district that had a 25 percent Asian CVAP and a 23 percent Latino CVAP. Royce announced his retirement, opening a seat in 2018 that has a Democratic registration of 32 percent and Republican of 39 percent.

What is the most striking in table 9.4 is that all 21 minority Congresspersons in the California delegation are Democrats. Not one is a Republican. Most minorities were elected in districts with overwhelming minority population (73 percent non-Anglo general population on average) and Democratic registration (24 points advantage on average). Ted Lieu was elected in a district with a minority population of only 31 percent and is, therefore, the exception. Every other minority official was elected in districts containing at least a minority population of 43 percent. But Ted Lieu benefitted from a 16-point advantage in Democratic registration. Also, it seems that a congressional district susceptible to elect a minority candidate needs to have a Democratic registration of at least 38 percent and a Republican registration rate lower than, or equal to, the Democratic one.

In 2016, the share of each minority group inside the California congressional delegation almost mirrored the share of each group in the electorate. The California delegation is 22 percent Latino, 15 percent Asian American, and 5

Table 9.4 Congressional Minority-won District Data

District	*Minority Representative*	*Party*	*Latino CVAP*	*AA CVAP*	*Asian CVAP*	*Min. Gen. Pop*[1]	*Democratic Registration*	*Republican Registration*
CD 6	Doris Matsui	D	16%	14%	13%	61%	50%	24%
CD 7	Ami Bara	D	10%	7%	10%	43%	39%	38%
CD 13	Barbara Lee	D	10%	23%	18%	64%	64%	8%
CD 17	Ro Khanna	D	13%	3%	38%	73%	44%	19%
CD 24	Salud Carbajal	D	17%	2%	4%	43%	38%	34%
CD 27	Judy Chu	D	23%	6%	32%	71%	42%	28%
CD 29	Tony Cardenas	D	50%	6%	9%	82%	55%	16%
CD 31	Pete Aguilar	D	35%	13%	6%	70%	41%	35%
CD 32	Grace Napolitano	D	50%	4%	15%	82%	47%	26%
CD 33	Ted Lieu	D	9%	3%	11%	31%	44%	28%
CD 34	Jimmy Gomez	D	50%	9%	21%	91%	58%	12%
CD 35	Norma Torres	D	52%	10%	6%	84%	48%	26%
CD 36	Raul Ruiz	D	27%	4%	3%	66%	39%	39%
CD 37	Karen Bass	D	21%	34%	9%	76%	65%	10%
CD 38	Linda Sánchez	D	51%	4%	14%	81%	49%	26%
CD 40	Lucille Roybal-Allard	D	73%	9%	4%	95%	61%	14%
CD 41	Mark Takano	D	37%	12%	6%	74%	42%	37%
CD 43	Maxine Waters	D	29%	33%	13%	85%	60%	16%
CD 44	Nanette Barragán	D	49%	28%	7%	93%	64%	12%
CD 46	Lou Correa	D	42%	3%	15%	82%	44%	30%
CD 51	Juan Vargas	D	51%	11%	9%	86%	49%	21%

Source: Data is provided by the CRC Final Report Appendix 3, August 15 2011, all figures based on 2010 U.S. Census expect for CVAP data based on 2005–2009 American Community Survey 5 yr estimates provided by statewide database.

1. Minority (non-White) General Population.

percent African American, while these three groups represented, respectively in the 2016 election, 23 percent, 13 percent, and 6 percent of the voting turnout, as shown in table 9.1. This, of course, is no coincidence and gives an idea of how careful and efficient the CRC (and its consultants) was about minority representation. But, as previously seen, this increase in minority representation came with an increase in the number of Democrats. This illustrates the consistent alignment of race, partisanship, and ideology that Cain and Zhang have called conjoined polarization.

Conjoined polarization is not a new phenomenon. As early as 2001, Justice Breyer, writing for the Court in *Easley v. Cromartie*, explained that "Caution is especially appropriate in this case, where the state has articulated a legitimate political explanation for its districting decision, and the voting population is one in which race and political affiliation are highly correlated."[11] But this case took place in the South between White and Black populations. What is new is that this polarization has spread through the country and is now visible in the West. The Republican Party has become more White and minorities have started to identify more strongly with the Democratic Party. So how strongly are race and partisanship correlated in today's California? According to a Public Policy Institute of California Survey, now only half of Democratic likely voters are White (50 percent).[12] Latinos voters equal 25 percent, 13 percent are Asian American, and 10 percent are African American. But an overwhelming majority of Republican likely voters are White (80 percent) and relatively few are Latino (10 percent), Asian American (6 percent), or African American (1 percent). Among likely independent voters, 57 percent are White, 17 percent are Asian American, 16 percent are Latino, and 5 percent are African American. The California Republican Party has become more racially homogenous as the California Democratic Party has become more racially heterogeneous. Furthermore, as the California Republican Party has become almost all White, its registration numbers have been declining (figures 9.2 and 9.3). The future of redistricting is therefore murky because of the evolution of the correlation between race and partisanship. Today, in California, African Americans, Latinos, and even Asian Americans display electoral behaviors that are distinct from Anglo Americans. In 2016, California Exit polls indicated these three minority groups preferred the Democratic candidate with rates of 88 percent, 71 percent, and 70 percent, while the rate for Anglos was 50 percent. This represents a racial electoral gap of at least 20 percent. These figures have been consistent over the past twenty years. Now, these three groups combined represent 60 percent of the population of the state and 50 percent of its registration. Conjoined polarization means that it is getting harder and harder to differentiate partisan gerrymandering from racial gerrymandering. If taking race into consideration is suspect then line drawers can claim partisan goals especially as long as the US Supreme Court cannot agree on a workable standard to prove partisan gerrymandering. As the Trump presidency has done little to improve the Republican brand's image among non-White, one can safely predict that this trend is not going to reverse any time soon. This has tremendous consequences for California politics and redistricting in particular. With Section 5 of the VRA not operative anymore and partisanship readily available to be used proxy for race, minority groups should be very concerned about 2021. The spectacular gains acquired over the past decade could be partially undone if the CRC process is not closely monitored. Section 5 was especially crucial as it had preemptive power and the burden of proof was on the state to prove that electoral change did not dilute minority vote. Section 2 litigation comes necessarily later in the process and can get very expensive and is usually quite long. The weakening of the VRA by the US Supreme Court makes 2021 a much crucial redistricting year.

This book has demonstrated throughout that, in California, any redistricting measure aiming at lowering or increasing minority representation has a partisan effect. That is because all manipulations of the electoral system are in essence partisan. But because redistricters' motives are never readily available, courts have relied on map drawing processes to deduct the authors' real motivations. If line drawers are a bit subtle, proving intent is generally quite difficult. And, as we have seen with the 2001 round of redistricting, even with a consultant protecting his brother's reelection, it can be quite tricky to convince judges to strike down a plan for discriminatory intent or effect.

The future of redistricting is very uncertain for many reasons. One of the main conundrums for redistricters is that taking race into consideration is a dangerous sport. The jurisprudence on racial gerrymandering is so opaque that a legislature or a commission can be sued for taking race too much, or not enough, into consideration. Before Section 5 was rendered inoperative by the *Shelby County* Supreme Court decision in 2013, line drawers had to take race into consideration especially for jurisdictions covered by the formula contained in Section 4. Because of Section 2 of the Voting Rights Act, race still needs to be taken into consideration but it is not clear how much leeway the courts will be willing to give to legislatures or commissions.

The second main problem faced by mapmakers is that some factors can be in direct contradiction of others. The post-*Shaw* jurisprudence puts the emphasis on the shape of districts.[13] During racial gerrymandering trials, courts have routinely considered districts' shapes as circumstantial evidence. In states, or areas within a state, where minorities are not neatly clustered, redistricters have to draw irregularly shaped districts to make sure a certain percentage of a district population belongs to a minority. But more importantly, neat, squarish districts do not guarantee that minorities have not been discriminated against or that they have the opportunity to elect the candidate of their choice. Since the courts have never established any standard for shape (and how could they?), it is anybody's guess what will constitute a suspicious-looking district. The absence of Section 5 preclearance, the erratic jurisprudence of the *Shaw*-line of cases, and the deficiency of any standard for partisan gerrymandering post-*Whitford* make redistricting unpredictable, and place the burden of redistricting enforcement on Section 2. However, Section 2 and its interpretation (the *Gingles* test) are from a different era when the main goal was to identify racial division inside the Democratic Party that controlled the South at the time. Today, conjoined polarization and the increase in diversity displayed by a state like California complicate all three parts of the *Gingles* test.

In California, because of the Citizens Redistricting Commission, the real fight to control redistricting outcome will take place during the commissioners' and the consultants' selection processes. In 2011, the stars aligned perfectly for the CRC in a way that is unlikely to be duplicated. One of the main differences will be that, this time around, parties and other agents have had time to study the process and prepare accordingly. Those who want to apply for a commissioner or a consultant position have probably either changed their voter registration or have modified their political behavior to eliminate any appearance of conflict of interest.[14] If the history of the professionalization of the referendum process in California has taught us anything is that political agents are very quick to adapt to new constraints and find ways around them. In 2011, the State Auditor's Office took the selection process very seriously but it relied on outside spending for public participation in addition to the estimated $10 million the CRC already cost. Lack of funds and time could limit the commission's capacity to educate the public, hear communities of interest grievances and take all those into account. The consultants' selection will also be very crucial especially because Section 5 will no longer have to be taken into consideration. In order to prevent retrogression under preclearance regime, jurisdictions were obligated to perform detailed voting analyses to be submitted to the US Department of Justice. Without these analyses line drawers can argue that minorities need majorities or super-majorities in a given district in order to have a real shot at electing the candidate of their choice. The very vague and ill-defined "community of interest" that was adopted by the CRC can also be used as justification for packing or cracking. Because "community of interest" is not clearly racial in nature it can potentially be used to disqualify racial gerrymandering suit.

The maps that were first released by the commission (that is before racial polarization studies were completed) looked quite different from the final ones. And the final maps can be challenged in courts or via referendum. Conjoined polarization will make any Republican challenge look like an attack on minorities' representation and any minority attack on the plan will look like a Democratic ploy for partisan gain. This confluence between race and partisanship has led the Republican Party in many states to consider that since its electorate was mainly White, any measure affecting minority turnout negatively was in its interest. The two fastest growing groups in the state, Latinos and Asian Americans, are also those with the lowest registration rates. In all logic, if both parties had a long-term strategy, both parties should try and tap into this potential electorate. Instead the Republican Party national strategy so far has been a short-term one. It has taken advantage of decentralized election administration laws and implemented in many states policies trying to prevent minorities from registering or voting: voter ID laws, purges of election rolls, and failure to implement the bilingual ballot provisions of Section 203. The two major parties now have opposed positions on something as fundamental as the right to vote: Democrats have adopted an expansive definition of voting rights while Republicans have embraced a more restrictive one. That is why Pamela Karlan called for a more affirmative conception of the right o vote.[15] In California, as recent election cycles have proven, this is not a viable strategy because the Republican Party is in the minority. Without federal protection such as Section 5 and with registration rates lower than Anglos, the stakes will be high again for minorities during the 2021 redistricting.

NOTES

1. California Secretary of State, "Report of Registration," October 24, 2016, http://www.sos.ca.gov/elections/report-registration/15day-general-2016/. The "Other" category is mostly composed of Decline to State. The "Other Party" registration rate has been stable in California at around 5 percent. "Other parties" were negligible since they amounted together to 4.8 percent of California's registrations. The breakdown of those parties was: the American Independent Party 2.6 percent, the Libertarian Party 0.72 percent, the Green Party 0.5 percent, the Peace and Freedom Party 0.39 percent, and "Other Parties" 0.59 percent.

2. Chris Wilson, "See How Trump's Approval Rating Stacks Up against Other Presidents after One Year," *Time*, http://time.com/5103776/donald-trump-approval-rating-graph/.

3. Mark Baldassare, Dean Bonner, David Kordus, and Lunna Lopes, "California's Independent Voters" (Washington, DC: Public Policy Institute of California, September 2016), http://www.ppic.org/publication/californias-independent-voters/.

4. According to the poll, the White population voted for the Republican Party at a rate of 52 percent. *New York Times*, "Election 2010, Senate Exit Polls," https://www.nytimes.com/elections/2010/results/senate/exit-polls.html.

5. This occurred mostly because Willard H. Murray (D-Paramount) unseated freshman Assemblyman Paul E. Zeltner (R-Lakewood) in AD 54 by 3 percentage points. Willie Brown had targeted that seat in an effort to maintain his speakership.

6. Kousser, "Has California Gone Color Blind?"

7. In 2012, they lost Joe Baca who lost to Gloria Negrete McLeod in the new Thirty-fifth District but Tony Cardenas, Raul Ruiz, and Juan Vargas were first elected to Congress hence a net total of 2 extra Latino-held seats.

8. Another example of the same type of district would be Linda Sanchez's CD 38 (61 percent Latino, 4 percent African American, 15 percent Asian American with 45 percent Democratic, 25 percent Republican, and 17 percent DTS registration rates).

9. He won 58–42 percent to Democrat John Hernandez, the head of the local Hispanic Chamber of Commerce.

10. In the San Fernando Valley Tony Cardenas in effect took the place of Howard Berman in the California delegation in a game of musical chairs when Schiff and Sherman survived. Waxman ran unopposed in 2012 but retired in 2014. Ted Lieu won his seat which means he won in a district that is only 15 percent Asian.

11. *Easley v. Cromartie* (532 U.S. 234 [2001]), at 242.

12. Mark Baldassare, Dean Bonner, David Kordus, and Lunna Lopes, "California Voter and Party Profile" (Washington, DC: Public Policy Institute of California, August 2017), http://www.ppic.org/publication/california-voter-and-party-profiles/.

13. Pildes and Niemi, "Expressive Harms."

14. Mac Donald, "Adventures," 487.

15. Pamela Karlan, "The Reconstruction of Voting Rights," in *Race, Reform, and Regulation of the Electoral Process*, eds. Guy-Uriel E. Charles, Heather K. Gerken, and Michael S. Kang (Cambridge: Cambridge University Press, 2011), 34–51.

Conclusion

In this case study of race and partisanship in California redistricting we have seen how the voting rights revolution in the 1960s, with the passage of the 1965 VRA and its subsequent amendments, along with the courts attempt to regulate elections, created great expectations for fair representation. The equal population standard established by the courts in the 1960s helped fight malapportionment and minorities were able to elect more representatives from their own community as metropolitan areas in California received a representation proportional to their population. The right to an undiluted vote led many to perceive fair representation as a form of descriptive representation in proportion to the electoral weight of particular groups or communities. At the same time, the Republican Party implemented its Southern Strategy, instrumentalizing racial animus for partisan gain in the southern states. This strategy participated in the partisan and racial realignment of the country. In the 1970s, Governor Reagan vetoed all three redistricting bills when the Democratic leadership refused to sacrifice an Assembly district susceptible to elect a Latino candidate. The Democrats were counting on Richard Alatorre's election in the Forty-eighth Assembly District (Los Angeles) to prove to the Latino community that they could protect most of their Anglo-incumbents and increase Latino representation. The Governor's vetoes triggered the intervention of the California Supreme Court. In a difficult attempt to thread the political needle, the Court reinstated the 1965 districts for the Assembly and the Senate in spite of the population discrepancies for the 1972 elections. Moreover, the Court decided to enforce, the bi-partisan congressional plan. In 1973, Governor Reagan vetoed again the redistricting plans and special masters were put in charge of drawing new electoral lines. As minority groups had hoped, the special masters protected and even tried to (modestly) increase minority representation. What made it easier for them to do so was the fact that they were not encumbered by incumbent protection. Incumbents suffered great losses in 1974. The plans contained a lot of marginal districts and from a partisan standpoint were not that much different from the ones created by the legislature. However, the Republicans' main problem was not redistricting. By that time the Watergate scandal had done so much damage to the Republican brand that no amount of redistricting creativity would have saved the GOP. It was not until the end of the decade and its fiscal revolution that the California Republican Party started making electoral gains again, but not enough to be in charge of redistricting in 1980.

So in 1980, the Democrats were in total control of redistricting as they had won the governorship and two majorities in both chambers of the legislature. The Democrats, in an attempt to lure the Latino community into its "rainbow coalition," dramatically increased the number of influence districts Latinos could hope to win. With minority elected officials such as African American Assembly Speaker Willie Brown and Latino Assembly member Richard Alatorre as Chairman of the Reapportionment Committee, Democrats were able to satisfy minorities' short-term interests while advancing their partisan gains. Having elected and appointed minorities in position of power really paid off for the Democrats. Meanwhile, the Republican strategy was to try and convince Latino activists to force the Democrats to create more majority-Latino districts to guarantee more Latino victories therefore concentrating Democrats in a few majority-minority districts to turn the adjacent districts safely Republican. In essence, they were trying to use the Voting Rights Act against their partisan foes. This was the strategy already used in regards to the African American community, by far the most faithful group of the traditional Democratic coalition at the national level. But Latino activists such as the Californios for Fair Representation remained outsiders to the legislative process making it difficult to really influence it. Besides, the risk was great for Latino organizations to be instrumentalized by the GOP for its partisan gains. Because there was no consensus as to what constituted a majority-Latino district or even if it was in the Latino community's long-term interest to align with a conservative party that sent mixed signals about Latino inclusion, Democrats were able to sell a redistricting deal that balanced Democratic and Latino gains. The blue districts lines of the Golden State were increasingly drawn with Black and Brown brushes.

By the end of the 1980s, Latino activists realized that elected officials numbers had stagnated. During the 1990s round of redistricting minority groups benefitted from the full power to the newly amended federal Voting Rights Act. Emboldened by legal victories such as the *Garza* case in Los Angeles County, MALDEF, the NAACP, and now CAPFIR intended to be players in the redistricting process yet that process, while more open to outside input, remained an insider's game. Minorities lacked resources and sometimes expertise to really weigh in. The second factor to consider is that Republicans controlled the governorship and were able to flip the majority on the State Supreme Court. Convinced that the courts would give them a better redistricting plan than any deal they could strike with the Democratic leadership, Republicans in Sacramento were in a confrontational mood, convinced that they had been fleeced in the 1980s by Phil Burton and his colleagues. Governor Wilson created a redistricting commission but could not use its plans since they blatantly diluted minority electoral power. The governor's strategy was, therefore, to take his chance with the court and he vetoed the redistricting bills presented by the legislature. The masters' plan increased minority opportunities even though activists were not entirely satisfied because they had lobbied for more. From a partisan standpoint Democratic incumbents were worse off and therefore the masters' plan seemed to benefit the GOP. But Democratic registration remained higher than Republican registration throughout the decade. With such a built-in advantage, associated with important residential segregation and other redistricting constraints, the most creative remapping can only generate limited electoral gains. Despite claims by scholars and journalists alike, redistricting plans in California have not produced partisan miracles. National waves produced large Democratic victories in 1992 and GOP victories in 1994. However, Wilson's gubernatorial victory in 1994 was linked to his support for Proposition 187. This anti-immigrant proposition was very instrumental in turning racial minorities, especially Latinos, away from the GOP. The Republican Party's attempt to lure Latinos as had been the case in the 1970s and 1980s was officially over. The Conservative Party now tried to capitalize politically on anti-immigration sentiment but it backfired in California. With great demographic and registration increases in the Latino community, and a willingness on the part of liberal Anglos to support minority candidates, their numbers spectacularly augmented in the 1990s. These ascending numbers in elected minority officials slowed down in 2000 due to a bipartisan plan that tampered minority and therefore Democratic gains in the 2000s.

In 2000, the memory of redistricting wars of the previous decades pushed the Democratic leadership to maintain the status quo. In theory, the Democrats could have rammed through a redistricting plan of their choice since they controlled the legislature and the governorship. Yet the intervention of the courts and the threat of a popular referendum was enough to discourage Democrats. Besides, they believed that they had maximized their electoral gains. They had not anticipated that the Republican brand image under the George W. Bush presidency would become very unpopular in California. To reach a referendum proof two-third majority, the Democrats protected every single incumbent. This was very consequential. Both parties' numbers remained the same throughout the decade, which in turn helped the Republican Party as it was immune to the unpopularity of its president and his ill-advised military interventions. But, perhaps most importantly, by striking an incumbent gerrymander, the Democrats alienated important parts of their coalition: Latinos and Asian American interest groups. Little did they know that these groups would team up with Republicans and "good government" groups to create an independent redistricting commission and take redistricting out of the hands of the legislative body.

As African Americans, Latinos, and Asian Americans joined the Democratic coalition in the 1980s and 1990s, their fight was no longer about access to the polls but about pushing out Anglo Democratic incumbents to increase *their* descriptive representation. Yet in a "winner-take-all" system with a high degree of racial polarization minority groups found that their electoral preferences were thwarted by racial, partisan, or incumbent interests, and did not lead to a body of representatives in the image of the population. This frustration in California was never as obvious as in 2000 when the US Supreme Court jurisprudence on racial gerrymandering had weakened the power of the VRA and the California legislature failed to find the appropriate balance between race and politics. In the 2000s, frustrated minority activists were able to push two important reforms. In 2002, a Latino civil rights lawyer was able to convince a Latino Senate majority leader to push through the legislative process the California Voting Rights Act that slowly eliminated at-large elections and forced local jurisdictions to adopt district elections. In 2008, and then in 2010, through the initiative process two former minority group lawyers were able to create the California Redistricting Commission which took redistricting out of the hands of the legislature. This commission in the 2011 round of redistricting eliminated the most blatant incumbent protection because among all the redistricting factors incumbent protection is the one that non-politicians can put on the proverbial back burner. Yet, many still believed that the resulting districts were not the most fair. Because they resulted in the Democrats winning two-third majorities in both chambers for the first time in decades the Commission was accused of partisan bias. And as the Democratic majorities reached record highs so did the number of minority elected officials.

Minority descriptive representation has expanded in California in parallel with Democratic partisan gains. As minorities became electoral pillars of the Democratic coalition they slowly pushed for more representation. These efforts were resisted by Anglo elected officials who were all for diversity but not if it meant losing their jobs. The fact that in California, as in many other states, the Democratic Party is the only one carrying the entire weight of diversity has led to tensions inside the Democratic coalition. In spite of these historic gains in California, minority organizations seem to be unsatisfied by these numbers in what is after all a majority-minority state. That is because fair representation of ethno-racial minorities is understood in California and in the US, in general, as descriptive representation in proportion to the minority's political weight. The creation of the CVRA and the CRC stems from this frustration on the part of minority groups in their quest for "fair representation." One may wonder if the minority representation conundrum can be solved without more electoral reform; or, if California may be the state to push for more institutional reform; or if the California model will be exported to other states. One thing is for sure: such a change will have to occur at the local level. Political reform at the national level has become virtually impossible.

Independent citizen commissions are not designed to boost minority representation, or do so indirectly only if they lift incumbent protection as a factor when they isolate line drawers from political pressure. These commissions are the result of a reform effort concentrated on limiting the conflict of interest implicit in legislative control over redistricting. The adoption of a redistricting commission by the state of California feels like a natural evolution in other democracies because most countries have tried to take redistricting out of the hands of legislatures to limit the conflict of interest. While in California, and in a few other US states, redistricting commissions have succeeded to a great degree in reaching that objective, they have not eliminated the inevitable partisan suspicions associated with redistricting and the correlated risk of commission gridlock. Moreover, redistricting commissions do not change the nature of redistricting in single-member plurality system. An independent commission still needs to find the right balance between race and politics. It needs to take race into consideration to comply with the federal Voting Rights Act and make sure minority electoral opportunities do not disappear. But if race is not used in the right way, that is if it is proven that race was the "predominant factor," the redistricting plan can be struck down by the courts. The same is true for partisanship but for different reasons. If a commission advantages one party over the other it might lose its credibility as a neutral buffer and the very reason for its existence. But redistricting is a partisan game. Legislature partisan gerrymanders only occur when one party is in complete control of the process. As we have seen in California, the partisan composition of the courts and the use of popular referendums give more options to the political party in the minority to force negotiation. Besides, redistricting is a zero-sum game and a partisan gerrymander is always risky. If a party overreaches and spreads its electors too thin it can backfire during the next round of elections and lead to electoral defeats. In a context of racial polarized voting, race can be used as a proxy for partisanship. After all, one of the characteristics of redistricting in the US is the extent to which it is litigated. And while partisan gerrymander challenges have not been successful it does not mean that the courts may not, in the future, come up with an acceptable standard.

But the larger issue might be whether such a standard is even desirable. It is, of course, tempting to believe that any one measure can be the ultimate standard of political fairness. The reality of redistricting is that political trade-offs have to be decided at some point. The decision takes place early in the process if the criteria are ordered by law or later in the process if the criteria are negotiated by bargaining among members of a legislature or another redistricting entity.[1] But a decision needs to be made at some point because redistricting is by nature a political trade-off activity centered on the question of what constitutes fair representation. Therefore, judges attempting to regulate the political process ought to be mindful of it especially in the context of conjoined polarization.

What this book has tried to show is that the redistricting process is becoming more complex due to the demographic evolution of the country. Party leaders not only need to navigate complex jurisprudence on racial gerrymandering (and potentially, in the future, partisan gerrymandering) but also satisfy minority groups wanting to be more involved in the redistricting process in order to increase their descriptive representation. As the American society is becoming more diverse, the population is expecting their elected bodies to reflect this diversity. This raises important issues for party leaders and minority groups that often need to negotiate with one another to avoid competition among non-White candidates especially in cosmopolitan metropolitan areas. However, with California's demographics and residential patterns, intra-minority electoral contests are bound to multiply.

One could argue that since the Democratic Party has become the only vehicle of minority group interests, pushing for Democratic majorities in other states will automatically help the cause of minorities. And that is true to some extent since partisan gerrymandering maintaining Republican control of a state usually limits minority groups' capacity to be heard since they are overwhelmingly Democratic voters. Republican drawn majority-minority districts are meant to weaken the Democratic Party. That is why so many minority groups have put the emphasis on the ills of partisan gerrymandering and their incapacity to seek judicial remedy. However, as the California example demonstrates, Democratic control of the redistricting process does not guarantee levels of representation satisfactory to minority group advocates. This is due, in part, to the shortcomings of the single plurality district system that is not well equipped to produce proportional representation. It is also due, in part, to the courts' position regarding the use race—refusing that race be used as a predominant factor in redistricting even though scholars have demonstrated how problematic this notion can be.[2] And also, in part, due to the fact that it is probably too much to expect one party to single-handedly be responsible for the descriptive diversity of all representative bodies. The Democratic Party is bound to resist this evolution as it did in California. Anglo-elected officials only reluctantly abandon favorable districts. Besides, minority candidates can also feel threatened by the emergence of another group's demographics. Party leaders need allies to keep their majorities and carry out their agenda. This resistance to minority group grievances can be costly if it is carried out in a confrontational manner as, in the end, California's parties were stripped of their control of the entire redistricting process. But unless the US adopts another voting system, and this is very unlikely, redistricting will continue to be more conflictual as minority groups grow in number and demand increases of *their* representation, that is to say in proportion to their demographic weight. The American concept of political representation is that of a body of elected officials that mirrors the diversity of the population. As long as redistricting is perceived as the main instrument to achieve ethno-racial diversity in a racially polarized environment it will concentrate all the tensions inherent to the political representation conundrum of the American society. Redistricting concentrates so many of the contradictions at the heart of representative democracy that redistricting reform is sometimes presented as the panacea for everything that hails American democracy: partisan polarization, incumbent advantage, lack of competition or underrepresentation of minority groups. It is neither negligible nor the key to electoral success that many elected officials believe it to be. Nor is it the source of all the shortcomings of democracy. If it generates so much passion it is because redistricting concentrates all the paradoxes and tensions inherent to representative democracy. And in California, as in the US generally, redistricting is so fundamental to any debate on representation because it occurs right at the confluence of race and politics. Moreover, far from having become post-partisan or post-racial, the American nation, and the state of California, face a situation where distinguishing between race and partisanship has become much more difficult than it used to be. Both have always been intertwined. But as partisan and racial polarization have increased, they have also aligned to the point that considering one without the other is, at least for the purpose of redistricting, simply untenable. The conflation of race and partisanship *is* the American political paradigm. And redistricting is at the heart of this conundrum as it keeps forcing American society to constantly think anew the question of representation.

NOTES

1. MacDonald and Cain, *op. cit.*, 2013, p. 619.
2. Daniel Hays Lowenstein, "You Don't Have to Be a Liberal to Hate Racial Gerrymandering," *Stanford Law Review*, 50, no. 3 (1998), 779–835.

Bibliography

Abramowitz, Alan, Brad Alexander, and Matthew Gunning. "Don't Blame Redistricting for Uncompetitive Elections." *PS: Political Science and Politics* 39, no. 1 (2006): 87–90.

Absoch, Yishaiya, Matt A. Barreto, and Nathan D. Woods. "An Assessment of Racially Polarized Voting For and Against Latino Candidates in California." In *Voting Rights Act Reauthorization of 2006: Perspectives on Democracy, Participation, and Power*, edited by Ana Henderson. Berkeley, CA: UC Berkeley Public Policy Press, 2007.

Adams, Florence. *Latinos and Local Representation: Changing Realities, Emerging Theories*. New York: Garland, 2000.

———. "Minority Representation in the New Millennium." In *Redistricting in the New Millennium*, edited by Peter F. Galderisi, 155–82. Lanham, MD: Lexington Books, 2005.

Adams, John. *Thoughts on Government*, Paper 4. April 1776. http://press-pubs.uchicago.edu/founders/documents/v1ch4s5.html.

Ahler, Dougls J., Jack Citrin, and Gabriel S. Lenz. "Do Open Primaries Improve Representation? An Experimental Test of California's Top-Two Primaries." *Legislative Studies Quarterly*, 41, no. 2 (2016): 237–68.

Aleinikoff, T. Alexander, and Samuel Issacharoff. "Race and Redistricting: Drawing Constitutional Lines after *Shaw v. Reno*." *Michigan Law Review* 92, no. 3 (1993): 588–651.

Allswang, John M. *The Initiative and Referendum in California 1898–1998*. Stanford, CA: Stanford University Press, 2000.

Altman, Micah, and Michael McDonald. "Redistricting and Polarization." In *American Gridlock: The Sources, Character and Impact of Political Polarization*, edited by James A. Thurber and Antoine Yoshinaka, 45–63. New York: Cambridge University Press, 2015.

Altman, Micah, Karin Mac Donald, and Michael McDonald. "From Crayons to Computers: The Evolution of Computer Use in Redistricting." *Sociological Science Computer Review* 23, no. 3 (2005): 334–46.

Amy, Douglas J. *Real Choices/New Voices: How Proportional Representation Elections Could Revitalize American Democracy*, 2nd ed. New York: Columbia University Press, 2002.

Ancheta, Angelo N. "Redistricting Reform and the California Citizens Redistricting Commission." *Harvard Law and Policy Review* 8 (2014): 109–40.

Anderson, Margo J., and Fienberg, Stephen E. *Who Counts?: The Politics of Census Taking in Contemporary America*. New York: Russell Sage Foundation, 1999.

Anderson, Nick. "Census Touchy Subject for State's GOP House Members." *Los Angeles Times*, March 31, 1999, 3.

Anderson, Totton J., and Eugene C. Lee. "The 1966 Election in California." *The Western Political Quarterly* 20, no. 2, pt. 2 (1967): 535–54.

Ansolabehere, Stephen, Nathaniel Persily, and Charles Stewart III. "Regional Differences in Racial Polarization in the 2012 Presidential Election: Implications for the Constitutionality of Section 5 of the Voting Rights Act." *Harvard Law Review Forum*, 126 (2013): 205–20.

Ansolabehere, Stephen, and James M. Snyder. "Candidate Positioning in US House Elections." *American Journal of Political Science* 45, no. 1 (2001): 136–59.

———. *The End of Inequality: One Person, One Vote and the Transformation of American Politics*. New York: Norton, 2008.

Apple, R. W. "Population Shift Likely to Give California GOP New Power." *New York Times*, September 27, 1970, 30.

Associated Press. "GOP Effort in Texas Fails in Bid to Redraw Districts." *New York Times*, July 26, 2003, A9.

———. "Hispanic Group Fights Remap." *San Francisco Chronicle*, December 18, 1991, A17.

———. "Texas Senate Approves Redistricting Plan." *New York Times*, September 24, 2003, A25.

———. "Texas Tries Anew on Redistricting." *New York Times*, September 9, 2003, A14.

Auchard, Eric. "Carving California with a Computer: The High-Tech Drawing of Districts." *California Journal* 22, no. 10 (1991).

Avila, Joaquin. "At-Large Elections Can Keep Chicanos off School Boards." *Un Nuevo Dia* 2, no. 4 (1976): 13.

Avila, Joaquin, Lee Eugene, and Terry M. Ao. "Report: Voting Rights in California: 1982–2006." *Southern California Review of Law & Social Justice* 17 (2007): 131–94.

Baker, Erwin. "*LA* Council's Plan for Redistricting Assailed." *Los Angeles Times*, September 7, 1972, OC6.

Baker, Gordon E. "Lessons from the 1973 California Master's Plan." In *Political Gerrymandering and the Court*, edited by Bernard Grofman, 296–317. New York: Agathon Press, 1990.

———. "Judicial Determination of Political Gerrymandering: A 'Totality of Circumstances' Approach." *Journal of Law and Politics* 3 (1986): 1–19.

———. "The California Senate: Sectional Conflict and *Vox Populi.*" In *The Politics of Reapportionment*, edited by Malcolm E. Jewell, 51–63. New York: Atherton Press, 1962.

Baldassare, Mark, Dean Bonner, David Kordus, and Lunna Lopes. "California's Independent Voters. Public Policy Institute of California," September 2016, http://www.ppic.org/publication/californias-independent-voters/.

———. "California Voter and Party Profile. Public Policy Institute of California," August 2017, http://www.ppic.org/publication/california-voter-and-party-profiles/.

Balinski M. L., and Peyton H. Young. *Fair Representation: Meeting the Ideal of One Man, One Vote*, 2nd ed. Washington, DC: Brookings Institution Press, 2001.

Ballotpedia, "Municipal Elections in Anaheim, California," 2016. https://ballotpedia.org/Municipal_elections_in_Anaheim,_California_(2016).

Balz, Dan. "California GOP Backs Redistricting Initiative." *Washington Post*, September 23, 1989, http://www.washingtonpost.com/archive/politics/1989/09/23/california-gop-backs-redistricting-initiative/53a95c3a-b3d5-494c-8167-0f4a68d7d263/.

Balzar, John. "Sebastiani Left Reeling but Won't Give Up." *Los Angeles Times*, September 16, 1983, B1.

———. "Sebastiani Revives Reapportionment: This Time He's Finding GOP Leaders Decidedly Cool to the Issue." *Los Angeles Times*, February 13, 1985, OC3.

———. "Sebastiani to Work for New Remap Effort." *Los Angeles Times*, October 3, 1983, B3.

———. "Stunned State GOP Looks to Voters for Rescue on Redistricting in '90." *Los Angeles Times*, January 18, 1989, LF21.

Banks, Sandy. "Latino Group to Press Redistricting Plan." *Los Angeles Times*, June 11, 1981, V18.

Barabak, Mark Z. "California to Gain only One congressional Seat." *Los Angeles Times*, February 26, 2001, A14.

———. "Democrats Rule the Redistricting Roost in California Politics." *Los Angeles Times*, July 25, 2001, A15.

Barreto, Matt A., and Loren Colinwood. "A Review of Racially Polarized Voting For and Against Latino Candidates in Los Angeles County 1994–2010." Report 1 of 2, in *Report on Legal Standard Pertaining to the Los Angeles County Redistricting Process*, edited by Justin Levitt, 82–165, August 9, 2011. http://file.lacounty.gov/SDSInter/bos/supdocs/62832.pdf.

———. "Latino Candidates and Racial Block Voting in Primary and Judicial Elections." Report Commissioned by: The Los Angeles County Chicano Employees Association. Alhambra, CA, October 31, 2009. http://mattbarreto.com/papers/laccea2008.pdf.

Barreto, Matt, Christian R. Grose, and Ana Henderson. "Redistricting: Coalition District and the Voting Rights Act." *The Chief Justice Earl Warren Institute on Law and Social Policy*, UC Berkeley Law School, Research Brief, May 2011, 7.

Barretto, Matt A., Gary M. Segura, and Nathan D. Woods. "The Mobilizing Effect of Majority-Minority Districts on Latino Turnout." *American Political Science Review* 98, no. 1 (2004): 65–75.

Baxton, Greg. "41st Altered Most in Redistricting Plan." *Los Angeles Times*, January 2, 1981, GB1.

Bebitch Jeffe, Sherry. "After Election, Comes the Dawn of Reality for Pete Wilson." *Los Angeles Times*, November 18, 1990, M5.

———. "Why Republicans May Rue Their Heartfelt Support for Term Limits." *Los Angeles Times*, December 8, 1991, M6.

Bergholtz, Richard. "38th District: Myriad of Choices: Pros, Youth, Wealth Vie for Democratic Congressional Nod." *Los Angeles Times*, May 13, 1972, B1.

———. "A Challenge: Fair Plan for Redistricting: College Group to Use Computer in Checking Efforts of Legislature." *Los Angeles Times*, December 7, 1980, A3.

———. "A District Ripe for Picking." *Los Angeles Times*, April 9, 1968, A4.

———. "Computer Maps Senate Redistricting: Draws Lines That Eluded Legislators." *Los Angeles Times*, July 20, 1965, A1.

———. "GOP Assemblyman Announces Petition Drive to Get Redistricting Plan on Ballot." *Los Angeles Times*, April 6, 1983, 22.

———. "GOP's Ballot Drive on Redistricting to Face Legal Challenge." *Los Angeles Times*, October 9, 1981, B3.

———. "GOP Will Take Aim at Ruling on Redistricting." *Los Angeles Times*, February 1, 1982, A12.

———. "Little Effect Seen in Redistricting." *Los Angeles Times*, November 29, 1973, 3.

———. "New GOP Strategy on Redistricting Develops." *Los Angeles Times*, February 4, 1983, B3.

———. "New Unit Urged to Handle State Redistricting; Rights Advisory Group Calls Legislature Unfair to Mexican-Americans." *Los Angeles Times*, April 27, 1971, 3.

———. "Redistricting Damned, Applauded by Critics." *Los Angeles Times*, September 10, 1981, A3.

———. "Reform Doesn't Mean 'Fair' Where Redistricting Is Concerned." *Los Angeles Times*, October 12, 1981, B3.

Bernstein, Sid. "3 Challenge Schabarum in Reelection Bid." *Los Angeles Times*, May 30, 1978, C1.

———. "Supervisors' Dispute Delays Redistricting Vote." *Los Angeles Times*, September 23, 1981, D1.

Berthelsen, Christian. "Dems Offer Redistricting Plan to Counter Governor's Plan. GOP Says It Leaves Legislature with Too Much Power." *San Francisco Chronicle*, June 29, 2005, B2.

Bialik, Kristen, and Jens Manuel Krogstad. "115th Congress Sets New High for Racial, Ethnic Diversity." Pew Research Center, January 24, 2017, http://www.pewresearch.org/fact-tank/2017/01/24/115th-congress-sets-new-high-for-racial-ethnic-diversity/.

Bickerstaff, Steve. *Drawing Lines in the Sand: Congressional Redistricting in Texas and the Downfall of Tom DeLay*. Austin: University of Texas Press, 2007.

Billiter, Bill. "Election Reform or Trojan Horse?: Partisan Storm Swirls about Plan to Revise Reapportionment Procedure." *Los Angeles Times*, October 14, E1.

Blacksher, James, and Lani Guinier. "Free at Last: Rejecting Equal Sovereignty and Restoring the Constitutional Right to Vote *Shelby County v. Holder*." *Harvard Law and Policy Review* 8, no. 1 (2014): 39–69.

Blacksher, James U., and Larry T. Menefee. "From *Reynolds v. Sims* to City of *Mobile v. Bolden*: Have the White Suburbs Commandeered the Fifteenth Amendment?" *Hastings Law Journal* 34, no. 1 (1982): 1–64.

Blake, Gene. "Brown Picks Woman, Black for High Court." *Los Angeles Times*, February 13, 1977, A1.

Blanchard, Robert M. "Assembly Unit Delays Vote on Redistricting." *Los Angeles Times*, June 11, 1965, 3.

———. "Brown Puts Off Decision on Redistricting Session." *Los Angeles Times*, June 4, 1965, B.

———. "Redistricting Battle Lines Taking Shape." *Los Angeles Times*, February 4, 1965, A4.

———. "Senators Seek Second Chance of Reapportion." *Los Angeles Times*, July 27, 1965, 3.

Block, A. G. "Putting the Puzzle Back Together." *California Journal* 32, no. 3 (2001): 10.

———. "The Reapportionment Failure: Legislature's Plans Fall to Wilson's Veto." *California Journal* 22, no. 10 (1991): 503–5.

Blood, Michael R. "Jackpot: Lawyers Earn Fees from Law They Wrote." *The Associated Press*, http://www.newsday.com/news/nation/jackpot-lawyers-earn-fees-from-law-they-wrote-1.1590856.

Blumenthal, Ralph. "After Bitter Fight, Texas Senate Redraws Congressional Districts." *New York Times*, October 13, 2003, A1.

———. "Texas Republicans Report a Deal on Hotly Disputed Redistricting." *New York Times*, October 9, 2003, A24.

Bluth, Alexa H. "Initiative Funding Limit Lifted for Lawmakers." *Sacramento Bee*, August 19, 2005, A1.

Borenstein, Daniel. "Political Winds in Big Shift." *Contra Costa Times*, December 3, 1991, 10F4.

Bowler, Shaun, Todd Donovan, and David Brockington. *Electoral Reform and Minority Representation: Local Experiments with Alternative Elections*. Columbus: Ohio State University Press, 2003.

Boyarsky, Bill, and Victor Merina. "Schabarum Raises $50,000 for Dana Attack on Burke." *Los Angeles Times*, October 30, 1980, D1.

Boyarsky, Bill. *Big Daddy Jesse Unruh: The Art of Power Politics*. Los Angeles: University of California Press, 2007.

———. "The Death of Gerrymandering?" *Los Angeles Times*, September 5, 1973, B6.

———. "Conservatives Win Control of Supervisors." *Los Angeles Times*, November 5, 1980, 1.

———. "Court Will Decide: Redistricting Plan: There Will Be Some New Faces in '74." *Los Angeles Times*, September 3, 1973, 1.

———. "Crossover Dreams: Richard Alatorre Calls the Shots in East LA, But to Succeed Citywide He'll Have to Woo the Westside." *Los Angeles Times*, October 22, 1989, http://articles.latimes.com/1989-10-22/magazine/tm-616_1_east-los-angeles/6.

———. "Lost Drama in Voting Rights Suit." *Los Angeles Times*, March 7 1990, B2.

———. "Mexican-Americans' Campaign for Legislative Power Begins; Chicano and Anglo Activists Join Forces to Gain Representation in Elective Offices through Redistricting." *Los Angeles Times*, January 21, 1967, C1.

———. "Mrs. Burke Becomes First Black, Woman Supervisor: Liberal Record May Make It Hard for Her to Hold Seat in Conservative, Largely White District." *Los Angeles Times*, June 15, 1979, B1.

———. "The Five Little Kings Who Are No More." *Los Angeles Times*, December 7, 1990, B2.

Broder, David S. "Calif. Democrats Seek Stability in Redistricting Plan." *Washington Post*, August 30, 2001, A2.

Broder, John M., and Dean E. Murphy. "A Recall Vote Seems Certain for California." *New York Times*, July 24, 2003, A1.

Brown, Anna, and Sara Atske. "Blacks Have Made Gains in US Political Leadership, But Gaps Remain." Pew Research Center, June 28, 2016, http://www.pewresearch.org/fact-tank/2016/06/28/blacks-have-made-gains-in-u-s-political-leadership-but-gaps-remain/.

Brownstein, Ronald. "2 States of Progress for Latinos." *Los Angeles Times*, August 1, 1990, OCA1.

———. "Quotas in Elections." *Los Angeles Times*, August 28, 1991, OCA1.

———. "Redrawing Rules and Boundaries." *Los Angeles Times*, March 5, 2005, A18.

Brunell, Thomas. *Redistricting and Representation: Why Competitive Elections Are Bad for America*. New York: Routledge, 2008.

Buchler, Justin. "Redistricting Reform Will Not Solve California's Budget Crisis." *California Journal of Politics and Policy* 1, no.1 (2009).

Bucy, Page E. "Sidebar to the New LA County Supervisorial Seat: Redistricting by Lawsuit." *California Journal* 22, no. 1 (1991): 22–28.

Bullock, Charles S. III. *Redistricting: The Most Political Activity in America*. Lanham, MD: Rowman & Littlefield, 2010.

Buntin, Glenn F. "Democrats Win 10-Seat Edge in Congressional Delegation." *Los Angeles Times*, November 5, 1992, SD A3.

Bustillo, Miguel, and Nicholas Riccardi. "Parties Rush to Overhaul Political Maps." *Los Angeles Times*, March 31, 2001, B1.

Butler, David, and Bruce E. Cain. *Congressional Redistricting: Comparative and Theoretical Perspectives*. New York: Macmillan, 1992.

Cain, Bruce E. *The Reapportionment Puzzle*. Los Angeles: University of California Press, 1983.

———. "Assessing the Partisan Effects of Redistricting." *The American Political Science Review* 79, no. 2 (1985): 320–33.

———. "Moving Past Section 5: More Fingers or a New Dike." *Election Law Journal* 13, no. 2 (2013): 338–40.

———. "Simple vs. Complex Criteria for Partisan Gerrymandering: A Comment on Niemi and Grofman." *UCLA Law Review* 33, no. 1 (1985): 214–16.

———. "The Contemporary Context of Ethnic and Racial Politics in California." In *Racial and Ethnic Politics in California*, edited by Bryan O. Jackson and Michael B. Preston. Berkeley, CA: Institute of Governmental Studies Press, 1991.

———. "Redistricting Commissions: A Better Political Buffer?" *Yale Law Journal* 121, no.7 (2012): 1808–44.

———. *Democracy More of Less: America's Political Reform Quandary*. New York: Cambridge University Press, 2015.

Cain, Bruce, John Hanley, and Thad Kousser. "Term Limits: A Recipe for More Competition?" In *The Marketplace of Democracy: Electoral Competition and American Politics*, edited by Michael McDonald and John Samples, 199–221. Washington, DC: Brookings Institution Press, 2006.

Cain, Bruce, and David Hopkins. "Mapmaking at the Grassroots: The Legal and Political Issues of Local Redistricting." *Journal of Election Law* 1, no. 4 (2002): 515–30.

Cain, Bruce E., and Thad Kousser. *Adapting to Term Limits: Recent Experiences and New Direction*. Berkeley: Public Policy Institute of California, 2004.

Cain, Bruce, Thad Kousser, and Karl T. Kurtz. "Institutional Imbalance: The Effects of Six-Year Term Limits in California." In *Legislating without Experience: Case Studies in Legislative Term Limits*, edited by Rick Farmer, Christopher Z. Mooney, Richard, J. Powell, and John C. Green, 17–42. Lanham, MD: Lexington Books, 2007.

Cain, Bruce, and Karin Mac Donald . "The Implications of Nesting in California Redistricting." Berkeley, CA: Institute of Governmental Studies, August 2007.

Cain, Bruce, Karin Mac Donald, and Iris Hui. "Competition and Redistricting in California: Lesson for Reform." Berkeley, CA: Institute for Governmental Studies, February 2006.

Cain, Bruce E., Karin Mac Donald, and Michael McDonald. "From Equality to Fairness: the Path of Political Reform since *Baker v. Carr*." In *Party Lines: Competition Partisanship and Congressional Redistricting*, edited by Bruce Cain and Thomas Mann. Washington, DC: Brookings Institution Press, 2005.

Cain, Bruce E., and Miller, Kenneth. "Voting Rights Mismatch: The Challenge of Applying the Voting Rights Act to 'Other Minorities.'" In *Voting Rights and Redistricting in the United States*, edited by Mark E. Rush. Westport, CT: Greenwood Press, 1998.

Cain, Bruce E., and Emily R. Zhang. "Blurred Lines: Conjoined Polarization and Voting Rights." *Ohio State Law Journal* 77, no. 4 (2016): 867–904.

California, Population of Counties by Decennial Census: 1900–90, compiled by Richard L. Forstall, US Bureau of the Census, http://www.census.gov/population/www/censusdata/cencounts/files/ca190090.txt.

California Citizens Redistricting Commission. *Final Report on 2011 Redistricting* (August 15, 2011), https://wedrawthelines.ca.gov/wp-content/uploads/sites/64/2011/08/crc_20110815_2final_report.pdf.

———. *Before the California Citizens Redistricting Commission,* In the matter of Full Commission Business Meeting, State Capital Building, Room 447, March 19, 2011.

———. *Before the California Citizens Redistricting Commission,* In the Matter of Full Commission Business Meeting, University of the Pacific, McGeorge School of Law, Classroom C 3200 Fifth Avenue Sacramento, California, July 29, 2011, full transcript, 15. http://wedrawthelines.ca.gov/downloads/transcripts/201107/transcripts_20110729_sacto.pdf.

California Journal. "Point/Counterpoint: Redistricting Challenge." *California Journal* 32, no. 1, (2002): 38.

California Journal. "Primary Election Results—Congress and Legislature." *California Journal* 34, no. 4 (2002): 29.

California Journal's Editors. "CJ's District-by-District—Congress." *California Journal*, 40, no. 11 (2002): 20.

California Judicial Council. Advisory Committee on Racial and Ethnic Bias in the Courts. *Final Report of the California Judicial Council Advisory Committee on Racial and Ethnic Bias in the Courts*. San Francisco, CA: The Committee, 1997.

California Legislative Analyst's Office. "Voters Empowerment Act." http://www.lao.ca.gov/ballot/2005/77_11_2005.htm.

California Secretary of State, Report of Registration. October 24, 2016, http://www.sos.ca.gov/elections/report-registration/15day-general-2016/.

———. California's Official Voter Guide 2008, Budget Summary, http://voterguide.sos.ca.gov/past/2008/general/titlesum/prop11-title-sum.htm.

———. Initiatives by Title and Year, http://elections.cdn.sos.ca.gov/ballot-measures/pdf/initiatives-by-title-and-summary-year.pdf.

———. Historical Voter Registration and Participation in Statewide General Elections 1910–2016, http://elections.cdn.sos.ca.gov/sov/2016-general/sov/04-historical-voter-reg-participation.pdf.

California State Advisory Committee to the United States Commission on Civil Rights Report, Palo Alto: Ernesto Galarza Collection, Department of Special Collections, Stanford University, 1967.

Calpeek. "Remap Wars: Court Plan Is Out and GOP Is All Smiles but Demos See Silver Lining." *Calpeek* 13, no. 45 (1991).

Cameron, Charles, David Epstein, and Sharyn O'Halloran. "Do Majority-Minority Districts Maximize Substantive Black Representation in Congress?" *American Political Science Review* 90, no. 4 (1996): 794–812.

Campbell, James E. *Polarized: Making Sense of a Divided America*. Princeton, NJ: Princeton University Press, 2016.

Cannon, Carl M. "California Divided." *California Journal* 32, no. 1 (2002): 8.

Cannon, Lou. *Ronnie and Jesse: A Political Odyssey*. New York: Doubleday, 1969.

Canon, David T. *Race, Redistricting, and Representation: The Unintended Consequences of Black Majority Districts*. Chicago: University of Chicago Press, 1999.

Capitol Weekly. "Republicans Likely to Abandon Referendum on Congressional Maps." *Capitol Weekly*, September 20, 2011, https://capitolweekly.net/republicans-likely-to-abandon-referendum-on-congressional-maps/.

Caress, Stanley M., and Todd T. Kunioka. *Term Limits and Their Consequences: Aftermath of Legislative Reform*. Albany, NY: SUNY Press, 2012.

Caress, Stanley M., Charles Elder, Richard Elling, Jean-Philippe Faletta, Shannon K. Orr, Eric Rader, Marjorie Sarbaugh-Thompson, John Strate, and Lyke Thompson. "Effect of Term Limits on the Election of Minority State Legislators." *State and Local Government Review* 35, no. 3 (2003): 183–95.

Cassey, Carol A. "The Nonpartisan Ballot in the US." In *Electoral Laws and Their Political Consequences*, edited by Grofman Bernard and Arend Lijphart, 226–41. New York: Algora Publishing, 2003.

Chang, Irene. "Asians, Latino Join in Proposal for Remapping." *Los Angeles Times*, August 31, 1991, B2.

Charles, Guy-Uriel. "Judging the Law of Politics." *Michigan Law Review* 103, no. 6 (2005): 1099–141.

Chávez, Lydia. *The Color Bind: California's Campaign to End Affirmative Action*. Los Angeles: University of California Press, 1998.

Chiang, Harriet, and Robert B. Gunnison. "How Wilson's Appointee May Affect Court. Appointment Surprised the Legal Experts." *San Francisco Chronicle*, July 31, 1991, A11.

———. "State High Court OKs Term Limits for Legislators." *San Francisco Chronicle*, October 11, 1991, A1.

———. "Wilson Picks Conservative as Supreme Court Justice. LA Judge Would Replace Retiring Liberal." *San Francisco Chronicle*, July 30, 1991, A1.

Choldin, Harvey M. *Looking for the Last Percent: The Controversy over Census Undercount*. New Brunswick, NJ: Rutgers University Press, 1994.

Christensen, Terry, and Larry N. Gerston. "Initiative as Catalysts for Racial Politics." In *Racial and Ethnic California: Continuity and Change*, edited by Sandra Bass and Bruce E. Cain, 121–37. Berkeley, CA: Berkeley Public Policy Press, 2008.

Chung, April. "Noncitizen Voting Rights and Alternatives: A Path toward Greater Asian Pacific American and Latino Political Participation." *UCLA Asian Pacific American Law Journal* 4 (1996): 163.

Churn, Steven. "Late Donations Boost Green's Senate Drive." *Los Angeles Times*, November 4, 1988, OC_A3.

Citrin, Jack, and Benjamin Highton. *How Race, Ethnicity and Immigration Shape the California Electorate*. Berkeley: Public Policy Institute of California, 2002.

City of Compton, General Municipal Election, June 4, 2013, Summary Report, June 10, 2013. http://www.comptoncity.org/civicax/filebank/blobdload.aspx?BlobID=25793.

Clark, George L. *Stealing Our Votes: How Politicians Conspire to Control Elections and How to Stop Them*. Pittsburgh, PA: Dorance, 2004.

Clymer, Adam. "Blacks Seen Retaining 17 Seats in the House Despite Census Losses." *New York Times*, June 21, 1981, 1.

———. "Democrats Warned of Districting Peril: Party Leaders Are Told of Efforts to Assist State Legislatures in Drawing Up New Lines." *New York Times*, February 14, 1981, 9.

———. "Would-Be 'Giant-Killer' on Coast Focusing on Burton's Personality." *New York Times*, October 23, 1982, 34.

Collins, William P. "Race as a Salient Factor in Nonpartisan Elections." *The Western Political Quarterly* 33, no. 3 (1980): 330–35.

Connel, Rich. "Art Snyder Again Beset by Political Turmoil." *Los Angeles Times*, December 14, 1992, OCA3.

Cook, Rhodes. "Do the Math, and the Result Is: Not Much of a Contest." *Washington Post*, October 6, 2002, B3.

Cox, Adam B., and Richard T. Holden. "Reconsidering Racial and Partisan Gerrymandering." *University of Chicago Law Review* 78, no. 2 (2011): 553–604.

Cox, Gary W. *Elbridge Gerry's Salamander: The Electoral Consequences of the Apportionment Revolution.* New York: Cambridge University Press, 2002.

Crum, Travis. "The Voting Rights Act Secret Weapon: Pocket Trigger Litigation and Dynamic Preclearance." *Yale Law Journal* 119, no. 8 (2010): 1992–2038.

Cuevas Ingram, Joanna E. "The Color of Change: Voting Rights in the Twenty-First Century and the California voting Rights Act." *Harvard Latino Law Review* 15 (2012): 183–231. http://harvardllr.com/wp-content/uploads/2012/09/HBK104.pdf.

Cummings, Judit. "Rousselot in Tight Race for New Seat." *New York Times*, October 31, 1982, 38.

Cushman, John H. Jr. "House reprimands Richardson." *New York Times*, August 2, 2012, https://thecaucus.blogs.nytimes.com/2012/08/02/house-reprimands-richardson/.

del Olmo, Franck. "Pro14 Endangers Latinos' Gains." *Los Angeles Times*, October 28, 1982, F11.

———. "3 Mexican-Americans Seeking 40th Assembly District Seat." *Los Angeles Times*, November 2, 1972, B1.

———. "Chicano Party Says It Defeated Alatorre in 48th District." *Los Angeles Times*, November 18, 1971, A3.

———. "Growing Latin Political Power Reflected in Election Results; Political Clout Shown by Mexican-Americans." *Los Angeles Times*, November 14, 1972, B1.

———. "Now Latinos Are in the Driver's Seat." *Los Angeles Times*, July 27, 2003, M5.

———. "Raza Unidad: Barrio Power?: Chicanos, Other Factions Weigh Effects of 48the District Upset." *Los Angeles Times*, December 13, 1971, D1.

———. "Redistricting Plays a Part in Budget Crisis." *Los Angeles Times*, July 6, 2003, M5.

———. "Snyder Syndrome Even Gets Snyder." *Los Angeles Times*, August 30, 1984, D5.

Deposition of Juan Vargas, April4 2002, *Cano v. Davis*, No.CV 01-08477 MMM (RCx).

DeSipio, Louis. "From Naturalized Citizen to Voter: The Context of Naturalization and Electoral Participation in Latino Communities." In *Immigration and the Border Politics and Policy in the New Latino Century*, edited by David L. Leal and José E. Limón, 149–81. Notre Dame, IN: University of Notre Dame Press, 2013.

Dixon, Robert G., Jr. *Democratic Representation: Reapportionment in Law and Politics*. New York: Oxford University Press, 1968.

Dolan, Maura. "Justice Says He's Sorry about Endorsement." *Los Angeles Times*, August 10, 1995, A3.

Dolan, Maura, and Mark Gladstone. "State High Court Pull Initiative off March Ballot." *Los Angeles Times*, December 14, 1999, A1.

Douzet, Frederick, Kenneth Miller, and Thad Kousser, eds. *The New Political Geography of California*. Berkeley, CA: Public Policy Institute Press, 2008.

Doyle, Jim. "US Judges Refuse to Block Remap Challenge to California's Plan Fails." *San Francisco Chronicle*, January 29, 1992, A11.

———. "Wilson to Go to Court in Remap Fight." *San Francisco Chronicle*, October 3, 1991, A23.

Drumond, Ayres B., Jr. "California Speaker Frustrates G.O. One Last Time." *New York Times*, June 6, 1995, http://www.nytimes.com/1995/06/06/us/california-speaker-frustrates-gop-one-last-time.html.

Editorial Staff. "Cheating Seating." *Wall Street Journal*, December 27, 2001, http://archive.fairvote.org/redistricting/reports/remanual/canews6.htm#cheating.

Editorial. "Dishonest Ads Again Sink Reapportionment." *San Francisco Chronicle*, June 7, 1990, A24.

Editorial. "Voting Rights in Whittier." *Los Angeles Times*, December 29, 2013, A25.

Edsall, Thomas B. "A political Fight to Define the Future: Latinos at Odds over California's Two New Democratic Congressional Districts." *Washington Post*, October 31, 2001, A8.

El Nasser, Haya. "Judge Puts Pro187 on Hold / Immigration Measure May Be Headed for Supreme Court." *USA Today*, November 17, 1994, A3.

Endicott, William. "Reapportionment Plan Favoring GOP Studied." *Los Angeles Times*, January 5, 1972, I24.

Engstrom, Richard L. "Race and Southern Politics: The Special Case of Congressional Districting." In *Writing Southern Politics: Contemporary Interpretations and Future Directions*, edited by Robert Steed and Laurence W. Moreland, 91–118. Lexington, KY: University of Kentucky Press, 2006.

———. "Influence Districts and the Court: A Concept in Need of Clarity." In *The Most Fundamental Right: Contrasting Perspective on the Voting Rights Act*, edited by Daniel McKool, 67–119. Bloomington: Indiana University Press, 2012.

———. "Racial Discrimination in the Electoral Process: The Voting Rights Act and the Vote Dilution Issue." In *Party Politics in the South*, edited by Robert Steed, Laurence Moreland and Ted Baker, 197–2013. New York: Praeger, 1980.

Engstrom, Richard, and Michael D. MacDonald. "The Effect of At-Large Versus District Elections on Racial Representation in US Municipalities." In *Electoral Laws and Their Political Consequences*, edited by Bernard Grofman and Arend Lijphart, 203–25. New York: Agathon Press, 1986.

Epstein, David L., and Sharyn O'Halloran. "Trends in Minority Representation, 1974 to 2000." In *The Future of the Voting Rights Act*, edited by David L. Epstein, Richard Pildes, Rodolfo De la Garza, and Sharyn O'Halloran, 61–80. New York: Russell Sage, 2006.

Epstein, David L., Richard H. Pildes, Rodolfo De la Garza, and Sharyn O'Halloran, eds. *The Future of the Voting Rights Act*. New York: Russell Sage 2006.

Epstein, Paige. "Addressing Minority Vote Dilution through State Voting Rights Acts." *University of Chicago Public Law and Legal Theory*, Working Paper No. 474, 2014.

Erickson, Robert S., Gerald C. Wright, and John P. McIver. *Statehouse Democracy: Public Opinion and Policy in American States*. New York: Cambridge University Press, 1993.

Escutia, Martha, and Gloria Romero. "MALDEF's Lawsuit Is Racially Divisive." *Los Angeles Times*, November 1, 2001, B13.

Fairbanks, Robert. "Redistricting Aids Moscone: Freshman S. F. Democrat New Force in State Senate." *Los Angeles Times*, January 29, 1968, 3.

Feng, Kathay, Keith Oaki, and Bryan Ikegami. "Voting Matters: APIAs, Latino/a and Post-2000 Redistricting in California." *Oregon Law Review* 81, no. 4 (2002): 889–916.

Fenichel Pitkin, Hanna. *The Concept of Representation*. Los Angeles: University of California Press, 1967.

Finnegan, Michael. "Latinos Blast ReBerman in Map Fight." *Los Angeles Times*, September 7, 2001, B3.

———. "Latinos May Gain Few Seats in Redistricting." *Los Angeles Times*, August 26, 2001, B1.

———. "Latinos May Gain Few Seats in Redistricting." *Los Angeles Times*, August 26, 2001, B1.

———. "Remapping Plan Fails to Appease Latinos." *Los Angeles Times*, September 11, 2001, B3.

———. "Neighboring LA Democrats Trade Barbs over Redistricting." *Los Angeles Times*, September 8, 2001, B3.

Fishkin, Joseph. "Equal Citizenship and the Equal Right to Vote." *Indiana Law Journal* 86, no. 4 (2011): 1289–360.

Fougere, Joshua, Stephen Ansolabehere, and Nathaniel Persily. "Partisanship, Public Opinion, and Redistricting." *Election Law Journal* 9, no. 4 (2010): 325–47

Fraga, Luis Ricardo, and Navarro, Sharon A. "Latinos in Latino Politics." In *Latino Politics: Identity, Mobilization and Representation*, edited by Roldfo Espino, David L. Leal, and Kenneth J. Meier. Charlottesville: University Press of Virginia, 2007.

Francis, Gerald. "Old Political Hands Adds New Face in the Race of Supervisor." *Los Angeles Times*, October 5, 1980, WS1.

Freund, Paul A. *Democratic Representation: Reapportionment in Law and Politics*. New York: Oxford University Press, 1968.

Gallagher, John F., and Louis F. Weschler. "California." In *Impact of Reapportionment in the Thirteen Western States*, edited by Eleonore Bushnell, 71–90. Salt Lake City: University of Utah Press, 1970.

Garret, Elizabeth. *Redistricting: Another California Revolution?* Initiative and Referendum Institute, University of Southern California, report 2005–1, February 2005.

Gay, Claudine. The Effect of Minority Districts and Minority Representation on Political Participation in California. Public Policy Institute of California, 2001.

Geiger, Kim. "Judge Knocks Redistricting Off Ballot in Loss for Rauner." *Chicago Tribune*, July 20, 2016, http://www.chicagotribune.com/news/local/politics/ct-illinois-redistricting-lawsuit-ruling-madigan-met-20160720-story.html.

Gelfand, David M. "Voting Rights Developments: Academic Reflections and Practical Projections for the 1990s." *Stetson Law Review* 21, no. 3 (1992): 707.

Gerken, Heather. "Keynote Address: What Election Law Has to Say to Constitutional Law." *Indiana Law Review* 44, no. 1 (2010): 7–22.

———. "Understanding the Right to an Undiluted Vote." *Harvard Law Review* 114, no. 6 (2001): 1663–743.

Gerken, Heather K., and Michael S. Kang. "The Institutional Turn in Election Law Scholarship." In *Race, Reform, and Regulation of the Electoral Process*, edited by Guy-Uriel E. Charles, Heather K. Gerken, and Michael S. Kang, 86–100. New York: Cambridge University Press, 2011.

Gerston, Larry N., and Christensen, Terry. *Recall! California's Political Earthquake*. Armonk, NY: M.E. Sharp Publisher, 2004.

Gillam, Jerry. "Assembly Redistricting Shelved by Democrats; Some Republicans Broke Word to Back Bill, Moretti Claims." *Los Angeles, Times*, March 9, 1973, 3.

———. "Break Seen in Senate Redistricting Dilemma." *Los Angeles Times*, February 10, 1965, 10.

———. "Democrats Unveil Redistricting Plan: Own Members, GOP Criticize Proposal for New Senate Lines." *Los Angeles Times*, October 7, 1971, A3.

———. "Reagan Veto Expected on Redistricting Law; Three Bills Merged into One Maneuver Designed to Enhance Override Chances." *Los Angeles Times*, June 15, 1973, 3.

———. "Reapportionment Delay Supported: Sen. Richardson Says GOP Could Gain under Plan." *Los Angeles Times*, February 4, 1981, 3.

———. "Redistricting Bill Clears Legislature: Reluctant Approval Given to Beat State Supreme Court Deadline." *Los Angeles Times*, December 6, 1967, 3.

———. "Redistricting Compromise Bid Fails; Issue May Go to Court; Reconvening of Special Legislative Session May Be Idle Gesture; Reinecke Panel Meets, Makes No Progress." *Los Angeles Times*, December 16, 1971, A3.

———. "Redistricting Plan Unveiled." *Los Angeles Times*, April 7, 1965, 1.

———. "Wilson Picks Redistricting Panel." *Los Angeles Times*, July 27, 1991, VCA 21.

Gladstone, Mark. "Democrats Win Senate Seat in Key Election." *Los Angeles Times*, May 13, 1987, 10.

Glazer, Amihai, Bernard Grofman, and Marc Robbins. "Partisan and Incumbency Effects of 1970s Congressional Redistricting." *American Journal of Political Science* 30, no. 3 (1987): 680–707.

Goff, Tom. "'Bipartisan' Redistricting Plan OKd by State Senate 25 to 13: Harmer-Zenovich Bill Would Maintain 20–20 Party Balance; May Be Combined with Assembly Measure." *Los Angeles Times*, May 24, 1973, A3.

———. "Democrats Unveil Plan to Redistrict Assembly." *Los Angeles Times*, October 29, 1971, A3.

———. "Divided Legislature: Passage of Key Bills May Be Tougher: Democrats Gain in Assembly but Lose Edge in Senate." *Los Angeles Times*, November 9, 1972, A1.

———. "Governor Urges Redistricting Plan without Partisan Politics." *Los Angeles Times*, January 21, 1972, I14.

———. "Legislature Still Faces Reapportionment Issue: Assembly Committee Moves Bill Setting Up Special Panel to Redraw District Lines." *Los Angeles Times*, June 18, 1972, B1.

———. "Reagan Veto of Redistricting Bills Seen as Legislators Recess; Bitter Special Session Ends as Assembly and Senate Democrats Adopt Plans on Straight Party-Line Vote." *Los Angeles Times*, December 21, 1971, A1.

———. "Reinecke Calls Disputed State Redistricting Panel into Session." *Los Angeles Times*, December 15, 1971, A3.

Gold, Matea, and Michael Finnegan. "No Consensus on Latino Vote Ruling; Politics: Some See Court Redistricting Decision as Sign of Progress. Others Fear It Will Halt Gains." *Los Angeles Times*, June 14, 2002, B1.

Gold, Matea, and Bettina Boxall. "Condit's Loss Brings Sense of Relief to Central Valley." *Los Angeles Times*, March 7, 2002, B1.

Gold, Scott. "Judges Uphold Texas' Contested Election Maps." *Los Angeles Times*, January 7, 2004, A10.

Goldmacher, Shane. "Battle Lines over Redistricting." *Los Angeles Times*, October 29, 2010, AA1.

———. "The Waxman-Berman Machine Finally Shuts Down." *The National Journal*, January 26, 2013, http://www.nationaljournal.com/magazine/the-waxman-berman-machine-finally-shuts-down-20130124.

Grant, David M., Melvin L. Oliver, and Angela D. James. "African-Americans: Social and Economic Bifurcation." In *Ethnic Los Angeles*, edited by Roger Waldinger and Mehdi Bozorgmehr, 379–411. New York: Russell Sage Foundation, 1996.

Greenbaum, Jon, Alan Martinson, and Sonia Gill. "Shelby County v. Holder: When the Rational Becomes Irrational." *Howard Law Journal* 57, no. 3 (2014): 811–67.

Greenber, Carl. "Democrats' Remapping Bills Vetoes by Reagan: Proposals Branded as Totally Partisan; Court Ruling Likely." *Los Angeles Times*, December 31, 1971, 3B.

———. "Election a 'Debacle' for GOP, Flournoy Says." *Los Angeles Times*, November 11, 1972, 24.

———. "Reagan Vetoes 3 Reapportioning Bills, Describes Them as Unfair." *Los Angeles Times*, December 30, 1971, 3.

———. "State Reapportion Foes See Last Hopes Fade." *Los Angeles Times*, August 5, 1965, 13.

Greenhut, Steven. "More Proof Dems Manipulated Redistricting." *Fox and Hounds*, December 22, 2011, http://www.foxandhoundsdaily.com/2011/12/propublica-ignores-worst-redistricting-lines/.

Grofman, Bernard. "Alternatives to Single-Member Plurality Districts: Legal and Empirical Issues." In *Representation and Redistricting Issues*, edited by Bernard Grofman, Arend Lijphart, Robert B. McKay, and Howard A. Scarrow, 875–98. Lanham, MD: Lexington Books, 1982.

———. "Criteria for Districting: A Social Science Perspective." *UCLA Law Review* 33, no. 1 (1985): 79–93.

Grofman, Bernard, and Lisa Handley, eds. *Redistricting in Comparative Perspective*. New York: Oxford University Press, 2008.

———. "Estimating the Impact of Voting-Rights-Act-Related Districting on Democratic Strength in the US House of Representatives." In *Race and Redistricting in the 1990s*, edited by Bernard Grofman, 51–67. New York: Agathon Press, 1998.

Grofman, Bernard, Lisa Handley, and Richard G. Niemi. *Minority Representation and the Quest for Voting Equality*. New York: Cambridge University Press, 1992.

Guerra, Fernando, and Luis Ricardo Fraga. "Theory, Reality and Perpetual Potential: Latinos in the 1992 California Elections." In *Ethnic Ironies: Latino Politics in the 1992 Elections*, edited by Rodolfo O. de la Garza and Louis DeSipio. Boulder, CO: Westview Press, 1996.

Guerra, Fernando J. "The Emergence of Ethnic Officeholders in California." In *Racial and Ethnic California*, edited by Bryan O. Jackson and Michael B. Preston, 117–31. Berkeley, CA: Institute of Governmental Studies Press, 1991.

Guinier, Lani. *The Tyranny of the Majority: Fundamental Fairness in Representative Democracy*. New York: Free Press, 1994.

Gunnison, Robert B. "Patchwork Power." *San Francisco Chronicle*, February 23, 1991, A14.

Haddock, Vicky. "Politics and Race." *San Francisco Chronicle*, September 28, 2003, D3.

Hager, Philipp. "Court Urged to OK Vote on Redistricting." *Los Angeles Times*, July 26, 1983, A3.

———. "Democrats Ask State Supreme Court to Stop Redistricting Vote." *Los Angeles Times*, July 20, 1983, A3.

———. "GOP-Backed Group Begins Drive to Unseat Justices Named by Brown." *Los Angeles Times*, October 11, 1982, C8.

———. "How Panel Redrew Political Maps." *Los Angeles Times*, December 8, 1991, VYA3.

———. "Redistricting Row in High Court Lap: Panel's Decision Could Affect Control of State Legislature for Years to Come." *Los Angeles Times*, August 28, 1983, A3.

Hager, Philipp, and Daniel M. Weintraub. "Redistricting Task Goes to State Justices." *Los Angeles Times*, September 26, 1991, A3.

Hajnal, Zoltan, and Mark Baldassare. *Finding Common Ground: Racial and Ethnic Attitudes in California*. Berkeley: Public Policy Institute of California, 2001.

Halberstam, Michael. "Process Failure and Transparency Reform in Local Redistricting." *Election Law Journal* 11, no. 4 (2012): 446–71.

Hall Barlow, Kimberly, and Marguerite Mary Leoni. "The California Voting Rights Act—An Update." League of California Cities Annual Conference, September 4, 2014.

Hallett, Joe. "Much Needed Redistricting Reform Isn't in the Cards for Ohio." *The Columbus Dispatch*, November 13, 2005, 5B.

———. "Schwarzenegger Wants Ohio Issue 4 to Pass." *The Columbus Dispatch*, November 6, 2005, 4A.

Handley, Lisa, and Bernard Grofman. "The Impact of the Voting Rights Act on Minority Representation: Black Officeholders in Southern State Legislatures and Congressional Delegations." In *Quite Revolution in the South*, edited by Chandler Davidson and Bernard Grofman, 335–50. Princeton, NJ: Princeton University Press, 1994.

Hanh, Kim, and Dena Bunis. "All Bow to Redistrict Architect Politics Secretive, Single-Minded Michael Berman Holds All the Crucial Cards." *Orange County Register*, January 21, 2001, 1.

Hardy, Leroy, and Charles P. Sohner. "Constitutional Challenge and Political Response: California Reapportionment, 1965." *The Western Political Quarterly* 23, no. 4 (December 1970): 733–51.

Hardy, Leroy C. "Congressional Redistricting in California, 1965–1967: The Quilting Bee and Crazy Quilts." *San Diego Law Review* 10 (June 1973): 757–92.

———. "Considering the Gerrymander." *Pepperdine Law Review* 4, no. 2 (1977): 243–84.

———. *Golden Betrayal: The Erosion of Representation and the Loss of Legitimacy in California*. Rose Institute of State and Local Government, 1993.

Hasen, Richard L. "Racial Gerrymandering's Questionable Revival." *Alabama Law Review* 67 (2016): 365–85.

———. "Race or Party: How Courts Should Think about Republican Efforts to Make It Harder to Vote in North Carolina and Elsewhere." *Harvard Law Review Forum* 127 (2014): 58–75

———. "Race or Party, Race as Party, or Party All the Time: Three Uneasy Approaches to Conjoined Polarization in Redistricting and Voting Cases." *William and Mary Law Review* 59, no. 5(2018): 1837.

———. "Shelby County and the Illusion of Minimalism." *William and Mary Bill of Rights Journal* 22, no. 3 (2014): 713–45.

———. *The Supreme Court and Election Law: Judging Equality from Baker v. Carr to Bush v. Gore*. New York: New York University Press, 2003.

Hayes, Danny, and Seth C. McKee. "The Intersection of Redistricting, Race, and Participation." *American Journal of Political Science* 56, no. 1 (January 2012): 115–30.

———. "The Participatory Effects of Redistricting." *American Journal of Political Science* 53, no. 4, (October 2009): 1006–1023.

Hill, Kevin A. "Does the Creation of Majority Black Districts Aid Republicans? An Analysis of the 1992 Congressional Elections in Eight Southern States." *Journal of Politics* 57, no. 2 (1995): 384–401.

Hill-Holzman, Nancy, and Jean O. Pasco. "California and the West: Doris Allen First Female Speaker of Assembly, Dies." *Los Angeles Times*, September 23, 1999, http://articles.latimes.com/1999/sep/23/news/mn-13311.

Hodson, Tim. "Disappearing Constraints: Voting Rights and Gerrymandering in 1991 and 2001." *Politics and Policy: A Journal of the Pat Brown Institute of Public Affairs* (Fall 1998).

———. "Is a Sacramento Mega-Deal in the Air?" *San Francisco Chronicle*, June 24, 2005, B9.

Hoeffel, John, and Rong-Gong Lin. "Taking a Risky Stand on Plans for Latino District." *Los Angeles Times*, September 15, 2011, A1.

Holland, Gale. "Pro187's Effects Ripple across Calif." *USA Today*, November 21, 1994, 2A.

Hollinger, David. *Postethnic America: Beyond Multiculturalism*. New York: Basic Books, 1995.

Hubler, Shawn. "Low Count of Minorities Not Justified, Court Says." *Los Angeles Times*, August 10, 1994, A1.

Hulse, Carl. "Colorado Court Rejects Redistricting Plan." *New York Times*, December 2, 2003, A26.

Hume, Ellen. "'Godfather of California Politics' May Be Mortal." *Los Angeles Times*, May 3, 1982, B1.

———. "Phil Burton Is Key Redistricting Figure." *Los Angeles Times*, July 23, 1981, A3.

Ingram, Carl. "Activists Upset by Central Coast Remap." *Los Angeles Times*, September 9, 2001, B6.

———. "Democrats Have Luck of Draw in Redistricting." *Los Angeles Times,* August 19, 2001, B7.

———. "LA Area Gets State's New Congressional Seat." *Los Angeles Times*, September 1, 2001, A1.

———. "Latinos, GOP Gain in Remap Plan." *San Francisco Examiner*, December 3 1991, 10F3.

———. "Plan to Redraw Districts Passes." *Los Angeles Times*, September 14, 2001, B8.

———. "Redistricting Plan Unveiled by Assembly." *Los Angeles Times*, August 30, 2001, B9.

———. "Remap to Uproot Politicians." *San Francisco Examiner*, December 17, 1991, A6.

———. "Revised Districts Hinder Minorities, Critics Say." *Los Angeles Times*, September 6, 2001, B8.

———. "State Redistricting Bill Passes Senate." *Los Angeles Times*, September 13, 2001, B6.

Impact 2000. Dotti Mavramattis (executive director), Peter Cari (Targeting/Analysis), Gerry Hebert (Legal Counsel), Mark Gersh (NCEC).

Issacharoff, Samuel. "Supreme Court Destabilization of Single-Member Districts." *University of Chicago Legal Forum* 1(1995): 205–39.

Jacobs, John. *A Rage for Justice: The Passions and Politics of Philip Burton*. Los Angeles: University of California Press, 1995, [1997].

Jacobson, Gary C. "All Quiet on the Western Front: Redistricting and Party Competition in California House Elections." In *Redistricting in the New Millennium*, edited by Peter F. Galderisi. Lanham: MD: Lexington Books, 2005.

———. "Competition in US Congressional Elections." In *The Marketplace of Democracy: Electoral Competition and American Politics*, edited by Michael McDonald and John Samples, 27–52. Washington, DC: Brookings Institution Press, 2006.

———. "Partisan and Ideological Polarization in the California Electorate." *State Politics and Policy Quarterly*4, no. 2 (Summer 2004): 113–39.

James R. Mills. *A Disorderly House: The Brown-Unruh Years in Sacramento*. Berkeley, CA: HeyDay Books, 1987.

Jarvis, Matthew G. "Redistricting Reform Could Save California from Itself." *California Journal of Politics and Policy* 1, no. 1 (2009).

Jennings Angel and Sewell Abby. "Aja Brown Elected Compton's Mayor." *Los Angeles Times*, June 6, 2013, AA1.

Jewell, Malcolm E. "The Consequences of Single and Multi-Member Districts." In *Representation and Redistricting Issues*, edited by Bernard Grofman, Arend Lijphart, Robert B. McKay and Howard A. Scarrow. Lanham, MD: Lexington Books, 1982.

Johnson, Douglas, Elise Lampe, Justin Lewitt, and Andrew Lee. "Restoring the Competitive Edge." The Rose Institute of State and Local Government, Claremont McKenna College, September 26, 2005.

Johnson, Kevin R. "An Essay on Immigration Politics, Popular Democracy, and California's Proposition 187: The Political Relevance and Legal Irrelevance of Race." *Washington Law Review* 70 (1995): 629–75.

Kang, Michael S. "Race and Democratic Contestation." *Yale Law Journal* 117, no. 5 (2008): 778–84, 787.

Karlan, Pamela. "The Fire Next Times: Reapportionment after the 2000 Census." *Stanford Law Review* 50, no. 3 (February 1998): 731–63.

Karlan, Pamela. "The Reconstruction of Voting Rights." In *Race, Reform, and Regulation of the Electoral Process*, edited by Guy-Uriel E. Charles, Heather K. Gerken, and Michael S. Kang, 34–51. New York: Cambridge University Press, 2011.

Karlan, Pamela S., and Daryl J. Levinson. "Why Voting Is Different." *California Law Review* 84, no. 4 (1996), 1201–32.

Katz, Ellen D. "Democrats at DOJ: Why Partisan Use of the Voting Rights Act Might Not Be So Bad After All." *Stanford Law and Policy Review* 23, no. 2 (2012): 415–30.

Kendall, John. "Yorty Kills Council Redistricting Plan." *Los Angeles Times*, September 16, 1972, 1.

Keppel, Bruce. "Voters Can Overhaul County's Government." *Los Angeles Times*, October 4, 1976, C1.

———. "$6.5 million for Props A, B Seen." *Los Angeles Times*, October 29, 1976, B30.

———. "County Mayor Plan Defeated." *Los Angeles Times*, November 4, 1976, 2.

Kershner, Vlae. "Court's Panel Reveals Its Plan for Redistricting. Republicans Expected to Gain Seats." *San Francisco Chronicle*, December 3, 1991, A1.

———. "Legislature Sends Wilson 3 Remap Plans. He Promises 3 Vetoes." *San Francisco Chronicle*, September 20, 1991, A1.

———. "Wilson Keeping Secret His Panel's Remap Plan. He Won't Reveal It until Issue Goes to Court." *San Francisco Chronicle*, September 25, 1991, A1.

Kertzer, David I., and Dominique Arel, eds. *Census and Identity: The Politics of Race, Ethnicity, and Language in National Censuses*. New York: Cambridge University Press, 2002.

Kimball, Brace, Bernard Grofman, and Lisa Handley. "Does Redistricting Aimed to Help Blacks Necessarily Help Republicans?" *Journal of Politics* 49, no. 1(1987): 169–85.

King, Wayne. "California GOP Plans Fight to Balk Redistricting: Petitions Due in a Week." *New York Times*, September 17, 1981, A17.

Klemanski, John S., David A. Dulio, and Michael Switalski. *Campaigns form the Ground Up: State Elections in a National Context*. New York: Routledge, 2015.

Kogan, Vladimir, and Eric McGhee. "Redistricting California: An Evaluation of the Citizens Redistricting Commission Final Plans." *Journal of California Politics and Policy* 4, no. 1 (2012).

Kousser, Morgan J. *Colorblind Injustice: Minority Voting Rights and the Undoing of the Second Reconstruction*. Chapel Hill: North Carolina Press, 1999.

———. Declaration of Expert Witness Kousser Morgan, *Cano v. Davis*, May 13, 2002.

———. "Do the Facts of Voting Right Support Justice Roberts's Opinion in Shelby County?" *Transatlantica*, 1(2015), https://transatlantica.revues.org/7462.

———. "Has California Gone Color Blind?" In *The New Political Geography of California*, edited by Frederick Douzet, Thad Kousser, and Kenneth Miller. Berkeley, CA: Berkeley Public Policy Press, 2008.

———. "How to Determine Intent: Lessons from LA." *Journal of Law and Politics* 7 (1991): 591–732.

———. "Racial Polarization in Compton Elections, 1994–2011, A Report for *Gonzalez v. City of Compton*."

———. "Redistricting: California 1971–2001." In *Governing California: Politics, Government, and Public Policy in the Golden State*, edited by Gerald C. Lubenow and Bruce E. Cain. Berkeley, CA: Institute of Governmental Studies, 1997.

———. "Redistricting Wars: Party, Race and Redistricting in California 1971–1992." In *Race and Redistricting in the 1990s*, edited by Bernard Grofman, 134–190. New York: Agathon Press, 1998.

Kousser, Thad. "The Top-Two, Take-Two: Did Changing the Rules Change the Game in Statewide Contests?" *The Journal of California Politics and Policy* 7, no. 1 (2015).

———. *Term Limits and the Dismantling of State Legislative Professionalism*. New York: Cambridge University Press, 2005.

Laguardia, Alan. "Ballot Watch: A Weekly Update on Proposed State Ballot Measures for a Special Election." *Sacramento Bee*, October 29, 2005, A3.

Landsberg, Mitchell. "Making Sure Minorities' Vote Counts." *Los Angeles Times*, January 4, 2009, B1.

Lauther, Claudia, and Jerry Gillam. "GOP Bloc Threatens to Delay Bills in Rift over Redistricting." *Los Angeles Times*, August 25, 1981, A 3.

Leadership California Institute, California Latino Legislative Caucus, National Association of Latino Elected and Appointed Officials (NALEO), The Status of Latinos in California: An analysis of the growing Latino population, voting trends and elected representation, (2015), http://leadershipcaliforniainstitute.org/sites/all/files/Status%20of%20Latinos%20Report%20Preview.pdf.

Lee, Eugene C. *The Politics of Nonpartisan Elections in California Cities*. Los Angeles: University of California Press, 1957.

Lembke, Dary E. "Supreme Court Issues Orders." *Los Angeles Times*, July 15, 1965, 3.

Liebert, Larry. "Doolittle in Washington." *California Journal* 22, no. 6 (July 1, 1991).

Lijphart, Arend. "Introduction to Part II." In *Representation and Redistricting Issues*, edited by Bernard Grofman, Arend Lijphart, Robert B. McKay and Howard A. Scarrow, 105. Lanham, MD: Lexington Books, 1982.

Lillis, Mike. "Deep in Minority, Dems Look for Redistricting for Hope." *The Hill*, August 29, 2015, http://thehill.com/homenews/house/252226-deep-in-minority-dems-look-to-redistricting-for-hope.

Lin, Rong-Gong. "Bid for More Latinos on Board Sets Up Fight." *Los Angeles Times*, August 6, 2011, A1.

Lindsey, Robert. "California Ballot Questions Dim Presidential Race." *New York Times*, October 8, 1984, B8.

———. "California Breaks Budget Deadlock as Redistricting Fight Shapes Up." *New York Times*, July 20, 1983, A20.

———. "Bradley Loses Close Contest on Coast." *New York Times*, November 4, 1982, A22.

Liptak, Adam. "*Bush v. Gore* Outlives Its Limited Warranty for Use in California." *New York Times*, September 16, 2003, A21.

Los Angeles Times. "Assembly Warned about Full Reapportionment." *Los Angeles Times*, May 4, 1965, 3.

———. "Bill Proposes Nonpartisan Redistricting." *Los Angeles Times*, August 14, 1973, 14.

———. "Congress Races: Burgener, Ketchum Get GOP Bids; Brown Edges Ayala." *Los Angeles Times*, June 8, 1972, A24.

———. "Congressional Redistricting." *Los Angeles Times*, October 10, 1967, A4.

———. "County Gains 2 Votes in Reapportionment: Congressional Incumbents Seen Helped by Registration Gains Under Redistricting." *Los Angeles Times*, December 7, 1967, OC1.

———. "Justice Denies GOP Plea on Redistricting." *Los Angeles Times*, March 11, 1982, A1.

———. "Latin Group to Push Redistricting Plan." *Los Angeles Times*, May 17, 1965, 3.

———. "Major Redistricting Losers: LA and S.F." *Los Angeles Times*, February 24, 1971, D4.

———. "Office Holders Satisfied with Redistricting: Boundary Changes Bring New Representatives into Area, Other Major Shifts." *Los Angeles Times*, December 16, 1973, CS1.

———. "Old Words Have Bearing on New Issue." *Los Angeles Times*, March 7, 1965, K6.

———. "Outrageous Back-Room Deal." *Los Angeles Times*, June 29, 1990, SDB6.

———. "Politicians Preparing for Redistricting Fight: GOP Fears Being 'Gerrymandered' Out of House Control; Extra Seats at Stake." *Los Angeles Times*, November 27, 1970, K5.

———. “Profile of the City Electorate.” *Los Angeles Times*, April 10, 1997, A27.

———. “Putting Chicanos on the Political Map.” *Los Angeles Times*, May 21, 1972, H1.

———. “State High Court Sets Up Redistricting Rules: But Decision Gives Legislature Third Chance to Do Job.” *Los Angeles Times*, March 24, 1973, C1.

———. “The Money Behind Proposition 13.” *Los Angeles Times*, October 22, 1948, A4.

———. “Wanted: A Better Reapportionment Plan.” *Los Angeles Times*, September 19, 1972, B6.

———. “Why the Bosses Favor Proposition 13.” *Los Angeles Times*, September 30, 1948, A4.

———. “Words and Dollars for Baxter Wards.” *Los Angeles Times*, June 27, 1980, C6.

Love, Keith. “Sebastiani Sets Political Bomb Ticking.” *Los Angeles Times*, July 10, 1983, 1.

Lowell, Frederick, and Teresa A. Craigie. “California’s Reapportionment Struggle: A Classic Clash Between Law and Politics.” *Journal of Law and Politics* 2 (1985): 245–62.

Lowenstein, Daniel H., and Jonathan Steinberg. “The Quest for Legislative Districting in the Public Interest: Elusive or Illusory?” *UCLA Law Review* 33, no. 1(1985): 12–35.

Lowenstein, Daniel Hays. “Brief of Petitioner Edmund G. Brown Jr.” In *Legislature v. Reinecke*, 6 Cal. 3d 595 (1972), Vol. II, Exhibit E, IGS Library, University of California Berkeley, 1972.

———. “The Message That Voters Sent in Rejecting Propositions 118 and 119.” *Los Angeles Times*, June 17, 1990, M5.

———. “You Don’t Have to Be a Liberal to Hate Racial Gerrymandering.” *Stanford Law Review* 50, no. 3 (February 1998): 779–835.

Lublin, David, and Michael McDonald. “Is It Time to Draw the Line?: The Impact of Redistricting on Competition in State House Elections.” *Election Law Journal* 5, no. 2, (2006): 144–57.

Lublin, David, and D. Stephen Voss. “Racial Redistricting and Realignment in Southern State Legislatures.” *American Journal of Political Science* 44, no. 4 (2000): 792–810.

Lublin, David. “The Election of African-Americans and Latinos to the US House of Representatives 1972–1994.” *American Politics Quarterly* 25, no. 3 (July 1997): 269–86.

———. *The Paradox of Representation: Racial Gerrymandering and Minority Interests in Congress*. Princeton, NJ: Princeton University Press, 1997.

Lucas, Greg. “Jackson in Redistricting Fight. He Says That Propositions 118 and 119 Would Hurt Minorities.” *San Francisco Chronicle*, May 22, 1990, A7.

———. “Voting Rights Act: A Free Generator for Lawyers?” *Calweekly*, May 5, 2011, http://capitolweekly.net/voting-rights-act-a-fee-generator-for-lawyers/

Luther, Claudia, and Richard Bergholz. “Campaign Launched for Remap Initiative.” *Los Angeles Times*, February 3, 1982, A3.

———. "Civil Rights Panel Opposes Redistricting Commission." *Los Angeles Times*, October 15, 1982, B11.

Luther, Claudia, and Jerry Gillam. "Democrats Could Gain Congress Seats in Redistricting Plan." *Los Angeles Times*, September 10, 1981, B3.

Luther, Claudia, and Ronald J. Ostrow. "Redistricting Clears US Legal Hurdle." *Los Angeles Times*, December 2, 1981, B3.

Luther, Claudia. "Hispanics Demand a Slice of the Redistricting Pie." *Los Angeles Times*, March 7, 1981, A5.

———. "Initiative to Create Redistricting Commission Qualifies for Ballot." *Los Angeles Times*, June 22, 1982, B3.

———. "New Redistricting Initiative Submitted: Would Strip the Legislature of Its Role, Create Commission." *Los Angeles Times*, December 17, 1981, B3.

Lyndsey, Robert. "California Becomes Melting Pot of 1980s." *New York Times*, August 23, 1981, 1.

Mai-Duc, Christine. "Legislative Races to Watch." *Los Angeles Times*, June 6, 2016, B4.

MALDEF, NAACPLDF, NAPALC. *The Impact of Redistricting in Your Community: A Guide to Redistricting.*

Mann, Thomas. "Redistricting Reform: What Is Desirable? Possible?" In *Party Line: Competition, Partisanship and Congressional Redistricting*, edited by Thomas Mann and Bruce Cain. Washington DC: Brookings Institution Press, 2005.

Marshall Manheim, Lisa. "Redistricting Litigation and the Delegation of Democratic Design." *Boston University Law Review* 93, no. 2 (March 2013): 563–620.

Martin, Mark. "Politics Intensify Budget Troubles. Redrawn Districts, Term Limits Decrease Compromise Incentive." *San Francisco Chronicle*, July 6, 2003, A1.

Matthews, Jon, and Llana DeBare. "GOP Could Seize Legislature." *Sacramento Bee*, December 4, 1991, A16.

Matthews, Jon. "Panel Remaps Puts Incumbents at Risk." *Sacramento Bee*, December 3,, 1991, A1.

Mayhew, David R. "Congressional Representation: Theory and Practice in Drawing the Districts." In *Reapportionment in the 1970s*, edited by Polsby, Nelson W. Berkeley: University of California Press, 1971.

McCarty, Nolan, Keith T. Poole, and Howard Rosenthal. *Polarized America: The Dance of Ideology and Unequal Riches*. Cambridge, MA: MIT Press, 2006.

McCool, Daniel, ed. *The Most Fundamental Right: Contrasting Perspectives on the Voting Rights Act*. Bloomington: Indiana Press University, 2012.

Mac Donald, Karin. "Adventures in Redistricting: A Look at the California Redistricting Commission." *Election Law Journal* 11, no.4 (2012): 472–89.

Mac Donald, Karin, and Bruce Cain. "Community of Interest Methodology and Public Testimony." *U.C. Irvine Law Review* 3, no. 3 (2013): 609–36.

McDonald, Michael. "Redistricting and Competitive Districts." In *The Marketplace of Democracy: Electoral Competition and American Politics*, edited by McDonald and Samples, 222–44. Washington, DC: Brookings Institution Press, 2006.

McGann, Anthony J., Charles Anthony Smith, Michael Latner, and Alex Keena. *Gerrymandering in America: The House of Representatives, the Supreme Court and the Future of Popular Sovereignty*. New York: Cambridge University Press, 2016.

McGee, Eric, and Jack Citrin. "Introduction: Democracy, California Style." *Journal of California Politics and Policy* 9, no. 2 (2017).

McGhee, Eric, and Daniel Krimm. California's New Electoral Reforms: The Fall Election. Public Policy Institute of California, 2012, http://www.ppic.org/main/publication_show.asp?i=1039

McGhee, Eric. Redistricting and Legislative Partisanship. Public Policy Institute, 2008, http://web.ppic.org/content/pubs/report/R_908EMR.pdf

———. Redistricting and Legislative Leadership, Public Policy Institute of California, 2008.

McGreevy, Patrick, and Melanie Mason. "A Time of Give and Take?" *Los Angeles Times*, December 1, 2014, P AA1.

———. "Gains in Legislature Not So Easy for Democrats." *Los Angeles Times*, June 5, 2014, AA4.

———. "GOP Has Early Lead in Key Legislature Races." *Los Angeles Times*, November 5, 2014, A9.

McGreevy, Patrick, and Richard Simon. "New Voting Maps Face Challenges." *Los Angeles Times*, August 15, 2011, AA1.

McGreevy, Patrick. "Brown OKs Redistricting Commission." *Los Angeles Times*, October 1, 2016, B3.

———. "Lawmakers Reject Measure Expanding County Boards of Supervisors." *Los Angeles Times*, September 10, 2015. http://www.latimes.com/local/political/la-me-pc-lawmakers-reject-supervisors-expansion-20150910-story.html.

———. "Secretary of State Debra Bowen Tells Her Struggle with Depression." *Los Angeles Times*, September 5, 2014, A1.

McKee, Seth, ed. *Jigsaw Puzzle Politics in the Sunshine State*. Gainesville: University of Florida Press, 2015.

McKenna, Kathleen Z. "Governor Supports Remapping." *Oakland Tribune*, December 4, 1991, A1.

McWilliams, Carey. *California: The Great Exception*. Santa Barbara, CA: Peregrine Smith and Co., 1976.

Mecoy, Lara. "Charges Mount in Remap Lawsuit." *Sacramento Bee*, October 31, 2001, http://archive.fairvote.org/redistricting/reports/remanual/canews6.htm#charges.

———. "House Remap Plan Boosts GOP." *Sacramento Bee*, December 4, 1991, A1.

Medsger, Betty. *Framed: The New Right Attack on Chief Justice Rose Bird and the Courts*. New York: Pilgrim Press, 1983.

Meheta, Seema. "California's Redistricting Panel Can't Escape Political Pressure." *Los Angeles Times*, March 19, 2011, AA3.

———. "Census Augurs Inland Power Shift." *Los Angeles Times*, March 9, 2011, A1.

Mendel, Ed. "Group Seeks Pro187-like Ballot Measure." *San Diego Union-Tribune*, December 3, 2003, A6.

Mendoza, Henry. "Speaker Brown's Views about Redistricting Hit." *Los Angeles Times*, May 5, 1981, B3.

Mercurio, John, and Ethan Wallison. "No Gold Rush in California: Democrats May Look for Gains Elsewhere." *Roll Call* (DC), September 10, 2001.

Mercurio, John. "Horn Retires after Losing District; Incumbents Protected by Redistricting Map." *Roll Call* (DC), September 6, 2001.

Merina, Victor. "Burke Aide Calls Dana's Busing Charge Racist." *Los Angeles Times*, September 13, 1980, D14.

———. "Burke Dana Clash on Busing in Final Debate." *Los Angeles Times*, October 29, 1980, D1.

———. "Racism Issue Marks Burke, Dana Contest." *Los Angeles Times*, October 31, 1979, D1.

———. "Yvonne Burke—No Opposition in Sight." *Los Angeles Times*, December 9, 1979, B1.

Merl, Jean. "Berman Loses His First Election—and His Seat." *Los Angeles Times*, November 8, 2012, AA9.

———. "Minority Districts on Dividing lines." *Los Angeles Times*, July 25, 2011, AA1.

———. "Officials in City Agree to District Voting." *Los Angeles Times*, May 7, 2015, B1.

Merl, Jean, and Patrick McGreevy. "Democrats Gain Big in the Legislature." *Los Angeles Times*, November 7, 2012, A1.

Mexican American Legal Defense Fund. *Proposed Legislative Districts United States Congress, Senate, State Assembly*. Submitted on September 4, 2001.

Miller, Alan C. "Parties Dig in for Redistricting War." *Los Angeles Times*, September 3, 1990, OCA3.

Mitchell, Alison. "Redistricting 2002 Produces No Great Shake-Ups." *New York Times*, May 13, 2002, A20.

Moncrief, Gary F. *Reapportionment and Redistricting in the West*. Lanham, MD: Lexington Books, 2011.

Morain, Dan, and Mark Z. Barabak. "Davis Sharpens Attack on Bush Energy Plan." *Los Angeles Times*, May 19, 2001, A1.

Morrison, Pat. "Congress Races Being Run on Road Full of Potholes." *Los Angeles Times*, October 13, 1992, A1.

Muir, Frederick M. "It's a New Race for Supervisors after Judge OKs Changes in 1st District." *Los Angeles Times*, August 4, 1990, SDA30.

Murphy, Dean E. "Who Should Draw the Lines." *New York Times*, October 23, 2005, http://www.nytimes.com/2005/10/23/magazine/who-should-redistrict.html.

Murphy, Dennis L. "*Garza v. County of Los Angeles*: The Dilemma over Using Elector Population as Opposed to Total Population in Legislative Apportionment." *Case Western Reserve Law Review* 41, no. 3 (1991): 1013–28.

Myers, John. "Democrats Wait to Reclaim Supermajority in Legislature." *Los Angeles Times*, November 10, 2016, B9.

Nagel, Stuart S. "Simplified Bipartisan Computer Redistricting." *Stanford Law Review* 17, no. 5 (1965): 863–99.

National Institute on Money in State Politics, PROPOSITION 011: Changes Authority for Establishing Assembly, Senate and Board of Equalization District Boundaries From Elected Representatives to 14 Member Commission. Follow the money.org, https://www.followthemoney.org/entity-details?eid=10246632.

———. Proposition 77. Followthemoney.org, http://www.followthemoney.org/entity-details?eid=10246412.

Navarro, Armando, and Emilio Lazarin. *The People of California: An Atlas of Latino Communities*. The Rose Institute of State and Local Government, 1990.

Navarro, Carlos. "A Report on California Redistricting and Representation for the Los Angeles Chicano Community." In *The Chicano Community and California Redistricting*, vol. 1, edited by Richard Santillan, Claremont, CA: The Rose Institute of State and Local Government, 1981.

Navarro, Carlos, and Richard Santillan. "The Latino Community and California Redistricting in the 1980s: Californios For Fair Representation." In *The Hispanic Community and Redistricting*, vol. 2, edited by Richard Santillan. Claremont, CA: The Rose Institute, 1984.

Nelson, Joe. "Former Claremont McKenna Official Pleads Guilty to Bribery Case." *San Gabriel Valley Tribune*, April 8, 2014, https://www.sgvtribune.com/2014/04/08/former-claremont-mckenna-official-pleads-guilty-in-bribery-case/.

Nicholas, Peter. "GOP Fears a Redistricting Backfire." *Los Angeles Times*, February 8, 2005, A1.

Nicholas, Peter. "Gov. to Call for Special Session; Legislature Will Be Asked to Consider New Ways to Rein in Spending and Draw Political Districts." *Los Angeles Times*, January 1, 2005, A1.

Nkanishi, Don T., and James Lai, eds. *National Asian Pacific Political Almanac*, 15th ed. (2014–2015). UCLA Asian American Studies Center Press, 2014.

O'Hare, William, ed. *Redistricting in the 1990s: A Guide to Minority Groups*. Population Reference Bureau, July 1989.

Ohio Secretary of State, State Issue 4: Amended Certified Ballot Language, http://www.sos.state.oh.us/sos/elections/Research/electResultsMain/2005ElectionsResults/05-1108Issue4/State%20Issue%204%20Amended%20Certified%20Ballot%20Language.aspx.

Ong, Paul M., and Doug Houston. "The 2000 Census Undercount in Los Angeles County." Working Paper #42, December 2002, http://164.67.121.27/files/Lewis_Center/Publications/LACensusUndercount.pdf.

Owens, John R., Edmond Costantini, and Louis F. Weschler, *California Politics and Parties*. New York: Collier-Macmillan, 1970.

Paddock, Richard. "Big Population Gains Drive Legislators in Redistricting State." *Los Angeles Times*, March 25, 1991, OCA3.

Paddock, Richard, and Mark Gladstone. "GOP Leader Nolan, Target in FBI Capitol Sting, Urged Colleagues to Keep Silent." *Los Angeles Times*, August 28, 1988, A3.

Panzar, Javier. "Ballot for Parts of LA County has GOP 'Dead Zone.'" *Los Angeles Times*, October 27, 2016, A1.

Payne, Gregory, J., and Scott Ratzan. *Tom Bradley: The Impossible Dream*. Santa Monica, CA: Roundtable, 1986.

Perlman, Jeffrey. "A Redistricting Plan GOP Can Love, Democrats Hate." *Los Angeles Times*, May 6, 1981, OC_A1.

———. "State Redistricting Taking Shape: Tentative New Districts Protect Incumbents, anger GOP." *Los Angeles Times*, August 22, 1981, OC_A1.

Persily, Nathaniel. "The Law of the Census: How to Count, What to Count, Whom to Count, and Where to Count Them." *Cardozo Law Review* 32, no. 3 (2011): 755–91.

———. "The Promises and Pitfalls of the New VRA." *Yale Law Journal* 117, no. 2 (2007): 174–253.

———. "When Judges Carve Democracies: A Primer on Court-Drawn Redistricting Plans." *George Washington Law Review* 73, no. 5 & 6 (2005): 1131–65.

———, ed. *The Real Y2K Problem: Census 2000 Data and Redistricting Technology*. New York: The Brennan Center for Justice, New York University School of Law, 2000.

Persily Nathaniel, and Melissa Cully Anderson. "Regulating Democracy through Democracy: The Use of Direct Legislation in Election Law Reform." *Southern California Law Review* 78, no. 4 (2005): 997–1034.

Pildes, Richard. "The Constitution and Political Competition." *Nova Law Review* 30 (2006): 269–94.

Pildes, Richard H. "Voting Rights the Next Generation." In *Reform and Regulation of the Electoral Process*, edited by Guy-Uriel E. Charles, Heather Gerken, and Michael Kang, 17–33. New York: Cambridge University Press.

Pildes, Richard H., and Richard G. Niemi. "Expressive Harms. "'Bizarre Districts,' and Voting Rights: Evaluating Election-District Appearances After *Shaw v. Reno*." *Michigan Law Review* 92, no. 2 (1993): 483–587.

Plendl, Lisa. "Are Voters Dissed by Redistricting?" *California Journal* 33, no. 1 (2002): 12–37.

Polsby, Daniel D., and Robert D. Popper. "Ugly: An Inquiry into the Problem of Racial Gerrymandering under the Voting Rights Act." *Michigan Law Review* 92, no. 3 (1993): 652–82.

Post, Robert. "Affirmative Action and Higher Education: The View from Somewhere." *Yale Law and Policy Review* 23, no. 25 (2005): 25–32.

Prewitt, Kenneth. "The Census Counts, the Census Classifies." In *Not Just Black and White: Historical and Contemporary Perspectives on Immigration, Race and Ethnicity in the United States*, edited by Nancy Foner and George M. Frederickson, 145–64. New York: Russell Sage, 2004.

Puente, Maria, and Gale Holland. "'Deep Vein' of Anger in California / Pro187 Reinforcing Divisions." *USA Today*, November 11, 1994, 8A.

Putnam, Jackson, K. *Jess: The Political Career of Jesse Marvin Unruh*. Lanham, MD: University Press of America, 2005.

Quach Hanh, Kim, and Dena Bunis. "All Bow to Redistrict Architect Politics Secretive, Single-Minded Michael Berman Holds All the Crucial Cards." *Orange County Register*, January 21, 2001, 1.

Quinn, Anthony. *Carving up California: A History of Redistricting 1951–1983*. PhD dissertation, Rose Institute of State and Local Government, Claremont, CA, n.d.

———. "Excluding the Public: Redistricting Commission Goes Dark." *Fox and Hounds*, July 11, 2011; http://www.foxandhoundsdaily.com/2011/07/9186-excluding-the-public-the-redistricting-commission-goes-dark/.

———. "Judging the Redistricting Commission." *The California Journal of State Politics and Policy* 3, no. 3 (2011).

———. "Leave Redistricting to These Judges?Absurd!." *Sacramento Bee*, March 13, 2005, E5.

———. "Opinion: Redistricting Commission showing Political Bias." *Mercury News*, April 5, 2011, http://www.mercurynews.com/2011/04/05/opinion-redistricting-commission-showing-political-bias/.

Rabin, Jeffrey. "Funds Flow for Knabe, Trickle in for Swanson." *Los Angeles Times*, October 13, 1996, http://articles.latimes.com/1996-10-13/local/me-53566_1_don-knabe.

Rainey, James. "Judge's Ruling on Remap Puts 1st District Race for Supervisor in Limbo." *Los Angeles Times*, July 1, 1990, SE_AJ5.

Rasky, Susan F. "Redistricting Defanged by Energy Crisis." *Los Angeles Times,* April 22, 2001, M1.

Regalado, James. "Conflicts over Redistricting in Los Angeles County: Who Wins, Who Loses." In *Racial and Ethnic Politics in California*, vol. 2, edited by Michael B. Preston, Bruce E. Cain, and Bass, Sandra Bass. Berkley, CA: Institute of Governmental Studies Press, 1998.

Reich, Kenneth. "Latino Group Sues over Redistricting." *Los Angeles Times*, October 2, 2001, B1.

———. "Yvonne Burk's Success Story: A Long Record of Being First." *Los Angeles Times*, June 15, 1979, B3.

Report and Recommendations of the Special Masters on Reapportionment to the Supreme Court of California, No S0228355, 1992.

Report of the Economy and Efficiency Commission, December 1974, http://eec.lacounty.gov/Portals/EEC/Reports/48_7412RepEEC.pdf.

Reynolds, Andrew. "Reserved Seats in National Legislatures: A Comparative Approach" In *Redistricting in Comparative Perspective*, edited Lisa Handley and Bernard Grofman, 115–22. New York: Oxford University Press, 2008.

Riccardi, Nicholas. "New Supervisorial Districts Just Like the Old." *Los Angeles Times*, June 27, 2001, BA.

Richard, Simon, and Merl Jean. "ReHorn to Retire." *Los Angeles Times*, September 5, 2001, B3.

Richardson, James. *Willie Brown: A Biography*. Berkeley: University of California Press, 1996.

Richardson, Lisa. "Foes Say Governor Targets Minorities. Schwarzenegger's Ballot Measure Would Weaken the Power of Blacks and Latinos, Critics Contend." *Los Angeles Times*, October 27, 2005, B8.

Robinson, Bert, and Robitaille, Stephen. "Minorities May Not Gain Quickly from Newly Drawn District Lines." *San Jose Mercury News*, December 8, 1991, 1A.

Rohrlich, Ted. "Coalition Attempts to Boost Latino Election Wins." *Los Angeles Times*, December 24, 1998, B1.

———. "Latino Voting in State Surged in 1996 Elections." *Los Angeles Times*, December 31, 1997, http://articles.latimes.com/1997/dec/31/news/mn-3813.

Rojas, Aurelio. "Federal Judge Rules AgainstPro187. State Cannot Regulate Immigration." *San Francisco Chronicle*, March 19, 1998, A17.

Rood, W. B. "Brown Approves Nov. 6 Vote on Busing, Spending." *Los Angeles Times*, July 3, 1979, B1.

Rosenbaum, Mark. "Drawing Fair Redistricting Lines." *Los Angeles Times*, September 27, 2011, http://articles.latimes.com/2011/sep/27/opinion/la-oe-rosenbaum-county-supervisors-redistricting-20110927.

Rosenzweig, David. "Judges Asked to Postpone Voting in 4 House Districts." *Los Angeles Times,* November 1, 2001, B7.

Rush, Mark, and Richard Engstrom. *Fair and Effective Representation: Debating Electoral Reform and Minority Rights*. Lanham, MD: Rowman & Littlefield, 2001.

Sahagun, Louis. "Newcomer in Challenge for Assembly Seat." *Los Angeles Times*, October 3, 1986, OC_A10.

Saito, Leland. *Race and Politics: Asian-Americans, Latinos and Whites in a Los Angeles Suburb*. Urbana: University of Illinois Press, 1998.

———. "The Politics of Race and Redistricting in California, 2000–2002." In *Remapping Asian American History*, edited by Sucheng Chan. Walnut Creek, CA: Alta Mira Press, 2003.

Salvato, Greg M. "New Limits on the California Initiative: An Analysis and Critique." *Loyola of Los Angeles Law Review* 19, no. 3 (1986): 1045–96.

Sanchez, Rene. "Divisive Pro187 Is Voided; Ruling Stands against Calif. Anti-Alien Law." *The Washington Post*, July 30, 1999, A03.

Sanders, Jim. "Ex-Judges Drawing Districts under Pro77 Likely Would Be Older White Males." *Sacramento Bee*, October 27, 2005, A3.

———. "GOP Ends Effort to Kill California Senate Districts, Won't Push Pro40." *Sacramento Bee*, July 13, 2012, 4A.

———. "Redistricting Revelations Spark Furor Letters Fly among Political Attorneys over Differences in Wording on Proposition 77." *Sacramento Bee*, July 16, 2005, A3.

———. "Ruling Settles Ballot Dispute; Discrepancies in Wording Shouldn't Have Stopped Vote on Pro77, Top Court Says." *Sacramento Bee*, February 17, 2006, A3.

Santillan, Richard. *California Reapportionment and the Chicano Community: An Historical Overview 1960–1980*. Claremont, CA: The Rose Institute, 1981.

———. "The Chicano Community and the Redistricting of the Los Angeles County Council." *Chicano Law Review* 6, no. 1 (1983): 122–43.

———. *The Chicago Community and California Redistricting*, The Rose Institute of State and Local Government, 1981.

Saunders, Debra J. "The Chicken Dinners Come Home to Roots." *San Francisco Chronicle*, April 2, 1999, http://www.sfgate.com/opinion/saunders/article/Chicken-Dinners-Come-Home-to-Roost-3318760.php.

Schaffner, Brian F., and Matthew J. Streb. "The Partisan Heuristic in Low-Information Elections." *Public Opinion Quarterly* 66, no. 4 (2002): 559–81.

Schaffner, Brian, Matthew Streb, and Gerald Wright. "Teams without Uniforms: The Nonpartisan Ballot in State and Local Elections." *Political Research Quarterly* 54, no. 7 (2001): 7–30.

Schleicher, David. "Why Is There No Partisan Competition in City Council Elections? The Role of Election Law." *Journal of Law and Politics* 23, no. 4 (2007): 419–73.

Schneider, William. "Voter Turnout Is Key to Sebastiani's Hopes." *Los Angeles Times*, August 21, 1983, E1.

Schrag, Peter. "Politicians Settled for 'Draw' in Redistricting." *Sacramento Bee*, February 17, 2002. http://statewidedatabase.org/resources/Redistricting_News/california/2002/february/politicians_settled_02_17_02.html.

———. "Pro77: Off Again, On Again, Gone Again." *Sacramento Bee*, August 17, 2005, B7. "Race and Gubernatorial Recall: Can They Be Linked?" *Sacramento Bee*, July 30, 2003, B7.

Schreiner, Tim. "LA Bias Trial Foreshadows State-wide Redistricting Fight." *San Francisco Chronicle*, January 29, 1990, A2.

Seabrook, Nicolas R. *Drawing the Lines: Constraints on Partisan Gerrymandering in US Politics*. Ithaca, NY: Cornell University Press, 2017.

Seelye, Howard. "Redistricting Plan to Cross County Lines: Incumbents Gain in Party Registration; State Senate Vote Due Today or Tuesday." *Los Angeles Times*, December 4, 1967, OC8.

———. "Incumbents Benefit in House Redistricting." *Los Angeles Times*, May 5, 1968, OC_B5.

Segura, Gary M. "An Evaluation of Hispanic Socio-Economic Conditions and Voter Registration and Turnout." In *Report on the Legal Standards Pertaining to the Los Angeles Redistricting Process*, Justin Levitt, Exhibit J. 2011. http://file.lacounty.gov/bos/supdocs/62832.pdf.

Sewel, Abby. "Gov. Jerry Brown Vetoes Expansion of State Voting Rights Act." *Los Angeles Times*, October 4, 2014, http://www.latimes.com/local/lanow/la-me-pc-governor-veto-voting-rights-20141001-story.html.

Sheppard, Harrison. "Moving the Lines of Power. Study: Redistricting could favor Latino in Congress." *The Daily News of Los Angeles*, September 27, 2005, N3.

———. "Pro77; Con: Measure Power Grab by GOP." *The Daily News of Los Angeles*, October 13, 2005, N1.

Shickler, Eric. *Racial Realignment: The Transformation of American Liberalism, 1932–1965*. Princeton, NJ: Princeton University Press, 2016.

Shogan, Robert. "90 California Governor Race Seen as Key to Redistricting." *Los Angeles Times*, October 26, 1989, A3.

Shotts, Kenneth W. "The Effect of Majority-Minority Mandates on Partisan Gerrymandering." *American Journal of Political Science* 45, no. 1 (2001): 120–35.

Shuit, Douglas. "Close Race Fought in Santa Barbara Area." *Los Angeles Times*, October 14, 1984, OC_A17.

———. "State GOP Betting on 1986 as Its Year to Gain Senate Seats." *Los Angeles Times*, March 23, 1986, SD3.

Shuit, Douglas, Jerry, Gillam. "GOP Gains 2 Senate, 3 Assembly Seats to Bolster Its Position." *Los Angeles Times*, November 6, 1986, A3.

Siegel, Jim. "Redistricting Amendment Proposal Could Means Less Black Legislators." *The Columbus Dispatch*, September 25, 2005, 1A.

Simon, Richard, and Dade Hayes. "Pro-Busing Stand Halted 20-Year Tenure." *Los Angeles Times,* August 31, 1997, 3.

Simon, Richard, and James Rainey. "Edelman Put in Latino District by Board Plan." *Los Angeles Times*, June 28, 1990, A1.

Simon, Richard. "Campaign Racial Overtones Raised in County Remapping Suit." *Los Angeles Times*, January 11, 1990, B3.

———. "County Board Ideology Yields to Politics." *Los Angeles Times*, March 18, 1990, B1.

———. "LA. County Remap Plan Gives Edelan Latino District." *Los Angeles Times*, June 28, 1990, SDA31.

———. "Molina Wins Historic Contest for Supervisor." *Los Angeles Times*, February 20, 1991, A1.

———. "Molina Elected to LA Supervisor's Seat." *Los Angeles Times*, February 20, 1991, SDA18.

———. "Ward Antonovitch Race Heats Up, Brings out Personal Attacks." *Los Angeles Times*, October 5, 1980, GB1.

Skelton, George. "Bush's Bumbling Won't Benefit State's Democrats." *Los Angeles Times*, August 14, 2006, B3.

———. "GOP's Prop.187 Wounds Healing, But Dems Are Bleeding." *Los Angeles Times*, May 11, 2006, B3.

———. "In the Ring with Contenders for Governor." *Los Angeles Times*, March 23, 1998, http://articles.latimes.com/1998/mar/23/news/mn-31902.

———. "Pro11 Foes Waging an Orwellian Campaign." *Los Angeles Times*, October 9, 2008, B1.

Skerry, Peter. *Counting on the Census: Race, Group Identity and the Evasion of Politics*. Washington, DC: Brookings Institution Press, 2000.

Skrentny, John D. *The Minority Rights Revolution*. Cambridge, MA: Harvard University Press, 2002.

Slingsby, Stephen. *The Gerrymander: Its Rise, Use, and Potential*. Claremont, CA: Claremont Graduate University, 1967.

Smith, Steven C. "Redistricting Confusion Triggers Wide Concern; Southeast Leaders Express Worries About Splintered Representation in the Legislature." *Los Angeles Times*, December 30, 1971, H1.

———. "Gains Sought by Mexican-Americans; Groups to Seek Strong Chicano Districts from Legislature during Reapportionment." *Los Angeles Times*, August 7, 1971, K1.

Sonenshein, Raphael J. *Politics in Black and White: Race and Power in Los Angeles*. Princeton, NJ: Princeton University Press, 1993.

———. "When the People Draw the Lines: An Examination of the California Citizens Redistricting Commission." 2013. https://cavotes.org/sites/default/files/jobs/RedistrictingCommission%20Report6122013.pdf.

Staff writer. "Two-Year Moratorium on Redistricting Asked." *Los Angeles Times*, January 20, 1965, 10.

Stall, Bill. "Political, Legal Battle over Redistricting Looms." *Los Angeles Times*, August 22, 1991, VCA3.

Stammer, Larry. "Deukmejian-Burke Race Issues Battle." *Los Angeles Times*, October 16, 1978, A3.

Stein, Mark. "One Latino Wins, 3 Others Lose in Watsonville Vote." *Los Angeles Times*, December 6, 1989, A3.

Stephanopoulos, Nicholas O. "Redistricting in the 2010s: Communities and the California Commission." *Stanford Law and Policy Review* 23, no. 281 (2012): 281–332.

Stephanopoulos, Nicholas O., and Eric M. McGhee. "Partisan Gerrymandering and the Efficiency Gap." *University of Chicago Law Review* 82, no. 2 (2015): 831–900.

Stewart, Jill. "*Terminator vs. Gerrymander*." *New York Times*, November 7, 2005, A23.

Stewart, Jocelyn Y. "Deane Dana, 78; Former LA County Supervisor Had Pro Business Stand." *Los Angeles Times*, April 22, 2005, http://articles.latimes.com/2005/apr/22/local/me-dana22.

Sullivan, Joseph W. "Massive Gerrymander Mapped in California by 38 Congressmen." *Wall Street Journal*, November 9, 1967, 1.

Swain, Carol M. *Black Faces, Black Interests: The Representation of African Americans in Congress*. Cambridge, MA: Harvard University Press, 1993.

Swain, John W., Stephen A. Borrelli, and Brian C. Reed. "Partisan Consequences of the Post-1990 Redistricting for the US House of Representatives." *Political Research Quarterly* 51, no. 4 (1998): 945–67.

Sweeney, James L. *The California Electricity Crisis*. Stanford, CA: Hoover Institution Press, 2002.

Takash, Paule Cruz, and Joaquin Avila. "Latino Political Participation in Rural California." Working Group on Farm Labor and Rural Poverty, Working Paper #8, February 1989.

Talev, Margaret. "New Districts to Solidify Position for Incumbents." *Los Angeles Times*, September 1, 2001, B3.

———. "Santa Paula Not Alone in Voting Issue." *Los Angeles Times*, September 26, 1999, 1.

Taryn, Luna. "How a High School Dropout Fought Her Way to the Pinnacle of California Politics." *Sacramento Bee*, November 1, 2016, http://www.sacbee.com/news/politics-government/capitol-alert/article111682772.html.

Testimony of The Mexican American Legal Defense and Educational Fund on the Voting Rights Act, Presented by Joaquin G. Avila, Associate Counsel, Before The Subcommittee on Civil Constitutional Fights of the Judiciary Committee US House of Representatives, June 5, 1981.

The New York Times, Election 2010, Senate Exit Polls, https://www.nytimes.com/elections/2010/results/senate/exit-polls.html.

The Redistricting Group at Berkeley Law, *California Redistricting Criterion: Communities of Interest* (*COI*) (2011), http://redistrictinggroup.org/wp-content/uploads/2011/04/Communities-of-Interest_2pagehandout_byTRGBL.pdf.

The Rose Institute of State and Local Government. *Facts and Figures about California's Latino Voters: 1988*. The Rose Institute of State and Local Government, 1988, Table 1.

Thurber, James A., and Antoine Yoshinaka, eds. *American Gridlocked: The Sources, Character, Impact of Political Polarization*. New York: Cambridge University Press, 2016.

Tokaji, Daniel P. "Responding to Shelby County: A Grand Election Bargain." *Harvard Law and Policy Review* 8, no. 1 (2014): 71–108.

Toobin, Jeffrey. "The Great Election Grab: When Does Gerrymandering Become a Threat to Democracy?" *The New Yorker* 79, no. 38 (2003): 63.

Totton, J. Anderson, and Charles G. Bell. "The 1970 Election in California." *The Western Political Quarterly* 24, no. 2 (1971): 262.

Trinh Võ, Linda. *Mobilizing an Asian American Community*. Philadelphia, PA: Temple University Press, 2004.

Tucker, James Thomas. *The Battle over Bilingual Ballot: Language Minorities and Political Access under the Voting Rights Act*. Burlington, VT: Ashgate 2009.

———. "The Politics of Persuasion: Passage of the Voting Rights Act Reauthorization Act of 2006." *Journal of Legislation* 33, no. 2 (2007): 205–67.

Turner, Wallace. "California Lawmaker Resigning 'to Come Home.'" *New York Times*, March 14, 1982, 29.

———. "Coast Democrats Spurn GOP Deal." *New York Times*, September 15, 1983, A23.

———. "GOP Favoring California Vote to Recall Judge." *New York Times*, February 1, 1982, A8.

———. "Rep. Philippe Burton, Democratic Liberal, Dies on Visit to California." *New York Times*, April 11, 1983, B6.

Ulloa, Jazmine. "Legislature Sees Rise in Diversity, Drop in Women." *Los Angeles Times*, November 26, 2016, B1.

US Census Bureau. "Black Elected Officials by Office, 1970 to 2002, and State, 2002." Statistical Abstract of the US 2011, table 413. http://www2.census.gov/library/publications/2010/compendia/statab/130ed/tables/11s0413.pdf.

Vallely, Richard. *The Two Reconstructions: The Struggle for Black Enfranchisement*. Chicago, IL: University of Chicago Press, 2004.

Vigil, Maurilio E. "Hispanics Gain Seats in the 98th Congress after Reapportionment." *International Social Science Review* 59, no. 1 (1984): 20–30.

———. *Hispanics in American Politics: The Search for Political Power*. Lanham, MD: University Press of America, 1987.

Vogel, Nancy. "Key Pro11 Donors Have GOP Ties." *Los Angeles Times*, October 24, 2008, B1.

———. "Looking to Design a Fairer Map." *Los Angeles Times*, February 13, 2005, B1.

———. "Modest Changes Seen under Pro77. Redistricting Would Create Some Closer Races, a Study Says, But a Power Shift Is Thought Unlikely." *Los Angeles Times*, September 27, 2005, B1.

———. "Pro11 Aims to Redo Map." *Los Angeles Times*, October 14, 2008, B1.

Walters, Dan. "New Era for State Politics." *San Francisco Daily Journal*, December 6, 1991, A4.

———. "New Redistricting Plan Whacks the Democrats." *San Jose Mercury News*, December 4, 1991, B11.

———. “Redistricting Panel Shows True Colors of Ideologies.” *Sacramento Bee*, March 25, 2011. https://wedrawthelines.ca.gov/wp-content/uploads/sites/64/2011/03/public_comment_20110325_walters.pdf.

Ward, Mike. “Six Incumbents Threatened by Redistricting Plan: Others in Valley in Good Reelection Position under Reapportionment Plan.” *Los Angeles Times*, September 16, 1973, SG1.

Ward, Mike, and Alan Maltun. “Redistricting Forces Hard Choices of GOP Congressmen: Rousselot, Moorhead May Have to Vie in Primary.” *Los Angeles Times*, September 27, 1981, SG1.

Waxman, Henry, A. “Waxman Gives Views on Chicano Redistricting.” *Los Angeles Times*, October 7, 1971, C7.

Way, Franck H. “Brutal Butchery in the Two-Party System.” In *The Politics of Reapportionment*, edited by Malcom E. Jewell, 249–64. New York: Atherton Press, 1962.

Weinberger, Caspar W. “Redistricting Ruling Was Bad.” *Los Angeles Times*, October 16, 1967, A4.

Weinstein, Henry. “Latinos Pushing Redistricting Plan: But LA Supervisors Are Expected to Oppose Major Changes.” *Los Angeles Times*, August 4, 1981, C1.

Weinstraub, Daniel M. “Voters May Redesign Redistricting.” *Los Angeles Times*, May 27, 1990, OCA38.

———. “Latino Group Seeks to Alter Remap Plan.” *Los Angeles Times*, December 17, 1991, A3.

———. “Chance fading for Bipartisan Deal on Reapportionment.” *Los Angeles Times*, September 17, 1991, VYA3.

———. “Democrats Pass Redistricting Plans.” *Los Angeles Times*, September 20, 1991, A3.

———. “Minorities Get GOP Support in Remap Battle.” *Los Angeles Times*, August 26, 1991, A3.

———. “Latinos Offer Own Plan for Redistricting.” *Los Angeles Times*, September 6, 1991, A3.

———. “Remap Could Bring Major Gains for GOP.” *Los Angeles Times*, December 4, 1991, A1.

———. “Wilson Asks Court to Takeover Redistricting.” *Los Angeles Times*, September 7, 1991, A1.

———. “Wilson Outlines Redistricting Strategy.” *Los Angeles Times*, July 19, 1991, A3.

———. “GOP Bid for Assembly Control Becomes a Long Shot.” *Los Angeles Times*, October 5, 1992, A1.

———. “Incumbents Come First in Redistricting, Speaker Says.” *Los Angeles Times*, August 30, 1991, A3.

———. “Infighting Dooms GOP Power Play.” *Los Angeles Times*, April 10, 1990, 0CA3.

———. “Lawmakers’ Fall Session Is Sure to Be Divisive.” *Los Angeles Times*, August 18, 1991, SBA3.

———. “Redistricting Measures Costliest on the Ballot.” *Los Angeles Times*, June 2, 1990, A29.

———. "When the Course of reapportionment." *Sacramento Bee*, December 16, 1991, B 15.

———. "Wilson Got His Wish in Remap Plan." *Los Angeles Times*, December 5, 1991, A3.

———. "Wilson Panel Remap Would Help Republicans." *Los Angeles Times*, October 12, 1991, A31.

West, Richard. "Latins Threaten to Form Third Party over Redistricting." *Los Angeles Times*, March 10, 1971, A1.

Weston, Margaret B. "One Person, One Vote: Staggered Elections, Redistricting and Disenfranchisement." *Yale Law Journal* 121, no. 7 (2012): 2013–30.

Wildermuth, John. "'Nonpartisan' Measure Draws Partisan Debate. Redistricting Plan Hotly Contested at Legislative Hearing." *San Francisco Chronicle*, September 27, 2005, B2.

———. "Redistricting Initiative Would Set State Apart. But Opponents Blast Proposition 77 as a 'Reckless Experiment.'" *San Francisco Chronicle*, October 7, 2005, B3.

———. "Redistricting Measure Could Drop Off Ballot." *San Francisco Chronicle*, July 7, 2005, B2.

———. "Redistricting Plan Thrown Off State Ballot" *San Francisco Chronicle*, July 22, 2005, A1.

———. "Redistricting: Incumbents Team Up to Oppose Schwarzenegger on Pro77." *San Francisco Chronicle*, August 26, 2005, B1.

———. "Voters Reject Attempt to Take Boundary-Drawing from the Hands of state Legislators." *San Francisco Chronicle*, November 9, 2005, A14.

———. "Wilson would Carry Plenty of Baggage in a Bid for Senate; Support for Pro187, utility Deregulation Could Cost Him Votes." *San Francisco Chronicle*, April 20, 2003, A25.

Wiley, Paul M. "Shelby and Section 3: Pulling the Voting Rights Act's Pocket Trigger to Protect Voting Rights After *Shelby County v. Holder*." *Washington and Lee Law Review* 71, no. 3 (2014): 2115–53.

Wilkening, David Lester. *The Political History of the California State legislative Reapportionment*, 1849–1977, Master's thesis. California State University Sacramento, 1977.

Willman, Martha L. "Some Incumbents Get Edge Under Redistricting: Redistricting Gives Incumbents Edge." *Los Angeles Times*, February 24, 1974, SF A1.

Wilson, Chris. "See How Trump's Approval Rating Stacks Up Against Other Presidents After One Year." *Time*, http://time.com/5103776/donald-trump-approval-rating-graph/.

Wilson, William J. *The Truly Disadvantaged: The Inner City, the Underclass and Public Policy*. Chicago: Chicago University Press, 1986.

Winburn, Jonathan. *The Realities of Redistricting: Following the Rules and Limiting Gerrymandering in State Legislatures*. Lanham, MD: Lexington Books, 2009.

Wood, Tracy. "Senate Quiet Fears, Passes Its Reapportionment Plan." *Los Angeles Times*, December 24, 1982, I3.

Yi, Daniel. "Political Mapping Process Is Redrawn." *Los Angeles Times*, August 11, 2001, B1.

Zeiger, Richard. "The Reapportionment Puzzle: Carving Up California." *California Journal* 22, no. 4 (1991): 204–6.

Zelman, Walter A. "Time's Up on Sacramento's Game-Playing." *Los Angeles Times*, September 19, 1983, C5.

Zeman, Ray. "Battle on Reapportionment Reopens Today in Assembly." *Los Angeles Times*, October 11, 1965, 3.

———. "State's Redistricting Struggle Heads for Conference Session." *Los Angeles Times*, November 16, 1967, 3.

———. "The Results of Redistricting." *Los Angeles Times*, June 23, 1966, A4.

Case List

Abrams v. Johnson, 521 U.S. 74, 100 (1997).
Aldasoro v. El Centro School District, 922 F. Supp. 339 (S.D. Cal. 1995).
Allen v. State Board of Elections, 393 U.S. 544 (1969).
Andal v. Davis (S101573); *Kennedy v. Davis* (S101719); and *Nadler v. Davis* (S101651).
Arizona State Legislature v. Arizona Independent Redistricting Commission, 576 US _ (2015).
Badham v. Eu, 694 F. Supp. 664 (N.D. Cal. 1988), aff'd mem. 109 S. Ct. 829 (1989).
Baker v. Carr, 369 U.S. 186 (1962).
Bartlett v. Strickland, 556 U.S. 1 (2009).
Beer v. United States, 425 U.S. 130 (1976).
Bethun-Hill v. Virginia Board of Election
Bush v. Vera, 517 U.S. 952 (1996).
Calderon v. City of Los Angeles, 4 Cal. 3d 251 (1971).
California Democratic Party v. Lungren, 919 F. Supp. 1397, 1399 (N.D. Cal. 1996).
Castorena v. City of Los Angeles, 34 Cal. App. 3d 902 (1973).
City of Mobile v. Bolden, 446 U.S. 55 (1980).
City of Petersburg v. United States, 93 S. Ct. 1441 (1973).
Colgrove v. Green, 328 U.S. 549 (1946).
Connerly v. State of California, 229 Cal. App. 4th 457 (2014).
Connor v. Johnson, 402 U.S. 690, 692 (1971).
Costa v. Superior Court, 128 P.3d 675, 690 (Cal. 2006).
Costa v. Superior Court, 32 Cal. Rptr. 3d 562, (Cal. App. 2005).
Costa v. Superior Court, Case No. S136296 (Cal. Aug. 12, 2005).
Davis v. Bandemer, 478 U.S. 109 (1986).
DeWitt v. Wilson, 856 F. Supp. 1409 (1994).
E. Carroll Parish Sch. Bd. v. Marshall, 424 U.S. 636, 639 (1976).
Easley v. Cromartie, 532 U.S. 234 (2001).
Gaffney v. Cummings, 412 U.S 735, (1973).

Garza v. County of Los Angeles, 756 F. Supp. 1298, 1341 (C.D. Cal. 1990).
Garza, v. County of Los Angeles, 918 F.2d 763 (9th Cir. 1990).
Georgia v. Ashcroft, 539 U.S. 461 (2003).
Gill v. Whitford, 585 US_(2018).
Gomez v. City of Watsonville, 863 F.2d 1407 (9th Cir. 1988).
Gomez v. Hanford Joint Union School District
Gomillion v. Lightfoot, 364 U.S. 339 (1960).
Gonzalez, et al. v. City of Compton, Case No. C45094 (LA County S. Ct. Cal. 2010).
Gray v. Sanders, 372 U.S. 368, 379 (1963).
Growe v. Emison, 507 U.S. 25, 34 (1993).
Jauregui v. City of Palmdale (Los Angeles County Super. Ct. No. BC483039). Upheld on appeal, B253713 (Cal. Ct. App. Jun.10, 2015).
Karcher v. Daggett, 462 U.S. 725 (1983).
Kirkpatrick v. Preisler, 394 U.S. 526 (1969)
League of United Latin Am. Citizens v. Wilson, 908 F. Supp. 755, 769 (C.D. Cal. 1995).
League of United Latin Am. Citizens, Council No. 4434 v. Clements, 999 F.2d 831, 865, 876 (5th Cir. 1993) (en banc) (LULAC II)
League of United Latin American Citizens v. Perry, 548 U.S. 399 (2006).
Legislature v. Reinecke IV, 10 Cal. 3d 396 (1973).
Legislature v. Reinecke I, 6 Cal. 3d. 595 (1972).
Legislature v. Reinecke, 110 Cal. Rptr. 718 (1973).
Legislature v. Reinecke, 516 P.2d 6 (Cal. 1973).
Lockyer v. McPherson, 2005 WL 1719252 (Cal. S. Ct. July 21, 2005).
Lucas v. Colo. Gen. Assembly, 377 U.S. 713, 731 (1964).
Mahan v. Howell, 410 U.S. 315, 332–33 (1973).
McCrory v. Harris.
Radanovich v. Bowen, No. S196852 (Cal. Sept. 29, 2011); *Radanovich v. Bowen,* No. S196852 (Cal. Oct. 26, 2011); *Radanovich v. Bowen,* No. 2:11-cv-09786-SVW-PJW (C.D. Cal. Feb. 9, 2012).
Reynolds v. Sims, 377 U.S. 533, 568 (1964).
Ruiz v. City of Santa Maria, 160 F.3d 543 (9th Cir. 1998).
Sanchez v. City of Modesto, 145 Cal. App. 4th 660, (Cal. Ct. App. 2007) cert. denied, 552 U.S. 974 (2007).
Sanchez v. City of Modesto, 51 Cal. Rptr. 3d 821 (2006).
Senate of the State of California v. Jones, 21 Cal. 4th 1142 (1999).
Silver v. Reagan, 67 Cal. 2d. 432; 62 Cal. Rptr. 424; 432 P.2d 26 (1967).
Terry v. Adams, 345 U.S. 461 (1953).
Thornburg v. Gingles, 478 U.S. 30 (1986).
United States Term Limits, Inc. v. Thornton, 514 U.S. 779 (1995).
Vandermost v. Bowen, 269 P.3d 446 (Cal. 2012).
Vieth v. Jubelirer, 541 U.S. 267 (2004).
Wesberry v. Sanders, 376 U.S. 1, 2 (1964).
Whitcombv. Chavis, 403 U.S. 124 (1971).
Wilson v. Eu, 54 Cal. 3d 471; 816 P. 2d 1306 (1991).

Wisconsin v. City of New York, 517 U.S. 1 (1996).
Wise v. Lipscomb, 437 U.S. 535, 540 (1978).
Yorty v. Anderson, 60 Cal. 2d 312, 33 Cal. Rptr. 97, 384 P.2d 417 (1963).
Yorty v. Jordan, Sac. No. 7543 (appealed to the US Supreme Court, October 1964 Term, Case No. 250, and dismissed for want of jurisdiction on October 12, 1964, 379 U.S. 8, 85 S. Ct. 68, 13 L.Ed.2d 22); and *Yorty v. Jordan, Sac.* No. 7582.

Index

Abrams v. Johnson, 521 U.S. 74, 100 (1997), 42, 63n41
Alatorre, Richard, 19, 20, 68, 70, 79, 80, 81, 86, 91, 106, 107, 109–12, 119, 124, 126, 128n9, 130n29, 190, 367–68
Aldasoro v. El Centro School District, 922 F. Supp. 339 (S.D. Cal. 1995), 284n12
Allen v. State Board of Elections, 393 U.S. 544 (1969), 29n61
Andal v. Davis (S101573); *Kennedy v. Davis* (S101719); and *Nadler v. Davis* (S101651), 261n75, 261n82
Arizona State Legislature v. Arizona Independent Redistricting Commission, 576 US _(2015), 337n136
Asian Pacific Legal Center, 178, 258n45
APLC. See Asian Pacific Legal Center
Avila, Joaquin, 22, 269–72, 279, 281–82, 284, 284n13, 284n15, 285n21, 287n50

Badham v. Eu, 694 F. Supp. 664 (N.D. Cal. 1988), aff'd mem. 109 S. Ct. 829 (1989), 128, 137n133
Baker v. Carr, 369 U.S. 186 (1962), 13–15, 19, 29n59, 33, 37, 59, 61n15
Baker, Gordon, 60n2, 89, 91, 103n83, 137n133
Bartlett v. Strickland, 556 U.S. 1 (2009), 262, 286n28, 334n107, 336n132
Beer v. United States, 425 U.S. 130 (1976), 26n33, 29n61
Berman, Michael, 6, 22, 72, 99n14, 106, 110, 116, 118, 123, 129n14, 130n32, 131n49, 137n128, 208n40, 209n52, 224, 233, 236–37, 241–42, 249, 261n80, 263n101, 297, 352
Berman, Howard, 22, 72, 77, 79, 83, 92, 106, 110, 116, 124–25, 128n7, 128n9, 133n69, 135n104, 172, 217n148, 234, 236–39, 241, 261n74, 261n80, 263n93, 263n101, 265n122, 292–93, 297, 314, 330n60, 366n10
Bethun-Hill v. Virginia Board of Election, 580_US (2017), 30n71
Brown, Edmund Gerald Jr. "Jerry", 82–84, 94, 105, 121–123, 133n73, 134n90, 144, 156, 322
Brown, Edmund Gerald Sr. "Pat," 36, 38, 42–43, 45, 47, 61n11, 61n19
Brown, Willie, 20, 49, 66n75, 66n76, 67n87, 72, 75, 79, 106–7, 109–111, 116, 118–19, 124, 126, 128n7, 129n10, 130n26, 130n31, 130n32,

167, 169, 175, 178, 182, 195–96, 201, 203, 211n68, 235, 366n5, 368

Burton, Philip, 52–53, 55, 59, 66n75, 72, 76–77, 81, 84, 85, 87, 94, 99n14, 100n31, 103n89, 116–119, 124, 131n51, 131n52, 132n64, 133n69, 133n71, 133n73, 135n102, 156, 167, 175, 352, 369

Burton, John, 72, 94, 116–19, 186, 199, 224, 232–33, 235, 265n154

Bush v. Vera, 517 U.S. 952 (1996), 188, 216n136

Cain, Bruce, 4, 13, 15, 24n15, 24n16, 28n50, 28n55, 30n70, 30n73, 31n82, 61n7, 99n13, 129n14, 130n25, 130n27, 130n33, 131n47, 137n133, 157n1, 160n51, 182–83, 202, 206n3, 207n11, 208n27, 209n53, 212n88, 213n101, 214n104, 221n186, 228, 243, 263n109, 266n137, 267n145, 267n149, 270, 281, 284n10, 303, 305, 327n18, 329n44, 329n52, 330n54, 332n84, 334n105, 335n116, 352, 362,
374n1

Calderon v. City of Los Angeles, 4 Cal. 3d 251 (1971), 142, 158n17

California Democratic Party v. Lungren, 919 F. Supp. 1397, 1399 (N.D. Cal. 1996), 285n23

California Coalition of Asian Pacific Americans for Fair Reapportionment (CAPAFR), 187, 231, 234–35, 258n45

California Statewide Database, 229, 256n30, 303, 333n95, 334n101, 358, 361

Californios for Fair Reapportionment, 108–9

Castorena v. City of Los Angeles, 34 Cal. App. 3d 902 (1973), 159n23

City of Mobile v. Bolden, 446 U.S. 55 (1980), 8, 26n29, 29n60, 162n85, 209n49, 242

City of Petersburg v. United States, 93 S. Ct. 1441 (1973), 64n54

Colgrove v. Green, 328 U.S. 549 (1946), 13, 28n57, 29n59

Connerly v. State of California, 229 Cal. App. 4th 457 (2014), 337n135

Connor v. Johnson, 402 U.S. 690, 692 (1971), 64n55

Costa v. Superior Court, 128 P.3d 675, 690 (Cal. 2006), 328n34

Costa v. Superior Court, 32 Cal. Rptr. 3d 562, (Cal. App. 2005); *Costa v. Superior Court*, Case No. S136296 (Cal. Aug. 12, 2005), 328n32

Davis v. Bandemer, 478 U.S. 109 (1986), 29n66, 137n134, 216n130, 251, 266n144

Deukmejian, George, 55, 65n61, 93, 105, 123, 126–28, 128n5, 136n115, 137n128, 144–45, 168, 187

DeWitt v. Wilson, 856 F. Supp. 1409 (1994), 216n133, 216n135

Dymally, Mervyn, 48–49, 58, 63n35, 65n70, 68n106, 72, 75–79, 83, 86–87, 90, 101n39, 118, 131n43, 214n108, 257n34

E. Carroll Parish Sch. Bd. v. Marshall, 424 U.S. 636, 639 (1976), 64n55

Easley v. Cromartie, 532 U.S. 234 (2001), 362, 366n11

Feng, Kathay, 22, 215n127, 230, 235, 258n44, 258n47, 258n48, 260n67, 260n70, 294–295, 297, 300, 314, 330n55

Gaffney v. Cummings, 412 U.S 735, (1973), 267n151

Garza, v. County of Los Angeles, 918 F.2d 763 (9th Cir. 1990); *Garza v. County of Los Angeles*, 756 F. Supp. 1298, 1341 (C.D. Cal. 1990), 6, 147, 151, 153–55, 162n70–72, 162n76,

162n78–80, 162n82–84, 173, 240, 368
Georgia v. Ashcroft, 539 U.S. 461 (2003), 9, 262n91
Gill v. Whitford, 585 US_(2018), 216n130, 364
Gomez v. City of Watsonville, 863 F.2d 1407 (9th Cir. 1988), 270, 283n6, 284n7, 284n9
Gomez v. Hanford Joint Union School District, Civ. Act. No. 04–Co284 (Cal. Super. Ct. 2004), 285n17–18
Gomillion v. Lightfoot, 364 U.S. 339 (1960), 29n58
Gonzalez et al. v. City of Compton, Case No. C45094 (LA County S. Ct. Cal. 2010), 278, 287n51, 288n53
Gray v. Sanders, 372 U.S. 368, 379 (1963), 14, 37, 61n16
Growe v. Emison, 507 U.S. 25, 34 (1993), 63n42

Hardy, Leroy, 43, 52, 55, 59, 60n5, 62n28, 63n46, 65n59, 66n71, 66n81, 67n86, 68n104, 68n107, 72, 77–78, 100n36, 131n49
Heslop, Alan, 72, 83, 108, 122, 132n57, 210n58, 304, 333n90–91
Hodson, Tim, 169, 176, 208n31, 209n46, 209n54, 210n60, 210n62, 212n75, 290, 326n8
Hofeller, Thomas, 72, 83, 85, 89, 108, 133n87, 186

Jauregui v. City of Palmdale (Los Angeles County Super. Ct. No. BC483039). Upheld on appeal, B253713 (Cal. Ct. App. Jun.10, 2015), 287n44
Johnson, Doug, 303–4, 326n8, 333n95

Karcher v. Daggett, 462 U.S. 725 (1983), 29n65
Kirkpatrick v. Preisler, 394 U.S. 526 (1969), 59
Kousser, Morgan, 25n21, 28n53, 30n76, 91, 99n17, 101n42, 101n45, 103n84, 103n91, 119, 128n1, 129n20, 131n47, 133n70, 134n94, 141, 149, 159n9–10, 158n15, 159n25, 160n40, 160n47, 161n54, 161n57–58, 161n63–65, 162n74, 183–184, 205, 209n47–48, 212n81–82, 213n90, 213n100, 214n103, 217n147, 221n188, 221n190, 240–41, 263n94, 263n97–99, 274, 279, 287n38, 288n53, 366n6

League of United Latin American Citizens, 178, 243
LULAC. *See* League of United Latin American Citizens,
League of United Latin Am. Citizens v. Wilson, 908 F. Supp. 755, 769 (C.D. Cal. 1995), 218n160
League of United Latin Am. Citizens, Council No. 4434 v. Clements, 999 F.2d 831, 865, 876 (5th Cir. 1993) (en banc) (LULAC II), 274, 286n34
League of United Latin American Citizens v. Perry, 548 U.S. 399 (2006), 29n66, 216n132, 262n91
Legislature v. Reinecke I, 6 Cal. 3d. 595 (1972), 101n44, 101n57
Legislature v. Reinecke, 110 Cal. Rptr. 718 (1973), 102n73
Legislature v. Reinecke, 516 P.2d 6 (Cal. 1973), 103n78–79, 114, 130n38
Legislature v. Reinecke IV, 10 Cal. 3d 396 (1973), 102n75, 103n82
Lockyer v. McPherson, 2005 WL 1719252 (Cal. S. Ct. July 21, 2005), 328n32
Lucas v. Colo. Gen. Assembly, 377 U.S. 713, 731 (1964), 64n56

Mahan v. Howell, 410 U.S. 315, 332–33 (1973), 64n56
Mexican American Legal Defense and Educational Fund, 21–22, 84, 98n9,

108, 119, 142–43, 148–49, 151–52, 171, 173, 178–79, 183–84, 186–87, 209n47, 211n70, 211n73, 212n76, 213n91, 214n108, 215n122, 229–31, 234–43, 257n38, 258n51, 260n63–64, 263n102, 269–70, 279, 284, 292, 295, 308–10, 331n71, 334n104, 352, 368
MALDEF. *See* Mexican American Legal Defense and Educational Fund
MacDonald, Karin, 214n104, 256n29, 303–5, 308, 313, 329n44–45, 330n54, 331n69, 332n78, 333n95–96, 334n105, 335n116, 337n137, 366n14, 374n1
McCrory v. Harris, 581 US_(2017), 30n71
McKaskle, Paul, 89, 104n95, 182
Moretti, Robert, 72, 74, 79–81, 83, 106

National Asian Pacific American Legal Consortium, 229, 257n38
National Association of Latino Elected Officials, 10, 27n40, 57, 271, 281, 287n47, 288n61, 301, 331n71
NALEO. *See* National Association of Latino Elected Officials,
National Association for the Advancement of Colored People, 149, 152, 173, 175, 187, 210n57, 216n128, 229, 231, 243, 257n38, 292, 295, 299, 331n71, 368
NAACP. *See* National Association for the Advancement of Colored People
NAACP LDF. *See* National Association for the Advancement of Colored People
Northwest Austin Municipal Utility District No. 1 v. Holder, 557 US 193 (2009), 10

Preclearance. *See* Voting Rights Act
Radanovich v. Bowen, No. S196852 (Cal. Sept. 29, 2011); *Radanovich v. Bowen,* No. S196852 (Cal. Oct. 26, 2011); *Radanovich v. Bowen*, No. 2:11–cv–09786-SVWPJW (C.D. Cal. Feb. 9, 2012), 335n120–21
Reagan, Ronald, 19, 44, 46–47, 50, 53, 55, 69, 71, 78, 80–88, 91, 93–94, 100n31, 105–6, 110, 116, 121, 127, 130n35, 153, 167–68, 236, 304, 349, 367
Reinecke, Howard Edwin "Ed", 82, 84, 89
Reno v. Bossier Parish School Board, 528 US 320 (2000), 9
Reynolds v. Sims, 377 U.S. 533, 568 (1964), 14, 37, 61n18, 62n21, 154
Rose Institute, 107–9, 125, 129n13, 120n20, 148, 154, 181, 302–5, 331n71, 332n83, 333n91, 336n133
Ruiz v. City of Santa Maria, 160 F.3d 543 (9th Cir. 1998), 284n12

Sanchez v. City of Modesto, 145 Cal. App. 4th 660 (Cal. Ct. App. 2007) cert. denied, 552 U.S. 974 (2007), 286n31
Sanchez v. City of Modesto, 51 Cal. Rptr. 3d 821 (2006), 272, 282, 285n19, 288n64
Section 2. *See* Voting Rights Act
Section 5. *See* Voting Rights Act
Senate of the State of California v. Jones, 21 Cal. 4th 1142 (1999), 327n29
Silver v. Reagan, 67 Cal. 2d. 432; 62 Cal. Rptr. 424; 432 P.2d 26 (1967), 67n89–90
Schwarzenegger, Arnold, 85, 135, 289–90, 293, 298–99, 328n37, 332n79
Shelby County v. Holder, 570 US 2 (2013), 10, 17, 31n80, 102n72, 155, 311, 363
Shumate, Joe, 125–26, 135, 181–84, 208n32, 260n67, 297

Terry v. Adams, 345 U.S. 461 (1953), 61n16
Thornburg v. Gingles, 478 U.S. 30 (1986), 26n31, 64n54, 147, 154,

161n53, 162n85, 240, 251, 259n52, 262n91, 283n3, 284n10, 286n28, 364

United States Term Limits, Inc. v. Thornton, 514 U.S. 779 (1995), 208n28
Unruh, Jesse, 36, 38–40, 43, 46–49, 53, 55, 63n35, 65n65, 66n74–76, 69, 72, 75, 92, 100n31, 131n43

Vandermost v. Bowen, 269 P.3d 446 (Cal. 2012), 336n125
Vieth v. Jubelirer, 541 U.S. 267 (2004), 29n66, 30n69, 216n130, 251, 267n146
Voting Rights Act, 1–22, 25n22–24, 26n30, 29n62, 33, 44–45, 48, 57, 60, 64n54, 80, 102n72, 112, 118, 130n35, 132n61, 143, 147, 151, 153, 155–56, 162n85, 170, 172–77, 180–81, 185, 188, 202, 205, 209n51, 216n132, 228–29, 236, 238, 253, 258n43, 262n91, 269, 271–72, 274–75, 282, 283, 285n18, 291–92, 296–97, 302, 305–7, 309–10, 324, 333n98, 336n132, 347, 351, 353, 356–57, 359, 363, 367–68, 370–71
VRA. *See* Voting Rights Act

Waxman, Henry, 72–74, 77, 79–80, 85, 94, 99n14, 104n95, 116–17, 119, 186, 244, 366n10
Wesberry v. Sanders, 376 U.S. 1, 2 (1964), 14, 37
West Virginia University Hospitals, Inc. v. Casey, 499 US 83 (1991), 9
Whitcomb v. Chavis, 403 U.S. 124 (1971), 64n57
William C. Velasquez Institute, 230, 263n101
Wilson, Pete, 21, 118, 169–70, 172–73, 177–78, 180–82, 185–86, 189, 194, 196–97, 212n80, 216n139, 218n159, 324, 347, 369
Wilson v. Eu, 54 Cal. 3d 471; 816 P. 2d 1306 (1991), 182–88
Wisconsin v. City of New York, 517 U.S. 1 (1996), 255n19
Wise v. Lipscomb, 437 U.S. 535, 540 (1978), 64n55

Yorty v. Anderson, 60 Cal. 2d 312, 33 Cal. Rptr. 97, 384 P.2d 417 (1963), 37
Yorty v. Jordan, *Sac*. No. 7543 1964 (379 U.S. 8, 85 S. Ct. 68, 13 L.Ed.2d 22); and *Yorty v. Jordan, Sac*. No. 7582, 62n21

About the Author

Olivier Richomme used to live in California and is a US history professor at the University of Lyon, France. He first moved to California in 1996 where he attended Sacramento City College and then California State University Sacramento. He received his PhD from the University of Paris—La Sorbonne in 2006. His dissertation was about the creation of racial statistics in the US and race-conscious public policies.

www.ingramcontent.com/pod-product-compliance
Lightning Source LLC
LaVergne TN
LVHW060009290926
849146LV00003B/63
9781498585927